THE EUROPEAN CONVENTION ON HUMAN RIGHTS

JACOBS, WHITE, AND OVEY

THE EUROPEAN CONVENTION ON HUMAN RIGHTS

ROBIN C A WHITE AND CLARE OVEY

Fifth edition

OXFORD

UNIVERSITY PRESS

OXFORD

UNIVERSITY PRESS

Great Clarendon Street, Oxford OX2 6DP

Oxford University Press is a department of the University of Oxford.
It furthers the University's objective of excellence in research, scholarship,
and education by publishing worldwide in

Oxford New York

Auckland Cape Town Dar es Salaam Hong Kong Karachi
Kuala Lumpur Madrid Melbourne Mexico City Nairobi
New Delhi Shanghai Taipei Toronto

With offices in

Argentina Austria Brazil Chile Czech Republic France Greece
Guatemala Hungary Italy Japan Poland Portugal Singapore
South Korea Switzerland Thailand Turkey Ukraine Vietnam

Oxford is a registered trade mark of Oxford University Press
in the UK and in certain other countries

Published in the United States
by Oxford University Press Inc., New York

British Library Cataloguing in Publication Data

Data available

Library of Congress Cataloging in Publication Data

Data available

Typeset by Newgen Imaging Systems (P) Ltd., Chennai, India
Printed in Great Britain
on acid-free paper by
Ashford Colour Press Ltd., Gosport, Hampshire

ISBN 978-0-19-954338-0

1 3 5 7 9 10 8 6 4 2

To human rights defenders everywhere

CONTENTS

PART 1 INSTITUTIONS AND PROCEDURES

PART 2 CONVENTION RIGHTS

PART 3   REFLECTIONS

FOREWORD

It is once again a great pleasure to welcome this new edition, a fully revised and up-to-date text on the European Convention on Human Rights.

Thoroughly revised by Robin White and Clare Ovey, this book is an extremely usable guide to the Strasbourg system, and a very clear survey of the case-law of the European Court of Human Rights. Avoiding excessive detail, it rightly concentrates on the principles derived from the case-law. As the book demonstrates, the Court has succeeded in treating the Convention as what it has called 'a living instrument', adapting it where appropriate to changing circumstances.

The Convention was fortunately drawn up in broad terms, which lend themselves to an evolving interpretation that can take account of social change and of the remarkable extension of the Convention system to virtually the whole of Europe.

Indeed this book, since it also traces the historical development of the Convention system and its case-law, also tells a remarkable story, recording as it does the extraordinary progress since my first edition was written 35 years ago. At that time, when the system was little known, when acceptance by Member States was optional and few had in fact accepted, it would not have seemed conceivable that there is today a Court of Human Rights with compulsory and automatic jurisdiction over an undivided Europe—and indeed beyond Europe, since the boundaries of the Council of Europe now extend deep into Asia. And the European system of protection of human rights has become a model which other regions of the world have sought to follow.

But, as the authors also show, the success of the European human rights system, reflected in its continuing expansion, has come to threaten its very future. The Council of Europe now has approaching 50 Member States with a total population of many hundreds of millions. While the Court continues to strive valiantly with its ever-increasing caseload, the system is near breaking-point.

Although, as the book relates, much has been done in recent years to improve the system, urgent reforms are still needed. More effective procedures are also needed within the Member States: the Strasbourg system is, after all, as the Court has stressed, a subsidiary one, to be used only where there is a failure at the national level.

It will not be easy to find the right package of reforms, but it is essential to do so if the system is to survive.

This book should therefore be seen as a spur to action, as well as a major contribution to the study of the European system of protection of human rights.

Francis G. Jacobs

September 2009

PREFACE TO THE FIFTH EDITION

Much of the work on the preparation of this fifth edition has coincided with the sixtieth anniversary of the founding of the Council of Europe, and the fiftieth anniversary of the establishment of the Strasbourg Court. There has also been something of an explosion in the case-law; the Court gave its 10,000th judgment in 2008. The Court has reached impressive levels of productivity, and yet also has a large backlog of cases. This indicates just how important the European Convention and its Court is for those within the jurisdiction of the Contracting Parties. A solution to the missing ratification by the Russian Federation to Protocol 14 has been found in the imaginative Protocol 14bis, which will enable the Court to make the most of its slender resources. There are two strands which can be identified from a global view of the applications made to the Court in recent years. For some States, most notably Russia, Turkey, Romania, and Ukraine, basic requirements of the Convention are not being met within the national legal orders, and they are producing very large numbers of applications. Elsewhere, the numbers are not so high, and many applications are concerned with novel questions relating to the interpretation and application of Convention rights. Yet overall probably something in the region of 70 per cent of admissible cases are repetitive and can be determined by the application of well-established Convention principles. Such cases could, and should, be resolved within the national legal orders. Such is the context in which this edition has been prepared.

As with previous editions, this book is explicitly about the European Convention as seen from Strasbourg rather than its implementation in any particular State. It continues to use as its main reference point the public voice of the Court in its judgments on the merits and its decisions on admissibility. Our overall aim has been to provide an accessible and readable account of the current state of Convention case-law, which focuses on the key principles which that case-law establishes. As the case-law grows, such synthesis strikes us as having an increasing role to play in ensuring an accurate overview of the content of Convention rights. In addition to the restructuring of the book, we have both been struck by the need to recast much material in the light of case-law developments. Inevitably, the book has increased in length, though we have strived to retain a length of text which does not overwhelm the reader with too much detail. We are both supporters of the Strasbourg Court, and have focused on the achievements of this pan-European system of adjudication of human rights questions. We hope our enthusiasm for the Court has not led us to be uncritical where the case-law is not in an entirely satisfactory state. It should be remembered that the role of the Strasbourg Court is casuistic in the sense that it does not control its case-law; it makes determinations on the merits of all those applications which it finds to be admissible. For big questions, it does have the mechanism of the Grand Chamber to bring the minds of a larger group of judges to such questions. It is perhaps not surprising that judgments of the Grand Chamber are less likely to be unanimous than decisions of Chambers.

In response to feedback from users of the book, for which we are grateful, and in response to the developing case-law, we have made some changes to the structure of the book. Institutional and procedural material has now been gathered together in the first part of the book. We have, however, drafted chapter 1 in such a way that it provides all the essential background for those who want to move directly from this overview to consideration of Convention rights, rather than to examine procedures in detail. There has also been some consolidation of material previously in chapters of their own; for example, the material on derogations and reservations has been brought together in a single chapter. The first chapter in the second part of the book, on Convention rights, is about Article 13, which requires Contracting Parties to have a system of remedies for arguable violations of Convention rights within their national legal orders. If all Contracting Parties fully ensured this Convention right, the burden of cases coming before the Strasbourg Court would be dramatically reduced. Its location as the first chapter on Convention rights also emphasizes the subsidiary role of the Strasbourg system. The continuing development of the case-law under Article 8 has led us to split this material over two chapters: the first deals with family life and the second with private life. It should, however, be remembered in reading these chapters that the Court still finds inspiration in reading Article 8 as a whole. One area informs the other in this field. Apart from these changes we have retained a structure which relates our synthesis and analysis to individual articles of the Convention and its Protocols. We continue to believe that this is the most effective way to present Convention rights to those coming to a study of the Convention as a whole for the first time.

The preparation of the first draft of every chapter of this new edition has fallen to Robin White, because of the time Clare Ovey had available given her work at the Court. Clare Ovey has, however, read and commented on every draft chapter, and provided significant input into the revision of those early drafts. We both take joint responsibility for the final text you have before you. Francis Jacobs continues to display a paternal pride in a work he started in 1975. His support and encouragement are much appreciated. We are both grateful to colleagues who have both consciously and unconsciously contributed to the preparation of this new edition through their responses to ideas we have tried out on them. It is important to stress that we both write in our personal capacities. Clare Ovey is a Head of Division at the Court and the views expressed in this book are her own and not in any sense those of the Court. Robin White holds a part-time judicial office as a Deputy Judge of the Upper Tribunal, and in so far as there are any matters which overlap with his judicial function, any views expressed are again purely personal and do not necessarily represent the views of the Upper Tribunal.

The text is intended to be up to date to 1 September 2009.

Robin White
Clare Ovey
Leicester and Strasbourg
September 2009

A NOTE ON CITATION CONVENTIONS

COMMISSION DECISIONS AND REPORTS

These are cited by application number in roman, followed by the names of the parties in italics and the date of the decision or report, and, where the decision or report is reported, the relevant report reference.

Example: App. 10581/83, *Norris and National Gay Federation v Ireland*, Decision of 16 May 1984, (1984) 44 DR 132.

COURT JUDGMENTS AND DECISIONS

JUDGMENTS

Older judgments of the Court were give a Series number, but for more modern judgments this practice has been abandoned.

In every case the date of the judgment is given. Where there is a Series number this is used. The application number is also given in parentheses and in roman after the names of the parties to the case. Judgments of the Grand Chamber are indicated by an annotation in square brackets after the date.

Where the case is reported in the *European Human Rights Reports*, a reference to those reports is also given. Where a case is also reported in the Court's official reports, published by Carl Heymanns Verlag KG, this reference is also given in the form recommended by the Strasbourg Court, namely ECHR [Year]-[Part] So a reference reading ECHR 2005-I would indicate that the judgment is reported in Part I of the official reports for the year 2005. A citation ending in 'nyr' means that the judgment will be reported in the official reports but that the case has not yet been allocated to a specific issue of the reports for that year.

Examples:

Cruz Varas v Sweden, (App. 15576/89), 20 March 1991, Series A No 201, (1992) 14 EHRR 1.

Mamatkulov and Askarov v Turkey, (Apps. 46827/99 and 46951/99), 4 February 2005 [GC], (2005) 41 EHRR 494, ECHR 2005-I.

DECISIONS

The Court is now responsible for admissibility decisions as well as judgments. Admissibility decisions are listed separately from judgments, but the structure of the reference follows the same principles: names of the parties followed by the application number and the date of the decision. If there is a report available that is given. The words 'Decision of' appear before the date to indicate that this is an admissibility decision rather than a judgment.

Example: Senator Lines v Austria, Belgium, Denmark, Finland, France, Germany, Greece, Ireland, Italy, Luxembourg, the Netherlands, Portugal, Spain, Sweden and the United Kingdom, (App. 56672/00), Decision of 10 March 2004 [GC] (2004) 39 EHRR SE3, ECHR 2004-IV

Note that nearly all Court decisions and judgments are available on the Court's database HUDOC; see http://echr.coe.int/echr/en/hudoc.

TABLE OF JUDGMENTS AND DECISIONS
OF THE COURT OF HUMAN RIGHTS

TABLE OF DECISIONS AND REPORTS OF THE COMMISSION OF HUMAN RIGHTS

TABLE OF TREATIES AND RELATED DOCUMENTS

References in **bold** indicate that the Article is reproduced in full

MISCELLANEOUS

EUROPE

CYPRUS

TABLE OF CASES

TABLE OF CASES BEFORE THE EUROPEAN COURT OF JUSTICE (ECJ)

ABBREVIATIONS

AC	Appeal Court
AJCL	*American Journal of Comparative Law*
AJIL	*American Journal of International Law*
BYIL	*British Yearbook of International Law*
CD	Collection of Decisions of the Commission of Human Rights
CLP	*Current Legal Problems*
CML Rev	*Common Market Law Review*
Contracting Parties	Parties to the European Convention on Human Rights
Crim LR	*Criminal Law Review*
CSCE	Conference on Security and Co-operation in Europe
CUP	Cambridge University Press
DH	*Droits de l'Homme*
DR	Decisions and Reports of the Commission of Human Rights
ELRev	*European Law Review*
EC	European Community
ECHR	European Convention on Human Rights
ECHR	(in citations to decisions and judgments) Reports of Judgments and Decisions of the European Court of Human Rights, Carl Heymanns Verlag KG.
ECR	European Court Reports
EEC	European Economic Community
EHRLR	*European Human Rights Law Review*
EHRR	European Human Rights Reports
EJIL	*European Journal of International Law*
ELJ	*European Law Journal*
EPL	*European Public Law*
ETS	European Treaty Series
European J of Int'l L	*European Journal of International Law*
EWHC	England and Wales: High Court
GC	Grand Chamber
HRLJ	*Human Rights Law Journal*
HRLRev	*Human Rights Law Review*
HRQ	*Human Rights Quarterly*
HUDOC	HUDOC database: http://echr.coe.int/echr/en/hudoc
ICCPR	International Covenant on Civil and Political Rights
ICLQ	*International and Comparative Law Quarterly*
ILJ	*Industrial Law Journal*

ILO	International Labour Organisation
KCLJ	*King's College Law Journal*
LIEI	*Legal Issues of European Integration*
LQR	*Law Quarterly Review*
Luxembourg Court	Court of Justice of the European Communities
Member States	Member States of the European Union
MJ	*Maastricht Journal of European and Comparative Law*
MLR	*Modern Law Review*
MUP	Manchester University Press
NATO	North Atlantic Treaty Organisation
NILR	*Netherlands International Law Review*
NQHR	*Netherlands Quarterly of Human Rights*
OUP	Oxford University Press
PKK	Parti Karkerani Kurdistan (Kurdistan Workers' Party)
PL	*Public Law*
SCR	Supreme Court Reports (Canada)
Strasbourg Court	European Court of Human Rights
Strasbourg organs	Commission, Court, and Committee of Ministers
UN GAOR	*United Nations General Assembly Official Records*
UNESCO	United Nations Educational, Scientific, and Cultural Organisation
WLR	Weekly Law Reports
Yearbook	*Yearbook of the European Convention on Human Rights*
YEL	*Yearbook of European Law*

PART 1

INSTITUTIONS AND PROCEDURES

1

CONTEXT, BACKGROUND, AND INSTITUTIONS

CONTEXT

Although the European Convention was a direct response to a global war which had included the horrors of the holocaust, its origins also belong to a line in the development of human rights which can be traced back much further.[1] It is linked to two centuries of political thought associated with the ideas expressed in the American Declaration of Independence and the French Declaration of the Rights of Man. But it can also be viewed in the context of the much longer struggle to secure respect for personal autonomy, the inherent dignity of persons, and the equality of all men and women.[2] The political philosophy and human rights agenda of the Allied Powers after the Second World War shaped both the selection of rights protected and the machinery for their protection. The United Nations Charter had taken a giant step forward in the protection of human rights in acknowledging in Articles 55 and 56 that the General Assembly should undertake responsibility for ensuring that all members of the United Nations kept the pledge in Article 55 to promote 'universal respect for, and observance of, human rights and fundamental freedoms for all without distinction as to race, sex, language or religion.' The recognition that the way in which a state treats its nationals is a matter for international concern and action was ground-breaking, and paved the way for the introduction of international human rights enforcement mechanisms. There was, however, no catalogue of human rights and fundamental freedoms. Within the United Nations, such a catalogue was established in the Universal Declaration of Human Rights.[3] The rights protected in the European Convention draw their

---

[1] See generally P. Lauren, *The Evolution of International Human Rights. Visions Seen* (University of Pennsylvania Press, Philadelphia 2003); M. Ishay, *The History of Human Rights. From Ancient Times to the Globalization Era* (University of California Press, Berkeley 2004); and C. Tomuschat, *Human Rights: Between Idealism and Realism* (OUP, Oxford 2003). See also J. Donnelly, 'Human rights: a new standard of civilization' (1998) 74 *International Affairs* 1.

[2] For a discussion of values and human rights, see D. Feldman, *Civil Liberties and Human Rights in England and Wales* (2nd edn OUP, Oxford 2002), Part I, and H. Fenwick, *Civil Liberties and Human Rights* (4th edn Routledge Cavendish, London 2007), ch.1, and the materials cited there. For a critical account of human rights adjudication under the Convention, see G. Beck, 'Human rights adjudication under the ECHR between value pluralism and essential contestability', [2008] EHRLR 214.

[3] See below, this chapter.

inspiration from the Universal Declaration, but do not simply duplicate the rights referred to there.

There were twin concerns which led the Council of Europe to seize the moment in preparing the European Convention. The first was to provide a means through which it was believed that the most serious human rights violations which had occurred during the Second World War could be avoided in the future. The second was to protect states from Communist subversion. This explains, in part, the constant references to values and principles that are necessary in a democratic society, though the precise nature of those values is nowhere described or defined in the Convention text itself. Seizing the moment and securing early agreement among the twelve States[4] which signed the European Convention on 4 November 1950 meant that compromises had to be made in the rights included in the main body of the Convention. Reading the *travaux préparatoires* provides a salutary reminder of the context in which the text of the Convention was prepared.[5] In order to secure speedy acceptance of the text, the rights selected for inclusion were broadly uncontroversial and were related directly to events of the then recent past. In the course of deliberations in the Consultative Assembly, Pierre-Henri Teitgen[6] said:

Who does not appreciate that these rights are fundamental, essential rights, and that there is no State which can, if it abuses them, claim to respect natural law and the fundamental principle of human dignity? Is there any State which can, by violating these rights and fundamental freedoms, claim that its country enjoys a democratic regime?[7]

The result was the production of a Convention containing civil and political rights considered essential to the provision of a bulwark against the spread of communism, and a guarantee against a repetition of the horrors of the Second World War. Further rights would be added later through a number of protocols.[8] But the organs charged with the interpretation and application of the rights set out in the Convention have never regarded them as static. The Convention is 'a living instrument'.[9] This has resulted in an interpretation which seeks to ensure that the requirements of the Convention are interpreted in a present day context and not locked into a moment in history following the Second World War.

---

[4] Belgium, Denmark, France, Germany, Iceland, Ireland, Italy, Luxembourg, Netherlands, Norway, Turkey and the United Kingdom.

[5] For a detailed consideration of the background to particular provisions of the Convention, see Council of Europe, *Collected Edition of the Travaux Préparatoires of the European Convention on Human Rights* (Martinus Nijhoff, The Hague 1975 to 1985). See also G. Marston, 'The United Kingdom's Part in the Preparation of the European Convention on Human Rights' (1993) 42 ICLQ 796; and A. W. Simpson, *Human Rights and the End of Empire. Britain and the Genesis of the European Convention* (OUP, Oxford 2004).

[6] One of the key figures involved in the drafting of the European Convention.

[7] Council of Europe, *Collected Edition of the Travaux Préparatoires,* Vol. I (Martinus Nijhoff, The Hague 1975), 268–70.

[8] For a more detailed but manageable discussion of the place of the European Convention in the development of the protection of human rights, see M. Janis, R. Kay, and A. Bradley, *European Human Rights Law. Text and Materials* (3rd edn OUP, Oxford 2008), 3–24.

[9] See particularly material on the interpretation of the Convention in ch.4 below.

THE STRUCTURE AND AIMS OF THE COUNCIL OF EUROPE

After the Second World War, European movements arose, simultaneously and spontaneously, throughout the European democracies. They arose in response to the threat to fundamental human rights and to political freedom which had all but overwhelmed the European continent in the War, and which reappeared after the War in new forms of totalitarianism. The International Committee of Movements for European Unity, and its Congress at The Hague in May 1948, were the foundation of the Council of Europe established on 5 May 1949 and the drafting by its Contracting Parties of the Convention for the Protection of Human Rights and Fundamental Freedoms of 4 November 1950,[10] generally known as the European Convention on Human Rights. The Convention reflected the concerns and objects of this novel international organization,[11] as set out in its Constitution, the Statute of the Council of Europe.[12] In the Preamble to the Statute, the Contracting States reaffirmed:

their devotion to the spiritual and moral values which are the common heritage of their peoples and the true source of individual freedom, political liberty and the rule of law, principles which form the basis of all genuine democracy.

The aim of the Council of Europe was, and remains, 'to achieve a greater unity between its Members for the purpose of safeguarding and realizing the ideals and principles which are their common heritage and facilitating their economic and social progress',[13] and this aim was to be pursued 'through the organs of the Council by discussion of questions of common concern and by agreements and common action in economic, social, cultural, scientific, legal and administrative matters and in the maintenance and further realization of human rights and fundamental freedoms.'[14]

The current political mandate of the Council of Europe was established at a summit which took place in Warsaw in 2005.[15] The agenda is:

- to protect human rights, pluralist democracy and the rule of law;
- to promote awareness and encourage the development of Europe's cultural identity and diversity;
- to find common solutions to the challenges facing European society: such as discrimination against minorities, xenophobia, intolerance, bioethics

---

[10] ETS 5. The Convention entered into force on 3 September 1953.

[11] See generally, Council of Europe, *Manual of the Council of Europe. Its Structure, Functions and Achievements* (Stevens, London 1970). See also www.coe.int.

[12] ETS 1.   [13] Art. 1(a) of the Statute.

[14] Art. 1(b). For recent material on the general contribution of the Council of Europe to the development of a common legal system for European states, see Council of Europe, *Towards a pan-European legal area* (Council of Europe Press, Strasbourg 2005); Council of Europe, *European judicial systems—facts and figures* (Strasbourg, 2005); and Council of Europe, *The early settlement of disputes and the role of judges* (Council of Europe Press, Strasbourg 2005).

[15] www.coe.int/t/dcr/summit/20050517_decl_varsovie_en.asp.

and cloning, terrorism, trafficking in human beings, organized crime and corruption, cybercrime, violence against children;

- to consolidate democratic stability in Europe by backing political, legislative and constitutional reform.

The Council operates through three organs. The decision-making body is the Committee of Ministers composed of the foreign ministers of the Contracting Parties. The Parliamentary Assembly,[16] composed of 318 representatives[17] drawn from the national parliaments, is the deliberative body whose debates can lead to recommendations made to the Committee of Ministers. The third organ was added in 1994 and is the Congress of Local and Regional Authorities of Europe, which has consultative functions and is composed of representatives of local and regional authorities. The work of these organs is supported by a Secretariat, headed by a Secretary-General appointed by the Parliamentary Assembly on the recommendation of the Committee of Ministers.[18]

Article 3 of the Statute requires that every Contracting Party 'must accept the principles of the rule of law and of the enjoyment by all persons within its jurisdiction of human rights and fundamental freedoms.' Under Article 8, a Contracting Party which has seriously violated Article 3 of the Statute may be suspended from its rights of representation and requested by the Committee of Ministers to withdraw from the Council of Europe under Article 7 and, if it does not comply, may be expelled.[19] The uniqueness of these provisions lay in the fact that questions of human rights fell traditionally within the domestic jurisdiction of States, and were of concern to international law only if the interests of another State were affected, as, for example, by the treatment of that State's nationals. History had demonstrated the inadequacy of those traditional concepts of international law and State sovereignty which made the protection of individuals the exclusive prerogative of the State of which they were nationals. Their rights may require protection, above all, against their own State. The creation of the Council of Europe and the adoption of the Convention on Human Rights are an acknowledgement that the protection of human rights is viewed as an indispensable element of European democracy.

The principle of respect for human rights had been established in international law by the Charter of the United Nations.[20] The Universal Declaration of Human Rights, adopted by the General Assembly of the United Nations on 10 December 1948, proclaims as a 'common standard of achievement' an extensive list of human rights, which, although the Declaration is not legally binding as such, is an authoritative guide to the interpretation of the Charter.[21] Further work in the United Nations, which led to the

---

[16] Referred to as the Consultative Assembly in the Statute of the Council of Europe, ETS 1: see Arts. 22–35. It styled itself the Parliamentary Assembly in 1974. In February 1994 the Committee of Ministers decided to use the denomination 'Parliamentary Assembly' in all future Council of Europe documents.

[17] With 318 substitutes.

[18] Statute of the Council of Europe, ETS 1, Arts. 36 and 37; and see below, this chapter.

[19] It was in consequence of proceedings started under this provision, following an initiative in the Consultative Assembly, that Greece announced in 1969 its withdrawal from the Council of Europe and denounced the Convention. Greece was readmitted in 1974.

[20] See, in particular, Arts. 55 and 56 of the United Nations Charter.

[21] While the Universal Declaration itself is not a binding instrument of international law, the principles it enshrines may acquire legal force as the 'general principles of law recognized by civilized nations' under

adoption in 1966 of two Covenants, the Covenant on Economic, Social and Cultural Rights and the Covenant on Civil and Political Rights, drew a distinction between two different classes of fundamental rights. Social and economic rights, although they appear in the Universal Declaration, are less universal in the sense that they constitute standards to be attained, depending on the level of economic development. They require action by governments, whereas civil and political rights often require protection against executive action. Within the Council of Europe, social and economic rights are mainly the concern of the European Social Charter,[22] which provides for progressive implementation and for supervision by the examination of periodic reports on progress achieved. The European Committee of Social Rights is the body responsible for monitoring compliance in the States party to the Charter under a collective complaints procedure which came into effect in 1998.[23]

The Council of Europe today consists of 47 countries.[24] There are five countries with observer status.[25] The membership of the Council of Europe is broad and now encompasses the new democracies of central and eastern Europe. New members of the Council of Europe are required to accede to the European Convention, which in its form as amended by Protocol 11 carries with it recognition both of an individual right of application to the Strasbourg Court and of a wholly judicial system for the protection of human rights.

THE CONTENT OF THE EUROPEAN CONVENTION

Human rights can be defined in terms of generations. This taxonomy was introduced by Karel Vasak, when he was Director of the Human Rights and Peace Division of UNESCO. First generation rights are civil and political rights, while second generation rights are social and cultural rights. The third generation of human rights consists of those rights that concern people collectively and include the right to development, to peace, and to a clean environment. Some commentators[26] now refer to a fourth generation of human rights, but there is no consistency over the content of this

Art. 38(1)(c) of the Statute of the International Court of Justice, or as customary law reflecting the general practice of States (see Art. 38(1)(b) of the Statute), or even as 'a peremptory norm of general international law' (*jus cogens*), that is, a norm accepted and recognized by the international community of States as a whole as a norm from which no derogation is permitted (see Art. 53 of the Vienna Convention on the Law of Treaties).

[22] The Charter entered into force on 26 February 1965. See generally D. Harris, *The European Social Charter* (University of Virginia Press, Charlottesville 1984); D. Gomien, D. Harris, and L. Zwaak, *Law and Practice of the European Convention on Human Rights and the European Social Charter* (Council of Europe Press, Strasbourg 1996); and *Fundamental Social Rights: Case Law of the European Social Charter* (Council of Europe Press, Strasbourg 2000).

[23] See www.coe.int/t/dghl/monitoring/socialcharter/default_EN.asp.

[24] There is one applicant country, Belarus, but its application for membership has been suspended because of concerns about human rights in the country.

[25] The Holy See, Canada, Japan, Mexico, and the United States.

[26] See, for example, D. Otto, 'Rethinking the "universality" of Human Rights Law' (1997) 29 *Columbia Human Rights Law Review* 1.

latest generational identification of human rights, save that they tend to relate to the impact of scientific and technological developments. Examples are communication and information rights, and rights relating to developments in biotechnology. It is sometimes said that it is the inter-generational character of these rights which constitutes the basis for their status as a generation of rights.[27]

The European Convention on Human Rights guarantees, for the most part, civil and political rights. However, Article 1 of the First Protocol, which protects property rights, and Article 2, which guarantees the right to education, are limited exceptions to this principle. Section I of the European Convention spells out, generally in more detailed form, most of the basic civil and political rights contained in the Universal Declaration, while the First, Fourth, Sixth, Seventh, Twelfth, and Thirteenth Protocols guarantee certain additional rights and freedoms. The remaining Protocols amended procedural provisions of the Convention. Finally, Protocol 14 paves the way for the next set of changes to improve the efficiency of the measures of implementation under the Convention.[28] The rights set out in the Convention and Protocols are thus derived essentially from the Universal Declaration. The content of these rights, and the circumstances in which limitations might legitimately be imposed on them, are often made more specific.

However, not every Contracting Party has ratified every provision of every protocol to the Convention. As at 1 September 2009, only 14 of the 47 Contracting Parties have ratified all substantive provisions of the Protocols to the Convention. This indicates that, although the provisions of the Convention and its Protocols may seem to be statements of the most basic human rights, they nevertheless present some issues which are controversial within certain Contracting Parties. For example, the United Kingdom has not even signed Protocol 7, which contains rights in relation to migration, the criminal law, and equality between spouses, or Protocol 12 on the general prohibition of discrimination. It has signed but not ratified Protocol 4 which is concerned with the prohibition of imprisonment for debt and with provisions related to migration. In both cases, it is concerns about migration rights which explain the absence of ratification of these protocols.

IS THERE A HIERARCHY OF RIGHTS?

There is no formal hierarchy of rights set out in the Convention; this means that the Convention text does not specify a system under which priority is given to one right over another if they are in conflict. But it has been accepted that there will be very many occasions when a balance has to be achieved between conflicting interests, usually those of the individual balanced against those of the community, but occasionally the

---

[27] Though that is true of rights relating to the environment. Such rights transcend the present generation; what is done now may have a significant impact on future generations.

[28] The Protocol has been ratified by all Contracting Parties except the Russian Federation. See now also Protocol 14bis, which seeks to implement certain provisions of Protocol 14 on a state by state basis. Both are discussed in more detail in ch.25.

rights of one individual must be balanced against those of another.[29] This is reflected in the internal structure of many of the Convention rights.[30]

Although there is no hierarchy of rights, the rights set out in the Convention can be split into two categories: unqualified rights, some of which are non-derogable, and qualified rights.

Unqualified rights are the right to life, subject to the exceptions listed in the article, in Article 2; the prohibition of torture, inhuman or degrading treatment in Article 3; the prohibition of slavery and forced labour as defined in Article 4; the right to liberty and security in Article 5; the right to a fair trial in Article 6; the prohibition on punishment without law in Article 7; the right to marry in Article 12; the right to an effective remedy in Article 13; the prohibition of discrimination in Article 14; the right to education and the right to free elections in Article 3 of Protocol 1; and the prohibition of the death penalty (except in time of war or of imminent threat of war) in Protocol 6; and the complete prohibition of the death penalty in Protocol 13.

Some of these rights are said to be absolute in the sense that no derogations under Article 15 are permitted; these are to be found in Articles 2, 3, 4, and 7, and in Protocols 6, 7, and 13. In addition the Strasbourg Court has referred to certain of the Convention rights as 'core' or 'fundamental' rights. These include the right to life, the right not to be tortured, and the right to liberty.[31] Interim measures to protect the position of the applicant are usually available only where there is a risk of irreparable damage to one of the 'core' Convention rights.[32]

Qualified rights arise where the Convention specifies a right, but goes on to indicate that a Contracting Party may interfere with it in order to secure certain interests. Such rights include the right to respect for private and family life in Article 8; freedom of thought, conscience, and religion in Article 9; freedom of expression in Article 10; freedom of assembly and association in Article 11; the protection of property in Article 1 of Protocol 1; and freedom of movement in Article 2 of Protocol 4.

Generally, the person alleging a violation of a right protected by the Convention has the burden of establishing the violation on the balance of probabilities,[33] but where an

---

[29] As in *Evans v United Kingdom* (App. 6339/05), 10 April 2007 [GC], (2008) 46 EHRR 728, ECHR 2007-IV, §73.

[30] See H. Fenwick, 'Clashing Rights, the Welfare of the Child and the Human Rights Act' (2004) 67 MLR 889; E. Brems (ed.), *Conflicts between Fundamental Rights* (Intersentia, Antwerp 2008); and J. Bomhoff, '"The rights and freedoms of others": the ECHR and its peculiar category of conflicts between individual fundamental rights', ssrn.com/abstract=1031682. For a discussion in a case of the balancing of rights, see *Von Hannover v Germany* (App. 59320/00), 24 June 2004, (2005) 40 EHRR 1, ECHR 2004-VI, §§58–81.

[31] *Aksoy v Turkey*, (App. 21987/93), 18 December 1996, (1997) 23 EHRR 553, ECHR 1996-VI, §§62 and 76; *A and others v United Kingdom*, (App. 3455/05), 19 February 2009 [GC], (2009) 49 EHRR 29, ECHR 2009-nyr, §§126 and 162; and *Jalloh v Germany*, (App. 54810/00), 11 July 2006 [GC], (2007) 44 EHRR 667, ECHR 2006-IX, §§104 and 107.

[32] See *Mamatkulov and Askarov v Turkey*, (Apps. 46827/99 and 46951/99), 4 February 2005 [GC], (2005) 41 EHRR 494, ECHR 2005-I, §108, and see further ch.2 below.

[33] Though where allegations relating to violations of Arts. 2 and 3 are concerned, the standard required is higher. The Court has, however, rejected the unqualified application of standards of proof applicable in the national legal orders.

interference can be shown with one of the qualified rights, it will be for the respondent State to establish on the balance of probabilities that its interference is justified. This will involve showing that the interference was in accordance with the law,[34] that the aim of the interference was to protect a recognized interest, and that the interference was necessary in a democratic society. This final criterion will require the respondent State to show that the interference with the qualified right was the minimum needed to secure the legitimate aim. This is the application of the doctrine of proportionality.[35]

THE SYSTEM OF PROTECTION

Protocol 11 to the Convention[36] entered into force on 1 November 1998 and restructured the institutional framework of the Convention. But an understanding of the system of protection prior to 1 November 1998 remains necessary because decisions made by the Strasbourg organs prior to the change continue to have an effect as authorities on the interpretation and application of the Convention.

THE 'OLD' SYSTEM OF PROTECTION

The Convention created two organs 'to ensure the observance of the engagements undertaken by the High Contracting Parties':[37] the European Commission of Human Rights and the European Court of Human Rights. The main function of these two part-time organs, sometimes collectively referred to as the Strasbourg organs,[38] was to deal with applications made by States and by individuals alleging violations of the Convention. Under former Article 24, any Contracting Party could refer to the Commission any alleged breach of the provisions of the Convention by another Contracting Party. Under former Article 25, the Commission could receive applications from any person, non-governmental organization, or group of individuals claiming to be the victim of a violation by one of the Contracting Parties of the rights set forth in the Convention and any relevant Protocols. Initially, acceptance of the jurisdiction of the Commission to receive individual petitions was optional, but in the 1990s came to be an expected requirement of participation in the Convention system.

---

[34] In the sense that there is a recognized legal basis in national law for the interference.

[35] See further chs.4 and 14 below.

[36] See N. Rowe and V. Schlette, 'The Protection of Human Rights in Europe after the Eleventh Protocol to the ECHR' (1998) 23 ELRev HR/1; A. Drzemczewski, 'The European Human Rights Convention: Protocol No 11—Entry into force and first year of application' (2000) 21 HRLJ 1; A. Drzemczewski, 'A major overhaul of the European Human Rights Convention control mechanism: Protocol No. 11' in *Collected Courses of the Academy of European Law,* Vol. VI (Martinus Nijhoff, Florence 1997) at 121; H. Schermers, 'The Eleventh Protocol to the European Convention on Human Rights' (1994) 19 ELRev 367; H. Schermers, 'Adaptation of the 11th Protocol to the European Convention on Human Rights' (1995) 20 ELRev 559; and H. Schermers, 'Election of Judges to the European Court of Human Rights' (1998) 23 ELRev 568.

[37] Former Art. 19 ECHR.

[38] Together with the Committee of Ministers: see below, this chapter.

The procedure differs depending on whether the application is made under Article 24 or 25; what follows describes the process in relation to individual applications under former Article 25.

Once an application was registered, the Commission first considered whether the application met the admissibility requirements, and made a *decision* on this question.[39] If the application was declared inadmissible, that was an end of the matter. If the application was declared admissible, the Commission went on to conduct an investigation into the merits of the complaint and to consider whether there had been a violation of the Convention. The result was a *report* from the Commission expressing an opinion[40] as to whether or not there had been a violation. The report was communicated on a confidential basis to the applicant and to the respondent State concerned and was delivered to the Committee of Ministers, the political organ of the Council of Europe. Throughout this time, attempts would have been made to secure a friendly settlement 'on the basis of respect for human rights'.[41]

Final decisions on cases on which the Commission had reported and which had not resulted in a friendly settlement were made by the Committee of Ministers, or the Court of Human Rights. Recognition of the jurisdiction of the Court was technically voluntary under former Article 46 of the Convention, but a clear expectation had arisen that Contracting Parties would recognize the competence of the Court.[42] Within three months of the transmission of the Commission report to the Committee of Ministers, the application could be referred to the Court by the Commission, the respondent State, or the Contracting Party whose national was alleged to be the victim.[43] The applicant had no standing to refer the application to the Court, unless the respondent State was a party to Protocol 9.[44] Where the respondent State had ratified Protocol 9, the applicant could refer the matter to the Court, but (unless it was also referred to the Court by the Commission or a State) it had first to be submitted to a panel of three judges, who could decide unanimously that the application should not be considered by the Court because it did not raise a serious question affecting the interpretation or application of the Convention.

If the case was referred to the Court and heard by it, there was a full judicial procedure, and even where Protocol 9 had not been ratified, some accommodations were made which allowed participation by the applicant, who could submit written pleadings and oral submissions at a hearing. The Court sat in plenary session or in Chambers of nine.[45] Decisions were made by a majority of the judges present and voting, with the President enjoying a casting vote if necessary. This was the judgment of the Court. Separate concurring or dissenting opinions could be attached to the judgment of the Court.

Those cases which were not referred to the Court within three months of transmission of the Commission's report to the Committee of Ministers were automatically

---

[39] See below, this chapter.   [40] This is not legally binding.
[41] Former Art. 28 ECHR.   [42] And this happened.   [43] Former Art. 48 ECHR.
[44] 24 Contracting Parties (not including the United Kingdom) ratified Protocol 9.
[45] Former Art. 43 ECHR.

decided by the Committee of Ministers. Latterly, the practice of the Committee of Ministers was to endorse the Commission report without any further investigation of the merits of the case. The use of a political organ was a compromise to ensure that all applications resulted in a final determination. In the early years, there were Contracting Parties which had not recognized the competence of the Court; even in respect of Contracting Parties who had accepted the Court's jurisdiction, a sizeable number of applications, particularly those involving repetitive violations (such as Italian length of proceedings cases), were not referred to the Court.

THE 'NEW' SYSTEM OF PROTECTION

Protocol 11 amended the Convention to make provision for a new wholly judicial system of determination of applications. The Commission and the Court were replaced from 1 November 1998 by a new permanent Court, which handles both the admissibility and merits phases of application. The Court is also charged with seeking to secure friendly settlement of matters before it.[46]

Inter-State complaints are made under Article 33. Since it was set up in 1959, the Court has delivered judgment in only three inter-State cases.[47] Such cases have invariably been politically motivated, and have had a highly-charged political content. The case brought by Ireland against the United Kingdom concerned the treatment of suspected terrorists in Northern Ireland.[48] The case brought by Cyprus against Turkey[49] raised questions concerning the Turkish intervention in Cyprus in July 1974. In March 2007, Georgia lodged an application against Russia concerning the alleged harassment of the Georgian immigrant population in Russia.[50] In August 2008, Georgia lodged a second inter-State application against Russian, complaining about the military intervention in South Ossetia.[51]

Individual applications are made to the Court under Article 34 and individuals have full standing before the Court. There has continued to be a filtering process by staff in the Registry of the Court before applications are registered. In the calendar year 2008, 49,850 applications were allocated to a decision body, and 14,800 disposed of administratively.[52] Applications which are registered are initially considered by a three-judge Committee which will consider whether the complaint meets the

---

[46] Art. 38(1)(b).

[47] *Ireland v United Kingdom*, (App. 5310/71), 18 January 1978, Series A No 25; (1979–80) 2 EHRR 25; ECHR 2001-IV; *Denmark v Turkey*, (App. 34382/97), 5 April 2000, (2000) 29 EHRR CD35; ECHR 2000-IV (struck out of the list); and *Cyprus v Turkey*, (App. 25781/94), 10 May 2001 [GC]; (2001) 35 EHRR 731; ECHR 2001-IV. A further seventeen inter-State applications were dealt with by the former Commission.

[48] *Ireland v United Kingdom*, (App. 5310/71), 18 January 1978, Series A No 25; (1979–80) 2 EHRR 25; ECHR 2001-IV.

[49] *Cyprus v Turkey* (App. 25781/94) 10 May 2001 [GC]; (2001) 35 EHRR 731; ECHR 2001-IV.

[50] *Georgia v Russia (I)*, (App. 13255/07), see Decision of 3 July 2009.

[51] *Georgia v Russia (II)*, (App. 38263/08).

[52] European Court of Human Rights, *Annual Report 2008* (Strasbourg 2009), 127.

Convention's admissibility criteria,[53] but the Committee can only rule an application to be inadmissible if it is unanimous.[54] The admissibility criteria have not changed with the amendments made by Protocol 11 and flow from the terms of Articles 34 and 35;[55] they involve the consideration of nine questions:

(1) Can the applicant claim to be a victim of a violation of a Convention right?

(2) Is the respondent State a party to the Convention?

(3) Have domestic remedies been exhausted?

(4) Is the application filed within the six-month time limit?

(5) Is the application signed?

(6) Has the application been brought before?

(7) Is the application compatible with the Convention?

(8) Is the application manifestly ill-founded?

(9) Is there an abuse of the right of petition?

Those cases which are not ruled inadmissible by the three-judge Committee are put before a seven-judge Chamber of the Court, which will include the judge sitting in respect of the respondent State. The Chamber will consider the written arguments of the parties, investigate the material facts if these are in contention, and may hear oral argument. This stage of the proceedings concludes with a decision whether the complaint is admissible[56] and whether a friendly settlement is possible.[57] There follows a consideration of the merits. In most cases the admissibility and merits phases are joined for reasons of judicial economy.

Certain cases of special difficulty can be relinquished or referred by a Chamber to a Grand Chamber of seventeen judges.[58]

The Contracting Parties undertake to abide by the final judgment[59] of the Court in any case to which they are parties.[60] The final judgment is transmitted to the Committee of Ministers whose sole role in the process is now to supervise the execution of judgments.[61]

---

[53] Arts. 27–8 ECHR. For a discussion of the conditions of admissibility, see ch.2.

[54] Art. 28 ECHR.

[55] Formerly Arts. 25 and 26.

[56] Note that it is open to the Chamber to conclude that the application is inadmissible by majority decision following the deliberations of the three-judge Committee which was not unanimous.

[57] Arts. 29 and 38, ECHR.

[58] Arts. 30–1 and 43 ECHR.

[59] A judgment by a Chamber becomes final (1) on expiry of the three-month period or (2) earlier if the parties announce that they have no intention of requesting a referral or (3) following a decision of the panel rejecting a request for referral to the Grand Chamber where an application for a referral is made.

[60] Art. 46(1).

[61] Art.46(2). There has in recent times been concern over the failure of Contracting States to implement final judgments. See T. Barkhuysen, M. van Emmerik, and P. van Kempen, *The Execution of Strasbourg and Geneva Human Rights Decisions in the National Legal Order* (Martinus Nijhoff, The Hague 1999).

THE ROLE OF THE SECRETARY-GENERAL
OF THE COUNCIL OF EUROPE

The Secretary-General is the senior official of the Council of Europe, elected for a period of five years by the Parliamentary Assembly from a list of candidates drawn up by the Committee of Ministers.[62] The Secretary-General is the depository for ratifications of the Convention[63] with all the duties that entails. Denunciations of the Convention and derogations permitted by the Convention, as well as any declarations required under Convention provisions, are filed with the Secretary-General.

The Secretary-General also has an important monitoring function under Article 52,[64] which provides:

On receipt of a request from the Secretary-General of the Council of Europe any High Contracting Party shall furnish an explanation of the manner in which its internal law ensures the effective implementation of any of the provisions of this Convention.

Reporting systems are, of course, common measures for securing implementation of human rights obligations.[65] Such procedures are proactive, requiring States to examine the state of their own law rather than reactive, requiring responses to alleged violations of international obligations. This kind of self-assessment or compliance audit can be very valuable if undertaken in the spirit required by the Convention.

Article 52 of the Convention is, however, silent on the circumstances in which the Secretary-General will exercise the powers given under the provision. The Secretary-General has stated that it is a matter entirely within 'his own responsibility and at his own discretion'.[66] Contracting Parties have acquiesced in this interpretation.

General practice to date has been to address requests to all Contracting Parties, but in recent years the Secretary-General has put individual questions to Moldova concerning Transdniestria, and to Russia concerning the situation in Chechnya. In October 1964 Contracting Parties were asked to report generally on how their legal

---

[62] Art. 36 of the Statute of the Council of Europe.

[63] Art. 59 ECHR.

[64] Formerly Art. 57. See generally, P. Mahoney, 'Does Article 57 of the European Convention on Human Rights serve any useful purpose?' in F. Matscher and H. Petzold (eds.), *Protecting Human Rights: The European Dimension. Studies in Honour of Gérard J. Wiarda* (Carl Heymanns Verlag, Köln 1988), at 373–93. See also J. Melander, 'Report on "Responses from the Organs of the European Convention including the Committee of Ministers"' and C. Zanghi, 'Written Communication on "Responsibilities Resulting for the Committee of Ministers and the Secretary General of the Council of Europe for the Implementation of the European Convention on Human Rights"' in Council of Europe, *Proceedings of the Sixth Colloquy about the European Convention on Human Rights, 13–16 November 1985* (Martinus Nijhoff, Dordrecht 1988), at 842–904 (esp. 892–904) and 920–64 (esp. 957–64) respectively. For a summary of activities under Article 52 of the Convention, see the annually produced *Yearbook of the European Convention on Human Rights*.

[65] See, for example, Art. 40 of the International Covenant on Civil and Political Rights; Arts. 16–22 of the International Covenant on Economic, Social and Cultural Rights; Arts. 22–3 of the Constitution of the International Labour Organisation; Arts. 42–3 of the American Convention on Human Rights; and Art. 62 of the African Charter on Human and Peoples' Rights.

[66] Statement of Secretary-General to the Legal Committee of the Consultative Assembly in Oslo on 29 August 1964, Council of Europe, *Collected Texts* (Council of Europe Press, Strasbourg 1987), 235–6.

systems guaranteed the rights protected in the Convention and First Protocol; in July 1970 on the implementation of the rights protected by Article 5(5); in April 1975 on the application of Articles 8, 9, 10, and 11; in March 1983 on the implementation of the Convention in respect of children and young persons placed in the care of institutions following a decision of the administrative or judicial authorities; and in July 1988 on the rights protected by Article 6(1) and (3).

The Secretary-General has compiled the responses received from the Contracting Parties and brought these to the notice of the Parliamentary Assembly, and more recently also to the Commission (until its abolition) and the Court.[67] The responses are not subject to any critical scrutiny.[68] The responses of the Contracting Parties are published, though each Contracting Party is consulted to seek its views on whether it would wish the information supplied by it not to be published. The Secretary-General has no standing to bring violations which might be evidenced in the responses from the Contracting Parties to the attention of the Court, though it would be open to any Contracting Party to the Convention to make a complaint under Article 33[69] provided that the admissibility conditions were met. In cases of the most serious violations, the matter could be referred to the Committee of Ministers with a view to its exercising its powers of suspension and expulsion under Articles 7 and 8 of the Statute of the Council of Europe.

A good example of a more recent initiative has been the enquiry into alleged secret detentions in the Contracting Parties of so-called 'high-value detainees' held by the United States. In November 2005, the Secretary-General, acting under Article 52, sent a questionnaire to all 46 Contracting Parties. The Article 52 inquiry was launched against the background of reports alleging involvement by Contracting Parties in unlawful deprivation of liberty of terrorist suspects and their transport in or through their territory by or at the instigation of foreign agencies; this has come to be known as 'secret detention', and 'extraordinary rendition'. In March 2006, the Secretary-General released his report based on the responses of 36 countries to the questionnaire, which was critical of the incomplete response of some Contracting Parties to the question enquiring whether any public officials had been involved in the unacknowledged deprivation of liberty of any individual, or transport of any individual while so deprived of their liberty. This prompted action within the Committee on Legal Affairs and Human Rights, and a detailed report was prepared for their consideration and presented in turn to the Parliamentary Assembly. The outcome, after further enquiries, was a recommendation of the Parliamentary Assembly declaring that it had established with a high degree of probability that secret detention centres operated by the Central Intelligence Agency of the United States had existed for some years in Poland

---

[67] Council of Europe, *Human Rights Information Sheet No. 21* H/INF(87)1, 95 and *Human Rights Information Sheet No. 23* H/INF(88)2, 59.

[68] Compare the procedure under Art. 40 of the International Covenant on Civil and Political Rights where the Human Rights Committee questions States on their responses. See generally, D. McGoldrick, *The Human Rights Committee* (OUP, Oxford 1991), ch.3.

[69] Formerly Art. 24.

and Romania. The recommendation also called on Contracting Parties to look into the need for democratic oversight of military intelligence services and foreign intelligence services operating on their territory.[70]

The role of the Secretary-General now overlaps to some extent with that of the Commissioner for Human Rights.

THE COMMISSIONER FOR HUMAN RIGHTS

The Commissioner for Human Rights is an office established by resolution of the Committee of Ministers.[71] The Commissioner[72] is elected by the Parliamentary Assembly and is charged with promoting education in, and awareness of, human rights in the territories of the Contracting Parties. Additionally the Commissioner helps to promote the effective observance and full enjoyment of human rights as embodied in a variety of Council of Europe instruments, as well as identifying possible shortcomings in the law and practice of the Contracting Parties in relation to the protection of human rights. But the Commissioner may not take up any individual complaints. Particular activities to date have included studies of the human rights situation in Georgia, in Chechnya, and in Kosovo. A substantial annual report is submitted to the Committee of Ministers and to the Parliamentary Assembly. The Commissioner may also issue recommendations, opinions,[73] and reports on any matters within his competence.[74]

The current Commissioner has adopted a number of major themes[75] coupled with the publication of a whole series of viewpoints on current issues.[76]

The Commissioner also makes both contact visits and assessment visits to countries who are members of the Council of Europe. Contact visits aim at strengthening the relationships with the authorities and looking into one or several specific issues, while the main goal of assessment visits is to give a comprehensive review of the effectiveness of human rights protection. Each assessment visit is completed by the publication

---

[70] Recommendation 1801 (2007); Text adopted by the Assembly on 27 June 2007 (23rd Sitting). For more detail see www.coe.int/T/E/Com/Files/Events/2006-cia/.

[71] Resolution (99) 50 of 7 May 1999, adopted by the Committee of Ministers at its 104th session.

[72] Currently Thomas Hammarberg, a Swedish national, elected in 2005 for a non-renewable term of six years beginning on 1 April 2006.

[73] See, for example, Opinion 1/2002 on certain aspects of the United Kingdom 2001 derogation from Article 5 paragraph 1 of the European Convention on Human Rights, 28 August 2002, Comm DH(2002)8 requested by the United Kingdom's Parliamentary Joint Committee on Human Rights.

[74] See generally www.coe.int/t/commissioner/About/welcome_en.asp.

[75] (1) Cooperation on national human rights structures; (2) eradicating discrimination; (3) the protection and development of an enabling environment for human rights defenders; and (4) the rights of migrants.

[76] Those written in 2007 have been collected in a compilation: T. Hammarberg, *Human Rights in Europe: no ground for complacency* (Council of Europe Press, Strasbourg 2008), and provide an interesting overview of some pressure points in relation to human rights protection in Europe.

of a report containing conclusions and relevant recommendations to help redress shortcomings.[77] Some of the reports are made public on the Commissioner's website.

Since he was appointed in April 2006, Thomas Hammarberg has carried out assessment visits in Albania, Germany, Armenia, Austria, Azerbaijan, Bosnia and Herzegovina, Ireland, 'The former Yugoslav Republic of Macedonia', San Marino, Ukraine, and Montenegro.

OTHER HUMAN RIGHTS INSTRUMENTS OF THE COUNCIL OF EUROPE

Mention has already been made of the European Social Charter as the Council of Europe instrument which addresses economic, social, and cultural rights. However, there are now 203 Council of Europe treaties, many of which address human rights issues[78]—the following are of particular significance:

- the European Agreement relating to persons participating in proceedings of the European Commission and Court of Human Rights of 6 May 1969;[79]
- the European Agreement relating to persons participating in proceedings of the European Court of Human Rights of 5 March 1996;[80]
- the European Convention for the Prevention of Torture and Inhuman and Degrading Treatment of 26 November 1987 and its two Protocols;[81]
- the European Charter for Regional or Minority Languages of 5 November 1992;[82]
- the Framework Convention for the Protection of National Minorities of 1 February 1995;[83]
- the Convention on Action against Trafficking in Human Beings;[84] and
- the Convention on the Protection of Children against Sexual Exploitation and Sexual Abuse.[85]

Though this work is concerned with the European Convention on Human Rights, the contribution of the Council of Europe to the protection of human rights goes far beyond this Convention. Conventions such as the European Convention for the Prevention of Torture are having a significant impact on the work of the Court in dealing with cases involving allegations of violations of Article 3 prohibiting torture, inhuman, and degrading treatment.[86]

---

[77] See T. Hammarberg, 'The Commissioner's Role' in Council of Europe, *Towards stronger implementation of the European Convention on Human Rights at national level* (Council of Europe Press, Strasbourg 2008), 111.

[78] For a full list, see www.conventions.coe.int.

[79] ETS 67.   [80] ETS 161.   [81] ETS 126, ETS 151, and ETS 152.   [82] ETS 148.

[83] ETS 157. See also Council of Europe, *Framework Convention for the Protection of National Minorities. Collected Texts* (Council of Europe Press, Strasbourg 2005).

[84] ETS 197.   [85] ETS 201.   [86] See ch.9 below.

RELATIONSHIP WITH OTHER INTERNATIONAL COURTS AND TRIBUNALS

A recent phenomenon has been the referral of the same issue to more than one process of international adjudication. There is a dispersal of responsibility for interpreting international human rights law among different judicial and quasi-judicial bodies. In addition to the International Court of Justice, there are the three major regional systems for the protection of human rights—in Africa, the Americas, and Europe—as well as the bodies responsible for the monitoring and implementation of the provisions of international human right instruments covering both general and particular aspects of human rights. Finally, there are the ad hoc bodies set up to address such matters as mass atrocities in the former Yugoslavia and in Rwanda.

Multiple referrals can happen in relation to the circumstances involved in individual applications, but can be most striking in relation to inter-State cases. The most dramatic contemporary example is the dispute between Georgia and the Russian Federation concerning South Ossetia, which is the subject of two inter-State applications filed with the Strasbourg Court. Contemporaneously Georgia instituted proceedings before the International Court of Justice alleging violations of the Convention on the Elimination of all Forms of Racial Discrimination. It is understood that consideration is also being given to a referral to the International Criminal Court.[87] The risk involved in referral to more than one system of consideration is that of a divergent approach to the same issues.[88] The Strasbourg Court has always stated that interpretation of the Convention must take account of relevant rules of international law.[89] But it has also referred to the special character of the Convention as an instrument of international human rights protection.[90] This can lead to perceived or real divergences of approach to central questions of international law. At a broad level of generality, it can certainly be said that the International Court of Justice and the Strasbourg Court take account of each other's case-law in determining such questions. Nevertheless, the risk of diverging interpretations remains.[91]

CONCLUDING REMARKS

The subject of this book brings together a number of threads which, however precariously, have brought developments in the ordering of international society that can

---

[87] But, since the Russian Federation is not a party to the founding Statute of the Court, an adjectival route to jurisdiction of the Court would need to be found.

[88] See generally R. Higgins, 'The International Court of Justice and the European Court of Human Rights: Partners for the Protection of Human Rights', Speech at the ceremony marking the fiftieth anniversary of the Strasbourg Court, 30 January 2009, available on the Court's website.

[89] *Loizidou v Turkey*, (App. 15318/89), 18 December 1996, (1996) 23 EHRR 513, ECHR 1996-VI, §43.

[90] *Cyprus v Turkey*, (App. 25781/94), 10 May 2001, (2001) 35 EHRR 731; ECHR 2001-IV, [GC], §78.

[91] On the relationship between the Strasbourg Court and the work of the European Union in the field of human rights, see comments in ch.25.

only be described as spectacular if compared with the situation in 1945. One of these threads is European integration on a level to serve not only technical needs and economic interests, but also to embody a system of liberal values which crystallize centuries of political development. The second is a continuing concern for the protection of human rights. The international protection of human rights has of course many other dimensions, but it has, arguably, been most fully and systematically developed under the law of the European Convention on Human Rights. European integration, also, has many other facets, but both the construction of the European Union, and cooperation in various fields among the States of western Europe, have been progressively based on a set of ideas and values of which the system described here is the most complete expression.[92] The third is the spread of democracy to the countries of central and eastern Europe and their embracing of the system of protection of human rights embodied in the European Convention on Human Rights, which has become a truly pan-European system offering a judicial approach to the protection of the fundamental rights and freedoms listed in the Convention and its Protocols.

---

[92] See A. Clapham, *Human Rights and the European Community: A Critical Overview* (Nomos, Baden Baden 1991); A. Casese, A. Clapham, and J. Weiler (eds.), *Human Rights and the European Community: Methods of Protection* (Nomos, Baden Baden 1991); and A. Casese, A. Clapham, and J. Weiler (eds.), *Human Rights and the European Community: The Substantive Law* (Nomos, Baden Baden 1991); P. Alston, *The EU and Human Rights* (Oxford, 1999); and A. Williams, *EU Human Rights Policies. A Study in Irony* (OUP, Oxford 2004).

2

PROCEEDINGS BEFORE THE COURT

INTRODUCTION

This chapter explains proceedings before the Strasbourg Court, including the application of the admissibility criteria, which results in over nine in every ten applications being rejected as inadmissible.[1]

On 1 November 1998 Protocol 11 to the European Convention came into effect, establishing a new permanent European Court of Human Rights. It has the largest territorial jurisdiction of any permanent court in the World, given that the combined population of the 47 Contracting Parties is over 800 million people; in addition, of course, non-nationals and non-residents can bring cases under the Convention concerning matters within a Contracting State's jurisdiction.[2]

The Strasbourg Court's principal role is to pronounce on applications, brought both by individuals and States, under the European Convention on Human Rights. Its judgments are legally binding on respondent States and are declaratory in nature: that is, the Court can announce that the facts of the application disclose a violation of one or more articles of the Convention, and, under Article 41 of the Convention, it can award monetary compensation to an individual victim of any such violation.

The Court's caseload is huge. In the calendar year 2008, 49,850 new applications were lodged; there were 1,881 judgments of the Court, including 21 judgments of a Grand Chamber. 30,163 admissibility decisions were made. Yet, as at 1 July 2009, the number of applications awaiting a determination stood at 108,350. The Court is faced with the difficult task of striking a balance between efficiency and speed in dealing with so many applications, while administering justice in each individual case and maintaining the quality of its judgments. Attempts to address some of these problems can be found in Protocol 14 and Protocol 14bis, which are discussed at the end of this chapter. The provisions of Protocol 14bis will apply to Contracting Parties from different dates. The standard procedure is described in the body of this chapter, and the variations which will apply under Protocol 14bis are dealt with in the discussion at the end of the chapter.

---

[1] A flow chart showing how cases are processed in the Strasbourg Court is included as an appendix to this chapter.

[2] See ch.5 below.

COMPOSITION AND GENERAL PROCEDURE

JUDGES

The Strasbourg Court consists of a number of judges equal to the number of Contracting Parties to the Convention.[3] The judges are elected by the Parliamentary Assembly from a list of three candidates nominated by each State.[4] They are required to be of high moral character and must either possess the qualifications required for appointment to high judicial office or be 'jurisconsults' of recognized competence.[5] Before electing a judge, the Parliamentary Assembly appoints delegates to interview the candidates, examine their résumés and report back to the Assembly. The judges are normally, but not necessarily, nationals of the Contracting Party in respect of which they are elected. They are, of course, independent. The judges are currently elected for a renewable period of six years.[6]

Attempts have been made to secure an appropriate gender balance among the judges of the Strasbourg Court. This became contentious in the context of the nominations of persons for consideration as successor to Judge Bonello as judge in respect of Malta, and resulted in an Advisory Opinion of the Court.[7] The Parliamentary Assembly had passed two resolutions seeking to secure better gender balance in the Court by requiring the nomination of at least one candidate of each sex. All the candidates proposed by the Maltese Government were men. Correspondence ensued between the representative of the Parliamentary Assembly and the Maltese Government. The Maltese Government argued that it had done its utmost to find a suitably qualified female candidate, but had failed to do so, and believed that its actions in nominating three men were in compliance with Article 21 of the Convention. The matter could not be resolved. At the request of the Maltese authorities, the Committee of Ministers requested an advisory opinion asking whether 'a list of candidates for the post of judge at the European Court of Human Rights, which satisfies the criteria listed in Article 21 of the Convention' could be refused 'solely on the basis of gender-related issues'. A second question asked whether the two resolutions of the Parliamentary Assembly were compatible with Article 22 of the Convention.[8] While stressing the importance of equality between the sexes in contemporary society, the Court noted that there had been no move to amend the Convention provisions on eligibility to serve as a judge

---

[3] Art. 20 ECHR. For an up-to-date list of judges, see www.echr.coe.int.

[4] Art. 22 ECHR.

[5] Art. 21(1) ECHR, which is based on Art. 2 of the Statute of the International Court of Justice.

[6] Art. 23 ECHR. Under this article, judges may be re-elected for more than one term. There is a retirement age of 70. When Protocol 14 comes into force, judges will serve for a single non-renewable nine year term.

[7] *Advisory Opinion on certain legal questions concerning the lists of candidates submitted with a view to the election of judges to the European Court of Human Rights*, 12 February 2008 [GC], (2009) 49 EHRR 29; see A. Mowbray, 'The Consideration of Gender in the Process of Appointing Judges to the European Court of Human Rights', (2008) 8 HRLRev 549. For further detail on the Court's jurisdiction to give advisory opinions, see below, this chapter.

[8] In the event, the Court did not find it necessary to provide an answer to this second question.

of the Strasbourg Court, and concluded that, where a Contracting Party shows that it has used all due care in seeking to nominate at least one candidate of each sex, it is not open to the Parliamentary Assembly to reject a Contracting Party's lists on the sole ground that no woman candidate is listed.

COMMITTEES, SECTIONS, CHAMBERS, AND GRAND CHAMBERS

Under Article 27 of the Convention, the Court may sit in Committees of three judges, Chambers of seven judges, or in a Grand Chamber of seventeen judges.

The Committees are competent only to declare applications inadmissible or strike them off the Court's list of cases,[9] and thus deal only with clearly inadmissible cases in the procedure outlined below.

The Court is divided into five Sections.[10] The composition of the Sections seeks to achieve geographic and gender balance and to reflect the different legal systems among the Contracting Parties. Within these Sections, the seven-judge Chambers examine the admissibility and merits both of individual applications, which are not prima facie inadmissible, and of inter-State cases.

Under Article 30 of the Convention, where a case pending before a Chamber raises a serious question affecting the interpretation of the Convention or Protocols, or where it appears that the Chamber is likely to reach a decision which would be inconsistent with earlier case-law, the Chamber may relinquish jurisdiction to the Grand Chamber unless one of the parties to the case objects. This proviso, requiring the consent of the parties to relinquishment, places considerable power in the hands of the applicant or respondent State to interfere with the working of the Court. Its force has been slightly mitigated by Rule 72(2), which states that the Registrar shall notify the parties of the Chamber's intention to relinquish jurisdiction, and sets a time limit of one month for objections, which must be 'duly reasoned'. An objection which does not meet these criteria will be considered invalid by the Chamber.

The Grand Chamber's other principal role is provided for by Article 43 of the Convention, which allows a party to a case to request that it be referred to the Grand Chamber after the Chamber has given judgment. The request must be submitted within three months of the date of judgment, and a panel of five judges of the Grand Chamber decides whether or not it should be accepted. Article 43(2) states that the panel 'shall accept the request if the case raises a serious question affecting the interpretation or application of the Convention or the protocols thereto, or a serious issue of general importance', but the panel's deliberations are secret and, to date, there has been little guidance as to the type of issues which it considers 'serious'. In 2008, the panel considered requests concerning a total of 295 cases, and accepted referral requests in ten cases.[11]

---

[9] Art. 28 ECHR.

[10] Up-to-date information on the composition of the Court and its Sections can be found at www.echr.coe.int.

[11] European Court of Human Rights, *Annual Report 2008* (Strasbourg 2009), 123.

The judge elected in respect of the respondent State automatically sits as a member of the Chamber or Grand Chamber,[12] and is often referred to as the 'national judge'. It is arguable that greater independence would be achieved by excluding the national judge, but the inclusion of the judge in respect of the respondent State has the advantage of ensuring acquaintance with the national legal order of that State.

PRESIDENCY

The Court has a President and two Vice-Presidents, and each Section has a President, elected by the plenary Court for three years. The President of the Strasbourg Court, at present the French judge Jean-Paul Costa, directs the work and administration of the Court and represents it. He sits in the Grand Chamber, but does not take part in the consideration of cases being heard by Chambers except where he is the national judge.[13]

PUBLIC NATURE OF PROCEEDINGS

The judges deliberate in private and details of their deliberations are secret.[14] Apart from that important exception, however, proceedings before the Court are generally public in character, with hearings held in open court.[15] All documents, with the exception of those deposited within the framework of friendly-settlement negotiations, are accessible to the public. In exceptional cases, however, the Rules of Court allow for confidentiality of hearings and documents.[16]

REGISTRY

Article 25 of the Convention states that 'The Court shall have a registry.' It consists of approximately 600 lawyers, translators, and administrative and clerical employees from the Contracting Parties, recruited by the Secretary-General of the Council of Europe.[17] The Registrar and Deputy Registrar are elected by the Court.[18] Because of the Court's heavy caseload, the registry has an important role in case management. Its main functions are to conduct correspondence with applicants and Contracting Parties, to prepare cases for examination, to advise the Court on questions of national law and the law of the Convention, and to assist in the drafting of judgments and decisions. The practice has been for an application to be assigned, as it comes in, to a lawyer in the registry, who will prepare the case for the judge chosen as rapporteur,[19] and attend sessions of the Chamber whenever the case is being examined. In a large measure the standard of the Court's work, and its effectiveness, depend on the quality of its registry.

---

[12] Art. 27(2).
[13] Rule 9 of the Rules of Court, which are available on the Court's website: www.echr.coe.int/echr/.
[14] Rule 22.   [15] Rules 33 and 63.   [16] Rule 63.   [17] Rule 18(3).   [18] Rules 15 and 16.
[19] Discussed in more detail later in this chapter.

PROCEDURE PRIOR TO THE DECISION
ON ADMISSIBILITY

INTRODUCTION OF AN APPLICATION

The Court's procedure is primarily a written one. Most applications originate in a letter to the Registrar setting out the complaint.[20] At this stage the case is given a file number and allocated to a lawyer in the registry from the State against which the complaint is made. Applicants may be represented by lawyers, but they have the option of acting in person until the case is communicated to the respondent State.[21] The Court's procedure in the early stages is designed to facilitate the position of litigants in person as far as possible. Thus, although the Court has only two official languages,[22] applicants may correspond with the Court in the State's official language before notice of the application has been given to the respondent State.[23]

Upon receipt of an introductory letter the registry lawyer will write to the applicant asking for further information and copies of documents and national judgments relevant to the application, and will send him or her an application form.[24] The form must be completed with details such as the applicant's name, age, occupation, and address and that of any representative, the name of the respondent State, the subject matter of the claim, as far as possible the provision of the Convention alleged to have been violated, and a statement of the facts and arguments on which the applicant relies.[25]

When the material submitted by the applicant is on its own sufficient to show that the application is inadmissible or should be struck of the Court's list of cases, a Committee will examine the file and decide whether or not to declare it inadmissible. Where the application does not appear to be clearly inadmissible, a judge rapporteur will be appointed to conduct an initial examination and to direct the future procedure.[26]

LEGAL AID

There are no fees or charges for applications to the Court and its expenses are met, under Article 50 of the Convention, by the Council of Europe. The Court may grant an applicant free legal aid at any stage of the proceedings after the respondent State's observations on admissibility have been received, or the time limit for their

---

[20] For an account of taking a case to the Court from an applicant's perspective, see P. Leach, *Taking a Case to the European Court of Human Rights* (OUP, Oxford 2005). See also K. Reid, *A Practitioner's Guide to the European Convention of Human Rights* (3rd edn Sweet & Maxwell, London 2008). A pilot project allowing online applications through the Court's internet site was launched in February 2009 for applicants using the Swedish or Dutch application forms.

[21] Rule 36.   [22] English and French: Rule 34(1).   [23] Rule 34.

[24] Available online: www.echr.coe.int.   [25] Rule 47.   [26] Rule 49.

submission has expired.[27] Applicants must submit a certified declaration of means, showing that they have insufficient means to meet their costs, and this is sent to the respondent State for comment. Legal aid may be granted to cover lawyers' fees, on a scale fixed by the Registrar, and also other necessary expenses.

INTERIM MEASURES AND THE RIGHT TO COMMUNICATE WITH THE COURT

The Strasbourg Court has no express power under the Convention to order interim or interlocutory measures to safeguard the position of the parties pending a final decision. However, in urgent cases, where there is 'an imminent risk of irreparable damage',[28] the Court may 'at the request of a party or of any other person concerned, or of its own motion, indicate to the parties any interim measure which it considers should be adopted in the interests of the parties or of the proper conduct of the proceedings before it'.[29] This power is most frequently used in deportation cases, where there is a possibility of immediate expulsion to a country where the applicant is likely to be tortured or killed,[30] but it has also been used, for example, to safeguard embryos created by *in vitro* fertilization that would otherwise have to be destroyed in accordance with domestic law.[31] In another case, the Court directed that an applicant detained in hospital as a person with a mental illness be seen by a lawyer.[32]

Initially the Court took the view that, in the absence of any relevant power contained in the Convention, such an indication gave rise to no binding obligation on the part of the State.[33] However, in the *Mamatkulov* case[34] the Grand Chamber overruled the earlier cases and, after making a survey of comparable human rights instruments, concluded that:

by virtue of Article 34 of the Convention Contracting States undertake to refrain from any act or omission that may hinder the effective exercise of an individual applicant's right of application. A failure by a Contracting State to comply with interim measures is to be regarded as preventing the Court from effectively examining the applicant's complaint

---

[27] Rules 91–6.

[28] See *Mamatkulov and Askarov v Turkey*, (Apps. 46827/99 and 46951/99), 4 February 2005 [GC], (2005) 41 EHRR 494, ECHR 2005-I, §104.

[29] Rule 39(1). In 2007, more than 1,000 requests were received, of which 262 were allowed: Speech by Jean-Paul Costa, President of the Court, Solemn hearing for the European Court of Human Rights on the occasion of the opening of the judicial year, 25 January 2008, 3.

[30] See the examples set out in *Mamatkulov and Askarov v Turkey*, (Apps. 46827/99 and 46951/99), 4 February 2005 [GC], (2005) 41 EHRR 494, ECHR 2005-I, §§104–7.

[31] *Evans v United Kingdom*, (App. 6339/05), 10 April 2007 [GC], (2008) 46 EHRR 728, ECHR 2007-IV.

[32] *Shtukaturov v Russia*, (App. 44009/05), 27 March 2008, §§31–40.

[33] For example, *Cruz Varas v Sweden*, (App. 15576/89), 20 March 1991, Series A No 201, (1992) 14 EHRR 1; and *Čonka and others v Belgium*, (App. 51564/99), Decision of 13 March 2001.

[34] *Mamatkulov and Askarov v Turkey*, (Apps. 46827/99 and 46951/99), 4 February 2005 [GC], (2005) 41 EHRR 494, ECHR 2005-I.

and as hindering the effective exercise of his or her right and, accordingly, as a violation of Article 34 of the Convention.[35]

This position has been reinforced by the Grand Chamber in the *Paludi* case.[36] The case concerned a Moldovan politician held in pre-trial detention. He had submitted medical reports to the Court which showed that he was seriously ill, and that he would not receive adequate medical treatment in prison. The Court indicated an interim measure to the Moldovan Government, requesting that the applicant should not be transferred from the clinic where he was being treated back to prison. There was a delay of approximately five days during which the interim measure was not complied with and the applicant was removed from the clinic to a prison, before being taken back to the clinic on the fifth day. There was no evidence that the applicant had suffered any irreversible harm to his health as a result of the delay. The Court in its judgment again emphasized the binding nature of interim measures and made it clear that any failure to comply would lead to a violation of Article 34 unless, in an exceptional case, the respondent State could demonstrate that there had been an 'objective impediment which prevented compliance and that the Government took all reasonable steps to remove the impediment and to keep the Court informed about the situation'.[37] The fact that the damage which the interim measure was designed to prevent subsequently turned out not to have occurred, despite the State's failure to act in full compliance with the interim measure, was irrelevant for the assessment of whether the State has fulfilled its obligations under Article 34.

It is not just a failure to comply with an interim measure which will give rise to a breach of Article 34. In the *Assenov* case,[38] for example, the Court found a violation of the right of application based on the fact that the Bulgarian police had visited the applicant's parents, at a time when the applicant was in custody, and put pressure on them to withdraw the application to Strasbourg.

In addition, freedom to correspond with the Court, even in the case of persons in detention whose correspondence is normally subject to control, is protected by the European Agreement relating to persons participating in proceedings of the European Commission and Court of Human Rights.[39] Under this Agreement, parties to the Convention undertake to respect the right of those involved in most capacities before the Court to correspond freely with the Court. Article 3(2) contains special provisions relating to those detained in custody. Article 4 guarantees free movement, subject to certain limitations, in connection with the proceedings. Finally, Article 2 offers immunity from legal process in respect of oral or written statements made before, and documents or other evidence submitted to, the Court.

---

[35] §128. Article 34 ECHR provides: The Court may receive applications from any person…claiming to be the victim of a violation…of the rights set forth in the Convention… . The High Contracting Parties undertake not to hinder in any way the effective exercise of this right.

[36] *Paladi v Moldova*, (App. 39806/05) 10 March 2009 [GC], ECHR 2009-nyr, §§87–92.

[37] §92.

[38] *Assenov and others v Bulgaria*, (App. 24760/94), 28 October 1998, (1999) 28 EHRR 652, ECHR 1998-VIII, §169.

[39] ETS 161.

EXAMINATION OF ADMISSIBILITY: PROCEDURAL ISSUES

COMMITTEE PROCEDURE

The admissibility criteria are set out in Article 35 of the Convention.[40] Given the large number of applications which it receives, the Court has had to devise an admissibility procedure which is economical and efficient, reserving as much time as possible for meritorious cases, but which still ensures that justice is done in each individual case. Thus, all applications which appear to the registry lawyer responsible for the case to be manifestly inadmissible are referred to a Committee of three judges.[41] At the end of 2008, of the 97,300 applications pending before a judicial body, 63,450 had been allocated to a Committee rather than a Chamber.[42]

The Committee's decisions, which are final with no possibility of appeal, must be taken unanimously.[43] Until 1 January 2002 applicants were sent a copy of the decision, which included very limited reasoning. Under the new procedure adopted by the Court, they receive only a letter from the registry stating that the application has been declared inadmissible and a brief outline of the grounds: for example, failure to comply with the six months' rule. The letter states that the registry is not able to give any further information or reasons in connection with the decision. Many applicants no doubt feel aggrieved to have their cases disposed of so summarily by the Court. However, given its vast caseload, it is arguable that the Court is justified in adopting a procedure which is as economic as possible in respect of hopeless applications. Other constitutional courts, such as the German Constitutional Court and the United States Supreme Court, adopt a similar practice.

More worrying, though perhaps inevitable given the Court's caseload, is the resulting absence of an easily consulted body of decisions clarifying the grounds of inadmissibility. The Court may rely on a particular line of reasoning in hundreds of cases, all declared inadmissible through the Committee procedure. There is a risk that no such case will ever be considered by a Chamber, and so the Strasbourg Court's stance in the matter will not become publicly known and accessible to lawyers and other interested parties.

CHAMBER PROCEDURE

Applications which are not dealt with in a Committee are considered by a Chamber, on the basis of a report prepared by the judge rapporteur. The Chamber can immediately decide to declare a case inadmissible,[44] but this happens rarely. Once an application has been declared inadmissible, whether by a Committee or a Chamber, that is the end of the matter. There is no possibility of appeal. However, almost all cases that

---

[40] See below in this chapter.   [41] Rule 49(2)(b).

[42] European Court of Human Rights, *Annual Report 2008* (Council of Europe Publishing, Strasbourg 2009), 127.

[43] Art. 28 ECHR, and Rule 53.   [44] Rule 54(1).

are referred to a Chamber appear to have some prima facie merit. The Chamber—or, increasingly frequently, for reasons of economy of procedure, the Chamber President acting alone—will usually decide to communicate the application to the respondent State, and request written observations.[45]

Again, to save judge time, the Court in most cases considers the admissibility and merits of a case jointly; thus reversing the exceptional rule contained in Article 29(3) of the Convention. Before coming to a conclusion on admissibility or the merits, the Chamber may decide to hold a hearing.[46]

The procedure for inter-State cases is broadly similar to that outlined above. However, any inter-State case is automatically communicated at once to the respondent State for its observations on admissibility.[47]

THIRD-PARTY INTERVENTION

A Contracting Party which is not the respondent State may intervene where an applicant is its national, and must be informed of any such application at the same time as it is communicated to the respondent State.[48]

Once the respondent State has been notified of an application, it is possible, subject to the leave of the President of the Chamber, for a third party to submit written comments or, occasionally, to intervene at the hearing.[49] Third-party comments are usually submitted by non-governmental organizations whose field of expertise touches on the subject matter of the application. However, it is possible for other States and interested individuals to intervene. In the *T and V* cases,[50] for example, which concerned the trial and sentencing of two children who had murdered another child, a non-governmental organization, Justice, was permitted to submit a written brief about the criminal responsibility of children, and the dead child's parents were allowed to submit written and oral comments. In *Saadi v Italy*,[51] which reconsidered and affirmed the rationale in *Chahal* case[52] that there was an absolute prohibition of treatment contrary to Article 3 which could not involve any weighing of the risk of ill-treatment against reasons of national security of the State in which the person was resident, the United Kingdom intervened to argue for a modification of the principles established in the *Chahal* case.[53]

ESTABLISHMENT OF THE FACTS

Article 38(1)(a) of the Convention provides:

If the Court declares the application admissible, it shall pursue the examination of the case, together with the representatives of the parties, and if need be, undertake an

---

[45] Rule 54(2).   [46] Rule 54(3).   [47] Rule 51.   [48] Rule 44(1).   [49] Rule 44.

[50] *T v United Kingdom*, (App. 24724/94); and *V v United Kingdom*, (App. 24888/94) 16 December 1999 [GC], (2000) 30 EHRR 121, ECHR 1999-IX.

[51] *Saadi v Italy*, (App. 37201/06), 28 February 2008 [GC], (2009) 49 EHRR 730, ECHR 2008-nyr.

[52] *Chahal v United Kingdom*, (App. 22414/93), 15 November 1996; (1997) 23 EHRR 413, ECHR 1996-V.

[53] For further examples of third-party submissions, see *Von Hannover v Germany*, (App. 59320/00), 24 June 2004, (2005) 40 EHRR 1, ECHR 2004-VI; *Vo. v France*, (App. 53924/00), 8 July 2004 [GC], (2005) 40 EHRR 259, ECHR 2004-VIII; *'Bosphorus Airways' v Ireland*, (App. 45036/98), 30 June 2005 [GC], (2006) 42 EHRR 1, ECHR 2005-VI; and *DH and others v Czech Republic*, (App. 57325/00), 13 November 2007 [GC], (2008) 47 EHRR 59, ECHR 2007-nyr.

investigation, for the effective conduct of which the States concerned shall furnish all necessary facilities.

In most cases, the facts will have been established by domestic courts and the task of the Strasbourg Court will be limited to examining these facts to assess compliance with the Convention. The Court also places increasing reliance on the report of the Committee on the Prevention of Torture in cases concerning the conditions of detention.[54] In some cases, however, particularly where the alleged violation arises wholly or in part from a deficiency in the administration of justice in the national legal order, or where, for example, the applicants are dispensed from exhausting domestic remedies,[55] and the facts are in dispute, the Court will be required to establish them itself.

Under Rule 42 of the Rules of Court, the Chamber may, at the request of a party to the case or a third party, or of its own motion, obtain any evidence which it considers capable of providing clarification of the facts of the case. It may request, but not order, the parties to produce documentary evidence and decide to hear as a witness or expert any person whose evidence or statements seem likely to be of assistance.[56]

Where necessary, the Court may appoint a delegation of judges to conduct an inquiry or carry out an investigation on the spot.[57] Under Article 38 of the Convention, the State concerned must 'furnish all necessary facilities' to enable the Court to conduct any such investigation. In the *Tanrikulu* case,[58] the Commission sent a delegation to south-east Turkey to investigate the alleged killing of the applicant's husband by security forces. The Commission repeatedly requested the Turkish authorities to give it a copy of the full investigation file, but this was not supplied.[59] In addition, the Commission requested the two State prosecutors who had investigated the case on the national level to appear before its delegates to give evidence. Neither of them appeared, and the Turkish authorities provided no satisfactory explanation for their failure to attend.[60] In its judgment, the Court made a separate finding that Turkey had fallen short of its obligations under Article 28 of the Convention (now Article 38).

The Court's approach to such matters is as follows:

The Court reiterates that it is of the utmost importance for the effective operation of the system of individual petition instituted under Article 34 of the Convention that States

---

[54] See, among the many examples, *Ostrovar v Moldova*, (App. 35207/03), 13 September 2005, (2007) 44 EHRR 378.

[55] *Akdivar and others v Turkey*, (App. 21893/93), 16 September 1996, (1997) 23 EHRR 143, ECHR 1996-IV, and see also below in this chapter.

[56] For example, in *Khokhlich v Ukraine*, (App. 41707/98), 29 April 2003, the Strasbourg Court decided that it needed a medical opinion to enable it to determine the truth of a complaint that the applicant had been infected with tuberculosis while detained on death row. The costs of the medical examination were borne by the Council of Europe under Rule 42(5).

[57] See the Annex to the Rules of Court. See also P. Leach, C. Paraskeva, and G. Uzelac, *International Human Rights and Fact-Finding. An analysis of the fact-finding missions conducted by the European Commission and Court of Human Rights* (London, 2009) available at www.londonmet.ac.uk/research-units/hrsj/.

[58] *Tanrikulu v Turkey*, (App. 23763/94), 8 July 1999 [GC], (2000) 30 EHRR 950, ECHR 1999-IV.

[59] §31.   [60] §39.

should furnish all necessary facilities to make possible a proper and effective examination of applications (see *Tanrıkulu v Turkey* [GC], no. 23763/94, § 70, ECHR 1999-IV). This obligation requires the Contracting States to furnish all necessary facilities to the Court, whether it is conducting a fact-finding investigation or performing its general duties as regards the examination of applications. Failure on a Government's part to submit such information which is in their hands, without a satisfactory explanation, may not only give rise to the drawing of inferences as to the well-foundedness of the applicant's allegations, but may also reflect negatively on the level of compliance by a respondent State with its obligations under Article 38 § 1 (a) of the Convention (see *Timurtaş v Turkey*, no. 23531/94, § 66, ECHR 2000-VI).[61]

An attempt of a delegation from the Strasbourg Court to visit Russia was frustrated in the *Shamayev* case, with the result that the Court abandoned its attempt to visit the applicants in Russia and proceeded on the basis of the evidence before it.[62]

CONDITIONS OF ADMISSIBILITY

PRELIMINARY REMARKS

Before the coming into force of Protocol 11, the Commission was primarily responsible for examining the admissibility of applications.[63] On 1 November 1998 the new permanent Court took over this function, and questions of admissibility are determined by judges sitting as a Committee or Chamber. The admissibility criteria, governed by Articles 34 and 35 of the Convention, have not, however, been altered by the provisions of Protocol 11, and the Court draws on the case-law of the Commission in this respect.[64] The principal criteria for admissibility are considered in the following paragraphs.

CAN THE APPLICANT CLAIM TO BE A VICTIM?

The first question to be considered is that of standing: who may bring an application to the Court? Article 33, on inter-State cases, presents no problem in this respect; an application may be brought only by a Contracting Party. Under Article 34, on individual applications, the Strasbourg Court may receive applications:

from any person, non-governmental organization or group of individuals claiming to be the victim of a violation by one of the High Contracting Parties of the rights set forth in this Convention or the protocols thereto.

---

[61] *Nolan and K v Russia*, (App. 2512/04), 12 February 2009, §55. See also M. Smith, 'The adjudicatory fact-finding tools of the European Court of Human Rights', [2009] EHRLR 206.

[62] *Shamayev and others v Georgia and Russia*, (App. 36378/02), 12 April 2005, ECHR 2005-III.

[63] See ch.1 above.

[64] See T. Zwart, *The Admissibility of Human Rights Petitions. The Case Law of the European Commission of Human Rights and the Human Rights Committee* (Martinus Nijhoff, Dordrecht 1994).

This formulation excludes the bringing of individual applications by governmental bodies or public corporations which are under the control of the State.[65]

The term 'person' (*personne physique* in the French text) appears to include only natural persons but an application may be brought also by any corporate or unincorporated body. Thus applications have been brought by companies, trade unions, churches, political parties, and numerous other types of body. A corporate body has some but not all of the rights of individuals; it has the right to a fair trial under Article 6, to protection of its correspondence under Article 8,[66] and is expressly granted property rights under Article 1 of the First Protocol, but it does not have the right to education under Article 2 of Protocol 1.

There are, of course, no restrictions based on residence, nationality, or any other status. Only if the individual applicant does not claim to be a victim, as for example where he or she complains generally of certain legislation, or where he or she simply alleges that a fellow-prisoner has been ill-treated, will the application be outside the Court's competence *ratione personae*. The Court has no jurisdiction on an individual application to review national law or practice in the absence of an alleged violation of a Convention provision. Similarly, associations have no capacity to raise general complaints,[67] though they may act in a representative capacity for specific individuals.[68]

Where a violation of the right to life is alleged, the Court must accept an application from close relatives of the dead person. In other cases close relatives have standing to bring an application only in relation to the effect of any alleged violation on themselves. So an application by close relatives of a person accused of crime who dies before final disposition of the case can make a claim based on the loss of reputation of the family.[69] In contrast, a complaint under Article 6 relating to the length and fairness of proceedings is personal to the litigant and an application by relatives will not be admitted.[70] Where the applicant dies in the course of the proceedings under the Convention, the Court will have regard to the wishes of the heirs of the deceased in deciding whether to permit the application to proceed.[71]

Cases concerning children will normally be brought by parents or guardians, but the Court will accept applications from minors if the complaint concerns action by

[65] See *Islamic Republic of Iran Shipping Lines v Turkey*, (App. 40998/98), 13 December 2007, (2008) 47 EHRR 573, ECHR 2007-nyr, §§78–84.

[66] App. 14369/88, *Noviflora Sweden AB v Sweden*; Decision of an unspecified date in 1992, (1993) 15 EHRR CD6.

[67] App. 10581/83, *Norris and National Gay Federation v Ireland*, Decision of 16 May 1984, (1984) 44 DR 132.

[68] App. 10983/84, *Confédération des Syndicats médicaux français and Fédération nationale des Infirmiers v France*, Decision of 12 May 1986, (1986) 47 DR 225; see also App. 10733/84, *Asociación de Aviadores de la República, Jaime Mata and others v Spain*, Decision of 11 March 1985, (1985) 41 DR 211.

[69] App. 10300/83, *Nölkenbockhoff and Bergemann v Federal Republic of Germany*, Decision of 12 December 1984, (1985) 40 DR 180.

[70] Ibid. But note observations in *Micallef v Malta*, (App. 17056/06), 15 January 2008, §§23–33 suggesting exceptions to this position. The Chamber judgment has been referred to the Grand Chamber: see now the judgment of the Grand Chamber of 15 October 2009.

[71] See, for example, *Aksoy v Turkey*, (App. 21987/93), 18 December 1996, (1997) 23 EHRR 553, ECHR 1996-VI, §2; and *Gładkowski v Poland*, (App. 29697/96), 14 March 2000.

the authorities affecting the relationship of child and parent or guardian.[72] A person who is neither a custodial parent, guardian, nor legal representative of a child will not have standing to make a complaint.[73] There is no bar to applications by persons under a disability.[74]

In certain cases, in order to give effective protection to human rights, the Strasbourg Court has had to give a wide interpretation to the notion of 'victim'. In the *Klass* case,[75] for example, where the applicants complained about legislation in Germany which allowed the State to intercept telephone calls without informing the person concerned, the Court concluded that the applicants could claim to be victims even though they were unable to establish that they had been the subjects of surveillance, since 'in the mere existence of the legislation itself there is involved, for all those to whom the legislation could be applied, a menace of surveillance', which must have placed a restriction on the applicants' confidence freely to use the telephone system. In that case, it would have been virtually impossible for the applicants to adduce evidence of specific measures taken against them—and indeed this very impossibility formed one of the bases of their complaints. However, where the legislation provides for notification of surveillance to a person concerned, a claim that there has been a violation of Article 8 will generally not succeed unless the applicant has received such notification.[76] Moreover, where the applicant complains of a specific instance of surveillance or telephone-tapping, the Court will require evidence establishing a 'reasonable likelihood' that some such measure was applied to him or her.[77]

In the *Norris* case the Court held that a homosexual man could 'claim to be a victim' of legislation in Ireland which criminalized consensual sex between men, because he either respected the law and suppressed his sexual preferences, or he indulged them and risked prosecution.[78] This was so even though the applicant himself had never been investigated by the police and there was evidence that the Irish authorities had a policy of not bringing prosecutions under the law.[79]

A person will not cease to be a victim by reason of some acknowledgment by the respondent State that there has been a violation of the Convention. The Grand Chamber has ruled:

The Court also reiterates that a decision or measure favourable to the applicant is not in principle sufficient to deprive him of his status as a 'victim' unless the national authorities have

---

[72] App. 10929/84, *Nielsen v Denmark*, Decision of 10 March 1986, (1986) 46 DR 55; *A. v United Kingdom*, (App. 25599/94), 23 September 1998, (1999) 27 EHRR 611, ECHR 1998-VI.

[73] App. 22920/93, *MB v United Kingdom*, Decision of 6 April 1994, (1994) 77-A DR 42.

[74] App. 527/62, *X v Austria*, Decision of 4 October 1962, (1962) 5 *Yearbook* 238.

[75] *Klass v Germany*, (App. 5029/71), 6 September 1978, Series A No 28, (1979–80) 2 EHRR 214; and see also *Malone v United Kingdom*, (App. 8691/79), 2 August 1984, Series A No 82, (1985) 7 EHRR 14.

[76] Joined Apps. 10439/83, 10440/83, 10441/83, 10452/83, and 10513/83, *Mersch and others v Luxembourg*, Decision of 10 May 1985, (1985) 43 DR 34.

[77] *Halford v United Kingdom*, (App. 20605/92), 25 June 1997, (1997) 24 EHRR 523, ECHR 1997-III.

[78] *Norris v Ireland*, (App. 10581/83), 26 October 1988, Series A No 142, (1991) 13 EHRR 186, §32.

[79] Further examples of where a person is virtually certain to be affected in the future by some national provision can be found in *Marckx v Belgium*, (App. 6833/74), 13 June 1979, Series A No 31, (1979–80) 2 EHRR 330; and *Burden v United Kingdom*, (App. 13378/05), 29 April 2008 [GC], (2007) 47 EHRR 857, ECHR 2008-nyr. Both cases concerned inheritance rights.

acknowledged, either expressly or in substance, and then afforded redress for, the breach of the Convention.[80]

In order to lose victim status, there must be a remedy which constitutes full redress for the violation which the victim has suffered. This will, obviously, require an exercise of judgment on the part of the Strasbourg Court.

WAS THE ALLEGED VIOLATION COMMITTED BY A CONTRACTING PARTY?

Under Articles 33 and 34 an application may be brought only against a Contracting Party, and only in respect of a breach for which the State is in some way responsible.[81] Otherwise the application will be rejected as being outside the Court's competence *ratione personae*.

The State is directly liable for the acts of the legislature, executive, and judiciary, and also for the acts of other public bodies, for example, public corporations with a certain measure of independence, such as a local health authority or a public corporation under the control of the State.[82] It cannot be held to account for the acts or omissions of private persons, such as private companies, lawyers or legal professional bodies like the Bar Council. As noted throughout this book, however, many of the substantive articles of the Convention impose positive obligations on a Contracting Party. Thus the State can, for example, be held responsible under Article 8 for failing to ensure that a privately owned factory does not dangerously pollute the surrounding area[83] or under Article 3 for the lack of adequate protection in its criminal law against violence carried out by a private individual.[84]

An application will be declared inadmissible as incompatible *ratione loci* with the Convention if it relates to an alleged violation of the Convention outside the State's territorial jurisdiction, and incompatible *ratione temporis* if it is based on events which occurred before the respondent State accepted the jurisdiction of the Court, or became a party to the Convention.

DO THE MATTERS COMPLAINED OF FALL WITHIN THE SCOPE OF THE CONVENTION OR PROTOCOLS?

The Court cannot deal with complaints concerning rights not covered by the Convention or Protocols, and a Contracting Party cannot be brought to task in respect of alleged violations of rights included in protocols which it has not ratified. Such

---

[80] *Scordino v Italy (No. 1)*, (App. 36813/97), 29 March 2006 [GC], (2007) 45 EHRR 207, ECHR 2006-V, §180; see also *Moscow Branch of the Salvation Army v Russia*, (App. 72881/01), 5 October 2006, (2007) 44 EHRR 912, ECHR 2006-XI, §§63–70.

[81] See also the discussion on jurisdiction in ch.5.

[82] App. 7601/76, *Young and James v United Kingdom*, Decision of 11 July 1977, (1977) 20 *Yearbook* 520; and App. 7866/76, *Webster v United Kingdom*, Decision of 3 March 1978, (1978) 12 DR 168.

[83] *López Ostra v Spain*, (App. 16798/90), 9 December 1994, Series A No 303–C, (1995) 20 EHRR 277.

[84] *A v United Kingdom*, (App. 25599/94), 23 September 1998, (1999) 27 EHRR 611, ECHR 1998-VI.

complaints are normally rejected under Article 35(3) as incompatible *ratione materiae* with the provisions of the Convention.

It is the duty of the Strasbourg Court to examine an application not only in relation to any rights that may have been invoked by the applicant, but also, of its own motion, in relation to any rights which, on the facts and submissions before it, may appear to have been infringed.

HAVE DOMESTIC REMEDIES BEEN EXHAUSTED?

Contracting Parties quite frequently raise objections that applicants have not exhausted the remedies available to them in the national legal order in order to remedy an alleged violation of Convention rights. According to Article 35(1):

The Court may only deal with the matter after all domestic remedies have been exhausted, according to the generally recognized rules of international law, and within a period of six months from the date on which the final decision was taken.

In the *Akdivar* case,[85] the Strasbourg Court explained the rationale for this rule:

[T]he rule of exhaustion of domestic remedies…obliges those seeking to bring their case against the State before an international judicial or arbitral organ to use first the remedies provided by the national legal system. Consequently, States are dispensed from answering before an international body for their acts before they have had an opportunity to put matters right through their own legal system. The rule is based on the assumption, reflected in Article 13 of the Convention—with which it has close affinity—that there is an effective remedy available in respect of the alleged breach in the domestic system whether or not the provisions of the Convention are incorporated in national law. In this way, it is an important aspect of the principle that the machinery of protection established by the Convention is subsidiary to the national systems safeguarding human rights.

But the Court has also said that the application of the requirement must be viewed in context:

The application of the rule of exhaustion must make due allowance for the fact that it is being applied in the context of machinery for the protection of human rights that the Contracting Parties have agreed to set up. Accordingly, the Court has recognized that Article 35(1) must be applied with some degree of flexibility and without excessive formalism. The rule is neither absolute nor capable of being applied automatically. In reviewing whether it has been observed it is essential to have regard to the particular circumstances of each case. This means, amongst other things, that the Court must take realistic account of the general legal and political context in which the remedies operate, as well as the personal circumstances of the applicant.[86]

Under Article 35(1), applicants are under an obligation to use the remedies provided by national law which are sufficient to afford redress in respect of the breaches alleged.

---

[85] *Akdivar and others v Turkey,* (App. 21893/93), 16 September 1996, (1997) 23 EHRR 143, ECHR 1996-IV.

[86] *Foka v Turkey,* (App. 28940/95), Decision of 9 November 2006, 11.

The complaint must be made to the appropriate judicial or administrative authorities, and should have been taken to the highest instance available. Applicants will not have complied with the rule if they have been unable to pursue national proceedings because of their own failure to comply with the domestic formal requirements and time limits.[87] In addition, applicants must have raised before the national authorities, if it is possible to do so, the particular complaints which they wish to make before the Court. If they raise only some of their complaints, only those will be admissible.[88]

There is, however, no obligation to attempt to use a remedy which is inadequate or ineffective,[89] but mere doubts will not suffice.[90] In addition, according to the 'generally recognized rules of international law' there may be special circumstances which absolve applicants from the obligation to exhaust the domestic remedies at their disposal. So, for example, in the *Akdivar* case, where the Kurdish applicants complained that their village had been destroyed by Turkish soldiers, and the respondent State was unable to provide evidence of damages having been awarded in a single similar case, the Strasbourg Court held that there was no need for the applicants to bring proceedings in the national courts before complaining in Strasbourg. Again, if the national case-law shows that a remedy, such as an appeal, has no reasonable chance of success, the applicant is not obliged to try it. The Court will accept a lawyer's formal opinion to this effect as a 'final decision' under Article 35.

The domestic remedies rule applies also to inter-State applications under Article 33, unlike the other grounds of inadmissibility specified in Article 35, which are expressly confined to individual applications under Article 34. The rule, however, has only a limited application in inter-State cases: domestic remedies must have been exhausted in respect of violations of the rights of particular individuals, but not where the scope of the application is to determine the compatibility with the Convention of legislative measures and administrative practices in general.[91]

The applicant must provide, in the application, information enabling it to be shown that the conditions laid down in Article 35 have been satisfied; if this is not done, the Court must examine the question of its own motion. If the respondent State raises the objection of non-exhaustion, it is for that State to prove the existence, in its municipal legal system, of remedies which have not been exercised.[92] If the existence of such a remedy is established, the applicant must show that it has been exhausted, or that it was unlikely to be effective and adequate in regard to the grievance in question, or that

---

[87] See, for example, *Yahiaoui v France*, (App. 30962/96), 14 January 2000, (2001) 33 EHRR 393.

[88] As in *A and others v United Kingdom*, (App. 3455/05), 19 February 2009 [GC], (2009) 49 EHRR 29, ECHR 2009-nyr, §122.

[89] Declarations of incompatibility under the Human Rights Act 1998 are not regarded as an effective remedy: *Burden v United Kingdom*, (App. 13378/05), 29 April 2008 [GC], (2007) 47 EHRR 857, ECHR 2008-nyr, §§40–4.

[90] *Daddi v Italy*, (App. 15476/09), Decision of 16 June 2009.

[91] App. 788/60, *Pfunders Case, Austria v Italy*, Decision of 11 January 1961, (1961) 4 *Yearbook* 116, at 146–50; and see, more recently, *Cyprus v Turkey*, (App. 25781/94), 10 May 2001 [GC]; (2002) 35 EHRR 30; ECHR 2001-IV. See further below in this chapter.

[92] *Akdivar and others v Turkey*, (App. 21893/93), 16 September 1996, (1997) 23 EHRR 143, ECHR 1996-IV.

in the special circumstances of the case he or she was absolved from compliance with the rule. The rules concerning the burden of proof are based, as is the substantive rule, on the generally recognized rules of international law referred to in Article 35.[93]

A particular issue has arisen in relation to the exhaustion of domestic remedies in cases involving complaints that judgment has not been given in a reasonable time. Several Contracting Parties have put special procedures in place to address the problem. The question arises as to whether such new procedures are effective and whether they must be exhausted before a complaint can be raised that there has been a violation of Article 6. Where Contracting Parties introduce such procedures in response to repeated judgments finding violations of the right to judgment within a reasonable time, the Strasbourg Court will examine such procedures with some care if a complaint is raised that an applicant has not exhausted domestic remedies, since:

It is also clear that for countries where length-of-proceedings violations already exist, a remedy designed to expedite the proceedings—although desirable for the future—may not be adequate to redress a situation in which the proceedings have clearly already been excessively long.[94]

ESCAPING THE REQUIREMENT TO EXHAUST DOMESTIC REMEDIES: TACKLING ADMINISTRATIVE PRACTICES

The exhaustion rule is inapplicable where an administrative practice is in issue, and this can have implications in both inter-State and individual applications. An administrative practice exists if there is repetition of acts and official tolerance, even if only at a subordinate level, and despite occasional reactions from the authorities.[95] In inter-State cases, there is no requirement in such cases that there should be a victim at all. Thus the rule does not apply if the applicant State can show that the treatment complained of constitutes an administrative practice. It did not apply, for this reason, in the *Irish* case,[96] to the Irish Government's complaints concerning the treatment of persons in custody in Northern Ireland. In applications by individuals, there will be a need for the applicant to show that he or she is a victim.[97] But it is not sufficient merely to allege the existence of such legislative measures or administrative practices; their existence must be shown by means of substantial evidence. On this ground, the complaints in the *Irish* case relating to deaths (as distinct from ill-treatment) allegedly caused by the respondent State's security forces were rejected.

---

[93] *Akdivar and others v Turkey*, (App. 21893/93), 16 September 1996, (1997) 23 EHRR 143, ECHR 1996-IV.

[94] *Scordino v Italy (No. 1)*, (App. 36813/97), 29 March 2006 [GC], (2007) 45 EHRR 207, ECHR 2006-V, §185; see also *Žunič v Slovenia*, (App. 24342/04), Decision of 18 October 2007.

[95] *Ireland v United Kingdom*, (App. 5310/71), 18 January 1978, Series A No 25; (1979–80) 2 EHRR 25.

[96] App. 5310/71, *Ireland v United Kingdom*, Decision of 1 October 1972, (1972) 15 *Yearbook* 76; see also Joined Apps. 9940–44/82, *France, Norway, Denmark, Sweden, and The Netherlands v Turkey*, Decision of 6 December 1983, (1984) 35 DR 143.

[97] Apps. 5577–83/72, *Donnelly and others v United Kingdom*, 5 April 1973, (1973) 16 *Yearbook* 212.

The reason for this exception is that, in cases where there is an administrative practice, proceedings to exhaust domestic remedies run the risk of tackling only a single instance of a Convention violation, whereas there is a systemic problem. In the *Caraher* case,[98] the Court summarized the case-law regarding the notion of an administrative practice as follows:

In the First Greek case (Yearbook 11 p.770), the Commission identified two elements necessary to the existence of an administrative practice: a repetition of acts and official tolerance. Repetition of acts was stated as referring to a substantial number of acts which were linked or connected in some way by the circumstances surrounding them (eg. time and place, or the attitude of persons involved) and which were not simply a number of isolated acts. The Court has stated that a practice incompatible with the Convention consists of an accumulation of identical or analogous breaches which are sufficiently numerous and inter-connected to amount not merely to isolated incidents or exceptions but to a pattern or system (Ireland v. the United Kingdom judgment of 18 January 1978, Series A no. 25, p. 64, §159). By official tolerance is meant that, though acts are plainly unlawful, they are tolerated in the sense that the superiors of those responsible, though aware of the acts, take no action to punish them or prevent their repetition; or that a higher authority, in the face of numerous allegations, manifests indifference by refusing any inadequate investigation of their truth or falsity; or that in judicial proceedings a fair hearing of such complaints is denied (*mutatis mutandis*, Application Nos. 9940-9944/82, France, Norway, Denmark, Sweden and the Netherlands v. Turkey, dec. 6.12.83, DR 35 p. 143 at p. 163, § 19). However, it may be noted that a practice may be found even where no official tolerance is established at the higher official levels and even where some acts have been prosecuted, since the higher authorities are under a responsibility to take effective steps to bring to an end the repetition of acts (see eg. Ireland v. the United Kingdom judgment, op. cit., § 159).[99]

Most cases involving allegations of an administrative practice have arisen in relation to allegations of violations of the prohibition of torture in Article 3. In certain length of proceedings cases under Article 6, the Strasbourg Court has referred to 'a practice which is incompatible with the Convention'.[100] The Court categorized the situation in the *Kauczor* case[101] in the same way in considering violations of Article 5 involving the length of pre-trial detention. In all three of these cases, this categorization was used more as the basis for ordering general remedial measures under Article 46[102] than as a reason to disapply the rule requiring exhaustion of domestic remedies.

HAS THE APPLICATION BEEN INTRODUCED WITHIN THE SIX-MONTH TIME LIMIT?

Article 35 prescribes a strict period of limitation: an application is inadmissible if it is not brought within six months from the date on which the final decision was taken.

---

[98] *Caraher v United Kingdom*, (App. 24520/94), 11 January 2000, ECHR 2000-I.   [99] p.18.

[100] *Bottazzi v Italy*, (App. 34884/97), 28 July 1999, ECHR 1999-V, §22; *Scordino (No. 1) v Italy*, (App. 36813/97), 29 March 2006 [GC], ECHR 2006-V, §§229–31.

[101] *Kauczor v Poland*, (App. 45219/06), 3 February 2009, §60.

[102] See further below in this chapter, and in ch.3.

Time starts running from the day after the applicant became aware of the act or decision of which he or she complains. Where domestic remedies have been completed,
this is usually the hearing at which the final domestic judgment is delivered,[103] but
where no domestic remedies are available, the six-month period runs from the date
of the act alleged to constitute the violation of the Convention. The applicant cannot reopen the period by, for example, subsequently applying for a retrial, as such an
application does not constitute an 'effective remedy' for the purposes of Article 35.
Where the complaint concerns a continuing situation, time runs from the end of the
situation, but as long as the situation continues, the six-months rule cannot bite.[104] The
Court has stated:

that the concept of a 'continuing situation' refers to a state of affairs which operates by continuous activities by or on the part of the State to render the applicants victims.[105]

But the Court went on to state:

The applicants' complaints have as their source specific events which occurred on identifiable dates.... These cannot be construed as a 'continuing situation' for the purposes of the
six-month rule. The fact that an event has significant consequences over time...does not
mean that the event has produced a 'continuing situation'.[106]

The concept of continuing violations of Convention rights has proved to be
problematic.[107] The Court seeks to distinguish instantaneous acts and continuing violations, but this is far from straightforward. Many instantaneous acts have continuing
effects. The taking of property provides an excellent example. If property is formally
expropriated and so the owner's title to the property has been extinguished, then
there is arguably an instantaneous act and time will start running to raise a complaint
under the Convention. But if a State acts in a way which adversely affects an owner's
enjoyment of their property, perhaps by the exercise of planning controls or threats of
compulsory purchase, then there may be a continuing violation of the right to peaceful enjoyment of property. The approach of the Commission was to seek to distinguish
between instantaneous acts which might give rise to enduring effects from violations
which continue. Only the latter prevent time from running. The Court has not yet
elaborated on the distinction. Loucaides is critical of the Court's current approach and
proposes a test in which the following factors are relevant considerations:

---

[103] *West v United Kingdom*, (App. 34728/97), Decision of 20 October 1997.

[104] *Papamichalopoulos and others v Greece*, (App. 14556/89), 24 June 1993, Series A No 260–B, (1993)
16 EHRR 440; and *Loizidou v Turkey* (App. 15318/89), 18 December 1996, (1996) 23 EHRR 513, ECHR
1996-VI.

[105] *Posti and Rahko v Finland*, (App. 27824/95), 24 September 2002, (2003) 37 EHRR 158, ECHR
2002-VII, §39.

[106] §40.

[107] See L. Loucaides, 'The concept of "continuing" violations of human rights' in P. Mahoney and
others (eds.), *Protecting Human Rights: The European Perspective. Studies in Memory of Rolv Ryssdal* (Carl
Heymanns, Köln 2000), 803.

(a) the nature of the complaint, i.e. the particular act or conduct alleged to be a violation;

(b) the effects of the act or conduct complained of on the rights of the applicant;

(c) the duration of such effects; and

(d) the prolongation of the operation of the relevant act or conduct or the maintenance of the effects in question through the involvement or conduct of the State.

Loucaides then proposes:

...there is a 'continuing' violation if the complaint is directed against a constant interference with a right safeguarded by the Convention, which is an extension of an interference caused by the initial instantaneous act whose effects still subsist as a result of a prolongation of the operation of the act or its effects through an involvement or conduct of the State.[108]

The six-months rule is applied strictly by the Court and cannot be waived by the respondent State.[109] In certain cases it may appear to create injustice—where an application is submitted late through the oversight of the applicant's lawyer, for example—but, like all limitation periods, it is intended to promote legal certainty and finality.

HAS THE APPLICATION BEEN BROUGHT BEFORE?

Article 35(2)(b) provides that an application is inadmissible if it:

is substantially the same as a matter which has already been examined by the Court or has already been submitted to another procedure of international investigation or settlement and contains no relevant new information.

There appears to be no decision of the Court or Commission rejecting an application on the ground that it has already been submitted to another procedure of international investigation or settlement. This is principally because the Commission and the Court have viewed the requirement of the alternative procedure as being judicial or quasi-judicial proceedings similar to those set up by the Convention.[110] It follows that the Resolution 1053 procedure before the United Nations Human Rights Commission is not a comparable procedure of international investigation.[111] The same conclusion has been reached in relation to complaints raised before the Human Rights Committee under the International Covenant on Civil and Political Rights.[112]

---

[108] 813–14.

[109] *Walker v United Kingdom* (App. 34979/97), Decision of 25 January 2000, ECHR 2001-I.

[110] *Mikolenko v Estonia*, (App. 16944/03), Decision of 5 January 2006.

[111] Ibid.

[112] *Folgerø and others v Norway*, (App. 15472/02), Decision of 14 February 2006. See also C. Phuong, 'The relationship between the European Court of Human Rights and the Human Rights Committee: has the "same matter" already been "examined"?' (2007) 7 HRLRev 385.

In many cases applicants seek to reopen proceedings after the application has been declared inadmissible, alleging errors in the Court's decision or introducing further details of the same complaints. Since there is no provision for reopening a case, it is necessary to treat the new material as a fresh application. Such an application will be doomed to failure if, for example, the new material does not affect the substance of the previous allegations. In other cases, the new material may remedy the ground on which the previous application was rejected. If, for example, an application is rejected for non-exhaustion of domestic remedies, the applicant may still be able to pursue the domestic remedies and then reintroduce the complaint.

IS THE APPLICATION MANIFESTLY ILL-FOUNDED?

Article 35(3) requires the Strasbourg Court to reject as inadmissible an application which is 'manifestly ill-founded'. This provision requires an initial assessment of the substance of the case and enables to Court to deal effectively with its immense caseload by weeding out at an early stage clearly unmeritorious applications. A complaint will be declared manifestly ill-founded if, for example, the applicant has made wholly unsubstantiated allegations or where the allegations, even if substantiated, would not suffice to establish a violation. For example, complaints by prisoners under Article 3 concerning the conditions of their detention have been rejected as manifestly ill-founded on the ground that, even if the matters complained of were established, they would not constitute 'inhuman or degrading treatment or punishment'. Similarly, complaints about issues which have already been examined by the Court and found not to constitute a violation can be declared inadmissible as manifestly ill-founded.

IS THERE AN ABUSE OF THE RIGHT OF APPLICATION?

Abuse of the right of application, as a ground of rejecting an application, must of course be distinguished from the principle of abuse of rights embodied in Article 17.[113] Article 17 lays down, in effect, that no one may be able to take advantage of the provisions of the Convention to perform acts aimed at destroying the rights guaranteed. It is thus concerned with preventing abuse of the substantive rights. Abuse of the right of application, on the other hand, may arise where an applicant makes improper use of the procedural rights under Article 34 to bring the complaint before the Court. For example, the Court is the recipient of multiple applications from a number of individuals who would have been (and frequently are), within the English system, subject to vexatious litigant orders. The Commission habitually declared such applications inadmissible for abuse of process, stating:

It cannot be the task of the Commission, a body which was set up under the Convention 'to ensure the observance of the engagements undertaken by the High Contracting Parties in the present Convention' to deal with a succession of ill-founded and querulous complaints,

---

[113] See ch.6 below.

creating unnecessary work which is incompatible with its real functions, and which hinders it in carrying them out.[114]

The presentation of incomplete and misleading information to the Court will constitute an abuse of the right of application, especially if the information concerns matter highly germane to the application,[115] as will the submission of forged documents.[116]

IS THE APPLICATION ANONYMOUS?

Article 35(2)(a) requires the Strasbourg Court to reject any application which is anonymous. The underlying purpose of this requirement is to preclude applications lodged for improper reasons, but it could be an inhibition to those who do not wish their identity to be revealed to a Contracting Party for fear of repercussions. Indeed the Court does ask applicants whether they are content for their identity to be disclosed to the respondent State, and will not disclose the applicant's identity if so requested.[117] This requirement has not proved to be problematic.

JUDGMENT

Judgments of the Strasbourg Court must contain, *inter alia*, a summary of the facts, the arguments and the reasons for the Court's decision.[118] Any judge who has taken part in the consideration of the case can annex a separate concurring or dissenting opinion. The names of the judges making up the majority and those annexing separate opinions must be stated. Judgments are structured around a common set of headings, which will typically be as follows:

- Procedure, which provides the details of the application and representation in the case.
- The Facts, which includes the circumstances of the case, and relevant national law and international law.
- The Law, which includes the alleged violation of the relevant Convention provision or provisions together with a summary of the arguments of the parties before concluding with the Court's assessment.
- Application of Article 41 on just satisfaction if that forms part of the Court's Judgment.[119]

---

[114] Joined Apps. 5070/71, 5171/71, and 5186/71, *X v Federal Republic of Germany*, Decision of 10 July 1971, (1971) 42 CD 58, 60; cited with approval in Joined Apps. 5145/71, 5246/71, 5333/72, 5586/72, 5587/72, and 5532/72, *Ringeisen v Austria*, Decision of 2 April 1973, (1973) 43 CD 152; and App. 13284/87, *M v United Kingdom*, Decision of 15 October 1987, (1987) 54 DR 214.

[115] *Hadrabová v Czech Republic*, (App. 42165/02), Decision of 25 September 2007.

[116] *Bagheri and Maliki v The Netherlands*, (App. 30164.06), Decision of 15 May 2007.

[117] Rule 47(3).   [118] Rule 74.

[119] See below in this chapter.

- The *dispositif*, that is, a summary of the Court's rulings on the alleged violations of the Convention.

- Any separate concurring opinions or dissenting opinions.

Chamber judgments are generally delivered in either English or French, although all judgments which are published in the Court's official series of report are translated into the other official language.[120] Grand Chamber judgments are translated into both official languages prior to adoption.

The Court's judgments may be delivered in open court or, more usually, communicated to the parties in writing.[121] Within three months of the date of a Chamber judgment, it is open to the parties to request that the case be referred to the Grand Chamber.[122] A judgment of the Grand Chamber is final. Judgments of the Chambers become final when (1) the parties declare that they will not be seeking a referral; or (2) the three-month period expires without any request having been made; or (3) the panel of the Grand Chamber refuses a request for referral.[123]

A finding by the Court in its judgment of a violation of the Convention or Protocols places an obligation on the respondent State to make the changes required to the domestic legal order to avoid a repetition of the breach. This is inherent in the obligation in Article 46(1) to abide by the decision of the Court in any case to which the State is a party. Where the Strasbourg Court issues a pilot judgments,[124] as in the *Kudła*[125] and *Broniowski*[126] cases, this may involve the introduction of new remedies in the national legal order where none exist, or the taking of steps to provide redress to a class of victims in the same position as the applicant in the case before the Court. Under Article 46(2) of the Convention, the Strasbourg Court's judgments are transmitted to the Committee of Ministers of the Council of Europe, which supervises their execution.[127]

PILOT JUDGMENTS PROCEDURE

Through development of its internal procedures, the Strasbourg Court has introduced pilot judgments as a means of addressing systemic problems in the Contracting Parties which result in multiple applications to the Court.[128] The slender legal base for

---

[120] Rule 76. For some reflections on the form of judgments in the Strasbourg Court, see R. White, 'Judgments in the Strasbourg Court: Some Reflections' in M. Andenas and S. Vogenhauer (eds.) *A Matter of Style? The Form of Judgments in the United Kingdom and Abroad: Essays in Honour of Lord Bingham of Cornhill* (Hart Publishing, Oxford 2010).

[121] Rule 77.

[122] Article 43 ECHR and Rule 73 of the Rules of Court.

[123] Article 44 ECHR.

[124] See below in this chapter.

[125] *Kudła v Poland*, (App. 30210/96), 26 October 2000 [GC], (2002) 35 EHRR 198, ECHR 2000-XI.

[126] *Broniowski v Poland*, (App. 31443/96), 22 June 2004 [GC], (2005) 40 EHRR 495, ECHR 2004-V.

[127] See ch.3 below.

[128] Endorsed by the Committee of Ministers in Resolution DH (2004) 3 of 12 May 2004. See generally E. Friberg, 'Pilot Judgments from the Court's Perspective' in Council of Europe, *Towards Stronger*

such judgments is Article 46 under which Contracting Parties agree to 'abide by the final judgment of the Court in any case to which they are parties'. The object of the pilot judgment is to set the environment in which the systemic problem can be addressed. Friberg says:

The specific feature of the PJP is that instead of dealing with each individual case, the Court singles out one or a small number of applications for priority treatment and adjourns all the other applications until the pilot case has been decided.[129]

In the judgment in the pilot case, the Strasbourg Court makes clear its expectations about how the respondent State should address the systemic problem and find a remedy not only for the individual applicant in the case, but also for all other applicants in look-alike cases. They would obtain a remedy under the new procedure established in the national legal order when the requirements of the pilot judgment are implemented. Friberg cites three important interests which are served by the use of pilot judgments: (1) speedier redress for victims; (2) the systemic problem is redressed within the national legal order under guidance from the Strasbourg Court; and (3) the removal from the Strasbourg Court's docket of large numbers of repetitive complaints.

The first pilot judgment was given in the *Broniowski* case,[130] which concerned the operation of a legislative scheme to enable purchases at a discount of land by those who had lost land in the redrawing of the eastern border of Poland after the Second World War.[131]

Variants on the procedure soon grew up to enable Chambers to address some of the issues, as in the *Lukenda* case,[132] though Judge Zagrebelsky, in a partly dissenting opinion, indicated that he believed that the case should have been relinquished in favour of a Grand Chamber.[133]

Implementation of the European Convention on Human Rights at National Level (Council of Europe Publishing, Strasbourg 2008), 86; V. Colandrea, 'On the Power of the European Court of Human Rights to Order Specific Non-Monetary Measures: Some Remarks in Light of the *Assanidze, Broniowski* and *Sejdovic* Cases' (2007) 7 HRLRev 396; and C. Paraskeva, 'Human Rights Protection Begins and Ends at Home: The "Pilot Judgment Procedure" Developed by the European Court of Human Rights' (2007) 3 *Human Rights Law Commentary*, www.nottingham.ac.uk/law/hrlc/publications/hrlc.php.

[129] E. Friberg, 'Pilot Judgments from the Court's Perspective' in Council of Europe, *Towards Stronger Implementation of the European Convention on Human Rights at National Level* (Council of Europe Publishing, Strasbourg 2008), 87.

[130] *Broniowski v Poland*, (App. 31443/96), 22 June 2004, (2005) 40 EHRR 495; ECHR 2004-X. See also *Hutten-Czapska v Poland,* (App. 35014/97), 19 June 2006 [GC], (2007) 45 EHRR 52, ECHR 2006-VIII.

[131] The so-called Bug River Claims. See below in ch.20.

[132] *Lukenda v Slovenia*, (App. 23032/02), 6 October 2005, (2008) 47 EHRR 728; ECHR 2005-X; and *Burdov v Russia (No. 2)*, (App. 33509/04), 15 January 2009, (2009) 49 EHRR 22.

[133] For further examples of variants on the pilot judgment procedure, see *Xenides-Arestis v Turkey*, (App. 46347/99), 22 December 2005; *Sejdovic v Italy*, (App. 56581/00), 1 March 2006 [GC], ECHR 2006-II; *Scordino v Italy (No. 1)*, (App. 36813/97), 29 March 2006 [GC], (2007) 45 EHRR 207; ECHR 2006-V; *Driza v Albania*, (App. 33771/02), 13 November 2007, (2009) 49 EHRR 779, ECHR 2007-XII; *Urbárska Obec Renčianske Biskupice v Slovakia*, (App. 74258/01), 27 November 2007, (2009) 48 EHRR 1139, ECHR 2007-nyr; *Gülmez v Turkey*, (App. 16330/02), 20 May 2008; and *Viaşu v Romania*, (App. 79951/01), 9 December 2008.

Friberg suggests that the Court could reduce the burden on itself even more if a more radical solution to repetitive cases was taken:

What one could envisage is that, instead of delivering judgments in repetitive cases, the Court would simply certify that the case is to be settled in the light of the previous decisive judgment. The follow-up cases would be referred directly to the Committee of Ministers, not as decided cases but certified to be enforced on the basis of that existing judgment.[134]

REMEDIES UNDER ARTICLE 41

Article 41 of the Convention[135] provides that:

If the Court finds that there has been a violation of the Convention or the protocols thereto, and if the internal law of the High Contracting Party concerned allows only partial reparation to be made, the Court shall, if necessary, afford just satisfaction to the injured party.

Respondent States are in principle free to choose the means whereby they will comply with a judgment in which the Court has found a breach. This discretion as to the manner of execution of a judgment reflects the freedom of choice attaching to the primary obligation of the Contracting States under Article 1 of the Convention to secure the rights and freedoms guaranteed. If the nature of the breach allows for *restitutio in integrum*, it is for the respondent State to effect it, the Court having neither the power nor the practical possibility of doing so itself.[136]

If, on the other hand, national law does not allow—or allows only partial—reparation to be made for the consequences of the breach, the Strasbourg Court can, under Article 41, afford the injured party such satisfaction as appears to it to be appropriate. The Court's case-law under Article 41 (formerly Article 50) has been criticized for the lack of clear principles as to when damages should be awarded and how they should be measured.[137] Nonetheless, it is possible to identify a few general rules which the Strasbourg Court applies in determining questions of just satisfaction. Awards of financial just satisfaction can be made under three heads: pecuniary loss, non-pecuniary loss, and costs and expenses.

---

[134] E. Friberg, 'Pilot Judgments from the Court's Perspective' in Council of Europe, *Towards Stronger Implementation of the European Convention on Human Rights at National Level* (Strasbourg 2008), 86, 93.

[135] See generally M. Mas, 'Right to Compensation under Article 50' in T. St. J. Macdonald, F. Matscher, and H. Petzold (eds.), *The European System for the Protection of Human Rights*, (Martinus Nijhoff, Dordrecht 1993), 775.

[136] See generally L. Loucaides, 'Reparation for violations of human rights under the European Convention and restitutio in integrum' [2008] EHRLR 182; and L. Wildhaber, 'Reparations for Internationally Wrongful Acts of States. Article 41 of the European Convention on Human Rights: Just Satisfaction under the European Convention on Human Rights' (2003) 3 *Baltic Yearbook of International Law* 1.

[137] See, for example, the report prepared jointly by the English and Scottish Law Commissions, *Damages under the Human Rights Act 1998*, Law Com. No. 266/Scot Law Com. No. 180, §§3.4 and following. See also A. Mowbray, 'The European Court of Human Rights' Approach to Just Satisfaction' [1997] PL 647.

The Court will award damages only in respect of losses which can be shown to have been caused by the violation in question. In the *Kingsley* case,[138] for example, the applicant, who had been stripped of his licence to run a casino by a tribunal which was not independent for the purposes of Article 6(1), claimed compensation for all the losses which he claimed to have resulted from the loss of the licence. The Grand Chamber pointed out that it could not be assumed that a tribunal in compliance with Article 6(1) would have reached a different conclusion and let the applicant keep the licence. It could not, therefore, award financial compensation to the applicant in respect of loss of procedural opportunity or any distress, loss or damage allegedly flowing from the outcome of the domestic proceedings.[139]

The most frequent award of just satisfaction beyond the declaration of a violation is the award of costs and expenses incurred in the case, either in the domestic proceedings or in Strasbourg. In either event, the costs must have been 'actually and necessarily incurred to prevent or redress the breach of the Convention, … [and] reasonable as to quantum'.[140]

ADVISORY OPINIONS OF THE EUROPEAN COURT OF HUMAN RIGHTS

Under Article 47 of the Convention[141] the Strasbourg Court has jurisdiction to give advisory opinions at the request of the Committee of Ministers[142] on legal questions concerning the interpretation of the Convention and its accompanying Protocols. The Court is required to sit as a Grand Chamber in considering such requests and must deliver a reasoned opinion on the questions referred; separate opinions are permitted.[143] Though a request for an Opinion was made in January 2002, no advisory opinion followed, since the Court decided that the request was outside its competence.[144] The first advisory opinion was delivered in February 2008 on the question of nominations for election as a judge at the Strasbourg Court.[145]

The paucity of advisory opinions is hardly surprising since Article 47(2) provides:

Such opinions shall not deal with any question relating to the content or scope of the rights or freedoms defined in Section I of the Convention and in the protocols thereto, or with any

---

[138] *Kingsley v United Kingdom* (App. 35605/97), 28 May 2002 [GC], (2002) 35 EHRR 177, ECHR 2002-IV.

[139] §43.   [140] §49.

[141] Formerly the Second Protocol which has been in force since 21 September 1970.

[142] Decisions to request an advisory opinion require a majority vote: Art. 47(3) of the Convention.

[143] Art. 31b of the Convention. See the Rules of Court for the procedural rules surrounding advisory opinions.

[144] *Decision on the competence of the Court to give an advisory opinion.* 2 June 2004 [GC], ECHR 2004-VI.

[145] *Advisory Opinion on certain legal questions concerning the lists of candidates submitted with a view to the election of judges to the European Court of Human Rights*, 12 February 2008 [GC], (2009) 49 EHRR 825, ECHR 2008-nyr. See above this chapter.

other questions which the Commission, the Court or the Committee of Ministers might have to consider in consequence of any such proceedings as could be instituted in accordance with the Convention.

On 2 June 2004 the Court decided that the request by the Committee of Ministers for an advisory opinion made in January 2002 concerning the coexistence of the European Convention and the Convention on Human Rights and Fundamental Freedoms of the Commonwealth of Independent States ('the CIS Convention') was outside its competence.[146] The CIS Convention was signed on 26 May 1995 and entered into force on 11 August 1998 on its ratification by Belarus, the Kyrgyz Republic, the Russian Federation, and Tajikistan. Among the Convention's measures of implementation is a CIS Commission with competence to examine individual and collective applications alleging breaches of the Convention provisions. As at the date of the Court's decision, the CIS Commission had not been set up. The existence of the CIS Convention machinery has troubled the Parliamentary Assembly and the Committee of Ministers for some time. Concern was expressed at the potential for conflict between the operation of the CIS Convention and of the European Convention. In January 2002 the Committee of Ministers accepted the recommendation of the Parliamentary Assembly which had stated:

The Assembly, taking into account the weakness of the CIS Commission as an institution for the protection of human rights (from the point of view of its control mechanisms; its political nature; the legal nature of its decisions; the impartiality, independence and competence of its members), and considering that the CIS Commission should not be regarded as 'another procedure of international investigation or settlement' in the sense of Article 35 paragraph 2.*b* of the European Convention on Human Rights, recommends that the Committee of Ministers request that the Court give an advisory opinion on the interpretation of Article 35 paragraph 2.*b* of the European Convention on Human Rights with regard to this specific issue.[147]

The Court adopted a narrow view of its jurisdiction to give advisory opinions, noting that the intention was to provide for advisory opinions on questions which could not arise from contentious proceedings. Examples given were such things as the election of judges and the procedure of the Committee of Ministers in exercising its role in the supervision of judgments. In deciding that it lacked competence to provide the requested opinion, the Court said:[148]

The Court considers that the purpose of the provisions excluding its advisory jurisdiction is to avoid the potential situation in which the Court adopts in an advisory opinion a position which might prejudice its later examination of an application brought under Articles 33 or 34 of the Convention and that it is irrelevant that such an application has not and may never be lodged.

---

[146] *Decision on the Competence of the Court to Give an Advisory Opinion*, 2 June 2004; ECHR 2004-VI.
[147] Recommendation 1519 (2001) of 23 May 2001.
[148] §33 of the Decision of 2 June 2004.

The Court concluded that it might be called upon in contentious proceedings to determine whether the procedures under the CIS Convention constituted 'another procedure of international investigation or settlement' and so it lacked the competence to respond to the request for an advisory opinion.

The restrictive framing of the conditions for advisory opinions of the European Court of Human Rights is unfortunate. The much broader advisory opinion procedure under the Inter-American Convention on Human Rights, which is open to Member States of the Organization of American States, has proved to be a particularly fruitful source of case-law under that Convention.[149] Advisory opinions of the International Court of Justice have also had a significant influence on the development of international law,[150] and the preliminary ruling procedure[151] under Article 234 of the EC Treaty[152] has been an outstanding success in securing both the development of European Community law and its uniform application throughout the Member States.[153]

PROTOCOL 14 AND PROTOCOL 14BIS

Protocol 14 was designed to enable to Strasbourg Court to streamline some of its procedures in order to make the most effective use possible of the judicial resources available to it. It was opened for signature on 13 May 2004. Its implementation has been frustrated by the continuing failure of the Russian Federation to ratify it. All other Contracting Parties had ratified it by October 2006.

THE KEY PROVISIONS OF PROTOCOL 14

This section examines only those provisions of Protocol 14 which affect the handling of cases by the Court.[154] Three approaches are adopted in Protocol 14 to enhance the effectiveness of the Court's work. First, there is reinforcement of the Court's ability to filter out unmeritorious cases. Secondly, a new admissibility criterion is introduced

[149] See Art. 64 of the American Convention on Human Rights of 22 November 1969, OAS Treaty Series No 36. As at 31 December 2004, the Inter-American Court had delivered 18 advisory opinions.

[150] See S. Rosenne, *The Law and Practice of the International Court 1920–1996*, Vol. I (3rd edn Martinus Nijhoff, The Hague 1997), ch.5.

[151] The jurisdiction of the Court of Justice is not advisory in the sense used above, though it does operate as an effective partnership between national courts and the Community court by providing national courts with authoritative interpretations of Community law which they must apply to the cases before them.

[152] Formerly Art. 177 of the EC Treaty.

[153] See generally L. Neville Brown and T. Kennedy, *The Court of Justice of the European Communities*, (5th edn Sweet & Maxwell, London 2000), ch.10.

[154] On Protocol 14, see L. Caflisch, 'The reform of the European Court of Human Rights: Protocol No. 14 and beyond' (2006) 6 HRLRev 403.

which would enable cases to be declared inadmissible where the applicant was not considered to have suffered significant disadvantage. Thirdly, new measures are introduced for dealing with repetitive cases.

An amendment to Article 27 gives single judges increased powers. Single judges, assisted by rapporteurs,[155] would be competent to take decisions on admissibility or decisions to strike a case out of the Court's list in clear cut cases. The inadmissibility would have to be manifest from the outset.

An amendment to Article 28 would permit Committees to declare individual applications admissible and to decide these cases on their merits, when the issues involved in the case can be determined by reference to well-established case-law of the Court. This will allow repetitive cases to be disposed of much more quickly than at present. The requirement for the national judge to be a member of any formation of the court determining a case against the State of that judge's nationality is removed in the case of judgments by Committees, although in appropriate cases where the presence of the national judge would be helpful, this is accommodated.

The most controversial provision is the introduction of a new admissibility criterion which would recast Article 35(3) to read:

The Court shall declare inadmissible any individual application submitted under Article 34 if it considers that:

- a. the application is incompatible with the provisions of the Convention or the Protocols thereto, manifestly ill-founded, or an abuse of the right of individual application; or
- b. the applicant has not suffered a significant disadvantage, unless respect for human rights as defined in the Convention and the Protocols thereto requires an examination of the application on the merits and provided that no case may be rejected on this ground which has not been duly considered by a domestic tribunal.

The operation of this provision is subject to three safeguards. The first two are to be found in the new provision itself. The Convention right raised must have been considered by a national court. Secondly, where respect for human rights requires the Strasbourg Court to consider the merits of the case, it must do so. The third safeguard is a transitional one to be found in Article 20 of the Protocol. Single-judge formations and Committees would not be able to apply the new inadmissibility criterion for the first two years of its operation. The obvious purpose is to enable Chambers and the Grand Chamber to establish some grounds rules on the application of the new criterion before smaller groupings of judges can make use of it. The provision has been viewed as controversial by some, since it appears to move away from a situation in which all admissible applications are subject to adjudication to one in which the Court itself can choose which cases it will hear.

---

[155] Who will be Registry lawyers.

PROTOCOL 14BIS

It had become increasingly clear that efforts to persuade the Russian Federation to ratify Protocol 14 were unlikely to succeed. The objective, however, remains to secure the ratification of Protocol 14, and Protocol 14bis will cease to operate when this happens. Protocol 14bis is an imaginative means of releasing judicial resources without requiring the changes to be ratified by every Contracting Party. So Protocol 14bis takes the judicial resource provisions of Protocol 14 and provides that they may apply to individual Contracting Parties. Thus, it is concerned only with the extension of the competence of single judges, and the extended competence of Committees which were contained in Protocol 14. It should be stressed that it does not make any changes to the current admissibility criteria.

Protocol 14bis will enter into force on the first day of the month following the expiration of a period of three months after the date on which three Contracting Parties ratify the Protocol. Its provisions will only take effect for those Contracting Parties who have ratified it. But under Article 7, it is possible for a Contracting Party to make a declaration applying the provisions of the Protocol on a provisional basis. Such declarations take effect on the first day of the month following the date of it receipt by the Secretary-General of the Council of Europe.[156] Once the Protocol is in force, its provisions will apply to Contracting Parties who subsequently ratify it from the first day of the month following the expiration of a period of three months from their ratification. The outcome will be that different procedures will apply to different Contracting Parties according to whether, and if so, from which date, they ratify Protocol 14bis. As at 1 September 2009 twelve Contracting Parties had signed the Protocol and six Contracting Parties had ratified it, while seven Contracting Parties had made declarations under Article 7 of the Protocol accepting the provisional application of Protocol 14. Protocol 14bis formally entered into force on 1 October 2009.

For Contracting Parties which have ratified Protocol 14bis or made declarations under Article 7,[157] there will be four formations of the Strasbourg Court: (1) single judges; (2) Committees of three judges; (3) Chambers of seven; and (4) a Grand Chamber of seventeen judges.

CONCLUDING REMARKS

To a certain extent, the Court has become a victim of its own success. Protocol 11 was adopted to assist the Strasbourg organs to deal effectively with the rapidly increasing

---

[156] In the second week of July 2009 the first 146 single-judge decisions were taken in respect of applications made against the United Kingdom, Germany, The Netherlands, Denmark, Switzerland, and Norway; these countries had made declarations under Article 7.

[157] See the Addendum to the Rules of Court of 1 July 2009 on the procedure in cases where the new procedures apply.

caseload, but only a few years after its coming into force, the Court has amended its Rules of Procedure to enable Committees to deal with inadmissible cases even more summarily. Furthermore Protocol 14 contemplates further changes, and discussions are taking place as to how the procedure should best be changed in the longer term, since it is recognized that Protocol 14 will not alone resolve the problems the volume of applications to the Strasbourg Court has produced.[158] The problem of the Russian Federation's intransigence over the ratification of Protocol 14 has been tackled by releasing judicial resources under the Protocol 14bis procedures. But in the longer term, further changes may be needed if the Court is to function as effectively in its second fifty years as it has in its first fifty years.

[158] See ch.25 below.

APPENDIX

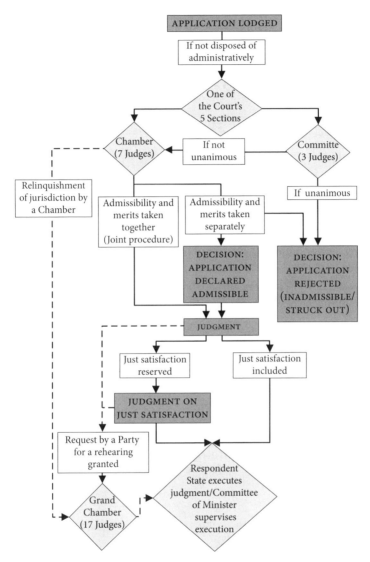

Figure 2.1 Case processing flow chart

Source: Reproduced with the permission of the European Court of Human Rights. This flow chart indicates the progress of a case through the different judicial formations. In the interests of readability, it does not include certain stages in the procedure—such as communication of an application to the respondent State, consideration of a re-hearing request by the Panel of the Grand Chamber and friendly settlement negotiations.

3

SUPERVISING THE ENFORCEMENT OF JUDGMENTS

INTRODUCTION

As mentioned in the preceding chapter, the Strasbourg Court's judgments are final[1] and binding on respondent States.[2] It is however evident that, without compliance or enforcement, even the best of judgments is of little value to the victims of human rights violations. As Leni Fischer, the President of the Council of Europe's Parliamentary Assembly, said at the new Court's inauguration ceremony on 3 November 1998:

What the new European Court of Human Rights needs most is unequivocal respect for and follow-up to its decisions in the Council of Europe member countries. This alone will provide the Court with the authority it needs in order to protect the fundamental rights of our people.[3]

The Committee of Ministers is the organ of the Council of Europe which is alone charged with the task of supervising the execution of these judgments.[4] The Committee of Ministers effectively 'signs off' judgments and friendly settlements;[5] and its manner of exercising this function has increased in rigour over time. It has recently begun producing very informative annual reports on the supervision of the execution of judgments.[6]

---

[1] Art. 44 ECHR.

[2] Art. 46(1) ECHR provides: 'The High Contracting Parties undertake to abide by the final judgment of the Court in any case to which they are parties'.

[3] Council of Europe Press Release No. 729/98. See also Committee of Ministers Recommendation CM/Rec(2008)2 on efficient domestic capacity for rapid execution of judgments of the European Court of Human Rights, 6 February 2008.

[4] Art. 46(2) of the Convention provides: 'The final judgment of the Court shall be transmitted to the Committee of Ministers, which shall supervise its execution'.

[5] See generally, E. Abdelgawad, *The execution of judgments of the European Court of Human Rights*, 2nd edn Human Rights Files No. 19 (Council of Europe Publishing, Strasbourg 2008), and J. Sims, 'Compliance without Remands: The Experience under the European Convention on Human Rights, (2004) 36 *Arizona State Law Journal* 639; and, rather more critical in tone, M. Marmo, 'The Execution of Judgments of the European Court of Human Rights—A Political Battle' (2008) 15 MJ 235.

[6] For the latest report, see Committee of Ministers, *Supervision of the Execution of Judgments of the European Court of Human Rights. Second Annual Report 2008* (Council of Europe Publishing, Strasbourg 2009) (referred to in this chapter as 'the *Second Annual Report*').

During the calendar year 2008, 1,384 new judgments finding a violation of a Convention provision were brought before the Committee for supervision of their execution. As at the end of the calendar year, there were 6,614 judgments still under active consideration by the Committee.[7]

COMPOSITION AND PROCEDURE

According to Article 14 of the Statute of the Council of Europe, each of the Contracting Parties is entitled to one representative on the Committee of Ministers, and each representative is entitled to one vote. In principle these representatives are the Ministers of Foreign Affairs of each Contracting Party, but the Ministers themselves usually meet only twice a year. At the bimonthly meetings which the Committee devotes to its tasks under the Convention, the Ministers act through their Deputies, namely their Permanent Representatives[8] in Strasbourg. The Committee is assisted by a Secretariat provided by the Secretary-General of the Council of Europe.

The Committee operates under Rules of Procedure adopted in May 2006 in the exercise of its supervisory function under Article 46(2) of the Convention.[9] Its functions include the supervision of the execution of friendly settlements as well as judgments of the Court. The Committee's deliberations remain confidential, although an increasing amount of information about the execution of judgments is made public, notably on the internet,[10] and through the annual reports.

The first section of the rules covers general provisions. Rules 1 and 2 are concerned with the organization and chairmanship of meetings. The Chair rotates among the Contracting Parties. Rule 3 provides that a judgment of the Court should be included on the Committee's agenda without delay; in practice, this is within six weeks of the Court's judgment. Rule 4 provides that violations which indicate a systemic problem should be given priority in the Committee's work, but not to the detriment of violations which have caused grave consequences for the injured party. Under Rule 5, the Committee adopts an annual report which is sent to the Court, the Secretary-General, the Parliamentary Assembly, and the Commissioner for Human Rights.

The second section of the rules concerns the supervision of the execution of judgments. Abdelgawad reports a trend in the Strasbourg Court of being more specific on the remedies which the respondent State must put in place.[11] The Committee invites

---

[7] Source: the *Second Annual Report*.

[8] Ambassadors.

[9] Rules of the Committee of Ministers for the supervision of the execution of judgments and of the terms of friendly settlements adopted by the Committee of Ministers on 10 May 2006 at the 964th meeting of the Ministers' Deputies, available on the Council of Europe's website dedicated to the supervision of the execution of the Court's judgments: www.coe.int/t/dghl/monitoring/execution/default_en.asp.

[10] www.coe.int/t/dghl/monitoring/execution/default_en.asp.

[11] E. Abdelgawad, *The execution of judgments of the European Court of Human Rights*, 2nd edn Human Rights Files No. 19 (Council of Europe Publishing, Strasbourg 2008), 46. See also V. Colandrea, 'On the Power of the European Court of Human Rights to Order Specific Non-monetary Measures: Some Remarks in the Light of the *Assanidze, Broniowski* and *Sejdovic* Cases' (2007) 7 HRLRev 396.

the respondent State to explain the measures taken as a consequence of the finding of a violation of Convention rights, and this will include the provision of any just satisfaction awarded by the Court. Of particular importance are general measures taken by the Contracting Party to avoid violations in the future in similar situations. Responses are expected promptly. If the respondent State informs the Committee that it is not yet in a position to provide information about measures taken in execution of the judgment, which, because of the shortness of the six-week delay, will frequently occur at the first meeting at which the judgment is placed on the agenda, the case will automatically return to the agenda of the following meeting. The Committee will then re-examine the case at each subsequent meeting until the required individual measures have been effected, and every six months until the general measures necessary to ensure compliance with the judgment have been taken. Though the deliberations of the Committee of Ministers on these issues are generally confidential, Rule 8 provides that, unless the Committee decides otherwise in order to protect legitimate public or private interests, the agenda of each meeting and certain information shall be accessible to the public, namely:

- information and documents provided by the respondent State; and
- information supplied by the victim,[12] by a non-governmental organization or national human rights bodies.

Rules 10 and 11 anticipate entry into force of the additions to Article 46 of the Convention made by Protocol 14.[13] Rule 10 will permit referral back to the Court for interpretation of the judgment. Such decisions require a majority vote of two thirds of the representatives entitled to sit on the Committee. Rule 11 contains the procedure for referring back to the Strasbourg Court a question of refusal to abide by a final judgment of the Court.

The third section of the rules concerns the supervision of the execution of the terms of friendly settlements, and largely parallels the provisions of the second section.

Rule 16 allows the Committee to make interim resolutions. An example would be for the respondent State to provide information on the progress of the execution of the judgment, or for the Committee to express concern or to make relevant suggestions with respect to the execution of the judgment. Rule 17 provides that:

After having established that the High Contracting Party concerned has taken all the necessary measures to abide by the judgment or that the terms of the friendly settlement have

---

[12] Whose anonymity will be preserved if anonymity has been granted under Rule 47(3) of the Rules of Court.

[13] Which would add two paragraphs to Article 46 as follows: (3) If the Committee of Ministers considers that the supervision of the execution of a final judgment is hindered by a problem of interpretation of the judgment, it may refer the matter to the Court for a ruling on the question of interpretation. A referral decision shall require a majority vote of two thirds of the representatives entitled to sit on the Committee. (4) If the Committee of Ministers considers that a High Contracting Party refuses to abide by a final judgment in a case to which it is a party, it may, after serving formal notice on that Party and by decision adopted by a majority vote of two thirds of the representatives entitled to sit on the Committee, refer to the Court the question whether that Party has failed to fulfil its obligations under paragraph 1.

been executed, the Committee of Ministers shall adopt a resolution concluding that its functions under Article 46, paragraph 2 . . . of the Convention have been exercised.

The Committee's resolutions are available from the Council of Europe and within HUDOC.

Since 1974, the Rules have permitted a quasi-adversarial process as regards the execution of individual measures, such as the payment of monetary compensation, the grant of a residence permit or the reopening of court proceedings. The victim of a violation may submit written comments and respond to those of the respondent State in connection with such issues.[14]

However, in a large number of cases brought before the Court, the prime concern of applicants is not just to ameliorate their personal situation, but also to achieve changes to existing domestic law or practice. There is no formal right of access to the Committee's decision-making process as regards the need for general measures, either for the victim or for interested non-governmental organizations or other third parties. It would, however, appear that in practice the Committee's Secretariat will, where necessary, seek and receive information from individual applicants, non-governmental and international organizations[15] to assist in determining the nature and extent of reforms needed to ensure compliance with the Court's judgment and the extent to which measures recommended to the respondent State through interim resolutions have been carried out. Any material received in this way by the Secretariat will not be used directly as a basis for discussion in the Committee, but will instead be forwarded to the respondent State for information.

The Committee's voting procedures are governed by the Statute of the Council of Europe. A quorum consisting of the representatives of two-thirds of the Contracting Parties is necessary before any meeting can proceed. For the adoption of a resolution or interim resolution a simple majority of all the Contracting Parties and a two-thirds majority of all the States present at the meeting is required. For certain matters unanimity is required.[16]

THE EXECUTION OF JUDGMENTS

JUST SATISFACTION

In every case where the Strasbourg Court finds a violation, it has the power under Article 41 of the Convention to award just satisfaction.[17] If the Court decides to make a monetary award, it will require the respondent State to pay the applicant within three months of the delivery of the judgment.[18] After the Committee's first examination

---

[14] Rules 9 and 15.

[15] The memorandum prepared by the Committee of Ministers' Secretariat on Cases concerning the action of security forces in Northern Ireland, CM/Inf (2004) 14, 29 October 2004, refers to comments received from, among others, the applicants' lawyers and from the Northern Ireland Human Rights Commission.

[16] Article 20 of the Statute.   [17] See ch.2 above.

[18] In 2008 €55.5 million was awarded to victims by way of compensation, costs, and expenses; source: the *Second Annual Report*.

at its meeting immediately following the delivery of the judgment, a case involving an award of just satisfaction will usually come up for renewed examination after the expiry of the three-month time limit. If the respondent State is unable to supply proof of payment, the case will return to the agenda at every subsequent meeting until the Committee is satisfied that the money has been paid in full. Since January 1996, to safeguard the value of an award in the case of delayed payment, the Court has included an order to States to pay simple interest, calculated on a daily basis, from the expiry of the three months until payment. To guard against inflation and for ease of comparison, the Court now expresses all monetary awards in euros, to be converted into the national currency at the date of payment.

Until the *Loizidou* case,[19] the most difficult case involving just satisfaction that the Committee of Ministers had had to deal with, and which was, indeed, largely responsible for the introduction of default interest, was the *Stran Greek Refineries* case.[20] The applicant company had entered into a contract with the Greek State (which at the time was governed by the military junta) to build an oil refinery, and had incurred considerable expenditure procuring goods and services for the construction of the refinery. When the democratic Government regained power, they decided that it was not in the national interest for the refinery to be built and they terminated the contract. The company started proceedings against the State for compensation for the expenditure it had incurred under the terms of the contract, and a substantial arbitration award was made against the Government, which appealed to the Court of Cassation. However, the State then asked for the hearing to be postponed on the ground that a draft law concerning the point in issue was just about to go through Parliament. The new legislation in fact made it inevitable that the Court of Cassation would find against the applicant. The Strasbourg Court unanimously found a violation of Article 6(1), and awarded pecuniary damages of almost US$30,000,000, together with simple interest at 6 per cent from 27 February 1984 (the date of the arbitration award) to the date of judgment.

Because of the size of the award, the Greek Government refused to pay within the three-month limit and asked the Committee if it could pay by instalments over a period of five years, without interest. This request was rejected by the Committee; the President at the time[21] wrote to the Greek Minister of Foreign Affairs, stressing that:

the credibility and effectiveness of the mechanism for the collective enforcement of human rights established under the Convention was based on the respect of the obligations freely entered into by the States and in particular in respect of the supervisory bodies.[22]

---

[19] *Loizidou v Turkey*, (App. 15318/89), 23 March 1995 (preliminary objections) Series A No 310, (1995) 20 EHRR 99, 18 December 1996 (merits), (1997) 23 EHRR 513, ECHR 1996-VI; and 28 July 1998 (just satisfaction), ECHR 1998-IV.

[20] *Stran Greek Refineries and Stratis Andreadis v Greece*, (App. 13427/87), 9 December 1994, Series A No 301-B, (1994) 19 EHRR 293.

[21] The Estonian Foreign Minister.

[22] Res. DH (1997) 184, 20 March 1997.

In the event, the case was not resolved until 17 January 1997, when, as a result of increasing pressure applied by the Committee, the Greek Government transferred US$30,863,828 to the applicants, corresponding to the just satisfaction awarded by the Court, increased in order to provide compensation for the loss of value caused by the delay in payment.[23]

OTHER INDIVIDUAL MEASURES

In addition to the payment of compensation, individual measures may be required to ensure that the injured party is put, as far as possible, in the same situation as he or she enjoyed prior to the violation of the Convention (*restitutio in integrum*). For example, where the Court has found a violation of Article 8 of the Convention caused by the refusal to allow adequate contact between a parent and a child in public care, the respondent State will be required to facilitate more frequent access visits; in a deportation case under Article 3 or 8, a residence permit should be granted; and so on.

The individual measure most commonly required for *restitutio in integrum* is the reopening of domestic legal proceedings. The need for such a measure arises primarily in respect of criminal proceedings, since problems with civil proceedings can frequently be remedied through financial compensation.[24] But a criminal conviction may need to be quashed, or a retrial ordered, in two types of situation: first, where the Court has found procedural injustice in the original trial giving rise to a violation of Article 6; or, secondly, where it has found that the substantive criminal law of a State is incompatible with one of the provisions of the Convention, for example, where an applicant has been tried and convicted for proselytism, contrary to Article 9,[25] or for exercising his or her right to freedom of expression in some way prohibited by national law.[26]

In its Recommendation No. R (2000) 2, adopted on 19 January 2000, the Committee asked Contracting Parties to provide means of reopening proceedings within their national legal systems following a finding of violation by the Strasbourg Court, particularly where the injured party continues to suffer very serious negative consequences because of the outcome of the domestic decision at issue, which are not adequately remedied by the just satisfaction and cannot be rectified except by re-examination or reopening, or where the judgment of the Court leads to the conclusion that the impugned domestic decision is on the merits contrary to the Convention, or the violation found is based on procedural errors or shortcomings of such gravity that a serious doubt is cast on the outcome of the domestic proceedings complained of.

Most Contracting Parties have now incorporated some mechanism into national law to permit criminal proceedings to be reopened in the circumstances outlined above.[27]

---

[23] Ibid.   [24] As in the *Stran Greek Refineries* case, above.

[25] For example, *Kokkinakis v Greece*, (App. 14307/88), 25 May 1993, Series A No 260-A, (1994) 17 EHRR 397: see ch.17 below.

[26] See ch.18 below.

[27] In Turkey, the Constitution was amended in 2003 to allow retrials following a finding of violation of Article 6 by the Strasbourg Court, but not for cases pending on that date before the domestic courts; it is

GENERAL MEASURES

The aim of general measures is to prevent the recurrence of similar violations of the Convention. There are many examples of States taking action as a result of findings of violations of the Convention, including, in the United Kingdom, changes in military policy to allow homosexuals to serve in the armed forces,[28] amendment of the law so that both men and women become entitled to free bus passes at the age of 60,[29] changes to rules on prisoners' correspondence,[30] the abolition of corporal punishment in schools,[31] and the decriminalization of consensual homosexual acts in Northern Ireland.[32] Sometimes the changes made are less salutary. For example, the Court held in the *Abdulaziz, Cabales and Balkandali* case[33] that immigration rules which permitted men to bring their non-national wives to live with them in the United Kingdom, but did not allow women in the same position to gain entry clearance for their husbands, gave rise to a violation of Articles 8 and 14 taken together. The respondent State's response—accepted, as it had to be, by the Committee of Ministers—was to bring an end to the discrimination by removing the right of entry for husbands and wives alike.

Over half of the general measures taken by respondent States involve changes to legislation. Other general measures include administrative reforms, changes to court practice or the introduction of human rights training for the police.

As mentioned above, the Committee's Rules provide that, until it is satisfied with the general measures taken by a respondent State to comply with a judgment of the Court, the case will return to the Committee's agenda every six months at least. On the whole, States are relatively quick to implement the recommendations of the Committee in respect of general measures, sometimes even adopting the necessary measures before the case in question comes before the Committee or even the Court.[34] When implementation is delayed, this is frequently caused by technical problems rather than political resistance in the respondent State. The case which has so far taken the longest time to be resolved to the Committee's satisfaction was the *Gaskin* case,[35]

---

thought that the latter exception was adopted to avoid having to give the Kurdish leader Öcalan a retrial: see *Öcalan v Turkey*, (App. 46221/99), 12 May 2005 [GC], (2005) 41 EHRR 985, ECHR 2005-IV.

[28] Following the judgment in *Smith and Grady v United Kingdom*, (Apps. 33985/96 and 33986/96), 27 September 1999, (2000) 29 EHRR 493, ECHR 1999-VI, the 'Armed Forces Code of Social Conduct' was brought into force on 12 January 2000, lifting the ban.

[29] *Matthews v United Kingdom*, (App. 40302/98), 15 July 2002 (friendly settlement).

[30] Following *Silver and others v United Kingdom*, (Apps. 5947/72, 6205/73, 7052/75, 7061/75, 7107/75, 7113/75, and 7136/75), 25 March 1983, Series A No 61, (1983) 5 EHRR 347.

[31] Following *Campbell and Cosans v United Kingdom*, (App. 7511/76, and 7743/76), 25 February 1982, Series A No 48, (1982) 4 EHRR 293.

[32] Following *Dudgeon v United Kingdom*, (App. 7525/76), 22 October 1981, Series A No 45, (1982) 4 EHRR 149.

[33] *Abdulaziz, Cabales and Balkandali v United Kingdom*, (Apps. 9214/80, 9473/81, and 9474/81), 28 May 1985, Series A No 94, (1985) 7 EHRR 471.

[34] For example, the Court 'noted with satisfaction' in *Findlay v United Kingdom*, (App. 22107/93) 25 February 1997; (1997) 24 EHRR 221, that the United Kingdom had implemented changes to its courts martial procedure following the Commission's Report indicating a violation of Article 6.

[35] *Gaskin v United Kingdom*, (App. 10454/83), 7 July 1989, Series A No 160, (1990) 12 EHRR 36.

where the Strasbourg Court found a violation based on the absence of any procedure to determine when the interests of an individual brought up in public care in having access to his or her medical and other records should outweigh the public interest in the confidentiality of such data. Almost immediately the respondent State enacted legislation to facilitate access to personal data,[36] but the new provisions did not have retroactive effect and did not, as required by the Court's judgment, provide for a fully independent review of a refusal to disclose information. According to the information provided by the respondent State to the Committee, the legislative work required to ensure full compliance with the judgment became increasingly complex because of a desire to create a general right of access by the public to documents held by the authorities. It was not until July 2000, following the coming into force of the Data Protection Act 1998, that the Committee adopted its final resolution in the case.[37]

In the *Modinos* case,[38] the Court found a violation of Article 8 of the Convention arising from the criminalization in Cyprus of private homosexual relations. Between 1995 and 1998 various draft laws were put before Parliament with a view to lifting the ban, but at each attempt the legislation was blocked following extensive debate. Finally, an Act was passed by the Cypriot Parliament on 21 May 1998.

Where there might be a delay in setting in place general measures in a national legal order, the Committee is increasingly expecting interim measures to be taken. To give just one example, the Committee approved interim measures taken in Cyprus in response to the Court's judgment in the *Egmez* case pending comprehensive legislative reforms.[39]

Perhaps more serious is the situation where measures are required to remedy a whole series of cases which highlight an ingrained and persistent problem within the respondent State. An example relates to the actions of the Turkish security forces in south-eastern Turkey. In well over 50 judgments, the Court found violations of Articles 2, 3, 5, 6, 8, and 13 of the Convention and Article 1 of Protocol 1, in respect of villages destroyed by security forces,[40] torture or serious ill-treatment of Kurds held in police custody,[41] and breaches of the right to life or disappearances.[42] In almost all of these cases the Court in addition found breaches of the Convention relating to the absence of adequate official investigations into the allegations in question, giving rise

---

[36] The Access to Personal Files Act 1987 and the Access to Personal Files (Social Services) Regulations 1989.

[37] Res. DH (2000) 106, 24 July 2000.

[38] *Modinos v Cyprus*, (App. 15070/89), 22 April 1993, Series A No 259, (1993) 16 EHRR 485.

[39] Res. DH (2006) 13, 12 April 2006.

[40] The first cases of this type were *Akdivar and others v Turkey*, (App. 21893/93), 16 September 1996, (1997) 23 EHRR 143; *Mentes and others v Turkey*, (App. 23186/94), 28 November 1997, (1998) 26 EHRR 595; and *Selçuk and Asker v Turkey*, (Apps. 23184/94 and 23185/94), 24 April 1998, (1998) 26 EHRR 477, ECHR 1998-II.

[41] The first findings of torture against Turkey were in *Aksoy v Turkey*, (App. 21987/93), 18 December 1996, (1997) 23 EHRR 553; *Aydin v Turkey*, (App. 23178/94), 25 September 1997, (1998) 25 EHRR 251, ECHR 1997-VI; and *Tekin v Turkey*, (App. 22496/93), 9 June 1998, (2001) 31 EHRR 95.

[42] The first cases of this type were *Kaya v Turkey*, (App. 22729/93), 19 February 1998; (1999) 28 EHRR 1; and *Kurt v Turkey*, (App. 24276/94), 25 May 1998; (1999) 27 EHRR 373, ECHR 1998-III.

to the virtual impunity of agents of the State and a lack of effective domestic remedies for their Kurdish victims.

The Committee started its examination of these problems in 1996, and they remain ongoing, although the Committee has decided to close its examination of a number of issues flowing from these cases. But it remains concerned about the procedures which might lead to prosecution of members of the security forces who exceed their official mandate, and has strongly encouraged the authorities to adopt a zero tolerance policy on the use of torture and other forms of ill-treatment.[43]

Another example of persistent and recurring human rights violations is the Italian length of proceedings cases which have persisted for over twenty years. It appears that the problems within the Italian legal system are so deep-rooted and pernicious that there is a limit to what the Italian Government can do to bring about effective reform. But continuing pressure from the Committee does appear to be beginning to bring results, not least in a frank acknowledgment by the highest courts of Italy of the seriousness of the problem for the operation of the rule of law.[44]

A third example relates to the implementation of judgments within Russia. The judgment in the *Burdov* case[45] found violations of Article 6 of the Convention and Article 1 of Protocol 1 because of the failure to enforce a domestic court judgment awarding damages to a Chernobyl rescue worker. The problem of non-enforcement of judgments is widespread in Russia, and is not limited to Chernobyl-related litigation. One result was the pilot judgment in the second *Burdov* case,[46] which required Russia to set up within six months an effective domestic remedy against such violations, and to provide redress within one year for all those awaiting enforcement of a judgment against the authorities in Russia. The Committee has welcomed statements of political will to address the problems, but is pressing for that political will to be matched by action on the ground.[47]

THE ROLE OF THE PARLIAMENTARY ASSEMBLY

The Parliamentary Assembly now includes on the agenda of one its four meetings each year the execution of judgments of the Strasbourg Court.[48] This has evolved from its earlier direction to the Committee on Legal Affairs and Human Rights to report problems which arise in compliance by Contracting Parties with judgments of the Strasbourg Court made against them. It will be recalled that the jurisdiction of the Parliamentary Assembly is purely consultative, but the use of such techniques as

---

[43] Res. DH (2008) 69, 18 September 2008.
[44] Res. DH (2009) 43,19 March 2009.
[45] *Burdov v Russia*, (App. 59498/00), 7 May 2002, (2004) 38 EHRR 639, ECHR 2002-III.
[46] *Burdov v Russia (No. 2)*, (App. 33509/04), 15 January 2009, (2009) 49 EHRR 22.
[47] Res. DH (2009) 43, 19 March 2009.
[48] See E. Abdelgawad, *The execution of judgments of the European Court of Human Rights*, 2nd edn Human Rights Files No. 19 (Council of Europe Publishing, Strasbourg 2008), 59–63.

written questions to the Committee of Ministers can raise the political temperature in relation to issues flowing from judgments of the Strasbourg Court. Abdelgawad says:

The significance of [involvement of the Parliamentary Assembly] lies above all in the ability of members of national parliaments to bring subsequent pressure to bear on the national legislature and executive to adopt the necessary measures, and also in their power to make formal recommendations to the national authorities in charge of policy making.[49]

SANCTIONS

Rolv Ryssdal, former President of the Court, once remarked:

[the Convention], as an international treaty that encroaches on domestic law, relies for its enforcement on a combination of binding legal obligation and the traditional good faith required of the signatories to an international agreement.[50]

However, in addition to good faith, a number of pressures and interests combines to encourage States to comply with the legal obligation to take measures of restitution created by a finding of a violation by the Court.

The first of these is the common interest in a stable Europe. The Convention was drafted and adopted in the aftermath of the Second World War, when European unity and the promotion and support of strong democracies throughout the continent were seen as essential to the security of all. The Convention system has played some part in the resolution of conflict in Northern Ireland and Cyprus, and in re-establishing democracy in Spain, Portugal, Turkey and Greece. However, its role in this respect became particularly relevant after the collapse of communism in central and eastern Europe in 1989, when it became apparent that Europe could no longer hope to rely on the Cold War fear of mutual annihilation to maintain order and stability. If the Contracting Parties of the Council of Europe aspire to strengthen democracy and the rule of law in the Balkans or in Turkey, for example, it is essential that every government is seen to comply willingly with the Court's judgments and the Committee's recommendations. This is the very basis of the collective enforcement of human rights.

In addition, in respect of those States which are not yet part of the European Union but that wish to join, a good record in Strasbourg is seen as an important precondition for membership. The Committee of Ministers' powers are thus reinforced by a certain indirect economic incentive.

There are a number of ways in which the Committee can attempt to influence a government. The first of these is confidential peer pressure: the ministers and their

---

[49] Ibid., at 61.
[50] Lecture given at Masaryk University, 20 March 1996; and see also R. Ryssdal, 'The Enforcement System set up under the European Convention of Human Rights' in M. Bulterman and K. Kuijer (eds.), *Compliance with Judgments of International Courts: proceedings of the symposium organized in honour of Professor Henry G. Schermers* (Martinus Nijhoff, The Hague 1996).

representatives are obliged to keep attending the Committee's meetings and will be reluctant to be seen—or rather, to have their governments seen—as unrepentant violators of human rights. The potency of this type of pressure should not be underestimated. In addition, on a more formal and public level, the Chairman of the Committee can make use of bilateral letters to notify the government concerned of the Committee's views on any particular matter.

In recent years the Committee has made increasing use of interim resolutions as a way of directly addressing the State authority competent to resolve the problems it is encountering in the enforcement of judgments. In addition, the Council of Europe's Parliamentary Assembly is taking a greater interest in the Committee's work under the Convention, and, through the use of Parliamentary questions, may elicit information about the progress of a case and highlight a State's failure adequately to cooperate.

The ultimate sanction available to the Committee is the threat of expulsion from the Council of Europe under Articles 3 and 8 of the Council's Statute.[51] So far, in the history of the Council, the Committee has never made use of its powers to suspend a Contracting Party, although it came close to doing so in 1970, when the military dictatorship which had seized power in Greece in 1967 declared that it considered the finding by the Commission in an inter-State case of a number of serious human rights violations, including torture, to be 'null and void' and that it '[did] not consider itself legally bound by the conclusions of the said report'.[52] In the event, however, Greece withdrew from the Council of Europe without being expelled, and did not join again until the dictatorship had been overthrown.

More recently, the Turkish Government repudiated the Court's judgment in the *Loizidou* case,[53] where the Court found that the denial to a Greek Cypriot of access to her property in northern Cyprus was a breach of Article 1 of the First Protocol to the Convention (right to peaceful enjoyment of property), imputable to Turkey, and ordered the payment of substantial compensation. For many years Turkey refused to pay the just satisfaction awarded by the Court. The Committee of Ministers adopted a number of interim resolutions, the last of which suggested a link between the failure to respect the judgment and Turkey's ambitions for closer relations with the European Union.[54] Turkey finally paid the money owing on 2 December 2003.[55]

Protocol 14 to the Convention provides the Committee with an interim sanction to deal with intractable States, short of expulsion. Under Article 16 of the Protocol, Article 46 of the Convention is amended so that, if a State refuses to abide by a final judgment against it, the Committee may, after serving formal notice on the respondent State, refer to the Court the question whether that State has failed to fulfil its obligation.

---

[51] See ch.1 above.　　　[52] Res. DH (1970) 1, 15 April 1970.

[53] *Loizidou v Turkey,* (App. 15318/89), 23 March 1995 (preliminary objections) Series A No 310; (1995) 20 EHRR 99; 18 December 1996 (merits), (1997) 23 EHRR 513, ECHR 1996-VI; and 28 July 1998 (just satisfaction), ECHR 1998-IV.

[54] Res. DH (2001) 80, 26 June 2001.

[55] Res. DH (2003) 190, 2 December 2003.

CONCLUDING REMARKS

In the first few decades of its existence, the organs of the European Convention system, in contrast to those of other regional and international systems for the protection of human rights,[56] were privileged in that their field of application extended, on the whole, to a relatively homogeneous region of Europe where democracy and the rule of law were well established. However, this region has now expanded to the borders of Asia, to incorporate new Contracting Parties which have developed very different cultures and traditions from those prevailing in western Europe. The Committee is increasingly being called upon to deal with grave and endemic breaches of human rights.

Historically, the Committee has largely relied on good faith and diplomatic pressure to ensure compliance with the Strasbourg Court's judgments. Apart from all-out expulsion from the Council of Europe, which risks being counter-productive to the protection of human rights in the offending State, the sanctions available are limited. However, the challenges of properly supervising the enforcement of judgments when there are so many more judgments than in earlier times, and when the range of systemic problems appears to be growing, should not be underestimated.

[56] Such as the Inter-American and African systems.

4

INTERPRETING THE CONVENTION

INTRODUCTORY REMARKS

The Convention, even with its Protocols, is a relatively short document. To be effective, it requires interpretation. The role of the Strasbourg Court is to interpret and apply the Convention.[1] An understanding of the development of the Convention case-law requires an understanding of the Court's approach to its interpretation.[2] The starting point for the Strasbourg Court was the rules of international law on the interpretation of treaties, since the Convention is an international treaty. When the Strasbourg Court first came to consider this question, the Vienna Convention on the Law of Treaties had not entered into force,[3] but the Strasbourg Court decided that its provisions represented customary international law and should be applied to the interpretation of the Convention.[4]

Two key themes have dominated the interpretation of the Convention. The first is a purposive interpretation,[5] drawn from the principles in the Vienna Convention which permit the application of meanings which are consonant with the object and purpose of the treaty. The second is the interpretation of the Convention as a living instrument, the so-called evolutive interpretation. The Strasbourg Court has summarized its approach as follows:

Under the Vienna Convention on the Law of Treaties, the Court is required to ascertain the ordinary meaning to be given to the words in their context and in the light of the object

---

[1] Article 32(1) ECHR.

[2] The material in this chapter draws in particular on material in J. Merrills, *The Development of International Law by the European Court of Human Rights* (MUP, Manchester, 1988); M. Delmas-Marty, *The European Convention for the Protection of Human Rights. International Protection versus National Restrictions* (Martinus Nijhoff, Dordrecht 1992), Part III; F. Matscher, 'Methods of Interpretation of the Convention' in R. Macdonald, F. Matscher, and H. Petzold, *The European System for the Protection of Human Rights* (Martinus Nijhoff, Dordrecht 1993), 63; S. Greer, *The European Convention on Human Rights. Achievements, Problems and Prospects* (CUP, Cambridge 2006); and G. Letsas, *A Theory of Interpretation of the European Convention on Human Rights* (OUP, Oxford 2007).

[3] It entered into force for the States Parties on 27 January 1980. As at 1 September 2009, there were 109 States Parties to the Convention.

[4] *Golder v United Kingdom*, (App. 4451/70), 21 February 1975, Series A No 18, (1979–80) 1 EHRR 524, §29; and *Al-Adsani v United Kingdom*, (App. 35763/97), 21 November 2001 [GC], (2002) 34 EHRR 273, ECHR 2001-XI, §55. See also L. Wildhaber, 'The European Convention on Human Rights and International Law' (2007) 56 ICLQ 217. Arts. 31–3 of the Vienna Convention are set out in the appendix to this chapter.

[5] Often referred to as a teleological interpretation.

and purpose of the provision from which they are drawn.... The Court must have regard to the fact that the context of the provision is a treaty for the effective protection of individual human rights and that the Convention must be read as a whole, and interpreted in such a way as to promote internal consistency and harmony between its various provisions.... The Court must also take into account any relevant rules and principles of international law applicable in relations between the Contracting Parties.... Recourse may also be had to supplementary means of interpretation, including the preparatory works to the Convention, either to confirm a meaning determined in accordance with the above steps, or to establish the meaning where it would otherwise be ambiguous, obscure or manifestly absurd or unreasonable....[6]

The Court has not adopted a hierarchical approach to the application of the principles of interpretation it uses. It has viewed the task of interpretation as a single complex operation, though reference to the object and purpose of the provision in the context of the Convention as a whole has been the most influential of the principles applied by the Court, and has been described as the 'sheet anchor of the Convention's principles of interpretation'.[7] There are, however, a number of supplementary aids to interpretation which have led some to question the coherence of the Strasbourg Court's approach to the interpretation of the Convention. Greer observes:

It is strange... that such an unstructured approach should have become so widely and uncritically accepted because some of the interpretive principles (for example, *democracy, effective protection* and *legality*) are obviously more intimately connected with the Convention's core purpose than others (for example, the *margin of appreciation* or *evolutive* and *autonomous* interpretation). This, in itself suggests a more formal and hierarchical structure than has yet been acknowledged.[8]

What no one denies is that the European Convention has a special character. It penetrates the national legal orders by requiring Contracting Parties to behave in a particular way towards their own citizens and those citizens of other countries who are within their jurisdiction. What was previously treated by international law as a matter within the domestic jurisdiction of States is brought within an international system of protection and supervision.

THE INFLUENCE OF THE VIENNA CONVENTION

In the *Golder* case[9] the Strasbourg Court had stated that Articles 31 to 33 of the Vienna Convention on the Law of Treaties of 23 May 1969, notwithstanding that the Vienna Convention was not then yet in force, should guide the Court in its

---

[6] *Saadi v United Kingdom*, (App. 13229/03), 29 January 2008 [GC], (2008) 47 EHRR 427, ECHR 2008-nyr, §62.

[7] S. Greer, *The European Convention on Human Rights. Achievements, Problems and Prospects* (CUP, Cambridge 2006), 195.   [8] Ibid., 194.

[9] *Golder v United Kingdom*, (App. 4451/70), 21 February 1975, Series A No 18, (1979–80) 1 EHRR 524, §29.

interpretation of the Convention since the principles contained in those articles were generally regarded as being declaratory of principles of customary international law.[10]

Examination of the principles to be found in Articles 31 to 33 suggests the following propositions.

(1) Terms used in the treaty should be accorded their ordinary meaning.

(2) Regard can be had to the context in which the words appear.

(3) Regard can be had to the object and purpose of the treaty.

(4) The *travaux préparatoires* may be used to help resolve an ambiguity in the text, to confirm a meaning attributed by the use of other rules, or to avoid an absurdity.

(5) The treaty is equally authentic in each official language and any differences of meaning are to be resolved by adopting the meaning which best accords with the object and purpose of the treaty.

How far do these general rules of treaty interpretation apply to the European Convention on Human Rights? While the relevant provisions of the Vienna Convention are sufficiently general to give some guidance, they must be applied with caution in view of the special features of the Convention. Although it is an international treaty, the Convention has a special character which goes beyond merely setting out the rights and obligations of the Contracting Parties. Some specific aspects of the application of principles in the Vienna Convention warrant further comment.

USE OF *TRAVAUX PRÉPARATOIRES*

The special nature of the European Convention means that particular caution is necessary in relying on the preparatory work of the Convention.[11] Preparatory work is notoriously unreliable as a general guide to treaty interpretation, and is hence treated only as a supplementary means of interpretation in Article 32 of the Vienna Convention. But because of the special features of the European Convention, it should be invoked, if at all, as a guide to the general intentions of the Contracting Parties, rather than to delimit strictly the scope of particular articles. This, too, is in accordance with the real purpose of the Convention. Caution is required in the use of the preparatory work because the Strasbourg Court has repeatedly confirmed that the Convention is a living instrument and has adopted a dynamic interpretation to

---

[10] Re-affirmed in *Banković and others v Belgium and 16 other Contracting States*, (App. 52207/99), Decision of 12 December 2001 [GC], (2007) 44 EHRR SE5, ECHR 2001-XII, §35.

[11] See the Report of the Commission of 29 August 1973 in the *Golder* case. See also *Banković and others v Belgium and 16 other Contracting States*, (App. 52207/99), Decision of 12 December 2001 [GC], (2007) 44 EHRR SE5, ECHR 2001-XII, especially §§17–21 and 58.

the substance of its provisions.[12] In the *Sigurjonsson* case[13] the Court noted that the use of the *travaux préparatoires* in the earlier *Young, James and Webster* case[14] was not decisive but merely provided a working hypothesis.[15]

The preparatory work was legitimately invoked by the Commission to show that the provision that 'Everyone shall be free to leave any country, including his own', does not entitle a convicted prisoner to leave the country in which he is lawfully detained. The contrary interpretation would lead, in the words of Article 32 of the Vienna Convention, to a result which is manifestly absurd or unreasonable. On the other hand, in the *Lawless* case, the Court refused to resort to the preparatory work to interpret a provision which was sufficiently clear.[16]

More recently, the Grand Chamber has relied on the *travaux préparatoires* in interpreting Article 3 of Protocol 1[17] on the right to free elections, which at first sight appears to give rise to obligations only between States.[18] In the *Banković* decision,[19] the Grand Chamber found confirmation of its view that the term 'jurisdiction' in Article 1 was an essentially territorial notion from the *travaux préparatoires*. The Expert Intergovernmental Committee had replaced the words 'all persons within their territories' with a reference to persons 'within their jurisdiction' indicating a wish to include those who were not physically present on the territory of a Contracting Party but had a sufficient legal connection with that Contracting Party. In the *Kudła* case,[20] the Strasbourg Court referred to the *travaux préparatoires* in support of its interpretation of Article 13 as requiring a domestic remedy for complaints about unreasonably long legal proceedings.

In recent years, reference to the *travaux préparatoires* has arisen more frequently in dissenting opinions than in the judgments of the Court.[21]

---

[12] See R. Bernhardt, 'Thoughts on the interpretation of human-rights treaties' in F. Matscher and H. Petzold, *Protecting Human Rights: The European Dimension* (Carl Heymanns, Köln 1990), 65, 68–9, and see further below in this chapter.

[13] *Sigurdur A. Sigurjonsson v Iceland*, (App. 16130/90), 30 June 1993, Series A No 264, (1993) 16 EHRR 462.

[14] *Young, James and Webster v United Kingdom*, (Apps. 7601/76 and 7801/77), 13 August 1981, Series A No 44, (1982) 4 EHRR 38.

[15] *Sigurdur A. Sigurjonsson v Iceland*, (App. 16130/90), 30 June 1993, Series A No 264, (1993) 16 EHRR 462, §§24–5.

[16] *Lawless v Ireland*, (App. 332/57), 1 July 1961, Series A No 2, (1979–80) 1 EHRR 13, §14.

[17] See ch.22 below.

[18] *Yumak and Sadak v Turkey*, (App. 10226/03), 8 July 2008 [GC], (2009) 48 EHRR 61, ECHR 2008-nyr, §109.

[19] *Banković and others v Belgium and 16 other Contracting States*, (App. 52207/99), Decision of 12 December 2001 [GC], (2007) 44 EHRR SE5, ECHR 2001-XII, §63.

[20] *Kudła v Poland*, (App. 30210/96), 26 October 2000 [GC], (2002) 35 EHRR 198, ECHR 2000-XI, §152.

[21] See, for example, *Ždanoka v Latvia*, (App. 58278/00), 16 March 2006 [GC], (2007) 45 EHRR 478, ECHR 2006-IV, dissenting opinion of Judge Rozakis; *Hutten-Czapska v Poland*, (App. 35014/97), 19 June 2006 [GC], ECHR 2006-VIII, partly concurring and partly dissenting opinion of Judge Zupančič; and *Kononov v Latvia*, (App. 36376/04), 24 July 2008 [GC], joint dissenting opinion of Judges Fura-Sandström, Björgvinsson, and Ziemele.

DIFFERENT LANGUAGE VERSIONS

The Convention is equally authentic in the English and in the French texts. Where these texts differ, the meaning which best reconciles the texts, having regard to the object and purpose of the treaty, must be adopted.[22] In the *James* case[23] the applicants sought to challenge provisions of the United Kingdom leasehold enfranchisement legislation as being inconsistent with Article 1 of Protocol 1. The issue raised required the Court to consider whether the deprivation of property suffered by the freeholders who were compelled under the legislation to sell the freehold to their tenants could be said to be 'in the public interest'. It appeared that the French text 'pour cause d'utilité publique' carried a somewhat different connotation from the English text. The Court adopted a definition which 'best reconciles the language of the English and French texts, having regard to the object and purpose of Article 1' and referred explicitly to Article 33 of the Vienna Convention in doing so.[24]

ORDINARY MEANING

The Strasbourg Court has frequently used the ordinary meaning of words in order to interpret provisions of the Convention. This may involve reference to dictionaries to determine the ordinary and natural meaning of the words.[25] In the *Johnston* case[26] the Court ruled that the ordinary meaning of the words 'right to marry' did not include a right to divorce; and, in the *Pretty* case,[27] that the right to life in Article 2 could not be read as including a right to die. In the *Lithgow* case[28] the Court ruled that the ordinary meaning of the reference to 'the general principles of international law' in Article 1 of Protocol 1 required that the phrase be given the same meaning as under Article 38(1)(d) of the Statute of the International Court of Justice. A similar approach was taken in the *Banković* case[29] in interpreting the notion of jurisdiction in Article 1 of the Convention, though here it was the ordinary meaning of the word in the context of international law that was adopted.[30]

---

[22] Article 33(4) of the Vienna Convention. See also the *Wemhoff* case, (App. 2122/64), 27 June 1968, Series A No 7; (1979–80) 1 EHRR 55.

[23] *James and others v United Kingdom*, (App. 8793/79), 21 February 1986, Series A No 98, (1986) 8 EHRR 123.

[24] §42. The Court had earlier taken exactly the same approach to the interpretation of the phrase 'prescribed by law' in Article 10(2) of the Convention in *The Sunday Times v United Kingdom*, (App. 6538/74), 26 April 1979, Series A No 30; (1979–80) 2 EHRR 245, §48.

[25] *Luedicke, Belkacem and Koç v Germany*, (Apps. 6210/73, 6877/75, and 7132/75), 28 November 1978, Series A No 29, (1981) 2 EHRR 149, §40.

[26] *Johnston v Ireland*, (App. 9697/82), 18 December 1986, Series A No 112, (1987) 9 EHRR 203.

[27] *Pretty v United Kingdom*, (App. 2346/02), 29 April 2002, (2002) 35 EHRR 1, ECHR 2002-III.

[28] *Lithgow and others v United Kingdom*, (Apps. 9006/80, 9262/81, 9263/81, 9265/81, 9266/81, 9313/81, and 9405/81), 8 July 1986, Series A No 102 (1986) 8 EHRR 329.

[29] *Banković and others v Belgium and 16 other Contracting States*, (App. 52207/99), Decision of 12 December 2001 [GC], (2007) 44 EHRR SE5, ECHR 2001-XII.

[30] §§56–8.

There is one area where the ordinary meaning of words takes on a special signifi-cance. Frequently the Convention uses terms which do not have identical scope in the national legal systems. Here a difficulty arises as to the precise scope of the Convention term. If the national definition is determinative of the meaning, there is a risk of vari-able application of the Convention among the Contracting Parties. Examples of such terms in the Convention are 'civil rights and obligations' and 'criminal charge' in Article 6. The Strasbourg Court has adopted its own rules for determining the mean-ing of such terms. This has come to be known as the independent classification of terms, or, more usually, as the autonomous meaning of terms. The Court has justified this approach by the need to secure uniformity of treatment among the Contracting Parties. Any other approach would result in the Convention's institutions having to defer to the classification adopted in a particular Contracting Party. The issue of defining 'criminal charge' arose in the *Engel* case[31] which concerned action against persons conscripted into the Netherlands armed forces. The action was classified as disciplinary. If the matter involved consideration of a criminal charge, it was squarely within the scope of Article 6. The Court ruled that a Convention definition must be applied to the proceedings; their classification in the national legal order was only one factor to be taken into account in determining their scope. In the *König* case[32] the applicant claimed a violation arising from proceedings of an administrative nature in which he had sought to challenge the withdrawal of his right to practise medicine. The Court concluded that the proceedings involved the determination of his civil rights and obligations despite the German classification of the proceedings as administra-tive in nature. The need to secure a uniform interpretation of the Convention in all the Contracting Parties clearly requires that differential application of the Convention protection arising from differences of terminology be avoided. The more controversial issue surrounds the criteria adopted by the Strasbourg Court for the determination of the meaning of the Convention term. Here there can be opportunities for judicial creativity.

The difference between the traditional international treaty and the Convention again becomes apparent. Many of the terms used belong essentially to the domestic legal order and so the Court has used comparative law techniques in assigning the Convention meaning to the terms.[33] Where common approaches or standards emerge from the comparative study, that meaning will be applied. Where common standards do not emerge, then a greater flexibility of standards is accepted which has come to be known as the 'margin of appreciation'.[34]

---

[31] *Engel and others v Netherlands*, (Apps. 5100/71, 5101/71, 5102/71, 5354/72, and 5370/72), 8 June 1976, Series A No 22, (1979–80) 1 EHRR 647.

[32] *König v Germany*, (App. 6232/73), 28 June 1978, Series A No 27, (1980) 2 EHRR 170.

[33] See L. Wildhaber, 'Judging in a modern constitutional democracy—Employing the comparative law method in constitutional decision-making', presentation by Judge Wildhaber in Johannesburg on 20 March 2004 to mark the inauguration of the new building for the Constitutional Court of South Africa.

[34] See further below in this chapter.

CONTEXT

In the *Golder* case, the Strasbourg Court said:

In the way in which it is presented in the 'general rule' in Article 31 of the Vienna Convention, the process of interpretation of a treaty is a unity, a single combined operation; this rule, closely integrated, places on the same footing the various elements enumerated in the four paragraphs of the Article.[35]

Context is defined in Article 31(2) of the Vienna Convention as the whole of the text together with its preamble and annexes, any agreement related to the treaty made by all the parties in connection with the conclusion of the treaty, and any instrument accepted by all the parties as one related to the treaty. In practice, the use of context enables a treaty to be read as a whole and assistance to be derived from the underlying objectives frequently set out in the preamble.

The use of context has most often arisen where applicants are faced with violations which are covered in some detail by provisions in a Protocol which has not been ratified by the respondent State. In such cases the respondent State often seeks to argue that the whole matter is governed by the Protocol, while applicants will argue that aspects of their claim nevertheless fall within articles of the Convention which are in force as against the respondent State. The Court has concluded in such cases that the presence of detailed rules in a Protocol does not bar the applicability of a more general provision to aspects of the case. So in the *Abdulaziz* case[36] the applicant was able to rely on the right to respect for family life in raising an issue concerning the United Kingdom immigration legislation, even though the United Kingdom is not a party to the Fourth Protocol. Similarly, the applicant in the *Rasmussen* case[37] was able to rely on Article 8 of the Convention in a case concerning paternity issues even though Denmark was not a party to the Seventh Protocol which sets out the rights of parents in relation to their children. In the *Guzzardi* case[38] the applicant was able to rely on Article 5 to challenge the requirement that he live on a small island under police supervision even though Italy had not recognized the rights of free movement contained in the Fourth Protocol.

The Court has said that interpretation of articles of the Convention 'must be in harmony with the logic of the Convention'.[39] So a finding that Article 8 did not require the disclosure of information held in a secret police register which accounted for the applicant's failure to secure employment near a naval base meant that a claim that there had been a failure to provide a remedy under Article 13 could not arise. The reverse situation may also arise; if a right is not part of a more specific provision, it cannot be part of a more general provision. So, since the right to divorce is not part of the right to

---

[35] *Golder v United Kingdom*, (App. 4451/70), 21 February 1975, Series A No 18, (1979–80) 1 EHRR 524, §30.

[36] *Abdulaziz, Cabales and Balkandali v United Kingdom*, (Apps. 9214/80, 9473/81, and 9474/81), 28 May 1985, Series A No 94, (1985) 7 EHRR 471.

[37] *Rasmussen v Denmark*, (App. 8777/79), 28 November 1984, Series A No 87, (1985) 7 EHRR 372.

[38] *Guzzardi v Italy*, (App. 7367/76), 6 November 1980, Series A No 39, (1981) 3 EHRR 333.

[39] *Leander v Sweden*, (App. 9248/81), 26 March 1987, Series A No 116, (1988) 9 EHRR 433, §78.

marry under Article 12, it cannot form part of the rights contained in Article 8, which is of more general purpose and scope.[40]

The *Maaouia* case illustrates how the Court uses context to determine the meaning of terms.[41] The applicant complained at the length of the proceedings for the rescission of the deportation order made against him. The question was whether such proceedings came within the terms 'civil rights and obligation' or constituted a 'criminal charge' against him.[42] The Court stressed that these were autonomous terms and that provisions of the Convention must be construed in the light of the entire Convention system including the Protocols to the Convention. Since Protocol 7 contained certain specific guarantees relating to procedures for the expulsion of aliens, they did not constitute proceedings relating to civil rights and obligations within Article 6(1). Nor did they constitute the determination of a criminal charge against the applicant. Consequently, Article 6(1) did not apply to such proceedings.

A further example can be found in the decision of the Grand Chamber in the *Stec* case.[43] Here the Court considered it to be in the interests of the Convention as a whole that the autonomous concept of possessions in Article 1 of Protocol 1 should be interpreted in a manner which was consistent with the concept of pecuniary rights under Article 6(1). For this reason, it included both contributory and non-contributory social security benefits as within the definition of possessions.

It is easy to make too much of the use of context, whereas examination of the case-law of the Court shows that the context used for reference in interpreting a term can vary considerably. In some cases, the context consists solely of paragraphs of the same article, while in others the whole Convention, including its Preamble and Protocols, is used. Selection of the context often merges into consideration of the object and purpose of the provision.

OBJECT AND PURPOSE

The Commission's Report on the *Golder* case suggests that particular account should be taken of two features of the European Convention when a question of interpretation arises. First, it provides for a system of international adjudication, while the general rules of treaty interpretation have evolved primarily as guides to interpretation by the parties themselves.[44] Hence, in the *Pfunders* case the Court stated that the Convention should be interpreted objectively:

...the obligations undertaken by the High Contracting Parties in the Convention are essentially of an objective character, being designed rather to protect the fundamental rights of

---

[40] *Johnston v Ireland*, (App. 9697/82), 18 December 1986, Series A No 112, (1987) 9 EHRR 203.

[41] *Maaouia v France*, (App. 39652/98), 5 October 2000 [GC], (2001) 33 EHRR 1037, ECHR 2000-X.

[42] See chs 12 and 13 below.

[43] *Stec and others v United Kingdom*, (Apps. 65731/01 and 65900/01), Decision of 6 July 2005 [GC], (2005) 41 EHRR SE18, ECHR 2005-X, §49.

[44] F. Jacobs, 'Varieties of Approach to Treaty Interpretation with Special Reference to the Draft Convention on the Law of Treaties before the Vienna Diplomatic Conference' (1969) 18 ICLQ 318, 341–3.

individual human beings from infringement by any of the High Contracting Parties than to create subjective and reciprocal rights for the High Contracting Parties themselves.[45]

Secondly, any general presumption that treaty obligations should be interpreted restrictively since they derogate from the sovereignty of States is not applicable to the Convention. This follows indeed from the last words of Article 31(1) of the Vienna Convention which provides that a treaty is to be interpreted in good faith in accordance with the ordinary meaning to be given to the terms of the treaty in their context and *in the light of its object and purpose*. Thus the Strasbourg Court stated in the *Wemhoff* case that it was necessary:

to seek the interpretation that is most appropriate in order to realise the aim and achieve the object of the treaty, not that which would restrict to the greatest possible degree the obligations undertaken by the Parties.[46]

These two features of the European Convention suggest that a further conclusion may be drawn as to the appropriate principles of interpretation: that the interpretation of the Convention must be 'dynamic' in the sense that it must be interpreted in the light of developments in social and political attitudes. Its effects cannot be confined to the conceptions of the period when it was drafted or entered into force.[47] Thus the concept of degrading treatment in Article 3 may be interpreted to include racial discrimination, even though this might not have entered the minds of the drafters of the Convention;[48] and the protection of privacy under Article 8 must be developed to meet new technological developments which were not envisaged fifty years ago.[49] But the dynamic or evolutive interpretation of the Convention will not justify reading new rights into the Convention. So the absence of any provision for divorce in the Convention could not be changed by reference to the increased incidence of marriage breakdown since the Convention was drafted. In the *Johnston* case, the Court said:

It is true that the Convention and its Protocols must be interpreted in the light of present-day conditions. However, the Court cannot, by means of an evolutive interpretation, derive from these instruments a right that was not included therein at the outset.[50]

Nor will a dynamic interpretation be used to ground an extension of the jurisdictional basis of the Convention.[51]

---

[45] App. 788/60, *Austria v Italy*, Decision of 11 January 1961, (1962) 4 *Yearbook* 116, 138.

[46] *Wemhoff* case, (App. 2122/64), 27 June 1968, Series A No 7, (1979–80) 1 EHRR 55, §8.

[47] See S. Prebensen 'Evolutive interpretation of the European Convention on Human Rights' in P. Mahoney and others, *Protecting Human Rights: The European Perspective. Studies in Memory of Rolv Ryssdal*, (Carl Heymanns, Köln 2000), 1123.

[48] See ch.9 below.

[49] See ch.16 below; and *The Belgian Linguistic* case, (Apps. 1474/62, 1677/62, 1691/62, 1769/63, 1994/63, and 2126/64), 9 February 1967 and 23 July 1968, Series A Nos 5 and 6, (1979–80) 1 EHRR 241 and 252.

[50] *Johnston v Ireland*, (App. 9697/82), 18 December 1986, Series A No 112, (1987) 9 EHRR 203, §53.

[51] *Banković and others v Belgium and 16 other Contracting States*, (App. 52207/99), Decision of 12 December 2001 [GC], (2007) 44 EHRR SE5, ECHR 2001-XII, §§64–5.

Perhaps the best example of the dynamic interpretation of the Convention can be found in the line of cases under Article 8 dealing with the rights of transsexuals to recognition of their gender identity.[52] Many other examples of a dynamic interpretation of the Convention will be met in subsequent chapters: changes in the concept of the family, of education, of forced labour, or of trade union freedom. This approach is necessary if effect is to be given to the general intentions of the drafters of the Convention. They did not intend solely to protect the individual against the threats to human rights which were then prevalent, with the result that, as the nature of the threats changed, the protection gradually fell away. Their intention was to protect the individual against the threats of the future, as well as the threats of the past. However, if no consensus emerges from a comparative interpretation[53] and if the issue is a controversial one, the Strasbourg Court will revert to respect for national margins of appreciation in recognizing a diversity of approaches.[54] One writer has described the dynamic or evolutive approach as 'firmly established in the Strasbourg jurisprudence as a flexible, albeit a limited, means of adaptation of the Convention law.'[55]

THE PRINCIPLE OF EFFECTIVENESS: THE BEDROCK OF EVOLUTIVE INTERPRETATION

Professor Merrills rightly notes[56] that the case-law of the Strasbourg Court supports the view that, in interpreting the Convention, the Court seeks to give the provisions of the Convention the 'fullest weight and effect consistent with the language used and with the rest of the text and in such a way that every part of it can be given meaning.'[57] It was use of the object and purpose provisions of the Vienna Convention in the context of the European Convention which opened the door to this approach to interpretation of the Convention. It was the *Tyrer* case[58] which first introduced the notion of the Convention as a 'living instrument' to be interpreted in the light of present-day conditions. The context was an application which raised a complaint that judicial corporal punishment in the form of 'birching' in the Isle of Man was degrading treatment prohibited by Article 3 of the Convention. The Court said:

[52] See especially *Goodwin v United Kingdom*, (App. 28957/95), 11 July 2002 [GC], (2002) 35 EHRR 447, ECHR 2002-VI; and *I v United Kingdom*, (App. 26580/94), 11 July 2002; (2003) 36 EHRR 967. See discussion of these cases in ch.16 below.

[53] See further below in this chapter.

[54] See, for example, *Vo v France*, (App. 53924/00), 8 July 2004 [GC], (2005) 40 EHRR 259, ECHR 2004-VIII, §§81–5, on the question of when the right to life begins.

[55] S. Prebensen 'Evolutive interpretation of the European Convention on Human Rights' in P. Mahoney and others, *Protecting Human Rights: The European Perspective. Studies in Memory of Rolv Ryssdal* (Carl Heymanns, Köln 2000), 1136.

[56] J. Merrills, *The Development of International Law by the European Court of Human Rights* (MUP, Manchester 1988), ch.5.

[57] Ibid., 98.

[58] *Tyrer v United Kingdom*, (App. 5856/72), 25 April 1978, Series A No 26, (1979–80) 12 EHRR 1.

The Court must also recall that the Convention is a living instrument which…must be interpreted in the light of present-day conditions. In the case now before it the Court cannot but be influenced by the developments and commonly accepted standards in the penal policy of the member States of the Council of Europe in this field.[59]

One of the most dramatic illustrations of the application of the principle of effectiveness arose in the *Airey* case.[60] Johanna Airey wished to seek a decree of judicial separation from her husband on the grounds of his alleged cruelty to her and their children. She is described as coming from a humble background and receiving low wages for her work. Mr Airey had left the matrimonial home, but Mrs Airey feared that he might return and wished to ensure that he had no right to do so. She was unable to find a lawyer to act for her, since no legal aid was available to assist her and she lacked the resources to fund such assistance on a fee-paying basis. She complained to the Commission which unanimously considered that there was a breach of Article 6(1) by reason of the effective denial of access to a court. The respondent State sought to argue, *inter alia*, that there was no bar to Mrs Airey appearing as a litigant in person before the Irish courts to seek a judicial separation. The Strasbourg Court, which by a majority of five to two decided that there was a violation of Article 6(1), considered it important to determine whether any remedy available to Mrs Airey was 'practical and effective' as distinct from being 'theoretical or illusory'.[61] The Court concluded that it was not 'realistic' for Mrs Airey to conduct her own case effectively.

While the *Airey* case is a dramatic illustration of an interpretation to secure effectiveness, the Court has contrasted rights which are practical and effective with those that are merely theoretical and illusory in a number of cases.[62] This principle can now be regarded as a general principle applicable whenever Convention rights are in issue.

The phrase "the Convention is a living instrument' has been used in around thirty cases.[63] The requirement that the Convention is interpreted as a living instrument

---

[59] §31.

[60] *Airey v Ireland*, (App. 6289/73), 9 October 1979, Series A No 32, (1979–80) 2 EHRR 305, §24. See also *Artico v Italy*, (App. 6694/74), 13 May 1980, Series A No 37, (1981) 3EHRR 1, §33.

[61] §24.

[62] See, for example, *The Belgian Linguistic* case, (Apps. 1474/62, 1677/62, 1691/62, 1769/63, 1994/63, and 2126/64), 23 July 1968, Series A No 6, (1979–80) 1 EHRR 252, §§3–4; *Golder v United Kingdom*, (App. 4451/70), 21 February 1975, Series A No 18, (1979–80) 1 EHRR 524, §35; *Luedicke, Belkacem and Koç v Federal Republic of Germany*, (Apps. 6210/73, 6877/75, and 7132/75), 28 November 1978, Series A No 29, (1980) 2 EHRR 433, § 42; *Marckx v Belgium*, (App. 6833/74), 13 June 1979, Series A No 31, (1979–80) 2 EHRR 330, §31; *Artico v Italy*, (App. 6694/74), 13 May 1980, Series A No 37, (1981) 3 EHRR 1, §33; *Kamasinski v Austria*, (App. 9783/82), 19 December 1989, Series A No 168, §65; *Matthews v United Kingdom*, (App. 24833/94), 18 February 1999 [GC], (1999) 28 EHRR 361, ECHR 1999-I, §34; *Podkolzina v Latvia*, (App. 46726/99), 9 April 2002, ECHR 2002-II, §35; *Folgerø v Norway*, (App. 15472/02), 29 June 2007 [GC], (2008) 46 EHRR 1147, ECHR 2007-VIII, §100; and *Mehmet Eren v Turkey*, (App.32347/02), 14 October 2008, §50.

[63] Recently in *EB v France*, (App. 43546/02), 22 January 2008 [GC], §92; and in *Saadi v United Kingdom*, (App 13229/03), 29 January 2008, §55 where the Court said: '[The Convention]…had to be interpreted in a manner which ensured that rights were given a broad construction and that limitations were narrowly construed, in a manner which gave practical and effective protection to human rights, and as a living instrument, in light of present day conditions and in accordance with developments in international law so as to reflect the increasingly high standard being required in the area of the protection of human rights.' A HUDOC search reveals that the phrase 'a living instrument' has been used in 47 cases.

means that it has to be given something of an activist interpretation. The Convention could not be a living instrument if its interpretation remained static; the content of the Convention rights will change over time. Most, but not all, commentators consider that this change must always operate to enhance the content of human rights.[64] Judicial activism is a label used to refer to a judicial approach which seeks to extend or modify existing law especially in cases where policy choices are before a court, while judicial restraint is a label used to refer to a judicial approach which focuses upon the judge applying existing case-law and avoiding developing the law beyond its clearly established parameters. It is sometimes suggested that judicial activism takes the judge into the realm of the policy-maker, while judicial restraint recognizes the separation of law-maker and law-applier. Mahoney comments:

Judicial activism raises the spectre of judges illegitimately enlarging their role in society to one of legislating on general policy matters and of exceeding their given functions of interpretation, whereas judicial self-restraint carries the risk of judges abdicating their responsibility of independent review of governmental action.[65]

Mahoney argues:

The conclusion of the present study is that, as far as the European Convention on Human Rights is concerned, the dilemma of activism versus restraint is more apparent than real, in that activism and restraint are complementary components of the methodology of judicial review inherent in the very nature of the Convention as an international treaty intended to secure effective protection of human rights and fundamental freedoms.[66]

Some commentators have observed that a new approach to the interpretation of the Convention can be discerned from some decisions in recent years which extends the evolutive approach.[67] This is an approach which seeks to integrate interpretation of the civil and political rights, which are traditionally considered to be the principal focus of the European Convention, and the interpretation of economic, social and cultural rights, which are traditionally considered to be the principal focus of the European Social Charter. The integrated approach limits the effect of the division created by two legal instruments. It recognizes that, on the one hand, the enjoyment of civil and political rights requires respect for and promotion of social rights, and, on the other hand, that social rights are not second best to civil and political rights.

Mantouvalou argues convincingly that the *Sidabras and Dziautas* case[68] is an illustration of this method of interpretation. The case concerned limitations on

---

[64] See discussion in P. Mahoney, 'Judicial Activism and Judicial Self-Restraint in the European Court of Human Rights: Two Sides of the Same Coin' [1990] HRLJ 57, 66–8.

[65] Ibid., 58.

[66] Ibid., 59. For a contrary and critical view, see L. Hoffmann, 'The Universality of Human Rights', Judicial Studies Board Annual lecture, delivered on 19 March 2009. But see also, disagreeing with these views, M. Arden, 'Human Rights and Civil Wrongs: Tort under the Spotlight', Hailsham Lecture 2009, 12 May 2009.

[67] For a useful summary, see V. Mantouvalou, 'Work and Private Life: *Sidabras and Dziautas v Lithuania*', (2005) 30 ELRev 573.

[68] *Sidabras and Dziautas v Lithuania* (Apps. 55480/00 and 593300/00), 27 July 2004, (2004) 42 EHRR 104, ECHR 2004-VIII. See also *Rainys and Gasparavicius v Lithuania* (Apps. 70665/01 and 74345/01), 7 April 2005.

the employment in Lithuania of former KGB employees. Complaints were made of breaches of Articles 8, 10, and 14 of the Convention. In finding by five votes to two, a violation of Article 14 when read in conjunction with Article 8, the Court appears to have been significantly influenced by conclusions of the European Committee on Social Rights in adjudicating on a claim under the European Social Charter, as well as concerns expressed within the International Labour Organisation framework concerning restrictions on access to employment in the public sector. According to the Court, it was proper to take a broad view of the scope of the Convention right in order to ensure its consistency with interpretations made in the context of the treaty frameworks concerned primarily with social rights. Mantouvalou concludes:

The adoption of the integrated approach has not been a matter of conscious choice for the ECtHR. That is why it is still unclear what exactly it entails and what outcomes it may lead to. It has been driven by applicants, who have genuinely believed that they had a claim under the Convention, and has been inspired by declarations that civil and political and economic and social rights are interdependent and indivisible.[69]

It is, however, possible to find authorities which go the other way. The Court's decision in the *N* case[70] finding that there would be no violation of Article 3 if the United Kingdom returned an AIDS sufferer to Uganda on the grounds that the circumstances were not wholly exceptional.[71] In coming to this conclusion, the Court had noted the advances which had been made in the availability of antiretroviral medication in Uganda, but also noted that the object of Article 3 was not to place an obligation on a Contracting Party to 'alleviate . . . disparities [in medical treatments] through the provision of free and unlimited health care to all aliens without a right to stay within its jurisdiction.'[72] This was seen to impose too great a burden on the Contracting Parties.

The Grand Chamber considered the practice of interpreting the Convention provisions in the light of other international texts and instruments in some detail in the *Demir and Baykara* case.[73] The context was consideration of the restriction in Turkey on municipal civil servants forming trade unions. The Turkish Government had argued that it was inappropriate for the Strasbourg Court to take account of international agreements to which it was not a party in interpreting Article 11 of the Convention. The Grand Chamber explores its practice in this area,[74] and concludes:

85. The Court, in defining the meaning of terms and notions in the text of the Convention, can and must take into account elements of international law other than the Convention, the interpretation of such elements by competent organs, and the

---

[69] V. Mantouvalou, 'Work and private life: *Sidabras and Dziautas v Lithuania*' (2005) 30 ELRev 573, 583.

[70] *N v United Kingdom*, (App. 26565/05), 27 May 2008 [GC], (2008) 47 EHRR 885, ECHR 2008-nyr.

[71] As they had been in *D v United Kingdom*, (App. 30240/96), 2 May 1997, (1997) 24 EHRR 423, ECHR 1997-III.

[72] §44.

[73] *Demir and Baykara v Turkey*, (App. 34503/97), 12 November 2008 [GC], (2009) 48 EHRR 1272, ECHR 2008-nyr.

[74] §§65–86.

practice of European States reflecting their common values. The consensus emerging from specialised international instruments and from the practice of Contracting States may constitute a relevant consideration for the Court when it interprets the provisions of the Convention in specific cases.

86. In this context, it is not necessary for the respondent State to have ratified the entire collection of instruments that are applicable in respect of the precise subject matter of the case concerned. It will be sufficient for the Court that the relevant international instruments denote a continuous evolution in the norms and principles applied in international law or in the domestic law of the majority of member States of the Council of Europe and show, in a precise area, that there is common ground in modern societies....

COMPARATIVE INTERPRETATION

One response to suggestions that the Strasbourg judges are too active and make law rather than interpret it has been resort to a the search for a common European standard. The standards adopted for interpreting the European Convention may sometimes differ from those applicable to other international instruments. This is because the interpretation of the European Convention may legitimately be based on a common tradition of constitutional laws and a large measure of legal tradition common to the countries of the Council of Europe.[75] Thus the Commission has relied as a guide to the scope of the rights guaranteed by the Convention, on comparative surveys of the laws of the Contracting Parties: the laws relating to vagrancy,[76] for example, or legislation on the right to respect for family life,[77] or on various aspects of criminal procedure,[78] or on the age of criminal responsibility,[79] or the law relating to recognition of the gender identity of transsexuals.[80]

Reference may be made to the general practice of the Contracting Parties in order to decide what is 'reasonable' or what is 'necessary'—two terms which occur frequently in the Convention—or what constitutes 'normal' civic obligations under Article 4.[81] There may thus be a conflict between two legitimate aims of interpretation: to avoid inconsistencies with other international instruments, and to develop the protection of human rights in Europe on the basis of a common European law.

The yardstick of democratic standards runs through the Convention and has proved to be an important source of inspiration in delimiting the requirements of the Convention. Certain key features of a democratic society emerge from a significant

[75] See generally A. Dremczewski, *European Human Rights Convention in Domestic Law* (OUP, Oxford 1983).

[76] See Appendix IV to the Commission's Report of 19 July 1969 on the *Vagrancy Cases*, entitled 'Outline of Vagrancy legislation in force in European countries'.

[77] See ch.15 below.

[78] See chs. 12 and 13 below.

[79] *V v United Kingdom*, (App. 24888/94), 16 December 1999, (2000) 30 EHRR 121, ECHR 1999-IX.

[80] *Goodwin v United Kingdom*, (App. 28957/95), 11 July 2002 [GC], (2002) 35 EHRR 447, ECHR 2002-VI; and *I v United Kingdom*, (App. 26580/94), 11 July 2002, (2003) 36 EHRR 967.

[81] See ch.10 below.

case-law in which the term has been relevant.[82] Democratic values require respect for the rule of law, which has been reflected in recognition by the Court of a right of access to the courts.[83] In one case, the Grand Chamber of the Court said:

> 89. As has been stated many times in the Court's judgments, not only is political democracy a fundamental feature of the European public order but the Convention was designed to promote and maintain the ideals and values of a democratic society. Democracy, the Court has stressed, is the only political model contemplated in the Convention and the only one compatible with it. By virtue of the wording of the second paragraph of Article 11, and likewise of Articles 8, 9 and 10 of the Convention, the only necessity capable of justifying an interference with any of the rights enshrined in those Articles is one that must claim to spring from 'democratic society'....

> 90. Referring to the hallmarks of a 'democratic society', the Court has attached particular importance to pluralism, tolerance and broadmindedness. In that context, it has held that although individual interests must on occasion be subordinated to those of a group, democracy does not simply mean that the views of the majority must always prevail: a balance must be achieved which ensures the fair and proper treatment of minorities and avoids any abuse of a dominant position....[84]

APPROACHES AND IDEOLOGIES, AND
THE MARGIN OF APPRECIATION

Fundamental differences of approach to interpretation of the Convention had emerged in the *Golder* case.[85] The Commission had argued that an important canon of interpretation of international treaties had only very limited application to the European Convention, namely consideration of the intention of the parties at the time of ratification. The Commission argued that the European Convention should not be interpreted in this subjective manner by reference to the intention of the parties, but should be interpreted objectively. The Commission argued:

The over-riding function of this Convention is to protect the rights of the individual and not to lay down as between States mutual obligations which are to be restrictively interpreted having regard to the sovereignty of these States. On the contrary, the role of the

---

[82] See further discussion in ch.14 below. See also J. Merrills, *The Development of International Law by the European Court of Human Rights* (MUP, Manchester 1993), ch.6. See also S. Marks, 'The European Convention on Human Rights and its "Democratic Society"' (1995) 66 BYIL 209; and C. Gearty, 'Democracy and Human Rights in the European Court of Human Rights: A Critical Appraisal' (2000) 51 NILQ 381.

[83] *Golder v United Kingdom*, (App. 4451/70), 21 February 1975, Series A No 18, (1979–80) 1 EHRR 524, §29.

[84] *Gorzelik and others v Poland*, (App. 44158/98), 17 February 2004, (2005) 40 EHRR 76, ECHR 2004-I, §§89–90.

[85] *Golder v United Kingdom*, (App. 4451/70), 21 February 1975, Series A No 18, (1979–80) 1 EHRR 524.

Convention and the function of its interpretation is to make the protection of the individual effective.[86]

This approach to interpretation was adopted by the majority of the Court in its 9–3 decision. The opposing view to interpretation of the Convention was championed by Sir Gerald Fitzmaurice throughout his term as a judge at the Court and an understanding of this approach helps to explain why he was so frequently in the minority in the Court. For Sir Gerald Fitzmaurice, the objective approach to interpretation was fundamentally flawed. Since the Convention made serious inroads into the domestic jurisdiction of States, a restrictive approach to its interpretation was required. He argued in his minority opinion in the *Golder* Case that a cautious and conservative approach should be adopted to the interpretation of the Convention, since extensive interpretation could impose on Contracting Parties obligations they had not intended to assume in ratifying the Convention. Therefore doubts should be resolved in favour of the State rather than the individual.

The resolution of doubts in favour of States has found its clearest exposition in the case-law of the Strasbourg Court in the concept of the 'margin of appreciation' which has been used extensively. But the term is used in more than one sense, as Letsas notes;[87] furthermore the Strasbourg Court is criticized for not always distinguishing between different meanings and contexts in which the term is used:

I propose to analyse the margin of appreciation doctrine, as it figures in the case-law, in a different way by drawing a distinction between two different ways in which it has been used by the Court. The first one, which I shall call the *substantive* concept is to address the relationship between individual freedoms and collective goals. The second one, which I shall call the *structural* concept, is to address the limits or intensity of review of the European Court of Human Rights in view of its status as an international tribunal. It amounts to the claim that the European Court should often *defer* to the judgment of national authorities on the basis that the ECHR is an *international* convention, not a national bill of rights. The ideas of subsidiarity and state consensus are usually invoked to support the structural use of the margin of appreciation.[88]

This is a helpful analysis which enables us to appreciate the different contexts in which the notion operates. In its first sense, it has its greatest application when balancing the rights contained in the first paragraphs of Articles 8 to 11 of the Convention against the permissible interferences which may be justified by resort to the limitations permitted by the second paragraphs of those provisions.[89] In the second sense, the easiest example is the approach of the Strasbourg Court to review of a Contracting Party's

---

[86] *Golder v United Kingdom*, Report of 1 June 1973. Series B, No 16, 40.

[87] G. Letsas, *A Theory of Interpretation of the European Convention on Human Rights* (OUP, Oxford 2007), ch.4.

[88] 80–1.

[89] For a further discussion of limitations in this context, see ch.14 below. The Strasbourg Court has interpreted certain other provisions of the Convention using the same methodology; so, for example, the right to property in Art.1 of Protocol 1 is now applied using this approach.

claim that there is a public emergency threatening the life of the nation which warrants derogation from one or more provisions of the Convention.[90]

Margins of appreciation are the outer limits of schemes of protection which are acceptable under the Convention.[91] The Court will not interfere with actions which are within the margin of appreciation. So in the *Brannigan* case,[92] the Court affirmed its earlier case-law in considering the validity of the United Kingdom's derogation under Article 15 excluding the application of Article 5(3) to the system of detention applicable under the prevention of terrorism legislation. The Court recognized that Contracting Parties are in a better position than the judges to decide both on the presence of an emergency threatening the life of the nation and on the nature and scope of the derogations necessary to avert it. It was therefore appropriate to leave 'a wide margin of appreciation...to the national authorities'.[93] However, even this wide margin of appreciation is subject to the supervision of the Convention organs, since it is for the Court to determine whether the derogation goes beyond the extent strictly required by the exigencies of the situation. It followed that:

in exercising its supervision the Court must give appropriate weight to such relevant factors as the nature of the rights affected by the derogation, the circumstances leading to, and the duration of, the emergency situation.[94]

The absence of judicial control over the extended period of detention was held not to be beyond the margin of appreciation in this case.

The use of margins of appreciation permits the Court to keep in touch with legal reality where there is scope for differential application of Convention provisions while retaining some control over State conduct.[95] As the concept has evolved in the case-law of the Court, it has become clear that the scope of the margin will vary according to the circumstances, subject matter, and background to the issue before the Court as well as the presence or absence of common ground among the States Parties to the Convention.[96]

---

[90] See ch.6 below.

[91] See G. van der Meersch, 'Le caractère "autonome" des termes et la "marge d'appreciation" des gouvernements dans l'interprétation de la Convention européenne des Droits de l'Homme' in F. Matscher and H. Petzold, *Protecting Human Rights: The European Dimension. Studies in honour of Gérard J. Wiarda* (Carl Heymanns, Köln 1989), 201; R. Macdonald, 'The margin of appreciation' in R. Macdonald, F. Matscher, and H. Petzold, *The European System for the Protection of Human Rights* (Martinus Nijhoff, Dordrecht 1993), 83; and J.G. Merrills, *The Development of International Law by the European Court of Human Rights* (MUP, Manchester 1993), ch.7.

[92] *Brannigan and McBride v United Kingdom*, (Apps. 14553/89, and 14554/89), 26 May 1993, Series A No 258–B, (1994) 17 EHRR 539.

[93] §43, affirming *Ireland v United Kingdom*, (App. 5310/71), 18 January 1978, Series A No 25, (1979–80) 2 EHRR 25, §207.

[94] *Brannigan and McBride v United Kingdom*, (Apps. 14553/89, and 14554/89), 26 May 1993, Series A No 258–B, (1994) 17 EHRR 539, §43.

[95] See generally Y. Arai-Takahashi, *The Margin of Appreciation Doctrine and the Principle of Proportionality in the Jurisprudence of the ECHR* (Intersentia, Antwerp 2002); and H. Yourow, *The Margin of Appreciation Doctrine in the Dynamics of European Human Rights Jurisprudence* (Martinus Nijhoff, Dordrecht 1996).

[96] See *Rasmussen v Denmark*, (App. 8777/79), 28 November 1984, Series A No 87, (1985) 7 EHRR 372.

Letsas has argued that a proper understanding of the margin of appreciation and of the limits of interpretation will avoid the Convention being extended into areas which are inappropriate for human rights protection; he calls this rights inflation. He uses the example of a right to sleep which he suggests was involved in the litigation concerning airport noise, where the Grand Chamber reversed the Chamber judgment, which had found a violation of Article 8.[97]

CONCLUDING REMARKS

Interpretation of the Convention builds on the rules of public international law on the interpretation of treaties and has remained broadly consistent with those principles. At the same time the approach taken to interpretation has recognized that both the nature of the obligations contained in the Convention and the regional limitation on its application legitimately permit the giving of a particular meaning to words and phrases in the Convention. There would appear to be two core principles of interpretation: that which seeks to effect the object and purpose of the Convention (the teleological approach), and that which seeks to give it a practical and effective application in the light of present-day conditions (the evolutive approach).

The role of the Strasbourg Court is casuistic; deciding individual cases does not lend itself to broad statements of theory, and the Court has never used practice statements or practice directions to set out its approach to interpretation. It has, accordingly, been left to commentators to synthesize from the case-law of the Strasbourg Court a set of principles which the Court uses in interpreting the Convention. Its overall approach can perhaps best be summarized as an evolutive approach based upon its understanding of the object and purpose of the Convention, but also reflective of its own role as an international human rights court conscious of its subsidiary role in the protection of human rights.

---

[97] G. Letsas, *A Theory of Interpretation of the European Convention on Human Rights* (OUP, Oxford 2007), esp. ch.6. See also *Hatton v United Kingdom*, (App. 36022/97), 8 July 2003 [GC], (2003) 37 EHRR 611, ECHR 2003-VIII, discussed in more detail in ch.16 below.

APPENDIX

EXTRACTS FROM THE VIENNA CONVENTION
ON THE LAW OF TREATIES

Article 31
General rule of interpretation

1. A treaty shall be interpreted in good faith in accordance with the ordinary meaning to be given to the terms of the treaty in their context and in the light of its object and purpose.

2. The context for the purpose of the interpretation of a treaty shall comprise, in addition to the text, including its preamble and annexes:

   (a) any agreement relating to the treaty which was made between all the parties in connection with the conclusion of the treaty;

   (b) any instrument which was made by one or more parties in connection with the conclusion of the treaty and accepted by the other parties as an instrument related to the treaty.

3. There shall be taken into account, together with the context:

   (a) any subsequent agreement between the parties regarding the interpretation of the treaty or the application of its provisions;

   (b) any subsequent practice in the application of the treaty which establishes the agreement of the parties regarding its interpretation;

   (c) any relevant rules of international law applicable in the relations between the parties.

4. A special meaning shall be given to a term if it is established that the parties so intended.

Article 32
Supplementary means of interpretation

Recourse may be had to supplementary means of interpretation, including the preparatory work of the treaty and the circumstances of its conclusion, in order to confirm the meaning resulting from the application of Article 31, or to determine the meaning when the interpretation according to Article 31:

   (a) leaves the meaning ambiguous or obscure; or

   (b) leads to a result which is manifestly absurd or unreasonable.

Article 33
Interpretation of treaties authenticated in two or more languages

1. When a treaty has been authenticated in two or more languages, the text is equally authoritative in each language, unless the treaty provides or the parties agree that, in case of divergence, a particular text shall prevail.

2. A version of the treaty in a language other than one of those in which the text was authenticated shall be considered an authentic text only if the treaty so provides or the parties so agree.

3. The terms of the treaty are presumed to have the same meaning in each authentic text.

4. Except where a particular text prevails in accordance with paragraph 1, where a comparison of the authentic texts discloses a difference of meaning which the application of Articles 31 and 32 does not remove, the meaning which best reconciles the texts, having regard to the object and purpose of the treaty, shall be adopted.

5

THE SCOPE OF THE CONVENTION

GENERAL SCOPE OF THE CONVENTION

This chapter explores a number of issues arising from the obligation in Article 1 of the Convention, which requires Contracting Parties to secure to everyone within their jurisdiction the Convention rights set out in Section I of the Convention. The whole of Section I, however, does not in terms impose any obligations on States; it takes the form of a declaration of rights. It is Article 1 which transforms this declaration of rights into a set of obligations for the Contracting Parties which ratify the Convention.

The overall approach of the Convention is based on the principles of solidarity and subsidiarity. Solidarity refers to the commitment of the Contracting Parties to secure effective protection of the rights enumerated in the Convention within their national legal orders, while subsidiarity[1] refers to the role of the Strasbourg Court as secondary to the institutions of national legal systems in adjudicating on claims that Convention rights have been violated. It is partly for this reason that a complaint cannot be made to the Strasbourg Court until all efforts to resolve the dispute have been undertaken within the national legal order. This principle also explains why the Strasbourg Court does not regard itself as a court of appeal from decisions of institutions within national legal orders.

Writers have differed on the nature of the guarantee in Article 1. Some have argued that there is an obligation to incorporate the actual text of the Convention, or of Section I at least, into national law.[2] A former President of the Court has spoken of the merits of incorporation in the following terms:

---

[1] See H. Petzold, 'The Convention and the Principle of Subsidiarity', in R. Macdonald, F. Matscher, and H. Petzold, *The European System for the Protection of Human Rights* (Martinus Nijhoff, Dordrecht 1993), 41.

2 See T. Buergenthal, 'The effect of the European Convention on Human Rights on the Internal Law of Member States' in *The European Convention on Human Rights*, British Institute of International and Comparative Law, Supplementary Publication No. 11, 1965, 57 *et seq.*, and for the opposite view T. Sørensen, 'Obligations of a State Party to a Treaty as regards its Municipal Law' in A. H. Robertson (ed.), *Human Rights in National and International Law* (MUP, Manchester 1968), 11–31. See also A.

Incorporation of the Convention into national law, as known in many States, is one of the most effective means of reducing the need for recourse to Strasbourg.[3]

The advantages of incorporation are spelled out in other speeches:

[Incorporation] has in fact two advantages: it provides the national court with the possibility of taking account of the Convention and the Strasbourg case-law to resolve the dispute before it, and at the same time it gives the European organs an opportunity to discover the views of the national courts regarding the interpretation of the Convention and its application to a specific set of circumstances. The dialogue which thus develops between those who are called upon to apply the Convention on the domestic level and those who must do so on the European level is crucial for an effective protection of the rights guaranteed under the Convention.[4]

There is, however, no dispute that national law must give full effect to the rights guaranteed by the Convention. Contracting Parties have in fact chosen to implement its guarantees by different methods, according to their own constitutional practices. Thus the Convention has the status of national law in Germany and of constitutional law in Austria. In France the Convention has an intermediate status, higher than ordinary legislation but lower than the Constitution. Prior to the Human Rights Act 1998, the Convention had not been enacted as part of the law of the United Kingdom and therefore did not have the force of law.[5] It was argued that the general law of the land guaranteed all the rights contained in the Convention. Convention rights[6] were enacted into United Kingdom law with the entry into force of the Human Rights Act 1998 on 2 October 2000. The Act is said to give 'further effect' to the Convention in United Kingdom law.[7]

Incorporation in some form is now the standard means by which effect is given to the Convention in the national legal orders. The protection of the individual is more effective if the substantive rights guaranteed by the Convention can be enforced by the national courts.[8] If the rights are not expressly enacted in national law, or cannot be

---

Drzemczewski, *European Human Rights Convention in Domestic Law. A Comparative Study* (OUP, Oxford 1983).

[3] R. Ryssdal, Speech to the Informal Ministerial Conference on Human Rights and Celebration of the 40th Anniversary of the European Convention on Human Rights, Rome, 5 November 1990, 2, Council of Europe document Cour (90) 289.

[4] R. Ryssdal, Speech at the ceremony for the 40th anniversary of the European Convention on Human Rights at Trieste, 18 December 1990, Council of Europe document Cour (90) 318, 2. See also dictum in *Ireland v United Kingdom*, (App. 5310/71), 18 January 1978, Series A No 25; (1979–80) 2 EHRR 25, §239; and J. Frowein, 'Incorporation of the Convention into Domestic Law' in J. P. Gardner (ed.), *Aspects of Incorporation of the European Convention of Human Rights into Domestic Law* (BIICL, London 1993).

[5] *R v Chief Immigration Officer, Heathrow Airport, ex parte Salamat Bibi*, [1976] 1 WLR 979, [1976] 3 All ER 843, CA; *R v Secretary of State for the Home Department, ex parte Brind*, [1991] 1 AC 696, [1991] 2 WLR 588, HL.

[6] With the exception of Art. 13.

[7] See below in this chapter.

[8] It also provides the possibility that national legal orders may more readily develop the protection of human rights beyond the minimum guarantees set out in the Convention.

invoked before the national courts, there is no alternative to the European procedure. The experience of statutory enactment into the law of the United Kingdom is that Convention rights gain a much higher profile within the national legal order, as public authorities determine the extent to which any action is compatible with the rights guaranteed in the Convention.

Whether or not Contracting Parties incorporate the actual text of the Convention into national law, they are obliged, by appropriate means, 'to ensure that their domestic legislation is compatible with the Convention and, if need be, to make any necessary adjustments to this end'.[9] Further, the terms of Article 52[10] show that national law must be such as to 'ensure the effective implementation' of all the provisions of the Convention. This does not, however, exhaust the effect of Article 1. Contracting Parties are liable for violations of the Convention which may result not only from legislation incompatible with it, but also from acts of all public authorities, at every level, including the executive and the courts.

Article 1 contains a double obligation. There is, on the one hand, the negative obligation which requires Contracting Parties not to infringe the rights protected in the Convention. There is also, on the other hand, the positive obligation to ensure that the rights protected by the Convention are guaranteed to those within the jurisdiction of Contracting Parties.[11] The extent to which a State may be liable for violations committed outside their territory is considered later in this chapter. But is the liability of a Contracting Party limited to its actions as the State exercising its public authority rather than its actions of a private nature, for example, as an employer?

In both the *Swedish Engine Drivers' Union* case[12] and the *Schmidt and Dahlström* case[13] the applicants' complaints under Articles 11 and 14 were arguably directed partly against the State as employer and partly against the State's exercise of public authority. The Swedish Government contended that the applicants were attacking not the Swedish legislative, executive, and judicial authorities, but rather the National Collective Bargaining Office and thus the 'State as employer'; and that, in the sphere of work and employment conditions, the Convention could not impose upon the State obligations that were not incumbent on private employers. According to the Commission, on the other hand, the disputed decision adopted by the Office could in principle be challenged under Article 11, even if the Office fulfilled typical employer functions. The Court concluded that the Convention was applicable in this situation.

---

[9] App. 214/56, *De Becker v Belgium*, Decision of 9 June 1958, (1958–9) 2 *Yearbook* 214, 234.

[10] Formerly Art. 57.

[11] See, for example, *Z and others v United Kingdom*, (App. 29392/95), 10 May 2001 [GC], (2002) 34 EHRR 97, ECHR 2001-V, §73.

[12] *Swedish Engine Drivers' Union v Sweden*, (App. 5614/72), 6 February 1976, Series A No. 20, (1979–80) 1 EHRR 617.

[13] *Schmidt and Dahlström v Sweden*, (App. 5589/72), 6 February 1976, Series A No 21, (1979–80) 1 EHRR 637.

TEMPORAL SCOPE

In the *Nielsen* case, the Commission said:

Under a generally recognized rule of international law, the Convention only governs for each Contracting Party those facts which are subsequent to the date of its entry into force with regard to the Party in question.[14]

The Convention has no retroactive effect. The Convention entered into force on 3 September 1953.[15] For any State ratifying the Convention and Protocols after these dates, they enter into force on the date of ratification. An application cannot relate back to an event earlier than the entry into force of the instrument in question in respect of a Contracting Party against which the application is brought, unless that event has consequences which may raise the question of a continuing violation.[16]

A different view was taken of the effect of declarations recognizing the competence of the Commission to consider individual applications. The general rule was that, unless the drafting of the recognition of competence precluded it, the Commission was competent to consider matters going back to the date of accession of the Contracting Party.[17] Similar considerations applied to declarations accepting the compulsory jurisdiction of the Court.[18]

An example of the Court's approach to jurisdiction *ratione temporis* can be found in the *Zana* case.[19] The case concerned a prosecution in relation to remarks made by the former mayor of a Turkish town to journalists expressing support for the PKK in August 1987. In March 1991 he was sentenced to a period of imprisonment. The Turkish Government had accepted the jurisdiction of the Strasbourg Court only in relation to facts and events subsequent to 22 January 1990, and objected to the Court's jurisdiction to decide Zana's application on this basis. But the Court decided that the principal fact which gave rise to the complaint of a violation of Article 10 was the judgment of the Turkish court in March 1991 rather than the applicant's statements

---

[14] App. 343/57, *Nielsen v Denmark*, Decision of 2 September 1959, (1959–60) 2 *Yearbook* 412, 454.

[15] The various Protocols entered into force on the following dates (not necessarily for all Contracting Parties): Protocol 1: 18 May 1954; Protocol 2: 21 September 1970; Protocol 3: 21 September 1970; Protocol 4: 2 May 1968; Protocol 5: 21 December 1971; Protocol 6: 1 March 1985; Protocol 7: 1 November 1988; Protocol 8: 1 January 1990; Protocol 9: 1 October 1994; Protocol 10: not in force (but rendered otiose since the entry into force of Protocol 11); Protocol 11: 1 November 1998; Protocol 12: 1 April 2005; Protocol 13: 1 July 2003; Protocol 14: not yet in force; and Protocol 14bis: 1 October 2009.

[16] As in App. 214/56, *De Becker v Belgium*, Decision of 9 June 1958, (1958–9) 2 *Yearbook* 214. See also ch.2 above for what constitutes a continuing violation.

[17] App. 6323/73, *X v Italy*, Decision of 4 March 1976, (1976) 3 DR 80 and App. 9587/81, *X v France*, Decision of 13 December 1982, (1983) 29 DR 228.

[18] But it was only necessary for the respondent State to have accepted the Court's competence for this purpose in the context of inter-State applications. A Contracting Party which has not accepted the competence of the Court for this purpose could nevertheless complain about the conduct of a Contracting Party which had: App. 788/60, *Austria v Italy*, Decision of 11 January 1961, (1962) 4 *Yearbook* 116.

[19] *Zana v Turkey*, (App. 18954/91), 25 November 1997, (1999) 27 EHRR 667, ECHR 1997-VII.

to journalists in August 1987. It was this event which interfered with the applicant's freedom of speech. The Turkish objection was rejected.[20]

Similarly in the *Witkowska-Toboła* case[21] the applicants complained about the breach of her property rights in relation to the operation of the compensation scheme for those who had lost land in Poland. Certain events had occurred prior to the entry into force of the Convention for Poland, but the Strasbourg Court ruled that:

the Court's jurisdiction *ratione temporis* covers the period following the date of ratification, the facts that occurred before that date being considered only inasmuch as they have created a situation extending beyond that date or are relevant for the understanding of the situation obtaining afterwards.[22]

The Grand Chamber reviewed the authorities and confirmed this approach in the *Blečič* case.[23] The key issue is to establish the date of the facts which constitute the interference with a Convention right. The subsequent failure of remedies aimed at addressing the interference cannot alone bring the matter within the temporal jurisdiction of the Strasbourg Court. In order to determine the date of the factual situation which gives rise to the alleged breach of Convention rights, the nature and scope of the Convention right in issue are relevant. In the *Šilih* case,[24] the Court observed that the procedural obligation to carry out an investigation under Article 2 into a death had evolved into 'a separate and autonomous duty'[25] and, in the particular circumstances of the case, the absence of an investigation into a death which had occurred before the date the Convention became binding for the respondent State did not take the matter outside the jurisdiction of the Court *ratione temporis*. But this was not unqualified. A significant proportion of the procedural steps required to meet the obligation in Article 2 needed to fall within the time frame after the Convention came into force for the Contracting Party.

Denunciation under Article 58[26] does not have immediate effect. When a State ratifies the Convention, there is an initial commitment for five years, and thereafter six months' notice is required to denounce the Convention. The obligations undertaken remain in full effect until the expiry of the period of notice. So the application made by Denmark, Norway, and Sweden against Greece in April 1970, some four months after Greece had denounced the Convention on 12 December 1969, was admissible since the six months' notice period did not expire until 13 June 1970.[27]

---

[20] Issues of the temporal scope of the Convention were also in issue in *Ilaşcu and others v Moldova and Russia*, (App. 48787/99), 8 July 2004 [GC], (2005) 40 EHRR 1030, ECHR 2004-VII discussed in detail later in this chapter. The Court followed the approach it had adopted in its earlier cases.

[21] *Witkowska-Toboła v Poland*, (App. 11208/02), Decision of 4 December 2007.

[22] §31.

[23] *Blečič v Croatia*, (App. 59532/00), 8 March 2006 [GC], (2006) 43 EHRR 1038, ECHR 2006-III, §§63–82, affirmed in *Šilih v Slovenia*, (App. 71463/01), 9 April 2009 [GC], (2009) 49 EHRR 996, ECHR 2009-nyr, §§139–47.

[24] *Šilih v Slovenia*, (App. 71463/01), 9 April 2009 [GC], (2009) 49 EHRR 996, ECHR 2009-nyr.

[25] §159.   [26] Formerly Art. 65.

[27] App. 4448/70, *Denmark, Norway and Sweden v Greece*, Decision of 26 May 1970, (1970) 13 *Yearbook* 108. This application was struck out of the Commission's list in 1976 after Greece had again become a party to the Convention: Report of Decision of 4 October 1976 (1976) 6 DR 6.

THE CONCEPT OF JURISDICTION IN ARTICLE 1 OF THE CONVENTION

The guarantee in Article 1 is to secure Convention rights to those 'within the jurisdiction' of a Contracting Party.[28] Establishing the jurisdiction of a Contracting Party is a threshold which must be reached before the Strasbourg Court can examine a complaint under the Convention.[29] Two principal questions have arisen in connection with the scope of jurisdiction under Article 1. First, to what extent is a State accountable under the Convention in respect of its acts or omissions which occur, or have effect, outside its territorial boundaries? Secondly, to what extent is a State accountable under the Convention in respect of acts or omissions which occur within its territorial borders but within a region over which the main State organs have no, or only limited, control?

THE EXTRA-TERRITORIAL SCOPE OF JURISDICTION

In its admissibility decision in the *Banković* case[30] the Grand Chamber held, unanimously, that 'jurisdiction' was essentially a territorial notion. The application was brought against the seventeen NATO States which were also parties to the European Convention by relatives of journalists killed by a NATO air strike on the offices of the Serbian national radio and television network in Belgrade during the Kosovo conflict in 1999. The applicants argued that, as a result of the air strike, the victims had been brought within the 'effective control' of the respondent States and that, in consequence, they were within the 'jurisdiction' of those States. They asked the Strasbourg Court to find that the obligation on those States under Article 1 to secure Convention rights outside their territories was proportionate to the level of control in fact exercised. The fact that the States exercised complete control over their military aircraft

---

[28] Compare Art. 2(1) of the International Covenant on Civil and Political Rights, which reads: Each State Party...undertakes to respect and to ensure to all individuals within its territory and subject to its jurisdiction the rights recognized in the present Covenant, without distinction of any kind, such as race, colour, sex, language, religion, political or other opinion, national or social origin, property, birth or other status.

[29] See M. Milanović, 'From Compromise to Principle: Clarifying the Concept of State Jurisdiction in Human Rights Treaties' (2008) 8 HRLRev 411.

[30] *Banković and others v Belgium and 16 other Contracting States*, (App. 52207/99), Decision of 12 December 2001 [GC], (2007) 44 EHRR SE5, ECHR 2001-XII. See R. Lawson, 'Life after *Banković*: On the Extraterritorial Application of the European Convention on Human Rights'; and M. O'Boyle, 'The European Convention on Human Rights and Extraterritorial Jurisdiction: A Comment on Life after *Banković*' both in F. Coomans and M. Kamminga (eds.) *Extraterritorial Application of Human Rights Treaties* (Intersentia, Antwerp 2004), 83 and 125. See also L. Loucaides, 'Determining the extra-territorial effect of the European Convention: facts, jurisprudence and the Banković case' [2006] EHRLR 391; M. Gondek, 'Extraterritorial Application of the European Convention on Human Rights: Territorial Focus in the Age of Globalization?' (2005) 52 *Netherlands International Law Review* 349; J. Altiparmak, '*Banković*: an obstacle to the application of the European Convention on Human Rights', (2004) 9 *Journal of Conflict and Security Law* 213.

and that the bomb dropped from the aircraft caused the deaths meant that the States should be held accountable under the Convention for this act.

The Court, however, rejected this argument and held that 'from the standpoint of public international law, the jurisdictional competence of a State is primarily territorial'[31] and that, since the Convention had to be interpreted in harmony with principles of international law, States could not normally be held to account under the Convention for acts or omissions of their agents outside their territorial borders.

The Court in *Banković* recognized that there were a small number of exceptions to the territorial principle, which included the activities of a State's diplomatic or consular agents abroad, and events on board craft and vessels registered in, or flying the flag of, that State; or situations where agents of the Convention State, with the consent of the Government of the territorial State, exercised public powers normally to be exercised by the territorial Government.[32] In addition, an exception had been established in two cases arising from the invasion of Cyprus by Turkish troops and the subsequent occupation and division of the island. In the *Loizidou (preliminary objections)* judgment,[33] the Strasbourg Court, examining a complaint by a woman living in southern Cyprus who was denied access to her property in northern Cyprus, had found that the responsibility of a Contracting Party was capable of being engaged when, as a consequence of lawful or unlawful military action, it exercised effective control of an area outside its national territory. On the merits,[34] the Court found that it was not necessary to determine whether Turkey actually exercised detailed control over the policies and actions of the authorities of the 'Turkish Republic of Northern Cyprus' ('TRNC'). It was obvious from the large number of troops engaged in active duties in northern Cyprus that Turkey's army exercised 'effective overall control over that part of the island'.[35] Such control, according to the relevant test and in the circumstances of the case, was found to entail the responsibility of Turkey for the policies and actions of the 'TRNC'. The Court concluded that those affected by such policies or actions therefore came within the jurisdiction of Turkey for the purposes of Article 1 of the Convention. Turkey's obligation to secure the rights and freedoms set out in the Convention was found therefore to extend to northern Cyprus. In its subsequent *Cyprus v Turkey* judgment,[36] the Court added that since Turkey had such 'effective control', its responsibility could not be confined to the acts of its own agents but was engaged by the acts of the local administration which survived by virtue of Turkish

---

[31] *Banković*, §57.

[32] This principle was first expressed in *Drozd and Janousek v France and Spain*, (App. 12747/87), 26 June 1992, Series A No 240, (1992) 14 EHRR 745, where the Court examined complaints arising from decisions of French and Spanish judges sitting in Andorran courts. In that case, however, the Court found that, when sitting in the Andorran courts, the French and Spanish judges were acting as Andorran judges and that no responsibility for their actions attached to France or Spain.

[33] *Loizidou v Turkey (Preliminary Objections)*, (App. 15318/89), 23 March 1995, Series A No 310, (1995) 20 EHRR 99.

[34] *Loizidou v Turkey (Merits)*, (App. 15318/89), 18 December 1996, (1996) 23 EHRR 513, ECHR 1996-VI.

[35] §56.

[36] *Cyprus v Turkey*, (App. 25781/94), 10 May 2001 [GC], (2002) 35 EHRR 731; ECHR 2001-IV.

support. Turkey's jurisdiction under Article 1 was therefore considered to extend to securing the entire range of substantive Convention rights in northern Cyprus.[37]

In the *Banković* case, the Strasbourg Court contrasted the situation created by the NATO bombing raids in Belgrade and held that, since the respondent States did not have 'effective' control of the area, it did not fall within their jurisdiction under Article 1 of the Convention. The Court did not find that the wording of Article 1 provided any support for the applicants' suggestion that the positive obligation in Article 1 to secure 'the rights and freedoms defined in Section I of this Convention' could be 'divided and tailored in accordance with the particular circumstances of the extra-territorial act in question'.[38] Moreover, the Court observed that:

> …the Convention is a multi-lateral treaty operating, subject to Article 56 of the Convention, in an essentially regional context and notably in the legal space (*espace juridique*) of the Contracting States. The FRY [former Republic of Yugoslavia] clearly does not fall within this legal space. The Convention was not designed to be applied throughout the world, even in respect of the conduct of Contracting States. Accordingly, the desirability of avoiding a gap or vacuum in human rights' protection has so far been relied on by the Court in favour of establishing jurisdiction only when the territory in question was one that, but for the specific circumstances, would normally be covered by the Convention.[39]

In subsequent cases, however, the Court has not applied the rule that Article 1 jurisdiction is limited to the European 'legal space'. The Convention has been considered to apply to the alleged acts of Turkish agents in northern Iraq,[40] Kenya,[41] Iran,[42] and in the UN neutral buffer zone in Cyprus.[43] It has been applied in relation to the acts of the Portuguese authorities having effects on a ship in international waters.[44] In a recent admissibility decision, a Chamber of the Court held that two Iraqi nationals who had been held in a British-run military detention facility in southern Iraq since the 2003 invasion fell within the United Kingdom's Article 1 jurisdiction.[45]

Nor has the Court been entirely consistent in applying the principle expressed in the *Banković* case that (apart from the limited 'embassies', 'ships', and 'aircraft' exceptions) jurisdiction under the Convention does not apply to acts or omissions of a Contracting State outside its territorial borders unless the State exercises 'effective control' over the region or area in question. The *Issa* judgment,[46] adopted after the Grand Chamber's unanimous decision in *Banković*, concerned claims by the relatives of Iraqi citizens living in Iraq that their husbands and sons had been killed by Turkish troops during an incursion into northern Iraq. While the Turkish Government confirmed that a sizeable military operation had taken place in northern Iraq at the material time

---

[37] §§75–7.   [38] *Banković*, §75.   [39] §80.

[40] *Issa and others v Turkey*, (App. 31821/96), Decision of 16 November 2004, (2005) 41 EHRR 567.

[41] *Öcalan v Turkey*, (App. 46221/99), 12 March 2003, (2005) 41 EHRR 985, ECHR 2005-IV.

[42] *Pad and Others v Turkey* (App. 60167/00), Decision of 28 June 2007.

[43] *Isaak v Turkey*, (App. 44587/98), 24 June 2008.

[44] *Women on Waves and Others v Portugal*, (App. 31276/05), 3 February 2009.

[45] *Al-Saadoon and Mufdhi v United Kingdom*, (App. 61498/08), Decision of 30 June 2009, (2009) 49 EHRR SE11.

[46] *Issa and others v Turkey*, (App. 31821/96), Decision of 16 November 2004, (2005) 41 EHRR 567.

aimed at pursuing and eliminating terrorists, it denied any military operations in the area where the applicants claimed their relatives had been killed. Ultimately the decision turned on the inability of the applicants to prove their assertion that the deaths were caused by Turkish military operations and the Court's observations on jurisdiction are, therefore, *obiter*. Nonetheless, it is striking that the Court expressly rejected the Turkish Government's submissions based on *Banković* and instead cited decisions of the Inter-American Commission on Human Rights and the United Nations Human Rights Committee[47] in support of the proposition that:

...a State may also be held accountable for violation of the Convention rights and freedoms of persons who are in the territory of another State but who are found to be under the former State's authority and control through its agents operating—whether lawfully or unlawfully—in the latter State.... Accountability in such situations stems from the fact that Article 1 of the Convention cannot be interpreted so as to allow a State party to perpetrate violations of the Convention on the territory of another State, which it could not perpetrate on its own territory....[48]

If this approach were to be followed in subsequent cases, it would expand the scope of the Convention dramatically beyond what was decided in the *Banković* case.

JURISDICTION OVER BREAK-AWAY OR AUTONOMOUS REGIONS

Since the Contracting States are required under Article 1 to secure the Convention rights and freedoms to everyone 'within their jurisdiction', and since the State's jurisdictional competence is primarily territorial, it follows that the State is generally under an obligation to apply the Convention in every part of its territory.

The Court has held that 'jurisdiction is presumed to be exercised normally throughout the State's territory.'[49] This presumption may, however, be limited in exceptional circumstances, particularly where a State is prevented from exercising its authority in part of its territory, as a result of military occupation by the armed forces of another State, acts of war or rebellion, or the acts of a foreign State supporting the installation of a separatist State within the territory of the State concerned.[50]

The *Ilaşcu* case[51] concerned the question whether either Moldova and/or Russia could be held accountable under the Convention for the arrest and detention of

[47] *Coard and others v United States*, Inter-American Commission on Human Rights, Decision of 29 September 1999, Report No 109/99, Case No 10.951, §§37, 39, 41, and 43; and the views adopted by the Human Rights Committee on 29 July 1981 in the cases of *Lopez Burgos v Uruguay and Celiberti de Casariego v Uruguay*, Nos 52/1979 and 56/1979, §§ 12.3 and 10.3 respectively.

[48] *Issa*, §71.

[49] See *Ilaşcu and others v Moldova and Russia*, (App. 48787/99), 8 July 2004 [GC], (2005) 40 EHRR 1030, ECHR 2004-VII, § 312.

[50] Ibid.

[51] *Ilaşcu and others v Moldova and Russia* (App. 48787/99), 8 July 2004 [GC], (2005) 40 EHRR 1030, ECHR 2004-VII. See also *Von Maltzan and others, von Zitzewitz and others, and Man Ferrostaal and Töpfer Stiftung v Germany*, (Apps. 1916/01, 71916/01 and 10260/02), Decision of 2 March 2005 [GC], (2006) 42 EHRR SE11, ECHR 2005-V.

four Moldovan nationals by the separatist regime which controls the region of Transdniestria, in the eastern part of Moldovan territory. In June 1990, as the Soviet Union began to break up, Moldova proclaimed its sovereignty. Three months later, the Transdniestrian separatist regime declared the existence of the 'Moldavian Republic of Transdniestria' (the 'MRT'). The 'MRT' has not been recognized by the international community. On 27 August 1991 the Moldovan parliament adopted the Declaration of Independence of the Republic of Moldova, whose territory included Transdniestria. Following this Declaration of Independence, the USSR began withdrawing its army and military equipment from Moldovan territory. Many of the Soviet soldiers who had been stationed in Transdniestria and who came from the region joined the separatist uprising and a large store of armaments fell into 'MRT' hands. During the winter of 1991–1992 there were violent clashes between Transdniestrian separatist forces and the Moldovan security forces. It was alleged that the separatists received military and economic support from Russia, both during the armed conflict, when the separatists were able to retain control over Transdniestria, and subsequently. The applicants were arrested in Transdniestria in June 1992 and subjected to severe ill-treatment. They were convicted by a Transdniestrian court of a number of offences, including offences against the 'national security' of 'the legitimate State of Transdniestria', and sentenced to long periods of imprisonment. The Supreme Court of Moldova quashed the convictions on the basis that they had been rendered by an unconstitutional court and ordered the applicants' release, but the authorities of the 'MRT' did not respond and the applicants remained in detention in appalling conditions.

In order to determine whether the applicants came within the jurisdiction of either Moldova or Russia, the Grand Chamber undertook a remarkable fact-finding mission. A delegation of four judges travelled to Chişinău and Tiraspol and heard evidence from 43 witnesses, including the President of Moldova at the time of the 1991–1992 conflict, a number of former Moldovan ministers, including the former Prime Minister, senior officials and diplomats, the commander of the Moldovan armed forces during the conflict, and a number of senior Russian military personnel.

The Strasbourg Court found, on the basis of all the material in its possession, that the Moldovan Government did not exercise authority over the part of its territory which was under the effective control of the 'MRT'. Nonetheless, the Court held that:

… even in the absence of effective control over the Transdniestrian region, Moldova still has a positive obligation under Article 1 of the Convention to take the diplomatic, economic, judicial or other measures that it is in its power to take and are in accordance with international law to secure to the applicants the rights guaranteed by the Convention.[52]

The Court concluded that Moldova had not complied with this positive obligation because, in its negotiations with Russia and representatives of the 'MRT' for the settlement of the situation in Transdniestria, no specific mention had been made of the applicants' plight with a view to securing their release.

---

[52] *Ilaşcu*, §331.

Even more controversially, the Court found that the applicants also fell within the jurisdiction of Russia. On the facts as found by the Court, the USSR, and particularly its 14th Army which had been stationed in Transdniestria, had given substantial support to the separatists during the fighting in 1991–1992. Moreover, following Russia's ratification of the Convention on 5 May 1998, the Russian army remained stationed in Transdniestria, in breach of Russia's undertakings to withdraw, and Russia had also provided considerable economic assistance to the 'MRT'. The Court concluded that 'that there is a continuous and uninterrupted link of responsibility on the part of the Russian Federation for the applicants' fate'.[53]

The Court concluded that there had been violations of Articles 3 and 5 of the Convention against both States and ordered each State to pay substantial awards of damages. The Russian judge was the only dissenter. In his separate opinion he expressed his 'deep disagreement' with the Court's findings and conclusions in respect of Russia.

In the *Assanidze* case,[54] the respondent State was Georgia, and the actions in issue were those of the Ajarian Autonomous Republic, a region of Georgia which enjoyed a high degree of self-government but which had no separatist ambitions. The applicant had been acquitted in a judgment of the Georgian Supreme Court, but remained in imprisonment in the Ajarian Republic. This was not a case in which a part of the territory of the respondent State was under the effective control of another State, and the Georgian Government accepted that the applicant fell within its jurisdiction. The Court found a violation against Georgia, holding that even where a State encountered real difficulties in securing compliance with the rights guaranteed by the Convention in all parts of its territory, it remained responsible for events occurring anywhere within its borders.

LIABILITY FOR ACTS OF
INTERNATIONAL ORGANIZATIONS

Questions have arisen as to whether a Contracting Party can violate the Convention by becoming party to another treaty. In one case, the Commission said:

If a State contracts treaty obligations and subsequently concludes another international agreement which disables it from performing its obligations under the first treaty, it will be answerable for any resulting breach of its obligations under the treaty.[55]

In another case, the Commission held that the transfer of powers by the Contracting States to an international organization is compatible with the Convention, provided that fundamental rights receive, within that organization, an equivalent protection.

---

[53] *Ilaşcu*, §393.

[54] *Assanidze v Georgia*, (App. 71503/01), 8 April 2004 [GC], (2004) 39 EHRR 653, ECHR 2004-II.

[55] App. 235/56, X *v Federal Republic of Germany*, Decision of 10 June 1958, (1958–9) 2 *Yearbook* 256, 300.

In the context of Article 1 of Protocol 1, the European Patents Convention contains detailed safeguards for the protection of intellectual property rights. The transfer of power which it entails is therefore compatible with the Convention. The application was outside the scope of the Convention *ratione personae*.[56]

In the *Matthews* case,[57] the Strasbourg Court was called upon to consider a complaint against the United Kingdom about participation in elections to the European Parliament which were set out in an act of the Community's institutions. The Community Act[58] establishing the rules for direct elections provided in Annex II that the United Kingdom would apply the provisions only in respect of the United Kingdom. Denise Matthews was a United Kingdom national living in Gibraltar, a dependent territory of the United Kingdom. She sought to register as a voter in respect of the elections to the European Parliament, but was refused on the grounds that the Community Act did not include Gibraltar within the franchise for these elections. She complained that this refusal violated her rights under Article 3 of Protocol 1 on free elections.[59] The Strasbourg Court decided that the United Kingdom remained responsible for securing the rights in Article 3 of Protocol 1 in respect of Community legislation in the same way as if the restriction on the franchise had been included in national law. The Court went on to find that Article 3 applied, since it was possible to interpret the European Parliament as being a legislature within the article, and concluded that there had been a violation of the article. The significance of the case is that the Strasbourg Court has stated in the clearest terms that the Contracting Parties remain responsible for guaranteeing the rights contained in the Convention even where they create an international organization and transfer competence to it in particular areas, and that, where no other judicial body is competent to review acts of the international organization, the Strasbourg Court will consider complaints of violations of the Convention's guaranteed rights.[60]

The relationship between obligations arising under European Community law and Convention law arose in the *Bosphorus Airways* case.[61] The context was the seizure in Ireland of an aircraft leased by Bosphorus Airways from Yugoslav Airlines[62] under

---

[56] App. 21090/92, *Heinz v Contracting Parties who are also Parties to the European Patent Convention*, Decision of 10 January 1994, (1994) 76-A DR 125. See also App. 13258/77, *M & Co. v Federal Republic of Germany*, Decision of 9 February 1990, (1990) 64 DR 138, 144, making the same point in connection with the EEC Treaty (as it then was).

[57] *Matthews v United Kingdom*, (App. 24833/94), 18 February 1999 [GC], (1999) 28 EHRR 361, ECHR 1999-I. see also Canor, 'Primus inter pares. Who is the ultimate guardian of fundamental rights in Europe?' (2000) 25 ELRev 3; T. King, 'Ensuring human rights review of intergovernmental acts in Europe' (2000) 25 ELRev 79; and H. Schermers, 'European Remedies in the Field of Human Rights' in C. Kilpatrick, N. Novitz, and P. Skidmore, *The Future of Remedies in Europe* (Hart, Oxford 2000), 205.

[58] This is a measure adopted by the Community institutions.

[59] See ch.22 below.

[60] For the 2004 elections to the European Parliament, Gibraltar was added to the constituency which included Cornwall!

[61] 'Bosphorus Airways' v Ireland, (App. 45036/98), 30 June 2005 [GC], (2006) 42 EHRR 1, ECHR 2005-VI.

[62] JAT.

the terms of EC Council Regulation 990/93[63] which was adopted as part of the United Nations sanctions regime against the Federal Republic of Yugoslavia (Serbia and Montenegro). The Strasbourg Court examined the nature of Regulations in European Community law, noting that they were binding in their entirety on the Member States of the European Union, and were directly applicable in the sense that they were immediately binding in the national legal order. The actions taken in pursuance of the Regulation were, however, an interference with property rights covered by Article 1 of Protocol 1. In determining whether such an act violated the Convention, the Grand Chamber took as a starting point that the protection of fundamental rights in European Community law was, at the relevant time, equivalent to that of the Convention system. There was therefore a rebuttable presumption that action taken in compliance with Community law met the requirements of the Convention.[64]

Events in Kosovo have also contributed to the case-law on the liability of international organizations. The decisions in the *Behrami* and *Saramati* cases[65] sit somewhat uneasily with the earlier case-law. These cases concerned claims in respect of alleged violations of the Convention by UNMIK[66] and KFOR.[67] UNMIK had been established by the United Nations Security Council acting under Chapter VII of the United Nations Charter. KFOR was part of the United Nations peace plan but was authorized by a Military Technical Agreement signed by the Federal Republic of Yugoslavia and Serbia in which the deployment and operation of KFOR in Kosovo was agreed. Principal contributors to KFOR were NATO members. The facts which gave rise to the cases were as follows. The two Behrami brothers were playing with unexploded cluster bombs; one exploded, killing one brother and seriously injuring the other. The father of the boys complained that the death and injuries had been caused by the failure of French KFOR troops to mark or defuse unexploded cluster bombs when they knew of their existence. Saramati's complaints related to his detention as a threat to the security of KFOR. His claims were made against France, Germany, and Norway as the relevant participating countries in KFOR.

The issue before the Strasbourg Court was whether the actions of which the applicants complained were within the jurisdiction of the Contracting Parties. This involved a consideration of the relationship between the Contracting Parties and the international groupings concerned. But the Strasbourg Court considered that the question concerned less the exercise of extra-territorial jurisdiction by the respondent States and more 'whether this Court is competent to examine under the Convention those States' contribution to the civil and security presences which did exercise the relevant

---

[63] [1993] *Official Journal of the European Communities* L102/1.

[64] '*Bosphorus Airways*' *v Ireland*, (App. 45036/98), 30 June 2005 [GC], (2006) 42 EHRR 1, ECHR 2005-VI, §§159–66. See below in ch.25 for further comment on the relationship between the Convention system and European Community law.

[65] *Behrami v France*, (App. 71412/01), Decision of 2 May 2007 [GC]; and *Saramati v France, Germany and Norway*, (App. 78166/01), Decision of 2 May 2007 [GC], (2007) 45 EHRR SE10; see A. Sari, 'Jurisdiction and International Responsibility in Peace Support Operations: The *Behrami* and *Saramati* Cases' (2008) 8 HRLRev 151, for a description of the Decision and criticism of it.

[66] United Nations Interim Administration Mission in Kosovo.

[67] Kosovo Force.

control in Kosovo'.[68] The Strasbourg Court concluded that the acts complained of were attributable to the United Nations, and so were outside the competence of the Strasbourg Court to review *ratione personae*.[69] The Court distinguished the *Bosphorus Airways* case[70] on the grounds that the Irish case had concerned an act of Ireland on its own territory and on the authority of its own Government, albeit in compliance with a Regulation of the European Union which was binding upon it. The Court's decision in distinguishing the *Bosphorus Airways* case would seem to close the door to review of any action by a Contracting Party where authority for the action is the United Nations. It assumes that responsibility can only be attributed to a single party; in reality it is difficult to see why there cannot be dual attribution of responsibility: that is, both to the international organization and to the individual participating States.

It should also be observed, particularly since the point has been raised regularly by Contracting Parties, that Article 103 of the UN Charter provides:

In the event of a conflict between the obligations of the Members of the United Nations under the present Charter and their obligations under any other international agreement, their obligations under the present Charter shall prevail.

The Strasbourg Court has alluded to this provision, but has not decided any case solely on its application. In its decision in the *Behrami* and *Saramati* cases, the Court said:

147. ... More generally, it is further recalled ... that the Convention has to be interpreted in the light of any relevant rules and principles of international law applicable in relations between its Contracting Parties. The Court has therefore had regard to two complementary provisions of the Charter, Articles 25 and 103, as interpreted by the International Court of Justice....

The Strasbourg Court recognized the importance of the United Nations system for the protection of international peace and security. Here measures under Chapter VII of the UN Charter had been authorized, and actions in connection with such measures were not susceptible to scrutiny by the Strasbourg Court. This would interfere to an unacceptable extent with the effective conduct of operations by the United Nations.[71]

OTHER ISSUES RELATING TO TERRITORIAL SCOPE

Under Article 1, the Contracting Parties guarantee the rights and freedoms defined in Section I to everyone within their jurisdiction. Many aspects of this issue have already been discussed in considering the scope of the concept of the term 'jurisdiction' as

---

[68] *Behrami v France*, (App. 71412/01), Decision of 2 May 2007 [GC], and *Saramati v France, Germany and Norway*, (App. 78166/01), Decision of 2 May 2007 [GC], (2007) 45 EHRR SE10, §71.

[69] §§144–52.   [70] See above this chapter.

[71] *Behrami v France*, (App. 71412/01), Decision of 2 May 2007 [GC], and *Saramati v France, Germany and Norway*, (App. 78166/01), Decision of 2 May 2007 [GC], (2007) 45 EHRR SE10, §§148–9.

used in Article 1. However, there remain one or two issues relating to the territorial scope of the Convention which should be noted.

The guarantee in Article 1 may be subject to certain territorial limits.[72] This follows from the so-called colonial clause in Article 56,[73] which provides that a Contracting Party may, by means of a declaration, extend the Convention to all or any of the territories for whose international relations it is responsible. But for this provision, the Convention would have extended, by the mere act of ratification, to all such territories. It has already been shown that the wording of Article 1 does not introduce any territorial limitation to the Convention. It is introduced, therefore, only by implication in former Article 63, which runs counter to the whole scheme of the Convention, and which can be explained by historical circumstances of little relevance today.[74]

Thus, a Contracting Party may be responsible for the acts of its officials abroad. It is responsible, for example, for the acts of its diplomatic and consular representatives. In one case, the Commission accepted that the acts of the German consul in Morocco could make the Federal Republic liable under the Convention.[75] It justified its decision on the narrow ground that the nationals of a State are, in certain respects, still within its jurisdiction, even when domiciled or resident abroad. The decision is certainly correct, but the reasoning is not satisfactory. No distinction should be made between nationals and others; it could not seriously be maintained that a Contracting Party is liable under the Convention for the acts of its diplomatic and consular officials abroad towards its nationals, but not towards aliens. As we have seen, the significance of the expression 'within their jurisdiction' in Article 1 is quite different. It does not mean that a Contracting Party is liable only for violations committed within its territory, or outside its territory if committed against its nationals. Such an interpretation would be contrary to the whole system of the Convention. Subject to Article 56, the State is responsible for breaches of the Convention wherever they are committed.

The United Kingdom has extended the Convention to a number of dependent overseas territories, and the Netherlands has extended it to Surinam[76] and the Netherlands Antilles. When such territories become independent, the declaration automatically lapses, and it is unnecessary to denounce the Convention in respect of the territory concerned under Article 58(4).[77] On independence, of course, the State which has made the declaration ceases to be responsible for the international relations of the new State;

---

[72] App. 1065/61, *X v Belgium*, Decision of 30 May 1961, (1961) 4 *Yearbook* 260, 268.

[73] Formerly Art. 63.

[74] See J. G. Merrills and A. H. Robertson, *Human Rights in Europe* (MUP, Manchester 2001), 26–7.

[75] App. 1611/62, *X v Germany*, Decision of 25 September 1965, (1965) 8 *Yearbook* 158, 168. See also Joined Apps. 6780/74 and 6950/75, *Cyprus v Turkey*, Decision of 26 May 1975, (1975) 18 *Yearbook* 82, and App. 8007/76, *Cyprus v Turkey*, Decision of 10 July 1978, (1978) 13 DR 85, 148–9, when Turkey was held to be responsible for acts of its armed forces, and Joined Apps. 7289/75 and 7349/79, *X and Y v Switzerland*, Decision of 14 July 1977, (1977) 9 DR 57, 73, when Switzerland was held to be responsible for official acts having effect in Liechtenstein.

[76] Until its independence in 1975.

[77] Formerly Art. 65(4).

and there can be no question of the new State remaining a party to the Convention by the law of State succession, since the Convention is confined, by Article 59(1),[78] to Members of the Council of Europe.[79]

A declaration under Article 56 may also lapse for a different reason. The Convention was extended by Denmark to Greenland, for whose international relations it was responsible at the time; but subsequently, in 1953, Greenland became part of metropolitan Denmark, so that the Convention automatically applied to Greenland irrespective of the declaration.

Article 56(3) provides that the provisions of the Convention apply to territories to which a declaration under Article 56(1) applies 'with due regard...to local requirements'. The interpretation of this phrase was considered in the *Tyrer* case[80] which concerned corporal punishment in the Isle of Man. The respondent State sought to argue that public opinion on the island which supported the practice of birching was a 'local requirement' which brought the practice within Article 63(3). The Court rejected this, saying that public opinion was insufficient to ground such a claim; positive and conclusive proof would be needed of the requirement.[81]

A number of provisions of the Convention may have extraterritorial effect. For example, in the *Soering* case,[82] the Court took the view that the extradition of Soering to the United States where he might be exposed to the so-called death row phenomenon would amount to a breach by the United Kingdom of its obligations under Article 3.

THE NATURE OF A STATE'S POSITIVE OBLIGATIONS

A difficult question is how far a Contracting Party is responsible for violations of the rights guaranteed by the Convention, committed within its territory by private persons. Where Section I of the Convention is enacted as part of national law, or can be invoked before the national courts, a limited effect on third parties[83] may be allowed,

---

[78] Formerly Art. 66(1).

[79] See M. Eissen, 'The Independence of Malta and the European Convention on Human Rights' (1965–6) 41 BYIL 401; and 'Malawi and the European Convention on Human Rights' (1968–9) 43 BYIL 190. Malta subsequently became a member of the Council of Europe and a party to the Convention, as did Cyprus.

[80] *Tyrer v United Kingdom*, (App. 5856/72), 25 April 1978, Series A No 26, (1980) 2 EHRR 1.

[81] §38. The Court's comments suggest that corporal punishment as a preventive measure could not be taken out of the application of Article 3 by reason of being a local requirement.

[82] *Soering v United Kingdom*, (App. 14038/88), 7 July 1989, Series A No 161, (1989) 11 EHRR 439. See further in ch.9 below.

[83] See for this effect on third parties *(Drittwirkung)* in national law, as well as on the European level, M. Eissen, 'The European Convention on Human Rights and the Duties of the Individual' in (1962) 32 *Acta Scandinavica Juris Gentium* 230; A. Drzemczewski, 'The domestic status of the European Convention on Human Rights. New Dimensions' [1977/1] LIEI 1–85; and E. A. Alkema, 'The third party applicability or "Drittwirkung" of the European Convention on Human Rights' in F. Matscher and H. Petzold, *Protecting*

since Section I does not itself confine liability to the State.[84] On the European level, however, the Strasbourg Court can only deal, under Article 34,[85] with an application by an individual claiming to be a victim of a violation by one of the Contracting Parties. If the violation is by a private individual, therefore, a State may have fulfilled its obligations if its law adequately protects the rights guaranteed and provides for an effective remedy in the event of such violation.

Positive obligations is a label used to describe the circumstances in which a Contracting Party is required to take action in order to secure to those within its jurisdiction the rights protected by the Convention.[86] Though positive obligations were once thought to be the exception rather than the rule, there are now hardly any provisions of the Convention under which positive obligations have not been recognized. Clearly one concern is the uncertainty which arises in defining the limits of such obligations, but the Strasbourg Court tends to allow a degree of latitude to Contracting Parties in this area of legal protection afforded by the Convention.

The requirement to act positively flows from the express terms of some Convention provisions, while in others it is implied and has required careful elaboration by the Strasbourg Court in its case-law. For example, Article 6 on the right to a fair trial expressly requires Contracting Parties to ensure that certain procedural safeguards exist in its national legal order in both civil and criminal procedure. In contrast, it took some time for the Strasbourg Court to read into Article 2 on the right to life an obligation to conduct an investigation into a death which was alleged to have occurred at the hands of the State or through failings of the State.

In the *Ilaşcu* case,[87] the Court summarizes the scope of a State's positive obligations in the following terms:[88]

In determining the scope of a State's positive obligations, regard must be had to the fair balance that has to be struck between the general interest and the interests of the individual, the diversity of situations obtaining in Contracting States and the choices which must be made in terms of priorities and resources. Nor must these obligations be interpreted in such a way as to impose an impossible or disproportionate burden.

This meant that, in circumstances where a Contracting Party had lost effective control of a part of its territory, that Contracting Party nevertheless had a duty to use all

---

Human Rights: The European Dimension. Studies in Honour of Gérard J. Wiarda (Carl Heymanns, Köln 1988), 33–45. See also A. Clapham, *Human Rights in the Private Sphere* (OUP, Oxford 1993).

[84] On the effect of incorporation and the notion of the horizontal effect of the Convention within a national legal order, see M. Hunt, 'The "horizontal effect" of the Human Rights Act' [1998] PL 423.

[85] Formerly Art. 25.

[86] See generally J.-F. Akandji-Kombe, *Positive obligations under the European Convention on Human Rights: a Guide to the implementation of the European Convention on Human Rights*, Human Rights Handbooks, No. 7 (Council of Europe Publishing, Strasbourg 2007); A. Mowbray, *The Development of Positive Obligations under the European Convention on Human Rights by the European Court of Human Rights* (Hart, Oxford 2004).

[87] *Ilaşcu and others v Moldova and Russia*, (App. 48787/99), 8 July 2004 [GC], (2005) 40 EHRR 1030, ECHR 2004-VII.

[88] §332.

appropriate legal and diplomatic means to continue to guarantee the protection of the rights and freedoms guaranteed by the Convention.[89] The decision of the majority in the *Ilaşcu* case attracted two partly dissenting opinions each joined by four other judges, a partly dissenting opinion, and a dissenting opinion. All these separate or dissenting opinions concerned the extent of positive obligations in situations such as that in this case. This indicates that, at least in the particular circumstances of that case, the conclusions of the majority in relation to Moldova's positive obligations are highly controversial.

Judge Bratza[90] dissented from the view expressed by the majority that the responsibility of a State suffering a loss of control of part of its territory such as that experienced by Moldova would depend upon its sufficient efforts on the legal and diplomatic plane to guarantee Convention rights. He did not see how the Court could make a determination as to the sufficiency of the efforts made by the State, as to the effectiveness of particular measures, and as to whether they were possible and were adequately implemented.

Judge Casadevall[91] also dissented on the question of Moldova's responsibility. But for him and his colleagues, the responsibility of Moldova should not be split but should be treated as existing continuously from the date of its ratification of the Convention in September 1997; any other approach would lead to the 'paradoxical and incoherent' conclusion of the majority which split liability before and after May 2001.

Judge Ress's dissenting opinion again related to the positive obligations of Moldova. Adding to the views of Judge Casadevall, whose partly dissenting opinion he had joined, Judge Ress notes that the scope of the jurisdiction of Moldova for the whole of its territory remained the same throughout. What may have fluctuated was its responsibility as a result of its inability to exercise effective control over a part of its territory. Ultimately, Judge Ress sees the circumstances of this case as being closer to those in the *Assanidze* case[92] than in the situation in the northern part of Cyprus. Hence Moldova remained responsible for the violations arising from the actions of the 'Moldavian Republic of Transdniestria'.

The partly dissenting opinion of Judge Loucaides followed his concurring opinion in the *Assanidze* case[93] to the effect that jurisdiction means actual authority:

The test should always be whether the person who claims to be within the 'jurisdiction' of a State, High Contracting Party to the Convention, in respect of a particular act can show that the act in question was the result of the exercise of authority by the State concerned.[94]

---

[89] §333.

[90] Whose partly dissenting opinion was joined by Judges Rozakis, Hedigan, Thomassen, and Panţiru.

[91] Joined by Judges Ress, Bîrsan, Tulkens, and Fura-Sandstrom.

[92] *Assanidze v Georgia*, (App. 71503/01), 8 April 2004 [GC], (2004) 39 EHRR 653, ECHR 2004-II.

[93] Ibid.

[94] *Ilaşcu and others v Moldova and Russia*, (App. 48787/99), 8 July 2004 [GC], (2005) 40 EHRR 1030, ECHR 2004-VII. Judge Loucaides quotes extensively from his concurring opinion in the *Assanidze* case in his partly dissenting opinion in the *Ilaşcu* case.

He develops this point in the *Ilaşcu* case asserting the proposition that a State may be accountable for a failure to meet its positive obligations if it was in a position to exercise its authority either directly or indirectly over those who had actual authority in the situation but did not do so.

However, the particular circumstances and difficulties of the *Ilaşcu* case should not deflect attention away from the pervasive influence of positive obligations under very many provisions the Convention. Indeed, it may be inappropriate to make too sharp a distinction between so-called negative obligations and positive obligations. The terms of many Convention provisions do not easily lend themselves to such analysis. Take Article 2 for example. Its first sentence provides that everyone's right to life shall be protected by law. That clearly requires some action on the part of the State, for example, by setting in place criminal sanctions for the taking of life. The difficulty is in determining the limits of such positive obligations. Does it extend to the provision of health services, and, if so, at what level? The second sentence, which is subject to certain exceptions, provides that no one shall be deprived of life intentionally. That is rather more in the nature of a prohibition than the first sentence of the Article. What is required is a careful analysis of each provision of the Convention. For this reason, the issue of positive obligations is addressed more specifically in the material in Part 2 of this book on Convention rights.

THE STATUS OF THE CONVENTION
IN THE UNITED KINGDOM

The enactment of the European Convention on Human Rights into national law in the United Kingdom under the Human Rights Act 1998[95] was an event of major constitutional significance. Statutory enactment means that Convention rights can be argued and considered in national courts and tribunals alongside other issues in cases before them. Incorporation has been followed by an energetic focus within the national legal order on compliance with Convention rights of many aspects of United Kingdom law. The Act was a clever and elegant piece of legislation which set in place a scheme which preserves the distinct roles of judges and politicians in the constitutional order of the United Kingdom.[96]

There is an improved system of pre-legislative scrutiny of legislation. Section 19 of the Act requires the Minister introducing a Bill in Parliament to state whether, in

---

[95] Which entered into force on 2 October 2000.

[96] For a description of preparations for implementation, see generally A. Finlay, 'The Human Rights Act: The Lord Chancellor's Department's Preparations for Implementation' [1999] EHRLR 512. For a judicial comment on the impact of incorporation, see Lord Steyn, 'The New Legal Landscape' [2000] EHRLR 549. For detailed commentaries on the operation of the Human Rights Act 1998, see R. Clayton and H. Tomlinson, *The Law of Human Rights* (2nd edn OUP, Oxford 2009); and B. Emmerson and J. Simor, *Human Rights Practice* (Sweet & Maxwell, London 2001) (with loose-leaf service updates). For an examination of the case-law of United Kingdom courts on the Convention, see A. Kavanagh, *Constitutional Review under the UK Human Rights Act* (CUP, Cambridge 2009).

his or her view, it is compatible with the European Convention, or to decline to do so but to indicate that the Government nevertheless wishes to proceed with the Bill. Critics have expressed concern that without the support of a national Human Rights Commission,[97] the level of scrutiny may well be inadequate to guarantee compliance with the Convention in every case.

The substantive articles of the Convention and Protocols to which the United Kingdom is party are restated in section 1 and Schedule 1 to the Act as provisions of United Kingdom law with the exception of Article 13 of the Convention.[98] The enacted rights are referred to as Convention rights.

Under section 6(1) of the Act, it is unlawful for any public authority to 'act in a way which is incompatible with a Convention right'. Public authorities include a court or tribunal, and 'any person certain of whose functions are of a public nature', but does not include either House of Parliament. There remains considerable uncertainty as to the ambit of the term 'public authority', and clearly flesh will need to be given to this term under national case-law.[99] Under section 7, any person who claims that a public authority has acted in a manner which is incompatible with a Convention right, may bring proceedings against the authority in a court or tribunal as determined by rules of court made under the Act. If the act complained of is that of a court or tribunal, the matter may only be raised on appeal. Furthermore, any party to proceedings can rely on a Convention right in legal proceedings. Applicants bringing judicial review proceedings will have standing if they are, or would be, considered a victim of a violation under Article 34 of the Convention.[100] Convention case-law has been generous over the matter of standing to raise a complaint of a violation.

Whenever Convention rights are in issue before public authorities, new rules of interpretation come into play. First, in determining whether there has been a violation of a Convention right, a court or tribunal must 'take into account' case-law of the Commission, Court of Human Rights, and the Committee of Ministers. In interpreting any primary or secondary legislation whenever enacted, the court or tribunal must 'so far as it is possible to do so, read and give effect to that legislation in a way which is compatible with the Convention rights.'[101]

---

[97] The work of the Joint Committee on Human Rights has been invaluable in considering a number of important issues in relation to compliance with the Convention in United Kingdom law. On 1 October 2007 a single Equality and Human Rights Commission was established under the Equality Act 2006 and combines the work of the Equal Opportunities Commission, the Commission for Racial Equality, and the Disability Rights Commission which it replaces. See www.equalityhumanrights.com.

[98] Article 13 guarantees an effective remedy before a national authority for a violation of a Convention right. Its omission is seen by some as controversial, see R. White, 'Remedies in a Multi-Level Legal Order: The Strasbourg Court and the UK' in C. Kilpatrick, T. Novitz, and P. Skidmore, *The Future of Remedies in Europe* (Hart, Oxford 2000), 191.

[99] See generally *The Meaning of Public Authority under the Human Rights Act*, Seventh Report of the Joint Committee on Human Rights of Session 2004–05. HL Paper 39 HC 382.

[100] See ch.2 above.

[101] s.3(1) of the Act. There is now a significant case-law on the proper role of the courts in interpreting legislation to secure compatibility: see in particular *Ghaidan v Godin-Mendoza*, [2004] UKHL 30, which

If a court or tribunal concludes that there has been a violation of a Convention right, 'it may grant such relief or remedy, or make such order, within its jurisdiction as it considers just and appropriate.'[102] This is an enabling provision giving courts and tribunals powers based on, but going beyond, those enjoyed by the Strasbourg Court under Article 41 of the Convention to afford just satisfaction to a victim of a violation.[103] However, damages can only be awarded by those courts or tribunals which have power to award damages, or to order the payment of compensation, in civil proceedings.[104]

The failure to incorporate Article 13, which guarantees a right to a remedy in national law, may be problematic here. The Government position in Parliamentary debates was that the whole Act meets the requirements of Article 13, and there was concern that its incorporation might give all courts and tribunals sweeping powers to grant remedies which would be inappropriate.

Where the new rules of interpretation do not enable a court or tribunal to read and give effect to primary legislation in a way which is compatible with the Convention rights, the declaration of incompatibility comes into play. Section 4(2) of the Act provides that a court which is satisfied that a provision in primary legislation is incompatible with a Convention right 'may make a declaration of incompatibility'.[105] For England and Wales, the following courts have power to make such a declaration: the High Court, Court of Appeal, House of Lords,[106] Judicial Committee of the Privy Council, and the Courts Martial Appeal Court. Where a lesser court or tribunal[107] is faced with such an issue, it must apply the 'incompatible' legislation and the matter will have to be taken on appeal until a court with the power is reached. All courts and tribunals, however, have the power to rule that subordinate legislation is incompatible with Convention rights unless the primary legislation prevents removal of the incompatibility.[108] The declaration of incompatibility is the solution to the dilemma of having judges declaring primary legislation invalid, which was seen to be an interference by judges in the role of the legislature. The declaration of incompatibility does not affect the validity, continuing operation or enforcement of the provision, and is not binding on the parties to the proceedings in which it is made.[109] Its effect is to prompt the legislature to consider making a remedial order under section 10 and Schedule 2 to the Act. This is a fast-track legislative procedure designed to remove the incompatibility at the heart of the court's declaration. Again critics of the Act argue that there

stresses the primacy of the rule of interpretation in securing the compatibility of United Kingdom law with Convention rights.

[102] s.8(1) of the Act.   [103] See ch.2 above.   [104] s.8(2) of the Act.

[105] In *Burden v United Kingdom*, (App. 13378/05), 29 April 2008 [GC], (2008) 47 EGRR 857, ECHR 2008-nyr, §§40–4, the Grand Chamber ruled that a declaration of incompatibility is not currently an effective remedy within the meaning of Article 35 of the Convention for the purpose of the rule requiring an applicant to exhaust domestic remedies.

[106] To be replaced by the Supreme Court in October 2009 under the Constitutional Reform Act 2005.

[107] And there are very many of these.

[108] s.4(3) and (4) of the Act.

[109] s.4(6) of the Act.

is a role for a national Human Rights Commission to assist in ensuring that any defect is fully corrected.

The incorporation of the Convention does not in any way deprive those who believe they are victims of violations of the Convention from making applications to the Court in Strasbourg, subject to the Convention's admissibility rules.

CONCLUDING REMARKS

The centrality of Article 1 to the multi-level system of protection set in place by the European Convention has been demonstrated by the material discussed in this chapter. The extension of the Convention to the countries of central and eastern Europe, the ramifications of international action in some parts of Europe, as well as the continuing failure to find a resolution to the division of Cyprus, have presented the Strasbourg Court with some very difficult factual situations with a heavy political content. It is to the credit of the Court that it has not ducked making decisions in the most difficult cases, though inevitably those judgments have proved to be controversial, and there are some developing inconsistencies in the lines of reasoning adopted by the Court in individual cases. In particular, the interaction of concepts such as 'effective control', '*espace juridique*', jurisdiction, and responsibility does not yet appear to have been fully worked out in the case-law of the Strasbourg Court.

6

RESERVATIONS AND DEROGATIONS

INTRODUCTION

This chapter brings together two principal means by which a Contracting Party can escape the full application of certain provisions of the Convention and two further provisions of the Convention designed to ensure that it is not used for a purpose for which it was not intended.

Article 57 of the Convention permits reservations to certain provisions to the extent that current law in force in the Contracting Party as at the date of ratification of the Convention is not compatible with the Convention. Reservations of a general character are not permitted. Reservations operate, so long as the reservation is in effect, as permanent variations of the obligations arising under the Convention for the Contracting Party making the reservation.

Article 15 of the Convention permits Contracting Parties to exclude on a temporary basis the operation of certain Convention rights in the limited circumstances provided by the article through the system of derogations.

Articles 17 and 18 seek to ensure that the Convention is not used to undermine the scheme of protection set out in it. Article 17 reflects a concern for the defence of democratic society and its institutions, and precludes actions which might undermine those principles. It is aimed at protection against totalitarian and other deeply offensive activities. The Strasbourg Court has consistently, and rightly, taken a very restrictive view of its application. Finally, Article 18 prohibits the use of the limitations permitted by the Convention provisions for any purpose other than that for which the Convention allows.

RESERVATIONS

International law recognizes that a State, in accepting a treaty, may in certain circumstances attach a reservation, that is, make its acceptance subject to some new term which limits or varies the application of the treaty to that State.[1] The extent to

---

[1] See Art. 19 *et seq.* of the Vienna Convention on the Law of Treaties.

which reservations are appropriate to a human rights instrument has been questioned. Frowein says:[2]

It is of crucial importance that the member States of the [European] Convention should be willing to exercise their collective responsibility in the matter of reservations and agree that reservations can only be a means whereby a new member can bring its law into line with the Convention. In fact, many of the reservations could easily be made superfluous by sometimes very minor amendments to the legislation in force. The Convention system has in recent years grown more and more into the role of a system of European integration in the sense of its preamble. Unilateral derogations are incompatible with the very idea of such a system.

Article 57[3] of the Convention permits certain reservations and provides:

1. Any State may, when signing this Convention or when depositing its instrument of ratification, make a reservation in respect of any particular provision of the Convention to the extent that any law then in force in its territory is not in conformity with the provision. Reservations of a general character shall not be permitted under this Article.

2. Any reservation made under this Article shall contain a brief statement of the law concerned.

Reservations must relate to a particular provision of the Convention and to a particular law in force at the time, and they must contain a brief statement of the law concerned. It should be noted that reservations are only permitted in relation to existing laws at the time of ratification; reservations are not permitted where a Contracting Party subsequently wishes to vary its commitments under the Convention.[4] A fair number of reservations have been made to the Convention and Protocols, but these are mainly very limited in scope.[5] Any far-reaching reservation would in any event be illegal as being incompatible with the object and purpose of the Treaty.[6]

Although there is no legal obligation in this respect, and no express provision for withdrawal of a reservation, it would be in accordance with the spirit of the Convention, and with its object and purpose, to envisage that laws which necessitated reservations would progressively be amended or repealed to ensure that the Contracting Parties complied without reservation with all the Convention's provisions. This has certainly happened on some occasions. When ratifying the Convention, Norway found it necessary to make a reservation in respect of Article 9, since the Norwegian Constitution of 1814 provided for a ban on Jesuits. In 1956 this provision was abrogated and the reservation withdrawn. Similarly in Switzerland, a reservation to the same article was

---

[2] J. Frowein, 'Reservations to the European Convention on Human Rights' in F. Matscher and H. Petzold (eds.), *Protecting Human Rights: The European Dimension. Studies in Honour of Gérard J. Wiarda* (Carl Heymanns, Köln 1990), 193–200, 200.

[3] Formerly Art. 64 of the Convention.

[4] Though Article 15 permits derogations from certain Convention provisions in time of war or other public emergency threatening the life of the nation.

[5] See http://conventions.coe.int for a full list of current reservations.

[6] Art. 19 of the Vienna Convention on the Law of Treaties. See also *Reservations to the Convention on Genocide*, [1951] ICJ Rep. 15.

considered necessary pending revision of the denominational articles of the Federal Constitution. When the revision was made, the reservation was withdrawn.

RESERVATIONS MADE BY CONTRACTING PARTIES

Article 57 of the Convention appears to permit only reservations in respect of those articles of the Convention which lay down substantive obligations, but Contracting Parties have attempted to qualify declarations relating to the procedural provisions of the Convention, that is, those provisions which dealt with the competence of the Strasbourg organs.

There is no such thing as a 'quasi-reservation'. The Latvian Government argued in the *Slivenko* case[7] that it had ratified the Convention on the assumption that it was entirely compatible with a treaty it had concluded with Russia of 30 April 1994, and so its ratification of the Convention and its Protocols was subject to a quasi-reservation in respect of that treaty. The Court did not share this view.

At the time of ratifying the Convention in 1990, Finland had lodged a reservation in respect to the right to a public hearing under Article 6(1), since Finnish law at that time did not provide for a public hearing in proceedings before certain courts, including the Supreme Administrative Court. In December 1996, when the law had been amended, Finland withdrew its reservation in respect of the lack of public hearings before the Supreme Administrative Court concerning decisions taken from 1 December 1996. In the *Helle* case,[8] the Court held that, in the light of the reservation, the failure to hold a hearing in relation to decisions reached in 1991 and 1992 did not give rise to a breach of Article 6.

Since recognition of the Court and acceptance of the right of individual petition are now mandatory requirements of the Convention, the matters raised in the following section are of largely historical interest. However, an understanding of the position adopted by some Contracting Parties may be helpful in reading certain significant cases in which the issue arose. There remained some doubt whether reservations could be made in declarations under former Article 25, accepting the competence of the Commission to receive applications from individuals, or under former Article 46, recognizing the compulsory jurisdiction of the Court. However, the Commission did accept that declarations under former Article 25 may be subject to the proviso that they have no retroactive effect. Former Article 46(1), providing for declarations recognizing the Court's jurisdiction 'in all matters', seems to exclude the possibility of a partial recognition, although the second paragraph provides that a declaration may be made on condition of reciprocity or for a limited period. Further, what is now Article 57 seems to envisage only reservations of a substantive character, relating to a specific law in force at the time of signature or ratification; and a reservation is not permissible

[7] *Slivenko and others v Latvia*, (App. 48321/99), Decision of 23 January 2002 [GC], ECHR 2002-II.
[8] *Helle v Finland*, (App. 20722/92), 19 December 1997, (1998) 26 EHRR 159. See also *Laukkanen and Manninen v Finland*, (App. 50230/99), 3 February 2004.

where a treaty provides for only specified reservations which do not include the reservation in question.[9]

The Turkish Government, however, filed two declarations under former Articles 25(1) and 46 to which conditions are attached that the Commission and Court would almost certainly consider to be attempted reservations. They appear to have been intended to exclude the Commission's competence in complaints concerning its conduct in the northern part of Cyprus, while others seek to exclude the right to complain about the activities of Turkish military personnel. The third, fourth, and fifth qualifications seek to limit the interpretation which may be placed on Articles 8 to 11 of the Convention. The Commission held all these 'qualifications' to be invalid in the *Chrysostomos* case.[10] These declarations were subsequently considered by the Court in the *Loizidou* case.[11] The Court ruled that a territorial limitation is not permissible, but that, notwithstanding the purported territorial restrictions, the declarations contained valid acceptances of the competence of the Commission and the Court.

INTERPRETATION OF RESERVATIONS

Applications which must be excluded because of a reservation made by the respondent State are outside the Strasbourg Court's competence *ratione materiae*. A reservation must be interpreted in the language in which it is made, not in its translation into one of the languages, English or French, of the authentic texts of the Convention.[12] The Commission gave rather extensive interpretations of those reservations which it had to consider, but its approach has now been overtaken by authority from the Court, which is much more robust.

The Commission had held that a reservation may serve to exclude not only measures expressly covered by the reservation, but also other related measures.[13] It may extend to exclude a new law which replaces the law in force at the time of the reservation, provided that the new law does not have the effect of enlarging the scope of the reservation.[14] It may extend to legislative and administrative measures to implement the purpose for which the reservation was made.[15] It may even extend to other provisions of the Convention than those expressly mentioned in the reservation if it is clearly intended to cover the entire operation of national law in the field concerned.[16] Quite apart from this point, it would seem that the Commission has departed from the evident intention of what was then Article 64. That article refers expressly to laws in

---

[9] Art. 19 of the Vienna Convention on the Law of Treaties.

[10] Apps. 15299–15311/89, *Chrysostomos v Turkey*, Decision of 4 March 1991, (1991) 12 HRLJ 113.

[11] *Loizidou v Turkey*, (App.15318/89), 23 March 1995, Series A No 310, (1995) 20 EHRR 99, §§65–98.

[12] App. 1047/61, *X v Austria*, Decision of 15 December 1961, (1961) 4 *Yearbook* 356; App. 1452/62, *X v Austria*, Decision of 18 December 1963, (1963) 6 *Yearbook* 268; App. 2432/65, *X v Austria*, Decision of 7 April 1967, (1967) 22 CD 124.

[13] App. 2432/65, *X v Austria*, Decision of 7 April 1967, (1967) 22 CD 124.

[14] Ibid. See also App. 3923/69, *X v Austria*, Decision of 14 December 1970, (1971) 37 CD 10.

[15] App. 2765/66, *X v Austria*, Decision of 15 December 1967, (1967) 10 *Yearbook* 412, 418.

[16] App. 3923/69, *X v Austria*, Decision of 14 December 1970, (1971) 37 CD 10; App. 4002/69, *X v Austria*, Decision of 29 March 1971, (1971) 14 *Yearbook* 178.

force at the time of signature or ratification, and clearly envisages that all subsequent legislation will be in conformity with the Convention. The Commission appears to have gone too far in accepting that a later law in the same field might be brought within the scope of a reservation.

However, both the Commission[17] and the Court have taken the view that it is for them to determine the legal validity of reservations. The Court has been rather more rigorous in its examination of these issues than the Commission. The leading authority is the *Belilos* case.[18] Marlène Belilos had been fined 120 Swiss francs for having taken part in an unauthorized demonstration. She raised a complaint under Article 6 of the Convention. This brought into play a *declaration* made by Switzerland in respect of this article:

The Swiss Federal Council considers that the guarantee of fair trial in Article 6, paragraph 1 of the Convention, in the determination of civil rights and obligations or any criminal charge against the person in question is intended solely to ensure ultimate control by the judiciary over the acts or decisions of the public authorities relating to such rights or obligations or the determination of such a charge.

The Strasbourg Court had to consider the effect of this declaration on the claim, which the respondent State argued amounted in substance to a reservation. The Court accepted this argument, noting that the Convention only made provision for reservations. As a reservation its validity fell to be determined against the requirements of former Article 64. The Court asserted jurisdiction relying on what were then Articles 19,[19] 45,[20] and 49.[21] The Court went on to say that reservations of a general character (which are not permitted by the reservations article of the Convention) were those 'couched in terms that were too vague or broad for it to be possible to determine their exact meaning and scope'.[22] The Court also noted that the validity of a reservation would be dependent upon its being accompanied by a brief statement of the law concerned. Since the Swiss reservation met neither of these conditions it was invalid. In international law, the position under the Vienna Convention in such circumstances would be that the provision in question would not be valid as between the parties.[23] However, the Court rightly, since this was not litigation between two States, decided

---

[17] Initially in App. 9116/80, *Telemtasch v Switzerland*, Decision of 5 May 1982, (1983) 31 DR 120.

[18] *Belilos v Switzerland*, (App. 10328/83), 29 April 1988, Series A No 132, (1988) 10 EHRR 466.

[19] Which charges the Court with ensuring the observance of the engagements undertaken by the High Contracting Parties.

[20] Giving the Court jurisdiction to consider all cases concerning the interpretation and application of the Convention referred by a State or the Commission under Art. 48.

[21] Providing that in the event of a dispute as to whether the Court has jurisdiction, the matter is to be settled by a decision of the Court.

[22] *Belilos v Switzerland*, (App. 10328/83), 29 April 1988, Series A No 132, (1988) 10 EHRR 466, §55.

[23] Art. 21(3) of the Vienna Convention provides: When a State objecting to a reservation has not opposed the entry into force of the treaty between itself and the reserving State, the provisions to which the reservation relates do not apply as between the two States to the extent of the reservation. See also J. Frowein, 'Reservations to the European Convention on Human Rights' in F. Matscher and H. Petzold (eds.), *Protecting Human Rights: The European Dimension. Studies in Honour of Gérard J. Wiarda* (Carl Heymanns, Köln 1990), 193–200, 197.

that the effect of holding the reservation invalid was that the full force of Article 6 applied in the case, and they went on to consider the merits of the case on that basis.

The Strasbourg Court has taken a tough line on the requirement to state the law concerned, and a number of purported reservations have been ruled invalid for a failure to state the law concerned.

A Swiss reservation was in issue in the *Weber* case.[24] Weber had been fined for breaching the confidentiality of a judicial investigation. He complained that his rights under Articles 6 and 10 had been violated. In relation to the complaint under Article 6, the respondent State sought to rely on a reservation in the following terms:

The rule contained in Article 6(1) of the Convention that hearing shall be in public shall not apply to proceedings relating to the determination...of any criminal charge which, in accordance with cantonal legislation, are heard before an administrative authority. The rule that judgment must be pronounced publicly shall not affect the operation of cantonal legislation on civil or criminal procedure providing that judgment shall not be delivered in public but notified to the parties in writing.

The Court found that this reservation was invalid because it was not accompanied by a brief statement of the law concerned; such an omission was not regarded as a purely formal requirement but a condition of substance. The Court proceeded to test the complaint against Article 6(1).

In a case concerning Austria,[25] a reservation to Article 5 was in issue. The Court noted that the national law in issue was all in force on the date when Austria ratified the Convention, and that its wording was sufficiently specific to meet the requirements of former Article 64(1). The reservation contained a reference to the Bundesgesetzblatt[26] by way of providing a brief statement of the laws affected. The Court amplified its earlier comments on the requirements of former Article 64(2):

According to the Court's case-law, the 'brief statement' as required by [Article 64(2)] 'both constitutes an evidential factor and contributes to legal certainty'; its purpose 'is to provide a guarantee—in particular for the other Contracting Parties and the Convention institutions—that a reservation does not go beyond the provisions expressly excluded by the State concerned.'...This does not mean that it is necessary under Article 64(2) to provide a description, even a concise one, of the substance of the texts in question.

In this instance, the reference to the Federal Official Gazette—preceded moreover by an indication of the subject-matter of the relevant provisions—makes it possible for everyone to identify the precise laws concerned and to obtain any information regarding them. It also provides a safeguard against any interpretation which would unduly extend the field of application of the reservation. Accordingly, that reservation complies with Article 64(2).[27]

A different Austrian reservation was in issue in the *Eisenstecken* case.[28] This reservation was broadly worded and concerned the right to a fair trial in Article 6; it read:

---

[24] *Weber v Switzerland*, (App. 11034/84), 22 May 1990, Series A No 177, (1990) 12 EHRR 508.

[25] *Chorherr v Austria*, (App. 13308/87), 25 August 1993, Series A No 266–B, (1994) 17 EHRR 358.

[26] Federal Official Gazette.   [27] §21.

[28] *Eisenstecken v Austria*, (App. 29477/95), 3 October 2000, (2002) 34 EHRR 860, ECHR 2000-X.

The provisions of Article 6 of the Convention shall be so applied that there shall be no prejudice to the principles governing public court hearings laid down in Article 90 of the 1929
version of the Federal Constitutional Law.

The applicant complained that there was no public hearing in a dispute concerning
real property transactions. The reservation had been considered in a number of earlier
cases,[29] and in a remarkably short section of one earlier judgment apparently accepted
as valid.[30] The Court in the *Eisenstecken* case observed that the compatibility of the
Austrian reservation with the requirements of what is now Article 57 had not previously been tested. The Court goes on to rule the reservation to be invalid for its failure
to contain a brief statement of the law which is said not to conform to Article 6 of the
Convention, and that it was not necessary to consider its compatibility with other
requirements of Article 57.

   In two cases against Lithuania,[31] the validity of a reservation in respect of
Article 5(3)[32] was in issue. Lithuania had made a reservation for one year after the
Convention entered into force in respect of Lithuania. The question was whether
on the expiry of the reservation, the obligation to bring a detained person promptly
before a judge arose, or whether the opportunity had been missed by reason of the
earlier detention. The Court is particularly accommodating (though there is logic in
the Court's position) in finding that the obligation arises immediately on entering
detention and cannot usefully be resurrected at some time later if the person is still in
detention on the expiry of the Lithuanian reservation. There was no renewed obligation after the expiry of the reservation.[33]

   Sometimes the reservation is not invalid but does not apply to the circumstances
in respect of which it is pleaded. This happened in the *Dacosta Silva* case[34] where the
Strasbourg Court determined that Spain's reservation in relation to Articles 5 and
6 in their application to military disciplinary rules did not apply to the disciplinary
rules of the Civil Guard, and so could not be relied upon to escape liability under the
Convention.

DEROGATIONS IN EMERGENCY SITUATIONS

Article 15 provides:

   1. In time of war or other public emergency threatening the life of the nation any High
      Contracting Party may take measures derogating from its obligations under this
      Convention to the extent strictly required by the exigencies of the situation, provided

---

[29] Eisenstecken §§24–6.

[30] *Ettl v Austria*, (App. 9273/81), 23 April 1987, Series A No 117, (1988) 10 EHRR 255, §42.

[31] *Jėčius v Lithuania*, (App. 34578/97), 31 July 2000, ECHR 2000-IX; and *Grauslys v Lithuania*,
(App. 36743/97), 10 October 2000.

[32] The entitlement of detained persons to be brought promptly before a competent judicial authority.

[33] *Jėčius v Lithuania*, (App. 34578/97), 31 July 2000, ECHR 2000-IX, §86.

[34] *Dacosta Silva v Spain*, (App. 69966/01), 2 February 2007, ECHR 2007-XIII.

that such measures are not inconsistent with its other obligations under inter-national law.

2. No derogation from Article 2, except in respect of deaths resulting from lawful acts of war, or from Articles 3, 4 (paragraph 1) and 7 shall be made under this provision.

3. Any High Contracting Party availing itself of this right of derogation shall keep the Secretary-General of the Council of Europe fully informed of the measures which it has taken and the reasons therefor. It shall also inform the Secretary-General of the Council of Europe when such measures have ceased to operate and the provisions of the Convention are again being fully executed.

It is greatly to the credit of the Contracting Parties that, as at 1 September 2009, not-withstanding the problems caused for a number of Contracting Parties by increases in terrorist activity, and the threats of such actions, there are no extant derogations in effect. To date it has been Articles 5 and 6 which have attracted almost all derogations; it is significant that these articles contain little scope for applying limitations on the sorts of grounds that are specified in, for example, Articles 8 to 11.[35]

Article 15 incorporates, in effect, the principle of necessity common to all legal systems. Most States have provisions for emergency legislation, empowering them to take measures in a state of emergency which would not otherwise be lawful.[36] However, under Article 15, such measures are subject to the control of the organs of the Convention. If a Contracting Party seeks to rely on a derogation in proceedings before the Strasbourg Court, it is for the Court to consider, first, whether a pub-lic emergency threatening the life of the nation could be said to exist at the mater-ial time; and secondly, whether the measures taken were in fact strictly required by the exigencies of the situation. Thirdly, such measures must be consistent with other obligations under international law. Finally, there must have been timely notification to the Secretary-General of the Council of Europe both of the introduction of dero-gating measures and of the reasons for them, and, where appropriate, of the lifting of those measures.

Issues relating to Article 15 have normally been examined on the merits and cannot usually be disposed of at the stage of admissibility. In inter-State cases, this is indeed inevitable, since such a case cannot be rejected as being manifestly ill-founded.[37] In the case brought by Ireland against the United Kingdom, the respondent State invoked, at the stage of admissibility, the notification of derogation which it had made in respect of Northern Ireland. The Irish Government accepted that a public emer-gency within the meaning of Article 15 existed in Northern Ireland, but denied that the measures taken by the respondent State were strictly required by the exigencies of

---

[35] See, in general, A. Mokhtar, 'Human Rights Obligations v Derogations: Article 15 of the European Convention on Human Rights', (2004) 8 *International Journal of Human Rights* 65; and J. Allain, 'Derogations from the European Convention on Human Rights in light of "Other Obligations under International Law"' [2005] EHRLR 480.

[36] See generally Pinheiro Farinha, 'L'article 15 de la Convention' in F. Matscher and H. Petzold (eds.), *Protecting Human Rights: The European Dimension. Essays in honour of Gérard Wiarda* (Carl Heymanns, Köln 1990), 521.

[37] See ch.2 above.

the situation. The Commission held that this question could not be determined at the stage of admissibility.[38] Indeed, even on an individual application, it would be difficult to justify a decision holding that all the conditions of Article 15 were fulfilled at the stage of admissibility; normally such an application should be examined at the merits phase if Article 15 is invoked.[39]

There would seem to be nothing objectionable in a Contracting Party making use of an Article 15 derogation to avoid granting rights under the Convention when it has been held to be in violation of the Convention. In the *Brogan* case[40] the United Kingdom was found to be in breach of Article 5(3) of the Convention in the period allowed for questioning before a suspect was brought before a judicial officer under the prevention of terrorism legislation. Prior to the judgment of the Court, it had considered that the legislation met the requirements of Article 5(3). In response to the judgment, instead of amending its legislation to ensure compliance with the period for bringing suspects before a judicial officer, the United Kingdom entered a derogation under Article 15. Obviously, that derogation could not apply retrospectively, and would be subject to assessment in the usual way by the Convention organs for compliance with the requirements of Article 15.[41] Any doubt about the validity of the derogation filed following the judgment in the *Brogan* case was resolved in the *Brannigan and McBride* case[42] in which the Court accepted the validity of the subsequent derogation.

NON-DEROGABLE RIGHTS

Certain rights under the Convention are not susceptible to derogation in any circumstances. Article 2 on the right to life is non-derogable, save to the extent that derogations are permitted 'in respect of deaths resulting from lawful acts of war'.[43] Article 2 itself does not include intentional deprivation of life in the execution of a sentence of a court following a conviction for a crime for which this penalty is imposed;[44] nor does it include deprivation of life in defence of any person from unlawful violence,[45] in order to effect a lawful arrest or to prevent the escape of a person lawfully detained,[46] and in action lawfully taken for the purpose of quelling a riot or insurrection.[47] Where Protocol 6 has been ratified, the prohibition of derogations in respect of the rights guaranteed by that Protocol contained in Article 3 of Protocol 6 applies. However, Article 2 of Protocol 6 permits Contracting Parties to

---

[38] Apps. 5310/71 and 5151/72, *Ireland v United Kingdom*, Decision of 1 October 1972, (1972) 41 CD 3, 88.

[39] But see App. 493/59, *X v Ireland*, Decision of 27 July 1961, (1961) 4 *Yearbook* 302, 310–16.

[40] *Brogan and others v United Kingdom*, (Apps. 11209/84, 11234/84, 11266/84, and 11386/85), 29 November 1988, Series A No 145–B, (1989) 11 EHRR 117.

[41] This is the view taken in J. Merrills, *Human Rights in Europe* (MUP, Manchester, 2001), 211.

[42] *Brannigan and McBride v United Kingdom*, (Apps. 14533/89, and 14554/89), 26 May 1993, Series A No 253–B, (1994) 17 EHRR 539.

[43] Art. 15(2).   [44] But see comments on Protocol 6 below.

[45] Art. 2(2)(a).   [46] Art. 2(2)(b).   [47] Art. 2(2)(c).

make provision in their law for the death penalty in respect of acts committed in time of war or imminent threat of war.[48] These provisions have now become largely otiose, since 41 Contracting Parties have ratified Protocol 13[49] which prohibits the use of the death penalty in all circumstances.

No derogations may be made in respect of the prohibition of slavery and servitude in Article 4(1); nor in respect of the requirement that there be no punishment without law under Article 7; nor in respect of the right not to be tried or punished twice under Article 4 of Protocol 7.

SUBSTANTIVE REQUIREMENTS

Permissible derogations under Article 15 must meet both the substantive requirements of Article 15(1) and the procedural requirements in Article 15(3). The substantive requirements require three conditions to be satisfied:

- there must be a public emergency threatening the life of the nation;
- the measures taken in response to it must be strictly required by the exigencies of the situation; and
- the measures taken must be in compliance with the Contracting Party's other obligations under international law.

The procedural requirements require that there is some formal or public act of derogation, and that notice of the derogation, measures adopted in consequence of it, and of the ending of the derogation, is communicated to the Secretary-General of the Council of Europe.[50]

The use of derogations under Article 15 arose for the first time in the *Cyprus* cases;[51] two applications were brought by Greece against the United Kingdom when Cyprus was still under British rule. The Commission considered that it was 'competent to pronounce on the existence of a public danger which, under Article 15, would grant to the Contracting Party concerned the right to derogate from the obligations laid down in the Convention.' The Commission also considered that it was 'competent to decide whether measures taken by a Party under Article 15 of the Convention had been taken to the extent strictly required by the exigencies of the situation.' It added that 'the Government should be able to exercise a certain measure of discretion in assessing the extent strictly required by the exigencies of the situation.'[52] Subsequently a

---

[48] Where this happens, the State must notify the Secretary-General of the Council of Europe of the relevant provisions of the law governing the death penalty: Art. 2 of Protocol 6. 46 of the 47 Member States of the Council of Europe have ratified Protocol 6: Russia has signed but not yet ratified the Protocol.

[49] Four further States have signed but not yet ratified the Protocol; Azerbaijan and Russia have not signed the Protocol.

[50] See Art. 15(3).

[51] App. 176/57, *Greece v United Kingdom*, (1958–9) 2 *Yearbook* 174 and 182; App. 299/57, *Greece v United Kingdom*, (1958–9) 2 *Yearbook* 178 and 186.

[52] App. 176/57, *Greece v United Kingdom*, (1958–9) 2 *Yearbook* 174, 176.

political solution to the Cyprus problem was reached, and the Committee of Ministers decided that no further action was called for. The notion of a government's 'measure of discretion'[53] was to have an influential career in this context. Its scope in relation to derogations is considered below. The existence of this control was confirmed by the Court in the *Lawless* case.[54] The Strasbourg Court considered, first, whether there could be said to be a public emergency threatening the life of the nation; second, whether the measures taken in derogation from obligations under the Convention were 'strictly required by the exigencies of the situation'; and third, whether the measures were consistent with other obligations under international law.

The Commission adopted the position that issues arising under Article 15 will not be examined unless they are raised by the respondent State. The *McVeigh* case[55] concerned the United Kingdom anti-terrorist legislation as it had been applied to the three applicants who had arrived in Liverpool on a ferry from Ireland. They were held for forty-five hours without charge, questioned, searched, finger-printed and photographed. They made complaints under Articles 5, 8, and 10. At the material time, various derogations were in effect in respect of the United Kingdom, but the United Kingdom did not seek to invoke them in respect of the situation in Great Britain, as distinct from Northern Ireland.[56]

THERE MUST BE A PUBLIC EMERGENCY THREATENING THE LIFE OF THE NATION

What constitutes a public emergency? In the *Lawless* case, the Strasbourg Court defined it as:

an exceptional situation of crisis or emergency which affects the whole population and constitutes a threat to the organized life of the community of which the State is composed.[57]

The danger must be exceptional in that the normal measures permitted by the Convention are plainly inadequate to deal with the situation. The Court found that the existence of a public emergency was 'reasonably deduced' by the Irish Government. The Court had regard in particular to three factors: the existence of a secret army (the Irish Republican Army—IRA); the fact that this army was also operating outside the territory of the Contracting Party; and the steady and alarming increase in terrorist activities in the period before the emergency was declared.[58]

---

[53] In French *marge d'appreciation*; the term 'margin of appreciation' is now used in preference to 'measures of discretion'.

[54] *Lawless v Ireland*, (App. 332/57), 14 November 1960, 7 April 1961, and 1 July 1961, Series A, Nos 1–3, (1979–80) 1 EHRR 1, 13, and 15, §22 of the judgment of 1 July 1961.

[55] Apps. 8022/77, 8025/77, and 8027/77, *McVeigh, O'Neil and Evans v United Kingdom*, Report of 18 March 1981, (1982) 25 DR 15.

[56] Derogations made by Turkey have frequently limited their application to parts of the country.

[57] *Lawless v Ireland*, (App. 332/57), 14 November 1960, 7 April 1961, and 1 July 1961, Series A, Nos 1–3, (1979–80) 1 EHRR 1, 13, and 15, §28 of the judgment of 1 July 1961.

[58] Ibid.

In the *Greek* case, the Commission had to consider the validity of a derogation by a revolutionary government. The respondent Government, which had seized power in Greece by a *coup d'état* on 21 April 1967 and had suspended parts of the Constitution, invoked Article 15 of the Convention. The Commission considered that the Convention applied in the same way to a revolutionary as to a constitutional government.[59] As regards the definition of a 'public emergency threatening the life of the nation', the Commission followed the definition given by the Court in the *Lawless* case.[60] Methodologically, too, the Commission followed the Court, but only in part. It sought to answer the question whether there was such a public emergency in Greece by examining the elements indicated by the respondent State as constituting in its view such an emergency.[61] These elements were examined by the Commission under three heads: the danger of a Communist take-over; the crisis of constitutional government; and the breakdown of public order in Greece.[62] The Commission considered that the burden lay upon the respondent State to show that the conditions justifying measures of derogation under Article 15 had been and continued to be met.[63] It concluded that the Greece had not satisfied it that there was on 21 April 1967 a public emergency threatening the life of the Greek nation.[64] However, in one respect the Commission did not follow the Court's earlier view of Article 15. The Commission, while referring to the Government's 'margin of appreciation', did not merely consider whether the Greek Government had sufficient reason to believe that a public emergency existed; it considered whether such an emergency existed in fact. This difference of approach is of great importance since it makes more stringent the requirements of Article 15.

In *Ireland v United Kingdom*[65] both the Commission and the Court readily accepted that there was a public emergency threatening the life of the nation because of the terrorist threat from the activities of the IRA. This issue was not contested by Ireland. No argument was made on the basis that—certainly at the time—the major threat related only to a part of the United Kingdom.

A rather different situation was presented in the *Sakik* case.[66] The Turkish Government sought, in responding to the applications alleging violations of Article 5 arising from the length of detention in police custody, to rely on derogations filed in respect of Article 5. But those declarations did not apply to the country as a whole, and did not apply to Ankara, where the facts alleged to have resulted in the violation of Article 5 had occurred. The Court confirmed that derogations would be strictly interpreted and could not extend to part of a territory not mentioned in the notice of derogation.[67]

The approach of the Court in reviewing whether there is a public emergency threatening the life of the nation is neatly summarized in the *Aksoy* case:

---

[59] App. 3321/67, *Denmark v Greece,* App. 3322/67, *Norway v Greece,* App. 3323/67, *Sweden v Greece,* and App. 3344/67, *Nertherlands v Greece,* ('the *Greek* case'), Report of 18 November 1969, (1969) 12 Yearbook 1, 32.

[60] Ibid., 71–2.

[61] Ibid., 44.   [62] Ibid., 45.   [63] Ibid., 72.   [64] Ibid., 76.

[65] *Ireland v United Kingdom,* (App. 5310/71), 18 January 1978, Series A No 25, (1979–80) 2 EHRR 25.

[66] *Sakik and others v Turkey,* (Apps. 23878/94–23883/94), 26 November 1997, (1998) 27 EHRR 662, ECHR 1997-VII.

[67] §39. See also *Abdülsamet Yaman v Turkey,* (App. 32446/96), 2 November 2004, §69.

The Court recalls that it falls to each Contracting State, with its responsibility for 'the life of [its] nation', to determine whether that life is threatened by a 'public emergency' and, if so, how far it is necessary to go in attempting to overcome the emergency. By reason of their direct and continuous contact with the pressing needs of the moment, the national authorities are in principle better placed than the international judge to decide both on the presence of such an emergency and on the nature and scope of the derogations necessary to avert it. Accordingly, in this matter a wide margin of appreciation should be left to the national authorities.[68]

The Court has been called upon to consider whether a United Kingdom derogation[69] in respect of Article 5(1) permitting detention without trial of foreign nationals suspected of involvement in terrorist activities was based upon a public emergency threatening the life of the nation in the *A and others* case.[70] The public emergency was said to flow from the terrorist attacks in New York, Washington DC, and Pennsylvania of 11 September 2001. However, no other party to the European Convention had felt it necessary to derogate from Convention rights in relation to those events, and there had, at the time, been no terrorist attacks in the United Kingdom attributable to those alleged to be responsible for the attacks of 11 September 2001 in the United States. United Kingdom support for the so-called war on terrorism has, however, had a high visibility, which clearly rendered the United Kingdom a *potential* target for such terrorist activity.[71] The House of Lords, by a majority of eight to one, concluded that there was a public emergency threatening the life of the nation, that imprisonment without trial would be a proportionate response to the threat faced, but that its limitation to foreign nationals was discriminatory, and the United Kingdom Government had only filed its derogation in respect of Article 5, and not of Article 14.[72] When the Grand Chamber came to consider whether there was a public emergency threatening the life of the nation, it observed that where there has been such a careful consideration of the validity of the derogation in the national courts, it would only interfere if the national court has misinterpreted or misapplied Article 15 as interpreted by the Strasbourg Court or had reached a conclusion which was manifestly unreasonable.[73]

To date, apart from the *Greek* case, which involved a derogation whose underlying purpose was to support a non-democratic government, the Strasbourg Court has accepted the existence of a Contracting Party's assessment of the existence of a public emergency threatening the life of the nation. Some dissenting judgments have suggested that the Strasbourg Court defers too readily to the judgment of Contracting Parties in this context.[74]

---

[68] *Aksoy v Turkey*, (App. 21987/93), 18 December 1996, (1997) 23 EHRR 553, ECHR 1996-VI, §68.

[69] See the Human Rights Act 1998 (Designated Derogation) Order 2001, SI 2001, No. 3644. The derogation was withdrawn with effect from 14 March 2005.

[70] *A and others v United Kingdom*, (App. 3455/05), 19 February 2009 [GC], (2009) 49 EHRR 29, ECHR 2009-nyr.

[71] Which, in fact, materialized in July 2005.

[72] *A and others v Secretary of State for the Home Department*; *X and another v Secretary of State for the Home Department*, [2004] UKHL 56.

[73] *A and others v United Kingdom*, (App. 3455/05), 19 February 2009 [GC], (2009) 49 EHRR 29, ECHR 2009-nyr, §174.

[74] See, for example, the dissenting opinion of Judge Walsh in *Brannigan and McBride v United Kingdom*, (Apps. 14533/89, and 14554/89), 26 May 1993, Series A No 258-B, (1994) 17 EHRR 539.

THE MEASURES TAKEN MUST BE STRICTLY REQUIRED

If it is established that this first condition of Article 15 is satisfied, it must next be asked whether the measures which are the subject of the application were 'strictly required by the exigencies of the situation'. In the *Aksoy* case, the Court said:

It is for the Court to rule whether, *inter alia*, the States have gone beyond the 'extent strictly required by the exigencies' of the crisis. The domestic margin of appreciation is thus accompanied by a European supervision. In exercising this supervision, the Court must give appropriate weight to such relevant factors as the nature of the rights affected by the derogation and the circumstances leading to, and the duration of, the emergency situation.[75]

In the *Lawless* case, the Strasbourg Court held, following the opinion of the Commission, that detention without trial was justified under Article 15. In considering whether such a measure was strictly required by the exigencies of the situation, the Court had particular regard, not only to the dangers of the situation, but also to the existence of a number of safeguards designed to prevent abuses in the operation of the system of administrative detention.[76] Examination of safeguards where there is a derogation has taken on great significance in cases where the Court is called upon to review the compatibility of derogations with the requirements of Article 15. In *Ireland v United Kingdom*[77] the Court made an independent examination of the circumstances, but in doing so placed considerable emphasis on the margin of appreciation to be accorded to the Contracting Party. The Court found that the system of extrajudicial deprivation of liberty was justified by the circumstances as perceived by the United Kingdom between August 1971 and March 1975.

The determination of whether measures taken are strictly required by the exigencies of the situation requires consideration of three elements. First, are the derogations necessary to cope with the threat to the life of the nation? Secondly, are the measures taken no greater than those required to deal with the emergency? This is a test of proportionality.[78] Finally, how long have the derogating measures been applied? There is no case-law in which duration of the measures has been a crucial issue, but it is certainly arguable that measures, which at their inception were clearly required, could cease to be so if they proved either to be ineffectual or if it could no longer be established that they were strictly required by the situation. The Court said in *Ireland v United Kingdom* that the interpretation of Article 15 must leave a place for progressive adaptation.[79]

---

[75] *Aksoy v Turkey*, (App. 21987/93), 18 December 1996; (1997) 23 EHRR 553, ECHR 1996-VI, §68, referring to *Brannigan and McBride v United Kingdom*, (Apps. 14533/89, and 14554/89), 26 May 1993, Series A No 258–B, (1994) 17 EHRR 539, §43.

[76] *Lawless v Ireland*, (App. 332/57), 14 November 1960, 7 April 1961, and 1 July 1961, Series A Nos 1–3, (1979–80) 1 EHRR 1, 13, and 15, §§31–8 of the judgment of 1 July 1961.

[77] *Ireland v United Kingdom*, (App. 5310/71), 18 January 1978, Series A No 25, (1979–80) 2 EHRR 25.

[78] For an example of its application, see *A and others v United Kingdom*, (App. 3455/05), 19 February 2009 [GC], (2009) 49 EHRR 29, ECHR 2009-nyr, §§182–90.

[79] §83. See also *Marshall v United Kingdom*, (App. 41571/98), Decision of 10 July 2001.

It is possible to detect in the *Brannigan and McBride* case[80] a greater willingness by the Court to question the effectiveness of the safeguards which the Contracting Party puts in place to compensate for suspension of the rights required by the Convention provision in respect of which the derogation is filed. This tougher stand on the safeguards required to ensure that the derogations do not go beyond what is strictly required by the exigencies of the situation is supported by the Court's approach in the *Aksoy* case, where the Court declined to accept that the situation required suspects to be held for fourteen days without judicial intervention, noting that the Turkish Government had not detailed any reasons why judicial intervention was impracticable.[81]

In the *A and others* case,[82] the Strasbourg Court upheld the House of Lords' landmark decision that the extended power of detention was disproportionate and therefore not 'strictly required' since it targeted only foreign nationals while there was evidence that a similar threat came from United Kingdom nationals involved with al-Qaeda and other linked groups. In particular the Court rejected the respondent State's argument that the assessment of what measures were needed to combat the threat was a matter of political rather than judicial judgment. It observed that, particularly where a derogating measure encroached upon a fundamental Convention right, such as the right to liberty, the Court had to be satisfied that it was a genuine response to the emergency situation, that it was fully justified by the special circumstances of the emergency and that adequate safeguards were provided against abuse.

THE MEASURES MUST COMPLY WITH OTHER OBLIGATIONS UNDER INTERNATIONAL LAW

Measures which may be taken by a Contracting Party under Article 15(1) must not be 'inconsistent with its other obligations under international law'. Thus, they must not conflict with its other treaty obligations, or obligations under customary international law. Any such measures are not permitted under Article 15. Hence, a Contracting Party could not avail itself of Article 15 to release itself from its obligations, for example, under other human rights instruments. This would in any event be precluded by Article 53 of the Convention,[83] which provides:

Nothing in this Convention shall be construed as limiting or derogating from any of the human rights and fundamental freedoms which may be ensured under the laws of any High Contracting Party or under any other agreement to which it is a Party.

The requirement of consistency with international obligations has played little part in the case-law of the Court on Article 15 so far. In the *Brannigan and McBride* case[84] it

---

[80] *Brannigan and McBride v United Kingdom*, (Apps. 14533/89, and 14554/89), 26 May 1993, Series A No 258-B, (1994) 17 EHRR 539.

[81] *Aksoy v Turkey*, (App. 21987/93), 18 December 1996; (1997) 23 EHRR 553, ECHR 1996-VI, §§78 and 84.

[82] *A and others v United Kingdom*, (App. 3455/05), 19 February 2009 [GC], (2009) 49 EHRR 29, ECHR 2009-nyr.

[83] Formerly Art. 60.

[84] *Brannigan and McBride v United Kingdom*, (Apps. 14533/89, and 14554/89), 26 May 1993, Series A No 253-B, (1994) 17 EHRR 539.

was argued that Article 4 of the United Nations International Covenant on Civil and Political Rights required the emergency to be 'officially proclaimed'. Without expressing a view on the precise content of this requirement, the Court observed that the statement of the Home Secretary in Parliament on 22 December 1988 was formal in character and made public the Government's reliance on Article 15, and was 'well in keeping with the notion of an official proclamation'.[85]

PROCEDURAL REQUIREMENTS

Two issues require consideration in addressing the procedural requirements of Article 15. First, is it an inherent requirement that there is some official proclamation of the public emergency threatening the life of the nation? Secondly, what are the notification requirements of Article 15(3), and what is the consequence of any failure to comply with those requirements?

There is no express requirement in Article 15 that there is an official proclamation of the public emergency in the national legal order. But it seems that some form of public proclamation of the public emergency is an implicit feature of Article 15.[86] Though there is no direct authority on this issue, the implications of the comments of the Court in the *Brannigan and McBride* case noted above are to this effect. At the very least, a Contracting Party which had not made any formal announcements within the national legal order might find itself facing greater difficulties in proving the existence of a public emergency before the Court.

Article 15(3) requires notification both of the introduction of derogations and of the lifting of them. The precise nature of the obligation in this paragraph was considered by the Court in the *Lawless* case where it was argued that notification to the Secretary-General in July 1957 did not meet the requirements of the paragraph for three reasons: first, it did not indicate expressly that it was a derogation under Article 15; secondly, it did not refer to the existence of a public emergency threatening the life of the nation; and, thirdly, the matter had not been made public in Ireland until October and so could not be relied upon in respect of acts occurring between July and October. The Court did not consider that any of these factors tainted the notification; it was couched in terms sufficient to enable the Secretary-General to understand the Irish Government's position. Furthermore the paragraph required the matter to be notified to the Secretary-General and did not impose any obligation to publish the derogation within the Contracting Party.[87] Nor did it regard a delay of twelve days between national adoption and notification outside the scope of a requirement of notification 'without delay'.[88]

In the *Greek* case, there was a four-month delay between the implementation of derogating measures and notification. Even though the derogation was held to be

[85] §72–3.
[86] Having regard, in particular, to the requirement under Art. 4 of the International Covenant on Civil and Political Rights.
[87] *Lawless v Ireland*, (App. 332/57), 1 July 1961, Series A No 1, (1979–80) 1 EHRR 15, 62.
[88] Ibid.

invalid because the Commission was not satisfied that there was a public emergency threatening the life of the nation, the Commission noted that late notification would not justify action taken before the actual notification.[89] In the *Aksoy* case,[90] the Court raised the question that the Turkish derogation notice did not appear to contain sufficient information about the measure in question, but found that it was not necessary to determine whether Turkey had complied with the formal requirements since the power to detain a suspect for fourteen days without charge was disproportionate in any event.

Three remarks should be added on the scope of derogations *ratione temporis*. First, in considering whether the measures were permissible under Article 15, regard must be had to the situation before the emergency is declared. This was of course done by the Court in the *Lawless* case and by the Commission in the *Greek* case, but arguably not in the *Brannigan and McBride* case. Secondly, notification under Article 15(3) may have a very limited retroactive effect. No time limit is laid down for notifications, but the Court appeared to consider in the *Lawless* case that communication without delay is an element in the sufficiency of information required by that provision.[91] In the *Greek* case the Commission considered that the initial notice of derogation was given within a reasonable time, but that there was undue delay in communicating the reasons for the measures of derogation.[92] Thirdly, it is evident that if the measures in question remain in force after the circumstances which justify them have disappeared, they represent a breach of the Convention.[93] In the *Greek* case, accordingly, the Commission examined the evolution of the situation from the date of the *coup* to the time of compiling its report.[94]

The paragraph contains no sanction, though, in practice, it may well be that a Contracting Party would find great difficulty in proving its case if it failed to notify the Secretary-General of the measures taken. After all, the essence of Article 15 is that the Contracting Party reviews its ability to sustain the protection of the rights guaranteed by the Convention and concludes that certain of them must be limited in order to deal with an extraordinary situation.

PROHIBITION OF ABUSE OF RIGHTS

Article 17 provides:

Nothing in this Convention may be interpreted as implying for any State, group or person any right to engage in any activity or perform any act aimed at the destruction of any of the

---

[89] App. 3321/67, *Denmark v Greece*, App. 3322/67, *Norway v Greece*, App. 3323/67, *Sweden v Greece*, and App. 3344/67, *Netherlands v Greece*, ('the *Greek* case'), Report of 18 November 1969, (1969) 12 Yearbook 1, 41–3.

[90] *Aksoy v Turkey*, (App. 21987/93), 18 December 1996, (1997) 23 EHRR 553, ECHR 1996-VI, §86.

[91] *Lawless v Ireland*, (App. 332/57), 14 November 1960, 7 April 1961, and 1 July 1961, Series A Nos 1–3, (1979–80) 1 EHRR 1, 13, and 15, §§42–7 of the Judgment of 1 July 1961.

[92] *The Greek Case*, (1969) 12 *Yearbook*, 42–3.

[93] App. 214/56, *De Becker*, Report of the Commission, Series B No 2, 133.

[94] *The Greek Case*, (1969) 12 *Yearbook*, 92–103.

rights and freedoms set forth herein or at their limitation to a greater extent than is provided for in the Convention.

In the *Norwood* case[95] the Court, in ruling the application inadmissible, referred to Article 17 in the following terms:

The general purpose of Article 17 is to prevent individuals or groups with totalitarian aims from exploiting in their own interests the principles enunciated by the Convention.[96]

THE EARLY COMMISSION DECISIONS

The Commission stated that Article 17 is designed to safeguard the rights listed in the Convention, by protecting the free operation of democratic institutions.[97] In an early case introduced by the German Communist Party, the Commission quoted, from the preparatory work, the statement that the object was to prevent adherents to totalitarian doctrines from exploiting the rights guaranteed by the Convention for the purpose of destroying human rights.[98] The object of Article 17, therefore, is to limit the rights guaranteed only to the extent that such limitation is necessary to prevent their total subversion, and it must be quite narrowly construed in relation to this object.

In the above case, the German Communist Party had, in 1956, been declared 'anti-constitutional' by the Federal Constitutional Court. The Court had consequently dissolved it and ordered the confiscation of its property. The Party challenged this decision as contrary to Articles 9, 10, and 11 of the Convention. The Commission, applying Article 17, rejected the application as incompatible with the provisions of the Convention. The avowed aim of the Communist Party, according to its own declarations, was to establish a communist society by means of a proletarian revolution and the dictatorship of the proletariat. Consequently, even if it sought power by solely constitutional methods, recourse to a dictatorship was incompatible with the Convention because it would involve the suppression of a number of rights and freedoms which the Convention guaranteed.

In a sequel to this case, a company incorporated under Swiss law, Retimag S.A., complained of the confiscation without compensation of two of its properties in Germany.[99] The German court which ordered the confiscation had held that the company was unquestionably a legal front which had the dual purpose of safeguarding real property belonging to the dissolved Communist Party and of continuing communist subversive activities. Article 17 was invoked by the German Government but the application was rejected for non-exhaustion of domestic remedies.

---

[95] *Norwood v United Kingdom*, (App. 23131/03), Decision of 16 November 2004, ECHR 2004-XI. See also *Witzsch v Germany*, (App. 7485/03), Decision of 13 December 2005.

[96] *Norwood v United Kingdom*, (App. 23131/03), Decision of 16 November 2004, ECHR 2004-XI, 4.

[97] App. 250/57, *Parti Communiste v Federal Republic of Germany*, 20 July 1957, (1955–7) 1 *Yearbook* 222, 224.

[98] Ibid.

[99] App. 712/60, *Retimag S.A. v Federal Republic of Germany*, Decision of 16 December 1961, (1961) 4 *Yearbook* 384.

The *Kühnen* case[100] concerned a German journalist, who was accused of trying to reinstitute the National Socialist Party, which was allegedly a neo-Nazi party. He sought to rely on Article 10. The Commission said that Article 17 covers essentially those rights which will facilitate the attempt to derive from them a right to engage personally in activities aimed at the destruction of any of the rights and freedoms set forth in the Convention. In particular, the Commission has found that the freedom of expression enshrined in Article 10 of the Convention may not be invoked in a sense contrary to Article 17.[101]

THE STRASBOURG COURT'S CASE-LAW

From the earliest decisions in which Article 17 has been raised, the Court has adopted a much more restrictive view of its application. In the *Lawless* case,[102] the Irish Government maintained that the activities of the IRA, in which Lawless was engaged, fell within the terms of Article 17, and that he was therefore not entitled to rely on Articles 5, 6, 7, or any other Article of the Convention. The Commission expressed the view that Article 17 was not applicable. It stated that the general purpose of Article 17 was to prevent totalitarian groups from exploiting the principles enunciated by the Convention. But to achieve that purpose, it was not necessary to deprive the persons concerned of all the rights and freedoms guaranteed in the Convention. Article 17 covered essentially those rights which, if invoked, would enable them to engage in the activities referred to in Article 17. The Court, in somewhat different language, followed in substance the view of the Commission.[103] Thus Article 17 applies only to rights, such as those in Articles 9, 10, and 11, which entitle a person to engage in activities; it prevents him from relying on those articles to engage in subversive activities. A person engaging in subversive activities does not, therefore, forfeit the right to a fair trial under Article 6; but he cannot claim the freedom to organize political meetings, for instance, if his or her purpose in using that freedom is to undermine all civil liberties. It is always a question of the purpose for which the rights are used; the principle is that 'no person may be able to take advantage of the provisions of the Convention to perform acts aimed at destroying the aforesaid rights and freedoms.'[104] Hence, Article 17 cannot be used to deprive an individual of his political freedom simply on the ground that he has supported a totalitarian government in the past.[105]

Even persons engaging in terrorist activities for subversive ends cannot be completely deprived of their protection under the Convention. In the result, those who pursue anarchy, for example, by organizing political meetings on a peaceful basis may

---

[100] App. 12194/86, *Kühnen v Federal Republic of Germany*, Decision of 12 May 1988, (1988) 56 DR 205.

[101] See also Apps. 8348/78 and 8406/78, *Glimmerveen and Hagenbeek v Netherlands*, Decision of 11 October 1979, (1980) 18 DR 187.

[102] *Lawless v Ireland*, (App. 332/57), 14 November 1960, 7 April 1961, and 1 July 1961, Series A Nos 1–3, (1979–80) 1 EHRR 1, 13 and 15.

[103] Ibid.   [104] §6 of judgment of 1 July 1961.

[105] See *De Becker*, Report of 8 January 1960, Series B No 2, 137–8.

in a sense be at a disadvantage compared with those who resort to violence. The former may lose, through the application of Article 17, the political freedoms guaranteed by Articles 9, 10, and 11; the latter, since they do not seek to exercise political activities, lose nothing. If, however, the scale of violence is such as to create a national emergency, the rights guaranteed under Articles 5 and 6 may also be suspended in application of Article 15.

The Strasbourg Court gave considerable attention to Article 17 in its judgment in the *Lehideux and Isorni* case.[106] The applicants had been convicted for 'public defence of war crimes or the crimes of collaboration' in relation to the publication of a one-page advertisement in the French newspaper, *Le Monde*, which spoke favourably about Philippe Pétain.[107] A criminal complaint had been filed by the National Association of Former Members of the Resistance, which had initiated the prosecution. The applicants complained of a violation of Article 10 of the Convention on freedom of expression, and the French Government responded by asking the Court to dismiss the application under Article 17. The Commission had concluded that there was nothing in the advertisement in *Le Monde* which constituted racial hatred or other statements calculated to destroy or restrict the rights and freedoms guaranteed by the Convention. Furthermore, it did not consider that the expression of ideas constituted an 'activity' within the meaning of Article 17. The Court first gave consideration to the complaint under Article 10, and ultimately found that there was a breach of Article 10 because the applicants' criminal conviction was disproportionate and, so, unnecessary in a democratic society. Having reached this conclusion, the Court decided that it was not appropriate to apply Article 17.[108]

A number of concurring and dissenting opinions are attached to the judgment. Judge Jambrek in a concurring opinion says:

In order that Article 17 may be applied, the aim of the offending actions must be to spread violence or hatred, to resort to illegal or undemocratic methods, to encourage the use of violence, to undermine the nation's democratic and pluralist political system, or to pursue objectives that are racist or likely to destroy the rights and freedoms of others.... Therefore, the requirements of Article 17 are strictly scrutinized, and rightly so.[109]

This appears to reflect the underlying approach adopted by the Court. The matter could be resolved by applying Article 10 and the repression of this type of publication through the use of criminal sanctions went beyond the requirements

---

[106] *Lehideux and Isorni v France*, (App. 24662/94), 23 September 1998, (2000) 30 EHRR 665, ECHR 1998-VIII.

[107] A national hero in France for his role in the First World War, who in June 1940 as Vice-Premier surrendered the north and west of France to Germany, but left the rest of France with its capital at Vichy ostensibly under his own control, whereas in reality he was a close collaborator with Germany. Pétain was subsequently convicted of treason and sentenced to death, but this was commuted to solitary confinement for life. Pétain died in July 1951.

[108] §58.

[109] §2 of concurring opinion.

of a democratic society. The defenders of Marshall Pétain could not be said to be undermining democracy in the way envisaged by Article 17. It was therefore inappropriate to permit the French Government to plead that provision to excuse their actions.

This approach seems to be confirmed by the way in which the ÖZDEP case[110] was argued. The case involved a court order dissolving a political party in Turkey. The Turkish Constitutional Court had concluded that the Freedom and Democracy Party's (ÖZDEP) activities were subject to the restrictions in Articles 11(2) and 17 of the Convention. The application to the Strasbourg organs did not raise issues under Article 17, but considered the matter solely under Article 11.[111]

However, some expression is regarded as beyond the pale. An example is denial of the Holocaust; in one case the Strasbourg Court said, 'Its proponents indisputably have designs that fall into the category of aims prohibited by Article 17 of the Convention.'[112] In that case the applicant could not rely on Article 10 on freedom of expression, and his application in this respect was ruled inadmissible.[113] By contrast merely wearing a red star as a totalitarian symbol was unrelated to racist propaganda and would not attract the exception in Article 17.[114]

The Court does not always seem to be consistent in its use of Article 17. In recent times, it has been used to dismiss an application without elaboration of possible justifications for a repressive measure taken by a Contracting Party. A good example is the *Norwood* case.[115] This concerned a complaint by a Regional Organizer for the British National Party[116] following his conviction under the public order legislation for the display of a large anti-Islamic poster in the window of his home. He had argued that this was an exercise of his right of freedom of expression. The Court noted that both the Court, and, previously, the Commission, had found that the freedom of expression guaranteed under Article 10 of the Convention may not be invoked in a sense contrary to Article 10. It concluded:

Such a general, vehement attack against a religious group, linking the group as a whole with a grave act of terrorism, is incompatible with the values proclaimed and guaranteed by the Convention, notably, tolerance, social peace and non-discrimination. The applicant's display of the poster in his window constituted an act within the meaning of Article 17, which did not, therefore, enjoy the protection of Articles 10 or 14.[117]

---

[110] *ÖZDEP v Turkey*, (App. 23885/94), 8 December 1999, (2001) 31 EHRR 675, ECHR 1999-VIII.

[111] Thus rendering it, in the view of the Court, unnecessary to consider the applicant's complaints under Article 9, 10, and 14.

[112] *Garaudy v France*, (App.65831/01), Decision of 24 June 2003, ECHR 2003-IX.

[113] See also to the same effect *Ivanov v Russia*, (App. 35222/04), Decision of 20 February 2007, ECHR 2007-II.

[114] *Vajnai v Hungary*, (App. 33629/06), Decision of 8 July 2008.

[115] *Norwood v United Kingdom*, (App. 23131/03), Decision of 16 November 2004, ECHR 2004-XI.

[116] An extreme right wing political party opposed to immigration into the United Kingdom.

[117] *Norwood v United Kingdom*, (App. 23131/03), Decision of 16 November 2004, ECHR 2004-XI, 4.

LIMITATION ON USE OF
RESTRICTIONS ON RIGHTS

Article 18 provides:

The restrictions permitted under this Convention to the said rights and freedoms shall not be applied for any purpose other than those for which they have been prescribed.

This provision shows that there can be no inherent or implied limitations on the rights guaranteed. Each limitation must be express and have an explicit purpose. Article 18 does not have an independent character and will only be relevant in conjunction with an article which contains limitations, though there does not need to be a violation of that other provision before Article 18 bites. It is not clear why Article 18 was included in the Convention. There is no equivalent provision in the Universal Declaration of Human Rights nor in the United Nations Covenant on Civil and Political Rights, though Article 30 of the American Convention provides:

The restrictions that, pursuant to this Convention, may be placed on the enjoyment or exercise of the rights or freedoms recognized herein may not be applied except in accordance with the laws enacted for reasons of general interest and in accordance with the purpose for which such restrictions have been established.

There is not much guidance in the preparatory work. Article 18 may seem to add little to the Convention except to make explicit what is either implicit in other provisions or else may be thought to be well established under the general principles recognized by international law. But it is useful as putting beyond doubt the scope of the restrictions permitted, and as making clear the requirement of good faith in the application of these restrictions.

Article 18 limits the area of discretion of the national authorities. In effect, it excludes *détournement de pouvoir*[118] or abuse of power, notions familiar in many systems of national law. The principle is that where the real purpose of the authorities in imposing a restriction is outside the purposes specified, one of the specified purposes cannot be used as a pretext for imposing that restriction. The restriction may be one which is legitimate in itself, and lawfully imposed in accordance with the proper procedure. But it will still be prohibited if imposed for an improper purpose. For example, where the right of a convicted prisoner to respect for family life is subject to a restriction on the grounds set out in Article 8(2), such a restriction may be imposed only for the purposes there specified, and not, for example, as a punishment.

One difficulty in using Article 18 is its dependence on showing a particular motivation. In the *Handyside* case[119] the applicant sought to argue that the purpose of

---

[118] See App. 753/60, *X v Austria*, Decision of 5 August 1960, (1960) 3 *Yearbook* 310; *Lawless v Ireland*, 14 November 1960, 7 April 1961, and 1 July 1961, Series A Nos 1–3, (1979–80) 1 EHRR 1, 13 and 15.

[119] *Handyside v United Kingdom*, (App. 5493/72), 7 December 1976, Series A No 24, (1979–80) 1 EHRR 737.

the seizure of *The Little Red Schoolbook* was not for the protection of morals, but 'to muzzle a small-scale publisher whose political leanings met with the disapproval of a fragment of the public opinion.'[120] The Commission concluded that there was no evidence to sustain this allegation, and the Court considered the matter solely on the limitations in Article 10(2) and did not consider the issue under Article 18. The Court has incorporated its consideration of motivation into its consideration of whether the limitations are necessary in a democratic society.

The provision is cited with some regularity by applicants, but the Court hardly ever finds the need to consider its terms. Other provisions of the Convention are usually sufficient for the application to be determined without recourse to this provision.[121] But the Strasbourg Court did find a violation of Article 18 in the *Gusinskiy* case.[122] The rather complicated saga involved the arrest and detention of the applicant, and an apparent agreement that the charges would be dropped if he sold his shares in a media company to Gazprom, a State-controlled company. The applicant complained that his detention was intended to force him to sell his share-holding on unfavourable terms and conditions and that this violated Article 18. The Strasbourg Court had already found that the applicant's detention had been in breach of Article 5. However, the Court concluded that 'it is not the purpose of such public-law matters as criminal proceedings and detention on remand to be used as part of commercial bargaining strategies'[123] and this further tainted the respondent State's actions; there was a violation of Article 18. It is interesting to note that the Court does not put forward any particular justification for using Article 18 in conjunction with Article 5; almost all the other cases involving Article 18 have been in the context of Articles 8 to 11 which contain specific internal limitations.[124]

---

[120] *Handyside*, §52.

[121] See, for example, *Quinn v France*, (App. 18580/91), 22 March 1995, (1996) 21 EHRR 529; *Lukanov v Bulgaria*, (App. 21915/93), 20 March 1997, (1997) 24 EHRR 121, ECHR 1997-II; *Kurt v Turkey* (App. 24276/94), 25 May 1998, (1999) 27 EHRR 373, ECHR 1998-III; and *Beyeler v Italy*, (App. 33202/96), 5 January 2000 [GC], (2001) 33 EHRR 1224, ECHR 2000-I.

[122] *Gusinskiy v Russia*, (App. 70276/01), 19 May 2004, (2005) 41 EHRR 281, ECHR 2004-IV.

[123] §76.   [124] See ch.14 below.

PART 2

CONVENTION RIGHTS

7

THE RIGHT TO AN
EFFECTIVE REMEDY

INTRODUCTION

The essence of Article 13 has been described by the Grand Chamber in the following terms:

The object of Article 13, as emerges from the *travaux préparatoires*, is to provide a means whereby individuals can obtain relief at national level for violations of their Convention rights before having to set in motion the international machinery of complaint before the Court.[1]

Article 13 provides:

Everyone whose rights and freedoms as set forth in this Convention are violated shall have an effective remedy before a national authority notwithstanding that the violation has been committed by persons acting in an official capacity.

There are significant differences between Article 13 and the corresponding provisions of other human rights instruments. For example, Article 8 of the Universal Declaration on Human Rights is wider in encompassing rights granted to an individual by the constitution or by law, but potentially narrower in only requiring effective remedies from competent national tribunals.[2]

Until comparatively recently, Article 13 occupied something of a twilight zone in the case-law of the Convention organs.[3] This is somewhat surprising for three reasons: first, the Convention is built upon an obligation that Contracting Parties guarantee to those within their jurisdiction the rights enumerated in the Convention and its Protocols; secondly, the engagement of the Strasbourg organs is subsidiary to the protection of these rights in the national legal orders; and, thirdly, the protection of rights in the national legal order must be dependent upon the remedies available there. These three reasons justify examining Article 13 in advance of other Convention rights, since Article 13 when read with Article 1 imposes an obligation on Contracting Parties to

---

[1] *Kudła v Poland*, (App. 30210/96), 26 October 2000 [GC], (2002) 35 EHRR 198, ECHR 2002-XI, §152.

[2] Art. 8 of the Universal Declaration reads: Everyone has the right to an effective remedy by the competent national tribunals for acts violating the fundamental rights granted him by the constitution or by law.

[3] See R. White, 'Remedies in a Multi-Level Legal Order: The Strasbourg Court and the UK' in C. Kilpatrick, T. Novitz, and P. Skidmore, (eds.), *The Future of Remedies in Europe* (Hart, Oxford 2000), 191.

provide remedies in the national legal order. If Contracting Parties accomplished this, then the Strasbourg Court's caseload would be reduced, and its work would become much more focused on big constitutional questions concerning the content of the rights protected by the Convention rather than in consideration of many routine violations of Convention rights which should have been put right within the national legal order.

One of the reasons for the slow development of this Convention right has been the ambiguities in the drafting of the provision. One ambiguity was whether Article 13 only applied *after* the Convention organs had determined that there had been a breach of the Convention rights.[4] The proper view is, however, that Article 13 is about guaranteeing a process within the national legal order by which a remedy for a violation can be provided at that level. This led to a further difficulty about the use of Article 13 by the Strasbourg organs. Since Article 13 only required a remedy in the national legal order where a person's rights and freedoms as set forth in the Convention are violated, was it necessary to prove a violation of one of the Convention rights before Article 13 could be pleaded? The question was answered in the *Klass* case in 1978, which ruled that Article 13 is an independent provision which can be violated even if there is no violation of another Convention right, although there must be an arguable violation of a Convention right.[5]

In its more recent judgments, the Strasbourg Court is increasingly taking issues of violations of Article 13 in conjunction with specific provisions of the Convention. In this regard, there are some similarities between the Court's approach to alleged violations of Articles 13 and 14, though, under Article 13, the test is whether the applicant has an 'arguable complaint' under one of the substantive articles.[6]

In the *Čonka* case[7] the Court found a violation of Article 13 when read in conjunction with Article 4 of Protocol 4, but not when taken in conjunction with Article 3 of the Convention; and, in the *Peck* case,[8] the Court found a violation of Article 13 when read in conjunction with Article 8. There are now many judgments reading Article 13 with Article 2 or 3 in finding that the respondent State has failed to conduct an investigation into allegations of a suspicious death or of ill-treatment.[9] The Court has summarized the position as follows:

---

[4] See J. Fawcett, *The Application of the European Convention on Human Rights* (OUP, Oxford 1987), 290–1.

[5] *Klass and others v Germany*, (App. 5029/71), 6 September 1978, Series A No 28, (1979–80) 2 EHRR 214, §63.

[6] Though this is probably not qualitatively that different from the question asked by the Court when dealing with alleged violations of Art. 14, namely, whether the complaint is within the material scope of one of the substantive articles. See ch.24 below.

[7] *Čonka v Belgium*, (App. 51564/99), 5 February 2002, (2002) 34 EHRR 1298, ECHR 2002-I.

[8] *Peck v United Kingdom*, (App. 44647/98), 28 January 2003, (2003) 36 EHRR 719, ECHR 2003-I.

[9] As, for example, *Abdurzakova and Abdurzakov v Russia*, (App. 35080/04), 15 January 2009 (Art. 13 in conjunction with Art. 2—disappearances in Chechnya); and *Muminov v Russia*, (App. 42502/06), 11 December 2008 (Art. 13 in conjunction with Art. 3—assessment of risk of ill-treatment of detainees if expelled to Uzbekistan). See further below in this chapter. See also P. van Dijk and others (eds), *Theory and Practice of the European Convention on Human Rights*, (4th edn Intersentia, Antwerp 2006), 1011–6.

The Court reiterates that Article 13 of the Convention guarantees the availability at the national level of a remedy to enforce the substance of the Convention rights and freedoms in whatever form they might happen to be secured in the domestic legal order. Given the fundamental importance of the right to protection of life, Article 13 requires, in addition to the payment of compensation where appropriate, a thorough and effective investigation capable of leading to the identification and punishment of those responsible for the deprivation of life and infliction of treatment contrary to Article 3, including effective access for the complainant to the investigation procedure leading to the identification and punishment of those responsible.... . The Court further reiterates that the requirements of Article 13 are broader than a Contracting State's obligation under Article 2 to conduct an effective investigation....[10]

Although the absence of a remedy before the national authorities will normally be a matter subsidiary to the principal complaint, it is appropriate that it should be examined separately where it is alleged that, as a general feature of the national law, there is no effective remedy. For example, it may be suggested that if an applicant complains of an invasion of privacy, and if national law affords no general remedy in such cases, the complaint should be examined under Article 13 as well as under Article 8.[11] On the other hand, where the essence of the principal complaint is the absence of an appropriate remedy required by another provision of the Convention, it is unnecessary to consider Article 13. Thus, in the *Vagrancy* cases,[12] where the Strasbourg Court found that the applicants did not have the necessary judicial guarantees under Article 5(4) to challenge the lawfulness of their detention, the Court did not consider that it had to examine separately the issue under Article 13.[13]

Article 13 does not offer any guarantee of a remedy allowing a State's primary legislation to be challenged before a national authority on the grounds that it is contrary to the Convention.[14]

It appeared from the early case-law that the requirements made of the national legal orders were at a relatively low level. It could almost be reduced to the question of whether there was some mechanism, or mechanisms taken together, which might lead to a remedy for the complaint. There are, however, signs in the more recent case-law that new life is being breathed into Article 13.[15]

There are two questions which must always be asked: whether there is an arguable complaint; and whether the remedy in the national legal order is effective.

---

[10] *Lyanova and Aliyeva v Russia*, (Apps. 12713/02 and 28440/03), 2 October 2008, §134.

[11] As in *Peck v United Kingdom*, (App. 44647/98), 28 January 2003, (2003) 36 EHRR 719, ECHR 2003-I.

[12] *De Wilde, Ooms and Versyp v Belgium*, (Apps. 2832/66, 2835/66, and 2899/66), 18 June 1971, Series A No 12, (1979–80) 1 EHRR 373.

[13] §95. And see below in this chapter on the relationship between Art. 13 and Art. 6 ECHR.

[14] *James and others v United Kingdom*, (App. 8793/79), 21 February 1986, Series A No 98, (1986) 8 EHRR 123, §85, confirmed in *Kudła v Poland*, (App. 30210/96), 26 October 2000 [GC], (2002) 35 EHRR 198, ECHR 2002-XI, §151.

[15] See discussion in ch.12 below on the Court's comments on the need for an effective remedy where there are violations of Art. 6 by reason of the excessive length of proceedings.

WHAT IS AN ARGUABLE COMPLAINT?

The Strasbourg Court requires the applicant to show only an arguable case in order to be able to complain of a violation of Article 13. The *Klass* case[16] concerned the availability of secret surveillance in Germany. The applicants complained that the legislation authorizing such surveillance violated Articles 6, 8, and 13. The Court differed from the Commission, which had concluded that it must be shown that a substantive provision had been violated before the Article came into play. The test, said the Court, is rather one of whether the applicant has an arguable case.

The precise delimitation of the arguability test remains difficult.[17] The Court itself has indicated that providing an abstract definition would not help and decides the issue on a case-by-case basis.[18] In the *Boyle and Rice* case[19] the Court addressed the tricky question of how a case could be viewed as arguable when the Commission had concluded that it was manifestly ill-founded; all but one of the applicants' complaints under Article 8 had been dismissed as manifestly ill-founded. The answer lies in there being two rather different tests. In deciding that a case is manifestly ill-founded, the Commission is making a judgment on the merits, in that, in effect, the finding means that examination of the merits is not required because the applicant has put forward insufficient evidence to justify doing so. In determining whether a case is arguable, the test is rather one of seeing whether there are the makings of a prima facie case. The Commission suggested before the Court in the *Boyle and Rice* case that to be arguable a case needed only to raise a Convention issue which merits further examination. That is a low threshold.[20] It follows from this that, in all those cases where the Court[21] finds that a complaint is admissible, the arguability threshold is met. The position adopted in the *Boyle and Rice* case was elaborated by the Court in the *Powell and Rayner* case,[22] which concerned complaints under Articles 6, 8, 13, and Article 1 of Protocol 1 in relation to excessive noise from air traffic in the vicinity of Heathrow Airport. The Court suggested that the coherence of the Convention system could be undermined if the test of arguability was set at so low a level that cases where the merits were so weak that the case could be regarded as manifestly ill-founded could nevertheless be considered under Article 13. The

---

[16] *Klass v Germany*, (App. 5029/71), 6 September 1978, Series A No 28, (1979–80) 2 EHRR 214.

[17] F. Hampson, 'The Concept of an "Arguable Claim" under Article 13 of the European Convention on Human Rights' (1990) 39 ICLQ 891.

[18] *Boyle and Rice v United Kingdom*, (App. 9659/82, and 9658/82), 27 April 1988, Series A No 131, (1988) 10 EHRR 425, §55.

[19] Ibid.

[20] See, for example, *Powell and Rayner v United Kingdom*, (App. 9310/81), 21 February 1990, Series A No 172, (1990) 12 EHRR 355.

[21] Note that, prior to 1 November 1998, admissibility decisions were made by the Commission.

[22] *Powell and Rayner v United Kingdom*, (App. 9310/81), 21 February 1990, Series A No 172, (1990) 12 EHRR 355, §33.

threshold should be the same. Now that both admissibility and merits questions are determined by the Strasbourg Court, any risk of inconsistencies of approach would seem to have been removed.

THE NATURE OF THE REMEDIES REQUIRED

BACKGROUND

The current position is neatly recapitulated in the *Iovchev* case:[23]

The Court reiterates that Article 13 of the Convention guarantees the availability at national level of a remedy to enforce the substance of the Convention rights and freedoms in whatever form they may happen to be secured in the domestic legal order. The effect of Article 13 is thus to require the provision of a domestic remedy to deal with the substance of an 'arguable complaint' under the Convention and to grant appropriate relief, although Contracting Parties are afforded some discretion as to the manner in which they conform to their Convention obligations under this provision. The scope of the obligation under Article 13 varies depending on the nature of the applicant's complaint under the Convention. Nevertheless, the remedy required by Article 13 must be 'effective' in practice as well as in law....

Article 13 offers a measure of respect for national procedural autonomy; this refers to the ability of each Contracting Party to determine the form of remedies offered to meet its obligations under the article. Those remedies need not be judicial, but must be effective. Ombudsman procedures and other non-judicial procedures will be included. Once a remedy is identified, it is not necessary to show the certainty of a favourable outcome.[24] National procedural autonomy does not, however, extend to the very existence of a remedy, since Article 13 requires that there is an effective remedy to enforce the substance of the Convention rights in the national legal order.[25] In the *Silver* case[26] the Court said that the remedy before the national authority should concern both the determination of the claim and any redress. The respondent State will be expected to identify the remedies available to the applicant and to show at least a prima facie case for their effectiveness. So, where respondent States cannot put forward an example of a

---

[23] *Iovchev v Bulgaria*, (App. 41211/98), 2 February 2006, §§142–3.

[24] *Pine Valley Developments v Ireland*, (App. 12742/87), 29 November 1991, Series A No 222, (1992) 14 EHRR 319, §66; *Costello-Roberts v United Kingdom*, (App. 13134/87), 25 March 1993, Series A No 247-C, (1995) 19 EHRR 112, §40; and *Lorsé v The Netherlands* (App. 52750/99), 4 February 2003, (2003) 37 EHRR 105, §96.

[25] See the discussion of what constitutes a domestic remedy for the purpose of the requirement to exhaust domestic remedies in ch.2 above.

[26] *Silver v United Kingdom*, (Apps. 5947/72, 6205/73, 7052/75, 7061/75, 7107/75, 7113/75, and 7136/75), 25 March 1983, Series A No 61, (1983) 5 EHRR 347, §113.

relevant remedy, they are unlikely to satisfy the Court that there is an effective remedy available.[27]

The process need not be judicial, but, if it is not, consideration should be given to its powers and the guarantees it affords. For example in the *Khan* case,[28] the Strasbourg Court held that the possibility of complaining to the Police Complaints Authority about alleged breaches of the Convention by the police was not an 'effective remedy', because the Authority was not sufficiently independent from either the police or the Home Secretary. Where the process is judicial, there will be a breach of Article 13 if an order of a court is not implemented by the authorities.[29]

ACCESS TO AN EFFECTIVE REMEDY

The tendency of respondent States has been simply to point to some procedure available within the national legal order for raising aspects of the matters covered by the applicant's complaint to the Strasbourg organs. The Court is, however, increasingly considering whether those remedies provide an effective means of raising the substance of the complaints of violations of the particular Convention rights in issue,[30] both as a matter of practice as well as of law.[31] Where irreversible harm might ensue, it will not be sufficient that the remedies are merely as effective as can be; they must provide much more certain guarantees of effectiveness.[32] The Court's position was summarized in its judgment in the *Čonka* case:

The scope of the Contracting Parties' obligations under Article 13 varies depending on the nature of the applicant's complaint; however, the remedy required by Article 13 must be 'effective' in practice as well as in law. The 'effectiveness' of a 'remedy' within the meaning of Article 13 does not depend on the certainty of a favourable outcome for the applicant. Nor does the 'authority' referred to in that provision necessarily have to be a judicial authority; but if it is not, its powers and the guarantees which it affords are relevant in determining whether the remedy before it is effective. Also, even if a single remedy does not by itself entirely satisfy the requirements of Article 13, the aggregate of remedies provided for under domestic law may do so.[33]

This approach is well illustrated in the facts of the *Keenan* case.[34] Keenan had been found hanged in his cell one day after the imposition of punishment of further imprisonment and segregation had been imposed on him. He had a history of mental illness.

---

[27] See, for example, *Vereinigung Demokratischer Soldaten Österreichs and Gubi v Austria*, (App. 15153/89), 19 December 1994, Series A No 302, (1995) 20 EHRR 56, §93.

[28] *Khan v United Kingdom*, (App. 35394/97), 12 May 2000, (2001) 31 EHRR 1016, ECHR 2000-V, §§43–7.

[29] *Iatridis v Greece*, (App. 31107/96), 25 March 1999 [GC], (2000) 30 EHRR 97, ECHR 1999-II.

[30] See *Chahal v United Kingdom*, (App. 22414/93), 15 November 1996, (1997) 23 EHRR 413, ECHR 1996-V.

[31] *Metropolitan Church of Bessarabia and others v Moldova*, (App. 45701/99), 14 December 2001, (2002) 35 EHRR 306, ECHR 2002-XII, §137; see also *Debelić v Croatia*, (App. 2448/03), 26 May 2005.

[32] *Chahal v United Kingdom*, (App. 22414/93), 15 November 1996, (1997) 23 EHRR 413, ECHR 1996-V, §§150–2.

[33] *Čonka v Belgium*, (App. 51564/99), 5 February 2002, (2002) 34 EHRR 1298, ECHR 2002-I, §75.

[34] *Keenan v United Kingdom*, (App. 27229/95), 3 April 2001, (2001) 33 EHRR 913, ECHR 2001-III.

His mother complained of violations of Articles 2, 3, and 13. No violation of Article 2 was found by the Court, but a violation of Article 3, in the form of inhuman and degrading treatment, was found because of a lack of effective monitoring and supervision of his mental state and the imposition of a punishment which threatened his physical and moral resistance having regard to the state of his mental health. In relation to remedies, the Court's enquiry focused on the availability of remedies to Keenan to complain of his ill-treatment in prison before his suicide, and of remedies to his next of kin in respect of his death. The respondent State argued that, during his detention, Mark Keenan had a number of possible remedies open to him: he could have sought judicial review; he could have made a complaint under the prison complaints procedure; he could have begun actions in tort; and he could have brought an action for misfeasance in the exercise of a public office. Furthermore, his mother could, after his death, have brought proceedings in tort in respect of any injury or exacerbation of his mental illness suffered prior to her son's death. The respondent State did, however, concede that an inquest was not an effective remedy since it did not furnish the applicant with the possibility of establishing the responsibility of the prison authorities or of obtaining damages.

The Court noted that there was no effective remedy available to Mark Keenan to challenge speedily the imposition of the punishment during which he killed himself. Such remedies as had been identified were not effective: it would not have been possible for Mark Keenan to have obtained legal aid and legal representation, and lodged an application for judicial review in a short period of time; similarly prison complaints typically took six weeks to adjudicate. In relation to the remedies available to the next of kin after the death, the Court notes the theoretical availability of the remedy, but did not accept that adequate damages would have been recoverable or that legal aid would have been available to pursue the claim. The Court indicates that in relation to a violation of Article 2 or Article 3, 'compensation for the non-pecuniary damage flowing from the breach should in principle be available as part of the range of possible remedies.'[35] Finally, the Court concluded that no effective remedy was available to the applicant which would have established where responsibility lay for the death of her son. This too was regarded as an essential element of a remedy under Article 13 for a bereaved parent. There was a violation of Article 13.

This case represents a degree of encroachment on national procedural autonomy in the interpretation of Article 13. The Strasbourg Court is increasingly indicating what constitutes effectiveness in the remedies available within the national legal order. The remedy must be one which enables the applicants to raise their Convention rights in a timely manner, and to have them considered in the national proceedings.[36] The Court has also indicated that, to be an effective remedy, a process may need to prevent the

---

[35] §129.

[36] *Hatton v United Kingdom*, (App. 36022/97), 8 July 2003 [GC], (2003) 37 EHRR 611, ECHR 2003-VIII, §140. On the limitations of the remedy of judicial review in England and Wales prior to the entry into force of the Human Rights Act 1998, see *Smith and Grady v United Kingdom*, (Apps. 33985/96 and 33986/96), 27 September 1999, (2000) 29 EHRR 493, ECHR 1999-VI; and *Peck v United Kingdom*, (App. 44647/98), 28 January 2003, (2003) 36 EHRR 719, ECHR 2003-I.

execution of measures contrary to the Convention. This means that it is not compatible with Article 13 for such measures to be put into effect before the national authorities have examined their compatibility with the Convention.[37]

The *Iovchev* case[38] provides a good example of where the Strasbourg Court will accept that there is a remedy which is effective in law but not in practice. The relevant Bulgarian legislation in principle did not exclude the possibility of compensation being paid where a person had suffered inhuman or degrading treatment while in detention, but the process by which this had to be established was so onerous in the particular circumstances of the case, coupled with the delays which had occurred, that the applicant could not be regarded as having at his disposal an effective remedy for his complaint about the conditions of his detention. There had been a violation of Article 13.[39]

In the *Klass* case[40] the Strasbourg Court indicated that the requirement of effectiveness had to be read in the context of the complaint. An effective remedy in respect of secret surveillance meant a remedy 'that was as effective as could be having regard to the restricted scope for recourse inherent in any system of secret surveillance'. The Court expanded on this in the *Leander* case[41] which concerned secret security checks, making clear that although no single remedy might itself entirely satisfy the requirements of Article 13, the aggregate of remedies under the system might do so.[42]

The *Al-Nashif* case[43] revisited the extent to which considerations of national security imposed limitations on the remedies required by Article 13 in the context of deportation proceedings. While accepting that there will be some limitations, especially where secret surveillance or secret checks are involved, there is nevertheless a minimum standard required by Article 13:

Even where an allegation of a threat to national security is made, the guarantee of an effective remedy requires as a minimum that the competent independent appeals authority must be informed of the reasons grounding the deportation decision, even if such reasons are not publicly available. The authority must be competent to reject the executive's assertion that there is a threat to national security where it finds it arbitrary or unreasonable. There must be some form of adversarial proceedings, if need be through a special representative after a security clearance. Furthermore, the question whether the impugned measure would interfere with the individual's right to respect for family life and, if so, whether a fair balance is struck between the public interest involved and the individual's rights must be examined.[44]

AN EFFECTIVE REMEDY FOR ALLEGED BREACHES OF ARTICLE 6

For many years, the Strasbourg Court concluded that the provisions of Articles 6 and 13 overlapped, so that if the matter was within Article 6, there was no need to consider any

---

[37] *Čonka v Belgium*, (App. 51564/99), 5 February 2002, (2002) 34 EHRR 1298, ECHR 2002-I, §79. The case concerned the expulsion of aliens.

[38] *Iovchev v Bulgaria*, (App. 41211/98), 2 February 2006.

[39] §§144–8.

[40] *Klass v Germany*, (App. 5029/71), 6 September 1978, Series A No 28, (1979–80) 2 EHRR 214.

[41] *Leander v Sweden*, (Apps. 9248/81), 26 March 1987, Series A No 116, (1987) 9 EHRR 433.

[42] *Chahal v United Kingdom*, (App. 22414/93), 15 November 1996, (1997) 23 EHRR 413, §145.

[43] *Al-Nashif v Bulgaria*, (App. 50963/99), 20 June 2002, (2003) 36 EHRR 655.   [44] §137.

alleged violations of Article 13. In the *Kamasinski* case,[45] the Court said, 'The requirements of Article 13 are less strict than, and are absorbed by, those of Article 6.'[46]

In the *Kudła* case,[47] the Grand Chamber decided that the case-law in this area should be reviewed in the light of the number of applications the Court received complaining of the failure to ensure a hearing within a reasonable time. The Court reiterated that excessive delays in the administration of justice presented a threat to the rule of law within the national legal order. In a significant development of the case-law on Article 13, the Grand Chamber concluded:

If Article 13 is, as the respondent State argued, to be interpreted as having no application to the right to a hearing within a reasonable time as safeguarded by Article 6(1), individuals will systematically be forced to refer to the Court in Strasbourg complaints that would otherwise, and in the Court's opinion more appropriately, have to be addressed in the first place within the national legal system. In the long term the effective functioning, on both the national and international level, of the scheme of human rights protection set up by the Convention is liable to be weakened.

In view of the foregoing considerations, the Court considers that the correct interpretation is that that provision guarantees an effective remedy before a national authority for an alleged breach of the requirements under Article 6(1) to hear a case within a reasonable time.[48]

It follows that the national legal orders must ensure that there is a remedy which either ensures that excessive delays are avoided, or provides redress where such delays arise.[49] In the context of the nature of the mischief being remedied, the remedy will almost certainly need to be judicial in nature.[50]

In areas other than the excessive length of proceedings, violations of Article 13 will continue to be largely absorbed by Article 6(1).[51]

THE RIGHT TO AN EFFECTIVE INVESTIGATION

In a number of cases,[52] the Court has stated that the exercise of remedies available within the national legal order must not be unjustifiably hindered by the acts or omissions of the authorities of the respondent State. In the *Keenan* case, the Court said:

Given the fundamental importance of the right to the protection of life, Article 13 requires, in addition to the payment of compensation where appropriate, a thorough and effective investigation capable of leading to the identification and punishment of those responsible

---

[45] *Kamasinski v Austria*, (App. 9783/82), 19 December 1989, Series A No 168, (1991) 33 EHRR 36.

[46] §110. See also *Kadubec v Slovakia*, (App. 27061/95), 2 September 1998, §64; and *Brualla Gomez de la Torre v Spain*, (App. 26737/95), 19 December 1997, (2001) 33 EHRR 1341, §41.

[47] *Kudła v Poland*, (App. 30210/96), 26 October 2000 [GC], (2002) 35 EHRR 198, ECHR 2000-XI.

[48] §§155–6.

[49] §159 refers to the relief being 'either preventive or compensatory'. See also *Krasuski v Poland*, (App. 61444/00), 14 June 2005, §66.

[50] Examples of violations of Art. 13 in conjunction with Art. 6(1) are: *Čiž v Slovakia*, (App. 66142/01), 14 October 2003; and *Kuzin v Russia*, (App. 22118/02), 9 June 2005.

[51] See, for example, *Mihajlović v Croatia*, (App. 21752/02), 7 July 2005, §49.

[52] See, for example, *Aksoy v Turkey*, (App. 21987/93), 18 December 1996; (1997) 23 EHRR 553, ECHR 1996-VI, §95; *Aydin v Turkey*, (App. 23178/94), 25 September 1997; (1998) 25 EHRR 251, ECHR 1997-VI, §103; and *Kaya v Turkey*, (App. 22729/93), 19 February 1998; (1999) 28 EHRR 1, ECHR 1998-I, §106.

for the deprivation of life, including effective access for the complainant to the investigation procedure.[53]

In the *Kaya* case,[54] the applicant's brother had been killed in disputed circumstances by the security forces. A violation of Article 2 was found by reason of the absence of an effective and independent investigation into the death, but the complaint that there was also a violation of Article 13 was then considered. The Court said:

In particular, where those relatives have an arguable claim that the victim has been unlaw-fully killed by agents of the State, the notion of an effective remedy for the purposes of Article 13 entails, in addition to the payment of compensation where appropriate, a thor-ough and effective investigation capable of leading to the identification and punishment of those responsible and including effective access for the relatives to the investigatory proced-ure. Seen in these terms the requirements of Article 13 are broader than a Contracting State's procedural obligation under Article 2 to conduct an effective investigation.[55]

A similar approach has been adopted in relation to certain claims falling within Article 3. The *Assenov* case[56] concerned, among other complaints, a complaint of vio-lations of Article 3 during police detention. No violation of Article 3 was found in respect of the alleged ill-treatment, but a violation was found by reason of the absence of an effective official investigation into the applicants' complaints.[57] A separate vio-lation of Article 13 was found in virtually identical terms to those quoted from the judgment in the *Kaya* case.[58]

The entitlement to an effective and independent investigation under Article 13 has also been applied to cases where the allegation is of an unlawful deprivation of liberty. In the *Kurt* case[59] the Court found a violation of Article 5 in circumstances where there was evidence of the applicant's son having being detained but where he had sub-sequently disappeared, but nevertheless went on to consider separately whether there had been a violation of Article 13. The absence of an effective and independent inves-tigation capable of leading to the identification and punishment of those responsible which included effective access for the relative to the investigatory process constituted a violation of Article 13. Again the Court stressed that the content of Article 13 is wider than the requirement for an investigation under Article 5.[60]

These judgments are to be welcomed, since they reflect the realities of the difficulties that are faced by individuals in building a case against powerful State agencies. Those agencies are best placed to collect the information required to determine whether there has been a violation of the rights guaranteed by the Convention. This development in

---

[53] *Keenan v United Kingdom*, (App. 27229/95), 3 April 2001, (2001) 33 EHRR 913, ECHR 2001-III, §122.

[54] *Kaya v Turkey*, (App. 22729/93), 19 February 1998; (1999) 28 EHRR 1, ECHR 1998-I. See also *Akdeniz v Turkey*, (App. 25165/94), 31 May 2005; and *Öneryildiz v Turkey*, (App. 48939/99), 30 November 2004 [GC], (2005) 41 EHRR 325, ECHR 2004-XII.

[55] §107. See also comment in ch.9 below.

[56] *Assenov and others v Bulgaria*, (App. 24760/94), 28 October 1998, (1999) 28 EHRR 652; ECHR 1998-VIII.

[57] See also comment in ch.9 below.

[58] *Assenov and others v Bulgaria*, (App. 24760/94), 28 October 1998, (1999) 28 EHRR 652, ECHR 1998-VIII, §117.

[59] *Kurt v Turkey*, (App. 24276/94), 25 May 1998, (1999) 27 EHRR 373, ECHR 1998-III.   [60] §140.

the ambit of Article 13 is an outstanding example of the Court seeking to ensure that Convention rights are practical and effective and not theoretical and illusory. Indeed, in one case,[61] the Court indicated that in some cases only court proceedings might be sufficient to offer sufficiency of redress, noting the strong guarantees of independence offered by such proceedings.

IS COMPENSATION AN INGREDIENT OF AN EFFECTIVE REMEDY?

It is clear that the obligation under Article 13 requires States to provide 'appropriate relief', and that there is some discretion afforded to the Contracting Parties in this regard. The Court has said that the 'nature of the right at stake has implications for the type of remedy' which the State is required to provide.[62] In some cases this must include the possibility of 'compensation for the non-pecuniary damage flowing from the breach' of the Convention. This is particularly so where breaches of Articles 2 and 3 are involved,[63] but would also appear to be a requirement of the remedies available where there has been excessive delay in the administration of justice.[64] The test is whether the remedy is effective in practice, as well as in law. In the *McGlinchey* case,[65] which concerned a death in prison, the respondent State had argued that internal prison remedies met its obligations under Article 13. The Court, however, noted that these would not provide any right to compensation, and that other possible remedies would be ineffective. This was a case in which there had been a breach of Article 3. In such cases compensation for the non-pecuniary damages flowing from the breach should be available as part of the range of possible remedies.[66] A violation of Article 13 in conjunction with Article 3 was found.

VIOLATIONS BY PERSONS IN AN OFFICIAL CAPACITY

The last words of Article 13, 'notwithstanding that the violation has been committed by persons acting in an official capacity', show that no defence of State privilege or immunity from suit may be allowed. It has been argued that they also show that the scope of the Convention is not limited to persons exercising public authority.[67]

What is, however, clear is that Article 13 is not concerned with challenges to legislation. Where the source of the grievance is the legislation itself, requiring an effective remedy would be tantamount to allowing judicial review of legislation. The Commission

---

[61] *Z and others v United Kingdom*, (App. 29392/95), 10 May 2001 [GC], (2002) 34 EHRR 97, ECHR 2001-V, §110.

[62] *Öneryildiz v Turkey*, (App. 48939/99), 30 November 2004 [GC], (2005) 41 EHRR 325, ECHR 2004-XII, §147.

[63] *Z and others v United Kingdom*, (App. 29392/95), 10 May 2001, (2002) 34 EHRR 97, ECHR 2001-V, §109. See also *McGlinchey v United Kingdom*, (App. 50390/99), 29 April 2003, (2003) 37 EHRR 821, ECHR 2003-V, §§62–3.

[64] *Kudła v Poland*, (App. 30210/96), 26 October 2000 [GC], (2002) 35 EHRR 198, ECHR 2000-XI; and *Krasuski v Poland*, (App. 61444/00), 14 June 2005.

[65] *McGlinchey v United Kingdom*, (App. 50390/99), 29 April 2003, (2003) 37 EHRR 821, ECHR 2003-V.

[66] §66.   [67] See ch.5 above.

had consistently held that Article 13 has no application in such situations, and the Court has not dissented from that view.[68] To read such a requirement into Article 13 would effectively require the incorporation of the Convention, but where the Convention has been incorporated, there will usually be some process by which the compatibility of legislation can be tested against the requirements of the Convention.[69]

CONCLUDING REMARKS

It has taken longer for real substance to be given to Article 13 through the case-law of the Strasbourg organs than to virtually any other provision of the Convention and its Protocols. In particular, the much more practical approach of the Strasbourg Court in recent years to the determination of whether the remedies allegedly available in the national legal order are, in fact, available as a means of dealing with the alleged violations of Convention rights is to be welcomed.

As Article 13 develops and the Contracting Parties respond, there is scope for its making a contribution to the reduction in the number of cases which result in applications to the Strasbourg Court. Wherever a remedy can be provided for a violation of Convention rights in the national legal order, the matter does not need to be raised at the supranational level. Greater emphasis on remedies in the national legal order will result in the deeper embedding of respect for Convention rights in the national legal orders.[70]

The potential for the development through interpretation of the rights contained in Article 13 remains high. Areas ripe for further interpretation include the determination of compensation where the Court has now said that Article 13 requires compensation to be available within national legal orders; and the extension of the requirement for investigations and remedies that have now been attached to Article 13, particularly in the context of violations of Articles 2, 3, and 5. This is all about measuring the sufficiency of the guarantees required within the national legal order in order to determine whether what is on offer there constitutes an effective remedy, not only in relation to the substance of the complaints made but also in relation to the relief granted in cases where a violation of a substantive provision is found.

---

[68] For example, App. 1080/184, *L v Sweden*, Report of the Commission, 3 October 1988, (1989) 61 DR 62, and see *Leander v Sweden*, (App. 9248/81), 26 March 1987, Series A No 116, (1987) 9 EHRR 433, §77; *Sigurdur Sigurjonsson v Iceland*, (App. 16130/90), 30 June 1993, Series A No 264, (1993) 16 EHRR 462, §77 of Commission Opinion, and §44 of the judgment; and *A v United Kingdom*, (App. 35373/97), 17 December 2002, (2003) 36 EHRR 917, ECHR 2002-X.

[69] See, for example, the possibility of obtaining a declaration of incompatibility in the United Kingdom under s. 4 of the Human Rights Act 1998. The Grand Chamber has confirmed that this does not constitute an effective remedy: *Burden v United Kingdom*, (App. 13378/05), 29 April 2008 [GC], (2008) 47 EHRR 857, ECHR 2008-nyr, §§40–4.

[70] L. Helfer, 'Redesigning the European Court of Human Rights: Embeddedness as a Deep Structural Principle of the European Human Rights Regime' (2008) 19 EJIL 125, esp 144–6.

8

THE RIGHT TO LIFE

INTRODUCTION

Article 2 provides:

1. Everyone's right to life shall be protected by law. No-one shall be deprived of his life intentionally save in the execution of a sentence of a court following his conviction of a crime for which this penalty is provided by law.

2. Deprivation of life shall not be regarded as inflicted in contravention of this Article when it results from the use of force which is no more than absolutely necessary:

   (a) in defence of any person from unlawful violence;

   (b) in order to effect a lawful arrest or to prevent the escape of a person lawfully detained;

   (c) in action lawfully taken for the purpose of quelling a riot or insurrection.

The Strasbourg Court observed in the *McCann* case that:

…as a provision which not only safeguards the right to life but sets out the circumstances when the deprivation of life may be justified, Article 2 ranks as one of the most fundamental provisions in the Convention…. As such, its provisions must be strictly construed.[1]

It was not until its judgment in the *McCann* case, in September 1994, that the Strasbourg Court had the opportunity to consider the right to life. However, since then an increasingly rich and diverse case-law has developed.[2] It emerges that a Contracting Party's obligation to safeguard life consists of three main aspects: the duty to refrain, by its agents, from unlawful killing; the duty to investigate suspicious deaths;[3] and, in certain circumstances, a positive obligation to take steps to prevent the avoidable loss of life.

---

[1] *McCann and others v United Kingdom*, (App. 18984/91), (App. 18984/91), 27 September 1995, Series A No 324, (1996) 21 EHRR 97, §97.

[2] See generally D. Korff, *The right to life: a Guide to the implementation of Article 2 of the European Convention on Human Rights*, Human Rights Handbooks, No. 8 (Council of Europe Publishing, Strasbourg 2006); and F. Ní Aoláin, 'The Evolving Jurisprudence of the European Court of Human Rights concerning the Right to Life' (2001) 19 NQHR 21.

[3] And, if required, to prosecute the perpetrators of an unlawful killing.

THE DEATH PENALTY AND THE EXTRATERRITORIAL APPLICATION OF THE RIGHT TO LIFE

In one respect, part of the text of Article 2 has, in practice, been overtaken by provisions in protocols. The second sentence of Article 2(1) reserves the right of Contracting Parties to subject convicted criminals to the death penalty.[4] However, Protocol 6 to the Convention abolishes the death penalty in peacetime and Protocol 13 abolishes it in all circumstances. Forty-six Contracting Parties have ratified Protocol 6,[5] and 41 Contracting Parties have ratified Protocol 13.[6] It is the policy of the Council of Europe to require all new Contracting Parties to undertake to abolish capital punishment in peacetime as a condition of their admission into the organization.

In the *Öcalan* case,[7] the Grand Chamber speculated whether the fact that almost all the Contracting States (at the time) had ratified Protocol 6, and 43 out of 44 of them had abolished capital punishment (with a moratorium on killings in the last remaining Contracting Party, Russia), could be taken as signalling their agreement to modify the second sentence of Article 2(1). However, it found it unnecessary finally to resolve the point because of its finding that it would be a breach of Article 2 to implement a death sentence after an unfair trial.

If a Contracting Party which has ratified Protocol 6 wishes to extradite an accused to a country where he or she would face judicial execution[8] there will be a risk of a violation of the Protocol,[9] and it may be necessary for the sending State to secure an agreement from the receiving State that the death penalty will not be applied before the extradition can go ahead.

Furthermore, Article 2 has a general extraterritorial application, to protect those liable to expulsion not just from the death penalty, but from any real risk of deliberate killing.[10]

---

[4] See, on the death penalty generally and human rights, R. Hood, *The Death Penalty. A World-Wide Perspective* (OUP, Oxford 1996); P. Hodgkinson and A. Rutherford (eds.), *Capital Punishment. Global Issues and Prospects* (Waterside Press, Winchester 1996); and Council of Europe, *Death Penalty. Beyond Abolition* (Council of Europe Publishing, Strasbourg 2004).

[5] Protocol 6 had entered into force on receiving five ratifications on 1 March 1985: see http://conventions.coe.int. Russia has signed but not yet ratified Protocol 6.

[6] A further four Contracting Parties have signed but not ratified Protocol 13. Azerbaijan and Russia have not signed the Protocol. Protocol 13 entered into force on 1 July 2003 on receiving ten ratifications.

[7] *Öcalan v Turkey*, (App. 46221/99), 12 May 2005 [GC], (2005) 41 EHRR 985, ECHR 2005-IV, §§163–166.

[8] As had been the case in *Soering v United Kingdom*, 7 July 1989, Series A No 161, (1989) 11 EHRR 439; see ch.9 below.

[9] See, for example, *Nivette v France*, (App. 44190/98), Decision of 3 July 2001, ECHR 2001-VII; and *Bader and Kanbor v Sweden*, (App. 13284/04), 8 November 2005, (2008) 46 EHRR 197, ECHR 2005-XI, §§41–2.

[10] See also the discussion of the extraterritorial application of Article 3 in ch.9.

PROHIBITION OF INTENTIONAL KILLING BY THE STATE

The first and most obvious element of a Contracting Party's obligation under Article 2 is to refrain, through its agents, from deliberate, unjustified killing.

This aspect was considered by the Strasbourg Court in the *McCann* case,[11] which was brought by the relatives of three Irish Republican terrorists who had been killed by members of the British security forces in Gibraltar. It was not disputed that the soldiers had intended to shoot and kill the terrorists; according to the briefing which the soldiers had been given, the terrorists had planted a car bomb in a crowded area and were likely to have been carrying a concealed detonator, which would have allowed them to explode the bomb at the touch of a button. The respondent State claimed that the facts fell within the ambit of paragraph 2(a) of Article 2: killings resulting from the use of force which was no more than absolutely necessary to defend a number of innocent bystanders from unlawful violence. The Court held that the use of the phrase 'absolutely necessary' in paragraph 2 indicated that the force used had to be strictly proportionate to the achievement of one of the aims set out in sub-paragraphs 2(a)–(c). Given this strict test, it was not sufficient for the person administering the force honestly to believe that his or her actions were valid; this belief had also to be based on reasonable grounds, in the light of the information available at the relevant time.

The Court accepted that the soldiers were not to blame, in that they honestly and reasonably believed that it was necessary to shoot the suspects to prevent them from detonating a bomb. However, the Court widened the field of scrutiny to look at the security operation in its entirety. The identities of the three members of the terrorist squad were known to the British authorities, and it would have been possible to arrest them as they entered Gibraltar, before there was any risk of their having set a car bomb. Looking at all the facts, therefore, the Court concluded that it had not been necessary to use lethal force and that the killings amounted to a violation of Article 2.

Similar principles may operate even where no death actually occurs. In the *Makaratzis* case,[12] the applicant, who drove his car through a red traffic light in the centre of Athens, was chased by several police cars and motorcycles. When he failed to stop, the police shot at his car, hitting him in the right arm, right foot, left buttock, and chest. The Strasbourg Court observed that it was only by sheer good luck that the applicant had not been killed, and that Article 2 therefore applied. It was prepared to accept that the use of lethal force had been reasonable in the circumstances, since the police appeared to believe that the applicant was himself armed and dangerous. However, the

---

[11] *McCann and others v United Kingdom*, (App. 18984/91), (App. 18984/91), 27 September 1995, Series A No 324, (1996) 21 EHRR 97.

[12] *Makaratzis v Greece*, (App. 50385/99), 20 December 2004 [GC], (2005) 41 EHRR 1092, ECHR 2004-XI.

Court was 'struck with the chaotic way in which the firearms were actually used', with a large number of officers acting erratically and uncontrollably, without a clear chain of command. The Court also found that the domestic law, as it then stood, contained insufficient guidance as to the use of firearms by the police.[13]

The *Ramsahai* case[14] is a classic case of a police shooting. Ramsahai had stolen a motor scooter from its owner at gunpoint and driven off. He was later seen on the scooter by two police officers. According to the police officers, he was challenged, but drew the gun and pointed it at the police officers. One of the police officers fired his own gun, and Ramsahai was hit in the neck, and died at the scene. The matter was investigated initially by the public prosecutor for the police area to which the officers were attached, but later by the State Criminal Investigation Department. The officers were exonerated, and a legal challenge to that decision by Ramsahai's family failed. The applicants complained of violations of Article 2. The Grand Chamber concluded that the firing of the shot which had killed Ramsahai was a use of force that was no more than was absolutely necessary.

Excessive use of force in all the circumstances of the case will result in a finding of a violation of Article 2, as in the *Nikolova and Velichkova* case,[15] in which a 63-year-old man was hit over the head by the police after being spotted by police testing a home-made metal detector; he died from severe cranial and cerebral trauma and internal brain haemorrhaging. It would also seem that suspect restraint techniques used by the police—being handcuffed in front of the body and immobilized by being pinned on the stomach by the use of the combined body weight of a number of officers—coupled with a failure to respond to a medical crisis which led to the death of the victim by slow asphyxia, can give rise to a violation of Article 2.[16]

It appears that the Court will itself examine the circumstances of a killing by State officials only where there is evidence that, for some reason, the domestic judicial system is inadequate or unable to uncover the truth. In the *Hugh Jordan* case,[17] it took into account the fact that civil proceedings brought by the applicant against the police regarding the killing of his son by a police officer in Northern Ireland were still pending, and explained that it would be inappropriate and contrary to its subsidiary role under the Convention to attempt to establish the facts of this case by embarking on a fact-finding exercise of its own by summoning witnesses. Such an exercise would duplicate the proceedings before the civil courts which are better placed and equipped as fact-finding tribunals.[18] The Strasbourg Court distinguished the case from those

---

[13] In *Andronicou v Cyprus*, (App. 25052/94), 9 October 1997, (1998) 25 EHRR 491, ECHR 1997-VI, the Court, differing from the Commission, found no violation of Article 2 where the police killed the hostage victim they were attempting to liberate. See also *Huohvainen v Finland*, (App. 57389/00), 13 March 2007, (2008) 47 EHRR 974.

[14] *Ramsahai and others v The Netherlands*, (App. 52391/99), 15 May 2007 [GC], (2008) 46 EHRR 983, ECHR 2007-nyr. See also *Giuliani and Gaggio v Italy*, (App. 23458/02), 25 August 2009.

[15] *Nikolova and Velichkova v Bulgaria*, (App. 7888/03), 20 December 2007, (2009) 48 EHRR 915.

[16] *Saoud v France*, (App. 9375/02), 9 October 2007, ECHR 2007-XI.

[17] *Hugh Jordan v United Kingdom*, (App. 24746/94), 4 May 2001, (2003) 37 EHRR 52, ECHR 2001-III.

[18] §111.

brought against Turkey where the Commission had embarked on fact-finding missions where there were pending proceedings against the alleged security force perpetrators of unlawful killings. The point of distinction was that those proceedings were criminal and had terminated, at first instance at least, by the time the Court was examining the applications. In those cases, it was an essential part of the applicants' allegations that the defects in the investigation were such as to render the criminal proceedings ineffective.[19] In the *Hugh Jordan* case, in contrast, there was no evidence to show that the civil courts would be unable to establish the facts and determine whether the killing had been lawful.

In two cases[20] concerning Greek Cypriots killed as a result of their involvement in demonstrations in the United Nations buffer zone in Nicosia directed towards Turkish Cypriots in the north of the island, the Strasbourg Court found that their deaths were at the hands of agents of the Turkish State. Isaak had become embroiled in a brawl with Turkish Cypriots and had been beaten to death; his fatal injuries were described as 'multiple head trauma'. Solomou had been shot five times when he climbed up a flagpole flying the Turkish flag. Both had been unarmed. The Strasbourg Court said that it could not be said that they were victims of force permitted by Article 2; they had been victims of unlawful force in violation of Article 2.

DEATH IN CUSTODY AND FORCED DISAPPEARANCE

History has shown that, in the absence of safeguards against abuse of power, it is all too easy for the State to cover up its own unlawful violence, particularly when that violence is carried out behind closed doors. The protection afforded by Article 2 would be of no value if a State could avoid international sanction by concealing the evidence of killings caused by its agents. Where an individual is known to have been taken into custody and subsequently disappears or is found dead, therefore, it is logical that a heavy burden should fall on the State to establish an innocent explanation.[21]

According to Amnesty International, following an analysis of the relevant international instruments, the crime of 'disappearances' has the following elements: (1) a deprivation of liberty, (2) effected by government agents or with their consent or acquiescence, followed by (3) an absence of information or refusal to acknowledge the deprivation of liberty or refusal to disclose the fate or whereabouts of the person, (4) thereby placing such persons outside the protection of the law.[22] The Inter-American

---

[19] See further below in this chapter.

[20] *Isaak v Turkey*, (App. 44587/98), 24 June 2008; and *Solomou v Turkey*, (App. 36832/97), 24 June 2008.

[21] See the judgment of the Inter-American Court of Human Rights in *Velásquez Rodríguez v Honduras*, 29 July 1988, Inter-Am. Ct. H. R. (Series C) No. 4 (1988).

[22] See Amnesty International's written submissions to the Strasbourg Court in connection with the case of *Kurt v Turkey* (App. 24276/94), 25 May 1998; (1999) 27 EHRR 373, ECHR 1998-III, §§68–71.

Court of Human Rights has held that 'the phenomenon of disappearances is a complex form of human rights violation', including breaches of the right to life and the right not to be subjected to ill-treatment, 'that must be understood and confronted in an integral fashion'.[23] The gravity of the violations of rights attendant on a disappearance has led the United Nations Human Rights Committee to conclude in relation to Article 6 of the International Covenant on Civil and Political Rights that State Parties should take specific and effective measures to prevent them occurring and thoroughly to investigate any case of a missing or disappeared person which may involve a violation of the right to life.[24] The UN Committee has subsequently held that the disappearance of a person is inseparably linked to treatment giving rise to a violation of Article 7 of the International Covenant, which mirrors Article 3 of the European Convention.[25]

Against this background, it is arguable that the Strasbourg organs were disappointingly timid in their treatment of the first case of a disappearance to come before them.[26] The Commission and Court both accepted that it had been proved beyond reasonable doubt that the applicant's son had last been seen some four and a half years earlier surrounded by soldiers during a security operation in his village in south-east Turkey. The Court moreover conceded that in these circumstances the applicant's fears that her son might have died in unacknowledged custody at the hands of his captors could not be said to be without foundation. Nonetheless, it declined to find a breach of Article 2 in the absence of concrete evidence that the young man had been killed by the authorities. Instead, it opted for 'a particularly grave violation of the right to liberty and security of person under Article 5 raising serious concerns about the welfare of [the applicant's son]'.

In more recent cases, however, the Court has been much more robust. In the *Timurtas* case,[27] the applicant alleged that his son had been taken into custody in August 1993 and had subsequently disappeared. He had filed a complaint with the Turkish authorities but the public prosecutor had decided not to investigate, because the applicant was unable to substantiate his allegations and because it was likely that his son was a member of a Kurdish terrorist organization. The respondent State denied that the applicant's son had ever been arrested and produced in support the custody records of the local police station, army headquarters, and interrogation centre—none of which contained any mention of the young man. A delegation from the Commission travelled to south-east Turkey to take evidence. The applicant was unable to find any eyewitness to testify to the arrest and detention of his son. He did, however, produce a photocopy of a document purporting to be an army post-operational report recording his son's arrest. The respondent State disputed the document's authenticity, claiming

[23] *Velásquez Rodríguez v Honduras*, 29 July 1988, Inter-Am. Ct. H. R. (Series C) No. 4 (1988).

[24] General Comment 6 (Sixteenth Session 1982), 37 UN GAOR, Supp. No. 40 (A/37/40) Annex V, para. 1.

[25] *Mojica v Dominican Republic*, Decision of 15 July 1994, Committee's views under Article 5(4) of the Optional Protocol to the ICCPR concerning Communication No. 449/1991; (1996) 17 HRLJ 18.

[26] *Kurt v Turkey*, (App. 24276/94), 25 May 1998, (1999) 27 EHRR 373, ECHR 1998-III.

[27] *Timurtaş v Turkey*, (App. 23531/94), 13 June 2000, (2001) 33 EHRR 121, ECHR 2000-VI.

that the reference number in truth belonged to another, quite different, document, but refusing to produce this second document for security reasons.

The Strasbourg Court acknowledged the risk inherent in relying for proof almost entirely on a photocopy. However, it held that the respondent State's failure, without satisfactory explanation, to disclose evidence which it claimed to hold gave rise to an inference that the photocopied report was genuine, and that the applicant's son had been arrested. The Court next considered whether, in the absence of a body, any issue could arise under Article 2, concluding that this would depend on all the facts of the case, in particular whether there was sufficient circumstantial evidence pointing towards death in custody. In this respect the length of time which had elapsed since the person had been placed in detention, although not decisive, was highly relevant, since the more time which passed without any news, the greater was the likelihood that he had died. Given that more than six and a half years had gone by since the applicant's son had been arrested and that the respondent State was unable to provide any explanation of what had happened to him, the Court found a violation of Article 2.[28]

The same principle applies *a fortiori* where there is clear evidence of a death in custody. In the *Salman* case,[29] the applicant's husband was arrested at midnight on 28 April 1992 on suspicion of aiding and abetting Kurdish terrorists. Twenty-four hours later he was taken to the State Hospital where he was declared dead on arrival. The hospital autopsy disclosed various marks and bruises, including a broken sternum, but did not determine the cause of death. The case was referred to the Istanbul Forensic Institute which concluded that the applicant's husband had died of a heart attack brought on by the effect of his arrest on a pre-existing heart condition. The applicant claimed that photographs of the corpse taken by the family showed that her husband had been beaten on the soles of his feet. Ten police officers were acquitted of homicide by the Adana Aggravated Felony Court on the basis that there was inadequate evidence of any use of torture. The Strasbourg Court observed that where a person was taken into custody in good health and then died, the obligation on the Contracting Party to provide a satisfactory account was particularly stringent. Since the respondent State was unable to explain how the applicant's husband had come by his injuries and since the evidence did not support the contention that he had died of a heart attack caused by the stress of arrest, the Court found the respondent State to have violated Article 2.

---

[28] The Chamber judgment of 10 January 2008 finding Turkey in continuing violation of Article 2 in respect of a failure to conduct an effective investigation into the disappearances of a number of Cypriot nationals captured and detained in July and August 1974 has been referred to the Grand Chamber: see *Varnava and others v Turkey*, (Apps. 16064–6/90, and 16068–73/90), 18 September 2009 [GC].

[29] *Salman v Turkey*, (App. 21986/93), 27 June 2000 [GC], (2002) 34 EHRR 425, ECHR 2000-VII. See also *Abdurrahman Orak v Turkey*, (App. 31889/96), 14 February 2002; and *Anguelova v Bulgaria*, (App. 38361/97), 13 June 2002, (2004) 38 EHRR 659, ECHR 2002-IV. In the latter case, the Court found a separate violation based on the failure of the police to get the applicant speedy medical assistance after he collapsed from a head injury.

RESPONDING TO INTERNAL ARMED INSURGENCY: THE CASE OF CHECHNYA

In recent years, the Strasbourg Court has delivered very many judgments arising from events in what has been labelled the second Chechen War.[30] The first Chechen War began in 1994 when Russian troops acted to restore constitutional order in Chechnya in the face of declared independence by Chechnya following the dissolution of the Soviet Union in 1991. A cease fire agreement in 1996 led to the withdrawal of Russian troops. The constitutional status of Chechnya remained that of part of the Russian Federation. There was no stability following the 1996 cease fire. There were serious concerns in Moscow that allowing Chechnya to become autonomous would result in a domino effect with further fragmentation of what was formerly the Soviet Union. A separatist president, Aslan Maskhadov, was elected in Chechnya in 1997. In August and September 1999, Russia conducted a campaign of aerial bombardment over Chechnya. There was significant civilian loss of life. A land offensive began in October 1999. There were offensives directed at the main city of Grozny, and at Gudermes, Chechnya's second largest city, as well as other parts of Chechnya. By the spring of 2000, Russian troops were largely in control of Chechnya; and in May 2000 President Putin established direct rule of Chechnya. This did not end the insurgency, which was continued by Chechen separatists. At no time did Russia seek to derogate from any provisions of the Convention; it could not in any event derogate in respect of its responsibilities under Article 2 on the right to life or Article 3 on the prohibition of torture. It characterized its actions as 'counter-terrorist operations'.

The human cost of the war was substantial loss of civilian life, displacement of hundreds of thousands of people, allegations of torture and war crimes from both sides in the conflict, and significant violations of international humanitarian law. The character of the Russian action has been described by the Strasbourg Court as a response to an illegal armed insurgency:

> 180. The Court accepts that the situation that existed in Chechnya at the relevant time called for exceptional measures by the State in order to regain control over the Republic and to suppress the illegal armed insurgency. Given the context of the conflict in Chechnya at the relevant time, those measures could presumably include the deployment of army units equipped with combat weapons, including military aviation and artillery. The presence of a very large group of armed fighters in Katyr-Yurt, and their active resistance to the law-enforcement bodies, which are not disputed by the parties, may have justified use of lethal force by the agents of the State, thus bringing the situation within paragraph 2 of Article 2.

---

[30] For a discussion of the case-law arising from this situation, see P. Leach, 'The Chechen conflict: analysing the oversight of the European Court of Human Rights' [2008] EHRLR 732. An appendix to the article lists the judgments of the Strasbourg Court up to 3 July 2008.

181. Accepting that the use of force may have been justified in the present case, it goes without saying that a balance must be achieved between the aim pursued and the means employed to achieve it. The Court will now consider whether the actions in the present case were no more than absolutely necessary for achieving the declared purpose ....[31]

The use of aerial bombardment of an area containing a civilian population requires special justification. The Strasbourg Court said:

> ...According to the servicemen's statements, bombs and other non-guided heavy combat weapons were used against targets both in the centre and on the edges of the village....

191. The Court considers that using this kind of weapon in a populated area, outside wartime and without prior evacuation of the civilians, is impossible to reconcile with the degree of caution expected from a law-enforcement body in a democratic society. No martial law and no state of emergency has been declared in Chechnya, and no derogation has been made under Article 15 of the Convention.... The operation in question therefore has to be judged against a normal legal background. Even when faced with a situation where, as the Government submit, the population of the village had been held hostage by a large group of well-equipped and well-trained fighters, the primary aim of the operation should be to protect lives from unlawful violence. The massive use of indiscriminate weapons stands in flagrant contrast with this aim and cannot be considered compatible with the standard of care prerequisite to an operation of this kind involving the use of lethal force by State agents.[32]

The applications to the Strasbourg Court raising violations of Article 2 have involved complaints of mass killings of civilians, disappearances, extra-judicial executions, and failures to investigate. The response of the Russian authorities has been to deny responsibility and to refuse to cooperate with the Court,[33] although in some cases the respondent State has suggested that the victims were members of paramilitary groups, but has failed to provide any credible evidence to establish this.

The *Imakayeva* case[34] is a typical disappearance case. The applicant complained of the disappearance of her son and husband. The day after the disappearance, the authorities were asked to assist and to investigate; efforts were made to find the missing men by visiting detention centres and prisons. The applicant was subsequently told that investigations had failed to establish the whereabouts of the missing men, although she was also told that her husband had been detained by military personnel but subsequently released, and her son had been detained on suspicion of being a member of a bandit group. The Strasbourg Court found violations of Article 2 both

---

[31] *Isayeva v Russia*, (App. 57950/00), 25 February 2005, (2005) 41 EHRR 791, §§180–1.

[32] §§190–1.

[33] And the respondent State has been found to be in breach of its duties under Article 38 to furnish the Court with all necessary facilities to enable it to pursue the examination of the case in many of the cases coming before the Court. This had led the Court to draw adverse inferences in many of the cases.

[34] *Imakayeva v Russia*, (App. 7615/02), 9 November 2006, (2008) 47 EHRR 139, ECHR 2006-XIII.

in respect of the disappearances,[35] and in respect of the failure to conduct an effective investigation into the circumstances in which they had disappeared.[36]

In the face of so many cases finding serious violations of Article 2, Leach nevertheless remains optimistic:

The growing corpus of Chechen cases is nevertheless significant because they deliver a degree of justice for the applicants and their families, they ensure that the international spotlight is intermittently directed at the region and its authorities, and they provide a measure of accountability. Depending on the outcome of the ongoing dialogue between the Committee of Ministers and the Russian Government, they should also lead directly to changes in domestic law, policy or practice.[37]

THE POSITIVE OBLIGATION TO PROTECT LIFE

In the *LCB* case,[38] the Strasbourg Court recognized for the first time that the first sentence of Article 2(1) enjoins a Contracting Party not only to refrain from the intentional and unlawful taking of life, but also to take appropriate steps to safeguard the lives of those within their jurisdiction. This was an important statement of principle, despite the fact that the applicant was unable to prove either that her father's service in the Royal Air Force during the United Kingdom's nuclear tests on Christmas Island in 1957–8 had been the cause of her childhood leukaemia or that, had the respondent State provided her family with more information about the tests and the possible health consequences, earlier medical intervention would have mitigated her illness.

More recent cases have demonstrated that the State's duty to safeguard life is extensive.[39] In the *Öneryildiz* case, the Grand Chamber went so far as to hold:

...that this obligation [to take appropriate steps to safeguard the lives of those within the State's jurisdiction] must be construed as applying in the context of any activity, whether public or not, in which the right to life may be at stake,....[40]

The obligation entails, at its most basic, a duty to put in place a legislative and administrative framework designed to provide effective deterrence against unlawful killing.[41] Thus, Turkey was at fault in cases involving the murder of a journalist working for a Kurdish separatist newspaper and a doctor known to have treated members of

---

[35] Described as 'life-threatening' in the particular circumstances.

[36] See further below in this chapter on the duty to investigate.

[37] P. Leach, 'The Chechen conflict: analysing the oversight of the European Court of Human Rights' [2008] EHRLR 732, 760.

[38] *LCB v United Kingdom*, (App. 23413/94), 9 June 1998; (1998) 27 EHRR 212, ECHR 1998-III.

[39] For a parallel obligation under Article 8, see *Guerra v Italy* (App. 14967/89), 19 February 1998, (1998) 26 EHRR 357, ECHR 1998-I; see ch.16 below.

[40] *Öneryildiz v Turkey*, (App. 48939/99), 30 November 2004 [GC], (2005) 41 EHRR 325, ECHR 2004-XII, §93.

[41] §89.

the Kurdish terrorist organization, the PKK.[42] In both cases the applicants alleged that their brothers had been assassinated by members of the State security forces, but this could not be proved. The Strasbourg Court did, however, find that the authorities were aware that journalists, doctors, and others associated with the PKK and Kurdish separatism had been the object of a campaign of serious attacks and threats, possibly emanating from or carried out with the acquiescence of the security forces. Although there was a framework of law in place aimed at the protection of life (criminal law, police, prosecutor, and courts), at the relevant time the implementation of the criminal justice system in south-east Turkey was seriously undermined by various Emergency Rule measures (including the transfer of jurisdiction away from the courts to councils of civil servants and a series of failures to investigate allegations of wrongdoing by the members of the security forces). This situation fostered a dangerous lack of accountability among members of the security forces and removed the protection which the applicants' brothers should have received by law.

In addition, an obligation to take action to avert a specific risk to a particular individual's life may arise in certain, limited circumstances. This can arise in both individual cases, and in more general situations, such as the planning of the policing of a known demonstration at an international event, such as a G8 summit.[43]

The *Osman* case[44] is an example of an individual situation. The applicants' family had become the target of a dangerous stalker, who eventually broke into their home and shot and killed their husband and father. Bearing in mind the difficulties in policing modern society, the unpredictability of human conduct, and the need for the police to act within the confines imposed on them by, *inter alia*, Articles 5 and 8 of the Convention, the Strasbourg Court defined this particular aspect of the duty to protect life rather narrowly. It considered that the authorities could be said to be in breach of Article 2 in this context only if it could be established that they knew or ought to have known at the relevant time of the existence of a real and immediate risk to the life of an identified individual or individuals from the criminal acts of a third party, and that they failed to take measures within the scope of their powers which, judged reasonably, might have been expected to avoid that risk. In the instant case, the applicants were not able to point to any decisive stage in the sequence of events leading to the shooting when it could be said that the police knew or ought or have known that the lives of the Osman family were at real and immediate risk, and the police could not be criticized for attaching weight to the presumption of innocence and the rights of the stalker in the absence of any concrete evidence against him.

---

[42] *Kiliç v Turkey*, (App. 22492/93), 28 March 2000, (2001) 33 EHRR 1357, ECHR 2000-III; and *Mahmut Kaya v Turkey*, (App. 22535/93), 28 March 2000, ECHR 2000-III.

[43] See *Giuliani and Gaggio v Italy*, (App. 23458/02), 25 August 2009, though no violation of the positive obligation to protect life was found in this case, which involved the policing of G8 protests in Genoa in July 2001.

[44] *Osman v United Kingdom*, (App. 23452/94), 28 October 1998, (1998) 29 EHRR 245, ECHR 1998-VIII. See also *Opuz v Turkey*, (App. 33401/02), 9 June 2009.

In the *Keenan* case,[45] the risk to life came from the victim himself, a young man with mental health problems who committed suicide in prison. The Strasbourg Court emphasized that prisoners are in a vulnerable position and that the authorities are under a duty to protect them,[46] and noted that this necessity is reflected in English law, where inquests are automatically held following all deaths in custody. In Keenan's case, the prison administration had acted reasonably to protect him from himself. They knew that he was prone to psychotic flare-ups, and during the periods when he appeared to be suicidal, they had placed him on the hospital wing and checked him every fifteen minutes. On the day when he killed himself, he had been returned to an ordinary cell because he did not appear to be in any particular trouble.[47]

The Court is showing much greater interest in the treatment of prisoners and the conditions of detention. It has confirmed that a State's obligation to protect life extends to the protection of the lives of persons in custody. This involves providing in a timely manner the medical care necessary to prevent death. Due diligence will be expected of the prison authorities to take account of a prisoner's medical condition.[48] The same approach is adopted where medical intervention is undertaken to treat those with alcohol substance abuse.[49]

The Strasbourg Court has summarized the positive obligations of the Contracting Parties in these circumstances as follows:

49.   The Court reiterates that the first sentence of Article 2 § 1 enjoins the State not only to refrain from the intentional and unlawful taking of life, but also to take appropriate steps to safeguard the lives of those within its jurisdiction.... This involves a primary duty on the State to secure the right to life by putting in place effective criminal-law provisions to deter the commission of offences against the person backed up by law-enforcement machinery for the prevention, suppression and punishment of breaches of such provisions. It also extends in appropriate circumstances to a positive obligation on the authorities to take preventive operational measures to protect an individual whose life is at risk from the criminal acts of another individual....

50.   Bearing in mind the difficulties in policing modern societies, the unpredictability of human conduct and the operational choices which must be made in terms of priorities and resources, the scope of the positive obligation must be interpreted in a way which does not impose an impossible or disproportionate burden on the authorities. Not every claimed risk to life, therefore, can entail for the authorities a Convention requirement to take operational measures to prevent that risk from materialising. For a positive obligation to arise, it must be established that the authorities knew or

---

[45]   *Keenan v United Kingdom*, (App. 27229/95), 3 April 2001, (2001) 33 EHRR 913, ECHR 2001-III.

[46]   See also *Paul and Audrey Edwards v United Kingdom*, (App. 46477/99), 14 March 2002, (2002) 35 EHRR 487, ECHR 2002-II, where the Court found a violation of Article 2 based on the prison authorities' negligence in locking the applicants' son in a cell with an extremely violent and mentally ill offender; and *Branko Tomašić and others v Croatia*, (App. 46598/06), 15 January 2009, §§49–51.

[47]   See also *Renolde v France*, (App. 5608/05), 16 October 2008, (2009) 48 EHRR 969.

[48]   *Gagiu v Romania*, (App. 63258/00), 24 February 2009.

[49]   *Mojsiejew v Poland*, (App. 11818/02), 24 March 2009.

ought to have known at the time of the existence of a real and immediate risk to the life of an identified individual from the criminal acts of a third party and that they failed to take measures within the scope of their powers which, judged reasonably, might have been expected to avoid that risk....[50]

Where the risk to life arises from an inherently dangerous, but basically lawful, activity, such as, for example, military tests,[51] or the operation of a factory involving toxic emissions,[52] or of a large waste disposal site,[53] there is a duty on the Contracting Party to provide an effective system of regulation, supervision and control, providing for the identification and correction of any dangerous shortcomings.[54] Where appropriate, the Contracting Party must ensure that people whose lives may be put at risk by the process in question are provided with sufficient information to allow them to assess the risk and take preventive measures.[55] These duties arise whether the activity is carried out by the Contracting Party or by private enterprise.

The *Öneryildiz* case[56] concerned a tragic accident at a huge rubbish tip operated by the local authorities on the outskirts of Istanbul. The relevant regulatory law had not been complied with, and no ventilation system was installed. This led to a build-up of methane and other gases, which exploded, causing a landslide which engulfed part of a shanty-town which had sprung up on the slope beneath the tip. The Strasbourg Court held that the Turkish authorities were to blame for the resulting loss of life, because an expert report produced several years before the accident had clearly identified the risk, but no action had been taken. Although the houses which were destroyed had been built illegally, the policy of the authorities was generally tolerant of such breaches of planning controls, and the inhabitants had been provided with an electricity and water supply and required to pay local taxes. Moreover, it would have been relatively simple to make the tip safe by building ventilation ducts.

The positive obligation will extend to natural disasters as well as those resulting from dangerous activities. The *Budayeva* case[57] concerned the response of the authorities to known risks of mudslides, which had occurred in the region every year since 1937. Mudslides in July 2000 caused considerable devastation, and the first applicant's husband had been killed when he had stayed behind in a block of flats to help his parents-in-law, and those flats had collapsed. The Strasbourg Court identified a string of deficiencies in the response of the authorities to the known risk, and found a violation

---

50 *Kontrová v Slovakia*, (App. 7510/04), 31 May 2007, ECHR 2007-VI, §§49–50.

51 *LCB v United Kingdom*, (App. 23413/94), 9 June 1998, (1998) 27 EHRR 212, ECHR 1998-III.

52 *Guerra v Italy* (App. 14967/89), 19 February 1998, (1998) 26 EHRR 357, ECHR 1998-I.

53 *Öneryildiz v Turkey*, (App. 48939/99), 30 November 2004 [GC], (2005) 41 EHRR 325, ECHR 2004-XII, §89.

54 §90.

55 *Öneryildiz v Turkey*, (App. 48939/99), 30 November 2004 [GC], (2005) 41 EHRR 325, ECHR 2004-XII.

56 Ibid.

57 *Budayeva and others v Russia*, (Apps 15339/02, 21166/02, 20058/02, 11673/02 and 15343/02), 20 March 2008.

of Article 2 because of the inadequacy of the defence system and the failure to establish any form of warning system. But the Strasbourg Court noted that the burden placed upon a Contracting Party must be reasonable:

> ... an impossible or disproportionate burden must not be imposed on the authorities without consideration being given, in particular, to the operational choices which they must make in terms of priorities and resources...; this results from the wide margin of appreciation States enjoy, as the Court has previously held, in difficult social and technical spheres.... This consideration must be afforded even greater weight in the sphere of emergency relief in relation to a meteorological event, which is as such beyond human control, than in the sphere of dangerous activities of a man-made nature.

136. ...

137. In the sphere of emergency relief, where the State is directly involved in the protection of human lives through the mitigation of natural hazards, these considerations should apply in so far as the circumstances of a particular case point to the imminence of a natural hazard that had been clearly identifiable, and especially where it concerned a recurring calamity affecting a distinct area developed for human habitation or use.... The scope of the positive obligations imputable to the State in the particular circumstances would depend on the origin of the threat and the extent to which one or the other risk is susceptible to mitigation.[58]

There must also be a proper judicial or administrative enquiry into alleged deficiencies which have led to a disaster of this nature.[59]

THE DUTY TO INVESTIGATE
SUSPICIOUS DEATHS

In the *McCann* case, the Strasbourg Court observed that any general legal prohibition of arbitrary killing by agents of the State would be ineffective in practice in the absence of a procedure for reviewing the lawfulness of the use of lethal force by State authorities:

The obligation to protect the right to life under this provision, read in conjunction with the State's general duty under Article 1 of the Convention to 'secure to everyone within their jurisdiction the rights and freedoms defined in [the] Convention', requires by implication that there should be some form of effective official investigation when individuals have been killed as a result of the use of force by, *inter alios*, agents of the State.[60]

---

[58] *Budayeva*, §§135 and 137.
[59] §§161–5.
[60] *McCann and others v United Kingdom*, (App. 18984/91), 27 September 1995, Series A No 324, (1996) 21 EHRR 97, §161.

In the *Ramsahai* case,[61] the Grand Chamber recapitulated the requirements of an investigation as follows:

323. The Court finds it opportune to clarify the scope and content of its examination of the effectiveness of the investigation.

324. In order to be 'effective' as this expression is to be understood in the context of Article 2 of the Convention, an investigation into a death that engages the responsibility of a Contracting Party under that Article must firstly be adequate. That is, it must be capable of leading to the identification and punishment of those responsible. This is not an obligation of result, but one of means. The authorities must have taken the reasonable steps available to them to secure the evidence concerning the incident. Any deficiency in the investigation which undermines its ability to identify the perpetrator or perpetrators will risk falling foul of this standard....

325. Secondly, for the investigation to be 'effective' in this sense it may generally be regarded as necessary for the persons responsible for it and carrying it out to be independent from those implicated in the events. This means not only a lack of hierarchical or institutional connection but also a practical independence.... What is at stake here is nothing less than public confidence in the state's monopoly on the use of force.[62]

The requirement for an effective investigation has formed a useful part of the Strasbourg Court's artillery, particularly in cases where the evidence is not sufficiently clear to justify a finding of deliberate killing by the State. In the *Kaya* case,[63] for example, the applicant's brother was found lying dead and riddled with bullets in a field near his village in south-east Turkey. The respondent State claimed that he was a terrorist who had been killed during a battle with security forces. Witnesses from the village—none of whom, however, were prepared to testify before the Commission's fact-finding delegation—allegedly said that he was an ordinary, unarmed farmer who had been shot by the soldiers without justification or provocation. Only a rudimentary post-mortem had been performed before the body was handed over for burial to the villagers, and the public prosecutor who subsequently took over the inquiry appeared to have accepted without question the military's version of events, omitting to take statements from witnesses or collect any forensic evidence. In these circumstances the Commission and Court, examining the case some years later and hampered by the reluctance of witnesses to come forward,[64] were unable to establish clearly what had taken place or to find for the applicant on his complaint that his brother had been deliberately killed by the soldiers. The Strasbourg Court did, however, find a breach of Article 2 on the basis that the domestic investigation into the death had been inadequate.[65]

---

61 *Ramsahai and others v The Netherlands*, (App. 52391/99), 15 May 2007 [GC], (2008) 46 EHRR 983, ECHR 2007-nyr.

62 §§323–5.

63 *Kaya v Turkey*, (App. 22729/93), 19 February 1998, (1999) 28 EHRR 1, ECHR 1998-I.

64 See ch.2 above for details of the Strasbourg organs' fact-finding powers.

65 See also *Akpinar and Altun v Turkey*, (App. 56760/00), 27 February 2007, ECHR 2007-III; *Osmanoğlu v Turkey*, (App. 48804/99), 24 January 2008; and *Beker v Turkey*, (App. 27866/03), 24 March 2009.

The Court has explained[66] that the essential purpose of such investigation is to secure the effective implementation of the domestic laws which protect the right to life and, in those cases involving State agents or bodies, to ensure their account-ability for deaths occurring under their responsibility. What form of investigation will achieve those purposes may vary in different circumstances. However, whatever mode is employed, the authorities must act of their own motion, once the matter has come to their attention. They cannot leave it to the initiative of the next of kin either to lodge a formal complaint or to take responsibility for the conduct of any investigative procedures. The procedural aspect of Article 2 can, in this way, be dis-tinguished from the obligation under Article 13 to provide an effective remedy. Put bluntly, Article 2 appears to be most concerned with an official investigation leading to the establishment of criminal liability, whereas the focus of Article 13 is the pro-vision of a civil remedy to the victim or his or her relatives, to enable them to seek compensation.[67]

For an investigation into alleged unlawful killing by State agents to be effective and to comply with Article 2, it must be carried out by someone who is fully independent of those implicated in the events[68] on the basis of objective evidence.[69] The investiga-tion must be capable of leading to a determination of whether the force used in such cases was justified in the circumstances and to the identification and punishment of those responsible.[70] This entails that the authorities must have taken the reason-able steps available to them to secure the evidence concerning the incident, includ-ing eyewitness testimony, forensic evidence, and, where appropriate, an autopsy which provides a complete and accurate record of injury and an objective analysis of clinical findings, including the cause of death.[71] Any deficiency in the investigation which undermines its ability to establish the cause of death or the person or persons responsible will risk falling foul of this standard. The investigation must be carried out promptly, in order to maintain public confidence in the authorities' adherence to the rule of law and to prevent any appearance of collusion in or tolerance of unlawful acts.[72] For the same reasons, the investigation must, to a certain degree, be open to

---

[66] See, for example, *Hugh Jordan v United Kingdom*, (App. 24746/94), 4 May 2001, (2003) 37 EHRR 52, ECHR 2001-III, §§105 and following.

[67] See *Öneryildiz v Turkey*, (App. 48939/99), 30 November 2004 [GC], (2005) 41 EHRR 325, ECHR 2004-XII.

[68] *Güleç v Turkey*, (App. 21593/93), 27 July 1998, (1999) 28 EHRR 121, ECHR 1998-IV; and *Ögur v Turkey*, (App. 21594/93), 20 May 1999; (2001) 31 EHRR 912, ECHR 1999-III.

[69] *Ergi v Turkey*, (App. 23818/94), 28 July 1998, (2001) 32 EHRR 388, ECHR 1998-IV.

[70] *Kaya v Turkey*, (App. 22729/93), 19 February 1998, (1999) 28 EHRR 1, ECHR 1998-I; and *Ögur v Turkey*, (App. 21594/93), 20 May 1999, (2001) 31 EHRR 912, ECHR 1999-III.

[71] *Salman v Turkey*, (App. 21986/93), 27 June 2000, (2002) 34 EHRR 425, ECHR 2000-VII; *Tanrikulu v Turkey*, (App. 23763/94), 8 July 1999 [GC], (2000) 30 EHRR 950, ECHR 1999-IV; and *Gül v Turkey*, (App. 22676/93), 14 December 2000, (2002) 34 EHRR 719.

[72] *Yasa v Turkey*, (App. 22495/93), 2 September 1998; (1999) 28 EHRR 408, ECHR 1998-VI; *Çakici v Turkey*, (App. 23657/94), 8 July 1999, (2001) 31 EHRR 133; *Tanrikulu v Turkey*, (App. 23763/94), 8 July 1999 [GC], (2000) 30 EHRR 950, ECHR 1999-IV; and *Mahmut Kaya v Turkey*, (App. 22535/93), 28 March 2000, ECHR 2000-III.

public scrutiny, and the relatives of the deceased must always have the opportunity to become involved.[73]

These requirements are illustrated by the *Ramsahai* case, which concerned the shooting of a suspect by the police.[74] Having found that the killings did not involve more force than was strictly necessary, the Strasbourg Court focused on aspects of the investigation which followed. Violations of Article 2 were found in only two respects: by thirteen votes to four that the investigation was inadequate; and by sixteen votes to one that the investigation was not sufficiently independent. On the former point, the Grand Chamber concluded that there had been a failure to test the hands of the police officers for gunshot residue, and to stage any reconstruction of the incident; no examination of the weapons or ammunition of the two officers had been undertaken. Furthermore there was no adequate photograph of the injuries suffered by Ramsahai; the officers had not been kept separate after the incident; and they had not been questioned until nearly three days later. The dissenting judges considered that a defect in the investigative procedure only gave rise to a violation of Article 2 if it was such as to undermine the capacity of the investigation to establish the facts surrounding the death or the liability of the person involved. That was not the case here. In respect of the second finding of a violation of Article 2, the Grand Chamber concluded that the delay of over fifteen hours before the investigation was handed over to someone unconnected with the police force to which the officers were attached meant that the investigation was not sufficiently independent. The dissenting judge did not consider that the delay had tainted the independence of the investigation, since it had not adversely impacted upon its effectiveness. There does not appear, on the facts of the case, to have been any suggestion that the Dutch police had acted in bad faith or were attempting to cover up any wrongdoing. What is striking from this judgment is the level of detail required of the process of investigation following the fatal shooting by the police.[75] This is standard-setting of a high order, and might prove to be impracticable or overly costly to apply, particularly in remote regions.

In the United Kingdom, investigations into suspicious deaths usually take the form of inquests, which are public hearings into the facts conducted by independent judicial officers (coroners), normally sitting with a jury. Judicial review lies from procedural decisions by coroners and in respect of any mistaken directions given to the jury. In the *McCann* case[76] the Strasbourg Court found that the inquest held into the deaths of three terrorists shot dead by British soldiers in Gibraltar satisfied the procedural obligation contained in Article 2, as it provided a detailed review of the events surrounding

---

[73] *Güleç v Turkey*, (App. 21593/93), 27 July 1998, (1999) 28 EHRR 121, ECHR 1998-IV; *Öğur v Turkey*, (App. 21594/93), 20 May 1999, (2001) 31 EHRR 912, ECHR 1999-III; and *Mojsiewiew v Poland*, (App. 11818/02), 24 March 2009.

[74] *Ramsahai and others v The Netherlands*, (App. 52391/99), 15 May 2007 [GC], (2008) 46 EHRR 983, ECHR 2007-nyr. See also *Giuliani and Gaggio v Italy*, (App. 23458/02), 25 August 2009.

[75] See *Ramsahai*, §§399–431.

[76] *McCann and others v United Kingdom*, (App. 18984/91), 27 September 1995, Series A No 324, (1996) 21 EHRR 97; see above in this chapter.

the killings and gave the relatives of the deceased the opportunity to examine and cross-examine witnesses involved in the operation. More recently, however, in a series of judgments concerning killings by the security forces in Northern Ireland,[77] the Strasbourg Court found violations of Article 2 based on flaws in the inquests.[78]

The son of the applicant in the *Hugh Jordan* case, for example, had been shot and killed by a British police officer. However, this police officer was not a compellable witness under the Northern Irish inquest rules, and declined to give evidence or to be cross-examined, thus seriously detracting from the inquest's power to establish the facts. Moreover, the Northern Irish system also differed from that used in Gibraltar in the *McCann* case (and applicable in England and Wales) in that the jury could not enter a verdict, such as 'unlawful killing'; all it could do was to give the identity of the deceased and the date, place, and direct cause of death. Since the inquest could not, therefore, play an effective role in the identification or prosecution of any criminal offences which might have occurred, the Strasbourg Court found that it fell short of the requirements of Article 2. The Court also criticized the lack of advance disclosure of witness statements to the deceased's family and the delay in the proceedings: over eight years after the death, the inquest had still not come to a conclusion. In the *Finucane* case,[79] the inquest was inadequate because it was limited to identifying the man who shot the applicant's husband (a lawyer who had represented a number of Republican suspects), and could not examine the evidence which suggested that members of the Royal Ulster Constabulary had in some way solicited the killing.[80]

It will apparently not breach Article 2 if soldiers who have been convicted of murder following the shooting of a civilian are, having regard to exceptional circumstances, retained as serving members of the armed forces on their release from custody.[81]

While the early cases have concerned investigations into deaths allegedly caused by a State's security forces, more recently the Court has dealt with cases concerning the investigation of deaths which have occurred in more routine circumstances. It has already been noted that a State is responsible for the proper medical care of prisoners,[82] and others who come into the State's care.[83] The Convention case-law on investigations apply as much to such circumstances as to cases involving the use of force by members of the security forces. Those requirements extend to a death following

---

[77] *Hugh Jordan v United Kingdom*, (App. 24746/94), 4 May 2001, (2003) 37 EHRR 52, ECHR 2001-III; *McKerr v United Kingdom*, (App. 28883/94), 4 May 2001, (2002) 34 EHRR 553, ECHR 2001-III; *Kelly and others v United Kingdom*, (App. 30054/96), 4 May 2001; *Shanaghan v United Kingdom*, (App. 37715/97), 4 May 2001; *McShane v United Kingdom*, (App. 43290/98), 28 May 2002, (2002) 35 EHRR 523; and *Finucane v United Kingdom*, (App. 29178/95), 1 July 2003, (2003) 37 EHRR 656, ECHR 2003-VIII.

[78] See M. Requa and G. Anthony, 'Coroners, controversial deaths, and Northern Ireland's past conflict' [2008] PL 443.

[79] *Finucane v United Kingdom*, (App. 29178/95), 1 July 2003, (2003) 37 EHRR 656, ECHR 2003-VIII.

[80] See, on the lack of independence of the Royal Ulster Constabulary (RUC) in relation to the investigation of certain deaths in Northern Ireland, *Reavey v United Kingdom*, (App. 34640/04), 27 November 2007.

[81] *McBride v United Kingdom*, (App. 1396/06), Decision of 9 May 2006, ECHR 2006-V.

[82] *Gagiu v Romania*, (App. 63258/00), 24 February 2009.

[83] *Mojsiejew v Poland*, (App. 11818/02), 24 March 2009.

treatment in hospital of an ordinary member of the public. The *Šilih* case[84] concerned a 21-year-old man who was being treated for urticaria. He had an allergic reaction to one of the drugs administered to treat his condition, and subsequently died. The case concerned the enquiries into the circumstances of the death, and any liability for it. In Slovenia, this can done through both criminal and civil proceedings. The man's parents used both processes, which proceeded at a snail's pace. This was not a case of absence of procedures, but of the way the procedures had operated in the case of this man's death. The Grand Chamber emphasized the need for a prompt response, especially to a sudden death in a hospital setting. In addition to the excessive length of both sets of proceedings, there were other deficiencies in the operation of the procedure and there was a violation of Article 2.

Despite early dicta to the contrary,[85] it now appears that the obligation to investigate is not confined to cases where it can be established that the death was caused by agents of the State, but also arises wherever life has been lost in circumstances potentially engaging the responsibility of the State.[86] In the *Menson* case,[87] the applicants' brother died after he had been set on fire by four white youths. The applicants did not allege that the State had in any way caused the death, or that the authorities knew, or should have known, that he was at risk of violence. The Strasbourg Court held, nonetheless, that the absence of any direct State responsibility for Menson's death did not exclude the applicability of Article 2. By requiring a Contracting Party to take appropriate steps to safeguard the lives of those within its jurisdiction,[88] Article 2(1) imposed a duty to secure the right to life by putting in place effective criminal law provisions to deter the commission of offences against the person, backed up by law enforcement machinery for the prevention, suppression, and punishment of breaches of such provisions. In the *Menson* case, since the applicants' brother sustained life-threatening injuries in suspicious circumstances, this obligation required by implication that there should be some form of effective official investigation, capable of establishing the cause of the injuries and the identification of those responsible with a view to their punishment. Despite serious shortcomings in the initial police reaction to the attack—which the applicants

---

84 *Šilih v Slovenia*, (App. 71463/01), 9 April 2009 [GC], (2009) 49 EHRR 996, ECHR 2009-nyr.

85 See, for example, *Kurt v Turkey*, (App. 24276/94), 25 May 1998; (1999) 27 EHRR 373, ECHR 1998-III, §107.

86 *Öneryildiz v Turkey*, (App. 48939/99), 30 November 2004 [GC], (2005) 41 EHRR 325, ECHR 2004-XII, §91.

87 *Menson and Others v United Kingdom*, (App. 47916/99), Decision of 6 May 2003, ECHR 2003-V. See also *Yasa v Turkey*, (App. 22495/93), 2 September 1998, (1999) 28 EHRR 408, ECHR 1998-VI, (death caused by unknown assailant); *Ögur v Turke,y* (App. 21594/93), 20 May 1999, (2001) 31 EHRR 912, ECHR 1999-IV, (death caused by warning shot fired into the air by a soldier); *Calvelli and Ciglio v Italy*, (App. 32967/96), 17 January 2002 [GC], ECHR 2002-I, (death caused by negligent medical treatment); *Öneryildiz v Turkey*, (App. 48939/99), 30 November 2004, (2005) 41 EHRR 325, ECHR 2004-XII, (death caused by the negligent operation of a waste disposal site); and *Dodov v Bulgaria*, (App. 59548/00), 17 January 2008, (2008) 47 EHRR 932, ECHR 2008-nyr, (presumed death following disappearance of woman with Alzheimer's disease from a State-run nursing home).

88 *LCB v the United Kingdom*, (App. 23413/94), 9 June 1998, (1998) 27 EHRR 212, ECHR 1998-III; see above in this chapter.

claimed to have arisen from the racist attitudes of the Metropolitan Police—the kill-ers had eventually been prosecuted and convicted. The respondent State's duty under Article 2 had, therefore, been satisfied.

By contrast, the respondent State in the *Angelova and Iliev* case[89] had not satisfied its duty to investigate and prosecute those who had committed murder. A 28-year-old man of Roma origin had been attacked by a group of teenagers and fatally stabbed. The initial action of the police was prompt and a number of youths were brought into custody. But the investigation was complicated by allegations from one of the suspects that the attack had been racially motivated; some of those arrested changed their evi-dence. The investigation stalled, and there was a period of nearly four years when nothing happened at all, and for which no reasonable explanation could be provided. The positive obligation to investigate, and where appropriate prosecute,[90] require 'promptness and reasonable expedition' especially where the death appeared to follow a racially motivated attack.[91]

MEDICAL TERMINATION OF PREGNANCY AND THE RIGHTS OF THE UNBORN CHILD

Unlike Article 4 of the American Convention on Human Rights, which provides that the right to life must be protected 'in general, from the moment of conception', Article 2 of the Convention is silent as to the temporal limitations of the right to life and, in particular, does not define 'everyone' ('*toute personne*') whose 'life' is protected by the Convention.

Having initially refused to examine *in abstracto* the compatibility of abortion laws with Article 2 of the Convention,[92] the Commission acknowledged in the *Brüggemann and Scheuten* case[93] that women complaining under Article 8 of the Convention about the Constitutional Court's decision restricting the availability of abortions had stand-ing as victims. It stated on that occasion: '... pregnancy cannot be said to pertain uniquely to the sphere of private life. Whenever a woman is pregnant her private life becomes closely connected with the developing foetus'. However, the Commission did not find it 'necessary to decide, in this context, whether the unborn child is to be considered as "life" in the sense of Article 2 of the Convention', or whether it could

---

[89] *Angelova and Iliev v Bulgaria*, (App. 55523/00), 26 July 2007, (2008) 47 EHRR 236, ECHR 2007-IX.

[90] See also *Nikolova and Velichkova v Bulgaria*, (App. 7888/03), 20 December 2007, (2009) 48 EHRR 915, §§58–64, and 75.

[91] §§97–8.

[92] See App. 867/60, *X v Norway*, Decision of 29 May 1961, (1961) 6CD 34; and App. 7045/75, *X v Austria*, Decision of 10 December 1976, (1976) 7 DR 87. See also C. Zampas and J. Gher, 'Abortion as a human right: international and regional standards', (2008) 8 HRLRev 249.

[93] App. 6959/75, *Brüggemann and Scheuten v Federal Republic of Germany*, Report of 12 July 1977, (1977) 10 DR 100.

be regarded as an entity which under Article 8(2) could justify an interference 'for the protection of others'. It expressed the opinion that there had been no violation of Article 8 of the Convention because 'not every regulation of the termination of unwanted pregnancies constitutes an interference with the right to respect for the private life of the mother', while emphasizing: 'There is no evidence that it was the intention of the Parties to the Convention to bind themselves in favour of any particular solution'.[94]

In *X v United Kingdom*[95] the Commission considered an application by a man complaining that his wife had been allowed to have an abortion on health grounds. While it accepted that the potential father could be regarded as the 'victim' of a violation of the right to life, it considered that the term 'everyone' as used in the Convention could not apply prenatally, but observed that 'such application in a rare case—e.g. under Article 6, paragraph 1—cannot be excluded'.[96] The Commission added that the general usage of the term 'everyone' and the context in which it was used in Article 2 of the Convention did not include the unborn. As to the term 'life' and, in particular, the beginning of life, the Commission noted a 'divergence of thinking on the question of where life begins' and added:

While some believe that it starts already with conception, others tend to focus upon the moment of nidation, upon the point that the foetus becomes 'viable', or upon live birth.[97]

The Commission went on to examine whether Article 2 was:

to be interpreted: as not covering the foetus at all; as recognising a 'right to life' of the foetus with certain implied limitations; or as recognising an absolute 'right to life' of the foetus.

Although it did not express an opinion on the first two options, it categorically ruled out the third interpretation, having regard to the need to protect the mother's life, which could not be separated from that of the unborn child:

The 'life' of the foetus is intimately connected with, and it cannot be regarded in isolation of, the life of the pregnant woman. If Article 2 were held to cover the foetus and its protection under this Article were, in the absence of any express limitation, seen as absolute, an abortion would have to be considered as prohibited even where the continuance of the pregnancy would involve a serious risk to the life of the pregnant woman. This would mean that the 'unborn life' of the foetus would be regarded as being of a higher value than the life of the pregnant woman.[98]

In the case of *H v Norway*,[99] concerning an abortion carried out on non-medical grounds against the father's wishes, the Commission added that Article 2 required a

---

[94] §§59–64 of the Report.

[95] App. 8416/79, *X v United Kingdom*, Decision of 13 May 1980, (1980) 19 DR 244.

[96] §7. For such an application in connection with access to a court, see App. 24844/94, *Reeve v United Kingdom*, Decision of 30 November 1994, (1995) 79-A DR 146.

[97] §12.

[98] §19.

[99] App. 17004/90, *H v Norway*, Decision of 19 May 1992, (1992) 73 DR 155.

Contracting Party not only to refrain from taking a person's life intentionally but also to take appropriate steps to safeguard life. It considered that it did not have to decide 'whether the foetus may enjoy a certain protection under Article 2, first sentence', but did not exclude the possibility that 'in certain circumstances this may be the case notwithstanding that there is in the Contracting Parties a considerable divergence of views on whether or to what extent Article 2 protects the unborn life.' It further noted that in such a delicate area the Contracting Parties had to have a certain discretion, and concluded that the mother's decision, taken in accordance with Norwegian legislation, had not exceeded that discretion. The Strasbourg Court followed this approach in a more recent case against Italy, also an application by a man complaining about his partner's decision to terminate her pregnancy.[100]

The *Vo* case[101] raised the new issue of whether, apart from cases where the mother has requested an abortion, harming a foetus should be treated as a criminal offence in the light of Article 2 of the Convention, with a view to protecting the right to life of the foetus. Hospital staff confused the identity of the applicant, who was six months pregnant and had come in for a routine check-up, with that of another woman with the same family name who wished to have her intra-uterine device (IUD) removed. As a result of the doctors' negligence the applicant lost her unborn child. She was unable to bring criminal proceedings against the doctors, because, under French law, a foetus could not be the victim of unintentional homicide.

The Strasbourg Court avoided coming to any firm conclusion on the question, observing that:

At European level...there is no consensus on the nature and status of the embryo and/or foetus..., although they are beginning to receive some protection in the light of scientific progress and the potential consequences of research into genetic engineering, medically assisted procreation or embryo experimentation. At best, it may be regarded as common ground between States that the embryo/foetus belongs to the human race. The potentiality of that being and its capacity to become a person—enjoying protection under the civil law, moreover, in many States, such as France, in the context of inheritance and gifts...—require protection in the name of human dignity, without making it a 'person' with the 'right to life' for the purposes of Article 2....[102]

The Court therefore concluded that it was neither desirable, nor even possible as matters stood, to answer in the abstract the question whether the unborn child is a person for the purposes of Article 2 of the Convention ('*personne*' in the French text). The

---

[100] *Boso v Italy*, (App. 50490/99), Decision of 5 September 2002, ECHR 2003-VII. Compare *Roe v Wade*, in the Supreme Court of the United States, 22 January 1973, (1973) 410 US 113, where the Supreme Court held that State laws which decriminalized abortion only where necessary to save the mother's life violated the Due Process Clause of the Fourteenth Amendment of the Constitution, which protects the right to privacy, including a woman's qualified right to terminate her pregnancy (a right which carries less and less weight as the pregnancy continues).

[101] *Vo v France*, (App. 53924/00), 8 July 2004 [GC], (2005) 40 EHRR 259, ECHR 2004-VIII.

[102] §84. Affirmed in *Evans v United Kingdom*, (App. 6339/05), 10 April 2007 [GC], (2008) 46 EHRR 728, ECHR 2007-IV, §§53–6.

State enjoys a margin of appreciation to decide, under its domestic law, when the right to life begins. The Court moreover considered it unnecessary to examine whether the abrupt end to the applicant's pregnancy fell within the scope of Article 2, since, even assuming that that provision was applicable, French law offered sufficient protection against such events, namely the criminal offence of unintentionally causing injury to the mother, and the possibility of bringing civil proceedings for damages.

EUTHANASIA AND THE QUALITY OF LIFE

Since the judgment in the *Pretty* case,[103] it is clear that the right to life in Article 2 does not include a 'right to die'. The applicant suffered from an untreatable motor-neurone disease. Her muscles were becoming progressively weaker, so that at the time of the application she was paralysed from the neck down, had virtually no decipherable speech, and had to be fed through a tube, although her intellect and capacity to make decisions were unimpaired. Her life expectancy was very poor, and the final stages of the disease were expected to be distressing and undignified. She wished her husband to be permitted to assist her suicide without risk of prosecution. The Strasbourg Court observed that the consistent emphasis in its case-law had been the obligation of the State to protect life. Article 2 was unconcerned with issues to do with the quality of life or self-determination.[104]

Assisted suicide[105] has been permitted in certain circumstances in the Netherlands since early 2001,[106] and in Switzerland, but there have not, to date, been any admissible cases under Article 2 brought by a friend or relative complaining about euthanasia carried out by a doctor or authorized by a Contracting Party.[107] The applicant in *Pretty*

---

[103] *Pretty v United Kingdom*, (App. 2346/02), 29 April 2002, (2002) 35 EHRR 1, ECHR 2002-III.

[104] See, on euthanasia generally, Council of Europe, *Euthanasia. Volume I: Ethical and human aspects* (Council of Europe Publishing, Strasbourg 2003); *Volume II: National and European perspectives*, (Council of Europe Publishing, Strasbourg 2004). See also J. Griffiths, H. Weyers, and M. Adams, *Euthanasia and Law in Europe* (Hart, Oxford 2008).

[105] See D. Morris, 'Assisted suicide under the European Convention on Human Rights: a Critique' [2003] EHRLR 65.

[106] The Dutch law provides that it is no longer a criminal offence for a doctor to assist a patient to die if the doctor is convinced that the patient is facing interminable and unendurable suffering and has made a voluntary and well-considered request to die, and as long as the doctor abides by certain safeguards, such as obtaining an independent medical opinion and keeping a written record of the treatment offered. The United Nations Human Rights Committee expressed criticism of this law in a Report published on 28 July 2001.

[107] In *Glass v United Kingdom*, (App. 61827/00), 9 March 2004, (2004) 39 EHRR 341, ECHR 2004-II, the applicants complained about the administration, against the wishes of his parents, of life-shortening morphine-based pain-killers to a very severely disabled child. The Court emphasized in its admissibility decision that there was no evidence that the doctors who prescribed the drugs intended to hasten the child's death; they wished only to alleviate his suffering; and indeed the child survived and was able to return home from hospital. For this reason the applicants' complaint under Article 2 was declared inadmissible and the complaint was examined only under Article 8. The Court found a violation of that provision, on the ground that the hospital authorities should have sought a court ruling before giving the child diamorphine.

case argued that a failure to acknowledge a right to die under the Convention would place such countries which do permit assisted suicide in breach of the Convention. The Strasbourg Court refused to consider this proposition in the abstract, and remarked that, even if circumstances prevailing in a particular country which permitted assisted suicide were found not to infringe Article 2 of the Convention, that would not assist the applicant in establishing 'the very different proposition—that the United Kingdom would be in breach of its obligations under Article 2 if it did not allow assisted suicide…'[108]

CONCLUDING REMARKS

After a slow start, the body of judgments concerning the right to life has now taken its place among the richest and most dynamic of all the Convention case-law. In recent years the scope of the Article, in so far as it relates to the life of the unborn child, and the right of the terminally ill to euthanasia, has been somewhat elucidated.[109] The broad lines, both procedural and substantive, of the prohibition on unlawful killing by agents of the State have been established, although no doubt further detail will emerge as different factual situations are placed before the Court. However, it is in connection with the positive obligation to take measures to safeguard lives that the greatest scope for innovation remains, and it will be interesting to see how far the Strasbourg Court considers it possible to extend the protection afforded by Article 2 without placing too great a burden on the State.

[108] *Pretty v United Kingdom*, (App. 2346/02), 29 April 2002, (2002) 35 EHRR 1, ECHR 2002-III. The Strasbourg Court also rejected the applicant's complaints under Articles 3, 8, and 14 about the ban on assisted suicide.

[109] Note that the Grand Chamber has pending before it *A, B and C v Ireland*, (App. 25579/05), in which three women who travelled to the United Kingdom for medical terminations of their pregnancies and are complaining about the restrictions on the possibility of such terminations in Ireland.

9

PROHIBITION OF TORTURE

INTRODUCTION

Article 3 is the shortest in Section I of the Convention stating simply: 'No one shall be subjected to torture or to inhuman or degrading treatment or punishment.' The fundamental character of the prohibition is affirmed by the fact that no derogation in respect of its provisions is permitted even in time of war or public emergency.[1]

The absolute nature of the prohibition is well illustrated by the *Chahal* case.[2] The United Kingdom wished to deport Chahal, a Sikh separatist, to India arguing that he had been involved in terrorist activities and posed a risk to the national security of the United Kingdom. The Strasbourg Court said:

Article 3 enshrines one of the most fundamental values of democratic society. The Court is well aware of the immense difficulties faced by States in modern times in protecting their communities from terrorist violence. However, even in these circumstances, the Convention prohibits in absolute terms torture or inhuman or degrading treatment or punishment, irrespective of the victim's conduct.[3]

Despite attempts to persuade the Strasbourg Court that the interests of the community as a whole may be taken into account in deciding whether to remove a person whose continued presence might be seen to be a threat to the host country, the Grand Chamber in the *Saadi* case has re-affirmed the absolute nature of the prohibition:

As the prohibition of torture and inhuman and degrading treatment or punishment is absolute, irrespective of the victim's conduct..., the nature of the offence allegedly committed by the applicant is therefore irrelevant for the purposes of Article 3....[4]

---

[1] On Article 3, see generally A. Reidy, *The prohibition of torture: a Guide to the implementation of Article 3 of the European Convention on Human Rights*, Human Rights Handbooks, No. 6 (Council of Europe Publishing, Strasbourg 2003; A. Cassese, 'Prohibition of Torture and Inhuman or Degrading Treatment or Punishment' in R. Macdonald, F. Matscher, and H. Petzold, *The European System for the Protection of Human Rights* (Martinus Nijhoff, Dordrecht 1993), 225; H. Danelius, 'Protection against Torture in Europe and the World' in R. Macdonald, F. Matscher, and H. Petzold, *The European System for the Protection of Human Rights* (Martinus Nijhoff, Dordrecht 1993), at 263; N. Rodley and M. Pollard, *The Treatment of Prisoners under International Law* (OUP, Oxford 2009); S. Levinson, *Torture. A Collection* (OUP, Oxford 2004); and J. Murdoch, *The treatment of prisoners. European standards* (Council of Europe Publishing Strasbourg 2006).

[2] *Chahal v United Kingdom*, (App. 22414/93), 15 November 1996, (1997) 23 EHRR 413, ECHR 1996-V.

[3] §80.

[4] *Saadi v Italy*, (App. 37201/06), 28 February 2008 [GC], (2009) 49 EHRR 730, ECHR 2008-nyr, §127.

The Strasbourg Court described the argument based on the balancing of the risk of harm if the person is removed against their dangerousness to the host State as 'misconceived'.[5] Nor was there any merit in the argument that the risk of ill-treatment should be stronger in those cases where the continued presence of the person in the host State presented a security risk; this was not compatible with the absolute nature of Article 3.[6] But the assessment of the real risk of ill-treatment in the country of destination will always be a rigorous one.[7]

After addressing the issues of definition which arise under Article 3, this chapter explores evidential issues connected with proving conduct falling within the article and the extraterritorial application of Article 3, before examining a number of specific areas where Article 3 has been applied by the Commission and the Court. One disappointing recent development is the frequency with which violations of Article 3 are found by the Court. This reflects only in part its increasing willingness to find violations in a broader range of situations than in earlier years.[8]

DEFINING THE TERMS

ARTICLE 3 IS ONLY CONCERNED WITH CONDUCT WHICH ATTAINS 'A MINIMUM LEVEL OF SEVERITY'

In order for conduct to fall within Article 3, it must 'attain a minimum level of severity'.[9] This test will apply whatever the category of conduct in issue. The effect of setting a significant threshold is that trivial complaints, and even activity which is undesirable or illegal, will not fall within the scope of the prohibition in Article 3 unless it causes sufficiently serious suffering or humiliation to the victim. However, in the *Selmouni* case,[10] the Strasbourg Court indicated that interpretation of the Convention as a living instrument could result in acts classified in the early case-law as inhuman or degrading treatment being classified as torture in the future. Presumably, it would follow that conduct which previously had not attained the threshold for categorization as inhuman or degrading treatment might be so categorized in the future.

In the *Jalloh* case,[11] the Grand Chamber restated the Court's long-standing view:

---

[5] *Saadi*, §139.

[6] §140. See, generally, D. Moeckli, '*Saadi v Italy*: The Rules of the Game Have *Not* Changed' (2008) 8 HRLRev 534.

[7] *NA v United Kingdom*, (App. 25904/07), 17 July 2008, (2009) 48 EHRR 337, ECHR 2008-nyr.

[8] Most notably in relation to various conditions of detention. See later in this chapter.

[9] *Ireland v United Kingdom*, 18 January 1978, Series A No 25, (1979–80) 2 EHRR 25, §162; and *Tyrer v United Kingdom*, 25 April 1978, Series A No 26, (1979–80) 2 EHRR 1, §30.

[10] *Selmouni v France*, (App. 25803/94), 28 July 1999 [GC], (2000) 29 EHRR 403, ECHR 1999-V, §101. See also M. Addo and N. Grief, 'Is there a policy behind the decisions and judgments relating to Article 3 of the European Convention on Human Rights?' (1995) 20 ELRev 178.

[11] *Jalloh v Germany*, (App. 54810/00), 11 July 2006 [GC], (2007) 44 EHRR 667, ECHR 2006-IX.

According to the Court's well-established case-law, ill-treatment must attain a minimum level of severity if it is to fall within the scope of Article 3. The assessment of this minimum level of severity is relative; it depends on all the circumstances of the case, such as the duration of the treatment, its physical and mental effects and, in some cases, the sex, age and state of health of the victim....[12]

So, for example, attacks on an applicant's honesty and way of life which were motivated by racial discrimination constitute an aggravating factor when considering whether treatment accorded to him reached the minimum level of severity.[13] But in another case, the Strasbourg Court found that strip searches of visitors (one of whom had a learning difficulty) to a prison, which were not carried out in accordance with national rules in a number of respects and caused the individuals significant distress, did not reach the minimum level of severity to fall within Article 3, though they did constitute a violation of Article 8.[14] The Strasbourg Court now subjects allegations of violations of Article 3 to a particularly thorough scrutiny even if there has been domestic proceedings and investigations into the allegations. The enquiries in the national legal order must themselves be very thorough, and represent a genuine attempt to find out what happened and who may be responsible for any reprehensible conduct.[15]

THE CONCEPT OF AN ADMINISTRATIVE PRACTICE

Where the factual evidence shows that the complained of action, even though it is unlawful, has been repeated time and again by agents of the State, and where there has been official tolerance of the conduct at more senior level, this has come to be known as an 'administrative practice.' In *Ireland v United Kingdom*, the Strasbourg Court characterized an administrative practice as

an accumulation of identical or analogous breaches which are sufficiently numerous and inter-connected to amount not merely to isolated incidents or exceptions but to a pattern or system....[16]

This has a double significance. First, at the stage of admissibility, the usual requirement to exhaust domestic remedies may well be disregarded.[17] Secondly, on consideration of the merits, the finding of an administrative practice, implying official tolerance of the pattern of conduct, is clearly far more serious than an isolated incident of improper conduct by individuals.

---

[12] §67. See also *Kafkaris v Cyprus*, (App.21906/04), 12 February 2008 [GC], (2009) 49 EHRR 877, ECHR 2008-nyr, §95.

[13] *Moldovan and others v Romania*, (Apps 41138/98 and 64320/01), 12 July 2005, (2007) 44 EHRR 302, ECHR 2005-VII, §111.

[14] *Wainwright v United Kingdom*, (App. 12350/04), 26 September 2006, (2007) 44 EHRR 809, ECHR 2006-X.

[15] See, for example, *Muradova v Azerbaijan* (App. 22684/05) 2 April 2009, §§99 and 101.

[16] *Ireland v United Kingdom*, 18 January 1978, Series A No 25, (1979–80) 2 EHRR 25, §159.

[17] Since legal action in respect of a single incident may not address the repetitive nature of the conduct: Apps. 5577–83/72, *Donnelly and others v United Kingdom*, 5 April 1973, (1973) 16 *Yearbook* 212. See further ch.2 above.

DEFINING TORTURE

The United Nations General Assembly's definition of torture in the 1975 Declaration provides a helpful starting point in stating that:

Torture constitutes an aggravated and deliberate form of cruel, inhuman and degrading treatment or punishment.[18]

Much space was taken up in the Commission's Report in the *Greek* case on the alleged violations of Article 3 by the Greek Government after the revolution of 21 April 1967.[19] However, the leading authority is the judgment of the Strasbourg Court in *Ireland v United Kingdom*, which concluded that:

... it was the intention that the Convention with its distinction between torture and inhuman treatment should by the first of these terms attach a special stigma to deliberate inhuman treatment causing very serious and cruel suffering.[20]

The distinction between torture and inhuman treatment is frequently one of degree. In every case the determination of whether there has been torture, inhuman or degrading treatment must be decided in the light of all the circumstances of the case. In *Ireland v United Kingdom*, the Strasbourg Court suggested that the following factors were relevant in determining the existence of inhuman treatment: the duration of the treatment, its physical or mental effects, and the sex, age and state of health of the victim.[21] In the *Tyrer* judgment, the Court said that the nature and context of the punishment itself, and the manner and method of its execution should be considered in determining whether a punishment constituted degrading treatment.[22] The threshold of seriousness required and the need to consider the relative nature of the conduct in context indicate that the prohibition in Article 3 is not a static one, but receives a living interpretation and must be considered in the light of present-day circumstances.[23]

In *Ireland v United Kingdom*,[24] the Irish Government alleged that persons in custody in Northern Ireland had been subjected to treatment which constituted torture and inhuman and degrading treatment and punishment within the meaning of Article 3 of the Convention and that such treatment constituted an administrative practice. In issue, in particular, were the five techniques for interrogating detained persons in depth, consisting of covering their heads with hoods, obliging them to stand for long periods against a wall with the limbs outstretched, subjecting them to intense noise, depriving them of sleep, and feeding them on a diet of bread and water. After a

---

[18] UNGA Res. 3452 (XXX) of 9 December 1975, Declaration on the protection of all persons from being subjected to torture and other cruel, inhuman or degrading treatment or punishment, Art. 1.

[19] App. 3321/67, *Denmark v Greece*; App. 3322/67, *Norway v Greece*; App. 3323/67, *Sweden v Greece*; and App. 3344/67, *Netherlands v Greece* ('the *Greek* case'), Report of 18 November 1969, (1969) 12 *Yearbook* 1, 186–510.

[20] *Ireland v United Kingdom*, 18 January 1978, Series A No 25, (1979–80) 2 EHRR 25, §167.

[21] §162.   [22] *Tyrer v United Kingdom*, 25 April 1978, Series A No 26, (1979–80) 2 EHRR 1, §30.

[23] *Selmouni v France*, (App. 25803/94), 28 July 1999, (2000) 29 EHRR 403, ECHR 1999-V, §101.

[24] *Ireland v United Kingdom*, 18 January 1978, Series A No 25, (1979–80) 2 EHRR 25.

committee of enquiry in the United Kingdom had looked into these techniques and consideration by Privy Counsellors, the Prime Minister announced in March 1972 that the interrogation techniques would be discontinued. The Commission's Report of February 1976 concluded that the five techniques amounted to torture and inhuman treatment in breach of Article 3.[25] The Irish Government referred the case to the Court which gave judgment in 1978. Rather to the surprise of many, it concluded that the five techniques did not amount to torture, though they did constitute inhuman and degrading treatment. The case is especially important for its contribution to the case-law on the definition of the terms used in Article 3, but it contains many mixed signals. While the majority limited the finding to inhuman and degrading treatment, several judges in the minority concluded that the five techniques amounted to torture and the British judge, Sir Gerald Fitzmaurice, in a powerful, but often considered partial, dissenting opinion concluded that they did not amount even to inhuman and degrading treatment.[26]

In the *Aksoy* case,[27] the Strasbourg Court, for the first time, found a Contracting Party guilty of torture. The applicant had been stripped naked, with his arms tied together behind his back, and suspended by his arms. The Court considered that this form of treatment must have been deliberately inflicted, and was of such a serious and cruel nature that it could only be described as torture.[28] In coming to this conclusion, the Court affirmed what it had said in *Ireland v United Kingdom* and noted:

In order to determine whether any particular form of ill-treatment should be qualified as torture, the Court must have regard to the distinction drawn in Article 3 between this notion and that of inhuman or degrading treatment. As it has remarked before, this distinction would appear to have been embodied in the Convention to allow the special stigma of 'torture' to attach only to deliberate inhuman treatment causing very serious and cruel suffering.[29]

Findings of torture have since been made in many other cases against a number of Contracting Parties. This greater willingness to categorize conduct as torture was signalled in the *Selmouni* case.[30] The case concerned ill-treatment in France of persons suspected of involvement in drug-trafficking. The applicant was, over a number of days, exposed to severe beatings, made to run along a corridor with police officers on either side to trip him up, invited to suck a police officer's penis, urinated upon, and threatened with a blowlamp and then a syringe. The Strasbourg Court concluded, unanimously, that the physical and mental violence, considered as a whole caused severe pain and suffering that was particularly serious and cruel, and was properly

---

[25] (1976) 19 *Yearbook* 512, 774–6.

[26] See M. O'Boyle, 'Torture and Emergency Powers under the European Convention on Human Rights' (1977) 71 AJIL 674; and D. Bonner, '*Ireland v United Kingdom*' (1978) 27 ICLQ 897.

[27] *Aksoy v Turkey*, (App. 21987/93), 18 December 1996, (1997) 23 EHRR 553, ECHR 1996-VI.

[28] §64.

[29] §63.

[30] *Selmouni v France*, (App. 25803/94), 28 July 1999, (2000) 29 EHRR 403, ECHR 1999-V, §101.

categorized as torture. It is almost certain that if similar facts to those in *Ireland v United Kingdom* came before the Strasbourg Court today, it would have no hesitation in categorizing the interrogation techniques as torture.

Unsurprisingly, repeated beating and rape of a witness by the police has been found to amount to torture.[31] It is particularly shocking that such conduct could happen in one of the Contracting Parties to the European Convention.

DEFINING INHUMAN TREATMENT

Inhuman treatment need not necessarily be deliberate.[32] All the circumstances of the case must be considered. The Strasbourg Court has repeatedly said:

Treatment has been held by the Court to be 'inhuman' because, *inter alia*, it was premeditated, was applied for hours at a stretch and caused either actual bodily injury or intense physical and mental suffering, and also 'degrading' because it was such as to arouse in its victims feelings of fear, anguish and inferiority capable of humiliating and debasing them. In order for a punishment or treatment associated with it to be 'inhuman' or 'degrading', the suffering or humiliation involved must in any event go beyond that inevitable element of suffering or humiliation connected with a given form of legitimate treatment or punishment. The question whether the purpose of the treatment was to humiliate or debase the victim is a further factor to be taken into account but the absence of any such purpose cannot conclusively rule out a finding of a violation of Article 3.[33]

It seems that beatings by the police will not attain the threshold to constitute torture where they occur 'over a short period of heightened tension and emotions' and where there are no aggravating factors, such as an aim to extract a confession, or conduct with racist motivation. Such conduct will, however, constitute inhuman treatment.[34]

The following situations have been found by the Court to amount to inhuman treatment:[35] ill-treatment in detention, deportation or extradition where there is a real risk of inhuman treatment in the proposed country of destination, anxiety caused by failure to carry out a proper investigation into a disappearance, and destruction of personal property.

Solitary confinement of a prisoner which involves complete sensory isolation would constitute a form of inhuman treatment, although restrictions on association with other prisoners for security reasons, and limitations on visits, would not, of themselves, constitute inhuman punishment or treatment. It might well be otherwise when

---

[31] *Maslova and Nalbandov v Russia*, (App. 839/02), 24 January 2008, ECHR 2008-nyr.

[32] *Labita v Italy*, (App. 26772/95), 6 April 2000 [GC], (2008) 46 EHRR 1228, ECHR 2000-IV, §120.

[33] *T & V v United Kingdom*, (Apps. 24888/94 and 24724/94), 16 December 1999 [GC], (2000) 30 EHRR 121, ECHR 1999-IX, §71. See also *Jalloh v Germany*, (App. 54810/00), 11 July 2006 [GC], (2007) 44 EHRR 667, ECHR 2006-IX, §68.

[34] See, for example, *Egmez v Cyprus*, (App. 30873/96), 21 December 2000, (2002) 34 EHRR 753, ECHR 2000-XII, §78.

[35] See further below in this chapter.

particular circumstances, such as the health of the individual or the duration of the restrictions, are considered.[36]

Sometimes the Strasbourg Court does not distinguish between inhuman and degrading treatment. So in the case of *II v Bulgaria*,[37] the Strasbourg Court categorized simply as 'inhuman and degrading treatment' the detention of an individual for three months in a very small cell without any natural light or satisfactory ventilation, coupled with poor sanitary facilities and no provision for spending time out of his cell.[38]

In the *Öcalan* case,[39] the Court concluded that the imposition of the death penalty after an unfair trial would constitute a breach of Article 2; and this conclusion informed their finding that the imposition of the death penalty after an unfair trial would also constitute inhuman treatment.[40]

DEFINING DEGRADING TREATMENT

As noted above, it has sometimes been said that degrading treatment requires the presence of gross humiliation before others or being driven to act against will or conscience. However, the Strasbourg Court has stated on several occasions that gross humiliation, as the purpose of the acts in issue, is not always a necessary ingredient of degrading treatment.[41] Nor is intention to humiliate.[42] But where humiliation or debasement is present, the threshold of severity would appear to require that the humiliation is severe. The process of investigation and discharge of homosexuals in the armed forces was found not to reach the requisite threshold in the *Smith and Grady* case.[43] The Court, however, noted that it would not exclude the possibility that treatment 'grounded upon a predisposed bias on the part of a heterosexual majority against a homosexual minority' could fall within the scope of Article 3.

The Commission has considered that racial discrimination could constitute degrading treatment.[44] In the *Marckx* case[45] the Court ruled that legal rules

---

[36] *Öcalan v Turkey*, (App. 46221/99), 12 May 2005 [GC], (2005) 41 EHRR 985, ECHR 2005-IV, §191.

[37] *II v Bulgaria*, (App. 44082/98), 9 June 2005. See also *Mayzit v Russia*, (App. 63378/00), 20 January 2005.

[38] On prison conditions, see further below in this chapter.

[39] *Öcalan v Turkey*, (App. 46221/99), 12 May 2005 [GC], (2005) 41 EHRR 985, ECHR 2005-IV.

[40] §169. Note that in *Ilaşcu and others v Moldova and Russia*, (App. 48787/99), 8 July 2004 [GC], (2005) 40 EHRR 1030, ECHR 2004-VII, §§434–42, the Court found that living in the 'constant shadow of death' for some years by reason of a death sentence which had no legal basis or legitimacy, coupled with the conditions of the applicant's detention, amounted to torture.

[41] See, for example, *Poltoratskiy v Ukraine*, (App. 38812/97), 29 April 2003, ECHR 2003-V, §131.

[42] *Peers v Greece*, (App. 28524/95), 19 April 2001, (2001) 33 EHRR 1192, ECHR 2001-III.

[43] *Smith and Grady v United Kingdom*, (Apps. 33985/96 and 33986/96), 27 September 1999, (2000) 29 EHRR 493, ECHR 1999-VI, §§120–3.

[44] Apps. 4403–19/70, 4422/70, 4434/70, 4476–8/70, 4486/70, 4501/70, 4526–30/70, *East African Asians v United Kingdom*, Decision of the Commission, 10 and 18 October 1970 (1970) 13 *Yearbook* 928; Report of the Commission, 14 December 1973 (1994) 78-A DR 5; Committee of Ministers Resolution DH (77) 2 of 21 October 1977 (1977) 20 *Yearbook* 642; and Committee of Ministers Resolution DH (94) 30 of 21 March 1994 (1994) 78-A DR 70, deciding to make the Report of the Commission public at the request of the United Kingdom Government; (1981) 3 EHRR 76, §§207–8 of the Report.

[45] *Marckx v Belgium*, 13 June 1979, Series A No 31, (1979–80) 2 EHRR 330.

discriminating against illegitimate children did not constitute degrading treatment within Article 3, though the case might be decided differently if the same situation arose today. In *Cyprus v Turkey*[46] the Strasbourg Court found that Greek Cypriots living in the Karpas region of northern Cyprus had been subject to discriminatory treatment which attained a level of severity which amounted to degrading treatment.[47]

The *Moldovan* case[48] concerned the treatment by Romania of Romanian nationals of Roma origin, whose homes were destroyed with the involvement of State officials, who had also mismanaged the reconstruction programme such that the applicants and their families had been forced to live for a considerable period of time in 'cellars, hen-houses, stables, burned out shells, or to move in with friends and relatives in such overcrowded conditions that illness frequently occurred.'[49] The Strasbourg Court considered that a particularly serious violation of Article 8 of a continuing nature aggravated by racial motives constituted degrading treatment, since it involved an interference with the applicants' human dignity.

The circumstances of arrest or detention in connection with court proceedings can fall within Article 3 where the humiliation or debasement to which it gives rise attains a special level which significantly differs from that inherent in the process.[50] Placing defendants who present no substantiated security risk in a metal cage in court for their trial will constitute a violation of Article 3.[51] The cumulative effect of the conditions of detention can also be relevant.[52] Applying these principles, the Court characterized as degrading treatment the repeated prosecution and sentence of a conscientious objector under the military penal code for refusal to wear a uniform.[53]

DISTINGUISHING PUNISHMENT AND TREATMENT

Punishment is given its ordinary meaning, but it is not normally necessary to distinguish between treatment and punishment. Punishment and treatment are often not subject to separate analysis, since in many cases punishment must involve treatment. Sometimes the Strasbourg Court simply categorizes the punishment as 'inhuman or degrading treatment' taken together.[54] Birching as a punishment of a juvenile on

---

[46] *Cyprus v Turkey*, (App. 25781/94), 10 May 2001, (2002) 35 EHRR 731, ECHR 2001-IV.
[47] §§302–11.
[48] *Moldovan and others v Romania*, (Apps 41138/98 and 64320/01), 12 July 2005, (2007) 44 EHRR 302, ECHR 2005-VII.
[49] §90.
[50] *Raninen v Finland*, (App. 20972/92), 16 December 1997, (1998) 26 EHRR 563, ECHR 1997-VIII, §55.
[51] *Ramishvili and Kokhreidze v Georgia*, (App. 1704/06), 27 January 2009, §§96–102.
[52] *Dougoz v Greece*, (App. 40907/98), 6 March 2001, (2002) 34 EHRR 1480, §46.
[53] *Ülke v Turkey*, (App. 39437/98), 24 January 2006.
[54] *II v Bulgaria*, (App. 44082/98), 9 June 2005. See also *Mayzit v Russia*, (App. 63378/00), 20 January 2005.

conviction of a crime was found to be degrading but not inhuman punishment.[55] In another case, requiring a person doing military service to undertake as a punishment an activity (350 knee bends) which severely exacerbated a known medical condition was found to constitute an inhuman punishment.[56]

The Court has said that a sentence whose severity bore no relationship to the offence could amount to an inhuman punishment.[57] Article 3 must, however, also be regarded as setting an absolute limit, based on respect for the human person, to what punishment is permissible, regardless of its label, and regardless also of the victim's own conduct. Article 3 should be considered as imposing an absolute prohibition of certain forms of punishment such as flogging, which are by their very nature inhuman and degrading. Within that limit, all the circumstances of the individual cases are relevant.

A particular issue has arisen in relation to life sentences, and whether the absence of any hope of release constitutes inhuman or degrading treatment. In the *Kafkaris* case,[58] the Strasbourg Court said that the imposition of a life sentence on an adult offender was not in itself incompatible with any provision of the Convention.[59] However, the existence of some system for consideration of release[60] is a factor to be taken into account in assessing the compatibility of the sentence with Article 3. Notwithstanding significant developments in penal policy among the Contracting Parties, the Grand Chamber[61] found no violation of Article 3 under the system in Cyprus under which early release of those sentenced to life imprisonment rested entirely on the discretion of the executive.

POSITIVE OBLIGATIONS

In the *Moldovan* case,[62] The Strasbourg Court said:

The obligation of the High Contracting Parties under Article 1 of the Convention to secure to everyone within their jurisdiction the rights and freedoms defined in the Convention, taken together with Article 3, requires States to take measures designed to ensure that

---

[55] *Tyrer v United Kingdom*, 25 April 1978, Series A No 26, (1979–80) 2 EHRR 1. See below on issues raised under Article 3 by the use of corporal punishment.

[56] *Chember v Russia*, (App. 7188/03), 3 July 2008, ECHR 2008-nyr.

[57] *Weeks v United Kingdom*, 2 March 1987, Series A No 114, (1988) 10 EHRR 293, §47.

[58] *Kafkaris v Cyprus*, (App. 21906/04), 12 February 2008 [GC], (2009) 49 EHRR 877, ECHR 2008-nyr. See also *Léger v France*, (App. 19324/02), 11 April 2006, referred to the Grand Chamber but struck out of the list on 30 March 2009 following the death of the applicant.

[59] *Kafkaris v Cyprus*, (App. 21906/04), 12 February 2008 [GC], (2009) 49 EHRR 877, ECHR 2008-nyr, §97.

[60] Which need not be a formal system of parole: §104–5.

[61] By ten votes to seven.

[62] *Moldovan and others v Romania*, (Apps 41138/98 and 64320/01), 12 July 2005, (2007) 44 EHRR 302, ECHR 2005-VII.

individuals within their jurisdiction are not subjected to ill-treatment, including ill-treatment administered by private individuals....[63]

Positive obligations under Article 3 would appear to involve two elements. First, there must be measures in the Contracting Party which constitute effective deterrence. This will involve the categorization of many forms of conduct as criminal activity; this issue alone seldom troubles the Strasbourg Court. It is more often the operation in practice of the law which gives rise to concerns. In the *Okkali* case,[64] a 12-year-old boy had been beaten by police interrogators. The Court found a violation of Article 3 because the application of the criminal law had lacked rigour and so did not have a dissuasive effect capable of ensuring effective protection from inhuman and degrading treatment. In the earlier *A* case,[65] which had concerned the availability of a defence of 'reasonable chastisement' in the context of the beating of a nine-year-old boy with a stick by his stepfather, the Court had ruled that children and other vulnerable individuals were entitled to State protection in the form of effective deterrence against beatings which constituted a serious breach of their personal integrity. Placing the burden of proof on the prosecution to establish beyond reasonable doubt that the beating went beyond the limits of reasonable chastisement, when the defence was raised, did not provide adequate protection.[66]

The second requirement is for an effective investigation capable of leading to prosecution of well-founded allegations of ill-treatment.[67] The investigation must be thorough, expedient, and independent,[68] with the capacity to lead to the identification of the perpetrators whether agents of the State, or private individuals.[69] This requirement has given rise to a significant case-law.

The Strasbourg Court has not been entirely consistent in spelling out the source of the obligation to conduct an effective investigation. In the *Aksoy* case,[70] the Court said that the obligation flowed from Article 13 requiring the State to provide an effective remedy in its national legal order.

In the *Sevtap Veznedaroglu* case[71] the Strasbourg Court recapitulated its case-law in the following terms, rooting the obligation more firmly within Article 3:

[T]he Court reiterates that, where an individual raises an arguable claim that he has been seriously ill-treated by the police or other such agents of the State unlawfully and in breach

---

[63] §98.   [64] *Okkali v Turkey*, (App. 52067/99), 17 October 2006, ECHR 2006-XII.

[65] *A v United Kingdom*, (App. 25599/94), 23 September 1998, (1999) 27 EHRR 611, ECHR 1998-VI.

[66] §§22–4; the need for amendment to the law as accepted by the respondent State before the Court. See also *Opuz v Turkey*, (App. 33401/02), 9 June 2009, where the Court found that the response of the authorities to complaints of domestic violence were 'manifestly inadequate'.

[67] The requirements of investigations under Articles 2 and 3 are similar: see ch.8 above.

[68] *Akkoç v Turkey*, (Apps. 22947/93 and 22948/93), 10 October 2000, (2002) 34 EHRR 1173, ECHR 2000-X, §118. See also *Mikheyev v Russia*, (App. 77617/01), 26 January 2006, §§107–10.

[69] See, for example, *Šečić v Croatia*, (App. 40116/02), 31 May 2007, (2009) 49 EHRR 408, ECHR 2007-nyr.

[70] *Aksoy v Turkey*, (App. 21987/93), 18 December 1996, (1997) 23 EHRR 553, ECHR 1996-VI, §98. See also *Assenov v Bulgaria*, (App. 24760/94), 28 October 1998, (1999) 28 EHRR 652, ECHR 1998-VIII, §§117–18.

[71] *Sevtap Veznedaroglu v Turkey*, (App. 32357/96), 11 April 2000, (2001) 33 EHRR 1412.

of Article 3, that provision, read in conjunction with the State's general duty under Article 1 of the Convention to 'secure to everyone within their jurisdiction the rights and freedoms defined in … [the] Convention' requires by implication that there should be an effective official investigation capable of leading to the identification and punishment of those responsible…. If this were not the case, the general legal prohibition of torture and inhuman and degrading treatment and punishment, despite its fundamental importance, would be ineffective in practice and it would be possible in some cases for agents of the State to abuse the rights of those within their control with virtual impunity.[72]

The obligation is later described as a 'procedural obligation' which devolves on the State under Article 3.[73] Failures of the judicial authorities to take up investigations will also engage the obligation in Article 3.[74]

Where the conduct complained of is that of private parties, rather different considerations apply. The leading authorities are the cases of *Costello-Roberts*[75] and *A*.[76] The *Costello-Roberts* case concerned the use of corporal punishment in private schools, while the *A* case concerned the beating of a child by his stepfather. The Strasbourg Court ruled in both cases that Contracting Parties had an obligation under Article 3 to ensure that those within their jurisdiction are not subjected to treatment prohibited by Article 3, even where that treatment was meted out by private individuals.

The Court has restated this view in the *Z and others* case,[77] which concerned four children who had been subject to severe parental abuse known to the authorities in October 1987. The children had, however, not been taken into care until 1992. The respondent State did not contest the Commission's finding that the suffering of the children amounted to inhuman and degrading treatment, nor that it had failed to provide the children with adequate protection against such treatment. The Strasbourg Court made clear that the positive obligation on States is to take measures:

to ensure that individuals within their jurisdiction are not subjected to torture or inhuman or degrading treatment, including such ill-treatment administered by private individuals…. These measures should provide effective protection, in particular, of children and other vulnerable persons and include reasonable steps to prevent ill-treatment of which the authorities had or ought to have had knowledge.[78]

EVIDENTIAL ISSUES

Because a finding that a Contracting Party is guilty of torture, or even of inhuman and degrading treatment, carries a certain stigma, the Convention organs have required a very high standard of proof of the conduct, even using the term 'beyond reasonable

---

[72] §32.   [73] §35.

[74] *Elci and others v Turkey*, (Apps. 23145 and 25091/94), 13 November 2003.

[75] *Costello-Roberts v United Kingdom*, 25 March 1993, Series A No 247-C, (1994) 19 EHRR 112.

[76] *A v United Kingdom*, (App. 25599/94), 23 September 1998, (1999) 27 EHRR 611, ECHR 1998-VI.

[77] *Z and others v United Kingdom*, (App. 29392/95), 10 May 2001 [GC], (2002) 34 EHRR 97, ECHR 2001-V.

[78] §73.

doubt' in the *Ireland v United Kingdom* case.[79] In the *Nachova* case,[80] the Grand Chamber explained in more detail what it meant in using the term 'beyond reasonable doubt'. This is not simply the transplantation of any similar notion from the national legal orders, and the Court has no preconceived notion of procedural barriers to the admissibility of evidence:

According to its established case-law, proof may follow from the coexistence of sufficiently strong, clear and concordant inferences or of similar unrebutted presumptions of fact. Moreover, the level of persuasion necessary for reaching a particular conclusion and, in this connection, the distribution of the burden of proof are intrinsically linked to the specificity of the facts, the nature of the allegation made and the Convention right at stake. The Court is also attentive to the seriousness that attaches to a ruling that a Contracting State has violated fundamental rights....[81]

There will often be considerable dispute as to the facts where allegations of violations of Article 3 are brought before the Court. The victim may well not be in as strong a position as the Contracting Party in relation to the collection and presentation of evidence. The Court has been sensitive to this problem, while also recognizing that there must be compelling proof of a Contracting Party's failure before condemning it under the Article.[82]

As already noted, an obligation on the authorities to conduct a proper, timely, and conscientious investigation of allegations of ill-treatment by agents of the State is a feature of Article 3.[83] Failure to meet this obligation also has evidential implications. The starting point is that any allegations of ill-treatment must be supported by appropriate evidence.[84] The State will then be expected to offer some explanation as to the cause of injuries of which there is cogent evidence.[85] If they cannot do so, the Court will draw appropriate inferences from evidence that an applicant had suffered unexplained injuries during, for example, a period of police custody.[86]

---

[79] *Ireland v United Kingdom*, 18 January 1978, Series A No 25, (1979–80) 2 EHRR 25, §161. See generally, R. Wolfrum, 'The Taking and Assessment of Evidence by the European Court of Human Rights' in S. Breitenmoser and others, *Human Rights, Democracy and the Rule of Law. Liber amicorum Luzius Wildhaber,* (Nomos, Baden-Baden 2007), 915.

[80] *Nachova and others v Bulgaria,* (Apps. 43577/98 and 43579/98), 6 July 2005 [GC], (2006) 42 EHRR 933, ECHR 2005-VII.

[81] §147.

[82] For a critical discussion of evidential issues, see U. Erdal, 'Burden and standard of proof in proceedings under the European Convention' (2001) 26 ELRev HR65.

[83] *Satik and others v Turkey,* (App. 31866/96), 10 October 2000.

[84] Reports by the Committee for the Prevention of Torture are increasingly being referred to by the Court in its judgments. See below in this chapter on the work of the Committee.

[85] *Tomasi v France,* 27 August 1992, Series A No 241-A, (1993) 15 EHRR 1, §109. See also *Selmouni v France,* (App. 25803/94), 28 July 1999, (2000) 29 EHRR 403, ECHR 1999-V, §87; and *Labita v Italy,* (App. 26772/95), 6 April 2000 [GC], (2008) 46 EHRR 1228, ECHR 2000-IV, §131.

[86] See, for example, *Klaas v Germany,* 22 September 1993, Series A No 269, (1994) 18 EHRR 305, §30; and *Mikheyev v Russia,* (App. 77617/01), 26 January 2006.

The Strasbourg Court's approach to internal investigations can, accordingly, have a double sting in the tail. A failure to conduct a proper and timely investigation may itself constitute a violation of the Convention, but the absence of such an investigation is likely to make it difficult to provide a plausible explanation for injuries suffered by applicants and, in effect, supports the evidence of applicants.[87]

EXTRATERRITORIAL EFFECT

In certain circumstances Article 3 can have an extraterritorial effect. In the *Soering* case,[88] the Strasbourg Court recognized that a Contracting Party may violate the obligations in Article 3 if its action exposes a person to the likelihood of ill-treatment in a place outside the jurisdiction of the Contracting Parties. The case concerned possible deportation to the United States where the 'death row phenomenon' was regarded as inhuman punishment. The Court made clear that the violation of the Convention in such circumstances is that of the sending State, and, by implication, the Court is not seeking to pass any judgment on a State which is not a party to the Convention.[89]

In the *Chahal* case,[90] the United Kingdom was precluded from returning a Sikh separatist to India, because the Court concluded that there would be a very real risk that the applicant would be the victim of ill-treatment at the hands of rogue elements within the Punjab Police. In the *Ahmed* case,[91] the Court found that the applicant, a Somali national living in Austria who was convicted of attempted robbery, would, if returned to Somalia where a civil war was raging, be exposed to a serious risk of being subjected to ill-treatment which would fall within the scope of Article 3.[92]

The Court in the *HLR* case[93] had to consider a claim by a convicted cocaine trafficker, who was a Colombian national and who had provided information to the authorities on the instigators of the traffic, that he should not be returned to Colombia, since 'he would be exposed to vengeance by the drug traffickers who had recruited him as a smuggler.'[94] While the Court did not exclude the possibility that the extraterritorial effect of Article 3 would apply where the serious threat of ill-treatment was at the hands of private parties, they were not convinced in this case that there was such a

---

[87] See, for examples, *Hasan Kiliç v Turkey*, (App. 35044/97), 28 June 2005; *Karakaş and Yeşilirmak v Turkey*, (App. 43925/98), 28 June 2005; and *SB and HT v Turkey*, (App. 54430/00), 5 July 2005.

[88] *Soering v United Kingdom*, 7 July 1989, Series A No 161, (1989) 11 EHRR 439. The case is discussed further below.

[89] §91.

[90] *Chahal v United Kingdom*, (App. 22414/93), 15 November 1996, (1997) 23 EHRR 413, ECHR 1996-V.

[91] *Ahmed v Austria*, (App. 25964/94), 17 December 1996, (1997) 24 EHRR 278.

[92] In *Othman v United Kingdom*, (App. 8139/09), a case pending before the Court, Abu Qatada is arguing that he should not be deported to Jordan since there is a real risk that torture evidence will be used against him there. On the use of evidence obtained by torture see ch.13 below.

[93] *HLR v France*, (App. 24573/94), 29 April 1997, (1998) 26 EHRR 29, ECHR 1997-III.

[94] §30.

serious risk. The six dissenting judges, in essence, disagreed with the assessment of the majority on the nature of the risk; their view is probably to be preferred.

The *D* case[95] presented a rather different set of circumstances, though the applicant was again a convicted drug smuggler. D was a national of St Kitts, who had been arrested at Gatwick Airport in possession of a large quantity of cocaine. While serving a prison sentence, he was discovered to be suffering from AIDS. As is normal, on completion of his prison sentence, he was subject to deportation back to St Kitts. He argued that he was in the advanced stages of the illness, medical services in St Kitts would be unable to provide treatment for his condition, and he had no relatives or friends in St Kitts who could care for him. This, he argued, would constitute treatment in breach of Article 3. The risk he had identified was, unlike the earlier cases, not a risk of intentional ill-treatment emanating from public authorities or private groups in his State of origin, but inherent inadequacies in the medical services in his home country. The Court emphasized the fundamental nature of the protection afforded by Article 3, and was clearly influenced by the consequences of the abrupt withdrawal of the medical and personal care afforded to him in the United Kingdom by the Terrence Higgins Trust, a leading AIDS charity. In the 'very exceptional circumstances'[96] of this case, the Court concluded that deportation to St Kitts would be a violation of Article 3 amounting to inhuman treatment.

In the *N* case,[97] the Grand Chamber clarified that the deportation of a person suffering from HIV or AIDS would not normally give rise to a violation of Article 3, even where the level of treatment available in the country of origin would be likely to fall far short of that enjoyed in the deporting State. The likelihood of a dramatically reduced life expectancy and the suffering attendant on dying from an AIDS-related disease would not amount to 'exceptional circumstances'. It would seem that only the removal of a person who was actually on the point of death, as in the *D* case, or possibly a pregnant woman whose child could be saved by anti-retroviral medication during pregnancy and immediately after birth, would give rise to a violation of Article 3. The Court in the *N* case stated that similar principles would apply in relation to the removal of a non-national suffering not just from AIDS or HIV but from any life-threatening physical or mental illness.[98]

However, there is no extraterritorial effect arising in circumstances where a national has been subjected to torture abroad.[99]

In the *Jabari* case,[100] the Court considered that the deportation to Iran of a woman, who had been found to have had an adulterous relationship in that country in respect

---

[95] *D v United Kingdom*, (App. 30240/96), 2 May 1997, (1997) 24 EHRR 423, ECHR 1997-III.

[96] §54.

[97] *N v United Kingdom*, (App. 26565/05), 27 May 2008, ECHR 2008-nyr.

[98] See also *Bensaid v United Kingdom*, (App. 44599/98), 6 February 2001, (2001) 33 EHRR 205, ECHR 2001-I, where no violation was found.

[99] *Al-Adsani v United Kingdom*, (App. 35763/97), 21 November 2001 [GC], (2002) 34 EHRR 273, ECHR 2001-XI, §§35–41.

[100] *Jabari v Turkey*, (App. 40035/98), 11 July 2000, ECHR 2000-VIII.

of which criminal proceedings had been instituted, would violate Article 3 because she would be at serious risk of punishment by stoning there. In an admissibility decision, the Court accepted that if a person deported to Nigeria could show a real risk of being subject to female genital mutilation, Article 3 would be engaged.[101]

There is nothing wrong in obtaining assurances from the receiving State that a person to be extradited will not be sentenced to death or life imprisonment, as in the *Olaechea Cahuas* case,[102] where Peru gave such an undertaking.

In determining whether there would be a risk that a person would be subject to treatment falling within Article 3 if removed to another country, the Strasbourg Court will take account of reports of non-governmental organizations (such as Amnesty International),[103] but may conclude that such findings constitute a description of the general situation and do not support specific allegations made by applicants to the Strasbourg Court,[104] which will require corroboration by other evidence. Present circumstances, rather than the historical position, will always be decisive. In the *Mamatkulov and Askarov* case, the Grand Chamber stated the requirements as follows:

In determining whether substantial grounds have been shown for believing that a real risk of treatment contrary to Article 3 exists, the Court will assess the issue in the light of all the material placed before it or, if necessary, material obtained *proprio motu*. Since the nature of the Contracting States' responsibility in cases of this kind lies in the act of exposing an individual to the risk of ill-treatment, the existence of the risk must be assessed primarily with reference to those facts which were known or ought to have been known to the Contracting State at the time of extradition; the Court is not precluded, however, from having regard to information which comes to light subsequent to the extradition. This may have value in confirming or refuting the appreciation that has been made by the Contracting Party of the well-foundedness or otherwise of an applicant's fears.[105]

Where the applicant has not been extradited or deported when the Court examines the case, the Court will assess the risk of ill-treatment at the time of the proceedings before the Court. This situation typically arises when deportation or extradition is delayed as a result of an indication by the Court of interim measures under rule 39 of the Rules of Court. Such an indication means more often than not that the Court does not yet have before it all the relevant evidence it requires to determine whether there is a real risk of treatment proscribed by Article 3 in the country of destination.[106] There has been an worrying increase in the number of occasions when a Contracting Party

---

[101] *Collins and Akaziebe v Sweden*, (App. 23944/05), Decision of 8 March 2007, ECHR 2007-nyr, though there was no such risk established on the facts of this application.

[102] *Olaechea Cahuas v Spain*, (App. 24668/03), 10 August 2006, (2009) 48 EHRR 572, ECHR 2006-X.

[103] *Saadi v Italy*, (App. 37201/06), 28 February 2008 [GC], (2009) 49 EHRR 730, ECHR 2008-nyr, §138. See also *NA v United Kingdom*, (App. 25904/07), 17 July 2008, (2009) 48 EHRR 337, ECHR 2008-nyr.

[104] As it did in *Mamatkulov and Askarov v Turkey*, (Apps. 46827/99 and 46951/99), 4 February 2005 [GC], (2005) 41 EHRR 494, ECHR 2005-I.

[105] §69.

[106] §69. See also *N v Finland*, (App. 38885/02), 26 July 2005.

fails to comply with these interim measures, which will frequently result in a finding of a violation of Article 34.[107]

In somewhat exceptional circumstances, the Strasbourg Court has ruled that removal of a person from Georgia to Russia[108] would constitute a violation of Article 3 given the evidence of persecution in Russia of individuals of Chechen origin who have lodged applications with the Strasbourg Court.[109]

Where deportation of an unaccompanied young child is involved, there must be proper arrangements for the welfare of the child both throughout the journey and on arrival at the destination. Failure to put such arrangements in place will violate Article 3.[110]

DISAPPEARANCES

A number of cases have addressed the application of Article 3 to situations where a close relative of the applicant has disappeared, and the events surrounding the disappearance have not been sufficiently investigated by the authorities.[111] The *Kurt* case,[112] which was an application by a mother in relation to her disappeared son, appears to be the first consideration by the Strasbourg Court of this issue under Article 3. The Court accepted that the uncertainty, doubt, and apprehension suffered by the applicant over a prolonged and continuing period caused her severe mental distress and anguish. The authorities failed to give serious consideration to her requests for information about his whereabouts. The Commission had concluded that this constituted inhuman and degrading treatment. The Court simply categorizes it as a breach of Article 3.

The Court in the *Çakici* case[113] established some general principles governing disappearance cases. The applicant claimed that his brother had been detained by the authorities in November 1993. He subsequently disappeared. The applicant said that

---

[107] For example, *Olaechea Cahuas v Spain*, (App. 24668/03), 10 August 2006, (2009) 48 EHRR 572, ECHR 2006-X; and *Paladi v Moldova* (App. 39806/05) 10 March 2009 [GC]. Note also the reported handover on 31 December 2008, in breach of interim measures ordered by the Strasbourg Court, to Iraqi authorities by British forces in Iraq of Faisal Al-Saadoon and Khalaf Mufdhi, who are accused of murdering two British soldiers: *Al-Saadoon and Mufdhi v United Kingdom*, (App. 61498/08), Decision of 30 June 2009 (2009) 49 EHRR SE11.

[108] Note that both States are Contracting Parties.

[109] *Shamayev and others v Georgia and Russia*, (App. 36378/02), 12 April 2005, ECHR 2005-III, §§366–8.

[110] *Mubilanzila Mayeka and Kaniki Mitunga v Belgium*, (App. 13178/03), 12 June 2006, (2008) 46 EHRR 449, ECHR 2006-XI.

[111] For a definition of the phenomenon of disappearances, see ch.8 above. For an account of the cases against Russia arising from its conduct in Chechnya, see P. Leach, 'The Chechen Conflict: Analysing the Oversight of the European Court of Human Rights' [2008] EHRLR 732.

[112] *Kurt v Turkey*, (App. 24276/94), 25 May 1998, (1999) 27 EHRR 373, ECHR 1998-III. The Court appears to have drawn some inspiration from the decision of the United Nations Human Rights Committee in *Quinteros v Uruguay*, 21 July 1983, Case 107/1981, (1983) 38 UNGAOR Supp. 40 Annex XXI, §14.

[113] *Çakici v Turkey*, (App. 23657/94), 8 July 1999 [GC], (2001) 31 EHRR 133, ECHR 1999-IV.

in May 1996 he was told by the authorities that his brother had been killed in a clash with security forces in February 1995. The respondent State claimed that the brother had not been taken into custody, that he was a militant member of the PKK, and had been killed in February 1995 in a clash with security forces. Evidence was adduced that the father of the applicant and the applicant had, in December 1993, submitted a petition to the authorities requesting information about the whereabouts of the disappearance of the brother. Enquiries continued to be made, notably by the applicant in September 1994. The response of the authorities was simply to verify whether records contained the name of the applicant's brother. The applicant complained that the lack of information about his brother's disappearance constituted inhuman treatment towards himself. The Court said:

Whether a family member is [a victim of treatment contrary to Article 3] will depend on the existence of special factors which gives the suffering of the applicant a dimension and character distinct from the emotional distress which may be regarded as inevitably caused to relatives of a victim of a serious human rights violation. Relevant elements will include the proximity of the family tie (in that context, a certain weight will attach to the parent–child bond), the extent to which the family member witnessed the events in question, the involvement of the family member in attempts to obtain information about the disappeared person and the way in which the authorities responded to those enquiries. The Court would further emphasize that the essence of such a violation does not so much lie in the fact of the 'disappearance' of the family member but rather concerns the authorities' reactions and attitudes to the situation when it is brought to their attention. It is especially in respect of the latter that a relative may claim directly to be a victim of the authorities' conduct.[114]

In the particular circumstances of this case, the Court concluded that there was no violation.[115]

The *Gongadze* case[116] is a shocking example of a violation of both Article 2 and Article 3 in relation to the disappearance of a political journalist in Ukraine. His widow reported his disappearance a day after he had gone missing. A decapitated corpse was subsequently found, but there were announcements and denials by officials that this was the body of the missing man. It was eventually established that this was indeed his corpse. A subsequent investigation established that the journalist had been kidnapped and killed with the collusion of the most senior parliamentarians. The Strasbourg Court found that the attitude of the investigating authorities towards the applicant and her family constituted degrading treatment.[117]

---

[114] *Çakici v Turkey*, (App. 23657/94), 8 July 1999 [GC], (2001) 31 EHRR 133, ECHR 1998-IV, §98.

[115] See also *Timurtaş v Turkey*, (App. 23531/94), 13 June 2000, (2001) 33 EHRR 121, ECHR 2000-VI, §§91–8; *Taş v Turkey*, (App. 24396/94), 14 November 2000, (2001) 33 EHRR 325, §§77–80; and *Cyprus v Turkey*, (App. 25781/94), 10 May 2001 [GC], (2002) 35 EHRR 731, ECHR 2001-IV, §§154–8.

[116] *Gongadze v Ukraine*, (App. 34056/02), 8 November 2005, (2006) 43 EHRR 967, ECHR 2005-XI.

[117] For further examples, see *Bazorkina v Russia*, (App. 69481/01), 27 July 2006, (2008) 46 EHRR 261; and *Varnava and others v Turkey*, (Apps. 16064–6/90 and 16068–73/90), 10 January 2008 (the Chamber judgment was referred to the Grand Chamber, see now judgment of 18 September 2009).

DESTRUCTION OF HOMES AND POSSESSIONS

In the *Bilgin* case,[118] the Strasbourg Court found that destruction of the applicant's house and his possessions during operations by the security forces constituted inhuman treatment. The acts were deliberate and the operations of the security forces had been conducted with complete disregard for the safety and welfare of the applicant.

In the *Moldovan* case[119] the Court found that the involvement of State agents in the destruction of the homes of those of Roma origin coupled with failures of State agencies to prosecute those responsible and to manage the reconstruction of the destroyed homes effectively were motivated by racial discrimination. This constituted a serious violation of Article 8 of the Convention, which in turn constituted degrading treatment in breach of Article 3.

CORPORAL PUNISHMENT

The extent to which corporal punishment constitutes conduct in breach of Article 3 has been considered by the Strasbourg Court in a number of cases. The *Tyrer* case[120] concerned the imposition of the penalty of birching in the Isle of Man on a 15-year-old who had been convicted of assault on a senior pupil at his school. The punishment was administered by a police constable in private in the presence of the boy's father and a doctor. In concluding that the punishment of Tyrer constituted degrading treatment, the Court had regard to its character as 'institutionalized violence', to the fact that the punishment constituted an assault on the applicant's dignity and physical integrity, which may have had adverse psychological effects, and to the anguish of anticipating the punishment.[121]

The *Campbell and Cosans* case[122] concerned the use of corporal punishment in schools. In one case, the parent was unable to obtain an assurance that her son would not be subject to corporal punishment, and in the other the son, on his father's advice, presented himself for punishment but refused to accept it and was immediately suspended from school until such time as he was willing to accept the punishment. The form of corporal punishment in issue was the striking of the hand with a leather strap known as a 'tawse'. The Commission concluded that there was no violation of Article 3 in these cases. The Court noted that neither child had been subjected to corporal punishment. Nevertheless, 'provided it is sufficiently real and immediate, a mere threat

---

[118] *Bilgin v Turkey*, (App. 23819/94), 16 November 2000, (2003) 35 EHRR 879.

[119] *Moldovan and others v Romania*, (Apps 41138/98 and 64320/01), 12 July 2005, (2007) 44 EHRR 302, ECHR 2005-VII.

[120] *Tyrer v United Kingdom*, 25 April 1978, Series A No 26, (1979–80) 2 EHRR 1.

[121] §33.

[122] *Campbell and Cosans v United Kingdom*, 25 February 1982, Series A No 48, (1982) 4 EHRR 293.

of conduct prohibited by Article 3 may itself be in conflict with the provision.'[123] The Court, however, concluded that the suffering resulting from the treatment of the two boys did not meet the level inherent in the notion of degrading treatment.[124] The Court went on to consider whether other provisions of the Convention had been violated.[125]

In the *Costello-Roberts* case[126] the Strasbourg Court ruled that the striking of the clothed buttocks of a seven-year-old boy with a rubber-soled gym shoe as an automatic punishment for accumulating five demerit points at his boarding school had no severe long-lasting effects and did not reach the level of severity necessary to bring the matter within Article 3. The Court did, however, have some misgivings about the automatic nature of the punishment and the delay of three days between the accumulation of the demerit points and the imposition of the penalty.

As in other cases, a careful judgment needs to be applied to the particular circumstances of each case. Corporal punishments which have a long-lasting effect and reach the threshold of severity required will violate Article 3, whether imposed in a public or a private school. The United Kingdom has responded to these judgments by passing legislation to prohibit corporal punishment in schools.

The *A* case[127] concerned the stepfather of a boy born in 1984, who in 1993 beat the boy with a garden cane using considerable force. The stepfather was prosecuted for assault occasioning actual bodily harm, but a jury acquitted him, apparently not accepting that the prosecution had proved that the beatings were other than for 'lawful correction' amounting to 'reasonable chastisement' which was a defence in English law. The Court concluded that the circumstances of this case meant that the applicant was not protected against treatment or punishment contrary to Article 3 by the United Kingdom, and consequently there was a violation of Article 3.

ACTS IN THE COURSE OF ARREST AND POLICE DETENTION

A number of cases have addressed conduct arising during the course of an arrest or detention as part of a police investigation. In some situations the conduct of the arresting and detaining officers will be subject to close scrutiny.[128] The use of handcuffs in connection with a lawful arrest or detention does not normally give rise to an issue under Article 3, provided that it does not entail the use of force or public exposure exceeding what is reasonably necessary in the particular circumstances of each case.[129]

---

[123] §26.   [124] See above in this chapter.   [125] See below in ch.16.

[126] *Costello-Roberts v United Kingdom*, 25 March 1993, Series A No 247-C, (1994) 19 EHRR 112.

[127] *A v United Kingdom*, (App. 25599/94), 23 September 1998, (1999) 27 EHRR 611, ECHR 1998-VI.

[128] As, for example, in *Olteanu v Romania* (App. 71090/01), 14 April 2009.

[129] *Raninen v Finland*, (App. 20972/92), 16 December 1997, (1998) 26 EHRR 563, ECHR 1997-VIII, §§52–9. See also *Erdoğan Yağiz v Turkey*, (App. 27473/02), 6 March 2007, ECHR 2007-nyr, where a violation was found.

All the circumstances must be considered including any reasonable belief that the person concerned would resist arrest or seek to escape, or be a danger to themselves or others. But even where the arrest and detention is unlawful, the Court will not always be convinced that being handcuffed so adversely affects the applicant that the minimum level of severity is reached for Article 3 to bite. However, the use of handcuffs in the particular circumstances must not be disproportionate to the security risk. Their use in transferring a sick prisoner in a weak condition from prison to hospital coupled with other aspects of his treatment constituted inhuman and degrading treatment in one case.[130]

In the *Tomasi* case[131] the applicant had been subjected to considerable ill-treatment over a period of nearly two days while in police custody. He had been slapped, kicked, punched, and given forearm blows, made to stand for long periods and without support, had his hands handcuffed behind his back, been made to stand naked in front of an open window, been deprived of food, and threatened with a firearm. The respondent State was unable to offer any explanation for the injuries suffered by the applicant. But they argued that the injuries suffered by the applicant did not meet the level of severity necessary to constitute a violation of Article 3, and that there were particular circumstances obtaining in Corsica where there was significant terrorist activity. The Court did not accept these arguments, and concluded that there had been a violation of Article 3.[132]

The *Ribitsch* case[133] might be regarded as the first of the modern cases on physical assault while in police custody, since it couples the failure of the authorities to provide an explanation for the applicant's injuries with its finding of a violation of Article 3. It was not disputed that the applicant's injuries had been sustained during police detention, and the respondent State was found not to have satisfactorily established that they were caused other than as a result of his treatment in custody. The Court found that the applicant had been the victim of inhuman and degrading treatment.[134]

The *Jalloh* case[135] addresses the limits of investigation methods following arrest. Jalloh was suspected of involvement in drug dealing, and had been seen to swallow a small plastic bag. While in detention, a prosecutor authorized the use of an emetic in order to secure the regurgitation of the item which had been swallowed. Jalloh resisted, but the medication was administered by force, and a bag of cocaine was regurgitated. The applicant argued that the forcible administration of the emetic amounted to a breach of Article 3, particularly in the light of considerable medical evidence of the dangers of such a procedure. The Strasbourg Court affirmed the obligation of the Contracting Parties to protect the physical well-being of those in detention

---

[130] *Mouisel v France*, (App. 67263/01), 14 November 2002, (2004) 38 EHRR 735, ECHR 2002-IX, §47.

[131] *Tomasi v France*, 27 August 1992, Series A No 241-A, (1993) 15 EHRR 1.

[132] §11. See also *Klaas v Germany*, 22 September 1993, Series A No 269, (1994) 18 EHRR 305.

[133] *Ribitsch v Austria*, 4 December 1995, Series A No 336, (1996) 21 EHRR 573.

[134] See also *Aksoy v Turkey*, (App. 21987/93), 18 December 1996, (1997) 23 EHRR 553, ECHR 1996-VI; and *Haci Özen v Turkey*, (App. 46286/99), 12 April 2007.

[135] *Jalloh v Germany*, (App. 54810/00), 11 July 2006 [GC], (2007) 44 EHRR 667, ECHR 2006-IX.

under suspicion of having committed offences. While any measure which is regarded as of therapeutic necessity cannot be regarded as inhuman or degrading, procedures designed to secure evidence from a suspect require further consideration. So, for example, the taking of blood or saliva samples contrary to a suspect's wishes will not constitute inhuman or degrading treatment. But procedures such as that in issue in the case require a weighing of all the risks of the procedure, its intrusiveness, the pain and suffering involved, the alternative procedures which may be available, the medical supervision involved, and the seriousness of the offence being investigated. In all the circumstances of this case, the Grand Chamber concluded by ten votes to seven that the procedure had amounted to inhuman and degrading treatment.[136]

CONDITIONS OF DETENTION

The fact and conditions of imprisonment are frequent sources of individual applications invoking Article 3. Few were considered by the Court in the early years, when the law was to be found in Commission decisions.[137] But the Strasbourg Court has now established a set of principles for determining when the conditions of detention might engage Article 3. In the *Poltoratskiy* case,[138] the Court, while acknowledging the inherent features of detention, said that conditions of detention must be compatible with respect for human dignity,[139] and that it is important that a detained person's health and well-being are adequately secured.[140] A similar approach is taken to the conditions of detention of those awaiting expulsion, or detained by the immigration authorities.[141]

In the *Valašinas* case,[142] the applicant made many claims about the shortcomings of the prison regime to which he was subject. The Court did not find that the undeniably tough regime violated Article 3 since it did not reach the minimum level of severity to amount to degrading treatment; this included a period of fifteen days when the applicant was detained in a solitary confinement cell.[143] However, a specific incident in which the applicant had been obliged to strip naked in the presence of a woman prison

---

[136] Contrast *Bogumil v Portugal*, (App. 35228/03), 7 October 2008, where a surgical procedure to remove a packet of drugs was regarded as a therapeutic necessity.

[137] See, generally, N. Rodley, *The Treatment of Prisoners under International Law* (OUP, Oxford 1999).

[138] *Poltoratskiy v Ukraine*, (App. 38812/97), 29 April 2003, ECHR 2003-V.

[139] On the concept of human dignity, see C. McCrudden, 'Human Dignity and Judicial Interpretation of Human Rights' (2008) 19 EJIL 655.

[140] §132, referring to *Kudła v Poland*, (App. 30210/96), 26 October 2000 [GC], (2002) 25 EHRR 198, ECHR 2000-XI, §§92–4.

[141] *Dougoz v Greece*, (App. 40907/98), 6 March 2001, (2002) 34 EHRR 1480, ECHR 2001-II. See also *SD v Greece*, (App. 53541/07, 11 June 2009.

[142] *Valašinas v Lithuania*, (App. 44558/98), 24 July 2001, ECHR 2001-VIII.

[143] Contrast *Nevmerzhitsky v Ukraine*, (App. 54825/00), 5 April 2005, ECHR 2005-II; and *Ostrovar v Moldova*, (App. 35207/03), 13 September 2005, where violations of Art. 3 were found.

officer, and in which his genitals and food were handled by a prison officer with bare hands, was considered to constitute degrading treatment.

In the *Aerts* case,[144] the applicant complained about the conditions in the psychiatric wing of the prison where he was in detention pending his trial for an assault on his ex-wife with a hammer. The Committee for the Prevention of Torture[145] had reported critically on the psychiatric and therapeutic care available in the prison psychiatric wing, but did not categorize them as degrading. The Court considered that prolonged periods in the psychiatric wing would carry with them the risk of deterioration in a person's mental health. There was, however, for the Court no convincing evidence that the applicant's mental health had suffered and it was not established that the applicant had suffered treatment which could be classified as inhuman or degrading. In extreme cases, a convicted person's health may make imprisonment of itself a violation of Article 3,[146] as in the case of prisoners suffering from Wernicke-Korsakoff Syndrome.[147]

Though there is as yet no direct authority on the point, placing a juvenile in an adult prison for any significant length of time may well constitute a breach of Article 3.[148] But the placing of a five-year-old in a Transit Centre, without facilities for children of this age, for two months pending her return from Belgium to the Democratic Republic of the Congo has been found to constitute inhuman treatment.[149]

In each case, as always, the facts must be viewed in the light of the circumstances as a whole. Thus the physical condition of the applicant may make treatment which would otherwise be lawful contrary to Article 3; conversely, the applicant's own conduct may exceptionally legitimize a degree of violence which would otherwise be prohibited. The case-law may conveniently be considered under a number of sub-headings.

PRISON CONDITIONS

The *Peers* case[150] concerned conditions in a prison in Greece. There had been a critical report by the Committee for the Prevention of Torture[151] in relation to the prison in question. It seemed that little had been done to improve the conditions in the prison. The Strasbourg Court concluded that confinement in a cell with no ventilation and no window at the hottest time of the year in circumstances where the applicant had to use the toilet in the presence of another and was present while the toilet was being used by his cell mate diminished his human dignity and amounted to degrading treatment.

---

[144] *Aerts v Belgium*, (App. 25357/94), 30 July 1998, (2000) 29 EHRR 50, ECHR 1998-V.

[145] See below in this chapter.

[146] *Tekin Yildiz v Turkey*, (App. 22913/04), 10 November 2005.

[147] A brain disorder involving loss of specific brain functions caused by a thiamine deficiency, which may be brought about following hunger strikes.

[148] See *Güveç v Turkey*, (App. 70337/01), 20 January 2009, where this situation resulted in serious psychological problems for the applicant.

[149] *Mubilanzila Mayeka and Kaniki Mitunga v Belgium*, (App. 13178/03), 12 June 2006, (2008) 46 EHRR 449, ECHR 2006-XI.

[150] *Peers v Greece*, (App. 28524/95), 19 April 2001, (2001) 33 EHRR 1192, ECHR 2001-III.

[151] See below in this chapter.

The poor state of prison facilities in some Contracting Parties remains a cause for concern. In the *Kadiķis* case,[152] the applicant complained that his cell, which had an area of six square metres, regularly held four or five people; it was poorly ventilated and had poor lighting; there were no exercise facilities; only one meal per day was provided; no drinking water was provided; there was no bedding or blankets; use of the toilet was restricted to three times a day and urgent needs were accommodated using a bottle and plastic bowl; and his family were allowed on only one occasion to provide him with items for personal hygiene and fresh clothing. The Strasbourg Court noted that the Committee for the Prevention of Torture had recommended a minimum of seven square metres of cell space per prisoner. The Court found these prison conditions to constitute degrading treatment in violation of Article 3.[153] In extreme cases, poor prison conditions, combined with aggravating circumstances, such as a failure to respond to a prisoner's mental health problems, could result in a finding that the overall prison regime constituted torture.[154]

The absence of facilities within a prison to meet the needs of a wheelchair user was found to constitute degrading treatment even though it was accepted that there was no intention to humiliate or debase the prisoner.[155]

TREATMENT OF DETAINEES, INCLUDING THE USE OF SOLITARY CONFINEMENT

Force-feeding a prisoner, where it could not be established that this was a medical necessity supported by genuine medical opinions, has been held to constitute torture.[156]

Strip searches which have no genuine relationship to security concerns and which are imposed on a prisoner can constitute degrading treatment.[157] Even where a process of strip searches can be justified for legitimate concerns over possession of prohibited articles or substances, the process must be administered in a manner which limits as far as possible the feelings of inferiority, anxiety, and humiliation which such procedures necessarily entail.[158]

A number of cases have questioned the practice of using solitary confinement. The Court's approach was explained in the *Van der Ven* case:

In this context, the Court has previously held that complete sensory isolation, coupled with total social isolation, can destroy the personality and constitutes a form of inhuman

---

[152] *Kadiķis v Latvia (No. 2)*, (App. 62393/00), 4 May 2006.

[153] See also *Ciorap v Moldova*, (App. 12066/02), 19 June 2007.

[154] *Sławomir Musiał v Poland*, (App. 28300/06), 20 January 2009, §95.

[155] *Vincent v France*, (App. 6253/03), 24 October 2006.

[156] *Nevmerzhitsky v Ukraine*, (App. 54825/00), 5 April 2005, ECHR 2005-II. See also *Ciorap v Moldova*, (App. 12066/02), 19 June 2007.

[157] See *Iwańczuk v Poland*, (App. 25196/94), 15 November 2001, (2004) 38 EHRR 148; *Lorsé and others v The Netherlands*, (App. 52750/99), 4 February 2003, (2003) 37 EHRR 105; *Van der Ven v The Netherlands*, (App. 50901/99), 4 February 2003, (2004) 38 EHRR 967, ECHR 2003-II; and *Frérot v France*, (App. 70204/01), 12 June 2007, ECHR 2007-nyr.

[158] *Frérot v France*, (App. 70204/01), 12 June 2007, ECHR 2007-nyr.

treatment which cannot be justified by the requirements of security or any other reason. On the other hand, the removal from association with other prisoners for security, disciplinary or protective reasons does not in itself amount to inhuman treatment or degrading punishment.... In assessing whether such a measure may fall within the ambit of Article 3 in a given case, regard must be had to the particular conditions, the stringency of the measure, its duration, the objective pursued and its effects on the person concerned....[159]

The *Ramirez Sanchez* case[160] is a particularly striking example of the permissible use of solitary confinement. Ramirez Sanchez, better known as 'Carlos the Jackal'[161] was kept in solitary confinement for eight years and two months. But this lengthy regime had been subject to a rigorous process of assessment every three months which prevented its being arbitrary. Those assessments had taken account of medical reports on the applicant, none of which gave rise to any cause for concern. The applicant had had regular contact with a doctor, a priest, and his lawyers, and there were no restrictions on visits from members of his family, although they had never requested a visit. There was no evidence to suggest any intention to humiliate or debase the applicant. He was eventually transferred to more normal detention. The Court ruled that solitary confinement could never be imposed upon a prisoner indefinitely, but that was not the case here. By twelve votes to five, the Grand Chamber concluded that there was no violation of Article 3. The dissenting judges felt that neither the applicant's physical robustness nor his mental stamina could make solitary confinement of the nature and duration he had experienced acceptable under Article 3.

In the *A and others* case,[162] a number of foreign nationals suspected of involvement in terrorist plots had been interned without trial[163] in the United Kingdom because they could not be deported. They complained that their detention had violated Article 3, arguing that the high security conditions were inappropriate and damaging to their health; they also claimed that there was abnormal suffering associated with the indeterminate nature of their detention. While accepting the impact of the detention on the mental health of some of the detainees, the Grand Chamber concluded that it could not be said that they had no hope of release. The Court, however, sidesteps the conclusions of the Committee on the Prevention of Torture's conclusions that, at the time of their visit, the conditions amounted to inhuman and degrading treatment, by noting that nearly all the applicants had failed to use domestic proceedings to challenge those conditions, and so had failed to exhaust domestic remedies in this regard.[164] The Court's overall finding was that the treatment of the detainees did not reach the threshold of inhuman and degrading treatment.

---

[159] *Van der Ven v The Netherlands*, (App. 50901/99), 4 February 2003, (2004) 38 EHRR 967, ECHR 2003-II, §51. See also *Rohde v Denmark*, (App. 69332/01), 21 July 2005.

[160] *Ramirez Sanchez v France*, (App. 59450/00), 4 July 2006 [GC], (2007) 45 EHRR 1099, ECHR 2006-IX. See also *Rohde v Denmark*, (App. 69332/01), 21 July 2005, (2006) 43 EHRR 325.

[161] Who was serving a life sentence for the murder of two police officers, and who claimed to be a revolutionary by profession. He was suspected of involvement in a series of terrorist attacks.

[162] *A and others v United Kingdom*, (App. 3455/05), 19 February 2009 [GC], (2009) 49 EHRR 29, ECHR 2009-nyr.

[163] Following the filing of a derogation in respect of the rights to be found in Article 5.

[164] §§132–3.

MEDICAL ATTENTION FOR DETAINEES

The Strasbourg Court has consistently ruled that all prisoners are entitled to conditions of detention which are compatible with human dignity. This includes having appropriate regard for their well-being.[165] Where mental health is in issue, Contracting Parties have been enjoined to take special account of the vulnerability of prisoners and their inability, in some cases, to complain coherently about their difficulties.[166] Very special measures will need to be put in place where a prisoner constitutes a suicide risk.[167] In one case, the Court ordered interim measures in the form of a requirement that the applicant be transferred from hospital to prison, somewhat controversially, found a violation where a transfer to prison took place and a transfer back to hospital took place three days later.[168]

In the *Price* case,[169] the conditions in which a thalidomide victim was kept in prison were found to amount to degrading treatment. The applicant had been committed to prison for seven days for contempt of court;[170] she was detained both in a police cell and in prison for three and a half days. She was seriously disabled by her condition, and used a wheelchair. The Court concluded that her detention in conditions where she was dangerously cold, risked developing sores because her bed was too hard or unreachable, and was unable to get to the toilet or keep clean without the greatest of difficulties amounted to degrading treatment. Judge Bratza in a separate concurring opinion is scathing of the judicial authorities in committing the applicant to prison without determining in advance whether there were adequate facilities for meeting her special needs.

A complaint of a violation of Article 3 might arise from a failure to respond promptly and effectively to a prisoner's medical needs. The *Mouisel* case[171] concerned a prisoner suffering from chronic lymphocytic leukaemia who had been sentenced to fifteen years' imprisonment for armed robbery, kidnapping, and fraud. He raised a complaint that his continued detention and the conditions in which he had been detained violated Article 3. The Court acknowledged that a failure to provide appropriate medical treatment could bring the conduct of the authorities within the positive obligations of Article 3.[172] So, for example, in the *McGlinchey* case,[173] the respondent State was found to have breached the prohibition of inhuman and degrading treatment in Article 3 in

---

[165] *Kudła v Poland*, (App. 30210/96), 26 October 2000 [GC], (2002) 35 EHRR 11, ECHR 2000-XI, §94; and *Paladi v Moldova* (App. 39806/05) 10 March 2009 [GC], §§71–2. For an example of a failure to provide an appropriate response to general medical needs, see *Khudobin v Russia*, (App. 59696/00), 26 October 2006, ECHR 2006-XII. For a pilot judgments relating to the lack of medical care in prisons in Georgia, see *Poghosyan v Georgia* (App. 9870/07) 24 February 2009.

[166] *Renolde v France*, (App. 5608/05), 16 October 2008, (2009) 48 EHRR 969, §120.

[167] *Rivière v France*, (App. 33834/03), 11 July 2006.

[168] *Paladi v Moldova* (App. 39806/05) 10 March 2009 [GC], §§84–106; the Grand Chamber was split 9–8 on the violation of Article 34.

[169] *Price v United Kingdom*, (App. 33394/96), 10 July 2001, (2002) 34 EHRR 1285, ECHR 2001-VII.

[170] Under the remission system she was only incarcerated for three and a half days.

[171] *Mouisel v France*, (App. 67263/01), 14 November 2002, (2004) 38 EHRR 735, ECIIR 2002-IX.

[172] §40.

[173] *McGlinchey and others v United Kingdom*, (App. 50390/99), 29 April 2003, (2003) 37 EHRR 821, ECHR 2003-V.

failing to respond to the applicant's deteriorating condition. She was eventually admitted to hospital as an emergency case when she collapsed, but later died. McGlinchey suffered from asthma and from heroin withdrawal.

In the *Herczegfalvy* case,[174] the applicant, who had been convicted of offences of fraud and violence, complained that the medical treatment to which he had been subjected amounted to degrading treatment. He had been diagnosed as suffering from a mental illness, and was forcibly administered food and neuroleptics, isolated, and attached with handcuffs to his security bed for several weeks. The Commission concluded that there had been a violation of Article 3. Their decision was based on the conclusion that the treatment accorded to the applicant went beyond what was strictly necessary, and that it extended beyond the period necessary to serve its purpose (including the period of a week when he was handcuffed to his bed despite being unconscious). The Court affirmed that mental patients remain under the protection of Article 3, but that the 'established principles of medicine are...decisive in such cases; as a general rule, a measure which is therapeutic cannot be regarded as inhuman or degrading.'[175] But the Court would need to be satisfied as to the medical necessity for any particular form of treatment. In the present case, the Court considered this test to be met. On the facts as presented, the conclusions of the Court are surprising and the opinion of the Commission is to be preferred.

In the *Keenan* case,[176] the Court took a particularly robust view of the needs of a prisoner who was suffering from mental illness which included a risk of suicide. Keenan had been found hanged in his cell, and his mother as his next of kin claimed a violation of Article 3. A combination of poor medical notes, lack of effective monitoring of Keenan's health when he was a known suicide risk, and the imposition on him of seven days' segregation in the punishment block and an additional twenty-eight days added to his sentence constituted inhuman and degrading treatment.[177] He had committed suicide on his second day in segregation.

EUROPEAN CONVENTION FOR THE PREVENTION OF TORTURE

The European Convention for the Prevention of Torture and Inhuman and Degrading Treatment[178] came into force in February 1989. The Convention creates a monitoring mechanism in the form of a Committee which may make visits to any establishment

---

[174] *Herczegfalvy v Austria*, 24 September 1992, Series A No 242-B, (1993) 15 EHRR 437.   [175] §82.

[176] *Keenan v United Kingdom*, (App. 27229/95), 3 April 2001, (2001) 33 EHRR 913, ECHR 2001-III.

[177] §§108–15.

[178] ETS 126, and Protocols 1 and 2, ETS 151 and 152. For a commentary, see M. Evans and R. Morgan, *Preventing Torture. A Study of the European Convention for the Prevention of Torture and Inhuman or Degrading Treatment* (OUP, Oxford 1998); A. Cassese, 'A New Approach to Human Rights: The European Convention for the Prevention of Torture' (1989) 83 AJIL 128.

in the territory of the Contracting Parties where persons are deprived of their liberty by a public authority. It aims at the prevention of torture rather than its repression and arises, according to the Preamble, from a conviction that:

the protection of persons deprived of their liberty against torture and inhuman and degrading treatment or punishment could be strengthened by non-judicial means of a preventive character based on visits.

Examination of the *travaux préparatoires* reveals that there was considerable concern about possible conflicts between the work of the Committee for the Prevention of Torture and the Commission and Court of Human Rights.[179] Happily this has not materialized, although there have been occasions where decisions of the Commission have taken the Committee by surprise.[180]

The existence of monitoring is designed to ensure that standards of treatment meet established human rights standards. The Committee has no judicial functions, but reports its findings and makes recommendations to the State concerned. These reports are confidential. They will remain unpublished unless the State requests their publication or the Committee by a two-thirds majority decides to make a public statement on a matter in the face of a State's failure to cooperate or refusal to make changes in the light of the Committee's recommendations. The Committee submits to the Committee of Ministers each year an overview report of its activities.

The norm has very much become for publication of the reports.[181] There is a growing tendency for the Strasbourg Court to refer to reports by the Committee in its decision-making. So in the *Aerts* case,[182] the Commission and the Court took note of the findings of the Committee in examining the conditions of detention in a particular psychiatric hospital. In a number of other cases, the Court has noted the conclusions of a report by the Committee, and has been influenced by those findings both in coming to its own conclusions on the facts and in giving content to the requirements of Article 3.[183]

---

[179] Evans and Morgan, n.178 above.

[180] For example, the decision of the Commission (subsequently reversed by the Court) that airport holding centres for aliens were not places of detention for the purposes of Article 5 ECHR in App. 19776/92, *Amuur v France*, 10 January 1995, reversed by the Court, 25 June 1996; (1996) 22 EHRR 533, ECHR 1996-III; see Evans and Morgan, n.178 above, 371–4.

[181] Evans and Morgan, n.178 above, 198–203 and 339–41.

[182] *Aerts v Belgium*, (App. 25357/94), 30 July 1998, (2000) 29 EHRR 50, ECHR 1998-V, §72 of the Commission's Report, and §§29–30, 42, and 62–5.

[183] See, for example, *Aksoy v Turkey*, (App. 21987/93), 18 December 1996, (1997) 23 EHRR 553, ECHR 1996-VI, §46; *Aydin v Turkey*, (App. 23178/94), 25 September 1997, (1998) 25 EHRR 251, ECHR 1997-VI, §§49–50; *Dougoz v Greece* (App. 40907/98), 6 March 2001, (2002) 34 EHRR 1480, ECHR 2001-II, §§40–1 and 46; *Peers v Greece*, (App. 28524/95), 19 April 2001, (2001) 33 EHRR 1192, ECHR 2001-III, §61 and 70–2; *Van der Ven v The Netherlands*, (App. 50901/99), 4 February 2003, (2004) 38 EHRR 967, ECHR 2003-II, §§32–4; *Mouisel v France*, (App. 67263/01), 14 November 2002, (2004) 38 EHRR 735, ECHR 2002-IX, §47; *II v Bulgaria*, (App. 44082/98), 9 June 2005, §§37–46; and *Salmanoğlu and Polattaş v Turkey* (App. 15828/03), 17 March 2009.

CONCLUDING REMARKS

It was only in December 1996 that the Strasbourg Court found a Contracting Party guilty of torture, but there has since been an upsurge in such findings.[184] Even more worrying has been the increase in findings of inhuman or degrading treatment. In 2008, there were findings of such treatment in 129 judgments against 15 Contracting Parties, with Bulgaria, Russia, and Turkey accounting for 104 of these judgments.[185] Some of these violations result from prison conditions, but many involve conduct which it is shocking should exist in Europe in the 21st century. The majority of the violations have been found against new Contracting Parties, who have some way to go to secure to those within their jurisdiction even the most basic of human rights guarantees.

The Strasbourg Court has kept faith with the absolute nature of the prohibition to be found in Article 3, and has resisted efforts by some Contracting Parties to introduce relative notions into the case-law relating to removal of persons to countries where there is a real risk that they will be exposed to ill-treatment. This is important in a climate where coping with terrorist threats puts respect for human rights under pressure.

The focus in recent years on improving prison conditions is also to be welcomed. There has been something of a sea change in this area. Early cases were somewhat dismissive of complaints by prisoners about the conditions of their detention, and to some extent about features of their own treatment in particular circumstances. However, prompted by important standard-setting work by the Committee for the Prevention of Torture, the Strasbourg Court has delivered judgments indicating the need for significant improvements in prison conditions which ensure the entitlement of prisoners to be treated with human dignity.

Perhaps the central message of the case-law examined in this chapter is the need for constant vigilance even among the countries of Europe in relation to one of the most fundamental of human rights.

---

[184] In 2008 the Strasbourg Court made findings of torture in 11 cases: one against Moldova, three against Turkey, and seven against Russia.

[185] Source: European Court of Human Rights, violation by article and country, January 2009.

10

PROTECTION FROM SLAVERY AND FORCED LABOUR

INTRODUCTION

Article 4 provides:

1. No one shall be held in slavery or servitude.

2. No one shall be required to perform forced or compulsory labour.

3. For the purposes of this Article the term 'forced or compulsory labour' shall not include:

    (a) any work required to be done in the ordinary course of detention imposed according to the provisions of Article 5 of this Convention or during conditional release from such detention;

    (b) any service of a military character or, in the case of conscientious objectors in countries where they are recognized, service exacted instead of compulsory military service;

    (c) any service exacted in case of an emergency or calamity threatening the life or well-being of the community;

    (d) any work or service which forms part of normal civic obligations.

Article 4(1) prohibits slavery and servitude; the wording shows that these are regarded as questions of status. Article 4(2), by contrast, prohibits forced or compulsory labour, and is intended to protect persons who are at liberty. Slavery and servitude are continuing—though not necessarily permanent—states, whereas forced labour may arise incidentally or on a temporary basis. The prohibitions of slavery and servitude are absolute (and outside any derogation under Article 15), but the prohibition of forced or compulsory labour is subject to the exemption for those forms of work or service expressly permitted under Article 4(3). No other substantive provision of the Convention is drafted in this way. The exceptions in Article 4(3)(a) and (b) are genuine exceptions, while the matters listed in Article 4(3)(c) and (d) are rather examples of obligations which cannot be said to fall within the definition of forced or compulsory labour.

The infrequency with which the Strasbourg Court has had to deal with this article justifies closer consideration of the decisions and reports of the Commission on the scope and application of Article 4 than is found in considering other articles of the Convention. It is, however, not uncommon for allegations of violations of Article 4 to be attached to applications alleging violations of other Convention provisions. So, in the *Šijakova* case,[1] the applicants sought to argue (without success) that their children over the age of 18 who had joined the monastic order of the Macedonian Orthodox Church were in slavery. In the *Pearson* case,[2] the applicant, who was complaining that women reached State pensionable age at 60 while men did not do so until 65, argued unsuccessfully that a consequence of this differential age for entitlement to a State pension was forced labour for men. In the *Solovyev* case,[3] the Strasbourg Court ruled as manifestly ill-founded a claim under Article 4(1) by a worker who had not received remuneration for the work he had done as an employee. He had secured a judgment for the unpaid wages, but the judgment remained unsatisfied.

Slavery and servitude are old-fashioned words suggesting practices which have long since ceased to exist. But the truth of the matter is that the modern manifestation of slavery and servitude is human trafficking, which exists on a significant scale worldwide. It exists within the Council of Europe countries in terms of countries of origin, transit, and destination.[4] The International Labour Organization has estimated that 2.45 million people are affected worldwide. The purpose of much of the traffic is sexual exploitation, but also includes forced labour or services. The practice affects women and children in particular.

SLAVERY OR SERVITUDE

DEFINITIONS

The prohibition of slavery and servitude is governed by numerous international treaties and there is now wide recognition that both are prohibited under customary international law.[5] The distinction between slavery and servitude is one of degree.[6] Slavery connotes being wholly in the legal ownership of another person, while servitude is more limited though still connoting conditions of work or service wholly outside the

---

[1] *Šijakova and others v FYRM* (App. 67914/01), Decision of 6 March 2003.

[2] *Pearson v United Kingdom* (App. 8374/03), Decision of 27 April 2004.

[3] *Solovyev v Ukraine*, (App. 4878/04), 14 December 2006.

[4] 'Council of Europe's action to combat trafficking in human beings' CM/Inf(2008)28 of 9 June 2008.

[5] See Article 4 of the Universal Declaration of Human Rights, and P. Sieghart, *The International Law of Human Rights* (OUP, Oxford 1983), 54–5.

[6] None of the major human rights instruments defines slavery and servitude. A definition of slavery can be found in Article 1 of the Slavery Convention of 1926 as follows: 'Slavery is the status or condition of a person over whom any or all of the powers attaching to the right of ownership are exercised.' Servitude is broadly defined in Article 7 of the Supplementary Convention on the Abolition of Slavery, the Slave Trade, and Institutions and Practices Similar to Slavery of 1956 by reference to a variety of practices listed in Article 1 of that Convention.

control of the individual. The Commission's Report in the *Van Droogenbroeck* case said that:

in addition to the obligation to provide another with certain services, the concept of servitude includes the obligation on the part of the 'serf' to live on another's property and the impossibility of changing his condition.[7]

The Strasbourg Court found that the situation in the *Siliadin* case[8] amounted to servitude but not slavery. The applicant had been brought to France from Togo by a relative of her father. She was then forced to work as a maid for some considerable time for fifteen hours a day, seven days a week. She had no personal resources, her papers had been confiscated, she was afraid of contacting the authorities because of her irregular immigration status, and was vulnerable and isolated. The Court considered that the applicant could not be said to be owned by the couple in the strict sense, but her lack of freedom and the requirement that she work such long hours on every day of the week meant that she had been held in servitude.

This case is particularly significant for its recognition of the modern phenomenon of trafficking in people, which in the form presented in the case constituted the victims being placed in a state of servitude.[9]

CONVENTION ON ACTION AGAINST TRAFFICKING IN HUMAN BEINGS

As a response to the growing problem of trafficking in human beings, the Council of Europe adopted the Convention on Action against Trafficking in Human Beings in 2005.[10] As at 1 September 2009, there were 25 ratifications, and 16 signatures not followed by ratification. Six countries had not even signed this Convention. The Convention is the first to recognize explicitly that human trafficking is a violation of human rights and an offence to the dignity and integrity of the human being. Parties to the Convention are required to implement national measures to prevent trafficking, particularly by ensuring that all activities linked to trafficking are made criminal offences, and to discourage demand, as well as to develop facilities to support victims of trafficking. Parties are also required to cooperate internationally to tackle the problem. The effectiveness of the Convention is secured through the monitoring

---

[7] *Van Droogenbroeck*, Report of 9 July 1980, Series B, No. 44.

[8] *Siliadin v France* (App. 73316/01), 26 July 2005, (2006) 43 EHRR 287, ECHR 2005-VII. See also V. Mantouvalou, 'Servitude and Forced Labour in the 21st Century: The Human Rights of Domestic Workers' (2006) 35 ILJ 395; and H. Cullen, '*Siliadin v France*: Positive Obligations under Article 4 of the European Convention on Human Rights' (2006) 6 HRLRev 585.

[9] The work of the ILO in the field of domestic labour is chronicled in V. Mantouvalou, 'Servitude and Forced Labour in the 21st Century: The Human Rights of Domestic Workers' (2006) 35 ILJ 395, 396–400. See also S. Scarpa, *Trafficking in Human Beings. Modern Slavery* (OUP, Oxford 2008).

[10] ETS 197, which entered into force on 1 February 2008. There is a particularly detailed Explanatory Report to the Convention. See also S. Egan, 'Protecting the victims of trafficking: problems and prospects' [2008] EHRLR 106.

mechanisms contained in Part VII. A Group of Experts on action against trafficking (GRETA) is established with responsibility for monitoring the activities of the Contracting Parties. There are also provisions ensuring that action by Council of Europe countries dovetails with international action to address the problem of human trafficking.

POSITIVE OBLIGATIONS

In addition to the question concerning whether the applicant was held in servitude in the *Siliadin* case, the Strasbourg Court was asked to consider whether France had afforded sufficient protection to the applicant under its positive obligations, since slavery and servitude were not classified as criminal offences under French criminal law. The couple who had kept the applicant in servitude had been acquitted when charged with the offences of wrongfully obtaining unpaid or insufficiently paid services from a vulnerable or dependent person. The Court noted a recommendation of the Parliamentary Assembly which had regretted the failure of Contracting Parties to make domestic slavery an offence under their criminal law in concluding that France had failed to meet its positive obligations under the Convention to afford the applicant effective protection against servitude.

In ruling that Article 4 requires Contracting Parties to take measures to suppress the problem of forced domestic labour, the Strasbourg Court took a significant step to breathe new life into Article 4. It connects the historical concepts of forced labour, servitude and slavery to the modern phenomenon of human trafficking.

FORCED OR COMPULSORY LABOUR

Article 4(2) provides that no one shall be required to perform forced or compulsory labour, but Article 4(3) provides for certain exceptions. The Strasbourg Court has said:

The Court reiterates that paragraph 3 of Article 4 is not intended to 'limit' the exercise of the right guaranteed by paragraph 2, but to 'delimit' the very content of that right, for it forms a whole with paragraph 2 and indicates what 'the term "forced or compulsory labour" shall not include' (ce qui 'n'est pas consideré comme "travail forcé ou obligatoire"'). This being so, paragraph 3 serves as an aid to the interpretation of paragraph 2. The four sub-paragraphs of paragraph 3, notwithstanding their diversity, are grounded on the governing ideas of the general interest, social solidarity and what is normal in the ordinary course of affairs.[11]

---

[11] *Karlheinz Schmidt v Germany*, 18 July 1994, Series A No 291-B; (1994) 18 EHRR 513, §22.

The expression 'forced or compulsory labour' is taken from a Convention of the International Labour Organisation, Convention No. 29 of 1930, subsequently supplemented by another ILO Convention, the Abolition of Forced Labour Convention of 1957. It seems reasonable to rely, for the interpretation of Article 4, on the work of the ILO organs in defining the term for the purposes of the ILO Conventions, and the Commission has in fact done so. The Commission has imported two key elements into the concept of forced or compulsory labour. First, the work must be performed by the worker involuntarily. Secondly, either the requirement to do the work must be unjust or oppressive or the work itself involves avoidable hardship.[12]

The issue of forced or compulsory labour was extensively examined by the Commission in the controversial *Iversen* case.[13] A law passed in Norway in 1956 provided that dentists might be required for a period of up to two years to take a position in a public dental service. Some members of the Opposition had objected to the Bill on the ground that it introduced a compulsory direction of labour which was contrary to the Norwegian Constitution and to Article 4 of the Convention. The respondent State, however, rejected these arguments and maintained that this direction of labour was necessary to implement a public dental service. The applicant, Iversen, was directed under the Act to take up for one year the position of dentist in the Moskenes district in northern Norway. He eventually accepted the post, but after some months he gave it up and left. He was subsequently convicted and sentenced under the Act, and his appeal was dismissed by the Supreme Court.

In his application to the Commission, he alleged that the Act, and the order assigning him to the district of Moskenes, were contrary to Article 4 of the Convention. Exceptionally, the Commission's decision on admissibility records a divided vote: it held by a majority of six votes to four that the application was inadmissible. The majority considered that the service of Iversen in Moskenes was not forced or compulsory labour within the meaning of Article 4 of the Convention. However, the majority was itself divided; four members of the majority considered that the service of Iversen in Moskenes was manifestly not forced or compulsory labour under Article 4(2), and therefore found it unnecessary to express any opinion on the applicability of Article 4(3), while the other two members of the majority considered that that service was reasonably required of him in an emergency threatening the well-being of the community and was therefore authorized under Article 4(3).

The concept of forced or compulsory labour was analysed by the four members of the majority as follows:

The concept cannot be understood solely in terms of the literal meaning of the words, and has in fact come to be regarded in international law and practice, as evidenced in part by the provisions and application of ILO Conventions and Resolutions on Forced Labour, as

---

[12] See App. 4653/70, *X v Federal Republic of Germany*, Decision of 1 April 1974 (1974), 17 *Yearbook* 148; App. 8410/78, *X v Federal Republic of Germany*, Decision of 13 December 1979, (1980) 18 DR 216; and App. 9322/81, *X v Netherlands*, Decision of 3 May 1983, (1983) 32 DR 180.

[13] App. 1468/62, *Iversen v Norway*, Decision of 17 December 1963, (1963) 6 *Yearbook* 278.

having certain elements...[namely] that the work or service is performed by the worker against his will and, secondly, that the requirement that the work or service be performed is unjust or oppressive or the work or service itself involves avoidable hardship.[14]

On this analysis the service required of Iversen was held not to be forced or compulsory labour under Article 4(2); the requirement to perform that service was not unjust or oppressive since the service, although obligatory:

...was for a short period, provided favourable remuneration, did not involve any diversion from chosen professional work, was only applied in the case of posts not filled after being duly advertised, and did not involve any discriminatory, arbitrary, or punitive application.

However, even if the element of oppressiveness could be said to be absent in this case, it is doubtful how far it is a necessary constituent of forced labour as generally under-stood in international law and practice. The ILO Forced Labour Convention No. 29 of 1930 in fact defines the term 'forced or compulsory labour', for the purposes of that Convention, simply as 'all work or service which is exacted from any person under the menace of a penalty and for which the said person has not offered himself voluntarily';[15] but that Convention did not prohibit such work or service if it forms part of normal civic obligations in a self-governing country, or is exacted in execution of a penal sen-tence, or exacted in an 'emergency requiring the mobilization of manpower for essen-tial work of national importance'. Article 4(3) of the European Convention, as seen above, contains similar provisions.

In the *Iversen* case, as already stated, the reasoning of the other two members of the Commission who voted for inadmissibility was based on Article 4(3); they held that the service of Iversen was service reasonably required of him in an emergency threatening the well-being of the community. The respondent State had made no sub-stantial submissions on this point but as part of the general background of the case had explained that the northern districts of Norway had a deplorable lack of social ser-vices, which seriously affected the social and health conditions of these communities; thus, while there was in Oslo in 1946 one dentist per 650 inhabitants, the ratio in three of the northern provinces was one dentist per 13,000, 6,000, and 5,500 inhabitants respectively. Moreover, adequate dental care was rendered even more difficult by the enormous distances, the difficulties of communication, and the arctic weather condi-tions prevailing during the winter months.

While these considerations may have made it difficult for the Norwegian authorities to find any alternative practical solution to the problem, it is by no means clear that they are relevant to the provisions of Article 4, which, unlike many of the later articles, contains no escape clause 'for the protection of health'. The opinion of the two mem-bers of the Commission referred to above is open to criticism; for it seems doubtful whether the situation in northern Norway could be described as an 'emergency' or

---

[14] (1963) 6 *Yearbook* 278, 328.

[15] Art. 2(1). See *Van der Mussele v Belgium*, 23 November 1983, Series A No 70, (1984) 6 EHRR 163, §§32–3.

'calamity' as required by Article 4(3)(c). These terms suggest some sudden overwhelming natural disaster, not the permanent social, climatic, and geographical conditions however serious they may be.

The minority of the Commission was rightly of the opinion that the application was not manifestly ill-founded, and that it should be declared admissible. The minority found that the conditions under which Iversen was required to perform his work, although it was paid and was only for a limited time, did not exclude the possibility of its being forced or compulsory labour, since it was imposed subject to penal sanctions; and that the question of the applicability of Article 4(3)(c) of the Convention required further examination.

It is hard to escape the conclusion that the Commission's decision to reject the application was influenced by political considerations. The case had caused considerable controversy in Norway and the decision coincided with a decision of the respondent State to renew its declaration accepting the Commission's competence under former Article 25 for a period of only one year.[16]

In the *Talmon* case,[17] the applicant complained that a requirement that he look for and accept employment deemed suitable for him as a condition of entitlement to unemployment benefit amounted to a requirement that he undertake forced or compulsory labour. He claimed that the only suitable employment for himself was work as an 'independent scientist and social critic'. The Commission declared the application manifestly ill-founded since it did not raise any issues under Article 4. Though this is an unremarkable case, the question may be posed as to the severity of the sanction for non-performance before something becomes compulsory or forced labour.

PRISON LABOUR

Article 4(3)(a) excludes from the term 'forced or compulsory labour' 'any work required to be done in the ordinary course of detention imposed according to the provisions of Article 5 of this Convention or during conditional release from such detention'.

In a group of applications[18] from persons detained in various prisons in Germany, the Commission examined the scope of this provision. The applicants complained that during their detention in prison they were subjected to forced and compulsory labour without receiving adequate payment and without being insured under the social security laws.

---

[16] (1963) 6 *Yearbook* 26. See also H. G. Schermers, 'European Commission of Human Rights: The Norwegian Dentist Case on Compulsory Labour' [1964] *Nederlands Tijdschrift voor International Recht* 366.

[17] App. 30300/96, *Talmon v Netherlands*, Decision of 26 February 1997; [1997] EHRLR 448.

[18] Apps. 3134/67, 3172/67 and 3188–3206/67, *Twenty-one Detained Persons v Federal Republic of Germany*, Decision of 6 April 1968, (1968) 11 *Yearbook* 528.

The Commission has regularly rejected applications by prisoners claiming higher payment for their work or claiming the right to be covered by social security systems.[19] The present applicants, however, raised a new point in complaining also that part of the work required of them during their detention was performed on behalf of private firms under contracts concluded with the prison administration; this system, they alleged, constituted a state of slavery for the prisoners concerned. However, the Commission examined this complaint primarily under Article 4(3)(a), that is, in relation to forced or compulsory labour. After an exceptionally detailed investigation of the background of this provision, and a survey of the practice in the Contracting Parties, the Commission found that the form of prison labour of which the applicants complained clearly appeared to fall within the framework of work normally required from prisoners within the meaning of Article 4(3)(a).

The Strasbourg Court has ruled as admissible an application by a man who had spent many years in prison complaining that the exclusion of prisoners from eligibility to be affiliated to the old-age pension system for work performed as a prisoner constituted unjustifiable discrimination when Article 4 is read with Article 14.[20]

It may be thought that the exemption under Article 4(3)(a) of 'work required to be done in the ordinary course of detention imposed according to the provisions of Article 5' can arise only if all the provisions of Article 5 have been observed. In the *Vagrancy* cases[21] the Commission had expressed the view that the work that the applicants were required to do was not justified under Article 4 because there had been a breach of Article 5(4). The Strasbourg Court, however, held that while there was a breach of Article 5(4), there was no breach of Article 4 because the vagrants were lawfully detained under Article 5(1)(e).[22] This is a perplexing decision since Article 5 must be read as a whole, and it would seem that any breach of paragraphs (1)–(4) would render the arrest or detention unlawful. It is not sufficient to say that the detention is justified under one provision of the Convention if it is unlawful under another provision. Nor does Article 4(3)(a) itself differentiate between the provisions of Article 5. On this point, therefore, the view of the Commission is to be preferred to that of the Court.

MILITARY SERVICE

Article 4(3)(b) excludes 'any service of a military character' from the prohibition of forced or compulsory labour.

---

[19] (1968) 11 *Yearbook* 528, 552.

[20] *Stummer v Austria*, (App. 37452/02), Decision of 11 October 2007.

[21] *De Wilde, Ooms and Versyp v Belgium*, 18 June 1971, Series A No 12, (1979–80) 1 EHRR 373. See ch.11 below.

[22] §89.

In the '*Sailor Boys*' case[23] four applicants aged 15 and 16 had joined the British army or naval forces for a period of nine years to be calculated from the age of 18. They had subsequently applied for discharge from the service but, in spite of repeated requests, discharge had been refused. They alleged, *inter alia*, a violation of their right under Article 4(1) not to be held in servitude.

The Commission also considered the case under Article 4(2) but found that any complaint that the applicants' service constituted 'forced or compulsory labour' must be rejected as being manifestly ill-founded in view of the express provision of Article 4(3)(b). That provision, according to the Commission, wholly excluded *voluntary* military service from the scope of Article 4(2); and, by the omission of the word 'compulsory' which appeared in the ILO Convention, 'it was intended to cover also the obligation to continue a service entered into on a voluntary basis.'[24]

The respondent State submitted that the exclusion of military service in Article 4(3)(b) was to be understood as applying equally to slavery and servitude in paragraph (1). Any argument to the contrary necessarily involved the anomalous conclusion that, although no service of a military character can be forced or compulsory labour under the Convention, military service may amount to the more oppressive condition of slavery or servitude. The applicants, however, rightly pointed out that the drafters of the article clearly intended that there should be an absolute prohibition against servitude or slavery, but only a qualified prohibition against forced or compulsory labour.

The Commission found that generally the duty of soldiers who enlist after the age of majority to observe the terms of their engagement, and the ensuing restriction of their freedom and personal rights, do not amount to an impairment of rights which could come under the terms 'slavery or servitude'; and that the young age at which the applicants entered the services could not in itself attribute the character of 'servitude' to the normal condition of a soldier.

With regard to the young age of enlistment, the applicants referred to the special protection of minors provided for in all legal systems in respect of 'their own possibly unconsidered engagements'. The Commission pointed out that the applicants' parents had given their consent and that:

the protection of minors in other fields of law consists exactly in the requirement of parental consent and also in the existence of the principle that an engagement entered into by the minor will be void without such consent but valid and binding if the consent has been duly given.

The Commission did not, however, refer to another element in the protection of minors, frequently found in domestic legal systems, which enables minors, in certain circumstances, to decide for themselves on reaching the age of majority whether to continue or to repudiate their undertaking.

---

[23] App. 3435–3438/67, *W, X, Y, and Z v United Kingdom*, Decision of 19 July 1968, (1968) 11 *Yearbook* 562.

[24] (1968) 11 *Yearbook* 562, 594.

The applications were thus finally rejected as inadmissible but subsequently revised Navy Service Regulations were introduced in the United Kingdom under which boy entrants could decide at the age of 18 to leave the navy after three years' adult service, that is, at the age of 21.

In addition to military service, Article 4(3)(b) also authorizes service required to be performed by conscientious objectors in lieu of compulsory military service.[25]

EMERGENCIES

Article 4(3)(c) takes outside the prohibition in Article 4(2) service exacted in case of an emergency or calamity threatening the life or well-being of the community. As noted above, in the *Iversen* case, some members of the Commission felt that this would encompass a shortage of dentists in remote parts of Norway. The better view is that it involves the work needed to deal with an acute and temporary emergency. Examples might be tackling a forest fire, or assisting in the evacuation of those threatened by some natural disaster. In requiring any service under this provision, the authorities would, of course, be required to have regard to a person's capacity for the work involved. In the absence of this exception, Contracting Parties would need to invoke Article 15 before the people could be required to assist in an emergency; the requirements of Article 15 are more strictly drawn than those set out in Article 4(3)(c). Nevertheless, the threshold for using the provision in Article 4(3)(c) does seem to be significant.

CIVIC OBLIGATIONS

Article 4(3)(d) authorizes 'any work which forms part of normal civic obligations'. This differs from the service encompassed within Article 4(3)(c) in that there need be no emergency. The test is one of normality in the sense of what might reasonably be expected of a particular individual in a particular situation. The distinction will usually be one of degree, but quite where the boundary is remains to be established. In one case[26] the Commission concluded that the obligation of the holder of shooting rights in a hunting district to take part in the gassing of fox holes could be justified either under paragraph (c) or (d). In another case, the Strasbourg Court was easily satisfied that jury service is a normal civic obligation.[27]

---

[25] Questions raised by this provision are discussed in ch.17 below in relation to App. 2299/64, *Grandrath v Federal Republic of Germany*, Report of Commission, 12 December 1966; Decision of Committee of Ministers, 29 June 1967, (1967) 10 *Yearbook* 626.

[26] App. 9686/82, *S v Federal Republic of Germany*, Decision of 4 October 1984 (1985) 39 DR 90.

[27] *Zarb Adami v Malta*, (App. 17209/02), 20 June 2006, (2007) 44 EHRR 49, ECHR 2006-VIII.

The question has been raised whether the Austrian system of legal aid was compatible with Article 4 of the Convention.[28] The applicant, a lawyer practising in Vienna, complained that he was compelled, contrary to Article 4, to act as unpaid defence counsel for a person who lacked the means to pay counsel's fees. Under the legal aid system, a lawyer was required to offer his services and was subject to disciplinary sanctions if he refused to do so. He was paid no fee and was reimbursed for practically none of his expenses. In return for these services, the respondent State paid annually to the Bar Association a fixed lump sum which was used for charitable purposes, especially for old-age pensions for lawyers no longer in practice; but there was no legal right to such benefits.

In the proceedings on admissibility, the respondent State submitted, *inter alia*, that lawyers, by voluntarily choosing their profession, accept the obligation to act under the legal aid system, and that consequently this was not compulsory labour, but a consequence of their own free decision. Further, even if it did constitute compulsory labour it formed part of normal civic obligations under Article 4(3)(d). The applicant replied that the obligation was limited to the legal profession, and within that profession applied only to counsel; consequently it could not be regarded as part of normal civic obligations. The Commission declared the application admissible, but there was subsequently a friendly settlement.

It would seem that the interpretation of 'normal' civic obligations requires a comparison with the practice in comparable professions in other Contracting Parties. Article 4(3)(d) contains the clearest invitation in the Convention to consider current practice as a standard of interpretation.

The issue of the normal incidents of professional work in the context of the free representation of indigents was considered by the Court in the *Van der Mussele* case.[29] The requirement in issue was that of Belgian law under which pupil barristers were required to represent indigent defendants without a fee or reimbursement of expenses. Failure to undertake this work could result in a refusal to admit the person to the Belgian Bar. The Strasbourg Court did not accept at face value the Commission's conclusion that the applicant had consented in advance to the situation. The Court's decision makes clear that the second requirement of forced or compulsory labour, namely that the character of the work to be performed must be unjust or oppressive, is very much a subsidiary criterion. The Court's approach is to have regard to all the circumstances of the case in the light of the purpose of Article 4. Having regard to the nature of the work which fell within the normal ambit of the work of an advocate, to the advantage to the pupil barrister of undertaking this work as part of professional training, and to the fact that the burden was not disproportionate, the Court concluded that there was no compulsory labour in this case for the purposes of Article 4(2) and so it did not need to consider whether the representation of indigents was a normal civic

[28] App. 4897/71, *Gussenbauer v Austria*, Decision of 22 March 1972, (1973) 42 CD 41 and App. 5219/71, *Gussenbauer v Austria*, Decision of 14 July 1972, (1973) 42 CD 94. See also App. 4653/70, *X v Federal Republic of Germany*, Decision of 1 April 1974, (1974) 17 *Yearbook* 148.

[29] *Van der Mussele v Belgium*, 23 November 1983, Series A No 70, (1984) 6 EHRR 163.

obligation for pupil barristers falling within Article 4(3)(d). The absence of any fee or reimbursement of expenses was regretted by the Court, but did not alone render the work forced or compulsory labour.

ARTICLE 4 AND ARTICLE 14

Article 14 of the Convention prohibits discrimination in areas within the ambit of the Convention.[30] This has caused particular difficulties in relation to Article 4.

The difficulty arises because of the unusual structure of Article 4. If the matters referred to in Article 4(3) are outside the scope of Article 4, can they ever be used as the basis for an argument that there has been discrimination in the way a Contracting Party regulates the activity?

In the *Van der Mussele* case,[31] the Strasbourg Court found that a requirement to undertake pro bono work without fee as a pupil advocate did not constitute forced labour under Article 4(2). But the Court went on to consider an argument based on discrimination between the groups required to undertake such legal work. The Court appears to have justified this by categorizing the work as 'abnormal' if there was discrimination in the groups or individuals required to undertake the work. In the event no such discrimination was found.

Karlheinz Schmidt v Germany[32] concerned an application complaining that a requirement in Germany that a person serve as a fireman or pay a fire service levy in lieu of service was discriminatory in that it applied to men but not to women, taking Article 4 together with Article 14.[33] Where the applicant lived, there was no shortage of volunteer firemen, and so the requirement was to pay the fire service levy. The Strasbourg Court considered that compulsory fire service constituted normal civic obligations within the meaning in Article 4(3)(d), and that the compensatory charge was so closely linked to compulsory fire service that it also fell within Article 4. The Court then went on to consider the issue of discrimination raised by the applicant. The Court found a violation of Article 14 read with Article 4(3)(d) despite that paragraph taking the matters included within its terms outside the protection afforded by Article 4.

In the *Zarb Adami* case,[34] the applicant successfully argued that practice in relation to the requirement to serve as a juror in Malta which resulted in very few women serving as jurors constituted unlawful discrimination when Article 4 was read together with Article 14, despite the categorization of jury service as a normal civic obligation. Judges Bratza and Garlicki, in two concurring opinions, express some dissatisfaction at the reasoning of the majority, and the reasoning of the Strasbourg Court in the

---

[30] See ch.24 below.
[31] *Van der Mussele v Belgium*, 23 November 1983, Series A No 70, (1984) 6 EHRR 163.
[32] *Karlheinz Schmidt v Germany*, 18 July 1994, Series A, No 291-B, (1994) 18 EHRR 513.
[33] See ch.24 below on Art. 14.
[34] *Zarb Adami v Malta*, (App. 17209/02), 20 June 2006, (2007) 44 EHRR 49, ECHR 2006-VIII.

earlier cases. Both judges, however, consider that there is a line of reasoning which permits these cases to be regarded as falling within the ambit of Article 4.[35] Judge Garlicki says:

...I believe that it is possible to read Article 4, taken as a whole, in a broader way, not only as prohibiting any forms of compulsory labour but also as regulating State prerogatives in establishing different forms of compulsory work and services. In other words, Article 4 may also be read as setting a general framework of duties which may be imposed on an individual. Article 4 empowers the State to establish such duties and services but—by the very fact of their enumeration—Article 4 absorbs (includes) them into the realm of the Convention. One of the consequences of such inclusion is that those duties and services must be formulated in a manner compatible with the Convention, its Article 14 included.[36]

CONSENT

Consent cannot make slavery or servitude which would otherwise be prohibited under Article 4(1) lawful. In the '*Sailor Boys*' case[37] the respondent State argued that an essential feature of servitude is that it has been forced upon a person against his will, in circumstances where he has no genuine freedom of choice.[38] However, Article 4(1) should be construed as prohibiting also the voluntary acceptance of servitude. As the Commission had observed, 'Personal liberty is an inalienable right which a person cannot voluntarily abandon.'[39] Indeed, a proposal to add the qualification 'involuntary' to servitude was rejected by the drafters of the Supplementary Convention on Slavery 1956 and of the United Nations Covenant on Civil and Political Rights precisely on the ground that 'it should not be possible for any person to contract himself into bondage.'[40] This interpretation is further supported by the judgment of the Strasbourg Court in the *Vagrancy* cases.[41]

However, it is less clear, in view of the terms 'forced' and 'compulsory', whether a voluntary undertaking would exclude the applicability of Article 4(2). It has already been seen that one of the elements of work which is prohibited is its performance by workers against their will; but the question remains whether a person who has voluntarily accepted an obligation can be compelled to continue in circumstances which, objectively viewed, would constitute forced or compulsory labour. The question raised

---

[35] Indeed Judge Bratza would have found the violation to be of Article 14 read in conjunction with Article 4, rather than Article 14 read in conjunction with Article 4(3)(d).

[36] Concurring Opinion of Judge Garlicki.

[37] App. 3435–3438/67, *W, X, Y, and Z v United Kingdom*, Decision of 19 July 1968, (1968) 11 *Yearbook* 562.

[38] (1968) 11 *Yearbook* 562, 576.

[39] Report of the Commission in the *Vagrancy Cases*, 19 July 1969, Series B No 10, 91.

[40] UN Doc. A/2929, 33.

[41] *De Wilde, Ooms and Versyp v Belgium*, 18 June 1971, Series A No 12, (1979–80) 1 EHRR 373. See ch.11 below.

is that of the severity of the sanction before the activity could be said to be compulsory or forced.

In the *Iversen* case the respondent State contended that the applicant had freely accepted the conditions of service, that he knew of the effect of the Norwegian legislation and voluntarily entered into an agreement with the competent authorities, and in particular that by his conversations with officials in the Ministry for Social Affairs and his consent to being posted in Moskenes, the relationship between the applicant and the Ministry had assumed a contractual nature which excluded any application of Article 4 of the Convention.[42] The Commission, however, did not refer to this aspect of the case in its decision.

In the '*Sailor Boys*' case, however, the Commission appeared to attach great importance to the fact that not only the applicants but also their parents had initially given their consent. This view, again, may be open to doubt in view of the Court's judgment in the *Vagrancy* cases and the issues of principle underlying that judgment, which were not fully apparent in the Commission's reasoning.

CONCLUDING REMARKS

In its unanimous decision in the *Siliadin* case,[43] the Strasbourg Court set its judgment in the context of a number of international conventions, including the Council of Europe Convention on Action against Trafficking in Human Beings, though it made no reference to this Convention in its judgment.[44] It rather located its judgment in questions of the definition of servitude in the light of international conventions, especially those to which France was a party. Now that the Trafficking Convention is in force for a substantial number of Contracting Parties, and has been signed by a further number, it is worth speculating whether the Strasbourg Court will expand on the principle set out in the *Siliadin* case in order to interpret Article 4 in the light of the obligations set out in the Trafficking Convention. That would be a welcome use of the principle of interpreting the Convention as a living instrument in order to strengthen efforts within the Council of Europe to combat the scourge of trafficking in human beings. At present, victims of trafficking seem to have little access to the courts, including the Strasbourg Court. If the opportunity presents itself, an explicit interpretation of Article 4 to address human trafficking could help to change that.

---

[42] App. 1468/62, *Iversen v Norway*, Decision of 17 December 1963, (1963) 6 *Yearbook* 278, 308.
[43] *Siliadin v France* (App. 73316/01), 26 July 2005, (2006) 43 EHRR 287, ECHR 2005-VII.
[44] The Convention had only been adopted on 16 May 2005.

11

PERSONAL LIBERTY
AND SECURITY

INTRODUCTION

The Strasbourg Court now frequently prefaces its consideration of Article 5 cases with the following words:

The Court stresses the fundamental importance of the guarantees contained in Article 5 for securing the right of individuals in a democracy to be free from arbitrary detention at the hands of the authorities. It has stressed in that connection that any deprivation of liberty must not only have been effected in conformity with the substantive and procedural rules of national law but must equally be in keeping with the very purpose of Article 5, namely to protect the individual from arbitrary detention. In order to minimize the risks of arbitrary detention, Article 5 provides a corpus of substantive rights intended to ensure that the act of deprivation of liberty be amenable to independent judicial scrutiny and secures the accountability of the authorities for that measure.[1]

The object of Article 5 is to guarantee liberty of the person,[2] and in particular to provide guarantees against arbitrary arrest or detention. It seeks to achieve this aim by excluding any form of arrest or detention without lawful authority and proper judicial control. Article 5(1) spells out exhaustively the only conditions under which a person may be deprived of his liberty, and these will be construed narrowly.[3] Article 5(2)–(5) sets out certain rights for persons who have been detained.[4] Derogations under Article 15 from the obligations in Article 5 are permitted.[5]

The first sentence of Article 5 provides that everyone has the right to liberty and security of person; the meaning of 'security' in Article 5 is, however, uncertain.[6] The

---

[1] Taken from *Bazorkina v Russia*, (App. 69481/01), 27 July 2006, (2008) 46 EHRR 261, §146.

[2] M. Mancovei, *The right to liberty and security of the person: a Guide to the implementation of Article 5 of the European Convention on Human Rights*, Human Rights Handbooks, No. 5 (Council of Europe Publishing, Strasbourg 2004).

[3] *Lexa v Slovakia*, (App. 54334/00), 23 September 2008, §§118–19.

[4] For a discussion of aspects of the protection afforded by Article 5 in criminal proceedings, see generally S. Trechsel, *Human Rights in Criminal Proceedings* (OUP, Oxford 2005).

[5] See ch.4 above. See also *A and others v United Kingdom*, (App. 3455/05), 19 February 2009 [GC], (2009) 49 EHRR 29, ECHR 2009-nyr.

[6] See R. Powell, 'The right to security of person in European Court of Human Rights jurisprudence' [2007] EHRLR 649.

question was raised, but not resolved, in the *East African Asians* cases.[7] On the normal principles of interpretation, the term 'security' should be given a meaning independent of 'liberty', but the remainder of the provision is concerned exclusively with deprivation of liberty. The matter appears to have been finally resolved in the *Bozano* case,[8] where the Strasbourg Court's reasoning indicated that the primary focus of Article 5 is the deprivation of liberty.[9] In cases involving the disappearance of prisoners, however, the Court has made greater use of the terminology of 'liberty and security of person', because of uncertainty as to the continuing detention of the disappeared person and the suspicion that he or she may have been executed.[10]

WHAT AMOUNTS TO A DEPRIVATION OF LIBERTY?

The second sentence of the provision states that no one shall be 'deprived of his liberty' save in the circumstances described. What constitutes a 'deprivation of liberty'? Confinement to a locked prison cell clearly constitutes such a deprivation, but less absolute forms of restriction can be more problematic. Article 2 of Protocol 4 protects the right to leave a country and to move freely within one,[11] so it has been necessary for the Strasbourg Court to draw a line between deprivations of liberty within the meaning of Article 5, and restrictions on freedom of movement. As the case-law shows, this distinction is more a matter of degree and intensity than of nature or substance.[12] In deciding whether a restriction on freedom falls within the scope of Article 5, the Strasbourg Court will look at such factors as the type, duration, effects, and manner of implementation of the measure in question.

The *Guzzardi* case[13] is the classic example of a borderline case. The applicant was ordered, on suspicion of being a member of the Mafia, to remain on a small island near Sardinia for sixteen months. Although there was no perimeter fence, he was not allowed to leave an area of two and a half square kilometres containing a village inhabited solely by other men subject to the same type of residence order, and he had to keep a curfew and report to the police twice a day. His wife and child were not prevented from living with him, but the available accommodation was cramped and dilapidated and thus unsuitable for a family. Although he was allowed to work, there were few

---

[7] App. 4626/70, *East African Asians v United Kingdom*, Decision of 6 March 1978, (1978) 13 DR 5.

[8] *Bozano v France*, 18 December 1986, Series A No 111, (1987) 9 EHRR 297.

[9] See especially §54.

[10] See, for example, *Timurtaş v Turkey*, (App. 23531/94), 13 June 2000, (2001) 33 EHRR 121, ECHR 2000-VI, §106; *Çiçek v Turkey*, (App. 25704/94), 27 February 2001, (2003) 37 EHRR 464, §169; and *Ibragimov and others v Russia*, (App. 34561/03), 29 May 2008, §117.

[11] See ch.23 below.

[12] *Guzzardi v Italy*, 6 November 1980, Series A No 39, (1981) 3 EHRR 333, §93.

[13] *Guzzardi v Italy*, 6 November 1980, Series A No 39, (1981) 3 EHRR 333.

employers on the island and he was unable to find a job. He had to seek the permission of the police before making a telephone call or seeing an outside visitor. Any breach of these conditions was punishable by incarceration. The Strasbourg Court, comparing Guzzardi's situation to that of a person kept in an open prison, found that there had been a deprivation of liberty for the purposes of Article 5.

In each case the Court must examine the concrete situation of the person involved. The applicant in the *HL* case[14] was severely autistic, unable to speak and prone to bouts of agitation and self-harm. His doctors decided that it was in his best interests to be admitted to hospital for a while; since he did not resist, he was admitted as an 'informal' patient, under no legal obligation to remain in hospital. He remained in the hospital on this basis for just over three months; thereafter, following national legal proceedings, he was compulsorily detained. He complained under Article 5(1) about his time as an 'informal' patient. The Court did not find it determinative that the applicant had been compliant and never attempted, or expressed the wish, to leave, considering that 'the right to liberty is too important in a democratic society for a person to lose the benefit of Convention protection for the single reason that he may have given himself up to be taken into detention'. Instead, it found the key factor to have been that the health care professionals treating and managing the applicant exercised complete and effective control over his care and movements, and he was not, in reality, free to leave, since had he made such an attempt there was evidence that the doctors would immediately have detained him under compulsory powers. There had, therefore, been a deprivation of liberty.[15]

The applicants in the *Amuur* case[16] were refugees from Somalia who had travelled via Kenya and Syria to Paris-Orly Airport. They were refused entry to France on the ground that their passports had been falsified and for twenty days, before being sent back to Syria, they were shuttled by the police between a nearby hotel, one of the floors of which had been let as a transit zone to the Ministry of the Interior, and the *Espace* lounge of the airport. The Court rejected the respondent State's argument that, since the applicants had been free at any time to return to Syria or any other country which would have accepted them, the holding measures to which they had been subjected did not amount to a deprivation of liberty.

Cases involving members of the armed forces have also thrown up some problems of definition. The *Engel* case[17] concerned the penalties which could be imposed on conscripted Dutch soldiers. There were grades of arrest: the lower grades involved confinement to barracks, while 'strict arrest' involved detention in locked cells. The

---

[14] *HL v United Kingdom*, (App. 45508/99), 5 October 2004, (2005) 40 EHRR 761, ECHR 2004-IX. See also *Ashingdane v United Kingdom*, 28 May 1985, Series A No 93, (1985) 7 EHRR 528.

[15] See also *Enhorn v Sweden*, (App. 56529/00), 25 January 2005, (2005) 41 EHRR 633, ECHR 2005-I, discussed later in this chapter. Contrast *HM v Switzerland*, (App. 39187/98), 26 February 2002, (2004) 38 EHRR 314, ECHR 2002-II.

[16] *Amuur v France* (App. 19776/92), 25 June 1996, (1996) 22 EHRR 533, ECHR 1996-III.

[17] *Engel and others v Netherlands*, (Apps. 5100/71, 5101/71, 5102/71, 5354/72, and 5370/72), 8 June 1976, Series A No 22, (1979–80) 1 EHRR 647.

Court considered that a different regime might well be applicable to the armed forces, and went on to find that the light forms of arrest did not amount to deprivations of liberty, although strict arrest would. Similarly, once an individual is detained in prison, additional restrictions on his or her liberty, imposed for disciplinary reasons, will not usually give rise to any issue under Article 5(1), although sufficiently severe cases could breach Article 3.[18]

Unacknowledged deprivation of liberty constitutes a serious violation of Article 5.[19] The Strasbourg Court now frequently says in such cases:

> The unacknowledged detention of an individual is a complete negation of these guarantees and discloses a most grave violation of Article 5. Bearing in mind the responsibility of the authorities to account for individuals under their control, Article 5 requires them to take effective measures to safeguard against the risk of disappearance and to conduct a prompt and effective investigation into an arguable claim that a person has been taken into custody and has not been seen since....[20]

The characteristics of unacknowledged deprivations are a failure by the State to account for the whereabouts of a person taken into their custody. This requires the formal recording of information as to the identity of the person detained and the person detaining him or her, the date, time, duration, and location of the detention, and the reasons for the detention.[21] Where complaints are made of unacknowledged detentions, there is a positive obligation on the State to conduct an investigation to determine the whereabouts of the missing person.[22]

THE CONCEPT OF ARBITRARINESS

It is axiomatic that the essence of Article 5 is to protect the individual against arbitrary detention. Even a detention which is lawful under national law will be a breach of Article 5 if it is arbitrary. Such a situation would arise where the authorities have acted in bad faith or used deception, as in the *Čonka* case,[23] where Romany families were tricked into presenting themselves at a police station with the promise that their asylum applications would be completed, only to be served with deportation papers and taken into immediate custody. The Grand Chamber has spelled out the key principles relating to arbitrariness in its judgment in the *Saadi* case.[24] The Court stressed

---

[18] See ch.9 above.

[19] *Timurtaş v Turkey*, (App. 23531/94), 13 June 2000, (2001) 33 EHRR 121, ECHR 2000-VI, §103.

[20] Taken from *Bazorkina v Russia*, (App. 69481/01), 27 July 2006, (2008) 46 EHRR 261, §146.

[21] *Çiçek v Turkey*, (App. 25704/94), 27 February 2001, (2003) 37 EHRR 464, §165.

[22] For an example of such cases arising from Russian conduct in Chechnya, see *Idalova and Idalov v Russia*, (App. 41515/04), 5 February 2009.

[23] *Čonka v Belgium*, (App. 51564/99), 5 February 2002, (2002) 34 EHRR 1298, ECHR 2002-I.

[24] *Saadi v United Kingdom*, (App. 13229/03), 29 January 2008 [GC], (2008) 47 EHRR 427, ECHR 2008-nyr, §§67–74.

the following points. Both the order to detain and the execution of the detention must genuinely conform with the purpose of detention as set out in Article 5(1); a failure to ensure that there is some relationship between the ground of permitted deprivation of liberty and the conditions of detention will render the deprivation arbitrary. The Strasbourg Court will also assess whether detention was necessary to achieve its stated aim. Detention should be seen as a remedy of last resort, and lesser measures must be considered and found to be insufficient to safeguard either the individual or the public interest. It follows that the duration of any detention will also be a relevant factor in considering whether it was, or has become, arbitrary in nature.

Where the detention is for the purpose specified in Article 5(1)(b), (d), or (e), the notion of arbitrariness requires an assessment to be made of the necessity of detention for the stated aim.[25] The requirement is somewhat different in relation to detention following conviction by a competent court under Article 5(1)(a), since the choice of detention as a sentence and its duration are matters for the national court rather than the Strasbourg Court.[26] The Court has adopted a similar position in relation to detention with a view to deportation in Article 5(1)(f), provided that the detention does not continue for an unreasonable length of time, and that deportation proceedings are conducted with due diligence.[27] The Court has said that the same consideration applies where the detention is for the purpose of preventing an unauthorized entry into the country.[28]

POSITIVE OBLIGATIONS

The development of positive obligations[29] under Article 5 has lagged somewhat behind its development under other articles of the Convention, most notably Articles 2, 3, and 8. That position has largely been remedied by the Strasbourg Court's judgment in the *Storck* case.[30] The applicant, who was born in 1958, had spent much of her life in hospitals and psychiatric institutions. One of the issues raised in her application concerned her detention in a locked ward in a private psychiatric clinic for nearly two years from July 1977 to April 1979. The police had assisted in her return to the clinic when she had escaped. An action for damages which she later instituted was, following appeals, unsuccessful. The Strasbourg Court found that the responsibility of the respondent State arose for three reasons: first, the police had assisted in her return to the clinic;

---

[25] §70.

[26] Provided that the detention follows and has a sufficient causal connection with a lawful conviction: §71.

[27] §72.   [28] §§73–4.

[29] Save for those expressly provided for in the provision: see A. Mowbray, *The Development of Positive Obligations under the European Convention on Human Rights by the European Court of Human Rights* (Hart, Oxford 2004), ch.4. Note also the requirements to record detentions, and to investigate unacknowledged detentions referred to earlier in this chapter.

[30] *Storck v Germany*, (App. 61603/00), 16 June 2005, (2006) 43 EHRR 96, ECHR 2005-V.

secondly, the courts had rejected her claims; and thirdly, the State had positive obligations under Article 5. The Court said:

Article 5(1), first sentence,... must... be considered as laying down a positive obligation on the State to protect the liberty of its citizens. Any conclusion to the effect that this was not the case would not only be inconsistent with the Court's case-law, notably under Articles 2, 3 and 8 of the Convention. It would, moreover, leave a sizeable gap in the protection from arbitrary detention which would be inconsistent with the importance of personal liberty in a democratic society. The State is, therefore, obliged to take measures providing effective protection of vulnerable persons, including reasonable steps to prevent the deprivation of liberty of which the authorities have or ought to have knowledge....[31]

To the extent that earlier pronouncements[32] might be taken to indicate that there are no, or only very limited, positive obligations arising under Article 5, those decisions should not be regarded as so deciding.[33]

NOTIFICATION OF THE REASONS FOR ARREST OR DETENTION

Article 5(2) embodies the elementary safeguard that those deprived of their liberty should know why. It provides:

Everyone who is arrested shall be informed promptly, in a language which he understands, of the reasons for his arrest and of any charge against him.

Consequently any person arrested or detained must be told promptly and in simple language the essential factual and legal basis for the detention. This will enable detainees to apply to challenge the lawfulness of the detention if they so wish. Whether the obligation is met will be determined in the light of all the circumstances of each case.[34] This provision applies in respect of *everyone* who is arrested or detained. It may be compared with Article 6(3)(a), which provides that everyone charged with a criminal offence must be informed promptly, in a language which he or she understands, and in detail, of the nature and cause of the accusation against him or her. The information to which a person is entitled under Article 6 is more specific and more detailed than that required by Article 5, because it is necessary to enable the accused to prepare a defence. For the purposes of Article 5(2), on the other hand, it is sufficient if detainees are informed in general terms of the reasons for the arrest and of any charge against them.[35]

---

[31] *Storck*, §102.

[32] *Nielsen v Denmark*, 28 November 1988, Series A No 144, (1989) 11 EHRR 175; *Koniarska v United Kingdom*, (App. 33670/96), Decision of 12 October 2000.

[33] See A. Campbell, 'Positive obligations under the ECHR: deprivation of liberty by private actors' (2006) 10 *Edinburgh Law Review* 399.

[34] *Kerr v United Kingdom*, (App. 40451/98), Decision of 7 December 1999.

[35] App. 343/57, *Nielsen v Denmark*, Decision of 2 September 1959, (1958–9) 2 *Yearbook* 412, 462.

The question of the timing of notification was raised in the *Murray* case.[36] The Strasbourg Court noted that whether the content and promptness of the information given to the detainee was sufficient depended on the special features of each case. An interval of a matter of hours between arrest and interrogation, during which the reasons for her arrest were brought to her attention, could not be regarded as failing to be prompt.

On occasion, however, the circumstances of the arrest may speak for themselves, as the Strasbourg Court found to have been the case in the *Dikme* case.[37] The applicant had presented false identity papers to the police and had been arrested immediately the police discovered the forgery. Whether or not the police gave reasons, the Court found that the applicant could not complain under Article 5(2) that he had been ignorant of the grounds for his arrest. In the *Kerr* case,[38] the applicant was informed at the time of his arrest of the anti-terrorist legislation under which he was detained. The Court held that a bare indication of the legal basis for an arrest could not, on its own, be sufficient for the purposes of Article 5(2), but that since, immediately after his arrest, the applicant was questioned about his suspected involvement in a recent bomb explosion at a military barracks, his membership of a proscribed organization, and about the use he had made of items seized by the police from his house, in particular computer equipment and the information stored on the computer, the reasons for his detention must have been sufficiently clear to him for the purposes of Article 5(2).

THE LAWFULNESS OF
THE DEPRIVATION OF LIBERTY

A deprivation of liberty which does not fall within one of the six categories listed in Article 5(1) will breach the Convention.[39] So, for example, in the *Riera Blume* case,[40] the Strasbourg Court found a violation of Article 5(1) arising from a court order releasing six members of a religious cult into the custody of their families who, assisted by the police, kept them confined in a hotel for ten days for 'deprogramming' by psychiatrists. Quite apart from the problems arising under Article 9 on freedom of religion, 'deprogramming' does not fall within one of the six permitted exceptions to the right to liberty.[41]

It is not, however, sufficient merely to come within one of the permitted grounds of detention. The deprivation of liberty must also be 'lawful' and carried out 'in

---

[36] *Murray v United Kingdom*, 28 October 1994, Series A No 300-A, (1995) 19 EHRR 193.

[37] *Dikme v Turkey*, (App. 20869/92), 11 July 2000, ECHR 2000-VIII.

[38] *Kerr v United Kingdom*, (App. 40451/98), Decision of 7 December 1999.

[39] *Saadi v United Kingdom*, (App. 13229/03), 29 January 2008, (2008) 47 EHRR 427, ECHR 2008-nyr, §67.

[40] *Riera Blume and others v Spain* (App. 37680/97), 9 March 1999, (2000) 30 EHRR 632, ECHR 1999-II.

[41] See below in this chapter.

accordance with a procedure prescribed by law'. The particular arrest or detention must have been carried out in compliance with the procedural and substantive rules of national law. Where, for example, a warrant is required for arrest, the warrant must be in the correct form or the arrest will not be lawful under Article 5.[42] Similarly, where force is used in order to effect an arrest, the degree of force used must not exceed that authorized in the circumstances by national law. Reviewing compliance with national law is not normally part of the Strasbourg Court's role, which tends to leave this job to the national courts in accordance with the principle of subsidiarity. However, since under Article 5(1) disregard of national law entails a breach of the Convention, the Court must satisfy itself that national law has been followed.[43] But a mere procedural defect, as distinct from a more serious irregularity, in national law will not be sufficient to constitute a failure to follow national law.[44]

In order for a deprivation of liberty to be 'lawful' within the meaning of Article 5(1) it is not sufficient for it simply to have been carried out in accordance with national law. In addition, the Convention requires that the national law be of a certain quality. First, it must contain clear and accessible rules governing the circumstances in which it is permissible for the State to deprive an individual of his or her liberty and the procedure which must be followed.[45] In the *Amuur* case,[46] guidelines under French law concerning the holding of asylum seekers in the international zone of an airport were contained in an unpublished Ministry of the Interior circular. This circular was not available to asylum seekers or their lawyers, contained no guarantees against arbitrary detention, and did not provide for review by the national courts. The law was not sufficiently clear and accessible. Similarly, in the *Baranowski* case,[47] the Court found deficiencies in the Polish law on pre-trial detention. In 1993, when the applicant was arrested, it was the practice in Poland that, once a bill of indictment had been lodged, the accused could continue to be detained on remand until trial without the need for a court order. The Court found that this practice of maintaining detention on the basis of the indictment was not founded on any specific legislative provision or case-law but stemmed from the absence of clear rules. It did not, therefore, satisfy the test of foreseeability.[48] Furthermore, the fact that without a court order the detention could continue for an unlimited and unpredictable period was contrary to the principle of legal certainty and open to arbitrariness and abuse.

---

[42] See, for example, *Rakevich v Russia*, (App. 58973/00), 28 October 2003.

[43] *Benham v United Kingdom* (App. 19380/92), 10 June 1996, (1996) 22 EHRR 293, ECHR 1996-III, §40; *Winterwerp v Netherlands*, 24 October 1979, Series A No 33, (1979–80) 2 EHRR 387, §46; *Steel and others v United Kingdom* (App. 24838/94), 23 September 1998, (1998) 28 EHRR 603, ECHR 1998-VII, §54.

[44] *Mooren v Germany*, (App. 11364/03), 9 July 2009 [GC], §§72–98.

[45] 'Lawfulness' in Article 5(1) thus carries the same meaning as 'in accordance with law' in Articles 8–11: see the *Steel and others v United Kingdom* (App. 24838/94), 23 September 1998, (1998) 28 EHRR 603, ECHR 1998-VII; and ch.14 below.

[46] *Amuur v France* (App. 19776/92), 25 June 1996, (1996) 22 EHRR 533, ECHR 1996-III.

[47] *Baranowski v Poland*, (App. 28358/95), 28 March 2000, ECHR 2000-III.

[48] See, similarly, *Hilda Hafsteinsdottir v Iceland*, (App. 40905/98), 8 June 2004.

As the *Baranowski* judgment indicates, even where the national law has been complied with, the deprivation of liberty will not be 'lawful' if national law allows for arbitrary or excessive detention. In the *Erkalo* case[49] the applicant was detained in a mental hospital pursuant to a court order. When the order expired there was, because of an administrative error, a period of two months during which the applicant continued to be detained before a new order was granted by the court. Although, under the Dutch Code of Criminal Procedure, the detention was not unlawful in these circumstances, the Court held that the lack of administrative and judicial safeguards—demonstrated by the fact that the absence of any legal basis for the detention came to light only when the applicant himself applied to court—rendered the detention arbitrary and thus unlawful under Article 5(1).[50]

PERMITTED PRE-TRIAL DETENTION

Article 5(1)(c) allows for the arrest and pre-trial detention of a person in the following terms:

the lawful arrest or detention of a person effected for the purpose of bringing him before the competent legal authority on reasonable suspicion of having committed an offence or when it is reasonably considered necessary to prevent his committing an offence or fleeing after having done so;

Article 5(3) adds to the safeguards for such persons by providing:

Everyone arrested or detained in accordance with the provisions of paragraph (1)(c) of this article shall be brought promptly before a judge or other officer authorized by law to exercise judicial power and shall be entitled to trial within a reasonable time or to release pending trial. Release may be conditioned by guarantees to appear for trial.

Article 5(1)(c) can be broken down into a number of separate conditions, all of which must be present in order for the arrest or detention to be acceptable under the Convention. Thus, the arrest or detention must be 'lawful'; it must be effected for the purpose of bringing the detainee 'before the competent legal authority'; and the detainee must reasonably be suspected of having committed an offence or of being about to commit an offence or abscond having committed an offence.

The expression 'competent legal authority' has been held to carry the same meaning as 'judge or other officer authorized by law to exercise judicial power' in Article 5(3);[51] this meaning is considered in more detail below in this chapter.

---

[49] *Erkalo v Netherlands*, (App. 23807/94), 2 September 1998, (1999) 28 EHRR 509, ECHR 1998-VI.

[50] The Court reached a similar conclusion in *HL v United Kingdom*, (App. 45508/99), 5 October 2004, (2005) 40 EHRR 761, ECHR 2004-IX.

[51] *Schiesser v Switzerland*, 4 December 1979, Series A No 34, (1979–80) 2 EHRR 417.

It has now been established that these provisions do not permit any form of preventive detention. It is not acceptable to detain someone for a crime not yet committed.[52]

As long as, at the time of the arrest or detention, the intention to bring the suspect to court is there, it is immaterial whether or not in the event he is actually brought to court or charged,[53] although too long a period of preliminary detention without judicial control may give rise to an issue under Article 5(3).

The word 'offence' in Article 5(1)(c) carries an autonomous meaning, identical to that of 'criminal offence' in Article 6,[54] and the 'offence' must be specific and concrete. Although the classification of the offence under national law is one factor to be taken into account, the nature of the proceedings and the severity of the penalty at stake are also relevant.[55] Thus, for example, detention under close arrest on charges of desertion from the British army,[56] carrying a maximum penalty of two years' imprisonment, falls within Article 5(1)(c), although such military offences lie outside the mainstream English criminal law.

There will, accordingly, be very few cases falling within the second two alternatives in paragraph 1(c). Since the words 'when it is reasonably considered necessary to prevent [the detained person] committing an offence' do not authorize general preventive detention, evidence of intention on the part of the detainee to commit a concrete offence will be necessary. However, in most European countries, acts preparatory to the commission of a crime are themselves categorized as offences. Such evidence would, therefore, usually be sufficient to bring the detainee within the first limb: arrest or detention upon 'reasonable suspicion of having committed an offence'. Similarly any arrest or detention falling within the third limb—'to prevent [the detainee]...fleeing after having [committed an offence]'—will also fall within the first.

The requirement that the arrest and detention must be dependent upon the existence of reasonable suspicion that an offence has been committed means that there must be facts or information which would satisfy an objective observer.[57] In the *Fox, Campbell and Hartley* case,[58] the applicants argued that the interpretation by the courts of emergency legislation as requiring only a subjective test of honest belief that the person detained was a terrorist was incompatible with Article 5(1)(c). The Strasbourg Court found that in the context of the special problems presented in combating terrorism a lower standard of 'reasonable suspicion' might be acceptable, but that some objectively realistic grounds would still be needed. Since the respondent State had not provided

[52] *Lawless v Ireland*, 1 July 1961, Series A No 3, (1979–80) 1 EHRR 15, §§13–14; and *Jėčius v Lithuania* (App. 34578/97), 31 July 2000, (2002) 35 EHRR 400, ECHR 2000-IX. For argument to the contrary, see C. Macken, 'Preventive Detention and the Right to personal Liberty and security under Article 5 ECHR' (2006) 10 *The International Journal of Human Rights* 195.

[53] *Labita v Italy*, (App. 26772/95), 6 April 2000 [GC], (2008) 46 EHRR 1228, ECHR 2000-IV, §155.

[54] See ch.12 below.

[55] *Benham v United Kingdom*, (App. 19380/92), 10 June 1996, (1996) 22 EHRR 293, ECHR 1996-III.

[56] *Hood v United Kingdom*, (App. 27267/95), 18 February 1999, (2000) 29 EHRR 365, ECHR 1999-I.

[57] *Erdagöz v Turkey*, (App. 21890/93), 22 October 1997, (2001) 32 EHRR 443, ECHR 1997-VI.

[58] *Fox, Campbell and Hartley v United Kingdom*, 30 August 1990, Series A No 182, (1991) 13 EHRR 157.

any evidence on which it could be shown that there was any basis for the suspicion that the applicants were terrorists, the Strasbourg Court found a violation of Article 5(1)(c). In the *Labita* case[59] it held that the uncorroborated hearsay evidence of an anonymous informant was not enough to found 'reasonable suspicion' of the applicant's involvement in Mafia-type activities. In the *O'Hara* case,[60] the applicant was arrested on suspicion of having committed a sectarian murder, and released without charge after six days and thirteen hours. The applicant complained of unlawful arrest, assault, and ill-treatment before the national courts, where the arresting officer gave evidence that he had made the arrest after having been told by a superior officer at a briefing that the applicant was suspected of the murder. It emerged during the Strasbourg proceedings that the briefing had been based on information from four separate informants, who had previously been proved reliable and whose information about the murder had been consistent. The Court held that this was sufficient to found a 'reasonable suspicion' that the applicant was involved.

Article 5(3) guarantees certain rights to persons arrested or detained in accordance with the provisions of Article 5(1)(c). The first part of Article 5(3) is concerned with rights immediately on arrest (the arrest period); the second part deals with detention on remand (the remand period), that is, following charge.[61]

THE ARREST PERIOD

According to Article 5(3), any person arrested on suspicion of having committed a criminal offence has the right to be brought 'promptly' before 'a judge or other officer authorized by law to exercise judicial power'. In contrast to the right to judicial review of the legality of the detention under Article 5(4), which may be conditional on the application of the detained person, the right under Article 5(3) is to be brought promptly before a judge: it is the duty of a Contracting Party on its own initiative to see that this is done.[62]

There has been considerable case-law on the meaning of 'promptly' in this context, particularly in connection with applicants detained on suspicion of involvement in terrorism.[63] States as diverse as the United Kingdom and Turkey have invoked the need to hold terrorist suspects *incommunicado* for some time following arrest, because of the risk that other members of the terrorist organization could destroy evidence or put the lives of witnesses or even judges in danger. Conversely, it can of course be argued that judicial safeguards are of particular importance in connection with emotive crimes of

---

[59] *Labita v Italy*, (App. 26772/95), 6 April 2000 [GC], (2008) 46 EHRR 1228, ECHR 2000-IV.

[60] *O'Hara v United Kingdom*, (App. 37555/97), 16 October 2001, (2002) 34 EHRR 812, ECHR 2001-X.

[61] These are distinct rights which are not necessarily temporally linked: *TW v Malta*, (App. 25644/94), 29 April 1999 [GC], (2000) 29 EHRR 185, §49; and *McKay v United Kingdom*, (App. 543/03), 3 October 2006 [GC], (2007) 44 EHRR 827, ECHR 2006-X, §§31–47.

[62] *McKay v United Kingdom*, (App. 543/03), 3 October 2006 [GC], (2007) 44 EHRR 827, ECHR 2006-X, §34.

[63] See E. Myjer, 'The plain meaning of the word "promptly"', in P. Mahoney and others, *Protecting Human Rights: The European Perspective. Studies in Memory of Rolv Ryssdal* (Carl Heymanns, Köln 2000), 975.

this nature, when the police and prosecution are likely to be under pressure to secure convictions and may be tempted to use unorthodox means to secure confessions.

The Strasbourg Court has never put a finite limit on the acceptable length of preliminary detention, since it considers that this must depend on the circumstances in each case. Some guidance is, however, provided by the *Brogan* case,[64] which indicates that the period is issue is a matter of a few days. The applicants were detained under special provisions enabling the Secretary of State for Northern Ireland to extend an initial forty-eight-hour period of detention. The shortest length of detention after arrest was four days and six hours and the longest was six days and sixteen hours. All the applicants were released without charge. Even taking account of the particular situation at that time in Northern Ireland, the Court regarded all cases as violations of the requirements of Article 5(3). The United Kingdom's response to the *Brogan* judgment was not to repeal the law allowing for extended periods of pre-charge detention; instead it filed a derogation under Article 15 of the Convention, claiming that, in view of the existence of 'an emergency threatening the life of the nation' this part of Article 5(3) should not be applied in Northern Ireland. When the same extended detention provisions came before the Court in the *Brannigan and McBride* case[65] the respondent State conceded that they were not consistent with Article 5(3), but the Court found that the derogation was valid and that there was no violation.[66]

Even where a Contracting Party has derogated from its Article 5(3) obligations the Court retains a power of review. The applicant in the *Aksoy* case[67] was arrested on suspicion of involvement with the PKK, and detained *incommunicado* for fourteen days under emergency provisions in force in south-east Turkey. The respondent State claimed that there was no violation because it had filed an Article 15 derogation in view of Kurdish separatist violence which had given rise to an 'emergency threatening the life of the nation'. The Court accepted that there was such an emergency, but ruled that, even taking into account the difficulty of investigating terrorist offences, fourteen days was too long to hold a suspect without judicial supervision and without access to a lawyer, doctor, or friend.

A number of cases have considered the character of the 'other officer authorized by law to exercise judicial power'.[68] The 'officer' need not be a judge but must display judicial attributes sufficient to protect the rights of the detained person. Most importantly, he or she must be independent of the executive and the parties to the case.[69] Thus a District Attorney who has been involved in indicting and prosecuting the accused

---

[64] *Brogan and others v United Kingdom*, 29 November 1988, Series A No 145-B, (1989) 11 EHRR 117.

[65] *Brannigan and McBride v United Kingdom*, 26 May 1993, Series A No 258-B, (1994) 17 EHRR 539.

[66] In February 2001 the United Kingdom lifted the derogation, in the light of the Northern Irish peace process. A new derogation to Art. 5(1)(f) was filed on 18 December 2001 following the September 11 attacks, which was lifted on 8 April 2005. See also *A and others v United Kingdom*, (App. 3455/05), 19 February 2009 [GC], ECHR 2009-nyr.

[67] *Aksoy v Turkey* (App. 21987/93), 18 December 1996, (1997) 23 EHRR 553, ECHR 1996-VI.

[68] Summarized in *McKay v United Kingdom*, (App. 543/03), 3 October 2006 [GC], (2007) 44 EHRR 827, ECHR 2006-X, §§35–40.

[69] *Schiesser v Switzerland*, 4 December 1979, Series A No 34, (1979–80) 2 EHRR 417.

cannot fulfil the role of judicial 'officer' under Article 5(3).[70] When assessing independence, the appearance of the situation from the viewpoint of an outside observer is decisive: if it appears that the 'officer' may intervene in subsequent criminal proceedings on behalf of the prosecution, his or her independence and impartiality may be open to doubt. In the *Assenov* case,[71] the Strasbourg Court therefore held that the prosecutor who authorized the applicant's continued detention on remand could not provide sufficient guarantees of independence, since he could in theory have taken over the prosecution of the subsequent criminal proceedings. Military disciplinary regimes in several countries have led to violations of Article 5(3), since the Strasbourg Court's autonomous interpretative approach brings many military offences within the scope of Article 5 paragraphs (1)(c) and (3). In the *Hood* case,[72] for example, the Court found that the British system whereby the accused soldier's commanding officer remanded him in close arrest was incompatible with Article 5(3) since the same officer was likely to play a central role in the ensuing prosecution and trial by court martial. Similarly, the lack of complete impartiality of the Dutch *auditeur militeur* and the Belgian counterpart took them outside the provision.[73]

The 'officer' must adopt a procedure which meets the normal requirements of due process. This includes hearing representations from the detainee at an oral hearing and deciding, by reference to legal criteria, whether or not the detention is justified.[74] If it is not justified, the 'officer' must have the power to order release.[75]

THE REMAND PERIOD: TRIAL WITHIN A REASONABLE TIME

Article 5(3) requires those kept in detention to be brought to trial within a reasonable time; there is a presumption in favour of release.[76] The drafting of Article 5(3) is ambiguous. Read together with Article 5(1) it appears to permit the detention on remand of any person reasonably suspected of having committed an offence—that is, any person likely to stand trial—as long as the trial takes place within a reasonable time, a right in any case guaranteed by Article 6(1). Such an interpretation would,

---

[70] *Huber v Switzerland*, (App. 12794/87), 23 October 1990, Series A No 188.

[71] *Assenov v Bulgaria* (App. 24760/94), 28 October 1998, (1998) 28 EHRR 652, ECHR 1998-VIII. And see also *Pantea v Romania*, (App. 33343/96), 3 June 2003, ECHR 2003-VI.

[72] *Hood v United Kingdom*, (App. 27267/95), 18 February 1999, (2000) 29 EHRR 365, ECHR 1999-I.

[73] *De Jong, Baljet and Van den Brink v Netherlands*, 22 May 1984, Series A No 77, (1986) 8 EHRR 20, *Van der Sluijs, Zuiderfeld and Klappe v Netherlands*, 22 May 1984, Series A No 78, (1991) 13 EHRR 461; *Duinhoff and Duif v Netherlands*, 22 May 1984, Series A No 79, (1991) 13 EHRR 478, and *Pauwels v Belgium*, 26 May 1988, Series A No 135, (1989) 11 EHRR 238. See also *Brincat v Italy*, 26 November 1992, Series A No 249-A, (1993) 16 EHRR 591, concerning the Italian deputy public prosecutor.

[74] *Assenov v Bulgaria* (App. 24760/94), 28 October 1998, (1999) 28 EHRR 652, ECHR 1998-VIII, §146; *Caballero v United Kingdom*, (App. 32819/96), 8 February 2000, (2000) 30 EHRR 643, ECHR 2000-II; *Sabeur ben Ali v Malta* (App. 35892/97), 29 June 2000, (2002) 34 EHRR 693.

[75] See, for example, *Aquilina v Malta* (App. 25642/94), 29 April 1999 [GC], (1999) 29 EHRR 185, ECHR 1999-III.

[76] *McKay v United Kingdom*, (App. 543/03), 3 October 2006 [GC], (2007) 44 EHRR 827, ECHR 2006-X, §41.

however, be at odds with the purpose of Article 5 which is, broadly, to limit detention to those circumstances where it is strictly necessary in the public interest and
to provide guarantees to detainees against arbitrariness. Moreover, it would mean
that the Convention allowed for pre-trial detention in many more cases than most
national European legal systems, where it is usually necessary to show some ground
such as a risk of absconding or tampering with evidence before it is possible to lock
up a person who, although accused of an offence, is innocent until proved guilty. The
Strasbourg Court has therefore rejected this reading and, in a clear example of the
purposive interpretative approach, has held in a series of judgments that not only the
initial arrest, but also the continuing *detention* must be justified, as long as it lasts, by
adequate grounds; and that, independently of those grounds, its *duration* must also
not exceed a reasonable time. Reasonableness will be assessed in the light of all the circumstances of the case, which will include examination of the reason put forward by
the respondent State.[77] It is also a requirement that the continuing need for detention
is considered, since a detention which is initially justified may cease to be so with the
passage of time.[78] Suspicion that the detained person has committed an offence, while
a necessary condition, does not suffice to justify detention continuing beyond a short
initial period, even where the accused is charged with a particularly serious crime and
the evidence against him is strong.[79] The Court has never elaborated an exhaustive list
of grounds which could justify pre-trial detention; each case is to be judged on its own
particular merits.

Thus, as far as the need for pre-trial detention is concerned, the Strasbourg Court
understands its role essentially as one of reviewing whether the reasons given by the
national courts for refusing release are adequate and sufficient.[80] In each case, the
national courts must assess the need for detention with reference to the particular
facts. For this reason a British law which automatically denied release on bail to a person charged with a serious violent crime if he had already been convicted of such a
crime was incompatible with Article 5(3).[81]

The ground most frequently relied upon by national courts is the risk of absconding. But the risk must be substantiated in each case. It is not sufficient for the national
authorities simply to point to the fact that the accused would receive a long prison sentence if convicted as evidence that he or she would be likely to disappear,[82] although
this may be a relevant consideration. The applicant in the *Barfuss* case[83] was charged
with fraudulently obtaining a number of large bank loans and faced a heavy sentence.
The decisions of the Czech courts refusing his applications for bail referred in addition to the fact that he had contacts in Germany, and that if he fled there it would

---

[77] *McKay*, §43.   [78] §44.

[79] *Tomasi v France*, 27 August 1992, Series A No 241-A, (1993) 15 EHRR 1; *Ječius v Lithuania*, (App.
34578/97), 31 July 2000, (2002) 35 EHRR 400, ECHR 2000-IX.

[80] *Prencipe v Monaco*, (App. 43378/06), 16 July 2009,§74.

[81] *Caballero v United Kingdom*, (App. 32819/96), 8 February 2000, (2000) 30 EHRR 643, ECHR 2000-II.

[82] See, for example, *Muller v France*, (App. 21802/93), 17 March 1997, ECHR 1997-II.

[83] *Barfuss v Czech Republic*, (App. 35848/97), 31 July 2000, (2002) 34 EHRR 948.

be impossible to continue with the prosecution because there was no extradition agreement between Germany and the Czech Republic. This reasoning was held by the Strasbourg Court to be sufficient for the purposes of Article 5(3).

Where the danger of absconding can be avoided by bail or other guarantees, the accused must be released, and there is an obligation on the national authorities to consider such alternatives to detention.[84] Moreover, in those countries which have the system of bail on financial sureties, the amount of the sureties must not be excessive, and must be fixed by reference to the purpose for which they are imposed, namely to ensure that this particular defendant appears for trial.[85] The sum must never be set exclusively by reference to the seriousness of the charge without considering the accused's financial circumstances.

Another common ground invoked to justify pre-trial detention is the risk of re-offending prior to trial. Again, the national court judgments must show that this risk was substantiated: reference to past crimes may not be sufficient.[86] There must be some evidence of a propensity to re-offend.[87] In the *Assenov* case[88] the authorities were entitled to rely on this ground since the applicant was charged with a long series of thefts, some of which had allegedly been committed subsequent to his initial arrest and questioning by the police.

Other grounds which have been accepted by the Strasbourg Court as capable of justifying detention are the risk of suppression of evidence,[89] and of collusion, that is, contacting other defendants or witnesses to agree on a false version of events.[90]

The right to trial within a reasonable time under Article 5(3) can be invoked only by those detained until trial. If a person is released at any stage before the trial, the situation is governed by Article 6(1) alone. Provided the relevant periods are sufficiently long, there is nothing to prevent a detainee from making claims under both provisions. The relevant period under Article 5(3) begins with arrest or detention. The question when the article ceases to apply is more complicated, since some European legal systems regard all detention as provisional until the conviction and sentence are confirmed by the final appeal court. In its judgment in the *B* case,[91] the Strasbourg Court ruled that, despite the provision of Austrian law that sentence becomes final only with the determination of any appeal, the applicant's detention on remand came to an end for the purposes of the Convention with the finding of guilt and sentencing at first instance.

---

[84] *Wemhoff v Germany*, 27 June 1968, Series A No 7, (1979–80) 1 EHRR 55, §15 of 'The Law'; *Jablonski v Poland* (App. 33492/96), 21 December 2000, (2003) 36 EHRR 455.

[85] *Neumeister v Austria*, 27 June 1968, Series A No 8, (1979–80) 1 EHRR 91, §§13–14 of 'The Law'; *Punzelt v Czech Republic* (App. 31315/96), 25 April 2000, (2001) 33 EHRR 1159.

[86] *Muller v France*, (App. 21802/93), 17 March 1997, ECHR 1997-II.

[87] *Matznetter v Austria*, 10 November 1969, Series A No 10, (1979–80) 1 EHRR 198, §9 of 'The Law'.

[88] *Assenov v Bulgaria* (App. 24760/94), 28 October 1998, (1999) 28 EHRR 652, ECHR 1998-VIII.

[89] *Wemhoff v Germany*, 27 June 1968, Series A No 7, (1979–80) 1 EHRR 55, §§13–14 of 'The Law'.

[90] *Ringeisen v Austria*, 16 July 1971, Series A No 13, (1979–80) 1 EHRR 455, §107.

[91] *B v Austria*, 28 March 1990, Series A No 175, (1991) 13 EHRR 20.

Just as the start and end points of the period to be considered under Article 5(3) are different from those relevant for Article 6(1), so the assessment of what length of time is 'reasonable' differs for the two articles. In its *Wemhoff* judgment the Court said:

It is…mainly in the light of the fact of the detention of the person being prosecuted that national courts…must determine whether the time that has elapsed, for whatever reason, before judgment is passed on the accused has at some stage exceeded a reasonable limit, that is to say imposed a greater sacrifice than could, in the circumstances of the case, reasonably be expected of a person presumed to be innocent.[92]

Consequently Article 5(3) requires that there must be 'special diligence' in bringing the case to trial if the accused is detained.[93] A detained person is entitled to have the case given priority and conducted with particular expedition.[94]

The Strasbourg Court applies a broad two-stage approach. It will first determine whether the grounds relied upon by the national authorities were adequate, until the very end, to justify remanding the accused in custody. If the detention was justified in principle, the Court will then examine the conduct of the prosecution to ensure that the pre-trial detention was not unnecessarily prolonged. Periods of inactivity by the national authorities lasting more than a few months are usually taken by the Court as a sign of lack of diligence, particularly if the overall duration of the detention was long. By way of example, the Court has found periods of pre-trial detention lasting from two and a half[95] to nearly five years[96] to be excessive.

THE REMAINING PERMITTED GROUNDS OF DETENTION

DETENTION AFTER CONVICTION BY A COMPETENT COURT: ARTICLE 5(1)(a)

Article 5(1)(a) permits 'the lawful detention of a person after conviction by a competent court'. It is the *detention* which must be 'lawful', not the *conviction*. The lawfulness of the detention ends when the term of imprisonment to which the person has been sentenced finishes. So continuing a person's detention beyond the period of their sentence will constitute a violation of Article 5.[97] Although many applications to the Strasbourg Court allege that they have been convicted of crimes they did not commit, the Court

---

[92] *Wemhoff v Germany*, 27 June 1968, Series A No 7, (1979–80) 1 EHRR 55, §5 of 'The Law' (emphasis added).

[93] *Stögmüller v Germany*, 10 November 1969, Series A No 9, (1979–80) 1 EHRR 155, §5 of 'The Law'.

[94] *Wemhoff v Germany*, 27 June 1968, Series A No 7, (1979–80) 1 EHRR 55, §17 of 'The Law'.

[95] *Punzelt v Czech Republic*, (App. 31315/96), 25 April 2000, (2001) 33 EHRR 1159. Compare *Pantano v Italy*, (App. 60851/00), 6 November 2003.

[96] *PB v France*, (App. 38781/97), 1 August 2000.

[97] *Pilla v Italy*, (App. 64088/00), 2 March 2006.

has no power under Article 5(1)(a) to examine whether the evidence adduced before the national courts was sufficient for a finding of guilt. Similarly, if an appeal against conviction is successful, the quashing of the conviction does not render the previous detention unlawful; and the same applies to acquittal following a retrial.[98]

The sentencing body must be a 'competent court'. 'Competent' means that it must have the power under national law to order the detention in question and 'court' carries the same meaning as in Article 5(4): the body must possess a judicial character and follow a fair procedure.[99]

In the *Ilaşcu* case,[100] the applicants were convicted and sentenced to detention pending execution by the Supreme Court of the break-away 'Moldavian Republic of Transdniestria', which was not recognized as a State under international law. The Strasbourg Court observed that in certain circumstances a court belonging to the judicial system of an entity not recognized under international law might be regarded as a tribunal 'established by law' provided that it formed part of a judicial system operating on a 'constitutional and legal basis' reflecting a judicial tradition compatible to the Convention, in order to enable individuals to enjoy the Convention guarantees. The Transdniestrian court, however, did not belong to such a system, and operated in a patently arbitrary and unfair manner. The Court accordingly found that none of the applicants had been convicted by a 'court', and that a sentence of imprisonment passed by a judicial body such as the 'Supreme Court of the MRT' at the close of proceedings like those conducted in the instant case, could not be regarded as 'lawful detention' ordered 'in accordance with a procedure prescribed by law'.

In cases where the 'court' is in a non-Convention State, it is not necessary for it to have followed the strict requirements of Article 6 when making the order for detention, as long as it has not acted in 'flagrant denial of justice'.[101]

'Conviction', like 'court', carries an autonomous meaning under the Convention, and can include a finding of guilt in respect of what is classified as a disciplinary or administrative offence under national law.[102] The deprivation of liberty must flow directly from the conviction. In the *Van Droogenbroeck* case[103] the sentence of the court involved imprisonment for two years followed by a further ten years following release during which the convicted person was 'placed at the Government's disposal', meaning that he could be detained by executive order. The Strasbourg Court considered that there was a sufficient causal connection between the original conviction and the recall during the ten-year period.

---

[98] App. 3245/67, *X v Austria*, Decision of 4 February 1969, (1969) 12 *Yearbook* 206, 236.

[99] *De Wilde, Ooms and Versyp v Belgium*, (Apps. 2832/66, 2835/66, and 2899/66), 18 November 1970, Series A No 12, (1979–80) 1 EHRR 373, §78; *Engel and others v Netherlands*, (Apps. 5100/71, 5101/71, 5102/71, 5354/72, and 5370/72), 8 June 1976, Series A No 22, (1979–80) 1 EHRR 647, §68.

[100] *Ilaşcu and others v Moldova and Russia*. (App. 48787/99), 8 July 2004 [GC], (2005) 40 EHRR 1030, ECHR 2004-VII.

[101] *Drozd and Janousek v France*, 26 June 1992, Series A No 240, (1992) 14 EHRR 745.

[102] *Engel and others v Netherlands*, (Apps. 5100/71, 5101/71, 5102/71, 5354/72, and 5370/72), 8 June 1976, Series A No 22, (1979–80) 1 EHRR 647.

[103] *Van Droogenbroeck v Belgium*, 24 June 1982, Series A No 50, (1982) 4 EHRR 443.

The applicant in the *Weeks* case[104] had been sentenced to life imprisonment following an assault because he was considered dangerous. He was released on licence, then
recalled to prison after becoming violent. The Strasbourg Court considered that the
deprivation of liberty which arose when Weeks's licence was revoked was sufficiently
closely linked to the original conviction to meet the requirements of Article 5(1)
(a). The same was not true in the *Stafford* case,[105] where the applicant, a convicted
murderer, was sentenced to life imprisonment, as is mandatory for all cases of murder in the United Kingdom. He was released on licence in 1979, after having served
the punitive element of the life sentence (the 'tariff'). Some fifteen years later he was
convicted of fraud and sentenced to a short term of imprisonment. On the expiry of
that sentence, the Home Secretary refused to allow his release, claiming that Stafford
should continue to be detained under the original life sentence, because there was a
risk that he would commit further offences of dishonesty. The Strasbourg Court abandoned its earlier case-law, which had held that the imposition of the mandatory life
sentence authorized the State to detain that person for any length of time, at any point,
throughout the rest of his or her life. Instead, it found that national law had evolved, to
the extent that it recognized that the mandatory life sentence did not impose imprisonment for life as a punishment. After the expiry of the tariff, only considerations of
dangerousness, linked to the original murder conviction, could justify the revocation of the licence. The Court could not accept that a decision-making power by the
executive to detain the applicant on the basis of perceived fears of future non-violent
criminal conduct unrelated to his original murder conviction accorded with the spirit
of the Convention, with its emphasis on the rule of law and protection from arbitrariness. The detention after the expiry of the fraud sentence was not, therefore, justified
under Article 5(1)(a).

The English provision permitting the Court of Appeal to determine that the time
spent in prison pending an unmeritorious appeal shall not form part of the sentence being served was in issue in the *Monnell and Morris* case.[106] The Commission
concluded that there had been a breach of Article 5, but the Court disagreed. The
rule created a disincentive to unmeritorious appeals, thereby assisting the speedier
handling of deserving cases; and trial within a reasonable time is one of the objectives of Article 6.[107] Possible loss of time was therefore an integral part of the criminal
appeal process following conviction of an offender and so was permissible under
Article 5(1)(a).

Again, since the Strasbourg Court is not an appeal court against decisions of national
courts, it will not substitute its own views on the appropriateness of a sentence for

---

[104] *Weeks v United Kingdom*, 2 March 1987, Series A No 114, (1988) 10 EHRR 293. A separate complaint
of a violation of Article 5(4) was successful: see below.

[105] *Stafford v United Kingdom*, (App. 46295/99), 28 May 2002 [GC], (2002) 35 EHRR 1121, ECHR
2002-IV.

[106] *Monnell and Morris v United Kingdom*, 2 March 1987, Series A No 115, (1988) 10 EHRR 205.

[107] See ch.12 below.

those of the national authorities. Thus, the applicants in the cases of *T* and *V*[108] failed to persuade the Strasbourg Court that their detention following their convictions, aged 11, for murdering a toddler when they were aged 10, was contrary to Article 5(1). In common with all children convicted of murder in England and Wales they were sentenced to an indeterminate period of detention ('during Her Majesty's pleasure'). It was argued on their behalf that to impose the same sentence on all child murderers, regardless of their age or circumstances, was arbitrary and therefore 'unlawful'. The Court, however, held that since the applicants' sentences complied with English law and followed conviction by a competent court, no issue arose under Article 5, although it did indicate that very long periods of detention in respect of juveniles might be inconsistent with Article 3 of the Convention.[109]

DETENTION OF A PERSON FOR FAILURE TO COMPLY WITH AN OBLIGATION PRESCRIBED BY LAW: ARTICLE 5(1)(b)

Article 5(1)(b) permits:

the lawful arrest or detention of a person for non-compliance with the lawful order of a court or in order to secure the fulfilment of any obligation prescribed by law;

The first limb authorizes detention for non-compliance with the lawful order of a court. This could mean, *inter alia*, arrest to secure attendance in court following a failure to comply with a summons,[110] or imprisonment for failure to pay a fine[111] or to comply with an injunction or a child custody or maintenance order.[112] In the *Steel* case,[113] the applicant hunt saboteurs had been ordered by the magistrates' court to agree to be bound over to keep the peace for a period of twelve months. Their imprisonment for refusing to enter into this promise of future good conduct was held by the Strasbourg Court to fall within the scope of the first limb of Article 5(1)(b).

The second limb authorizes detention to secure the fulfilment of any obligation prescribed by law. In the *Benham* case[114] the applicant's imprisonment for failing to pay local taxes was held to fall within this part of Article 5(1)(b).

Detention under this ground must always be proportionate to the aim pursued. In the *Vasileva* case,[115] the applicant, a 65-year-old woman, was arrested following a dispute with an inspector on a bus as to whether or not she had a valid ticket, and

---

[108] *T v United Kingdom* (App. 24724/94); and *V v United Kingdom* (App. 24888/94) 16 December 1999 [GC], (2000) 30 EHRR 121, ECHR 1999-IX.

[109] See ch.9 above.

[110] App. 32206/96, *GK v Austria*, Decision of 16 October 1996.

[111] App. 28188/95, *Tyrell v United Kingdom*, Decision of 4 September 1996.

[112] App. 26109/95, *Santa Cruz Ruiz v United Kingdom*, Decision of 22 October 1997.

[113] *Steel and others v United Kingdom* (App. 24838/94), 23 September 1998, (1998) 28 EHRR 603, ECHR 1998-VII.

[114] *Benham v United Kingdom*, (App. 19380/92), 10 June 1996, (1996) 22 EHRR 293, ECHR 1996-III.

[115] *Vasileva v Denmark*, (App. 52792/99), 25 September 2003, (2005) 40 EHRR 681. See also Apps. 8022/77, 8025/77, 8027/77, *McVeigh and others v United Kingdom*, Decision of 18 March 1981, (1982) 25 DR 15.

detained in police custody for over twenty-four hours because she refused to give them her name and address as required by Danish law. The moment she complied with this obligation, she was released. The Strasbourg Court accepted, therefore, that the applicant had been detained in order to 'secure the fulfilment' of an obligation as required by Article 5(1)(b) of the Convention. It went on, however, to examine 'whether in the circumstances of the present case a reasonable balance was struck between the importance of securing the fulfilment of the obligation in general and the importance of the right to liberty'. Taking into account (1) the nature of the obligation arising from the relevant legislation including its underlying object and purpose; (2) the characteristics of the person being detained and the particular circumstances leading to the detention; and (3) the length of the detention, it concluded that a proper balance had not been struck between the need to secure the fulfilment of the obligation and the right to personal liberty.[116]

Imprisonment for debt may be permitted by Article 5(1)(b). However, for those Contracting Parties which have ratified the Fourth Protocol to the Convention, a restriction on detention in such cases is introduced by Article 1 of that Protocol.[117]

DETENTION OF MINORS: ARTICLE 5(1)(d)

Article 5(1)(d) permits:

the detention of a minor by lawful order for the purpose of educational supervision or his lawful detention for the purpose of bringing him before the competent legal authority;

This clause authorizes detention in two distinct sets of circumstances. The first limb covers orders requiring compulsory attendance at school which might otherwise amount to a deprivation of liberty under Article 5(1). There is no requirement that the order should be that of a court; the making of such orders by an administrative authority is not excluded. In such cases however the person subject to the order will be entitled to seek a review of that order under Article 5(4).[118] The second limb of paragraph (1)(d) allows minors to be brought before the judicial or administrative authority which is to decide whether or not to order their detention. The paragraph thus clearly authorizes the exercise of the jurisdiction of juvenile courts in non-criminal cases.

The age at which a person ceases to be a minor has not been definitively established. The Council of Europe has adopted a resolution recommending Member States in principle to reduce the age of majority from 21 to 18,[119] but the adoption of the age of 18 as the age of majority has not been universal under national legal systems. In the *Koniarska* case,[120] the Strasbourg Court held that the applicant was a minor until the

---

[116] Contrast *Novotka v Slovakia*, (App. 47244/99), Decision of 4 November 2003.

[117] Which provides: 'No one shall be deprived of his liberty merely on the ground of inability to fulfil a contractual obligation.'

[118] See below in this chapter.

[119] Resolution CM(72) 29 of the Committee of Ministers of the Council of Europe.

[120] *Koniarska v United Kingdom*, (App. 33670/96), Decision of 12 October 2000.

age of 18 and that Article 5(1)(d) permitted her detention for educational supervision up to that age, even though the school-leaving age in the United Kingdom is 16. It would appear, therefore, that 'minor' is to be given an autonomous meaning under the Convention, independent of the age of majority under national law.

The *Bouamar* case[121] concerned the detention of a 16-year-old boy with a disturbed personality. He had displayed behavioural problems and was detained in an adult prison for nine periods each of up to fifteen days because the authorities had been unable to find a suitable juvenile institution able to accept him immediately. The Belgian Government sought to argue that the detention was for educational supervision, but this argument failed since no genuine educational facilities had been made available for him. The Court concluded that an interim custody measure prior to placement involving supervised education was not precluded by Article 5(1)(d) but that the shuttling between prison and other arrangements totalling 119 days of detention in a 291-day period did violate the provision.[122]

In contrast, the applicant in the *Koniarska* case,[123] a 17-year-old girl, had been diagnosed as suffering from a psychopathic disorder and was placed in a specialist, secure, residential facility for seriously disturbed young people. She submitted that this detention was not for the purpose of educational supervision, but was instead ordered as a containment measure, any education offered being purely incidental. However, the Strasbourg Court held that the words 'educational supervision' should not be equated rigidly with notions of classroom teaching but could also be seen as embracing other aspects of local authority care, particularly where, as was the case with the applicant, an extensive range of classes was made available.

The specific provisions relating to minors in Article 5(1)(d) do not preclude the application to them of arrest and detention under any of the other sub-paragraphs of Article 5(1), such as detention consequent upon conviction or as persons of unsound mind.

VULNERABLE GROUPS: ARTICLE 5(1)(e)

Article 5(1)(e) permits:

the lawful detention of persons for the prevention of the spreading of infectious diseases, of persons of unsound mind, alcoholics or drug addicts or vagrants;

Article 5(1)(e) draws together a disparate group[124] whose detention might be justified on grounds of social protection: those with infectious diseases, persons of unsound mind, alcoholics, drug addicts, and vagrants. There is no requirement that the detention should be imposed by a court; it may be ordered by an administrative authority, although such an order will be subject to judicial control under paragraph (4).

---

121   *Bouamar v Belgium*, 29 February 1988, Series A No 129, (1989) 11 EHRR 1.
122   §§51–3. See, similarly, *DG v Ireland*, (App. 39474/98), 16 May 2002.
123   *Koniarska v United Kingdom*, (App. 33670/96), Decision of 12 October 2000.
124   Using labels that now look somewhat dated.

VAGRANTS

Since the judgment of the Strasbourg Court in the *Vagrancy* cases in 1971,[125] there have been few cases concerning this permitted ground of detention, probably because as standards evolve in Europe it appears increasingly repugnant forcibly to detain people merely because they are homeless. It is difficult to imagine many such cases where the detention would not in reality be prompted by some other aspect of the vagrant's conduct or condition, such as criminal offending, addiction, or mental illness.

The case of vagrancy is exceptional because 'vagrants' are detained for their *previous* rather than *present* condition, so that there is no obvious trigger for release. In the *Vagrancy* cases, two of the applicants had been placed at the disposal of the respondent State for the astonishingly long period of two years (they were both released earlier), while the third was placed at its disposal indefinitely (although in practice under Belgian law this meant one year). Unless a general limit to the length of detention can be inferred from the practice of the Contracting Parties, so as to render longer periods 'arbitrary', the only control in the Convention would appear to be that the detention must not be so lengthy as to constitute inhuman or degrading treatment under Article 3. It is, however, likely that if another such case were to come before the Strasbourg Court today, in line with the case-law on the detention of mental patients and alcoholics, it would read into this provision an implied requirement that the detention be proved strictly necessary for the welfare of the vagrant or the public.

MENTAL ILLNESS

The approach adopted by the Strasbourg Court to provide protection for persons detained by reason of mental illness has been to establish a framework of procedural tests which must be satisfied. In the *Winterwerp* case[126] the Court established three tests. First, the presence of 'unsound mind' must be determined by objective medical evidence; secondly, the mental illness must result in a condition making detention necessary for the protection of the patient or others; thirdly, the detention must be justified on a continuing basis. It has since added a fourth requirement: there must be some relationship between the ground of detention relied upon under Article 5(1) and the place and conditions of detention. Thus, persons detained because of mental illness must be held in a hospital or clinic, and not in a prison where the treatment and therapy required is unavailable.[127]

In the *Varbanov* case,[128] the Strasbourg Court found a violation based on the fact that the applicant, who had a history of threatening behaviour, had been committed to psychiatric hospital for a period of twenty days on the order of a prosecutor in the

---

[125] *De Wilde, Ooms and Versyp v Belgium*, (Apps. 2832/66, 2835/66, and 2899/66), 18 November 1970, Series A No 12, (1979–80) 1 EHRR 373.

[126] *Winterwerp v Netherlands*, (App. 6301/73), 24 October 1979, Series A No 33, (1979–80) 2 EHRR 387.

[127] *Aerts v Belgium* (App. 25357/94), 30 July 1998, (1999) 29 EHRR 50, ECHR 1998-V.

[128] *Varbanov v Bulgaria*, (App. 31365/96), 5 October 2000, ECHR 2000-X.

absence of any medical evidence of mental illness. Although the Court observed that in an urgent case where immediate committal was believed to be necessary for safety reasons it might be acceptable under Article 5(1)(e) to arrest the patient first and get a medical appraisal shortly thereafter,[129] in Varbanov's case there was no evidence of danger and no psychiatric evaluation was ever undertaken throughout the time of his detention.

The developing nature of medical understanding of mental illness, together with the fact that individuals suffering from certain psychiatric conditions, if released, may pose a danger not only to themselves but also to the community, has meant that there is a certain deference to national authorities in their evaluation of the medical evidence in connection with the second and third limbs of the *Winterwerp* test.[130] Even where the evidence shows that the detained person is no longer suffering from mental illness, it does not automatically follow that he or she should immediately and unconditionally be released back into the community. The Court made this approach clear in the *Johnson* case,[131] although it also emphasized that the exercise of official caution cannot justify delaying release indefinitely. The applicant had been properly detained, but his condition improved and he was found on the medical evidence no longer to be mentally ill. But the authorities considered that he was not yet ready to live on his own in the community. His discharge from hospital was made conditional on his residence under supervision in a hostel. However, because of a combination of the limited number of hostel places and the applicant's negative attitude, which deterred the few available hostels from taking him, no place was found for him and his release from hospital was delayed for four years, until the Tribunal ordered his unconditional release. The applicant argued that from the time of the review at which he was found no longer to be suffering from mental illness, his detention had not been in conformity with Article 5(1)(e) and he should have been immediately and unconditionally released. The Court rejected this submission, declaring that such a rigid approach to the interpretation of the third *Winterwerp* condition would place an unacceptable degree of constraint on the national authorities' discretion, given that the assessment of full recovery from mental illness was not a certain science and that premature, unsupervised release might be risky in some cases. The national authorities had based their decision on the medical evidence before it and it had not been unreasonable to make the applicant's release conditional on residence in a hostel. However, once this condition had been imposed, the onus was on the authorities to make sure that a hostel place was available. In fact, the lack of a hostel place and the continuing insistence that the applicant could only be released to a hostel led to the indefinite deferral of his release, until he was unconditionally discharged four years after the authorities had first found him free of mental illness. This delay, together with the lack of adequate

---

[129] As occurred in, for example, *Herz v Germany*, (App. 44672/98), 12 June 2003.

[130] See *Luberti v Italy*, 23 February 1984, Series A No 75, (1984) 6 EHRR 440, §27. The criteria also apply to recall of patients who have been detained in mental hospitals: see *X v United Kingdom*, 24 October 1981, Series A No 46, (1982) 4 EHRR 188.

[131] *Johnson v United Kingdom*, (App. 22520/93), 24 October 1997, (1997) 27 EHRR 296, ECHR 1997-VII.

procedural safeguards—it was not possible for the applicant to petition the authorities between annual reviews—gave rise to a violation of Article 5(1).

Because of the need for specialist expertise and the near impossibility of the Strasbourg Court itself attempting to assess medical evidence, the requirement of procedural 'lawfulness' is particularly important in connection with the detention of the mentally ill. In the *Varbanov* case,[132] as well as finding the applicant's detention unlawful for lack of supporting medical opinion, the Strasbourg Court found an additional ground of violation in that, at the time of the committal, Bulgarian law did not contain any express provision empowering a prosecutor to order compulsory confinement for the purpose of psychiatric evaluation. There was an instruction issued by the Minister of Health, implying that prosecutors had such powers, but this lacked the requisite clarity to conform with the standard of 'lawfulness' under the Convention.

Persons detained as being mentally unsound are normally detained for an indefinite period, although often with a right to periodical review. Article 5(4), discussed below, is therefore of great importance for mental patients, for it will frequently be the case that initial detention in hospital is justified, but the need for continuing detention may be more questionable.

ALCOHOLICS AND THOSE SUFFERING FROM INFECTIOUS DISEASE

As with all the other terms describing vulnerable groups in Article 5(1)(e), the word 'alcoholic' carries an autonomous Convention meaning. The Court gave some indication as to how it should be interpreted in the first case to come before it concerning detention for drunkenness.[133] The applicant, a partially sighted pensioner, was apprehended by the police at a post office where he was complaining that his post box had been opened and emptied. He was taken to a sobering-up centre, where he was certified by a doctor as being 'moderately intoxicated' and held for six and a half hours. The Court observed that in common usage the word 'alcoholic' denotes a person who is addicted to alcohol. There was, however, a link with the other categories in sub-paragraph (e), in that the detention of individuals in these groups could be justified only where it was necessary for medical treatment or on grounds of social policy to prevent a risk of danger to themselves or to the public. Having regard to the rule in the Vienna Convention on the Law of Treaties that in interpreting a treaty it is necessary to look at its object and purpose,[134] the Court found that this purpose would be defeated if the provision allowed for the detention only of those suffering from the clinical condition of alcoholism, but not for non-alcoholics whose conduct under the influence of drink

---

[132] *Varbanov v Bulgaria*, (App. 31365/96), 5 October 2000, ECHR 2000-X.
[133] *Witold Litwa v Poland*, (App. 26629/95), 4 April 2000, (2001) 33 EHRR 1267, ECHR 2000-III.
[134] See ch.4 above.

gave rise to a danger to the safety of themselves or others. This approach was confirmed by the *travaux préparatoires*, which included reference to 'drunkenness'. The applicant's arrest and detention therefore in principle fell within the scope of Article 5(1)(e). However, the Court found that there had been a violation of Article 5(1) because there was no evidence that the applicant had behaved in such a way as to pose a threat to himself or others or that the draconian measure of detention was necessary in the light of the rather trivial facts of the case. An individual could not be deprived of his liberty for being an 'alcoholic' unless other, less severe, measures had been considered and found to be insufficient to safeguard the individual or public interest.

The Court followed these principles in its first judgment concerning detention 'for the prevention of the spreading of infectious diseases'.[135] The applicant, who was HIV positive, was ordered to be held in compulsory hospital isolation over a period of almost seven years; because he kept escaping, he was in fact deprived of his liberty for about eighteen months. Under the Swedish Infectious Diseases Act, the county medical officer had issued the applicant with various instructions aimed at preventing the spread of the disease, such as a requirement to inform all medical practitioners and prospective sexual partners that he was HIV positive and to abstain from consuming such an amount of alcohol that his judgement would thereby be impaired and others put at risk of being infected with HIV. The applicant claimed that as soon as he found out about his condition he stopped having sex, and although he continued drinking, there was no evidence that he did so to excess. He did, however, refuse voluntarily to see a psychiatrist. The national courts ordered his confinement because they considered there was reasonable cause to suspect that the applicant, if released, would fail to comply with the medical officer's instructions. The Court found that the essential criteria when assessing the 'lawfulness' of the detention of a person 'for the prevention of the spreading of infectious diseases' were whether the spreading of the infectious disease was dangerous for public health or safety, and whether detention of the person infected was the last resort in order to prevent the spreading of the disease, less severe measures having been considered and found to be insufficient to safeguard the public interest. Given that the applicant had, to a large extent, complied with the medical officer's instructions, his detention was not held to have been essential and there had been a violation of Article 5(1).

DETENTION IN CONNECTION WITH DEPORTATION OR EXTRADITION: ARTICLE 5(1)(f)

Article 5(1)(f) permits:

the lawful arrest or detention of a person to prevent his effecting an unauthorized entry into the country or of a person against whom action is being taken with a view to deportation or extradition.

---

135 *Enhorn v Sweden*, (App. 56529/00), 25 January 2005, (2005) 41 EHRR 633, ECHR 2005-I.

The first limb is for the prevention of an unauthorized entry into the country, and the second is where detention is required where action is being taken to deport or extradite someone.

The Grand Chamber considered the first limb for the first time only in 2008 in the *Saadi* case.[136] The Court concluded that the presence of an asylum seeker in a country was not authorized on presentation of a claim for asylum to the authorities. The consequence is that a Contracting Party could detain an asylum seeker, or indeed any person seeking immigration, until that person's entry has been authorized. However, such detention must remain compatible with the overall purpose of Article 5 and not be arbitrary. The Grand Chamber said:

> To avoid being branded as arbitrary...such detention must be carried out in good faith; it must be closely connected to the purpose of preventing unauthorized entry of the person to the country; the place and conditions of detention should be appropriate, bearing in mind that 'the measure is applicable not to those who have committed criminal offences but to aliens who, often fearing for their lives, have fled from their own country...; and the length of the detention should not exceed that reasonably required for the purpose pursued.[137]

Applying these principles, the Strasbourg Court found no violation of Article 5(1) where the respondent State had initially not detained an applicant for asylum, but subsequently detained him in a reception centre for asylum seekers for seven days.[138]

In order to comply with the second limb of this provision, the detained person must be the object of action 'with a view to deportation or extradition'. There is no need for the State to establish that the detention was reasonably considered necessary in order to prevent the person from absconding or from committing an offence—in contrast to the position of a person detained under Article 5(1) paragraphs (c), (b), or (e).[139]

In the *A and others* case,[140] the Grand Chamber was not satisfied that the detention of a number of the applicants fell within Article 5(1)(f), as claimed by the respondent State, since it could not be said that they were being detained with a view to deportation or extradition. As the Grand Chamber noted, the derogation which the United Kingdom had filed in respect of Article 5(1) was based on the proposition that deportation or extradition was not possible because of the risk of ill-treatment in the country of destination.

In addition, as long as the *detention* is 'lawful', it is immaterial for the purposes of Article 5(1)(f) whether the underlying *decision to expel* can be justified under

---

[136] *Saadi v United Kingdom*, (App. 13229/03), 29 January 2008 [GC], (2008) 47 EHRR 427, ECHR 2008-nyr, §§61–6.

[137] §74.

[138] See also *Riad and Idiab v Belgium*, (Apps. 29787/03 and 29810/03), 24 January 2008, ECHR 2008-nyr, for an example of a case where the Court decided that the respondent State had not acted in good faith.

[139] *Chahal v United Kingdom*, (App. 22414/93), 15 November 1996, (1997) 23 EHRR 413, ECHR 1996-V, §112; *Čonka v Belgium*, (App. 51564/99), 5 February 2002, (2002) 34 EHRR 1298, ECHR 2002-I, §38.

[140] *A and others v United Kingdom*, (App. 3455/05), 19 February 2009 [GC], (2009) 49 EHRR 29, ECHR 2009-nyr, §§161–72.

national or Convention law.[141] This interpretation follows from the wording of Article 5(1)(f) and is consistent with the principle that in assessing compliance with Article 5(1)(a) the Strasbourg Court will not itself examine whether there was sufficient evidence to support the applicant's conviction. Thus in the *Chahal* case,[142] even though the Court found that the decision to expel the applicant to India was contrary to Article 3 of the Convention because he would run a real risk of torture or illegal killing, his detention for six years prior to the Court's judgment was permissible under Article 5(1)(f).

It follows that, in the absence of any procedural irregularity or official arbitrariness such as to render the detention unlawful,[143] the only way for an applicant to establish a breach of this provision is to show that, throughout or for some part of his detention, he was not truly the object of deportation or extradition action. One way of establishing this is to show that the authorities did not pursue the expulsion proceedings with 'due diligence' and that they thereby allowed the detention to be unnecessarily prolonged. In the *Kolompar* case[144] delays of over two years and eight months awaiting deportation were found not to constitute a violation of Article 5 since the delays were not attributable to the action of the authorities. Even more strikingly, as mentioned above, the Court found no violation of Article 5(1) in the *Chahal* case,[145] where the applicant, a Sikh separatist accused of terrorism by the British Government, had been detained for over six years pending the completion of the national and Strasbourg proceedings. This period included a delay of over seven months while the Home Office considered and rejected an application for refugee status and a further six months for the Home Office to make a fresh decision after the first had been quashed by judicial review. The Court found that these delays were justified in view of the importance of the issues in the case—the respondent State alleged that intelligence information showed that Chahal's continued residence in England raised a threat to British national security, whereas Chahal denied these accusations and claimed that he would run a risk of torture or illegal execution if returned to India. Hasty decision-making in such a case would not, in the Court's view, benefit either the applicant or the general public. However, perhaps the *Chahal* case should be regarded as exceptional; six years does seem a very long time to imprison a person who has not been proved to have committed even the most insignificant criminal offence, and in such circumstances it is arguable that a high standard of speed and diligence should be expected of the authorities.

[141] *Chahal v United Kingdom*, (App. 22414/93), 15 November 1996, (1997) 23 EHRR 413, ECHR 1996-V, §112.

[142] Ibid.

[143] See, for example, *Čonka v Belgium*, (App. 51564/99), 5 February 2002, (2002) 34 EHRR 1298, ECHR 2002-I, where the Roma applicants' arrest and detention pending deportation was in breach of Article 5(1) because the authorities had tricked them into reporting to the police station by issuing them with a summons stating that their attendance was necessary 'to complete the asylum process'; and see the discussion of arbitrariness in *Chahal*.

[144] *Kolompar v Belgium*, 24 September 1992, Series A No 235-C, (1993) 16 EHRR 197, §§37–43.

[145] *Chahal v United Kingdom*, (App. 22414/93), 15 November 1996, (1997) 23 EHRR 413, ECHR 1996-V.

TESTING THE LEGALITY OF THE DETENTION

Article 5(4) provides for a legal review of the legality of any detention:

Everyone who is deprived of his liberty by arrest or detention shall be entitled to take proceedings by which the lawfulness of his detention shall be decided speedily by a court and his release ordered if the detention is not lawful.

The right to judicial review under Article 5(4) covers all forms of arrest and detention. The 'court' to which the detained person has access for the purposes of Article 5(4) does not have to be a 'court of law of the classic kind integrated within the standard judicial machinery of the country'.[146] It must, however, be a body of a 'judicial character' offering certain procedural guarantees.[147] Thus the 'court' must be independent both of the executive and of the parties to the case.[148] It must have the power to order release if it finds that the detention is unlawful; a mere power of recommendation is insufficient.[149]

THE NATURE OF THE JUDICIAL REVIEW

The scope of the proceedings required by Article 5(4) was the subject of comment in the *E* case:

Article 5(4) does not guarantee a right to judicial review of such a scope as to empower the court on all aspects of the case, including questions of pure expediency, to substitute its own discretion for that of the decision-making authority. The review should, however, be wide enough to bear on those conditions which are essential for the 'lawful' detention of a person according to Article 5(1).[150]

It follows, therefore, that if a person is detained under Article 5(1)(c) of the Convention, the 'court' must be empowered to examine whether or not there is sufficient evidence to give rise to a reasonable suspicion that he or she has committed an offence, because the existence of such a suspicion is essential if detention on remand is to be 'lawful' under the Convention.[151] Similarly, in the case of a person detained on grounds of

---

[146] *Weeks v United Kingdom*, 2 March 1987, Series A No 254, (1988) 10 EHRR 293, §61.

[147] *De Wilde, Ooms and Versyp v Belgium*, (Apps. 2832/66, 2835/66, and 2899/66), 18 November 1970, Series A No 12, (1979–80) 1 EHRR 373.

[148] *Neumeister v Austria*, 27 June 1968, Series A No 8, (1979–80) 1 EHRR 91, §24 of 'The Law'.

[149] See, for example, *Singh v United Kingdom* (App. 23389/94), 21 February 1996, ECHR 1996-I, §65; *Curley v United Kingdom* (App. 32340/96), 28 March 2000; *Benjamin and Wilson v United Kingdom*, (App. 28212/95), 26 September 2002; (200) 36 EHRR 1.

[150] *E v Norway*, 29 August 1990, Series A No 181, (1990) 17 EHRR 30, §50.

[151] See, for example, *Nikolova v Bulgaria*, (App. 31195/96), 25 March 1999 [GC], (2001) 31 EHRR 64, ECHR 1999-II; *Grauslys v Lithuania* (App. 36743/97), 10 October 2000, (2002) 34 EHRR 1084; and *A and others v United Kingdom*, (App. 3455/05), 19 February 2009 [GC], ECHR 2009-nyr.

mental ill-health, the reviewing 'court' must assess the legality of the detention in the light of the *Winterwerp* criteria discussed above.[152]

The scope of review required with regard to a person detained under paragraph 5(1)(f) appears uncertain. In the *Chahal* judgment,[153] as has been seen, the Court held that all that was needed to ensure that the detention was 'lawful' under this provision was proof that action was being taken with a view to deportation; absent arbitrariness, it was immaterial for the purposes of Article 5(1) whether or not the underlying decision to expel was justified or whether there was any evidence that the detention was necessary to prevent the proposed deportee from absconding or committing a crime, for example. It might be assumed, therefore, that all that could be expected from the 'court' reviewing the legality of the detention under Article 5(4) would be a determination of the fact that deportation proceedings were genuinely under way. However, the Court went on to hold in the *Chahal* judgment that the bail and habeas corpus proceedings brought by the applicant in the English courts were deficient under Article 5(4) because the courts were unable to look behind the Secretary of State's assertions that national security would be at risk if Chahal was at liberty so as to determine the question themselves in the light of all the available evidence. The Court went so far as to refer to a procedure used in Canada in such cases, which it suggested would ensure compliance with Article 5(4), whereby all evidence relating to national security was aired before the court deciding on the legality of the detention in the presence of a security-cleared counsel instructed by the detainee.

In the *A and others* case,[154] the Grand Chamber found a violation of Article 5(4) in relation to two of the detainees. The Strasbourg Court considered the arrangements under which the Special Immigration Appeals Commission (SIAC) could consider both open material, which was disclosed to the detainee, and closed material which was disclosed neither to the detainee nor to his or her legal advisers. Instead the closed material was disclosed to a special advocate appointed by the respondent State's Solicitor General to act on behalf of the detainee, and who could make submissions to SIAC on both matters of procedure and substance. Once the special advocate had seen closed material, he or she was not permitted to have any contact with the detainee. The essence of the special advocate procedure was accepted as balancing the need for disclosure and the risk of compromising national security. However, the operation of the system must not leave a detainee in the position of being unable to challenge the allegations against them because the open material was of such a general nature that it lacked sufficient specificity to enable this to be done. That was the case in relation to the two detainees in respect of whom a violation of Article 5(4) was found.

---

[152] Habeas corpus and judicial review proceedings in the High Court are therefore insufficient for the purposes of Article 5(4): *HL v United Kingdom*, (App. 45508/99), 5 October 2004, (2005) 40 EHRR 761, ECHR 2004-IX.

[153] *Chahal v United Kingdom*, (App. 22414/93), 15 November 1996; (1997) 23 EHRR 413, ECHR 1996-V, §112.

[154] *A and others v United Kingdom*, (App. 3455/05), 19 February 2009 [GC], (2009) 49 EHRR 29, ECHR 2009-nyr, §§202–24.

As far as procedural requirements are concerned, Article 5(4) does not always require the same guarantees as would be necessary under Article 6(1) for criminal or civil litigation. The proceedings must generally be capable of commencement on the application of the person deprived of his or her liberty,[155] though automatic reference to review of a judicial character will also suffice. The form of procedure followed may vary depending on the nature of the detention under review and the relevant issues before the 'court'.[156] An adversarial oral hearing with legal representation is always required, however, in cases of detention under Article 5(1)(c) or where the continued legality of the detention depends on an assessment of the applicant's character or mental state.[157] In the *Lamy* case,[158] the Court considered that the failure to make documents available promptly to the applicant's lawyer precluded the possibility of an effective challenge to statements which formed the basis of the decision to detain, giving rise to a violation of Article 5(4).

The requirement for review by a 'court' prompted a spate of applications from former Communist countries where under the old regime it was common for the prosecuting authorities to be empowered to decide virtually all questions relating to pre-trial detention, with the possibility of only limited recourse to a court. In Bulgaria, for example, in the mid-1990s, a person detained on remand on the decision of the prosecutor was entitled to contest his detention in court only once, even if the detention continued for two years or more. Since the frequency of this periodic review was inadequate, and since the prosecution was not an independent 'court' for the purposes of Article 5(4), the Court found a violation in the *Assenov* case.[159] During the same period in Poland, although a person detained on remand could apply to a court, neither the detained person nor his lawyer was entitled to attend the hearing or be informed of the prosecutor's reasons for opposing release, leading the Strasbourg Court to find violations in a number of cases.[160]

WHEN ARE REVIEWS REQUIRED?

Article 5(4) provides that 'the lawfulness of [the] detention shall be decided *speedily*' (emphasis added). There are two aspects to this requirement: first, the opportunity for legal review must be provided soon after the person is taken into detention

---

[155] There was a violation of Article 5(4) in *Rakevich v Russia*, (App. 58973/00), 28 October 2003, because under Russian law the applicant, a mental patient, was unable herself to apply to have her continuing detention judicially reviewed, but had instead to rely on the initiative of the hospital authorities.

[156] See, for example, *Niedbała v Poland*, (App. 27915/95), 4 July 2000, §66.

[157] *Assenov v Bulgaria* (App. 24760/94), 28 October 1998, (1999) 28 EHRR 652, ECHR 1998-VIII; *Niedbala v Poland* (App. 27915/95), 4 July 2000; *Grauslys v Lithuania* (App. 36743/97), 10 October 2000; *Wloch v Poland*, (App. 27885/98), 19 October 2000, (2002) 34 EHRR 229.

[158] *Lamy v Belgium*, 30 March 1989, Series A No 151, (1989) 11 EHRR 529.

[159] *Assenov v Bulgaria* (App. 24760/94), 28 October 1998, (1999) 28 EHRR 652, ECHR 1998-VIII.

[160] *Niedbała v Poland*, (App. 27915/95), 4 July 2000, (2000) 33 EHRR 1137; *Trzaska v Poland* (App. 25792/94), 11 July 2000; *Wloch v Poland* (App. 27785/95), 19 October 2000, (2002) 34 EHRR 229; and see *Grauzinis v Lithuania*, (App. 37975/97), 10 October 2000, (2002) 35 EHRR 144, for a similar problem in Lithuania.

(and thereafter, as discussed below, at reasonable intervals if necessary); secondly, the review proceedings must be conducted with due diligence.

In each case, the question whether the review has been completed sufficiently 'speedily' depends on all the circumstances. In a case of a straightforward bail application by a man detained on suspicion of drug-trafficking, for example, the Court held that three weeks was too long.[161] Longer periods might be acceptable in more complex cases—for example, where it is necessary to seek medical reports in respect of a detained mental patient—but, given the importance of the right to liberty, there is still a pressing obligation on the authorities to deal quickly with such applications for release. In the *Baranowski* case,[162] for example, the fact that it took a court deciding a bail application six weeks to obtain a report from a cardiologist and a further month to obtain evidence from a neurologist and a psychiatrist was evidence of lack of due diligence and gave rise to a violation of Article 5(4).

In many cases, the examination carried out by the court which first makes the order for detention is sufficient for the purposes of Article 5(4). This is so, for example, where a person convicted of a criminal offence is sentenced to a determinate term of imprisonment.

Where, however, the justification for a prolonged period of detention is liable to vary over time, the detained person is entitled under Article 5(4) to apply for judicial review of the detention's continued legality at intervals. This proposition was first enunciated in cases of indefinite detention under mental health legislation, but has been extended to cases where continuing detention is conditioned upon a view that the person is dangerous in a broader sense, and even to cases of detention on remand.[163]

Thus, in the United Kingdom, all prisoners serving life sentences (either mandatory life imprisonment for murder or a discretionary life sentence for some other offence), are entitled, once the punitive part of the sentence (the 'tariff') has expired,[164] to periodic review to determine whether they are still too dangerous to be released into the community.[165] The same applies to juveniles sentenced to be detained 'during Her Majesty's pleasure'.[166] The review must be effective, in the sense of taking proper

---

[161] *Rehbock v Slovenia*, (App. 29462/95), 28 November 2000, ECHR 2000-XII; and see also *GB v Switzerland*, (App. 27426/95), 30 November 2000, (2002) 34 EHRR 265 (32 days to decide the bail application of terrorist suspect was too long).

[162] *Baranowski v Poland*, (App. 28358/95), 28 March 2000, ECHR 2000-III.

[163] *De Jong, Baljet and van der Brink v Netherlands*, (Apps. 8805/79, 8806/79, and 9242/81), 22 May 1984, Series A No 77, (1986) 8 EHRR 20; and *Bezicheri v Italy*, (App. 11400/85), 25 October 1989, Series A No 164, (1990) 12 EHRR 210.

[164] And the 'tariff' itself must be set by a judge: *Stafford v United Kingdom*, (App. 46295/99), 28 May 2002 [GC], (2002) 35 EHRR 1121, ECHR 2002-IV; *T v United Kingdom* (App. 24724/94); and *V v United Kingdom* (App. 24888/94), 16 December 1999 [GC], (2000) 30 EHRR 121, ECHR 1999-IX.

[165] *Thynne, Wilson and Gunnell v United Kingdom*, (Apps. 11787/85, 11978/86, and 12009/86), 25 October 1990, Series A No 190, (1991) 13 EHRR 666; *Stafford v United Kingdom*, (App. 46295/99), 28 May 2002 [GC], (2002) 35 EHRR 1121, ECHR 2002-IV; *Benjamin and Wilson v United Kingdom*, (App. 28212/95), 26 September 2002, (2003) 36 EHRR 1.

[166] *Hussain v United Kingdom*, (App. 21928/93), 21 February 1996, (1996) 22 EHRR 1, ECHR 1996-I; *Singh v United Kingdom* (App. 23389/94), 21 February 1996, ECHR 1996-I.

account of the original concerns which led to the detention, and it should also be conducted judicially, in a procedurally fair manner, and speedy. In the *Oldham* case[167] the Court held that a two-year interval between reviews of detention following the applicant's recall to prison was too long to be 'speedy'.

AN ENFORCEABLE RIGHT TO COMPENSATION

Article 5(5) provides that:

Everyone who has been the victim of arrest or detention in contravention of the provisions of this article shall have an enforceable right to compensation.

It is not clear why special provision is made for compensation for a breach of Article 5(1)–(4), when there is no such special provision in relation to the other rights guaranteed by the Convention, and when there is a general provision under Article 13 requiring an effective remedy for any violation.

Although any breach of Article 5 established by national courts or by Convention organs will, in the absence of an enforceable right to compensation under national law, give rise in addition to a breach of Article 5(5),[168] relatively few applicants invoke this provision before the Court, perhaps because by the time they get to Strasbourg most applicants are more interested in seeking damages under Article 41.

In the *Fox, Campbell and Hartley*[169] and *Brogan*[170] cases, for example, the Court found this provision to have been breached since there was no rule of Northern Irish law which would have provided compensation for the arrest and prolonged initial detention of the applicants under the prevention of terrorism legislation. More recently, the Court came to the same conclusion in the *Hood* case,[171] where the applicant, a soldier, was unable to claim compensation before the English courts in respect of the fact that his commanding officer, who was not sufficiently independent for the purposes of Article 5(3), had authorized his detention in close arrest.

CONCLUDING REMARKS

The right to liberty is of fundamental importance. As well as the value to the individual of liberty in itself, many of the other rights protected by the Convention are to a certain extent conditional upon it. It becomes possible to interfere with and place limitations

---

[167] *Oldham v United Kingdom*, (App. 36273/97), 26 September 2000, (2001) 31 EHRR 34, ECHR 2000-X.

[168] See, for example, *Houtman and Meeus v Belgium* (App. 22945/07), 17 March 2009; and *A and others v United Kingdom*, (App. 3455/05), 19 February 2009 [GC], ECHR 2009-nyr.

[169] *Fox, Campbell and Hartley v United Kingdom*, (Apps. 12244/86, 12245/86, and 12383/86), 30 August 1990, Series A No 182, (1991) 13 EHRR 157.

[170] *Brogan and others v United Kingdom*, (Apps. 11209/84, 11234/84, 11266/84, and 11386/85), 29 November 1988, Series A No 145-B, (1989) 11 EHRR 117.

[171] *Hood v United Kingdom*, (App. 27267/95), 18 February 1999, (2000) 29 EHRR 365, ECHR 1999-I.

on the autonomy of detainees in every imaginable way; for example, they may only send and receive letters if this is allowed by those holding them, and their detention may leave them vulnerable to torture and execution.[172] It is, therefore, regrettable that the text of Article 5 of the Convention is rather confused and unclear. Instead of using a multiplicity of expressions—'competent court' in 5(1)(a), 'court' in 5(1)(b) and 5(4), 'competent legal authority' in 5(1)(c), and 'judge or other officer authorized by law to exercise judicial power' in 5(3)—would it not have been possible for those drafting this provision to use one term consistently? And what is to be made of the apparent overlap of limitations on pre-trial detention in paragraphs 1(c) and 3, and of the rights to judicial review in paragraphs 3 and 4?

In their approach to the interpretation of Article 5, the Strasbourg Court has done much to overcome these problems. Most of the basic principles under Article 5 are now clearly established. Nonetheless, this is a Convention article that is repeatedly violated by many Contracting Parties. Corruption and political pressure on judges can in some countries mean that individuals are detained pre-trial even where there is no reasonable suspicion of criminal conduct. In parts of central and eastern Europe, Soviet traditions have been hard to dispel, and criminal suspects are still detained almost as a matter of course, even where the national court has not clearly identified any real ground for refusing bail. Under-resourced legal systems and long delays in coming to trial can mean that individuals who have not been convicted of any wrongdoing are detained for year after year.[173] Those States which have bad records in relation to unjustified and excessively lengthy pre-trial detention under Article 5(3), moreover, are frequently also States which the Strasbourg Court has found under Article 3 to provide inhuman and degrading conditions of detention. The problems are clearly linked, both in terms of the suffering caused to detainees and the solution available to those Contracting Parties.

The interpretation and application of the right to compensation in Article 5(5) remains undeveloped.

---

[172] See *Aksoy v Turkey* (App. 21987/93), 18 December 1996, (1997) 23 EHRR 553, ECHR 1996-VI, §76.
[173] As in, for example, *Kauczor v Poland*, (App. 45219/06), 3 February 2009.

12

THE RIGHT TO A FAIR TRIAL IN CIVIL AND CRIMINAL CASES

INTRODUCTION

Article 6 is an omnibus provision, which has been described as 'a pithy epitome of what constitutes a fair administration of justice'.[1] The rights protected by the article occupy a central place in the Convention system. A fair trial, in civil and criminal cases alike, is a basic element of the notion of the rule of law and part of the common heritage, according to the Preamble, of the Contracting Parties.

While Article 6(2) and (3)[2] contain specific provisions setting out 'minimum rights' applicable only in respect of those charged with a criminal offence, Article 6(1) applies both to civil and criminal proceedings.

The text of Article 6(1) reads:

In the determination of his civil rights and obligations or of any criminal charge against him, everyone is entitled to a fair and public hearing within a reasonable time by an independent and impartial tribunal established by law. Judgment shall be pronounced publicly but the press and public may be excluded from all or part of the trial in the interests of morals, public order or national security in a democratic society, where the interests of juveniles or the protection of the private life of the parties so require, or to the extent strictly necessary in the opinion of the court in special circumstances where publicity would prejudice the interests of justice.

Article 6 is the provision of the Convention most frequently invoked by applicants to Strasbourg.[3] As with other provisions of the Convention, many of the terms used

---

[1] N. Mole and C. Harby, *The right to a fair trial: a Guide to the implementation of Article 6 of the European Convention on Human Rights,* Human Rights Handbooks, No. 3 (Council of Europe Publishing, Strasbourg 2006). See also J. Cremona, 'The public character of trial and judgment in the jurisprudence of the European Court of Human Rights' in F. Matscher and H. Petzold, *Protecting Human Rights: The European Dimension: Studies in Honour of Gérard J. Wiarda* (Carl Heymanns, Köln 1990), 107. See also L. Loucaides, 'Questions of Fair Trial under the European Convention on Human Rights' (2003) 3 HRLRev 27.

[2] Considered in ch.13 below.

[3] In 2008, out of 1,423 judgments finding a violation of at least one Convention provision, 493 concerned the right to a fair trial and a further 456 concerned the length of proceedings: European Court of Human Rights, *Annual Report 2008* (Council of Europe Publishing, Strasbourg 2009), 132.

in Article 6(1) bear 'autonomous' meanings and require interpretation. It is therefore hardly surprising that there is substantial case-law on the provision's application. It would not be possible, within the scope of this book, to give a comprehensive account of this case-law, and the present chapter is intended only to provide an overview of some of the more important and interesting aspects.

THE SCOPE OF ARTICLE 6(1)

THE 'FOURTH INSTANCE' DOCTRINE

Every month the Strasbourg Court receives many hundreds of letters complaining about the decisions reached by national courts in civil and criminal trials. Many of these applications are, however, based on a fundamental misconception of the Convention system. The Court has no jurisdiction under Article 6 to reopen national legal proceedings or to substitute its own findings of fact, or the application of national law to them, for the conclusions of national courts.[4] The Court's task with regard to a complaint under Article 6 is to examine whether the proceedings, taken as a whole, were fair and complied with the specific safeguards stipulated by the Convention. Unlike a national court of appeal, it is not concerned with the questions whether the conviction was safe, the sentence appropriate, the award of damages in accordance with national law, and so on. And a finding by the Court that an applicant's trial fell short of the standards of Article 6 does not have the effect of quashing the conviction or overturning the judgment, as the case may be.[5]

The Court calls this principle the 'fourth instance' doctrine, because it is *not* to be seen as a third or fourth instance of appeal from national courts. It is important to bear the doctrine in mind when considering whether a particular factual situation based on criminal or civil proceedings raises any issue under Article 6.

WHAT IS A 'CRIMINAL CHARGE'?

Article 6(1) applies 'in the determination of [a person's] civil rights and obligations or of any criminal charge against him'. As with other key expressions used in the Convention, the Court has ruled that the concept of a 'criminal charge' must bear an 'autonomous' meaning, independent of the categorizations employed within the national legal orders. In this way, it is possible to achieve uniformity of approach throughout Europe and prevent States from avoiding Convention controls by classifying offences as disciplinary, administrative or civil matters.

---

[4] It follows, therefore, that an application pending before the Strasbourg Court is not a ground for a stay of execution in national proceedings: see the English decision in *Locabail (UK) Ltd v Waldorf Investment Corp and others*, [2000] HRLR 623, 25 May 2000, Chancery Division.

[5] See ch.13 below.

The *Engel* case[6] concerned action taken against members of the armed forces in respect of offences, such as insubordination, classified in the Netherlands as disciplinary in nature. The Court stated that relevant considerations in establishing whether the matter should be seen as involving the determination of a 'criminal charge' for the purposes of Article 6 were threefold: (1) the classification of the proceedings under national law; (2) the essential nature of the offence; and (3) the nature and degree of severity of the penalty that could be imposed having regard in particular to any loss of liberty, a characteristic of criminal liability.

The Court also considered the group to whom the legislation applied (small and closely defined groups of potential offenders are suggestive of a disciplinary or administrative procedure rather than a mainstream criminal offence). Short periods of imprisonment are not sufficient in themselves to bring Article 6 into play: Engel's punishment of two days of strict arrest was insufficiently severe, in the absence of other criminal characteristics, to be regarded as a criminal penalty. The national classification is however important. If a matter is classed as criminal under national law, this will be enough to bring it within the scope of Article 6, even if it is relatively trivial.

The Grand Chamber has endorsed and applied this methodology in the *Ezeh and Connors* case.[7] The applicants were convicted rapists serving sentences of imprisonment who committed offences contrary to the Prison Rules—threatening to kill a probation officer, in one case, and colliding with a prison officer during exercise in the other. They were tried by the Prison Governor, without legal aid or representation, and sentenced to additional days of custody—40 for the first applicant and seven days for the second applicant. The Court, applying the *Engel* criteria, noted that the offences were classified as disciplinary under national law and applied only to prisoners, although they also corresponded to the offences of making a threat to kill and assault under the mainstream criminal law. The nature and severity of the punishment were decisive in leading the Court to hold that the offences were 'criminal' for the purposes of Article 6: under national law there was a legal right to remission, and the loss of remission or additional days of imprisonment amounted to new deprivations of liberty over and above the rape sentences.[8] The Court emphasized in this connection that what was important in deciding whether the applicant faced a 'criminal charge' was the penalty that was 'liable to be imposed', which could be determined with reference to the statutory maximum, which was forty-two days for each offence. In these circumstances, the deprivations of liberty which were liable to be, and which

---

[6] *Engel and others v Netherlands*, (Apps. 5100/71, 5101/71, 5102/71, 5354/72, and 5370/72), 8 June 1976, Series A No 22, (1979–80) 1 EHRR 647.

[7] *Ezeh and Connors v United Kingdom*, (Apps. 39665/98 and 400086/98), 9 October 2003 [GC], (2004) 39 EHRR 1, ECHR 2003-X.

[8] The Court in effect overruled *Campbell and Fell v United Kingdom*, (Apps. 7819/77, and 7878/77), 28 June 1984, Series A No 80, (1985) 7 EHRR 165. See also *Findlay v United Kingdom*, (App. 22107/93), 25 February 1997, (1997) 24 EHRR 221, ECHR 1997-I; *Hood v United Kingdom*, (App. 27267/95), 18 February 1999 [GC], (2000) 29 EHRR 365, ECHR 1999-I; *Benham v United Kingdom*, (App. 19380/92), 10 June 1996, (1996) 22 EHRR 293, ECHR 1996-III; and *Steel and others v United Kingdom*, (App. 24838/94), 23 September 1998, (1998) 28 EHRR 603, ECHR 1998-VII.

actually were, imposed on the applicants were not sufficiently inconsequential as to displace the presumed criminal nature of the charges against them.[9] The Court did not give a fixed lower limit at which a sentence of imprisonment would be too short to bring a disciplinary charge into the criminal sphere, although it did refer to the decision in the *Engel* case that two days was not enough.[10]

In the *Ezeh and Connors* case, the respondent State argued that the special need to maintain discipline in prisons entailed that prison governors should be allowed a certain flexibility in awarding punishment of loss of remission, following proceedings which need not necessarily comply with Article 6. The Court took note of these submissions, but considered that there were other sanctions available to prison governors which would be adequate to keep up discipline without bringing Article 6 into operation.

The *Matyjek* case[11] concerned the nature of the proceedings in which the applicant had been found to have lied in making a declaration about his involvement with Poland's security services between 1944 and 1990 under lustration laws. The underlying purpose of lustration legislation is to require declarations about such prior involvement so that such matters cannot be the source of the blackmailing of public officials. A final judgment that a person had lied in a lustration declaration disqualified them from public office for a period of ten years. In its admissibility decision, the Strasbourg Court reiterated its earlier case-law, but emphasized that the second and third criteria established in the *Engel* case were alternative and not necessarily cumulative. A cumulative approach remained appropriate, however, where separate analysis of each criterion did not make it possible to reach a clear conclusion.[12] Applying these criteria, the Court concluded that the lustration proceedings in issue constituted criminal charges.

In the *Öztürk* case[13] the German authorities had decided as a matter of policy to take certain less serious motoring offences, punishable by fine, out of the criminal sphere. The majority of the Court found, applying the *Engel* criteria, that the purpose of the fine was both deterrent and punitive and this sufficed to show the criminal nature of the matter for Convention purposes. The process of decriminalization in the national law did not affect the classification under the Convention.[14] A strong dissenting group of five felt, however, that the decision did not adequately reflect the trend towards

---

[9] §129. [10] §129.

[11] *Matyjek v Poland*, (App.38184/03), Decision of 30 May 2006, ECHR 2006-VII; 24 April 2007, ECHR 2007-nyr.

[12] §47. In its consideration of the merits, the Court found a violation of Art. 6(1), taken in conjunction with Art. 6(3).

[13] *Öztürk v Germany*, (App. 8544/79), 21 February 1984, Series A No 73, (1984) 6 EHRR 409.

[14] The Court has similarly found, against other States, that motoring and other offences, despite local classification as 'administrative', are 'criminal' for the purposes of Article 6: *Lutz v Germany*, (App. 9912/82), 25 August 1987, Series A No 123, (1988) 10 EHRR 163; *Schmautzer v Austria*, (App. 15523/89), 23 October 1995, Series A No 328-A, (1995) 21 EHRR 511; *Malige v France*, (App. 27812/95), 23 September 1998, (1999) 28 EHRR 578; and see also *Lauko v Slovakia*, (App. 26138/95), 2 September 1998 (nuisance); *Bendenoun v France*, 24 February 1994, Series A No 284, (1994) 18 EHRR 54; and *AP, MP and TP v Switzerland*, (App. 19958/92), 29 August 1997, (1998) 26 EHRR 541 (tax offences).

decriminalization of minor offences in several European countries and the fact that it was in the interests of the accused to remove certain types of conduct from the stigma of criminality. Recognizing the legitimacy of these significant changes would, for them, take such matters outside the ambit of criminal law.

AT WHAT STAGES OF CRIMINAL PROCEEDINGS DOES ARTICLE 6(1) APPLY?

The protection of Article 6 starts from the time when a person is charged with a criminal offence. This is not, however, necessarily the moment when formal charges are first made against a person suspected of having committed an offence. For, as previously noted, the protection of Article 6 does not depend on the particular features of the system of criminal investigation and prosecution, which may and do vary considerably between the Contracting Parties. Moreover, as the object of Article 6 is to protect a person throughout the criminal process, and since formal charges may not be brought until a fairly advanced stage of an investigation, it is necessary to find a criterion for the opening of criminal proceedings which is independent of the actual development of the procedure in a specific case.

The Court has defined a 'charge' for the purposes of Article 6(1) as 'the official notification given to an individual by the competent authority of an allegation that he has committed a criminal offence.'[15] It may, however, 'in some instances take the form of other measures which carry the implication of such an allegation and which likewise substantially affect the situation of the suspect.'[16]

Article 6(1) covers the whole of the proceedings in issue, including appeal proceedings and the determination of sentence.[17]

Thus, in the *Delcourt* case,[18] Article 6(1) was found to be applicable to proceedings before the Belgian Court of Cassation. The respondent State had argued that the Court of Cassation did not deal with the merits of cases submitted to it, but the Court found that although the judgment of the Court of Cassation could only confirm or quash a decision, and not reverse or replace it, it was still 'determining' a criminal charge.

The cases of *T* and *V*[19] raised questions about the applicability of Article 6(1) to a sentencing procedure. The applicants had been convicted at the age of eleven of murdering a two-year-old the year before. As with all children convicted in England and Wales of murder, they were sentenced to be detained 'during Her Majesty's pleasure'. This is an indeterminate sentence: a period of detention, 'the tariff', is served to satisfy

---

[15] *Eckle v Germany*, (App. 8130/78), 15 July 1982, Series A No 51, (1983) 5 EHRR 1, §73.

[16] *Foti v Italy*, (Apps. 7604/76, 7719/76, 7781/77, and 7913/77), 10 December 1982, Series A No 56, (1983) 5 EHRR 313, §52.

[17] *Eckle v Germany*, (App. 8130/78), 15 July 1982, Series A No 51, (1983) 5 EHRR 1, §§76–7; *Phillips v United Kingdom*, (App. 41087/98), 5 September 2001, ECHR 2001-VII.

[18] *Delcourt v Belgium*, (App. 2689/65), 17 January 1970, Series A No 11, (1979–80) 1 EHRR 355.

[19] *T v United Kingdom*, (App. 24724/94); and *V v United Kingdom* (App. 24888/94), 16 December 1999 [GC], (2000) 30 EHRR 121, ECHR 1999-IX.

the requirements of retribution and deterrence, and thereafter it is legitimate to continue to detain the offender only if this appears to be necessary for the protection of the public. At the time of the applicants' conviction, the tariff was set by the Home Secretary. The Court held that the tariff-fixing procedure amounted to the fixing of a sentence and that there had been a violation of Article 6(1) since the Home Secretary was not 'an independent and impartial tribunal'.

Proceedings which take place after conviction and sentence have become final fall outside Article 6. Thus this provision does not cover an application by a convicted prisoner for release on probation or parole,[20] or for a new trial,[21] or for review of his sentence after the decision has become *res judicata*.[22] Nor does Article 6(1) apply on an application for provisional release pending trial[23] nor to proceedings following a decision that an applicant is unfit to plead to a criminal charge.[24]

WHAT ARE 'CIVIL RIGHTS AND OBLIGATIONS'?

The definition of 'civil rights and obligations' has proved more problematic.

First, it is clear that there must be a 'right' (or an 'obligation'). Thus, for example, questions relating to the making of an *ex gratia* payment by the State would not attract the protection of Article 6 because there is no 'right' to such a payment. Secondly, the right (or obligation) must exist under national law: this point is dealt with in more detail below in the section on 'access to court'. Thirdly, the right (or obligation) must be 'civil' in nature, and it is in connection with this aspect of the definition that the real difficulties arise.

It is evident that this phrase covers ordinary civil litigation between private individuals, relating, for example, to actions in tort, contract, and family law. It is more difficult, however, to determine whether Article 6(1) should apply also to disputes between individuals and the State concerning rights which, under some systems of law, fall under administrative rather than private law. If, for example, a public authority expropriates my land, do I have the right to a court hearing? Does the term cover only private rights to the exclusion of public law matters?[25]

From the start, the Court and Commission took the view that, as with the definition of 'criminal charge', the question whether a dispute relates to 'civil rights and

---

[20] App. 606/59, *X v Austria*, Decision of 19 September 1961 (1961) 4 *Yearbook* 340; App. 1760/63, *X v Austria*, Decision of 23 May 1966, (1966) 9 *Yearbook* 166; App. 4133/69, *X v United Kingdom*, Decision of 13 July 1970, (1970) 13 *Yearbook* 780.

[21] *Fischer v Austria*, (App. 27569/02), Decision of 6 May 2003.

[22] App. 1237/61, *X v Austria*, Decision of 5 March 1962 (1962) 5 *Yearbook* 96, 102.

[23] *Neumeister v Austria*, (App. 1936/63), 27 June 1968, Series A No 8, (1979–80) 1 EHRR 91, §§22 and 23 of 'The Law'; *Matznetter v Austria*, (App. 2178/64), 10 November 1969, Series A No 10, (1979–80) 1 EHRR 198, §13 of 'The Law'.

[24] *Antoine v United Kingdom*, (App. 62960/00), Decision of 13 May 2003.

[25] For a detailed consideration of the legislative history of the provision, see P. Van Dijk, 'The interpretation of "civil rights and obligations" by the European Court of Human Rights—one more step to take' in F. Matscher and H. Petzold, *Protecting Human Rights: The European Dimension: Studies in Honour of Gérard J. Wiarda* (Carl Heymanns, Köln 1990), 131–43.

obligations' could not be answered solely by reference to the way in which it is viewed under the national law of the respondent State; the concept has an 'autonomous' mean-ing under the Convention.[26] Any other approach would have allowed Contracting Parties to circumvent fair trial guarantees under Article 6(1) simply by classifying various areas of the law as 'public' or 'administrative' and would have risked creating disparity in the protection of human rights throughout Europe.

While this refusal to be tied by national law definitions is no doubt correct, it does give rise to uncertainty as to whether a particular type of dispute is included. Although the Court has, from time to time, appeared to base itself on various elements such as the economic nature of the right concerned, it has never attempted to elaborate uni-versal criteria, comparable to the *Engel* criteria for a 'criminal offence',[27] by which to identify 'civil rights and obligations', preferring instead to decide the matter on a case-by-case basis. The closest it has come to giving general guidance is to repeat that while the national law position is not totally without importance, the substantive content, character, and effects of the right concerned are more decisive.

The Strasbourg Court first considered the interpretation of 'civil rights and obli-gations' in the *Ringeisen* case.[28] The dispute in question involved an application by Ringeisen for approval of the transfer to him, from a private person, of certain plots of land in Austria. He alleged that the Regional Real Property Transactions Commission which had heard his appeal against the decision of the District Commission, was biased, and consequently that it was not an impartial tribunal as required by Article 6(1).

The majority of the Commission concluded that Article 6(1) did not apply because the expression 'civil rights and obligations' should be construed restrictively as includ-ing only disputes between private individuals and not any proceedings in which the citizen is confronted by a public authority. In contrast, the Court held that Article 6(1) was applicable (although it had not been violated because there was no evidence of bias). As to the interpretation of Article 6(1), it held as follows:[29]

For Article 6, paragraph (1), to be applicable to a case ('contestation') it is not necessary that both parties to the proceedings should be private persons, which is the view of the majority of the Commission and of the Government. The wording of Article 6, paragraph (1), is far wider; the French expression 'contestations sur (des) droits et obligations de caractère civil' covers all proceedings the result of which is decisive for private rights and obligations. The English text, 'determination of...civil rights and obligations', confirms this interpretation.

The character of the legislation which governs how the matter is to be determined (civil, commercial, administrative law, etc.) and that of the authority which is invested

---

[26] App. 1931/63, *X v Austria*, Decision of 2 October 1964, (1964) 7 *Yearbook* 212 at 222; *König v Germany*, (App. 6232/73), 28 June 1978, Series A No 27, (1979–80) EHRR 170; and see, more recently, *Maaouia v France*, (App. 39652/98), 5 October 2000 [GC], (2001) 33 EHRR 1037, ECHR 2000-X, §34.

[27] See above in this chapter.

[28] *Ringeisen v Austria*, (App. 2614/65), 16 July 1971, Series A No 13, (1979–80) 1 EHRR 455.

[29] §94.

with jurisdiction in the matter (ordinary court, administrative body, etc.) are therefore of little consequence.

When Ringeisen purchased property from the Roth couple, he had a right to have
the contract for sale which they had made with him approved if he fulfilled, as he
claimed to do, the conditions laid down in the Act. Although it was applying rules
of administrative law, the Regional Commission's decision was to be decisive for the
relations in civil law ('de caractère civil') between Ringeisen and the Roth couple. This
is enough to make it necessary for the Court to decide whether or not the proceedings in the case complied with the requirements of Article 6, paragraph (1), of the
Convention.

Following its decision in the *Ringeisen* case, the Strasbourg Court has adopted an
increasingly liberal interpretation of the concept of civil rights and obligations. Thus,
in another early case,[30] it held that proceedings which involved the withdrawal of
an authority to run a medical clinic and an authorization to practise medicine were
within the scope of Article 6(1). This was so even though the function of the body
which had taken the decision was to act in the interests of public health and to exercise
responsibilities borne by the medical profession towards society at large. Similarly,
in the *Pudas* case,[31] where the applicant's licence to operate a taxi on specified routes
was revoked as part of a programme of rationalization which would have involved the
replacement of one of his routes by a bus service, the Court rejected the respondent
State's argument that, since the revocation of the licence depended essentially on an
assessment of policy issues not capable of, or suited to, judicial control, the matter did
not involve the determination of civil rights and obligations. Instead the Court held,
unanimously, that the public law features of the case did not exclude the matter from
the scope of Article 6(1), which applied since the revocation of the licence affected the
applicant's business activities.

Questions relating to children taken into public care;[32] the expropriation of property
by public authorities;[33] objections to and the enforcement of planning and decisions
and the environment;[34] the withdrawal of licences to serve alcohol[35] and to work a
gravel pit; disciplinary proceedings resulting in suspension from medical[36] and legal[37]

---

[30] *König v Germany*, (App. 6232/73), 28 June 1978, Series A No 27, (1979–80) 2 EHRR 170. See also
Kraska v Switzerland, (App. 13942/88), 19 April 1993, Series A No 254-B, (1994) 18 EHRR 188.

[31] *Pudas v Sweden*, (App.10426/83), 27 October 1987, Series A No 125, (1988) 10 EHRR 380.

[32] *McMichael v United Kingdom*, (App. 16424/90), 24 February 1995, Series A No 307-B, (1995) 20 EHRR
205.

[33] *Sporrong and Lönnroth v Sweden*, (Apps. 7151/75, and 7152/75), 23 September 1982, Series A No 52,
(1983) 5 EHRR 35; and *Bodén v Sweden*, (App.10930/84), 27 October 1987, Series A No 125, (1988) 10 EHRR
36; *Zanatta v France* (App. 38042/97), 28 March 2000.

[34] *Mats Jacobsson v Sweden*, (App. 11309/84), 28 June 1990, Series A No 180-A, (1991) 13 EHRR 79; *Bryan
v United Kingdom*, (App. 19178/91), 9 September 1997, Series A No 335-A, (1995) 21 EHRR 342; *Taskin v
Turkey*, (App. 49517/99), Judgment of 4 December 2003, ECHR 2003-X.

[35] *Tre Traktörer AB v Sweden*, (App. 10873/84), 7 July 1989, Series A No 159, (1991) 13 EHRR 309.

[36] *Fredin v Sweden*, (App. 12033/86), 18 February 1991, Series A No 192, (1991) 13 EHRR 784.

[37] *Le Compte, van Leuven and de Meyere v Belgium*, (App. 6878/75, and 7238/75), 23 June 1981, Series A
No 43, (1982) 4 EHRR 1.

practice; conditions of detention[38] and even an application for release from detention in a prison psychiatric wing[39] have all been held to be sufficiently 'civil' in nature to fall within the scope of Article 6(1).

Disputes concerning liability to tax, despite their pecuniary consequences, have been held to be public law issues to which Article 6(1) does not apply.[40] It might be thought that social security is another such issue. However, in the *Feldbrugge* case,[41] which concerned a claim for sickness benefits, the Strasbourg Court concluded by a majority of ten to seven that Article 6(1) applied. It considered that, although the character of the legislation, the compulsory nature of insurance against certain risks, and the assumption by public bodies of responsibility for ensuring social protection were public law characteristics, these were outweighed by the personal and economic nature of the asserted right by the applicant, the connection with a contract of employment, and the similarities with insurance under ordinary law. In the *Deumeland* case,[42] decided the same day, the Court reached the same conclusion as regards the right to a widow's supplementary pension following the death of her husband in an industrial accident.[43]

Until the *Salesi* judgment,[44] it was not clear whether this interpretation would extend to non-contributory types of social assistance, which are not based on any 'contract' between the State and the individual and are harder to compare to private law insurance schemes. In the *Salesi* case, however, which concerned a dispute over entitlement to a disability allowance financed entirely from public funds and not dependent on the payment of contributions, the Court found that Article 6(1) applied.[45] It appeared to rely on two factors: first, the fact that entitlement to the allowance was a right under national law, derived from statute, which the applicant could assert in an ordinary civil court and which was not dependent on an exercise of State discretion; secondly, the fact that, as a result of being denied the allowance, the applicant had suffered an interference with her means of subsistence. This second factor was sufficient to make the right 'civil' for the purposes of the Convention.

---

[38] *Ganci v Italy*, (App. 41576/98), 30 October 2003, ECHR 2003-XI; *Musumeci v Italy*, (App. 33695/96), 11 January 2005.

[39] *Aerts v Belgium*, (App. 25357/94), 30 July 1998, (2000) 29 EHRR 50, ECHR 1998-V.

[40] *Charalambos v France*, (App. 49210/99), Decision of 8 February 2000; *Vidacar S.A. and Obergrup S.L. v Spain*, (Apps. 41601/98, 41775/98), Decision of 20 April 1999.

[41] *Feldbrugge v Netherlands*, (App. 8562/79), 29 May 1986, Series A No 99, (1986) 8 EHRR 425.

[42] *Deumeland v Germany*, (App. 9384/81), 29 May 1986, Series A No 100, (1986) 8 EHRR 448. See also *Schouten and Meldrum v Netherlands*, (Apps. 19005/91, and 19006/91), 9 December 1994, Series A No 304, (1995) 19 EHRR 432.

[43] See also, similarly, *Schuler-Zgraggen v Switzerland*, (App. 14518/89), 24 June 1993, Series A No 263, (1993) 16 EHRR 405, relating to invalidity pension.

[44] *Salesi v Italy*, (App. 13023/87), 23 February 1993, Series A No 257-A, (1998) 26 EHRR 187, §19. For a similar progression in the scope of the notion of 'possessions' under Article 1 of Protocol 1 to encompass claims for non-contributory benefits see *Stec and others v United Kingdom*, (Apps. 65731/01 and 65900/01), Decision of 6 July 2005 [GC], (2005) 41 EHRR SE18, ECHR 2005-X.

[45] See also *Mennitto v Italy*, (App. 33804/96), 3 October 2000 [GC], (2002) 34 EHRR 1122, ECHR 2000-X.

The same arguments could perhaps be applied to certain rights of aliens to enter and stay in States of which they are not nationals. Rights such as the right to asylum are governed by international and national law and are not within the discretion of the State to withhold; moreover, a decision to expel an alien can have the most serious consequences on his or her economic and personal welfare. However, the Commission consistently rejected all such applications as inadmissible under Article 6(1),[46] and this approach was confirmed by the Strasbourg Court in the *Maaouia* case.[47] The applicant, a Tunisian national, complained about the length of the proceedings he had brought to overturn an order excluding him from France. In this case the Court did not consider the economic or personal effect of exclusion on the individual concerned, but instead attempted to determine the intention of the Contracting Parties who had drafted and signed the Convention. Despite the fact that Protocol 7 to the Convention was adopted only in November 1984, after the Commission had already expressed the view that a decision to deport a person does 'not involve a determination of his civil rights and obligations or of any criminal charge against him' within the meaning of Article 6(1), the Court decided that the creation of this Protocol, which contains procedural guarantees applicable to the expulsion of aliens, indicated that the Contracting Parties did not regard such proceedings as being governed by Article 6.

Disputes about access to election documentation raised by election observers are not proceedings concerned with the determination of civil rights and obligations.[48]

The Court's emphasis on the character of the right in question and its effects on the individual has created difficulties in classifying employment-related claims brought by civil servants against their employer, the State. The Court initially held that 'disputes relating to the recruitment, careers and termination of service of civil servants are as a general rule outside the scope of Article 6(1)'.[49] This principle was soon perceived as unsatisfactory, however, since it left everyone working in the public sector without the protection of Article 6(1) and led to disparity between the Member States of the Council of Europe because the type of employees categorized as 'civil servants' varies from State to State; in some countries, for example, teachers are 'civil servants' whereas they are assimilated with private sector employees in others.

The Court's case-law, therefore, witnessed a gradual whittling away of this sweeping exclusion. In a series of cases involving, for example, pension[50] and salary[51] disputes, it was held that where the claim in issue related to a 'purely' or 'essentially' economic right, Article 6(1) applied. Where, however, the claim principally called into question the authorities' discretionary powers, Article 6(1) did not apply.

---

[46] See the citations in the *Maaouia v France*, (App. 39652/98), 5 October 2000 [GC], (2001) 33 EHRR 1037, ECHR 2001-X, §35.

[47] *Maaouia v France*, (App. 39652/98), 5 October 2000 [GC], (2001) 33 EHRR 1037, ECHR 2000-X.

[48] *Geraguyn Khorhurd Patgamavorakan Akum v Armenia*, (App. 11721/04), Decision of 11 May 2009.

[49] *Massa v Italy*, (App. 14399/88), 24 August 1993, Series A No 265-B, (1994) 18 EHRR 266, §26.

[50] *Massa v Italy*, (App. 14399/88), 24 August 1993, Series A No 265-B, (1994) 18 EHRR 266; and *Francesco Lombardo v Italy*, (App. 11519/85), 26 November 1992, Series A No 249-B, (1996) 21 EHRR 188.

[51] *De Santa v Italy*, (App. 25574/94); *Lapalorcia v Italy*, (App. 25586/94); *Abenavoli v Italy*, (App. 25587/94), 2 September 1997.

Once again, the Court's approach proved unworkable. Almost any employment dispute will have economic consequences for the employee and it proved difficult to draw the line between cases falling within Article 6(1) and those excluded without creating uncertainty and injustice. In the *Neigel* case,[52] for example, the proceedings brought by the applicant centred on the authorities' refusal to reinstate her to a permanent post in the civil service, but the Court held that it concerned her recruitment and career and that Article 6(1) was not applicable; her claim for lost salary was insufficient to bring it within the scope of that provision because in order to succeed with this claim she needed first to prove that the refusal to reinstate her had been unlawful.

One of the first acts of the new Court was to attempt to rectify this situation. In the *Pellegrin* judgment[53] the Grand Chamber set out a new test for determining the application of Article 6(1) to civil service employment disputes, based on the nature of the employee's duties and responsibilities. The only disputes now excluded from the scope of Article 6(1) are 'those which are raised by public servants whose duties typify the specific activities of the public service in so far as the latter is acting as the depository of public authority responsible for protecting the general interests of the State or other public authorities'.[54] This principle allows the State to protect its interests by giving it virtually a free hand (as far as Article 6 is concerned) in hiring and firing core civil servants, such as diplomats, policy-makers, policemen, and soldiers,[55] while protecting the rights of the thousands of others (cleaners, nurses, teachers, and so on) whose jobs, to all intents and purposes, are identical to those of their counterparts in the private sector.[56]

That judgment, however, is not the end of the story, since the application of the functional criterion was acknowledged by the Court in a later case to be capable of anomalous results.[57] Accordingly the Strasbourg Court extended its decision in the *Pellegrin* case as follows:

To recapitulate, in order for the respondent State to be able to rely before the Court on the applicant's status as a civil servant in excluding the protection embodied in Article 6, two conditions must be fulfilled. First, the State in its national law must have expressly excluded access to a court for the post or category of staff in question. Secondly, the exclusion must be justified on objective grounds in the State's interest. The mere fact that the applicant is in a sector or department which participates in the exercise of power conferred by public law is not in itself decisive. In order for the exclusion to be justified, it is not enough for the State

[52] *Neigel v France*, (App. 18725/91), 17 March 1993.
[53] *Pellegrin v France*, (App. 28541/95), 8 December 1999 [GC], (2001) 31 EHRR 651, ECHR 1999-VIII.
[54] §66.
[55] See, for example, *Batur v Turkey*, (App. 38604/97), Decision of 4 July 2000.
[56] See, for example, *Frydlender v France*, (App. 30979/96), 27 June 2000 [GC], ECHR 2000-VII; *Procaccini v Italy*, (App. 31631/96), 30 March 2000; *Satonnet v France*, (App. 30412/96), 2 August 2000; *Castanheira Barros v Portugal*, (App. 36945/97), 26 October 2000; *Lambourdière v France* (App. 37387/97), 2 August 2000; *Martinez-Caro de la Concha Casteneda and others v Spain*, (App. 42646/98), Decision of 7 March 2000; *Kajanen and Tuomaala v Finland*, (App. 36401/97), Decision of 18 October 2000.
[57] *Eskelinen and others v Finland*, (App. 63235/00), 19 April 2007 [GC], (2007) 45 EHRR 985, ECHR 2007-IV, §51.

to establish that the civil servant in question participates in the exercise of public power or that there exists, to use the words of the Court in the *Pellegrin* judgment, a 'special bond of trust and loyalty' between the civil servant and the State, as employer. It is also for the State to show that the subject matter of the dispute in issue is related to the exercise of State power or that it has called into question the special bond. Thus, there can in principle be no justification for the exclusion from the guarantees of Article 6 of ordinary labour disputes, such as those relating to salaries, allowances or similar entitlements, on the basis of the special nature of relationship between the particular civil servant and the State in question. There will, in effect, be a presumption that Article 6 applies. It will be for the respondent Government to demonstrate, first, that a civil-servant applicant does not have a right of access to a court under national law and, second, that the exclusion of the rights under Article 6 for the civil servant is justified.[58]

In conclusion, then, it can be seen that the expression 'civil rights and obligations' has come to encompass many areas which are frequently regarded by national systems as part of public or administrative law. While this extension of the protection offered by Article 6(1) can only be welcomed, it is on occasion difficult to discern any consistent principle in the Court's case-law. This lack of principle can make it difficult for Contracting Parties to determine the extent of their obligations under Article 6(1) and for citizens to know their rights. Moreover, certain inconsistencies can appear difficult to defend. What, for example, is the fundamental difference between entitlement to a tax allowance and entitlement to a social security benefit which could justify holding the latter to fall within the scope of 'civil rights and obligations' but not the former?

THE NEED FOR A DISPUTE

Article 6(1) requires not only that the matter concern civil rights or obligations, but that there be a dispute (*contestation*, from the French text of Article 6(1)) concerning the particular rights or obligations. In the *Benthem* judgment[59] the Strasbourg Court reviewed the case-law on this requirement and summarized its content as follows:

(a) Conformity with the spirit of the Convention requires that the word 'contestation' (dispute) should not be 'construed too technically' and should be 'given a substantive rather than a formal meaning'…

(b) The 'contestation' (dispute) may relate not only to 'the actual existence of a…right' but also to its scope or the manner in which it may be exercised…It may concern both 'questions of fact' and 'questions of law'…

(c) The 'contestation' (dispute) must be genuine and of a serious nature…

(d) …'the…expression "contestations sur (des) droits et obligations de caractère civil" [disputes over civil rights and obligations] covers all proceedings the result of which is decisive for [such] rights and obligations'.…. However, 'a tenuous connection or

---

[58] §62. For an example of the application of the new criteria, see *Czetković v Serbia*, (App. 17271/04), 10 June 2008, §§36–8.

[59] *Benthem v Netherlands*, (App. 5548/80), 23 October 1985, Series A No 97, (1986) 8 EHRR 1, §32.

remote consequences do not suffice for Article 6(1)...: civil rights and obligations must be the object—or one of the objects—of the 'contestation' (dispute); the result of the proceedings must be directly decisive for such a right.

Thus, for example, in the *Fayed* case,[60] the Court held that an investigation by inspectors appointed by the Department of Trade and Industry into the applicants' take-over of Harrods did not attract the protection of Article 6, despite the applicants' argument that their reputations (a civil right) had been at stake. The Court found that the purpose of the inquiry had been to ascertain and record facts which might subsequently be used as the basis for action by other competent authorities—prosecuting, regulatory, disciplinary, or even legislative. It was satisfied that the functions performed by the inspectors were essentially investigative and that they had not been empowered to make any legal determination as to criminal or civil liability concerning the Fayed brothers.

Article 6(1) continues to apply to all stages of legal proceedings for the 'determination of... civil rights and obligations', not excluding stages subsequent to judgment on the merits. For example, in the *Robins* case[61] the Court held that proceedings to determine the costs liability of the unsuccessful party to civil litigation should be seen as a continuation of the principal dispute, and had therefore to be decided within a reasonable time.

RIGHT OF ACCESS TO COURT

One of the rights which has been developed out of the provisions of Article 6 is the right of access to a court for the determination of a particular civil issue.

The Court first recognized this right in the *Golder* case in 1975.[62] In a clear application of the 'effective rights' interpretation technique, it held that the detailed fair trial guarantees under Article 6 would be useless if it were impossible to start court proceedings in the first place. The applicant was detained in an English prison where serious disturbances broke out. He was accused of assault by a prison officer and wished to bring proceedings for defamation in order to have his record cleared, but this was precluded by the Prison Rules. Though not without limitation, the Court concluded that Article 6(1) contained an inherent right of access to court, observing:

In civil matters one can scarcely conceive of the rule of law without there being a possibility of access to the courts.... The principle whereby a civil claim must be capable of being submitted to a judge ranks as one of the universally recognized fundamental principles of law; the same is true of the principle of international law which forbids the denial of justice. Article 6(1) must be read in the light of these principles.[63]

---

[60] *Fayed v United Kingdom*, (App. 17101/90), 21 September 1994, Series A No 294-B, (1994) 18 EHRR 393.

[61] *Robins v United Kingdom*, (App. 22410/93), 23 September 1997, (1998) 26 EHRR 527, ECHR 1997-V.

[62] *Golder v United Kingdom*, (App. 4451/70), 21 February 1975, Series A No 18, (1979–80) 1 EHRR 524.

[63] §§34–5.

The right of access to court is not absolute: it is open to States to impose restrictions on would-be litigants, as long as these restrictions pursue a legitimate aim and are not so wide-ranging as to destroy the very essence of the right.[64] For example, orders preventing vexatious litigants from commencing or pursuing claims without leave are not usually in breach of Article 6(1), since such orders pursue the aim of preserving court time and resources for deserving cases and since the litigant would be granted leave to pursue a meritorious action.[65] But it is not open to a Contracting Party to refuse to accept process starting actions by electronic means whether its code of civil procedure permits this. In the *Lawyer Partners* case[66] the respondent State refused to accept details on DVDs as a means of starting multiple actions claiming that it lacked the resources to process actions submitted in this way notwithstanding the permissibility of filing action by electronic means. The case was clear cut, partly because the national constitutional court had also concluded that the authorities could not refuse to accept actions filed in this way.

In the *Stubbings* case,[67] the Strasbourg Court ruled that the provisions of the Limitation Act 1960, requiring actions for damages for trespass against the person to be started within three years of the alleged injury or the victim's 18th birthday, were not a disproportionate restriction on the right of access to court, even though the applicants, victims of child sexual abuse, had been unable to bring proceedings within the time limit because of the effects of repressed memory syndrome. Limitation periods were held to pursue the legitimate aim of ensuring legal certainty and finality, while still allowing litigants some opportunity to come to court. However, their application to particular facts can result in their being a disproportionate response.[68]

The right of access to a court must not only exist in theory, it must also be effective. This means, for example, that if a poor litigant wishes to bring court proceedings which are meritorious but so complex as to be impossible to pursue without professional legal assistance, the State must provide legal aid if this is 'indispensable for an effective access to court'.[69] A similar principle applies where the needy party is the defendant to the action. The Court explained in a case brought by two environmental protesters sued for libel by the hamburger chain McDonald's:

The question whether the provision of legal aid is necessary for a fair hearing must be determined on the basis of the particular facts and circumstances of each case and will depend *inter alia* upon the importance of what is at stake for the applicant in the proceedings, the

---

[64] *Ashingdane v United Kingdom*, (App. 8225/78), 28 May 1985, Series A No 93, (1985) 7 EHRR 528; see for a more recent restatement of this approach *Markovic and others v Italy*, (App. 1398/03), 14 December 2006 [GC], (2007) 44 EHRR 1045, ECHR 2006-XIV.

[65] App. 11559/85, *H v United Kingdom*, Decision of 2 December 1985, (1985) 45 DR 281.

[66] *Lawyer Partners AS v Slovakia*, (Apps 54252/07 and 14 others), 16 June 2009.

[67] *Stubbings and others v United Kingdom*, (Apps. 22083/93 and 22095/93), 22 October 1996; (1997) 23 EHRR 213, ECHR 1996-IV.

[68] *Stagno v Belgium*, (App. 1062/07), 7 July 2009.

[69] *Airey v Ireland*, (App. 6289/73), 9 October 1979, Series A, No 32, (1979–80) 2 EHRR 305, §26.

complexity of the relevant law and procedure and the applicant's capacity to represent him or herself effectively...[70]

Because the 'McLibel Two' were defending their freedom of expression, a right considered important under the Convention system, and risked having a substantial sum of damages awarded against them, and because the case was extraordinarily complex and cumbersome to defend, the above criteria were fulfilled and there was a violation of Article 6(1).[71]

The right to bring a claim to court applies only in respect of rights provided for by the national law; it is not possible through Article 6(1) to challenge the substantive *content* of national law. Sometimes, however, it can be difficult to decide whether a particular rule of national law negates a substantive right, or simply forms a procedural impediment to access to court such as to raise an issue under Article 6(1). This has been the case with the rules under English law providing that certain professions are immune from civil suit. In the *Osman* case[72] a member of the applicants' family was shot and killed by a stalker. The applicants claimed that the police had negligently failed to protect them, despite the presence of clear warning signs from the killer. They started negligence proceedings against the police in the English courts, but these were struck out by the Court of Appeal which held that, in light of House of Lords case-law, no action could lie against the police in negligence in the investigation and suppression of crime because public policy (the desire to save police resources for fighting crime rather than fighting court cases) required an immunity from suit. Before the Strasbourg Court, the British Government argued that Article 6(1) did not apply, because the exclusionary rule applied by the Court of Appeal meant that the applicants had no substantive right under national law against the police.

In a controversial decision, the Strasbourg Court held that Article 6(1) was applicable. It observed that English common law had long accorded a plaintiff the right to bring proceedings in negligence. Faced with such a claim, it was for the national court to determine whether the defendant owed the plaintiff a duty of care; in other words, whether the damage caused had been foreseeable, whether there existed a relationship of proximity between the parties, and whether it was fair, just, and reasonable to impose a duty of care in the circumstances. The rule applied by the Court of Appeal—giving the police a certain, limited immunity from suit on policy grounds—did not automatically doom the proceedings to failure from the start, but instead in principle allowed the national court to make a considered assessment as to whether or not the rule should be applied in that particular case. The Court therefore concluded that that applicants had a right under English law, derived from the law of negligence, to seek an adjudication on the admissibility and merits of their claim against the police, but

---

[70] *Steel and Morris v United Kingdom*, (App. 68416/01), 15 February 2005, (2005) 41 EHRR 403, ECHR 2005-II, §61.

[71] This finding should be contrasted with that in *McVicar v United Kingdom*, (App. 46311/99), 7 May 2002; (2002) 35 EHRR 566; ECHR 2002-III, where the Court found that the journalist defending libel proceedings was able to mount an effective case without legal representation.

[72] *Osman v United Kingdom*, (App. 23452/94), 28 October 1998, (2000) 29 EHRR 245, ECHR 1998-VIII.

that the rule giving the police immunity from suit acted as a watertight, irrebuttable defence and was thus disproportionate.

In the later *Z and others* case,[73] the Court, while not expressly overruling its judgment in *Osman*, conceded that its reasoning there 'was based on an understanding of the law of negligence... which has to be reviewed in the light of the clarifications subsequently made by the domestic courts'.[74] The applicants were five children who had been badly neglected and abused by their parents. During a period of over five years, despite being aware of the situation, the local authority took no steps to remove the children from their parents' care. The applicants subsequently started proceedings against the local authority, claiming damages for negligence and/or breach of statutory duty and arguing that the local authority's failure to act had resulted in their psychological damage. The proceedings were struck out as revealing no cause of action, and the applicants appealed to the Court of Appeal and, finally, the House of Lords.[75] In its judgment the House of Lords examined, *inter alia*, whether the local authority had owed the applicants a duty of care. It was accepted that the damage to the applicants had been foreseeable, and that there was a relationship of proximity between the parties. The House of Lords did not, however, consider that it would be just and reasonable to impose a duty of care in the circumstances, in view of the interdisciplinary nature of the statutory system of child protection, and the extraordinarily difficult and delicate task faced by social services in such situations. If liability in damages were to be imposed, it was feared that local authorities would adopt a more cautious and defensive approach to their duties, which would not be in the interests of children generally.

The Strasbourg Court found that Article 6(1) applied, since, prior to the judgment of the House of Lords, there had been no national decision indicating whether or not a local authority owed children a duty of care in such circumstances; until that judgment, therefore, the applicants had had an arguable claim to a civil right under English law. This aspect of the Court's reasoning alone would appear to contradict its *Osman* judgment, since by the time the applicants in *Osman* started proceedings the House of Lords had already established that no negligence action could lie against the police in respect of their acts and omissions in the investigation and suppression of crime. Moreover, when the Court in *Z and others* went on to examine whether there had been a violation of Article 6, it found that the applicants had not in fact been deprived of access to court, since they had been able to bring their claims before the national courts, culminating in a detailed consideration by the House of Lords as to whether a novel category of negligence actions should be developed.[76]

---

[73] *Z and others v United Kingdom*, (App. 29392/95), 10 May 2001 [GC], (2002) 34 EHRR 97; ECHR 2001-V.

[74] §100.

[75] *X and others v Bedfordshire County Council*, [1995] 2 AC 633.

[76] The Court did, however, find violations of Articles 3 and 13 based on the local authority's failure to act and the lack of any effective domestic remedy. The distinction between the absence of a substantive national legal right (when Article 6(1) does not apply) and a procedural restriction on a litigant's ability to sue on the

The Grand Chamber had the opportunity to review its approach to the right of access to a court in the *Markovic* case.[77] The case concerned claims made in Italy by relatives of citizens of Serbia and Montenegro who had been killed in a NATO air strike on Belgrade. Italy had provided the air bases from which the aircraft had taken off in order to carry out the bombing raids in which the relatives of the applicants were killed. The Italian Court of Cassation concluded that it had no jurisdiction to consider the claims. The applicants then argued that they had been denied access to a court in breach of Article 6. The Strasbourg Court affirmed that the distinction between substantive limitations and procedural bars determines the scope of the guarantees under Article 6.[78] The Court continued:

Where…the superior national courts have analysed in a comprehensive and convincing manner the precise nature of the impugned restriction, on the basis of the relevant Convention case-law and principles drawn therefrom, this Court would need strong reasons to differ from the conclusion reached by those courts by substituting its own views for those of the national courts on the question of interpretation of domestic law…and by finding, contrary to their view, that there was arguably a right recognized by domestic law.[79]

Applying these principles, the Grand Chamber concluded by ten votes to seven that there was no violation of Article 6. The effect is that the guarantee of a fair trial in Article 6 does not extend to the determination of claims for damages which national law classifies as political acts which are not justiciable before the national courts. The seven dissenting judges concluded that, in contrast to the detailed considerations which had been given to the arguments of the parties in the litigation in the *Z and others* case,[80] the Italian courts had not sought to balance the competing interests at stake and had not explained with sufficient clarity why the fact that the acts complained of were of a political nature should defeat their civil action. This lack of consideration and explanation meant that there had not been a proper consideration of the issues in the national legal order. The minority judgment does not mean that the Italian courts did have jurisdiction, but simply that they had failed to analyse the claims in a comprehensive and convincing manner.

The right of access to court has a more limited application in the criminal sphere. There is no right under Article 6 to have criminal proceedings brought against a suspected offender, for example, and no right as such to an appeal. Where, however, an appeal procedure is provided by national law, it must comply with Article 6[81] and

basis of an existing right (when Article 6(1) applies and may be violated where the restriction is disproportionate) was re-examined in *Roche v United Kingdom*, (App. 32555/96), 19 October 2005 [GC], (2006) 42 EHRR 599; ECHR 2005-X. This was a case brought by conscripts who participated in medical tests during the 1950s and have been unable to claim damages because the State enjoys immunity under s. 10 of the Crown Proceedings Act 1947.

[77] *Markovic and others v Italy*, (App. 1398/03), 14 December 2006 [GC], (2007) 44 EHRR 1045, ECHR 2006-XIV.

[78] §94.   [79] §95.

[80] *Z and others v United Kingdom*, (App. 29392/95), 10 May 2001 [GC], (2002) 34 EHRR 97, ECHR 2001-V, and see above in this chapter.

[81] *Delcourt v Belgium*, (App. 2689/65), 17 January 1970, Series A No 11, (1979–80) 1 EHRR 355.

access to it must not be blocked disproportionately or unfairly. Thus the rule under French law that a convicted person may bring an appeal in cassation only if he surrenders to custody was found to be a disproportionate restriction on access to court in the *Papon* case.[82] The Court also found a violation of this right in a case against the Netherlands,[83] where the applicant company had been persuaded to withdraw its appeal against sentence on the basis of assurances from the Advocate General that the penalty would, in any event, be reduced. By the time the company discovered that these assurances would not be followed through, the withdrawal of the appeal had become irrevocable.

THE EFFECTIVENESS OF COURT PROCEEDINGS

Linked to the principle of access to court is another fundamental aspect of the rule of law: that a final court judgment should be effective.

This is obviously true in criminal as in civil cases. The Grand Chamber found a violation of Article 6 in the *Assanidze* case[84] where the applicant, the former mayor of Batumi, the capital of the Ajarian Autonomous Republic, was convicted of a number of criminal offences and imprisoned in the Ajarian Autonomous Republic. Even when he had subsequently been acquitted of all charges by the Georgian courts, the Ajari authorities refused to release him. The Court observed that:

The guarantees afforded by Article 6 of the Convention would be illusory if a Contracting State's national legal or administrative system allowed a final, binding judicial decision to acquit to remain inoperative to the detriment of the person acquitted. It would be inconceivable that paragraph 1 of Article 6, taken together with paragraph 3, should require a Contracting State to take positive measures with regard to anyone accused of a criminal offence...and describe in detail procedural guarantees afforded to litigants—proceedings that are fair, public and expeditious—without at the same time protecting the implementation of a decision to acquit delivered at the end of those proceedings. Criminal proceedings form an entity and the protection afforded by Article 6 does not cease with the decision to acquit...[85]

The non-execution of civil judgments appears to be an endemic problem in much of eastern Europe—particularly in cases where the State is the judgment debtor—and there have been many judgments finding violations of Article 6 on this ground.[86]

---

[82] *Papon v France*, (App. 54210/00), 25 July 2002, (2004) 39 EHRR 217, ECHR 2002-XII.

[83] *Marpa Zeeland B.V and Metal Welding B.V v The Netherlands*, (App. 46300/99), 9 November 2004, (2005) 40 EHRR 407, ECHR 2004-X.

[84] *Assanidze v Georgia*, (App. 71503/01), 8 April 2004 [GC], (2004) 39 EHRR 653, ECHR 2004-II.

[85] §182.

[86] See, among many examples, *Hornsby v Greece*, (App. 18357/91), 19 March 1997, (1997) 24 EHRR 250; *Burdov v Russia*, (App. 59498/00), 7 May 2002, (2004) 38 EHRR 639, ECHR 2002-III; *Jasuniene v Lithuania*, (App. 41510/98), 6 March 2003; *Shmalko v Ukraine*, (App. 60750/00), 20 July 2004; and *Popov v Moldova*, (App. 74153/01), 18 January 2005. In *Pini, Bertani, Manera and Atripaldi v Romania*, (Apps. 78028/01 and

In the second *Burdov* case,[87] the Strasbourg Court adopted a pilot judgment follow-ing the finding of a violation of Article 6(1) and of Article 1 of Protocol 1 on account of the prolonged failure of the Russian authorities to enforce certain national judgments ordering monetary payments by the authorities. The respondent State was required to set up an effective domestic remedy to secure adequate redress for non-enforcement or delayed enforcement of judgments, and to grant such redress within one year for all victims of non-payment of judgment debts.

The right to effective court proceedings also entails that once a civil judgment or a criminal acquittal has become final and binding, there should be no risk of its being overturned. Many former Communist countries have retained in their codes of pro-cedure a power enabling a State official, such as a prosecutor, to bring an extraordinary appeal at any time.[88] In the *Ryabykh*[89] case the Court explained:

> ...One of the fundamental aspects of the rule of law is the principle of legal certainty, which requires, among other things, that where the courts have finally determined an issue, their ruling should not be called into question.... Legal certainty presupposes respect for the principle of *res judicata*..., that is the principle of the finality of judgments. This principle insists that no party is entitled to seek a review of a final and binding judgment merely for the purpose of obtaining a rehearing and a fresh determination of the case. Higher courts' power of review should be exercised to correct judicial errors and miscarriages of justice, but not to carry out a fresh examination. The review should not be treated as an appeal in disguise, and the mere possibility of there being two views on the subject is not a ground for re-examination. A departure from that principle is justified only when made necessary by circumstances of a substantial and compelling character.

THE OVERALL REQUIREMENTS OF
A FAIR HEARING

Much of what will be said later in this chapter will deal with the specific features of a fair trial set out in Article 6(1), but there is also an overriding requirement that the proceedings should be fair. Compliance with specific rights set out in Article 6 will not alone guarantee that there has been a fair trial. It is not possible to state in the abstract the content of the requirement of a fair hearing; this can be considered only

---

78030/01), 22 June 2004, (2005) 40 EHRR 312; ECHR 2004-V, where the Court found a violation where the State had not acted to enforce a judgment requiring a private children's home to hand children over to their adoptive parents.

[87] *Burdov v Russia (No. 2)*, (App33509/04), 15 January 2009, (2009) 49 EHRR 22, ECHR 2009-nyr.

[88] See, for example, *Brumarescu v Romania*, (App. 28342/95), 28 October 1999 [GC], (2001) 33 EHRR 862, ECHR 1999-VII; and *Ryabykh v Russia*, (App. 52854/99), 24 July 2003, (2005) 40 EHRR 615, ECHR 2003-IX.

[89] *Ryabykh v Russia*, (App. 52854/99), 24 July 2003, (2005) 40 EHRR 615, ECHR 2003-IX; §§51–2.

in the context of the proceedings as a whole, including any appeal proceedings.[90] A number of specific ingredients of a fair trial have, however, emerged from the case-law.

PROCEDURAL EQUALITY

The concept of 'equality of arms' (*égalité des armes*) was first mentioned in the *Neumeister* case,[91] and has been a feature of Article 6(1) ever since. It requires a fair balance between the parties and applies to both civil and criminal cases.[92] In the context of civil cases between private parties, 'equality of arms' does not have to be absolute. There is no duty on the State, for example, to provide legal aid to an impecunious litigant to such a level as to bring him or her into total parity with a wealthy opponent.[93] What matters is that parties are afforded a reasonable opportunity to present their case—including their evidence—under conditions that do not place them at a substantial disadvantage *vis-à-vis* the other side.[94] Thus, in criminal proceedings, if the prosecution enjoys a significant procedural advantage—such as the chance for the *avocat général* to make submissions to the Court of Cassation in the absence of representatives of the defence—there will not be a reasonable equality of arms between the parties.[95] By way of another, rather glaring, example, the Court found a violation of Article 6(1) in criminal proceedings where the defence lawyer was made to hang around for fifteen hours before finally being given a chance to plead his case in the early hours of the morning.[96]

AN ADVERSARIAL PROCESS AND DISCLOSURE OF EVIDENCE

Closely related to equality of arms is the right to have an adversarial trial. This means 'the opportunity for the parties to have knowledge of and comment on the observations filed or evidence adduced by the other party'.[97]

In order for the adversarial process to work effectively, it is important, in civil and criminal proceedings, that relevant material is available to both parties. Security considerations will not justify blanket restrictions on the availability of such evidence where it affects the interests of a litigant, since there are means which can

---

[90] *Fedje v Sweden*, (App. 12631/87), 26 September 1991, Series A No 212-C, (1994) 17 EHRR 14; and *Kostovski v Netherlands*, (App. 11454/85), 20 November 1989, Series A No 166, (1990) 12 EHRR 434.

[91] *Neumeister v Austria*, (App. 1936/63), 27 June 1968, Series A No 8, (1979–80) 1 EHRR 91.

[92] *Steel and Morris v United Kingdom*, (App. 68416/01), 15 February 2005, (2005) 41 EHRR 403, ECHR 2005-II, §59.

[93] §62.

[94] *Dombo Beheer BV v Netherlands*, (App. 14448/88), 27 October 1993, Series A No 274-A, (1994) 18 EHRR 213, §33.

[95] *Borgers v Belgium*, (App. 12005/86), 30 October 1991, Series A No 214, (1993) 15 EHRR 92.

[96] *Makhfi v France*, (App. 59335/00), 19 October 2004.

[97] *Ruiz-Mateos v Spain*, (App. 12952/87), 23 June 1993, Series A No 262, (1993) 16 EHRR 505, §63.

accommodate legitimate security concerns while offering a substantial measure of procedural justice to a litigant.[98]

The Court explained the principle as it applies in criminal proceedings in its *Rowe and Davis* judgment:[99]

It is a fundamental aspect of the right to a fair trial that criminal proceedings, including the elements of such proceedings which relate to procedure, should be adversarial and that there should be equality of arms between the prosecution and defence. The right to an adversarial trial means, in a criminal case, that both prosecution and defence must be given the opportunity to have knowledge of and comment on the observations filed and the evidence adduced by the other party.... In addition Article 6(1) requires...that the prosecution authorities should disclose to the defence all material evidence in their possession for or against the accused.

The entitlement to disclosure of relevant evidence is not, however, an absolute right. In criminal (and sometimes also in civil) proceedings there may be competing factors, such as national security, or the need to protect witnesses at risk of reprisals, or to keep secret police methods of investigation of crime, which must be weighed against the rights of the accused. In some cases it may be necessary to withhold certain evidence from the defence so as to preserve the fundamental rights of another individual or to safeguard an important public interest. However, as the Court emphasized in *Rowe and Davis*, only such measures restricting the rights of the defence which are strictly necessary are permissible under Article 6(1).

In accordance with the 'fourth instance' doctrine, the Court will not itself review whether or not an order permitting non-disclosure was justified in any particular case. Instead, it examines the decision-making procedure to ensure that it complied, as far as possible, with the requirements of adversarial proceedings and equality of arms and incorporated adequate safeguards to protect the interests of the accused.

In the *Rowe and Davis* case the prosecution had unilaterally decided, without consulting the trial judge, to withhold evidence in its possession about the existence and role of an informer. This man, who was one of the main prosecution witnesses at the applicants' trial on charges of armed robbery and murder, had, unbeknown to the defence or the judge, received a substantial reward for assisting the prosecution authorities. The applicants were convicted and appealed, and at this stage the prosecution notified the Court of Appeal about the withheld material. The Court of Appeal inspected it and held a hearing to decide whether it should be disclosed, but the defence were not permitted to attend this hearing and were never allowed to see the evidence or informed of its nature or content.

The Strasbourg Court decided that the procedure before the Court of Appeal was not sufficient to satisfy the requirements of Article 6(1). The rights of the defence

---

[98] *Dağtekin and others v Turkey*, (App. 70516/01), 13 March 2008.
[99] *Rowe and Davis v United Kingdom*, (App. 28901/95), 16 February 2000 [GC], (2000) 30 EHRR 1, ECHR 2000-II, §60.

would have been adequately protected if the trial judge had had the opportunity to examine the withheld evidence and make the decision on disclosure.[100] However, the Court took the view that, unlike the trial judge, who saw the witnesses give their testimony and was fully versed in all the evidence and issues in the case, the judges in the Court of Appeal were dependent for their understanding of the possible relevance of the undisclosed material on transcripts of the Crown Court hearings and on the account of the issues given to them by prosecuting counsel. In addition, the first instance judge would have been in a position to monitor the need for disclosure throughout the trial, assessing the importance of the undisclosed evidence at a stage when new issues were emerging, when it might have been possible through cross-examination seriously to undermine the credibility of key witnesses and when the defence case was still open to take a number of different directions or emphases. In contrast, the Court observed, the Court of Appeal was obliged to carry out its appraisal *ex post facto* and might even, to a certain extent, have unconsciously been influenced by the jury's verdict of guilty into underestimating the significance of the undisclosed evidence.

In the *Edwards and Lewis* case,[101] it was the trial judge who reviewed all the evidence which the prosecution sought not to disclose. In the particular circumstances of the case, however, this created a problem of inequality of arms. Each applicant had applied to have the prosecution case against him struck out for abuse of process on the ground that he had been entrapped into committing the offence by undercover police officers. As a matter of English procedural law, the trial judge must determine, as a question of fact and taking into account such matters as the accused's past criminal record and any evidence concerning his dealings with the police, whether or not it is established on the balance of probabilities that the police improperly incited the offence. The problem arose under Article 6 because the same trial judge had already examined, in the absence of any representative of the defence, the prosecution's undisclosed evidence, which had to be disclosed only if it was likely to be of assistance to the defence case. Because of the secret nature of this procedure the defence were unable to know whether or not the undisclosed evidence was in fact harmful to the accused's allegations of entrapment, and, if so, whether the evidence was accurate or could have been rebutted. For example, it was subsequently revealed in the case of Edwards that the undisclosed evidence suggested that he had for some time before the police operation been involved in drug trafficking: an allegation which was of material relevance to the judge's decision on entrapment and one which the defendant strongly denied.

---

[100] As occurred in the cases of *Jasper v United Kingdom*, (App. 27052/95), 16 February 2000, (2000) 30 EHRR 97; and *Fitt v United Kingdom*, (App. 29777/96), 16 February 2000, (2000) 30 EHRR 223, ECHR 2000-II, where the Court found no violation.

[101] *Edwards and Lewis v United Kingdom*, (Apps. 39647/98 and 40461/98), 27 October 2004 [GC], (2005) 40 EHRR 593, ECHR 2004-X.

A REASONED DECISION

A reasoned decision, while not expressly required by Article 6, is implicit in the requirement of a fair hearing, which has been recognized by the Court.[102] If a court gives some reasons, then prima facie the requirements of Article 6 in this respect are satisfied, and this presumption is not upset simply because the judgment does not deal specifically with one point considered by an applicant to be material. On the other hand, if, for example, an applicant were to show that the court had ignored a fundamental defence, which had been clearly put before it and which, if successful, would have discharged him in whole or in part from liability, then this would be sufficient to rebut the presumption of a fair hearing. Refusal to address a ground of appeal submitted by an appellant, which is cogent and relevant, and could have an effect on the outcome of the case, will also constitute a breach of Article 6(1).[103]

This analysis applies *a fortiori* to criminal proceedings. Thus, where a convicted person has the possibility of an appeal, the lower court must state in detail the reasons for its decision, so that on appeal from that decision the accused's rights may be properly safeguarded.[104]

In the *Gorou* case,[105] the Grand Chamber indicated that the elaboration of reasons must be related to the nature of the dispute before the court, and that the Strasbourg Court will take account of judicial practice in the national legal orders. This would justify only a brief decision in cases where a civil party joined in criminal proceedings was seeking to secure the filing of an appeal by the public prosecutor following an acquittal in the criminal proceedings.

APPEARANCE IN PERSON

It depends on the nature of the proceedings whether a failure to allow the individual accused or civil litigant to attend in person will constitute a violation of Article 6(1).[106] In the *Kremzow* case,[107] the applicant was represented by a lawyer at the hearing of his appeal against sentence, but was not himself brought to court from prison. The Strasbourg Court made it clear that, as a general rule, accused persons should always be present at their trial. It further held that the applicant should have been enabled to attend the hearing of his appeal against sentence, since an increase from twenty years to life imprisonment was in issue, and an assessment of the applicant was to take place. The Court said:

---

[102] *Van de Hurk v Netherlands*, (App. 16034/90), 19 April 1994, Series A No 288, (1994) 18 EHRR 481, §61. See also *Ruiz-Torija v Spain*, (App. 18390/91), 9 December 1994, Series A No 303-A, (1994) 19 EHRR 553; and *Hiro Balani v Spain*, (App. 18064/91), 9 December 1994, Series A No 303-B, (1994) 19 EHRR 566.

[103] *Luka v Romania*, (App. 34197/02), 21 July 2009.

[104] App. 1035/61, *X v Federal Republic of Germany*, Decision of 17 June 1963 (1963) 6 *Yearbook* 180, 192.

[105] *Gorou v Greece (No. 2)*, (App. 12686/03), 20 March 2009 [GC], ECHR 2009-nyr.

[106] And, in criminal cases, Article 6(3)(c): see ch.14 below.

[107] *Kremzow v Austria*, (App. 12350/86), 21 September 1993, Series A No 268-B, (1994) 17 EHRR 322.

These proceedings were thus of crucial importance for the applicant and involved not only an assessment of his character and state of mind at the time of the offence but also his motive. In circumstances such as those of the present case, where evaluations of this kind were to play such a significant role and where their outcome could be of major detriment to him, it was essential to the fairness of the proceedings that he be present during the hearing of the appeals and afforded the opportunity to participate in it together with his counsel.[108]

In contrast, no issue arose under Article 6 by virtue of Kremzow's absence during the appeal court's consideration of his plea of nullity, since he was represented and the nature of the hearing did not require him to be there.

The same principles apply in civil proceedings. Thus the individual concerned should be allowed to attend where, for example, an assessment of his or her character or state of health is directly relevant to the formation of the court's opinion, as in the case of a parent seeking access to a child[109] or a claimant seeking disability benefits.[110]

EFFECTIVE PARTICIPATION

It is not, however, sufficient that the criminal defendant or civil party is present in court. He or she must, in addition, be able effectively to participate in the proceedings. In one criminal case,[111] the applicant was slightly deaf and had not been able to hear some of the evidence given at trial. The Strasbourg Court did not, however, find a violation of Article 6(1) in view of the fact that the applicant's counsel, who could hear all that was said and was able to take his client's instructions at all times, chose for tactical reasons not to request that the accused be seated closer to the witnesses.

The applicants in the T and V cases[112] were eleven years old at the time of their trial for the murder of a two-year-old child. The proceedings were held in a blaze of publicity, in a packed courtroom, and there was medical evidence to show that both boys were suffering from post-traumatic stress at the time. The Strasbourg Court found violations of Article 6(1), commenting that it was highly unlikely that the applicants would have felt sufficiently uninhibited, in the tense courtroom and under public scrutiny, to have consulted with their lawyers during the trial. A later case[113] involved an 11-year-old boy with a long history of offending who was tried for robbery in the Crown Court. In contrast to the T and V trial, the case had attracted no publicity and a modified procedure had been adopted in an attempt to make the trial less intimidating; for example, the judge and barristers left off their wigs and gowns, plenty of breaks were taken and the applicant was allowed to sit with his social worker. The Strasbourg Court nonetheless found a violation of Article 6(1) on the ground that the

---

[108] §67.

[109] App. 434/58, *X v Sweden*, Decision of 30 June 1959 (1958–9) 2 *Yearbook* 354, at 370.

[110] *Salomonsson v Sweden*, (App. 38978/97), 12 November 2002.

[111] *Stanford v United Kingdom*, (App. 16757/90), 23 February 1994, Series A No 282-A.

[112] *T v United Kingdom*, (App. 24724/94); and *V v United Kingdom*, (App. 24888/94), 16 December 1999 [GC], (2000) 30 EHRR 121, ECHR 1999-IX.

[113] *SC v United Kingdom*, (App. 60958/00), 15 June 2004, (2005) 40 EHRR 226, ECHR 2004-IV.

applicant had been found to have the intellectual capacity of a child aged six to eight, and appeared to have little understanding of the nature of the proceedings or what was at stake. The Court concluded that:

> …when the decision is taken to deal with a child, such as the applicant, who risks not being able to participate effectively because of his young age and limited intellectual capacity, by way of criminal proceedings rather than some other form of disposal directed primarily at determining the child's best interests and those of the community, it is essential that he be tried in a specialist tribunal which is able to give full consideration to and make proper allowance for the handicaps under which he labours, and adapt its procedure accordingly.[114]

THE SPECIFIC REQUIREMENTS OF ARTICLE 6(1)

AN INDEPENDENT AND IMPARTIAL TRIBUNAL ESTABLISHED BY LAW

Article 6(1) guarantees the right to a fair trial before 'an independent and impartial tribunal established by law'. There cannot be a fair criminal or civil trial before a court which is, or appears to be, biased against the defendant or litigant, and the fair trial guarantees are meaningless if the tribunal's decision is liable to be overturned by some other authority which does not offer such guarantees.[115]

The Strasbourg Court is concerned both with the subjective and objective elements of independence and impartiality. The subjective element involves an enquiry into whether the personal conviction of a judge in a particular case raises doubts about his or her independence or impartiality. The judge's lack of bias is presumed unless there is evidence to the contrary and there are exceedingly few cases where subjective bias has been established since in practice such evidence can be very hard to come by. The objective element involves determination of whether, in terms of structure or appearance, a party's doubts about the tribunal's independence and impartiality may be legitimate.[116]

In the *Salaman* case[117] the Court was called upon to consider the effect of a judge's membership of the Freemasons. The applicant had brought proceedings to challenge the codicil of a will, made by a Freemason, which revoked an earlier will in favour of the applicant and left the property instead to a man claimed by the applicant also to be a Freemason. The applicant referred before the Strasbourg Court to popularly held suspicions about the secretive, pervasive, and corrupting nature of Freemasonry.

---

[114] §35.

[115] *Van de Hurk v Netherlands*, (App. 16034/90), 19 April 1994, Series A No 288, (1994) 18 EHRR 481.

[116] See generally *Piersack v Belgium*, (App. 8692/79), 1 October 1982, Series A No 53, (1983) 5 EHRR 169, and *Hauschildt v Denmark*, (App. 10486/83), 24 May 1989, Series A No 154, (1990) 12 EHRR 266.

[117] *Salaman v United Kingdom*, (App. 43505/98), Decision of 15 June 2000; and see also *Kiiskinen and Kovalainen v Finland*, (App. 26323/95), Decision of 3 June 1999.

The Strasbourg Court, however, did not consider that membership of a judge in the Freemasons in the United Kingdom could in itself raise doubts as to his impartiality where a witness or party in a case was also a Freemason; in particular, there was no reason to fear that a judge would not regard his oath on taking judicial office as taking precedence over any other social commitments or obligations. The applicant's doubts as to the lack of impartiality of the judge were not objectively justified.

The Strasbourg Court commented that whether or not a problem could arise, for example, due to a judge's personal acquaintance with a fellow Freemason or due to the interests of a Freemason institution being in issue in a case would depend on all the circumstances. The same applies whenever a member of a tribunal knows one of the parties to or witnesses at a trial. In the *Pullar* case,[118] for example, by sheer coincidence one of the jurors selected to try a case of corruption had previously been employed by the leading prosecution witness. The Strasbourg Court did not consider that this gave rise to a problem under Article 6(1), because a detailed examination of the juror's relationship with the witness—who had dismissed him from his job—did not demonstrate that the juror would be predisposed to believe his testimony.[119]

Care is also required, particularly in Continental criminal justice systems, where a judge has had some involvement in the pre-trial stages of the process. If this is routine pre-trial supervision of the case, there will be no breach of Article 6(1), but if the nature of the decision could suggest some pre-judging of the substantive issue, a violation of Article 6(1) could arise.[120]

In one case,[121] five of the nine jurors who served in the trial of a defamation action brought by way of private prosecution were members of the political party which was the principal target of the allegedly defamatory material. The jury selection procedures complied with the requirements of Swedish law; attempts by the applicant to have those jurors disqualified who were members of the political party failed. The Strasbourg Court found that the links between the defendants and the five jurors could give rise to misgivings as to their objective independence and impartiality; this in turn rendered the independence and impartiality of the court questionable and there was a violation of Article 6(1).

This judgment may be less far-reaching than at first sight appears.[122] In essence, there was a failure by the national procedures to achieve their objective of removing from the jury those with an interest in the outcome of the litigation. Wider applications, such as complaints about trial by a jury whose composition does not correspond

---

[118] *Pullar v United Kingdom*, (App. 22399/93), 10 June 1996, (1996) 22 EHRR 391, ECHR 1996-III.

[119] See also *Langborger v Sweden*, (App. 11179/84), 22 June 1989, Series A No 155, (1990) 12 EHRR 416.

[120] As in *Hauschildt v Denmark*, (App. 10486/83), 24 May 1989, Series A No 154, (1990) 12 EHRR 266; see also *De Cubber v Belgium*, (App. 9186/80), 26 October 1984, Series A No 86, (1985) 7 EHRR 236; *Ben Yaacoub v Belgium*, (App. 9976/82), 27 November 1987, Series A No 127-A, (1991) 13 EHRR 418; *Fey v Austria*, (App. 14396/88), 24 February 1993, Series A No 255, (1993) 16 EHRR 387; and *Nortier v Netherlands*, (App. 13924/88), 24 August 1993, Series A No 267, (1993) 17 EHRR 273.

[121] *Holm v Sweden*, (App. 14191/88), 25 November 1993, Series A No 279-A, (1994) 18 EHRR 79.

[122] And see, in contrast, *AB Kurt Kellermann v Sweden*, (App. 41579/98), 26 October 2004; and *Pabla KY v Finland*, (App. 47221/99), 22 June 2004, ECHR 2004-V.

to the ethnic origin of the defendant, are unlikely to succeed unless the particular facts of the case show that the defendant's concerns about racism in the tribunal are objectively justified.

In the *Sander* case,[123] for example, the defendant was Asian. In the course of his trial in the Crown Court a member of the jury sent a note to the judge alleging that two fellow jurors had been making openly racist remarks and jokes and expressing the fear that the defendant would be convicted, not on the evidence, but because he was Asian. The judge adjourned the case, asking each member of the jury to consider overnight whether he or she felt able to try the case without prejudice. The following morning the judge received two letters from the jury. The first, signed by all the jurors including the one who had sent the complaint, refuted the allegation of racism. The second letter was written by a single juror who explained that he might have been the one responsible for making the racist jokes. He apologized for causing offence and declared that, in truth, he was not in the slightest racially biased. The judge decided not to dismiss the jury—despite a request from the defence—but instead directed them on the importance of their task and the trial continued, culminating in the applicant's conviction.

The Strasbourg Court, finding a violation of Article 6(1), held that, viewed object-ively, the collective letter from the jury could not have been sufficient to dispel the applicant's fears, because the jurors would have been unlikely openly to admit to racism. Nor could his fears have been allayed by the judge's direction, however tren-chant, because racist views could not be changed overnight. This judgment demon-strates, perhaps, the evolution of the Court's understanding of racism: in the earlier *Gregory* case,[124] with almost identical facts, the Court found that the judge's direction had been adequate to guarantee the jury's impartiality.

In other cases, the defect in the tribunal derives not from the personality, behaviour or prior involvement of one particular member, but from more formal concerns about the body's structure, powers, and composition. Relevant factors here are the manner of appointment and duration of office of the adjudicators[125] and the existence of guar-antees against outside interference,[126] as well as the appearance of independence.[127] The use of lay judges sitting with legally qualified judges is not, of itself, objectionable, particularly where the expertise which the lay judges bring to the proceedings can be helpful. But the system must offer sufficient guarantees of the independence of the lay judges. They must not be removable from office at will, and their other roles must not conflict with their judicial functions.[128]

---

[123] *Sander v United Kingdom*, (App. 34129/96), 9 May 2000, (2001) 31 EHRR 1003, ECHR 2000-V.

[124] *Gregory v United Kingdom*, (App. 22299/93), 25 February 1997, (1998) 25 EHRR 577.

[125] *Le Compte, van Leuven and de Meyere v Belgium*, (Apps. 6878/75, and 7238/75), 23 June 1981, Series A No 43, (1982) 4 EHRR 1, §55.

[126] *Piersack v Belgium*, (App. 8692/79), 1 October 1982, Series A No 53, (1983) 5 EHRR 169, §27.

[127] *Delcourt v Belgium*, (App. 2689/65), 17 January 1970, Series A No 11, (1979–80) 1 EHRR 355.

[128] *Luka v Romania*, (App34197/02), 21 July 2009.

In the *Findlay* case[129] the Strasbourg Court examined the independence and impartiality of an army court martial. Under the legislation then in force, a court martial in the United Kingdom was convened on an ad hoc basis by a senior officer in the defendant's regiment. The convening officer not only appointed all the officers who sat as judges in the court martial, he also appointed the prosecuting and defending officers, prepared the evidence against the accused, and had the power to quash or vary the court's decision. It is not, therefore, surprising that Strasbourg Court found that the court martial was not 'independent and impartial'.[130]

The *Incal* case[131] was also concerned with the effect of the participation of military personnel in the criminal justice system. The applicant, a civilian, was convicted of disseminating Kurdish separatist propaganda by a National Security Court. These courts, composed of two civilian judges and a legally trained army officer, were set up specifically to deal with offences against Turkey's territorial integrity and national security. The Strasbourg Court found a violation of Article 6(1) on the basis that, given the nature of the charges against him and the fact that he was a civilian, the applicant could legitimately fear that the reason for including a military judge on the tribunal was to lead it to be unduly influenced by considerations which had nothing to do with the evidence in the case. The presence of a military judge on the panel determining Abdullah Öcalan's culpability for numerous terrorist offences led the Grand Chamber to find a violation of Article 6(1), even though the military judge had been replaced, before the verdict was reached, by a civilian who had sat as a substitute.[132]

The requirements of independence and impartiality apply equally in civil cases. In a group of related cases,[133] the Strasbourg Court found that the presence of civil servants on adjudicating tribunals did not, of itself, taint the tribunal provided that there were appropriate guarantees of their independence, including a prohibition on public authorities from giving them instructions concerning the exercise of the judicial function.[134] Moreover, in certain circumstances even where the first instance tribunal is not sufficiently independent, the availability of judicial review by an Article 6-compliant court will remedy the earlier defect.[135]

---

[129] *Findlay v United Kingdom*, (App. 22107/93), 25 February 1997, (1997) 24 EHRR 221, ECHR 1997-I.

[130] The Grand Chamber found in 2003 that the new procedure, as amended by the Army Act 1998, complies with Article 6: see *Cooper v United Kingdom*, (App. 48843/99), 16 December 2003 [GC], (2004) 39 EHRR 171, ECHR 2003-XII; compare *Grieves v United Kingdom*, (App. 57067/00), 16 December 2003, (2004) 39 EHRR 51, ECHR 2003-XII.

[131] *Incal v Turkey*, (App. 22678/93), 9 June 1998; (2000) 29 EHRR 449, ECHR 1998-IV.

[132] *Öcalan v Turkey*, (App. 46221/99), 12 May 2005 [GC], (2005) 41 EHRR 985, ECHR 2005-IV.

[133] *Ettl and others v Austria*, (App. 9273/81), 23 April 1987, Series A No 117, (1988) 10 EHRR 255; *Erkner and Hofauer v Austria*, (App. 9616/81), 23 April 1987, Series A No 117, (1987) 9 EHRR 464; and *Poiss v Austria*, (App. 9816/82), 23 April 1987, Series A No 117, (1988) 10 EHRR 231; compare *Sramek v Germany*, (App. 8791/79), 22 October 1984, Series A No 84, (1985) 7 EHRR 351.

[134] *Tsfayo v United Kingdom*, (App. 60860/00), 14 November 2006, (2009) 48 EHRR 457, §§40–9.

[135] Compare, for example, *Edwards v United Kingdom*, (App. 13071/87), 16 December 1992, Series A No 247-B, (1993) 15 EHRR 417, and *Rowe and Davis v United Kingdom*, (App. 28901/95), 16 February 2000 [GC], (2000) 30 EHRR 1, ECHR 2000-II; or *Bryan v United Kingdom*, (App. 19178/91), 22 November 1995, Series A

PUBLIC HEARINGS

Publicity is seen as one guarantee of the fairness of trial; it offers protection against arbitrary decisions and builds confidence by allowing the public to see justice being administered.[136] To answer the question whether there has been a public hearing within the meaning of Article 6(1), it is necessary to consider the proceedings as a whole. For example, the absence of a public hearing on appeal or cassation raises an issue under Article 6(1) only if the superior court is 'determining' an issue, which is not the case in legal systems where the appeal or cassation court carries out a supervisory role, in the sense that decisions of earlier hearings can be overturned only on points of law, requiring a further hearing in the court below.[137] In the *Axen* case,[138] for example, there was a public first instance hearing of a personal injuries claim, but the appeal was heard *in camera*, pursuant to a scheme to reduce the workload of the courts. This did not violate Article 6(1), since the proceedings taken as a whole could be regarded as public. The role of the appeal court was limited to dismissal of the appeal on points of law, thus making the decision of the first instance court final.[139]

In England and Wales, applications for leave to appeal against conviction or sentence are normally heard in private, and the position is similar in other countries. It would seem that this is permissible if such applications can be regarded as a step in the appellate process, and if there is a right to an appeal, heard in public, against the refusal of the application. Similarly, in civil cases, interlocutory proceedings which are held in private may be permissible subject to corresponding conditions.[140]

Article 6(1) contains a list of limitations to the right to a public hearing on grounds of public policy, national security, privacy, or where strictly necessary in the interests of justice, but these are to be tightly construed. The applicant in the *Riepan* case[141] was tried for offences committed in prison in a special hearing room in the prison. The public was not excluded, but no steps were taken to let anyone know that the hearing would take place. The Strasbourg Court held that only in rare cases could security concerns justify excluding the public. It observed that a trial would comply with the requirement of publicity only if the public was able to obtain information about its date and place and if this place was easily accessible. In many cases these conditions would be fulfilled by holding the hearing in a normal courtroom large enough to accommodate spectators. The holding of a trial outside a regular courtroom, in particular in a place like a prison to which the general public usually has no access, presented a serious obstacle to its public character, and the State was under an obligation to take

---

No 335-A, (1996) 21 EHRR 342; with *Kingsley v United Kingdom*, (App. 35605/97), 7 November 2000, (2001) 33 EHRR 288, ECHR 2000-IV.

[136] *Pretto and others v Italy*, (App. 7984/77), 8 December 1983, Series A No 71, (1984) 6 EHRR 182.
[137] Ibid.
[138] *Axen v Germany*, (App. 8273/88), 8 December 1983, Series A No 72, (1984) 6 EHRR 195.
[139] See also *Sutter v Switzerland*, (App. 8209/78), 22 February 1984, Series A No 74, (1984) 6 EHRR 272.
[140] App. 3860/68, *X v United Kingdom*, Decision of 16 May 1969 (1970) 30 CD 70.
[141] *Riepan v Austria*, (App. 35115/97), 14 November 2000, ECHR 2000-XII, §34.

compensatory measures to ensure that the public and the media were informed and granted effective access.

By way of contrast, the hearings at issue in the *P and B* case[142] were to determine the residence of children. According to the Family Proceedings Rules applicable in England and Wales, the presumption is that such hearings should be held in chambers, although the judge has a discretion to hold a public hearing if one of the parties requests this and shows that there are strong grounds for doing so. The respondent State relied on the proviso in Article 6(1) that 'the press and public may be excluded from all or part of the trial … where the interests of juveniles or the private life of the parties so require, or to the extent strictly necessary in the opinion of the court in special circumstances where publicity would prejudice the interests of justice.' The Strasbourg Court agreed, commenting that proceedings concerning the residence of children were:

prime examples of cases where the exclusion of the press and public may be justified in order to protect the privacy of the child and parties and to avoid prejudicing the interests of justice. To enable the deciding judge to gain as full and accurate a picture as possible of the advantages and disadvantages of the various residence and contact options open to the child, it is essential that the parents and other witnesses feel able to express themselves candidly on highly personal issues without fear of public curiosity or comment.

PUBLIC JUDGMENTS

Article 6(1) also gives a right, in civil and criminal cases, to the public pronouncement of the judgment. There have been a number of cases concerning the precise meaning to be given to the words 'pronounced publicly'.[143] Fairly early on, the Strasbourg Court decided that it was not necessary for the judgment actually to be read out in open court and that States enjoyed a discretion as to the manner in which judgments would be made public. In the leading case of *Pretto*,[144] for example, the applicant complained that the judgment of the Court of Cassation on appeal had not been pronounced at a public hearing. The Strasbourg Court stressed the need to take account of the entirety of the proceedings. Furthermore, although the Court of Cassation's decision had not been pronounced in open court, anyone could consult or obtain a copy of it. There had therefore been no violation of Article 6(1). The form of publicity to be given to a judgment had to be assessed in the light of the special features of the proceedings in question and by reference to the object and purpose of Article 6(1).[145]

The requirement in Article 6(1) for public pronouncement of judgments, unlike that for a public hearing, is not expressed to be subject to any limitations. In the *P and B*

---

[142] *P and B v United Kingdom*, (Apps. 36337/97 and 35974/97), 24 April 2001, (2002) 34 EHRR 529, ECHR 2001-III.

[143] In the French text, 'doit être rendu publiquement.'

[144] *Pretto and others v Italy*, (App. 7984/77), 8 December 1983, Series A No 71, (1984) 6 EHRR 182.

[145] §26.

case,[146] however, the Strasbourg Court agreed with the respondent State that it would frustrate the purpose of holding child residence hearings in private—namely, to protect the privacy of the children and their families and to promote justice—if judgments were freely available to the public. It held that the requirements of Article 6(1) were satisfied in child residence cases because anyone who could establish an interest could, with the leave of the court, consult or obtain a copy of the full text of the orders and/or judgments of first instance courts, and that the judgments of the Court of Appeal and of first instance courts in cases of special interest were routinely published, thereby enabling the public to study the manner in which the courts generally approach such cases and the principles applied in deciding them.

JUDGMENT IN A REASONABLE TIME

Excessive length of legal proceedings is the single most common complaint received by the Strasbourg Court. The Grand Chamber has encapsulated the requirements of judgment within a reasonable time as follows:

> 43. …[The Court] reiterates that the 'reasonableness' of the length of proceedings must be assessed in the light of the circumstances of the case and with reference to the following criteria: the complexity of the case, the conduct of the applicant and of the relevant authorities and what was at stake for the applicant in the dispute.…
>
> …
>
> 45. The Court reiterates that it is for the Contracting States to organize their legal systems in such a way that their courts can guarantee to everyone the right to a final decision within a reasonable time in the determination of his civil rights and obligations.…[147]

The right under Article 6(1) to 'a fair and public hearing within a reasonable time' may be compared with the right under Article 5(3) to trial within a reasonable time. However, while the right guaranteed under Article 5(3) applies only to persons detained on remand on a criminal charge, the scope of Article 6(1) is wider, extending to civil and criminal cases alike, and in criminal cases it applies whether the accused is detained or at liberty. The latter factor is important in assessing the reasonableness of the period, since, as stated above, Article 5(3) requires that there must be 'special diligence' in bringing the case to trial if the accused is detained. The object of the provision in Article 6(1) is to protect the individual concerned from living too long under the stress of uncertainty and, more generally, to ensure that justice is administered without delays which might jeopardize its effectiveness and credibility.[148]

In civil cases there is usually no problem in deciding when the period to be taken into consideration started: this is usually the date on which proceedings were initiated,

---

[146] *P and B v United Kingdom*, (Apps. 36337/97 and 35974/97), 24 April 2001, (2002) 34 EHRR 529, ECHR 2001-III; see also above, in relation to 'public hearings'.

[147] *Frydlender v France*, (App. 30979/96), 27 June 2000 [GC], (2001) 31 EHRR 1152, ECHR 2000-VII, §§43 and 45.

[148] *Bottazzi v Italy*, (App. 34884/97), 28 July 1999, ECHR 1999-V.

for example by the issuing of a summons or writ.[149] In criminal cases, time begins to run as soon as the accused is officially notified of an allegation that he has committed a criminal offence; this may occur on a date prior to the case coming before the trial court, such as the date of arrest, the date when the person concerned was officially notified that he would be prosecuted, or the date when preliminary investigations were opened.[150] The period to be taken into consideration lasts until the final determination of the case, and therefore includes appeal or cassation proceedings, proceedings to assess damages or sentence, and enforcement proceedings.[151] The State can be held responsible only for delays which are attributable to it; if the parties to the litigation or the defendant in a criminal case have caused or contributed to the delay, those periods of time are not taken into account.

As noted above, the reasonableness of the length of proceedings is assessed in the light of all the circumstances of the case, having regard in particular to the complexity of the issues before the national courts, the conduct of the parties to the dispute and of the relevant authorities, and what was at stake for the applicant.[152] For example, in a case where the applicant sought compensation from the State for having negligently infected him with HIV, 'special diligence' was required in view of the fact that the applicant was dying of AIDS.[153] Similarly, delays are less likely to be tolerable where the dispute concerns access between a parent and child, given the irreversible damage which can be done to such a relationship through lack of contact.[154]

The Court is called upon to determine more complaints about the unreasonable length of proceedings than any other type of case under the Convention. In the *Bottazzi* case[155] in 1999 it observed that the frequency with which violations of this provision were found against Italy reflected a continuing situation that had not been remedied, constituting a practice of systematic human rights breaches incompatible with the Convention.[156]

Applications complaining about the excessive length of proceedings in the national legal order are among the most numerous before the Strasbourg Court.[157] The result is that the Strasbourg Court's docket gets clogged up with repetitive cases which require formal adjudication. One response to such cases has been the use of variants of the pilot judgment procedure.[158] In the *Lukenda* case[159] the length of proceedings in Slovenia was identified as a systemic problem. The Strasbourg Court urged Slovenia to

---

[149] *Šakanovič v Slovenia*, (App. 32989/02), 13 March 2008, §§35–6.

[150] *Eckle v Germany*, (App. 8130/78), 15 July 1982, Series A No 51, (1983) 5 EHRR 1.

[151] *Crowther v United Kingdom*, (App. 43741/00), 9 February 2005, §24.

[152] *Frydlender v France*, (App. 30979/96), 27 June 2000, (2001) 31 EHRR 1152, ECHR 2000-VII, §43; and *Davies v United Kingdom*, (App. 42007/98), 16 July 2002, (2002) 35 EHRR 720, §26.

[153] *A and others v Denmark*, (App. 20826/92), 8 February 1996, (1996) 22 EHRR 458.

[154] *H v United Kingdom*, (App. 9580/81), 8 July 1987, Series A No 120, (1988) 10 EHRR 95.

[155] *Bottazzi v Italy*, (App. 34884/97), 28 July 1999, ECHR 1999-V.

[156] See also developments under Art. 13 noted in ch.7 above.

[157] Venice Commission, *Can excessive length of proceedings be remedied?* (Council of Europe Publishing, Strasbourg 2007).

[158] Described in ch.2 above.

[159] *Lukenda v Slovenia*, (App. 23032/02), 6 October 2005, (2008) 47 EHRR 728, ECHR 2005-X.

address the problem 'that has resulted from inadequate legislation and inefficiency in the administration of justice.'[160] The Court added:

To prevent future violations of the right to a trial within a reasonable time, the Court encourages the respondent State to either amend the existing range of legal remedies or add new remedies so as to secure genuinely effective redress for violations of that right.[161]

This is a variant of the pilot judgment procedure since other pending cases before the Strasbourg Court were *not* adjourned while remedies were found within the national legal order for the look-alike cases. Indeed the Strasbourg Court subsequently produced around 200 further judgments against Slovenia in the look-alike cases where application had been made to the Strasbourg Court.[162] Following the judgment in the *Lukenda* case, the Slovenian Government established the Lukenda Project to address the problem, and passed legislation in 2006 to this end. In a later case, the Strasbourg Court expressed itself satisfied that the 2006 legislation did address the problem and required future applicants complaining of failure to deliver judgment in a reasonable time to use the remedies provided under the new legislation. Failure to do so would result in dismissal of their applications for failure to exhaust domestic remedies.[163]

In the *Scordino* case[164] the Strasbourg Court laid down certain conditions which it would expect national courts to establish in order to address problems about the speed of judicial proceedings.[165] The best solution is prevention, but where concerns arose, there should be a remedy designed to expedite proceedings which are lingering. This is more satisfactory than a system of compensation for proceedings which go on too long. States with systemic problems[166] are praised for introducing procedures both for seeking the expediting of proceedings and for awarding compensation where delays are excessive. But it may not be necessary to introduce both types of procedure.[167]

EXTRATERRITORIAL EFFECT

In the *Soering* judgment the Court observed that:

The right to a fair trial in criminal proceedings, as embodied in Article 6 holds a prominent place in a democratic society. The Court does not exclude that an issue

---

[160] *Lukenda*, §93.   [161] §98.

[162] E. Friberg, 'Pilot Judgments from the Court's Perspective' in Council of Europe, *Towards Stronger Implementation of the European Convention on Human Rights at National Level* (Council of Europe, Strasbourg 2008), 86, 91. See also *Scordino v Italy (No. 1)*, (App. 36813/97), 26 March 2006 [GC], (2007) 45 EHRR 207; ECHR 2006-V.

[163] *Korenjak v Slovenia*, (App. 463/03), Decision of 15 May 2007.

[164] *Scordino v Italy (No. 1)*, (App. 36813/97), 29 March 2006 [GC], (2007) 45 EHRR 207, ECHR 2006-V.

[165] §§182–9.

[166] Austria, Croatia, Spain, Poland, and the Slovak Republic are named: §186.

[167] For a study of the effectiveness of national remedies in respect of excessive length of proceedings, see Venice Commission, *Can Excessive Length of Proceedings be Remedied?* (Council of Europe Publishing, Strasbourg 2007).

might exceptionally be raised under Article 6 by an extradition decision in circumstances where the fugitive has suffered or risks suffering a flagrant denial of a fair
trial....[168]

It appears, therefore, that the extraterritorial application of Article 6 is limited to the
criminal sphere.

The applicants in the *Mamatkulov and Askarov* case[169] were charged with terrorist
offences in Uzbekistan and fled to Turkey, where they were arrested and extradited.[170]
After their return to Uzbekistan they were tried and convicted in private, without
being given any access to their lawyers, and sentenced to long terms of imprisonment. They argued before the Strasbourg Court that, in extraditing them, Turkey
had violated Article 6. The Grand Chamber held that, in principle, the extraditing
State's responsibility could be engaged under Article 6 in these circumstances, but
then bizarrely went on to find that since the risk of a flagrant denial of justice in the
receiving State had to be assessed at the date of extradition, and since there was at
that point—but only because Turkey rushed through the extradition contrary to the
Court's request to wait until it had decided the case—very little available evidence
about what awaited the applicants in Uzbekistan, there had been no violation. The
view of the four dissenting members of the Grand Chamber is much to be preferred.
They clarified that:

What constitutes a 'flagrant' denial of justice has not been fully explained in the Court's
jurisprudence but the use of the adjective is clearly intended to impose a stringent test
of unfairness going beyond mere irregularities or lack of safeguards in the trial procedures such as might result in a breach of Article 6 if occurring within the Contracting
State itself.... In our view, what the word 'flagrant' is intended to convey is a breach of
the principles of fair trial guaranteed by Article 6 which is so fundamental as to amount
to a nullification, or destruction of the very essence, of the right guaranteed by that
Article.

The minority went on to find that documents available from Amnesty International
before the extradition took place demonstrated substantial grounds for concluding
that self-incriminating evidence extracted by torture was routinely used to secure
guilty verdicts in Uzbekistan and that suspects were frequently detained and inter-
rogated for many days without being given access to a lawyer. Given that the Turkish
Government had not sought or received any assurances from Uzbekistan that the
applicants would be given a fair trial, the Court should have found Turkey to have been
in breach of Article 6.

---

[168] *Soering v United Kingdom*, (App. 14038/88), 7 July 1989, Series A No 161, (1989) 11 HRR 439,
§113.
[169] *Mamatkulov and Askarov v Turkey*, (Apps. 46827/99 and 46951/99), 4 February 2005 [GC], (2005) 41
EHRR 494, ECHR 2005-I.
[170] Contrary to the Court's request to Turkey under Rule 39 of the Rules of Court: see further ch.2
above.

WAIVING RIGHTS

It is possible to waive some, but probably not all, of the rights under Article 6. One example is the right of a criminal defendant to be present at trial.[171] In a case involving a criminal trial, the Strasbourg Court said:

Neither the letter nor the spirit of Article 6 of the Convention prevents a person from waiving of his own free will, either expressly or tacitly, the entitlement to the guarantees of a fair trial.... However, if it is to be effective for Convention purposes, a waiver of the right to take part in the trial must be established in an unequivocal manner and be attended by minimum safeguards commensurate to its importance.... Furthermore, it must not run counter to any important public interest....[172]

An accused who absconds before trial cannot, for example, be said to have impliedly, through his conduct, waived the right to trial in his presence unless this was a clearly foreseeable consequence of his actions. Thus, in the *Jones* case,[173] where the possibility of trying a defendant *in absentia* had not been clearly established under English law at the time of the trial, the applicant, as a layman, could not have been expected to appreciate that his failure to attend on the date set for the start of the trial would result in his being tried and convicted in his absence and in the absence of legal representation.

CONCLUDING REMARKS

The Strasbourg Court's case-law on the right to a fair trial is extensive and has had a significant impact. For the individual concerned, a finding of a violation by the Court can lead to criminal proceedings being reopened or, in civil cases, the award of damages.[174] Perhaps more importantly, States all over Europe have amended and improved their legal procedures to comply with the Court's rulings. The perennial problem of excessive length of proceedings is beginning to be addressed in a systematic fashion in a number of Contracting Parties.

There are, however, limitations to the scope of the Court's review under Article 6. First, like the rest of the Convention, this provision protects only against violations imputable to the State; if unfairness is caused in legal proceedings by the negligence or misconduct of a lawyer (a private person), rather than, for example, the courts, no

---

[171] For a similar waiver in a civil case, see *Zumtobel v Austria*, (App. 12235/86), 21 September 1993, Series A No 268-A, (1994) 17 EHRR 116.

[172] *Sejdovic v Italy*, (App. 56581/00), 1 March 2006 [GC], ECHR 2006-II, §86. See also *Jones v United Kingdom*, (App. 30900/02), Decision of 9 September 2003.

[173] *Jones v United Kingdom*, (App. 30900/02), Decision of 9 September 2003. See also *Sejdovic v Italy*, (App. 56581/00), 1 March 2006 [GC], ECHR 2006-II.

[174] See ch.2 above.

issue can arise.[175] Secondly, in accordance with the principle of subsidiarity and the 'fourth instance' doctrine, the Strasbourg Court has no power under Article 6 to substitute its own assessment of the evidence in a case for that of the national courts, and in connection with certain procedural matters, such as the need to call a particular witness, it will take issue with national courts only in exceptional circumstances.[176] Article 6 cannot be used as a vehicle to criticize the *content* of national law. And the Court's interpretation of the expressions 'criminal charge' and 'civil rights and obligations', though extensive, does not embrace all types of legal proceedings.

Some of these lacunae are filled by other provisions in the Convention and Protocols. Article 1 of Protocol 7, for example, provides certain procedural rights to an alien lawfully resident in the territory of a State and facing expulsion. In addition, the Strasbourg Court has read procedural guarantees into some of the substantive rights under the Convention—the right to family life under Article 8, for example, requires that a fair procedure be followed when a child is taken into public care and, in accordance with Article 13, an effective domestic remedy must be provided in respect of all arguable breaches of the Convention.[177]

The following chapter is concerned with certain additional rights which arise in the context of criminal law and procedure.

---

[175] *Tripodi v Italy*, (App. 13743/88), 22 February 1994, Series A No 281-B, (1994) 18 EHRR 295.

[176] *Thomas v United Kingdom*, (App. 19354/02), Decision of 10 May 2005.

[177] See *Z and others v United Kingdom*, (App. 29392/95), 10 May 2001 [GC], (2002) 34 EHRR 97, ECHR 2001-V, and, in respect of the procedural guarantees available to asylum seekers, *Chahal v United Kingdom*, (App. 22414/93), 15 November 1996, (1997) 23 EHRR 413, ECHR 1996-V. See also ch.7 above.

13

ASPECTS OF THE CRIMINAL PROCESS

INTRODUCTION

This chapter examines the fair trial guarantees specific to criminal proceedings.[1] These are principally contained in paragraphs (2) and (3) of Article 6, although certain aspects of the right to a fair trial in Article 6(1) which apply only in criminal proceedings are also considered here. The second part of the chapter is concerned with the rule against retrospective legislation in Article 7 of the Convention, and a number of additional rights connected with the criminal process introduced by Articles 2 to 4 of Protocol 7.

THE SCOPE OF ARTICLE 6(2) AND (3)

Article 6, paragraphs (2) and (3) provide:

2. Everyone charged with a criminal offence shall be presumed innocent until proved guilty according to law.

3. Everyone charged with a criminal offence has the following minimum rights:

    (a) to be informed promptly, in a language which he understands and in detail, of the nature and cause of the accusation against him;

    (b) to have adequate time and facilities for the preparation of his defence;

    (c) to defend himself in person or through legal assistance of his own choosing or, if he has not sufficient means to pay for legal assistance, to be given it free when the interests of justice so require;

    (d) to examine or have examined witnesses against him and to obtain the attendance and examination of witnesses on his behalf under the same conditions as witnesses against him;

    (e) to have the free assistance of an interpreter if he cannot understand or speak the language used in court.

---

[1] See S. Trechsel, *Human Rights in Criminal Proceedings* (OUP, Oxford 2005).

Articles 6(2) and (3) apply to 'everyone charged with a criminal offence'. As with the expression 'in the determination ... of any criminal charge against him' in Article 6(1),[2] the Court has adopted an autonomous interpretation, independent of the categorization of legal proceedings under national law.

In order to decide whether a person can be said to be 'charged with a criminal offence' within the meaning of Article 6, paragraphs (2) and (3), the Strasbourg Court has regard to the same *Engel* criteria[3] that it applies when assessing whether proceedings are 'in the determination of any criminal charge' in paragraph (1). Indeed, there does not appear to be any significant difference between the scope of the two expressions except as regards the duration of the proceedings covered. In the *Phillips* case[4] the Court explained:

[W]hilst it is clear that Article 6(2) governs criminal proceedings in their entirety, and not solely the examination of the merits of the charge ... the right to be presumed innocent under Article 6(2) arises only in connection with the particular offence 'charged'. Once an accused has properly been proved guilty of that offence, Article 6(2) can have no application in relation to allegations made about the accused's character and conduct as part of the sentencing process, unless such accusations are of such a nature and degree as to amount to the bringing of a new 'charge' within the autonomous Convention meaning.

It can be presumed that the same is true of the application of Article 6(3). In contrast, Article 6(1) applies throughout criminal proceedings in their entirety, including sentencing.[5]

FAIR TRIAL GUARANTEES IN CRIMINAL CASES

In addition to the safeguards discussed in the preceding chapter, which are necessary to a greater or lesser degree in both civil and criminal proceedings, the Strasbourg Court has held that a person charged with a criminal offence enjoys, *inter alia*, certain additional rights, some of which are considered below. The five rights set out in Article 6(3) are stated to be minimum rights in criminal cases.

POLICE METHODS OF INVESTIGATION

Even before charges are brought against an accused, unfairness on the part of the police responsible for the investigation against him or her may be sufficient to give rise to a violation of Article 6(1). In the *Teixeira de Castro* case,[6] for example, the applicant

---

[2] See ch.12 above.
[3] *Engel and others v Netherlands*, (Apps. 5100/71, 5101/71, 5102/71, 5354/72, and 5370/72), 8 June 1976, Series A No 22, (1979–80) 1 EHRR 647; and see ch.12 above.
[4] *Phillips v United Kingdom*, (App. 41087/98), 5 September 2001, ECHR 2001-VII.
[5] See ch.12 above.
[6] *Teixeira de Castro v Portugal*, (App. 25829/94), 9 June 1998, (1999) 28 EHRR 101, ECHR 1998-IV.

was offered money by undercover police officers to supply them with heroin. Although he had no previous criminal record, the applicant did have contacts who were able to get hold of drugs, and, tempted by the money, he complied with the officers' request. He was subsequently charged and convicted of a drugs offence. There was no evidence that the trial proceedings in themselves were unfair, but the Strasbourg Court held that, since the police officers appeared to have instigated the offence, which would not otherwise have been committed, from the outset the applicant was deprived of a fair trial in breach of Article 6(1). The Court contrasted the officers' actions with those of 'true' undercover agents, who conceal their identities in order to obtain information and evidence about crime, without actively inciting it; the second type of situation would not normally in itself give rise to any issue under Article 6.[7]

It is only in rare and extreme cases that the Strasbourg Court considers unlawful behaviour by the police or investigators sufficient in itself to bring the trial into breach of Article 6. If the domestic courts choose to accept the prosecution evidence, the Strasbourg Court will usually accept that decision,[8] unless the abuse of process has been fundamental (as in *Teixeira de Castro* and the other cases on entrapment) or has in some way rendered the evidence against the accused unreliable (as in the cases about the breach of the right to silence, considered below).

So, for example, in the *Khan* case,[9] the police had installed a hidden listening device in a hotel and obtained a recording of the applicant discussing a drugs deal. At the time of the investigation and trial there was no legislation in the United Kingdom governing the use of such apparatus by the police; in consequence, the Court found that Article 8 of the Convention had been violated.[10] It declined, however, the applicant's invitation to find that Article 6(1) had also been breached by virtue of the unlawful methods employed during the investigation. Instead, the Court examined the fairness of the proceedings as a whole and found no violation of Article 6(1), referring to the fact that the applicant had been afforded the opportunity to contest the authenticity of the recording and its admission in evidence. It had reached a similar conclusion in the *Schenk* case[11] where the obtaining of a tape recording by the police was unlawful not only according to the Convention, but also under domestic law.

The applicant in the *Allan* case[12] was suspected of shooting the manager of a convenience store during a robbery. During his interviews with the police he elected to remain silent. The police, frustrated with the lack of evidence, began secretly recording

---

[7] See *Lüdi v Switzerland*, (App. 12433/86), 15 June 1992, Series A No 238, (1993) 15 EHRR 440; *Eurofinacom v France*, (App. 58753/00), Decision of 17 September 2004, ECHR 2004-VII; and *Gorgievski v FYR of Macedonia*, (App. 18002/02), 16 July 2009.

[8] In accordance with the 'fourth instance' doctrine: see *Allan v United Kingdom*, (App. 48539/99), 5 November 2002, (2003) 36 EHRR 143, ECHR 2002-IX, §42.

[9] *Khan v United Kingdom*, (App. 35294/97), 12 May 2000, (2001) 31 EHRR 1016; see also *Chalkley v United Kingdom*, (App. 63881/00), 12 June 2003, (2003) 37 EHRR 680; and *Perry v United Kingdom*, (App. 63737/00), 17 July 2003, (2004) 39 EHRR 76, ECHR 2003-IX.

[10] The procedure was not 'in accordance with law': see ch.14 below.

[11] *Schenk v Switzerland*, (App. 10862/84), 12 July 1988, Series A No 140, (1991) 13 EHRR 242.

[12] *Allan v United Kingdom*, (App. 48539/99), 5 November 2002, (2003) 36 EHRR 143, ECHR 2003-IX.

the applicant's conversations in prison with his girlfriend and co-accused. When it appeared that the recordings, although containing some incriminating statements, would not be enough to convict the applicant, they put him in a cell with a long-standing informant, whom they had carefully coached in the art of extracting information. After four months of shared custody, the informant was able to produce a 60-page statement regarding his conversations with the applicant, which was used at the latter's trial for murder.

The Strasbourg Court, following its *Khan* judgment, found that since the domestic courts had considered the recordings of the applicant's conversations with his girlfriend and co-accused to be reliable, their use at trial was not in breach of Article 6. Interestingly, however, the Court found that, in contrast to the position in *Khan*, the admissions allegedly made by the applicant to his informant cell-mate, and which formed the main or decisive evidence against him at trial, were not spontaneous and unprompted statements volunteered by the applicant, but were induced by persistent questioning. The informant, at the insistence of the police, had channelled their conversations into discussions of the murder in circumstances which could be regarded as the functional equivalent of interrogation, without any of the safeguards which would attach to a formal police interview, including the attendance of a solicitor and the issuing of the usual caution, and in circumstances where the applicant was feeling vulnerable and open to pressure. The Court concluded that the information gained by the informant had been obtained in defiance of the applicant's will and its use at trial impinged on his right to silence:

While the right to silence and the privilege against self-incrimination are primarily designed to protect against improper compulsion by the authorities and the obtaining of evidence through methods of coercion or oppression in defiance of the will of the accused, the scope of the right is not confined to cases where duress has been brought to bear on the accused or where the will of the accused has been directly overborne in some way. The right, which the Court has previously observed is at the heart of the notion of a fair procedure, serves in principle to protect the freedom of a suspected person to choose whether to speak or to remain silent when questioned by the police. Such freedom of choice is effectively undermined in a case in which, the suspect having elected to remain silent during questioning, the authorities use subterfuge to elicit, from the suspect, confessions or other statements of an incriminatory nature, which they were unable to obtain during such questioning and where the confessions or statements thereby obtained are adduced in evidence at trial.[13]

The following section is concerned with further aspects of the right to silence.

THE RIGHT TO SILENCE, THE PRINCIPLE AGAINST SELF-INCRIMINATION, AND THE PRESUMPTION OF INNOCENCE

Although it is not specifically mentioned in Article 6 of the Convention, the Strasbourg Court has held[14] that the right to silence and the right not to incriminate oneself are

---

[13] §51.
[14] *Saunders v United Kingdom*, (App. 19187/91), 17 December 1996, (1997) 23 EHRR 313, ECHR 1996-VI.

generally recognized international standards which lie at the heart of the notion of a fair criminal procedure under Article 6(1). These rights are closely linked to the principle enshrined in Article 6(2), that a person accused of a crime is innocent until proved guilty according to law.

As Lord Mustill has observed,[15] the 'right to silence' is a composite term which in fact encompasses a number of separate rights. He identified the following as protected, to a greater or lesser degree, by English law:

(1) A general immunity, possessed by all persons and bodies, from being compelled on pain of punishment to answer questions posed by other persons or bodies.

(2) A general immunity, possessed by all persons and bodies, from being compelled on pain of punishment to answer questions the answers to which may incriminate them.

(3) A specific immunity, possessed by all persons under suspicion of criminal responsibility whilst being interviewed by police officers or others in similar positions of authority, from being compelled on pain of punishment to answer questions of any kind.

(4) A specific immunity, possessed by accused persons undergoing trial, from being compelled to give evidence, and from being compelled to answer questions put to them in the dock.

(5) A specific immunity, possessed by persons who have been charged with a criminal offence, from having questions material to the offence addressed to them by police officers or persons in a similar position of authority.

(6) A specific immunity...possessed by accused persons undergoing trial, from having adverse comment made on any failure (a) to answer questions before the trial, or (b) to give evidence at the trial.

The right not to incriminate oneself can include protection against the requirement to produce documents, as well as the right not to make statements or admissions.[16]

In the *Saunders* case[17] the applicant had been forced, through the threat of imprisonment for failure to answer questions, to give evidence to government-appointed investigators about an allegedly illegal share-support scheme. Transcripts of his interviews with the inspectors were subsequently used by the prosecution in criminal proceedings against him. The Strasbourg Court, which had found in an earlier judgment[18] that Article 6 did not apply to investigations of this kind, did not find any breach of the Convention arising from the inspectors' compulsory powers *per se*. However, it

---

[15] *R. v Director of Serious Fraud Office, ex parte Smith*, [1992] 3 WLR 66.

[16] *JB v Switzerland*, (App. 31827/96), 3 May 2001, ECHR 2001-III. See also *Funke and others v France*, (App. 10828/84), 25 February 1993, Series A No 256-A, (1993) 16 EHRR 297.

[17] *Saunders v United Kingdom*, (App. 19187/91), 17 December 1996; (1997) 23 EHRR 313, ECHR 1996-VI.

[18] *Fayed v United Kingdom*, (App. 17101/90), 21 September 1994, Series A No 294-B, (1994) 18 EHRR 393.

held that the subsequent use by the prosecution at the applicant's criminal trial of transcripts of the interviews violated his right to silence.

In its *Saunders* judgment the Court observed that the rationale of the right to silence and the principle against self-incrimination lies in the protection of the accused against improper compulsion by the authorities, thereby contributing to the avoidance of miscarriages of justice. The right not to incriminate oneself, in particular, presupposes that the prosecution in a criminal case should seek to prove its case against the accused without resort to evidence obtained through methods of coercion or oppression in defiance of the will of the accused. On the basis of this explanation, the Court drew a distinction between the right of an accused person to remain silent, which is protected by the Convention, and the use in criminal proceedings of material which might be obtained from the accused through the use of compulsory powers but which has an existence independent of the will of the suspect, such as documents acquired pursuant to a warrant, breath, blood and urine samples, and bodily tissue for the purpose of DNA testing, which is not inconsistent with Article 6.[19]

This distinction between documents, which can be said to have an 'independent existence' and statements or admissions was revisited by the Grand Chamber in the *Jalloh* case.[20] On his arrest on suspicion of dealing in drugs, Jalloh was seen to swallow a plastic bag. On authorization of the public prosecutor, an emetic was forcibly administered which resulted in Jalloh's regurgitating one bag which was found to contain cocaine. He complained that the use at his trial of this evidence violated his rights under Article 6 not to incriminate himself. The Grand Chamber noted that it could be said that the bag of cocaine was evidence which had an existence independent of the will of the accused, but found a number of features of the case which distinguished it from that line of authority. The compulsory administration of emetics was used to retrieve the material against the will of the accused, and the degree of force required was considerable, and was found to violate Article 3.[21] Summarizing its position the Strasbourg Court said:

In order to determine whether the applicant's right not to incriminate himself has been violated, the Court will have regard, in turn, to the following factors: the nature and degree of compulsion used to obtain the evidence; the weight of the public interest in the investigation and punishment of the offence at issue; the existence of any relevant safeguards in the procedure; and the use to which any material so obtained is put.[22]

By eleven votes to six, the Grand Chamber found that Article 6 had been violated.

---

[19] This distinction was adopted and applied by the Privy Council in *Brown v Stott*, [2001] 2 WLR 817 where it held that a statutory requirement to provide a breath specimen when suspected of driving with excess alcohol, with a maximum penalty of a £1,000 fine or six months' imprisonment for non-compliance, was not incompatible with Article 6(2). See also App. 8239/78, *X v Netherlands*, (1979) 16 DR 184, where the Commission came to a similar conclusion.

[20] *Jalloh v Germany*, (App. 54810/00), 11 July 2006 [GC], (2007) 44 EHRR 667, ECHR 2006-IX.

[21] The prohibition of torture, and inhuman or degrading treatment. See ch.9 below.

[22] *Jalloh v Germany*, (App. 54810/00), 11 July 2006 [GC], (2007) 44 EHRR 667, ECHR 2006-IX, §117.

There is also considerable case-law under paragraphs (1) and (2) of Article 6 on the extent to which a criminal court may draw an inference of guilt from an accused's silence. This is the aspect of the right to silence referred to at point (6) in Lord Mustill's list above, and the question is also relevant to the presumption of innocence, which requires that the burden of proving an offence lies on the prosecution.

The applicant in the *Telfner* case[23] was convicted of an offence involving a hit-and-run driving incident. The victim of the incident had been able to give the police the make and registration number of the car, but could not identify the driver. The applicant elected not to give evidence at trial, and the prosecution case relied almost entirely on the findings of the police that the applicant was the principal user of the car (registered in his mother's name) and had not been at home at the time of the accident. The Strasbourg Court held that, although it might be permissible for a court to draw an inference of guilt from an accused's silence, where the evidence adduced was so strong that the only common-sense inference to be drawn was that the accused had no answer to the case against him, in the instant case the evidence for the prosecution was extremely weak. In requiring the applicant to provide an explanation, without having first established a convincing prima facie case against him, the courts in effect shifted the burden of proof from the prosecution to the defence, giving rise to a violation of Article 6(2).

The *O'Halloran and Francis* case[24] concerned requirements under English legislation that the registered keeper must provide evidence of who was the driver of a vehicle caught by a roadside speed camera. Failure to comply is an offence. The question before the Strasbourg Court was whether the compulsion to make statements which might incriminate a person or lead to their incrimination is compatible with Article 6 of the Convention. The Court, relying on the test it had laid down in the *Jalloh* case,[25] concluded that there was no violation of this provision. Owners of motor vehicles know they are subject to a regulatory regime, and only limited information was required under the legislation in issue.

In the *John Murray* case[26] the Court found that it was compatible with Article 6(1) for the trial judge (who sat alone, without a jury) to draw an inference of guilt from the fact that the applicant had remained silent under police questioning and at trial. The evidence against him was strong and, in accordance with Article 3 of the Criminal Evidence (Northern Ireland) Order 1988, he had been warned at the time of his arrest that he did not have to say anything, but that his failure to mention any fact which he subsequently relied on in his defence might be treated in court as supporting the case against him.

---

[23] *Telfner v Austria*, (App. 33501/96), 20 March 2001, (2002) 34 EHRR 207.

[24] *O'Halloran and Francis v United Kingdom*, (Apps. 15809/02 and 25624/02), 29 June 2007 [GC], (2008) 46 EHRR 397, ECHR 2008-nyr.

[25] *Jalloh v Germany*, (App. 54810/00), 11 July 2006 [GC], (2007) 44 EHRR 667, ECHR 2006-IX, see above in this chapter.

[26] *Murray (John) v United Kingdom*, (App. 18731/91), 8 February 1996, (1996) 22 EHRR 29, ECHR 1996-I.

It is clear, therefore, that the Court does not consider that the drawing of inferences from an accused's silence is in itself incompatible with Article 6, as long as judicial safeguards operate to ensure fairness. In the *Condron* case[27] it found a violation of Article 6(1), because the trial judge failed to direct the jury that they could draw an adverse inference only if satisfied that the applicants' silence at the police interview could only sensibly be attributed to their having no answer to the accusations against them, or none that would stand up to cross-examination. The applicants were heroin addicts and suffering from withdrawal at the time of their interviews with the police on suspicion of drug dealing. Although they were cautioned by the investigating officers that it might harm their defence if they failed to mention something which they might later rely on in court, and were found by a police doctor to be fit for questioning, they made no comment on the advice of their solicitor, who disagreed with the doctor's assessment.

This case illustrates the Court's tendency to assess the fairness of proceedings looked at as a whole, rather than to formulate rigid procedural rules. If the trial judge had exercised his discretion properly, no unfairness would have been caused to the accused. It was, however, impossible for the Court of Appeal to rectify the problem (without ordering a retrial) because of the difficulty of assessing the extent to which the jury had been influenced by the misdirection.

In the *Salabiaku* case,[28] the Court was asked to consider the compatibility with Article 6(2) of a law reversing the burden of proof in respect of certain elements of an offence. The applicant had been found in possession of illegal drugs at a Paris airport. He was not, however, charged with and convicted of an offence of simple possession, but instead with offences of smuggling and importation, which include an element of knowledge or intent. The French Customs Code setting out the offences stated generally that 'the person in possession of contraband goods shall be deemed liable for the offence.' The Court rejected the Commission's opinion that Article 6(2) merely provided a procedural guarantee to be observed by the courts, and held that the provision also placed a duty on legislators to respect the rights of the accused when framing offences. It observed, generally, that:

Presumptions of fact or of law operate in every legal system. Clearly, the Convention does not prohibit such presumptions in principle. It does, however, require the Contracting States to remain within certain limits in this respect as regards criminal law.

The Court underlined that it was not its task to consider legislation *in abstracto*, and instead examined the facts of the particular case. It found that the presumption created by the Code and applied to the applicant was not irrebuttable, since the courts which had dealt with the applicant had followed case-law to the effect that once the

---

[27] *Condron v United Kingdom*, (App. 35382/97), 2 May 2000, (2001) 31 EHRR 1, ECHR 2000-IV.

[28] *Salabiaku v France*, (App. 10519/83), 7 October 1988, Series A No 141-A, (1991) 13 EHRR 379. See also *Hoang v France*, (App. 13191/87), 25 September 1992, Series A No 243, (1993) 16 EHRR 53; *Radio France and others v France*, (App. 53984/00), 30 March 2004, (2005) 40 EHRR 706, ECHR 2004-X; and *Phillips v United Kingdom*, (App. 41087/98), 5 September 2001, ECHR 2001-VII.

fact of possession had been established by the prosecution, the burden shifted to the defence to prove, if they could, that the accused was the victim of '*force majeure*' or for some reason could not have been expected to know about the goods in his possession, in which case he would have been acquitted. The courts had examined all the evidence, including evidence that the applicant had shown no surprise when the drugs were discovered in his suitcase, and had found him guilty without relying on the statutory presumption. In these circumstances, there had been no violation of Article 6(2).

It is interesting to speculate as to what type of reversed burden of proof the Court would find inconsistent with Article 6. The *Telfner, John Murray* and *Condron* cases underline that Article 6(1) and (2) require the prosecution at least to establish prima facie that the accused has committed an offence, and that it is permissible for a court to draw an inference of guilt from the accused's failure to provide an explanation only where this is the sole common-sense conclusion to be drawn. The legislation under examination in the *Salabiaku* case placed the onus on the prosecution to establish possession of prohibited goods, and then required the court to infer that the accused had knowledge of them, in the absence of proof to the contrary. Again, particularly having regard to the way in which this law was actually applied in the applicant's case, it might be said that the reversal of the burden of proof only went so far as to permit the court to draw a 'common-sense' inference.

In the *Phillips* case which concerned confiscation of assets from a convicted drug trafficker, the statutory presumption came into operation once the prosecution had established (1) that the accused had derived some benefit from drug-trafficking (which must in many cases follow almost automatically from his or her conviction for the offence which triggers the confiscation procedure); and (2) that the accused had owned property or incurred expenditure at any time since his conviction or during the period of six years before the date on which the criminal proceedings were commenced. The burden then passed to the accused to prove that the property or expenditure did not represent the proceeds of drug-trafficking.

Owning property and spending money are activities undertaken by almost everyone in western society and, unlike possessing illegal drugs, are not prima facie unlawful. In finding no violation of Article 6(1), the Court appears to have been influenced by the fact that had the applicant's account of his financial dealings been true, it would not have been difficult for him to rebut the statutory assumption; most people who, for example, buy a house, are able to show where the money came from without great difficulty. The Court indicated that 'an issue relating to the fairness of the procedure might arise in circumstances where the amount of a confiscation order was based on the value of assumed hidden assets', presumably because of the difficulty which would be involved in disproving the existence and source of unspecified and unsubstantiated articles. The Court's acceptance of the reversed burden of proof in this case might also be explained by the fact that it operated in the context of a procedure analogous to sentencing, to enable the national court to assess the amount at which a confiscation order should properly be fixed. It is possible that if a similarly sweeping presumption were applied to facilitate a court in finding a person guilty of an offence, this might give rise to a violation of Article 6(1) and (2).

USE OF EVIDENCE OBTAINED BY TORTURE

Article 15 of the United Nation's Convention against Torture provides:[29]

Every State Party shall ensure that any statement which is established to have been made as a result of torture shall not be invoked as evidence in any proceedings, except against a person accused of torture as evidence that the statement was made.

There is no corresponding provision in the European Convention, but it would be surprising if the Strasbourg Court did not read such an obligation into Article 6. The issue was touched on in the *Jalloh* case,[30] although that case concerned not statements, but physical evidence: cocaine regurgitated following the forcible administration of an emetic. In the course of its judgment, the Strasbourg Court said:

...different considerations apply to evidence recovered by a measure found to violate Article 3. An issue may arise under Article 6 § 1 in respect of evidence obtained in violation of Article 3 of the Convention, even if the admission of such evidence was not decisive in securing the conviction (see *İçöz v. Turkey* (dec.), no. 54919/00, 9 January 2003; and *Koç v. Turkey* (dec.), no. 32580/96, 23 September 2003). The Court reiterates in this connection that Article 3 enshrines one of the most fundamental values of democratic societies. Even in the most difficult circumstances, such as the fight against terrorism and organised crime, the Convention prohibits in absolute terms torture and inhuman or degrading treatment or punishment, irrespective of the victim's conduct. Unlike most of the substantive clauses of the Convention, Article 3 makes no provision for exceptions and no derogation from it is permissible under Article 15 § 2 even in the event of a public emergency threatening the life of the nation....[31]

But the Court goes on to say:

The right not to incriminate oneself, in particular, presupposes that the prosecution in a criminal case seek to prove their case against the accused without resort to evidence obtained through methods of coercion or oppression in defiance of the will of the accused....[32]

The Court found a violation of Article 3, but the conduct did not constitute torture. The Court's reasoning in finding a violation of Article 6(1) is replete with difficulties and unresolved questions, and roots its conclusions in the distinction between the right to silence and the ability to use evidence which has an existence independent of the will of the suspect. The principal basis for finding a violation of Article 6(1) was that the public interest in the conviction of the applicant was not of such weight as to warrant allowing the evidence of the regurgitated cocaine to be used at this trial. The

---

[29] See generally, T Theniel, 'The admissibility of evidence obtained by torture under international law' (2006) 17 EJIL 349.

[30] *Jalloh v Germany*, (App. 54810/00), 11 July 2006 [GC], (2007) 44 EHRR 667, ECHR 2006-IX.

[31] §99.   [32] §100.

joint dissenting opinion of Judges Ress, Pellonpää, Baka, and Sikut stresses that the proscription in Article 15 of the UN Convention relates to evidence obtained through torture, and that caution needs to be exercised where the evidence may have been obtained as a result of inhuman or degrading treatment.

The use of evidence obtained by torture also arises where it is not the defendant who is tortured, but some other person whose evidence is then used in the defendant's trial. In the *Osmanağaoğlu* case,[33] the applicant complained that he had been convicted on the basis, in part, of evidence obtained from two of his co-defendants by torture. The judgment sidesteps the question of the admissibility of such evidence in determining that there had been a violation of Article 6(1) and (3)(d) because the trial judges had not assessed the effect of the admission of the contested statements and had not provided an opportunity for the applicant to question the versions of events contained in those statements.

In the *Gäfgen* case,[34] the applicant complained that his conviction was based, in part, on evidence obtained from him under duress. He had been threatened by two police officers with serious violence to his person in an interaction lasting about ten minutes. In response to these threats, he had led the police to the place where a body had been left. In its Chamber judgment, the Strasbourg Court considered that the use of evidence obtained under duress could render the trial unfair. The Court said:

As to the use during the trial of real evidence recovered as a direct result of ill-treatment in breach of Article 3, the Court has considered that incriminating real evidence obtained as a result of acts of violence, at least if those acts had to be characterised as torture, should never be relied on as proof of the victim's guilt, irrespective of its probative value. Any other conclusion would only serve to legitimate indirectly the sort of morally reprehensible conduct which the authors of Article 3 of the Convention sought to proscribe or, in other words, to 'afford brutality the cloak of law' (see *Jalloh,* ... §§ 105–107).[35]

But in the light of all the other evidence against him, including his own subsequent confession, the Court concluded that the applicant's right to a fair trial had not been compromised and that there was no violation of Article 6(1) and (3). The Chamber judgment has been referred to the Grand Chamber, whose judgment is expected in the last quarter of 2009.

The issue of torture evidence is also raised in an application to the Court made by Abu Hamza, who claims that the background knowledge about al-Qaeda which led the United States investigators to charge him and seek his extradition from the United Kingdom came from torture in Camp X-Ray at Guantanamo Bay and/or secret CIA prisons elsewhere.[36] Press reports also indicate that at least some of those convicted of conspiring to mount an al-Qaeda inspired bomb attack in the United Kingdom are

---

[33] *Osmanağaoğlu v Turkey*, (App. 12769/02), 21 July 2009.
[34] *Gäfgen v Germany*, (App. 22978/05), 30 June 2008, which involved the kidnap for ransom of a child, who was subsequently murdered.
[35] §99.
[36] *Mustafa v United Kingdom*, (App. 36742/08), pending before the Court.

to make applications to the Strasbourg Court arguing that their detention for some months by the Inter-Services Intelligence Directorate in Pakistan and the torture to which they were subject there during interrogation, with the alleged complicity of the British Government, compromised the fairness of their trials.

OTHER ASPECTS OF THE PRESUMPTION OF INNOCENCE

Article 6(2) is not merely concerned with the burden of proof. It also prohibits the authorities from saying or doing anything which indicates that they believe a person is guilty of an offence, unless or until guilt is proven.[37] This does not prevent the authorities from informing the public about criminal investigations in progress, but it does require them to be discreet and circumspect in order to preserve the presumption of innocence. So reference, without qualification, at a press conference conducted by senior officials that a person was an accomplice to murder amounted to a declaration of guilt in breach of Article 6(2).[38] In this case the Strasbourg Court for the first time indicated that the protection of Article 6(2) may be infringed not only by a judge or a court, but also by other public authorities.

In a group of related cases,[39] statements were made, after criminal proceedings had been discontinued and where the defendants were seeking reimbursement of expenses, indicating some probability that the defendants were guilty. On close analysis, the Court concluded that the terms used by the judges described a state of suspicion rather than a finding of guilt. Article 6(2) had not been violated. This issue was taken up in the *Sekanina* case.[40] Sekanina had been tried and acquitted for the murder of his wife, then brought proceedings for reimbursement of costs and compensation for detention on remand for just over a year. The claim for compensation was dismissed on the ground that his acquittal had not dispelled the suspicion of his having committed the murder. The respondent State argued that the indications given by the court merely referred to the continued existence of suspicion, which had been accepted in earlier cases, and did not reflect the opinion that Sekanina was guilty. The Court unanimously distinguished the earlier cases which concerned the discontinuance of proceedings before a final determination, whereas the present case concerned proceedings following an acquittal. The statements made by the national court were inconsistent with the presumption of innocence.[41]

---

37 *Borovský v Slovakia*, (App. 24528/02), 2 June 2009.

38 *Allenet de Ribemont v France*, (App. 15175/89), 10 February 1995, Series A No 308, (1996) 22 EHRR 582. See, more recently, *Lavents v Latvia*, (App. 58442/00), 28 November 2002; and *YB and others v Turkey*, (Apps. 48173/99 and 48319/99), 28 October 2004; compare *Zollmann v United Kingdom*, (App. 62902/00), Decision of 27 November 2003.

39 *Lutz v Germany*,(App. 9912/82) 25 August 1987, (1988) 10 EHRR 182; *Nölkenbockhoff v Germany*, (App. 10300/83), 25 August 1987, (1988) 10 EHRR 163.

40 *Sekanina v Austria*, (App. 13126/87), 25 August 1993, Series A No 266-A, (1994) 17 EHRR 221.

41 See, in a similar vein, *Baars v Netherlands*, (App. 44320/98), 28 October 2003, (2004) 39 EHRR 538; *Del Latte v Netherlands*, (App. 44760/98), 9 November 2004; and *Capeau v Belgium*, (App. 42914/98), 13 January 2005. ECHR 2005-I.

PROMPT NOTIFICATION OF THE CHARGES
AND INTERPRETATION

The possibility for an accused to know the case against him is essential to the preparation of a defence. The duty on the State under Article 6(3)(a) is more explicit than the requirement of notification of the reason for detention in Article 5(2), and demands prompt information in a language the accused understands and in detail. Article 6(3)(e) grants the right to free interpretation if a person cannot understand or speak the language used in court. This issue has often been raised in conjunction with the right to notification of the charges and the two issues will be considered together.

Whereas the right to publicly funded legal assistance does not arise in every case, interpretation, where necessary, must be provided free regardless of the means of the defendant and must extend to the translation or interpretation of all documents or statements in the proceedings which it is essential for the defendant to understand in order to have the benefit of a fair trial.[42]

The applicant in the *Cuscani* case[43] was the Italian manager of 'The Godfather Restaurant' in Newcastle. He was prosecuted for serious tax offences, carrying a substantial prison sentence, and pleaded guilty. At the sentencing hearing the applicant's counsel told the judge that the applicant's 'English is poor and his Italian is very Southern'. The proceedings were adjourned, but at the next hearing no interpreter was present, contrary to the judge's order. The applicant's counsel, however, informed the judge that he thought it would be all right to proceed because the applicant's brother was present and had quite good English, and they would 'make do and mend'. The Court, finding a violation of Article 6(1)(e), held that the judge was 'the ultimate guardian of the fairness of the proceedings' and should not have been satisfied with the defence counsel's assurances, particularly since it was apparent that counsel himself had difficulty in communicating with his client.

The *Kamasinski* case[44] concerned an American charged with offences in Austria. He was provided with an interpreter during the pre-trial stages of the criminal process and a lawyer who was a registered English language interpreter was appointed to represent him at his trial. He nevertheless complained that he had not received English translations of the indictment. The Court held that Article 6(3)(a) did not require that the notification of the charge be given in writing nor translated in written form. In some cases, a difficulty could arise under the provision if no written translation of the indictment was provided, but in the circumstances of the present case, it was clear that the oral explanations provided to the applicant in his first language constituted sufficient information of the charges against him.

---

[42] *Luedicke, Belkacem and Koç v Germany*, (Apps. 6210/73, 6877/75, and 7132/75), 28 November 1978, Series A No 29, (1979–80) 2 EHRR 149. See also *Öztürk v Germany*, (App. 8544/79), 21 February 1984, Series A No 73, (1984) 6 EHRR 409 and *Kamasinski v Austria*, (App. 9783/82), 19 December 1989, Series A No 168, (1991) 13 EHRR 36.

[43] *Cuscani v United Kingdom*, (App. 32771/96), 24 September 2002, (2003) 36 EHRR 11. See also *Brozicek v Italy*, (App. 10964/84), 19 December 1989, Series A No 167, (1990) 12 EHRR 371.

[44] *Kamasinski v Austria*, (App. 9783/82), 19 December 1989, Series A No 168, (1991) 13 EHRR 36.

An accused person whose own conduct has been the principal cause of his not receiving notification of the charges against him cannot complain under Article 6(3)(a).[45] Discrepancies resulting from a clerical error in the statement of the provision which is the basis of the charge will not amount to a violation of the provision.[46]

TIME AND FACILITIES TO RUN A DEFENCE

The obligation in Article 6(3)(b) that those charged with a criminal offence are to have adequate time and facilities for the preparation of a defence is linked to the right in Article 6(3)(c) to personal representation or legal assistance. There are comparatively few cases in which Article 6(3)(b) alone has resulted in a violation of the Convention.

A pragmatic view is taken of the nature of the right. For example, where an accused person's lawyer has access to documentation, but not the accused himself, there will be no breach of the provision,[47] and a failure by the court to comply with a procedural request will not give rise to a breach if it seems that the procedure would not have served a useful purpose.[48]

The applicant in the *Hadjianastassiou* case[49] wished to challenge in the Court of Cassation the legality of proceedings in the Court of Appeal. The Court of Appeal's decision had been read out in summary form on 22 November 1985, but the full reasons were not disclosed until 10 January 1986. The time limit for applying to the Court of Cassation was five days from the date of the Court of Appeal's judgment (in November), and after the expiry of the time limit applicants were barred from expanding upon any legal argument. The Strasbourg Court concluded that the rights of the defence had been restricted to such a degree that there had been a violation of Article 6(3)(b) taken in conjunction with Article 6(1).

LEGAL ASSISTANCE

Article 6(3)(c) provides that 'everyone charged with a criminal offence' has three minimum rights: (1) to defend himself in person, or (2) to defend himself through legal assistance of his own choosing, and (3) if he has not sufficient means to pay for legal assistance, to be given it free when the interests of justice so require. The aim of this provision is to ensure that defendants have the possibility of presenting an effective defence.[50]

---

[45] *Hennings v Germany*, (App. 12129/86), 16 December 1992, Series A No 215-A, (1993) 16 EHRR 83, §26.

[46] *Gea Catalán v Spain*, (App. 19160/91), 10 February 1995, Series A No 309, (1995) 20 EHRR 266.

[47] *Kamasinski v Austria*, (App. 9783/82), 19 December 1989, Series A No 168, (1991) 13 EHRR 36.

[48] *Bricmont v Belgium*, (App. 10857/84), 7 July 1989, Series A No 158, (1990) 12 EHRR 217.

[49] *Hadjianastassiou v Greece*, (App. 12945/87), 16 December 1992, Series A No 252-A, (1993) 16 EHRR 219.

[50] *Goddi v Italy*, (App. 8966/80), 9 April 1984, Series A No 76, (1984) 6 EHRR 457.

Only shortcomings in legal representation which are imputable to the State authorities can give rise to a violation of Article 6(3)(c). In the *Tripodi* case,[51] the applicant's lawyer was ill and unable to attend a hearing before the Court of Cassation, which refused his request for an adjournment and determined the matter in his absence, on the basis of written pleadings. It appeared that the lawyer had done little to ensure that he was replaced for the day of the hearing but the Strasbourg Court, looking at the proceedings as a whole, found no violation.

The rights in Article 6(3)(c) are capable of applying pre-trial, since absence of legal representation at this stage could in certain circumstances affect the fairness of the proceedings as a whole.[52] In the *Öcalan* case[53] the applicant, the leader of the PKK, was detained on a small island in the Marmara Sea near Istanbul pending trial for numerous terrorist offences. The island was declared a military zone and access to it was strictly controlled. The applicant was denied contact with his lawyers for the first week of his detention, during which time he was extensively questioned and made a number of admissions. Subsequently, the applicant was allowed to consult with his lawyers, but for two one-hour periods a week, and only within hearing of the prison guards. Neither the applicant nor his lawyers were given sight of the voluminous case-file until very shortly before the hearing. The overall effect of these difficulties so restricted the rights of the defence that the principle of a fair trial was contravened, giving rise to a violation of Article 6(1), taken together with Article 6(3)(b) and (c).

The right to see a lawyer in the early stages of a police investigation is not absolute, and, where there is a good reason, can be subjected to restrictions. In the *John Murray* case[54] the respondent State argued that the problems involved in investigating terrorist offences justified the denial of contact between the applicant and a lawyer during the first forty-eight hours of police questioning, but the Court disagreed. Since Northern Irish law permitted an inference of guilt to be drawn from the applicant's silence under police questioning, the refusal of a lawyer had deprived him of a fair trial.

The *Poitrimol* case[55] concerned a rule of criminal procedure which allowed the appeal courts to refuse to hear an appeal against conviction where the accused was a fugitive from justice and declined to attend. The Strasbourg Court ruled that a person does not lose his right to the benefit of legal assistance by virtue of his own absence from court. Although it was permissible to have sanctions to secure the attendance of the accused in court, in Poitrimol's case the refusal to hear his lawyer was disproportionate and there was a violation of Articles 6(1) and 6(3)(c) taken together.

---

[51] *Tripodi v Italy*, (App. 13743/88), 22 February 1994, Series A No 281-B, (1994) 18 EHRR 295.
[52] *Imbrioscia v Switzerland*, (App. 13972/88), 24 November 1993, Series A No 275, (1994) 17 EHRR 441.
[53] *Öcalan v Turkey*, (App. 46221/99), 12 May 2005 [GC], (2005) 41 EHRR 985, ECHR 2005-IV.
[54] *Murray (John) v United Kingdom*, (App. 18731/91), 8 February 1996; (1996) 22 EHRR 29, ECHR 1996-I.
[55] *Poitrimol v France*, (App. 14032/88), 23 November 1993, Series A No 277-A, (1994) 18 EHRR 130. See also *Lala v Netherlands*, (App. 14861/89), 22 September 1994, Series A No 297-A, (1994) 18 EHRR 586 and *Pelladoah v Netherlands*, (App. 16737/90), 22 September 1994, Series A No 297-B, (1994) 19 EHRR 81.

The Strasbourg Court has held that 'where the deprivation of liberty is at stake, the interests of justice in principle call for legal representation', and if the defendant cannot afford to pay for this himself, public funds must be available as of right.[56] It will normally be in the interests of justice for a person to receive representation on an appeal where a substantial prison sentence is involved and there is a real issue to be considered.[57] Where an initial refusal of legal aid has taken place, and such an issue emerges, there should be a procedure for further considering the grant of legal assistance.[58] Where an appeal court is called upon to make a full assessment both factually and legally of the defendant's guilt or innocence on a serious charge, personal attendance as well as representation will be required for the proceedings to comply with Article 6(3)(c).[59]

While the national authorities 'should, as a rule, endeavour to choose a lawyer in whom the defendant places confidence',[60] the accused does not have an unlimited veto where his legal representation is publicly funded. In the *Croissant* case,[61] the national court had appointed three lawyers to assist in the defence of the applicant, who was charged with various criminal offences arising out his activities as lawyer to various members of the Red Army Faction; the trial had political overtones. Croissant objected to the assignment of one of the lawyers, whom he alleged had been assigned to ensure that the trial proceeded without interruption rather than to protect his interests. There was no evidence to show that the relationship was so strained as to make a proper defence impossible, and the Strasbourg Court found no violation of Article 6(3)(c) either in the appointment of multiple counsel nor in the appointment of counsel against the wishes of the defendant.

In the *Sejdovic* case,[62] the Strasbourg Court has elaborated the Convention requirements for representation by counsel where defendants are tried in their absence. It stressed the fundamental importance of adequate defence even for those not present at their trial. While it is appropriate to discourage unwarranted absences, any sanctions for failure to attend must not be disproportionate in the circumstances of the case. Sejdovic had been declared a fugitive by the Italian courts and tried in his absence; it appeared that he had not been given notice of the case against him. He was furthermore deprived of the opportunity to ask for the proceedings against him to be reopened. There had been a violation of Article 6.

---

[56] *Benham v United Kingdom*, (App. 19380/92), 10 June 1996; (1996) 22 EHRR 293, ECHR 1996-III.

[57] *Granger v United Kingdom*, (App. 11932/86), 28 March 1990, Series A No 174, (1990) 12 EHRR 469; *Boner v United Kingdom*, (App. 18711/91), 28 October 1994, (1995) 19 EHRR 246; and *Maxwell v United Kingdom*, (App. 18949/91), 28 October 1994, Series A No 300–C, (1995) 19 EHRR 97. See also *Quaranta v Switzerland*, (App. 12744/87), 24 May 1991, Series A No 205.

[58] Ibid.

[59] *Sibgatullin v Russia*, (App. 32156/02), 23 April 2009.

[60] *Croissant v Germany*, (App. 13611/88), 25 September 1992, Series A No 237-B, (1993) 16 EHRR 135, §7.

[61] Ibid.

[62] *Sejdovic v Italy*, (App. 56581/00), 1 March 2006 [GC], ECHR 2006-II.

WITNESSES AND EVIDENCE

Article 6(3)(d) grants a number of rights in respect of defence witnesses: to secure their attendance and to examine their evidence on the same basis as the witnesses against the accused. This provision must be considered in the context of both the accusatorial system—where it is for the parties, subject to the control of the court, to decide which witnesses they wish to call—and the inquisitorial system—where the court decides for itself which witnesses it wishes to hear. In the former system, the witnesses are examined and cross-examined by the parties or their representatives, although additional questions may be put by the judge, while in the latter system witnesses are examined by the court.

Article 6(3)(d) is intended to ensure, under each system, that the accused is placed on a footing of equality with the prosecution as regards the calling and examination of witnesses,[63] but it does not give defendants a right to call witnesses without restriction.[64] Moreover, in accordance with the 'fourth instance' doctrine, it is normally for the national courts to decide whether it is necessary or advisable to call a witness, and, provided the principle of equality has been respected, the Strasbourg Court would find a violation only in exceptional circumstances.[65] A court can therefore refuse to hear a witness for the reason that his statement would be irrelevant,[66] and, even where the evidence is relevant, the court fulfils its obligation if it takes all appropriate steps to try to ensure the appearance of the witness.[67]

The Strasbourg Court has been called upon to decide a number of cases in which the prosecution in criminal trials has relied upon the evidence of anonymous witnesses. The applicant in the *Doorson* case[68] had been convicted of drugs offences on the evidence of a number of anonymous witnesses. He had not been permitted to see these witnesses since they claimed to be frightened of reprisals, but during the course of the appeal proceedings his lawyer had been present while they were questioned by the investigating judge and had had an opportunity to put questions to them himself, and the investigating judge had drawn up a full report for the Court of Appeal explaining her reasons for considering that the witnesses could be relied upon. The Court found that it was justifiable to protect the rights of the witnesses to respect for their life, liberty, and security of person (as secured by various provisions in the Convention) by preserving their anonymity and that the difficulties this caused for the defence had been adequately counterbalanced by the procedures followed by the investigating judge. Nonetheless, the Court observed that it would never be acceptable for a conviction to be based solely or to a decisive extent on anonymous statements.[69]

---

[63] *Bönisch v Austria*, (App. 8658/79), 6 May 1985, Series A No 92, (1987) 9 EHRR 191.

[64] Or to have hearsay statements admitted in evidence when the witness is no longer able to remember crucial events: *Thomas v United Kingdom*, (App. 19354/02), Decision of 10 May 2005.

[65] *Bricmont v Belgium*, (App. 10857/84), 7 July 1989, Series A No 158, (1990) 12 EHRR 217.

[66] App. 1404/62, *Wiechert v Federal Republic of Germany*, Decision of 7 March 1964 (1964) 7 *Yearbook* 104, 112.

[67] *Thomas v United Kingdom*, (App. 19354/02), Decision of 10 May 2005.

[68] *Doorson v Netherlands* (App. 20524/92), 26 March 1996, (1996) 22 EHRR 330.

[69] See also *Saidi v France*, (App. 14647/89), 20 September 1993, Series A No 261-C, (1994) 17 EHRR 251.

A similar issue arose in the *Van Mechelen* case.[70] Here the applicants were convicted of attempted murder and robbery after a trial at which the prosecution evidence included the uncorroborated statements of several police officers who refused to reveal their names and were identified only by numbers. The defence were given a chance to question the officers in the following conditions: each officer was confined in a closed room with the investigating judge and a registrar, while the defendants, their lawyers, and an advocate general sat in another room. There was a sound-link between the two rooms, so that the defence could hear all the questions put to the officers and their answers, but they could not observe their demeanour under questioning and thus test their reliability.

The Court distinguished this case from the *Doorson* case in view of the particular problems which arise where police officers give evidence anonymously. Although their interests—and those of their families—also deserved protection under the Convention, it had to be recognized that their position was different from an ordinary disinterested witness or a victim, since they owed a general duty of obedience to the State's executive authorities and usually had links to the prosecution. The Court was not satisfied that the measures in question had been strictly necessary—for example, the national court had not made a sufficient effort to assess whether the threat of reprisals which had been made against the police officers could be taken seriously. It therefore found a violation of Articles 6(1) and 3(d) taken together.

A further variant was before the Strasbourg Court in the *Al-Khawaja and Tahery* case.[71] In the first case the evidence in question was the read statement of the victim of an alleged sexual assault who had subsequently committed suicide. In the second case, the evidence which was read out was not of an anonymous witness, but of an identified witness who had been too scared to attend the trial and give evidence. In neither case could this evidence be subject to cross-examination. The Strasbourg Court indicated that in all cases, the starting point for the Court's assessment is whether the defendant has had an opportunity to test or to have evidence tested, whether during the investigation or at trial, in circumstances where the conviction is based solely or to a decisive degree on that evidence.[72] In the case before them, the two statements which were read out were regarded as the decisive basis for the conviction. In neither case were there sufficient counterbalancing safeguards (such matters as the judge's warning to the jury, or the ability of the defendant to rebut the evidence by giving evidence himself) to avoid a violation of Article 6(1) read with Article 6(3)(d).[73]

The *Perna* case[74] applied similar principles to the admission of documentary evidence, as well as requests that particular persons are called to give evidence. The Grand

---

[70] *Van Mechelen and others v Netherlands* (Apps. 21363/94, 21364/94, 21427/93, and 22056/93), 23 April 1997, (1998) 25 EHRR 647, ECHR 1997-III.

[71] *Al-Khawaja and Tahery v United Kingdom*, (Apps. 26766/05 and 22228/06), 20 January 2009, (2009) 49 EHRR 1. A request for referral to the Grand Chamber is pending.

[72] §36, referring to *Lucà v Italy*, (App. 33354/96), 27 February 2001, ECHR 2001-II, §40.

[73] The judgment of the Court of Appeal in *R v Horncastle and Blackmore and two other cases*, [2009] EWCA Crim 964 would appear to repudiate the judgment in the *Al-Khawaja* case.

[74] *Perna v Italy*, (App. 48898/99), 6 May 2003 [GC], (2004) 39 EHRR 563, ECHR 2003-V.

Chamber, in a unanimous decision, affirmed that the admissibility of evidence is primarily a matter for regulation by national law. In dealing with complaints relating to such matters the Strasbourg Court is concerned to ascertain whether the proceedings as a whole were fair.[75] It will be for the person complaining that a trial has been unfair to show why it is important for the witnesses concerned to be heard and their evidence must be necessary for the establishment of the truth. The applicant had not established these matters and the Grand Chamber unanimously found no violation of Article 6(1) and (3)(d) of the Convention.

In criminal proceedings concerning accusations of sexual abuse, particularly where the complainant is a child, the Court has held that certain measures may be taken to protect him or her, provided that such measures can be reconciled with an adequate and effective exercise of the rights of the defence. Thus in the *SN* case[76] the Court found no violation of Article 6 paragraphs 1 and 3(d) taken together where a schoolteacher had been convicted of sexually assaulting her 10-year-old pupil virtually solely on the basis of a videotaped interview of the boy with a specially trained police officer. Under Swedish law in such cases child complainants are rarely called to give evidence in court because of the traumatizing effect this might have on them. The Court found that it was sufficient for the purposes of Article 6 that the applicant's counsel could have attended the interview or given the police officer any questions which the defence wanted to be put to the boy.

THE PRINCIPLE OF LEGALITY

The Convention is not merely concerned with the procedural fairness of criminal trials. Article 7 is concerned with the substantive criminal law and embodies the principle of legality, which stipulates that no one should be convicted or punished except in respect of a breach of a pre-existing rule of law.[77] There are two main aspects to this principle. First, Article 7 prohibits legislatures and courts from creating or extending the law so as to criminalize acts or omissions which were not illegal at the time of commission or omission, or to increase a penalty retroactively. Secondly, it requires that the criminal law should be clearly defined;[78] this second aspect of the principle is almost a precondition of the first, since the more precisely drafted an offence is, the less scope there is for creative judicial interpretation and nasty courtroom surprises for defendants.

---

[75] *Perna*, §29.

[76] *SN v Sweden*, (App. 34209/96), 2 July 2002, ECHR 2002-V; see also *Magnusson v Sweden*, (App. 53972/00), Decision of 6 December 2003.

[77] *Nullum crimen, nulla poena sine lege*; best paraphrased in English as: only the law can define a crime and prescribe a penalty.

[78] The Strasbourg Court has said that 'the criminal law must not be extensively construed to an accused's detriment': *Achour v France*, (App. 67335/01), 29 March 2006 [GC], (2007) 45 EHRR 9, ECHR 2006-IV, §41.

Article 7 states:

1. No one shall be held guilty of any criminal offence on account of any act or omission which did not constitute a criminal offence under national or international law at the time when it was committed. Nor shall a heavier penalty be imposed than the one that was applicable at the time the criminal offence was committed.

2. This Article shall not prejudice the trial and punishment of any person for any act or omission which, at the time when it was committed, was criminal according to the general principles of law recognised by civilised nations.

APPLICABILITY OF ARTICLE 7

The terms 'criminal offence' and 'penalty' in Article 7 carry autonomous meanings independent of the characterization under domestic law. The question whether any particular act amounts to a conviction for a 'criminal offence' is determined by reference to the '*Engel* criteria':[79] principally the classification in domestic law, the nature of the offence itself, and the nature and severity of the sentence which can be imposed.[80] Similar considerations apply in deciding whether a measure amounts to a 'penalty'. As the Strasbourg Court observed in the *Welch* case:[81]

The wording of Article 7(1), second sentence, indicates that the starting point in any assessment of the existence of a penalty is whether the measure in question is imposed following conviction for a 'criminal offence'. Other factors that may be taken into account as relevant in this connection are the nature and purpose of the measure in question; its characterisation under national law; the procedures involved in the making and implementation of the measure; and its severity.

The applicant in that case was arrested for drugs offences committed in November 1986. The Drug Trafficking Offences Act 1986 came into force in January 1987; it introduced confiscation orders intended to ensure that those convicted of drugs offences could not retain the profits of drugs-related activity. The retroactive effect of the confiscation order imposed on the applicant was not in dispute; the only question before the Strasbourg Court was whether such an order could properly be described as a 'penalty'. The Court rejected the respondent State's argument that the order was preventive, rather than punitive, observing that 'the aims of prevention and reparation are consistent with a punitive purpose and may be seen as constituent elements of the very notion of punishment.' It concluded that Welch faced more 'far-reaching detriment' as a result of the confiscation order than that to which he would have been exposed at the time he committed the offences, and that there had, therefore, been a violation of Article 7.

In the *Adamson* case[82] the Court was called upon to decide whether inclusion on a register of known sex offenders constituted a 'penalty'. Under the Sex Offenders Act

---

[79] See ch.12 above.
[80] *Brown v United Kingdom*, (App. 38644/97), Decision of 24 November 1998.
[81] *Welch v United Kingdom*, (App. 17440/90), 9 February 1993, Series A No 307-A.
[82] *Adamson v United Kingdom*, (App. 42293/98), Decision of 26 January 1999.

1997, which entered into force on 1 September 1997, any person convicted after that date of one of the sexual offences listed in the Act, or any person already serving a sentence of imprisonment for such an offence at the date of commencement, was required, after his release, to register with the police and keep them informed of any change of name or address. In holding that this requirement did not amount to a 'penalty', the Court found it relevant that its purpose was not to punish sex offenders, but to contribute towards a lower rate of re-offending. It noted that the obligation to register was imposed as a matter of law, with no additional procedure, following conviction of a sexual offence. Although failure to register constituted a criminal offence, punishable by imprisonment, independent proceedings would have to be brought against a defaulter in which his degree of culpability in defaulting would be taken into account in sentencing. Finally, the Court did not consider that the obligation to notify the police of the information required by the Act could, in itself, be regarded as severe. The applicant had expressed the fear that his inclusion on the register would lead to vigilante-style attacks on him or his family, but the Court dismissed this concern because it had not been provided with any evidence to suggest that the applicant would be put at risk in this way.

RETROACTIVE CRIMINALIZATION

The Convention was drafted in the aftermath of the Second World War, and presumably those responsible for framing Article 7 had in mind events in Germany and other parts of Europe in the 1930s, when newly imposed totalitarian regimes promulgated retroactive laws, making criminal without warning acts which had been lawful under democratic rule. Following the fall of the Berlin Wall in November 1989, the change of administration in many eastern and central European countries was almost as extreme, with democratic governments being elected in the place of Communist dictatorships. Quite naturally, these changes were frequently accompanied by a strong desire to bring to justice those responsible for the worst excesses of the old regimes.

Faced with a similar situation following the fall of Nazi Germany in 1945, the international community developed the 'Nuremberg principles', which permitted individuals to be prosecuted for acts so heinous as to be classified as 'crimes against humanity', even if these same acts had not been criminal according to Nazi legislation and practice. These principles are reflected in the second paragraph of Article 7.[83]

In two applications against Germany the Strasbourg Court was required to examine whether it was compatible with Article 7(1) for the courts of the unified Federal Republic to convict men in respect of acts which, in the submission of the applicants,

---

[83] In *Papon v France*, (App. 54210/00), Decision of 15 November 2001, ECHR 2001-XII, the Court rejected the applicant's argument that at his trial for war crimes it had been a breach of Article 7 for the national court to reverse its case-law and adopt a broader interpretation of Article 6 of the Nuremberg Statute, removing the need to prove intent on the part of an accessory to such an offence to serve as an instrument of the Nazis' totalitarian policy. See also *Kononov v Latvia*, (App. 36376/04), 24 July 2008, for an example of a war crimes case.

had not been criminal according to the law and practice of the German Democratic Republic (GDR). The three applicants in the case of *Streletz, Kessler and Krenz v Germany*[84] had occupied senior positions in the GDR State apparatus. After unification, the first two applicants were convicted of incitement to commit intentional homicide and the third applicant was convicted of intentional homicide as an indirect principal on the grounds that, as they had participated in high-level decisions on the GDR's border-policing regime, they shared responsibility for the deaths of a number of young people who had attempted to flee to West Berlin between 1971 and 1989 and had been killed by landmines or by shots fired by East German border guards. The applicant in the case of *K-HW*[85] had served as a soldier in the GDR border guard and, in 1973, when he was twenty years old, had shot and killed a fugitive attempting to swim to West Berlin.

The German courts which convicted the applicants did not rely on the argument that the acts in question had amounted to 'crimes against humanity' or had been criminal according to the general principles of international law. Instead they held that the acts had been prohibited by GDR law on the dates they were committed. They relied on the fact that the GDR had ratified the United Nations' International Covenant on Civil and Political Rights (which guarantees, *inter alia*, the right to life and the right to freedom of movement) and enacted a number of statutory provisions protecting the right to life and restricting the use of lethal force to the prevention of serious crime. The practice of the East German authorities, however, for which the applicants in the *Streletz* case had been partly responsible, was to encourage border guards to disregard the legislation and to annihilate border violators. In the event of a successful crossing, the guards on duty could expect to be the subject of an investigation by the military prosecutor.

In the *Streletz* case the Strasbourg Court observed that GDR statute law, together with the provisions of the international treaties ratified by it, had provided a clear prohibition on disproportionate and arbitrary killing. It was not open to the applicants to argue that, in the light of GDR State practice, their convictions as accessories to murder had not been foreseeable, since they themselves had to a large extent been responsible for the disparity between the legislation and the practice.

The Court's finding of no violation of Article 7 in the *K-HW* case appears somewhat harsher (and three of the seventeen judges in the Grand Chamber dissented from it). The applicant had been a young and junior soldier; he had undergone a process of indoctrination and had been ordered to protect the border 'at all costs'; he knew that he would be subject to investigation if he allowed a fugitive successfully to escape from East Germany. However, the Court held that the GDR statute law was accessible to all, and that 'even a private soldier could not show total, blind obedience to orders which

---

[84] *Streletz, Kessler and Krenz v Germany*, (Apps. 34044/96, 35532/97, and 44801/98), 22 March 2001 [GC], (2001) 33 EHRR 751, ECHR 2001-II.

[85] *K-HW v Germany*, (App. 32701/97), 22 March 2001, (2003) 36 EHRR 1081, ECHR 2001-II.

flagrantly infringed not only the GDR's own legal principles but also internationally recognized human rights'.[86]

Perhaps more convincing is the argument put by Sir Nicolas Bratza in his concurring opinion:

I accept…that the situation in the GDR was such that the applicant could hardly have foreseen at the time that his actions would result in his prosecution for the offence of intentional homicide. But this is a very different question from the one facing the Court, namely whether the applicant could reasonably have foreseen that his actions amounted to such an offence. While this question may be open to differing opinions, I can find no reason to depart from the considered opinion of the national courts that opening fire on a defenceless person, who was attempting to swim away from East Berlin and who posed no threat to life or limb, so clearly breached any principle of proportionality that it was foreseeable that it violated the legal prohibition on killing.

The issue of war crimes has troubled the Strasbourg Court in recent years. Such cases can turn on detailed consideration of the factual conclusions.[87] In the *Korbely* case,[88] the Strasbourg Court was called upon to consider whether events in October 1956 in Budapest in which the applicant was involved constituted with sufficient accessibility and foreseeability crimes against humanity under the Geneva Convention. The Strasbourg Court re-affirmed the requirement that an offence must be clearly defined in law:

This requirement is satisfied where the individual can know from the wording of the relevant provision—and, if need be, with the assistance of the courts' interpretation of it and with informed legal advice—what acts and omissions will make him criminally liable. The Court has thus indicated that when speaking of 'law' Article 7 alludes to the very same concept as that top which the Convention refers elsewhere when using that term, a concept which comprised written as well as unwritten law and implies qualitative requirements, notably those of accessibility and foreseeability.[89]

The Grand Chamber concluded that the law in the Geneva Convention was accessible since the Geneva Conventions had been proclaimed in Hungary by a national legislative measure. But whether the requirement of foreseeability was met turned on the meaning of a crime against humanity in 1956. Careful analysis of the provision and its understanding in Hungary suggested that it was 'open to question whether the constituent elements of a crime against humanity were satisfied in the present case'.[90]

The Strasbourg Court has also been called upon to consider prosecutions flowing from events in Bosnia. In the *Jorgic* case,[91] the applicant took issue with his conviction for genocide, arguing that the German courts had adopted an interpretation of genocide which did not have a basis either in German law or international law. The Strasbourg Court concluded that the interpretation adopted by the national

---

[86] *K-HW*, §75.   [87] As in *Kononov v Latvia*, (App. 36376/04), 24 July 2008.
[88] *Korbely v Hungary*, (App. 9174/02), 19 September 2008 [GC], ECHR 2008-nyr.
[89] §70.   [90] §85.
[91] *Jorgic v Germany*, (App. 74613/01), 12 July 2007, ECHR 2007-IX.

court was supported both by the Genocide Convention and by a number of German scholars. Furthermore the interpretation was reasonably foreseeable on receipt of proper advice. There was no violation of Article 7. A second area of enquiry was also needed in order to ascertain whether one of the victims of the killing by the applicant was 'taking no active part in the hostilities' which was a requirement to bring him within the protection of the Geneva Convention. This issue had not been fully addressed by the national courts. This meant that it could not be shown that it was foreseeable that the applicant's acts constituted a crime against humanity under international law, and there had been a violation of Article 7 of the Convention.

CLARITY OF CRIMINAL LEGISLATION

It follows from the rule against retrospective legislation under Article 7 that legal provisions which interfere with individual rights must be adequately accessible and formulated with sufficient precision to enable the citizen to regulate his conduct. The Strasbourg Court's approach towards such cases under Article 7 is identical to that used to determine whether a provision authorizing an interference with the right to private and family life under Article 8 or to freedom of religion or expression under Articles 9 and 10 is sufficiently precise as to render the interference 'in accordance with the law'.[92] The condition is satisfied where the individual can know from the wording of the relevant provision and, if need be, with the assistance of the national courts' interpretation of it, what acts and omissions will make him liable.[93]

While has been argued that certain offences known to English law, such as those based on dishonesty, public mischief, or conspiring to corrupt public morals may be inconsistent with Article 7,[94] the Strasbourg case-law shows that a crime has to be very loosely defined indeed before the Court will find a violation of this provision.[95]

In the *Kokkinakis* case,[96] for example, the applicant, a Jehovah's witness, was convicted under a Greek law which prohibited proselytism. 'Proselytism' was defined in the statute as meaning:

in particular, any direct or indirect attempt to intrude on the religious beliefs of a person of a different religious persuasion, with the aim of undermining those beliefs, either by any kind of inducement or promise of an inducement or moral support or material assistance, or by fraudulent means or by taking advantage of his inexperience, trust, need, low intellect or naïvety.

---

[92] See ch.14 below, and see *Custers, Deveaux and Turk v Denmark*, (Apps. 11843/03, 11847/03, and 11849/03), 3 May 2007.

[93] *Kokkinakis v Greece*, (App. 14307/88), 25 May 1993, Series A No 260-A, (1994) 17 EHRR 397, §52.

[94] See *Shaw v Director of Public Prosecutions*, [1962] AC 220; *Knuller (Publishing, Printing and Promotions) Limited v Director of Public Prosecutions*, [1973] AC 435; *R. v Pattni, Dhunna, Soni and Poopalarajah*, [2001] Crim LR 570.

[95] For an examples, see *Liivik v Estonia*, (App. 12157/05), 25 June 2009.

[96] *Kokkinakis v Greece*, (App. 14307/88), 25 May 1993, Series A No 260-A, (1994) 17 EHRR 397, §52.

The applicant contended that this provision was so widely defined that it could encompass almost any attempt to convert a person to another religious faith. The Strasbourg Court noted that the wording of many statutes is not absolutely precise and that the need to avoid excessive rigidity and to keep pace with changing circumstances means that many laws were inevitably couched in fairly vague terms. However, the settled national case-law interpreting the statute was sufficiently clear to enable Kokkinakis to regulate his conduct in the matter.[97]

Article 7 does not merely prohibit retrospective law-making by the legislature or executive, it also prohibits extension of the application of the criminal law by the judiciary.[98] Nonetheless, the Strasbourg Court has shown itself prepared to give national courts considerable leeway in this respect, recognizing that:

> however clearly drafted a legal provision may be, in any system of law, including criminal law, there is an inevitable element of judicial interpretation. There will always be a need for elucidation of doubtful points and for adaptation to changing circumstances. Indeed, in the...Convention States, the progressive development of the criminal law through judicial law-making is a well entrenched and necessary part of legal tradition. Article 7 of the Convention cannot be read as outlawing the gradual clarification of the rules of criminal liability through judicial interpretation from case to case, provided that the resulting development is consistent with the essence of the offence and could reasonably be foreseen.[99]

The applicant in the *CR* case[100] was convicted of the attempted rape of his wife. At the time he tried to force her to have sex, and indeed until the judgments of the Court of Appeal and House of Lords in his case, it was an established rule of common law that a man could not rape his wife, because in getting married a woman was deemed to have consented once and for all to intercourse with her husband. A number of exceptions to this principle had been developed—for example, where the couple had separated by court order or deed of agreement—but these did not apply in the applicant's case. The Court of Appeal and House of Lords both refused his appeal against conviction, holding that the rule was unacceptable in modern Britain and should be held inapplicable.

Despite the fairly overwhelming evidence that the domestic courts' judgments represented a reversal, rather than a clarification, of the law, the Strasbourg Court rejected the applicant's complaint under Article 7, holding that 'judicial recognition of the absence of immunity had become a reasonably foreseeable development of the law'.

---

[97] See also *Baskaya and Okçuoglu v Turkey*, (Apps. 23536/94 and 24408/94), 8 July 1999, (2001) 31 EHRR 292, ECHR 1999-IV.

[98] App. 1852/63, *X v Austria*, Decision of 22 April 1965 (1965) 8 *Yearbook* 190, 198.

[99] *CR v United Kingdom*, (App. 20190/92), 2 November 1995, Series A No 335-C, (1996) 21 EHRR 363, §34.

[100] Ibid.

Perhaps the true explanation for the Court's decision was its understandable repugnance for the rule conferring immunity from rape charges to husbands. As it observed:

The essentially debasing character of rape is so manifest that the result of the decisions of the Court of Appeal and the House of Lords—that the applicant could be convicted of attempted rape, irrespective of his relationship with the victim—cannot be said to be at variance with the object and purpose of Article 7 of the Convention, namely to ensure that no one should be subjected to arbitrary prosecution, conviction or punishment.... What is more, the abandonment of the unacceptable idea of a husband being immune against prosecution for rape of his wife was in conformity not only with a civilised concept of marriage but also, above all, with the fundamental objectives of the Convention, the very essence of which is respect for human dignity and human freedom.[101]

The Court's reasoning appears to overlook the fact that most criminal laws are directed at behaviour which offends against human dignity and freedom. While the removal of the immunity from English law is to be welcomed, the rule of law would have been better respected if Parliament had carried out the reform with purely prospective effect.[102]

The issue of the quality of the law is well illustrated in the *Kafkaris* case.[103] Kafkaris had been convicted of a contract killing; he had placed explosive beneath a car which had killed a man and his two children. He was sentenced to life imprisonment under the provisions of the Cyprus Criminal Code. Regulations on the effect of the sentence indicated that this would be for a term of twenty years with the possibility of early release for good behaviour. In litigation not involving the applicant, the Regulations were declared unconstitutional. The effect was to increase operative length of the applicant's sentence to a whole life term without the possibility of early release. By fifteen votes to two, the Grand Chamber found a violation of Article 7 by reason of the deficiency in the quality of the law applicable at the material time, and by sixteen votes to one that there had been no violation in relation to the complained of retrospective application of a longer sentence and removal of the possibility of remission. The Grand Chamber considered that the sentence of life imprisonment was provided for in the Criminal Code and was the only basis for the imposition of this sentence. By contrast, the Regulations in issue concerned the manner in which the sentence would be executed. The penalty of life imprisonment under the Criminal Code could not be regarded at the time as amounting only to twenty years in prison.[104] However, at the material time, the distinction between the scope of a life sentence and its manner of execution was 'not immediately apparent'[105] and this constituted a breach of Article 7.

---

[101] §42.

[102] Rather than the matter being dealt with by judicial decisions on the content of the common law.

[103] *Kafkaris v Cyprus*, (App. 21906/04), 12 February 2008 [GC], (2009) 49 EHRR 877, ECHR 2008-nyr.

[104] §149. There is a particularly trenchant criticism of the reasoning of the majority in the dissenting opinion of Judge Borrego.

[105] §148.

RECIDIVISM

The *Achour* case[106] concerned French legislation which provided that those committing a second offence of the same nature would incur a longer sentence. Prior to 1 March 1994 the period within which the second offence had to be committed for a person to be regarded as a recidivist was five years from the expiry of a prison sentence. From 1 March 1994 the period was extended to ten years. Achour had completed a sentence for drug trafficking on 12 July 1986. He was sentenced for a further offence in respect of which proceedings had begun on 11 December 1995. This was outside the five-year period provided for in the earlier law, but within the ten-year period in the later law. He argued that this violated Article 7.

The Strasbourg Court noted that 'matters relating to the existence of [rules on recidivism], the manner of their implementation, and the reasoning behind them' was a matter for policy decisions in the respondent State.[107] The Court concluded, by sixteen votes to one, that, notwithstanding the extension of the period within which the second offence was committed, it was foreseeable that the applicant could be regarded as a recidivist with the consequences for the length of his sentence on committing the repeat offence. It seems significant that recidivism was seen as an aggravating factor in relation to a particular individual and not in relation to the nature of the offence committed.[108]

PROTOCOL 7

Protocol 7 includes a number of additional rights in respect of the criminal process: a rule against double jeopardy, the right to an appeal, and the right to compensation following a miscarriage of justice.[109]

THE RULE AGAINST DOUBLE JEOPARDY

Article 4 of Protocol 7 provides:

1. No one shall be liable to be tried or punished again in criminal proceedings under the jurisdiction of the same State for an offence for which he has already been finally acquitted or convicted in accordance with the law and penal procedure of that State.

2. The provisions of the preceding paragraph shall not prevent the reopening of the case in accordance with the law and penal procedure of the State concerned, if there

---

[106] *Achour v France*, (App. 67335/01), 29 March 2006 [GC], (2007) 45 EHRR 9, ECHR 2006-IV.

[107] §44.

[108] *In personam* rather than *in rem* in the words of the Court. There is a helpful concurring opinion of Judge Zupančič.

[109] The United Kingdom is not a signatory to this Protocol. For an up-to-date list of ratifications see http://conventions.coe.int.

is evidence of new or newly discovered facts, or if there has been a fundamental defect in the previous proceedings, which could affect the outcome of the case.

3. No derogation from this Article shall be made under Article 15 of the Convention.

The Explanatory Memorandum to Protocol 7 resolves some aspects of the wording of the provision. A conviction or acquittal becomes final, according to the Memorandum, when 'no further ordinary remedies are available or when the parties have exhausted such remedies or have permitted the time limit to expire without availing themselves of these.'

There is no intention in the wording of the Article to preclude cases being reopened in favour of the convicted person, but the prohibition on double jeopardy does not preclude a person being subject to several different types of procedure in relation to the same conduct, for example, to civil proceedings for compensation in addition to a criminal trial.

The application of the Article is limited to proceedings in a single State. The Explanatory Memorandum notes that the international application of the prohibition is adequately covered in the European Convention on Extradition of 1957, the European Convention on the International Validity of Criminal Judgments of 1970, and the European Convention on the Transfer of Proceedings in Criminal Matters of 1972.

The Strasbourg Court has stated that the aim of Article 4 of Protocol 7 'is to prohibit the repetition of criminal proceedings that have been concluded by a final decision.'[110] The scope of Article 4 has been clarified by the Grand Chamber in the *Sergey Zolotukhin* case.[111] The Grand Chamber was influenced by the text of corresponding provisions in the Covenant on Civil and Political Rights, and the American Convention on Human Rights, in concluding that the Article should be interpreted as prohibiting the prosecution or trial of an individual for a second offence where that second prosecution or trial arose from 'identical facts or facts which are substantially the same, and the guarantee comes into play where a new set of proceedings is instituted after a prior acquittal or conviction has acquired the status of *res judicata*.'[112]

THE RIGHT TO AN APPEAL

Article 2 of Protocol 7 provides:

1. Everyone convicted of a criminal offence by a tribunal shall have the right to have his conviction or sentence reviewed by a higher tribunal. The exercise of this right, including the grounds on which it may be exercised, shall be governed by law.

---

[110] *Nikitin v Russia*, (App. 50178/99), 20 July 2004, (2005) 41 EHRR 149, ECHR 2004-VIII, §35; followed in *Fadin v Russia*, (App. 58079/00), 27 October 2006; and *Xheraj v Albania*, (App. 37959/02), 29 July 2008. See also *Ruotsalainen v Finland*, (App. 13079/03), 16 June 2009.

[111] *Sergey Zolotukhin v Russia*, (App. 14939/03), 10 February 2009 [GC], ECHR 2009-nyr.

[112] §§82–3.

2. This right may be subject to exceptions in regard to offences of a minor character, as prescribed by law, or in cases in which the person concerned was tried in the first instance by the highest tribunal or was convicted following an appeal against acquittal.

The explanatory report indicates that the reference to a tribunal in paragraph (1) is designed to exclude from its ambit any conviction resulting from a decision of a non-judicial organ. There is no explanation as to the relationship of this provision with Article 6, which would seem to require that the determination of criminal charges is by an independent tribunal. Paragraph (2) allows limitations to be placed on the right, and excludes it altogether in certain situations. It is unclear how the provision accommodates systems, like that of England and Wales, which in many cases require leave to be obtained before an appeal may be pursued. The explanatory report indicates that the intention was to view application for leave to appeal as a form of review under the provision, though it is at least arguable that the words of the text do not achieve this.

The *Galstyan* case[113] concerned a prosecution and conviction for a public order offence. The applicant claimed that he had no right of appeal under Article 2 of Protocol 7, while the respondent State argued that a procedure for review did exist. The Strasbourg Court indicated that where an offence is found to be of a criminal character within Article 6 of the Convention, it also attracts the provisions of Article 2 of Protocol 7.[114] The procedure on which the respondent State relied lacked 'any clearly defined procedure or time limits and consistent application in practice.' Such a review was not compatible with the requirements of Article 2 of Protocol 7.[115]

COMPENSATION FOR A MISCARRIAGE OF JUSTICE

Article 3 of Protocol 7 provides:

When a person has by final decision been convicted of a criminal offence and when subsequently his conviction has been reversed, or he has been pardoned, on the ground that a new or newly discovered fact shows conclusively that there has been a miscarriage of justice, the person who has suffered punishment as a result of such conviction shall be compensated according to the law or the practice of the State concerned, unless it is proved that the non-disclosure of the unknown fact in time is wholly or partly attributable to him.

The right to compensation is narrowly drafted, but the provision is reasonably self-explanatory. It is intended only to cover the clearest cases of miscarriages of justice where the miscarriage cannot be said to be wholly or partly the fault of the person punished. The scope of the reference to the 'practice' of the State in the provision is unclear. It suggests that *ex gratia* arrangements may be permissible. The

---

[113] *Galstyan v Armenia*, (App. 26986/03), 15 November 2007.
[114] §120.   [115] §126.

right to compensation for victims of arrest or detention in breach of the requirements of Article 5 refers to 'an enforceable right to compensation', which is an altogether clearer phrase.

It is clear that the Strasbourg Court will require the conditions set out in the Article to be fully met, especially that the conviction has been reversed on the grounds that a new or newly discovered fact shows conclusively that there has been a miscarriage of justice.[116]

---

[116] See *Matveyev v Russia*, (App. 26601/02), 3 July 2008.

14

LIMITATIONS COMMON TO ARTICLES 8–11

INTRODUCTION

This chapter is about the express limitations to be found in the second paragraphs of Articles 8 to 11, but it also reports the historical debate on whether there are inherent limitations to some of the rights protected by the Convention arising as a consequence of particular circumstances in which individuals might find themselves. Brief consideration of the restrictions on the political activities of aliens which may arise under Article 16 is also included in this chapter.

The Convention does not contain a single approach to limiting the scope of the rights it protects; rather it uses a number of different techniques. There is provision in Article 15 for derogating from some of the protected rights in times of war or public emergency threatening the life of the nation.[1] Secondly, some of the articles themselves define conduct as outside the protection of the article in which the right is enumerated when it might otherwise be viewed as within it. So, Article 2(2) excludes deprivation of life from the scope of the right to life when it results from the use of force which is no more than absolutely necessary in one of three defined situations.[2] Similarly Article 4(3) provides that certain types of work, and military service, do not constitute forced or compulsory labour.[3] Article 5 spells out exhaustively the circumstances in which a deprivation of liberty will be permissible.[4] The third technique adopted for limiting the scope of Convention rights can be found in Articles 8 to 11 which make provision for limitations where certain qualifying conditions are satisfied.[5]

Each of Articles 8–11 sets out a Convention right in the first paragraph, but then qualifies it by listing limitations, or restrictions as the Court sometimes describes them, in the second paragraph. Though there are some differences of detail in the nature of the limitations arising under each article, there is sufficient commonality of approach to justify a collective consideration of these limitations before examining the substantive rights protected under each of these articles.[6] The justification for

---

[1] See ch.6 above.   [2] See ch.8 above.   [3] See ch.10 above.   [4] See ch.11 above.

[5] Similar or analogous limitations can be found elsewhere in the Convention; for example, in Article 2 of Protocol 4 and Article 1 of Protocol 7. It can also be argued that the Strasbourg Court has construed the protection of property rights in Article 1 of Protocol 1 as requiring a similar approach: see ch.20 below.

[6] See generally, S. Greer, *The Exceptions to Articles 8 to 11 of the European Convention on Human Rights* (Council of Europe Publishing, Strasbourg 1997); J. Viljanen, 'The European Court of Human Rights as a

these limitations is sometimes said to arise because of the need to balance the interest of the community against the interests of the individual. This has led some to characterize the exceptions as public interest exceptions to Convention rights. One commentator has observed:

The relationship between human rights and public interest exceptions is one of the most important issues in contemporary human rights jurisprudence. Not only is the interpretation given to exceptions a key determinant of the utility of rights in practice, but this is also the area in which the political or value-laden nature of the choices facing the court is most obvious, raising questions as to the legitimacy of judicial rather than democratic decision-making.[7]

INHERENT LIMITATIONS

The principle that only the restrictions expressly provided by the Convention are allowed has not always been accepted. In the early days the Commission appeared to accept that there were certain situations, notably those involving prisoners and other detained persons, in which there were inherent limitations arising from the applicant's situation. The notion has also been supported by some writers on the Convention.[8] The Strasbourg Court did not follow the Commission in this regard, and the Commission abandoned the notion many years ago.

The Commission's doctrine that certain restrictions are an 'inherent feature' of detention seems to have been disapproved by the Strasbourg Court in the *Vagrancy* cases.[9] In that case, the Court held:

[I]n the light of the information given to it, that the competent Belgian authorities did not transgress in the present cases the limits of the power of appreciation which Article 8(2) of the Convention leaves to the Contracting States: even in cases of persons detained for vagrancy, those authorities had sufficient reason to believe that it was 'necessary' to impose

---

Developed of General Doctrines of Human Rights Law. A Study of the Limitations Clauses of the European Convention on Human Rights (Tampereen yliopisto, Tampere 2003); B. Hovius, 'The Limitations Clauses of the European Convention on Human Rights and Freedoms and Section 1 of the Canadian Charter of Rights and Freedoms: A Comparative Analysis' (1987) 6 YEL 1; A. McHarg, 'Reconciling Human Rights and the Public Interest: Conceptual Problems and Doctrinal Uncertainty in the Jurisprudence of the European Court of Human Rights' (1999) 62 MLR 671; L. Wildhaber, 'The "Margin of Appreciation" in National Law and the Law of the Strasbourg Institutions', Address to Conference of Presidents of the Supreme Courts and Attorneys General of the Member States of the European Union, London 1 June 2000; S. Greer, 'Constitutionalizing Adjudication under the European Convention on Human Rights' (2003) 23 OJLS 405; S. Greer, '"Balancing" and the European Court of Human Rights: a Contribution to the Habermas-Alexy Debate' (2004) 63 CLJ 412; and J. Sweeney, 'Margins of Appreciation: Cultural Relativity and the European Court of Human Rights in the Post-Cold War Era' (2005) 54 ICLQ 459.

[7] A. McHarg, 'Reconciling Human Rights and the Public Interest: Conceptual Problems and Doctrinal Uncertainty in the Jurisprudence of the European Court of Human Rights' (1999) 62 MLR 671, 695.

[8] J. Fawcett, The *Application of the European Convention on Human Rights* (OUP, Oxford 1987), 232–3.

[9] *De Wilde, Ooms & Versyp v Belgium*, (Apps. 2832/66, 2835/66, and 2899/66), 18 June 1971, Series A No 12, (1979–80) 1 EHRR 373.

restrictions for the purpose of the prevention of disorder or crime, the protection of health or morals, and the protection of the rights and freedoms of others.[10]

In the *Golder* case, the Strasbourg Court held that there was unquestionably an interference with the right to respect for correspondence; it thus rejected the notion that there was no need to find justification under paragraph (2), and went on to say explicitly that the restrictive formulation of Article 8(2) 'leaves no room for the concept of implied limitations'.[11] The same conclusion applies in relation to Articles 9–11 of the Convention.

Any lingering doubt has been removed by the statements of the Grand Chamber in the *Hirst* case:

> 69. …the Court would begin by underlining that prisoners in general continue to enjoy all the fundamental rights and freedoms guaranteed under the Convention save for the right to liberty, where lawfully imposed detention falls within the scope of Article 5 of the Convention… . Any restrictions on [Convention] rights require to be justified, although such justification may well be found in the considerations of security, in particular the prevention of crime and disorder, which inevitably flow from the circumstances of imprisonment… .
>
> 70. There is, therefore, no question that a prisoner forfeits his Convention rights merely because of his status as a person detained following conviction… .[12]

The current position is that any limitation on the rights guaranteed by Articles 8–11 must be justified under the provisions of the second paragraph of the article in issue. The notion of inherent limitations is of purely historical interest.

EXPRESS LIMITATIONS: SOME GENERAL POINTS

The second paragraphs of Articles 8–11 allow for interference by the authorities with the protected rights under certain prescribed conditions. There are two basic principles concerning the restrictions on the rights guaranteed. The first principle is that only the restrictions expressly authorized by the Convention are allowed. That principle is nowhere stated explicitly, but it is presupposed by the whole system of the Convention. Further, it is presupposed, in particular, by the second basic principle, which is expressly stated by Article 18. This principle is that 'the restrictions permitted under this Convention to the said rights and freedoms shall not be applied for any purpose other than those for which they have been prescribed.'

---

[10] *De Wilde, Ooms & Versyp*, §93.

[11] See also *Golder v United Kingdom*, (App. 4451/70), 21 February 1975, Series A No 18, (1979–80) 1 EHRR 524, §44.

[12] *Hirst v United Kingdom (No. 2)*, (App. 74025/01), 6 October 2005 [GC], (2006) 42 EHRR 849, ECHR 2005-IX, §§69–70, re-affirmed in *Dickson v United Kingdom*, (App. 44362/04), 4 December 2007 [GC], (2008) 46 EHRR 927, ECHR 2007-XIII, §§67–8.

The importance of requiring that restrictions must, in every case, be justified by an express provision of the Convention is very great. It enables the Strasbourg Court to control the alleged interference by reference to those express provisions. In dealing with exceptions to Convention rights, the Court adopts a narrow interpretation.[13] In the *Sidiropoulos* case, which concerned the limitations to Articles 11, the Strasbourg Court noted that 'exceptions to freedom of association must be narrowly interpreted, such that the enumeration of them is strictly exhaustive and the definition of them necessarily restrictive.'[14] The same is true of all the limitations to Articles 8 to 11.

Greer has suggested that the justifications for the limitations expressed in these articles can be divided into those which protect public interests (national security, territorial integrity, the economic well-being of the nation, health and morals, and disorder or crime) and those which protect private interests (maintaining the authority and impartiality of the judiciary, protecting the rights and freedoms of others, and preventing the disclosure of information received in confidence, protecting the rights and freedoms of others).[15] Such a distinction is, however, somewhat artificial, since some of the interests said to be private interests are clearly intended to serve a public purpose, such as maintaining the authority and impartiality of the judiciary. Most commentators agree that there is a considerable diversity of treatment of individual cases by the Strasbourg organs,[16] and that the Strasbourg Court's decisions tend to be very fact specific.

The Strasbourg Court adopts a three-part enquiry where a Contracting Party seeks to rely on a limitation in one of the Convention articles. First, it determines whether the interference is in accordance with, or prescribed by, law, then it looks to see whether the aim of the limitation is legitimate in that it fits one of the expressed heads in the particular article, and finally it asks whether the limitation is in all the circumstances necessary in a democratic society. In making this assessment, the Strasbourg Court will consider whether a Contracting Party has based its decision 'on an acceptable assessment of the relevant facts.'[17] Central to this determination is the proportionality of the interference in securing the legitimate aim. Only the minimum interference with the right which secures the legitimate aim will be permitted. The essence of each of the restrictions is that the interests of society as a whole override the interests of the individual. In cases involving this balancing of values, the question frequently before

---

[13] See, for example, *Klass v Germany*, (App. 5029/71), 6 September 1978, Series A No 28, (1979–80) 2 EHRR 214, §42; and *The Observer and The Guardian v United Kingdom*, (App. 13585/88), 26 November 1991, Series A No 216, (1992) 14 EHRR 153, §59.

[14] *Sidiropoulos and others v Greece*, (App. 26695/95), 10 July 1998, (1999) 27 EHRR 633, ECHR 1998-IV, §38.

[15] S. Greer, *The Exceptions to Articles 8 to 11 of the European Convention on Human Rights* (Council of Europe Publishing, Strasbourg 1997).

[16] For example, A. McHarg, 'Reconciling Human Rights and the Public Interest: Conceptual Problems and Doctrinal Uncertainty in the Jurisprudence of the European Court of Human Rights' (1999) 62 MLR 671, 683–4.

[17] *Gorzelik and others v Poland*, (App. 44158/98), 17 February 2004 [GC], (2005) 40 EHRR 76, ECHR 2004-I, §96.

the Strasbourg Court will be whether the interference goes beyond what is necessary in a democratic society.

The Strasbourg Court does not always follow this three-part enquiry. In some cases, it moves directly to the question of whether an interference can be regarded as necessary in a democratic society without determining whether the complained-of measure was taken in accordance with law for a legitimate aim. In such cases, the Strasbourg Court will indicate that its decision does not require it to determine whether a State measure was in accordance with law or served a legitimate aim.[18] The reason for this approach would seem to be twofold. Sometimes it is difficult for the Court to call into question a respondent State's good faith in imposing restrictions on a Convention right; and sometimes it is hard for the Court to find a breach of national law if the national authorities have acted on the basis that national law has been complied with.

A REQUIRED LEGAL BASIS FOR THE INTERFERENCE

First it must be shown that any restriction imposed on one of the Convention rights is in each case 'in accordance with the law',[19] or 'prescribed by law'.[20] The difference in the language used in Article 8 when compared with Articles 9–11 is immaterial;[21] the French text of the Convention reads *prévue(s) par la loi* in all cases.[22]

The Strasbourg Court, building on the Commission's case-law, has established a threefold test for determining whether an interference is in accordance with law. First, it must be established that the interference with the Convention right has some basis in national law.[23] Secondly, the law must be accessible; and, thirdly, the law must be formulated in such a way that a person can foresee, to a degree that is reasonable in the circumstances, the consequences which a given action will entail. This is known as the test of foreseeability.[24] The requirements of accessibility and foreseeability have been described as the 'quality of law' requirements.[25]

---

[18] For a clear example of such an approach, see *Christian Democratic People's Party v Moldova*, (App. 28793/02), 14 February 2006, (2007) 45 EHRR 392, ECHR 2006-II.

[19] Art. 8(2) of the Convention. The same language is used in Arts. 2(3) and (4) of Protocol 4, and Art. 1(1) of Protocol 7. What is said here is relevant to consideration of those provisions of the Convention.

[20] Arts. 9(2), 10(2), and 11(2). The same language is used in Art. 2(2) of Protocol 7. What is said here is relevant to consideration of those provisions of the Convention.

[21] See *Sunday Times v United Kingdom*, (App. 6538/74), 26 April 1979, Series A No 30, (1979–80) 2 EHRR 245, §48.

[22] Art. 1 of Protocol 1 requires interferences to be 'subject to the conditions provided for by law', which raises similar issues to those discussed in this section.

[23] For an example of a case in which the Court could find no relevant law, see *Djavit An v Turkey*, (App. 20652/92), 20 February 2003, (2005) 40 EHRR 1002, ECHR 2003-III.

[24] See, for example, *Huvig v France*, (App. 11105/84), 24 April 1990, Series A No 176-B, (1990) 12 EHRR 528, §26; and *S and Marper v United Kingdom*, (Apps. 30562/04 and 30566/04), 4 December 2008 [GC], (2009) 48 EHRR 1169; ECHR 2008-nyr, §99.

[25] For example, *Al-Nashif v Bulgaria*, (App. 50963/99), 20 June 2002, (2003) 36 EHRR 655, §121.

The references to 'law' are, of course, to national law, and the Strasbourg Court must accept the interpretation of national law adopted by the national courts, unless there are very strong reasons for disagreeing.[26] This is not because the Court is not a 'fourth instance', or higher court of appeal above the national courts. It is rather because questions of national law are for the Court simply questions of fact.

There is no requirement that the law be statutory; it can be unwritten law. In the *Sunday Times* case[27] it was the common law of contempt that was in issue. In the *Barthold* case[28] it was the rules of the Veterinary Surgeons' Council, which had authority to make professional rules. In the *Slivenko* case[29] it was a Treaty between Latvia and Russia relating to the withdrawal of Russian troops from the country. In the *'Bosphorus Airways'* case[30] it was a European Community Regulation.

The character of the law imposing the limitations was considered in the *Sunday Times* case.[31] It is not alone enough that the law qualifies as such in the national legal system (though if it does not, any defence a Contracting Party seeks to mount is certain to fail), it must also display additional qualities. First, the law must be adequately accessible: the citizen must be able to have an indication that is adequate in the circumstances of the legal rules applicable to a given case. Secondly, a norm cannot be regarded as 'law' unless it is formulated with sufficient precision to enable citizens to regulate their conduct: they must be able—if need be with appropriate advice—to foresee, to a degree that is reasonable in the circumstances, the consequences which a given action may entail.[32] The Strasbourg Court went on to explain that the requirement of foreseeability was not designed to secure absolute certainty, so that no interpretation would be required in determining the scope of application of the law. However, a certain level of clarity is required. In the *Vogt* case[33] the Court said that the level of precision required:

depends to a considerable degree on the content of the instrument in question, the field it is designed to cover and the number and status of those to whom it is addressed.[34]

These requirements can be problematic in cases where they relate to the interests of national security. In the *Malone* case,[35] the Strasbourg Court stressed that the law must indicate the scope of any discretion of the executive with regard to the interception of

---

[26] *Roche v United Kingdom*, (App. 32555/96), 19 October 2005 [GC], (2006) 42 EHRR 599; ECHR 2005-X, §120. This was a case on restrictions to access to a court under Article 6, but the same principles must apply under Articles 8 to 11.

[27] *Sunday Times v United Kingdom*, (App. 6538/74), 26 April 1979, Series A No 30, (1979–80) 2 EHRR 245.

[28] *Barthold v Germany*, (App. 8734/79), 23 March 1985, Series A No 90, (1985) 7 EHRR 383.

[29] *Slivenko v Latvia*, (App. 48321/99), 9 October 2003 [GC], (2004) 39 EHRR 490, ECHR 2003-X.

[30] *'Bosphorus Airways' v Ireland*, (App. 45036/98), 30 June 2005 [GC], (2006) 42 EHRR 1, ECHR 2005-VI.

[31] *Sunday Times v United Kingdom*, (App. 6538/74), 26 April 1979, Series A No 30, (1979–80) 2 EHRR 245.

[32] §49.

[33] *Vogt v Germany*, (App. 17851/91), 26 September 1995, (1996) 21 EHRR 205.   [34] §48.

[35] *Malone v United Kingdom*, (App. 8691/79), 2 August 1984, Series A No 82, (1985) 7 EHRR 14; and *Liberty v United Kingdom*, (App. 58243/00), 1 July 2008, (2009) 48 EHRR 1.

communications and the manner of its exercise with sufficient clarity to give the individual protection against arbitrary interference. The law of England and Wales was so obscure and subject to such differing interpretations, particularly in respect of the dividing line between conduct covered by legal rules and that covered by executive discretion that it lacked the minimum degree of legal protection required to qualify as 'law' for the purposes of the Convention. In the *Halford* case,[36] there was no regulation of interceptions of calls made on telecommunications systems outside the public network. Telephone calls made on a private network by Alison Halford when Assistant Chief Constable with the Merseyside Police were intercepted; this constituted a violation of Article 8, since the interference with respect for her private life and correspondence was not in accordance with the law.

In the *Leander* case,[37] which concerned security checks on certain government personnel, the Strasbourg Court recognized that the requirement of foreseeability could not be the same in the context of security checks on personnel as in other fields. Nevertheless, the law had to be sufficiently clear in regard to the circumstances and conditions which justified secret checks. The Swedish law met these standards.

Two further cases against the United Kingdom illustrate the application of the requirement of identifiability, accessibility and foreseeability in determining whether an interference is 'prescribed by law'. The *Steel* case[38] concerned the imposition of a requirement to be bound over to keep the peace on those charged with, and convicted of, breaches of the peace. The Strasbourg Court concluded that a liability to be bound over to keep the peace was sufficiently clear where such a requirement was imposed after a finding that a person had committed a breach of the peace, despite its being couched in vague and general terms. In the particular circumstances it would be clear that those bound over were agreeing to refrain from causing further, similar, breaches of the law for the period for which they agreed to be bound over.[39] The facts before the Strasbourg Court in the *Hashman and Harrup* case[40] were, arguably, significantly different. The applicants had been involved in activities designed to disrupt a fox-hunt. They were brought before the magistrates' court by way of complaint that they should be required to enter into a recognizance to keep the peace and be of good behaviour. They were so bound over. On a complaint that the measures constituted an interference with their freedom of expression, the Court considered whether binding over to keep the peace as a means of controlling anti-social behaviour was 'prescribed by law'. Here the Court regarded the law as being too vague; the binding over orders were not in the nature of a sanction for past unlawful conduct; the notion of conduct *contra bonos*

---

[36] *Halford v United Kingdom*, (App. 20605/92), 25 June 1997, (1997) 24 EHRR 523, ECHR 1997-III.

[37] *Leander v Sweden*, (App. 9248/81), 26 March 1987, Series A No 116, (1987) 9 EHRR 433.

[38] *Steel and others v United Kingdom*, (App. 24838/94), 23 September 1998, (1999) 28 EHRR 603, ECHR 1998-VII.

[39] §§76 and 94.

[40] *Hashman and Harrup v United Kingdom*, (App. 25594/94), 25 November 1999, (2000) 30 EHRR 241, ECHR 1999-VIII.

mores[41] was too vague to meet the requirement of predictability of application. It could not be said that what the applicants were being bound over not to do must have been apparent to them. The dissenting judge disagreed, noting that the binding over order placed an 'unmistakable obligation on the applicants, namely to refrain from any offensive and deliberate action which would disturb the lawfully organized activity of others engaged in fox-hunting.'[42] The distinction between a case where there is conduct of which the applicants were convicted which rendered the binding over foreseeable, and one where there is conduct leading to a complaint but no conviction, is a particularly narrow one.

SPECIFIED LEGITIMATE AIMS

Table 14.1 maps the legitimate aims to be found in the second paragraphs of Article 8–11 of the Convention. Article 10 on freedom of expression has the longest list of limitations, and Article 9 on freedom of thought, conscience, and religion the shortest list of limitations. In modern times, it looks anomalous that the interests of national security are not listed in Article 9. There is also considerable overlap between some of the restrictions. There are also some differences of wording which do not appear to be particularly significant.

For example, national security is almost certainly broad enough to incorporate territorial integrity, though that is only mentioned in Article 10. It is also interesting to note that the economic well-being of the country is only listed in Article 8, which suggests that economic considerations cannot base restrictions on the rights protected by Articles 9–11. Given the case-law on trade union rights under Article 11, that omission might be questioned by some. Articles 8, 10, and 11 refer to the prevention of disorder or crime, whereas Article 9 alone refers to the protection of public order and does not mention the prevention of disorder or crime. But the concepts of protecting public order, and preventing disorder and crime, are probably much the same in terms of a Contracting Party's aims in imposing restrictions on the rights contained in Articles 8 to 11.

Once the Court is satisfied that any restriction has a legal basis which meets the requirements of 'law' under the Convention provisions, it will go on to consider whether the restriction is for one of the specified legitimate aims.[43] The justifications set out in the Convention provisions are exhaustive, but also quite comprehensive in the range of interests which may be brought into play. It has proved very easy for

---

[41] Defined as behaviour which is 'wrong rather than right in the judgment of contemporary fellow citizens': §38.

[42] Dissenting opinion of Judge Baka.

[43] See generally P. Kempees, ' "Legitimate aims" in the case-law of the European Court of Human Rights' in P. Mahoney and others, *Protecting Human Rights: The European Perspective. Studies in Memory of Rolv Ryssdal* (Carl Heymanns, Köln 2000), 659.

Table 14.1 Express limitations in Articles 8–11

Article 8 *Right to respect for private and family life*	Article 9 *Freedom of thought, conscience and religion*	Article 10 *Freedom of expression*	Article 11 *Freedom of assembly and association*
in accordance with law	prescribed by law	prescribed by law	prescribed by law
necessary in a democratic society	necessary in a democratic society	necessary in a democratic society	necessary in a democratic society
interests of national security		interests of national security	interests of national security
		interests of territorial integrity	
interests of public safety	interests of public safety	interests of public safety	interests of public safety
interests of economic well-being of the country			
prevention of disorder or crime	protection of public order	prevention of disorder or crime	prevention of disorder or crime
protection of health or morals	protection of health or morals	protection of health or morals	protection of health or morals
		protection of the reputation of others	
protection of the rights and freedoms of others	protection of the rights and freedoms of others	protection of the rights of others	protection of the rights and freedoms of others
		preventing the disclosure of information received in confidence	
		maintaining the authority and impartiality of the judiciary	

a Contracting State to bring its action within one of the stated exceptions, and the Strasbourg Court seldom has to spend much time analysing the nature of the limitation to satisfy itself that it falls within one of them;[44] indeed, it frequently finds that a measure is justified by reference to several specific aims. Kempees reports that there is no case in which the Strasbourg Court has found a violation of one of Articles 8 to 11 purely on the basis of the failure of a respondent State to satisfy the requirement for a legitimate aim underlying the interference raised before the Strasbourg Court.[45] Sometimes the Strasbourg Court states a legitimate aim which is not expressly listed in the second paragraph of the relevant article. An example is the *Nnyanzi* case,[46] in which the Strasbourg Court described the applicant's proposed removal from the United Kingdom to Uganda as 'motivated by a legitimate aim, namely the maintenance and enforcement of immigration control.'[47] But there are also cases where the Strasbourg Court doubts the applicability of a claim by a Contracting Party. So, in the *Sidiropoulos* case,[48] Greece sought to justify refusal to register an association on the grounds that it was 'upholding Greece's cultural traditions and historical and cultural symbols.'[49] The Strasbourg Court was not persuaded that such a ground fell within the legitimate aims set out in Article 11(2), but was nevertheless able to find other legitimate aims served by the measures adopted by the respondent State.

The Court does, however, adopt a rigorous, though variable, approach to the issues of necessity and proportionality in relation to the measures taken to secure the legitimate aim. What follows are simply some illustrations of cases in which reliance has been placed on a particular ground.

THE INTERESTS OF NATIONAL SECURITY

The interests of national security are listed in Articles 8, 10, and 11, but omitted from Article 9.[50] National security is a broad concept. Kempees summarizes the scope of this limitation as measures protecting 'the safety of the state against enemies who might seek to subdue its forces in war or subvert its government by illegal means' including those features which make it a democracy.[51]

---

[44] Claims by the respondent State are only rarely contested by applicants.

[45] P. Kempees, '"Legitimate aims" in the case-law of the European Court of Human Rights' in P. Mahoney and others, *Protecting Human Rights: The European Perspective. Studies in Memory of Rolv Ryssdal* (Carl Heymanns, Köln 2000), 659.

[46] *Nnyanzi v United Kingdom*, (App. 21878/06), 8 April 2008, (2008) 47 EHRR 461.

[47] §76.

[48] *Sidiropoulos and others v Greece*, (App. 26695/95), 10 July 1998, (1999) 27 EHRR 633, ECHR 1998-IV.

[49] §37.

[50] See *Nolan and K v Russia*, (App. 2512/04), 12 February 2009.

[51] P. Kempees, '"Legitimate aims" in the case-law of the European Court of Human Rights' in P. Mahoney and others, *Protecting Human Rights: The European Perspective. Studies in Memory of Rolv Ryssdal* (Carl Heymanns, Köln 2000), 662.

In the *Zana* case[52] the Strasbourg Court regarded measures taken by Turkey to deal with the security situation in south-east Turkey as measures for the protection of national security.

The *Klass* case[53] concerned the legitimacy of secret surveillance. The Strasbourg Court accepted that the German measures fell within the national security exception, since democratic societies found themselves threatened by highly sophisticated forms of espionage and by terrorism, and needed to undertake secret surveillance to counter such threats.

In the *Rekvényi* case[54] the Court accepted, in the context of a challenge that the provisions violated Article 10, that a constitutional ban on political activities and party affiliation by police officers could be imposed 'for the protection of national security and public safety and the prevention of disorder'.

THE INTERESTS OF TERRITORIAL INTEGRITY

This ground, which is surprisingly only mentioned specifically in Article 10, is often linked to national security as in the *Zana* case.[55] The Court has chosen to couple territorial integrity closely with issues of national security, thus reducing the effect of its specific mention only in Article 10. The interests of territorial integrity would seem to require some threat of violence or disorder before resort can be made to this ground. Turkish arguments that a limitation justified on grounds of territorial integrity involved issues relating to the preservation of national unity as an idea[56] were rejected.

THE INTERESTS OF PUBLIC SAFETY

Few cases have raised questions of limitations based solely on public safety, and the Strasbourg Court does not appear to have relied exclusively on this head, though frequently, as in the *Rekvényi* case above, reliance is placed on public safety alongside national security and the prevention of disorder. In one case,[57] the Commission upheld resort to public safety in a case where it was argued that married people should be able to continue their married life in prison. A more easily sustained case could be made under the prevention of disorder or crime head.

The ground was raised and accepted in the *Buckley* case,[58] which concerned the refusal of planning permission to a gypsy for caravans to be used as homes. The

---

[52] *Zana v Turkey* (App. 18954/91), 25 November 1997, (1999) 27 EHRR 667, ECHR 1997-VII, §49.

[53] *Klass v Germany*, (App. 5029/71), 6 September 1978; Series A No 28, (1979–80) 2 EHRR 214.

[54] *Rekvényi v Hungary*, (App. 25390/94), 20 May 1999, (2000) 30 EHRR 519, ECHR 1999-III, §41.

[55] *Zana v Turkey*, (App. 18954/91), 5 November 1997, (1999) 27 EHRR 667, §49.

[56] And so justifying restrictions on freedom of expression, see, for example, *Arslan v Turkey*, (App. 23462/94), 8 July 1999, (2001) 31 EHRR 264.

[57] App. 8166/78, *X and Y v Switzerland*, 3 October 1978, (1979) 13 DR 241, 243.

[58] *Buckley v United Kingdom* (App. 20348/92), 25 September 1996, (1997) 23 EHRR 101, ECHR 1996-IV, §§62–3.

requirement of planning permission was said in this case to be 'aimed at furthering highway safety, the preservation of the environment and public health'. The Court accepted that these came within the exceptions relating to public safety, the economic well-being of the country, the protection of health, and the protection of the rights of others.

Public safety is often viewed as being synonymous with public order. In the *Metropolitan Church of Bessarabia* case, which concerned the system in Moldova under which only recognized religions could be practised, the Strasbourg Court said:

> The Court considers that States have the power to inquire into whether a movement or association is using supposedly religious aims in order to pursue activities that may harm the population or public safety.
>
> In view of the circumstances of the case, the Court holds that the impugned interference did in this case pursue a legitimate aim under Article 9(2) namely the protection of order and public safety.[59]

FOR THE ECONOMIC WELL-BEING OF THE COUNTRY

This legitimate aim is mentioned only in Article 9, which suggests that economic considerations may not underpin limitations to the rights in Articles 8, 10, and 11. The omission of this specific head from Article 11 is worth noting.[60]

The protection of the economic well-being of the country was referred to in the *Gillow* case,[61] which concerned the requirement to have permission from the authorities to occupy a home in Guernsey. The Strasbourg Court accepted the respondent State's arguments that it was permissible to 'maintain the population within limits that permit the balanced economic development of the island'.[62] In the *Berrehab* case, the Strasbourg Court concluded that the deportation of a Moroccan citizen on his divorce from a Dutch national could legitimately be based on the economic well-being of the country since the respondent State was concerned 'because of population density, to regulate the labour market.'[63]

The *Miailhe* case[64] concerned the exercise of search and seizure powers of people's homes by customs authorities. The applicants argued that there had been a violation of Article 8. The Strasbourg Court considered that the interferences with the rights protected in Article 8 were in the interests of the economic well-being of the country.

---

[59] *Metropolitan Church of Bessarabia v Moldova*, (App. 45701/99), 14 December 2001, (2002) 35 EHRR 306, ECHR 2001-XII, §113. See also *Leela Förderkreis EV v Germany*, (App.58911/00), 6 November 2008, (2009) 49 EHRR 117, §94 (an Article 9 case).

[60] Nor is it mentioned in Article 2 of Protocol 4, although Article 2(4) of that Protocol does include limitations 'justified by the public interest'; this is a phrase not used in Articles 8 to 11 and may be wide enough to include economic interests.

[61] *Gillow v United Kingdom*, (App. 9063/80), 24 November 1986, Series A No 109, (1986) 11 EHRR 355.

[62] §54.

[63] *Berrehab v Netherlands*, (App. 10730/84), 21 June 1988, Series A No 138, (1989) 11 EHRR 322, §26.

[64] *Miailhe v France*, (App. 12661/87), 25 February 1993, Series A No 256-C, (1993) 16 EHRR 332.

Similarly in the *Funke* case[65] the Court was faced with a complaint of a violation of Article 8 arising from searches of the applicant's home in connection with enquiries into financial dealings with foreign countries contrary to French law. The Court concluded that the interferences pursued a legitimate aim of being in the interest of the economic well-being of the country.

In the *Hatton* case,[66] the Strasbourg Court seems to have accepted that night flights 'contribute at least to a certain extent to the general economy', though it was acknowledged that it was difficult to draw a clear line between the interests of the airlines and that of the economic interests of the country as a whole.

THE PREVENTION OF DISORDER OR CRIME

Articles 8, 10, and 11 refers to the prevention of disorder or crime, whereas Article 9 refers to the prevention of public disorder. Little seems to turn on the difference of wording,[67] since the concept of order, of which the opposite is disorder, is probably somewhat wider than the concept of 'public order'.[68] What is, however, clear is that disorder and crime are different concepts. But the phrase is 'the prevention of crime' and not 'the detection of crime'; any measures based upon this limitation must be aimed at preventing crime. The limitation does not permit interferences with the rights protected in paragraph 1 of Articles 8, 10, and 11 for the sole purpose of detecting criminal conduct. The distinction may be a fine one in some cases. So in the *S and Marper* case, the Strasbourg Court accepted that a system of retaining DNA samples and fingerprints served the aim of preventing crime, although it found that the scheme in place in the United Kingdom was too far-reaching and disproportionate.[69]

The prevention of disorder or crime is the most frequently raised justification before the Strasbourg Court, and the most frequently accepted by it. This is unsurprising since many complaints involve penal measures, whose underlying purpose is the prevention of disorder or crime.

In the *Otto-Preminger Institute* case[70] the Strasbourg Court accepted that the provisions of the Austrian Penal Code which permitted seizure of a film considered to offend the religious sensibilities of Roman Catholics were 'intended to suppress behaviour directed against objects of religious veneration that is likely to cause "justified indignation"'[71] and so operated to prevent public disorder.

---

[65] *Funke v France*, (App. 10828/84), 25 February 1993, Series A No 256-A, (1993) 16 EHRR 297.

[66] *Hatton v United Kingdom* (App. 36022/97), 8 July 2003 [GC], (2003) 37 EHRR 611, ECHR 2003-VIII, §126.

[67] Article 1 of Protocol 7 refers to 'public order', and Article 2 of Protocol 4 uses the French phrase *ordre public*.

[68] See *Engel and others v Netherlands*, (Apps. 5100/71, 5101/71, 5102/71, 5354/72, and 5370/72), 8 June 1976, Series A No 22, (1979–80) 2 EHRR 647, §98.

[69] *S and Marper v United Kingdom*, (Apps 30562/04 and 30566/04), 4 December 2008 [GC], (2009) 48 EHRR 1169; ECHR 2008-nyr. See further below in this chapter, and the discussion of the case in ch.16.

[70] *Otto-Preminger Institute v Austria*, (App. 13470/87), 20 September 1994, Series A No 295-A, (1995) 19 EHRR 34.

[71] §48.

THE PROTECTION OF HEALTH OR MORALS

This limitation is frequently cited as the justification for interferences with Convention rights.[72] Once again, two rather disparate interests are combined, but it is clear that the limitation may operate for the protection of health or for the protection of morals; it does not have to be for the protection of both. It is also clear that the protection of health refers to individual health and not just to the protection of public health.[73]

The notion of the protection of morals seems to have been regarded as referring to sexual morality, when that is not a necessary constraint of the language used. The classic example is the seizure of *The Little Red Schoolbook* which gave rise to the *Handyside* case.[74] The Strasbourg Court was called upon to consider whether the conviction of individuals who had published a reference book targeted at children of school age containing advice on sexual and other matters violated the guarantee of freedom of expression in Article 10. The Court readily accepted that the issues raised here related to the protection of morals in the sense that the protection of morals entailed the safeguarding of the moral standards of society as a whole. A similar view was taken in a case involving the confiscation of a number of sexually explicit paintings.[75]

Perhaps a different approach was adopted in the *Dudgeon* case,[76] in which the Court was called upon to decide whether the continuing criminalization, in Northern Ireland, of certain sexual activities between consenting male adults in private constituted a breach of Article 8 of the Convention. Elsewhere in the United Kingdom, such acts no longer constituted criminal offences. In its judgment the Strasbourg Court said:

The Convention right affected by the impugned legislation protects an essentially private manifestation of the human personality.... There is now a better understanding, and in consequence an increased tolerance, of homosexual behaviour to the extent that in the great majority of the member States of the Council of Europe it is no longer considered to be necessary or appropriate to treat homosexual practices of the kind now in question as in themselves a matter to which the sanctions of the criminal law should be applied.... Although members of the public who regard homosexuality as immoral may be shocked, offended or disturbed by the commission by others of private homosexual acts, this cannot on its own warrant the application of penal sanctions when it is consenting adults alone who are involved.[77]

The Strasbourg Court could not see that criminalization of the acts in question was required to preserve moral standards, though it is equally the case that the Court was able to find a common European standard in relation to the conduct in question. The

---

[72] See generally C. Nowlin, 'The Protection of Morals under the European Convention for the Protection of Human Rights and Fundamental Freedoms' (2002) 24 HRQ 264.

[73] *Eriksson v Sweden*, (App.11373/85), 22 June 1989, Series A No 156, (1990) 12 EHRR 183, §§66–7.

[74] *Handyside v United Kingdom*, (App. 5493/72), 7 December 1976, Series A No 24, (1979–80) 1 EHRR 737.

[75] *Müller and others v Switzerland*, (App. 10737/84), 24 May 1988, Series A No 132, (1991) 13 EHRR 212.

[76] *Dudgeon v United Kingdom*, (App. 7525/76), 22 October 1981, Series A No 45, (1982) 4 EHRR 149.

[77] §60.

case may be contrasted with the Court's judgment in the *Laskey, Jaggard and Brown* case.[78] This case concerned sado-masochistic practices undertaken by men in private, and arguably was on all fours with the circumstances in the *Dudgeon* case in terms of private manifestations of human personality. Nevertheless, the Strasbourg Court did not regard the criminalization of acts of a sado-masochistic nature[79] as in breach of Article 8. The Court failed to grasp the nettle of considering the limits of State interference in private consensual conduct as a breach of respect for the personal autonomy of individuals. It may have been influenced by the arguments relating to the protection of health having regard to the nature of the injuries inflicted by the participants upon one another. In a later case (not involving concerns about 'public health considerations'), the Court followed the approach in the *Dudgeon* case in confirming that there was a violation of Article 8 in applying criminal sanctions to consensual sexual conduct between men in private.[80]

THE PROTECTION OF THE REPUTATION OF OTHERS

The protection of the reputation of others is only mentioned in Article 10,[81] which concerns freedom of expression. Articles 8 and 9 refer to the protection of the rights and freedoms of others, while Article 10 refers to the protection of the reputation or rights of others. Little seems to turn on the different form of wording, but the subordination of freedom of expression for the protection of the reputation of others probably justifies specific reference in Article 10. It is commonly cited in Article 10 cases.[82]

In the *Lindon* case,[83] writers and publishers of a book presented as a novel were convicted of defamation or complicity in defamation. The book tells the story of the trial of Ronald Blistier, a *Front National* militant, for the killing of a young man of North African descent. The book is based on a real-life trial for murders of black men. Jean-Marie Le Pen[84] had declared that the case was a put-up job to discredit the *Front National*. It was not contested in the case that the French legislation on which the convictions of the writers and publishers were based was for the protection of the reputation of others.[85] It is accordingly clear that the protection of the reputation of others is not simply that of individuals but also of various kinds of organization.[86]

---

[78] *Laskey, Jaggard and Brown v United Kingdom* (Apps. 21627/93, 21826/93, and 21974/93), 19 February 1997, (1997) 24 EHRR 39, ECHR 1997-I.

[79] And the refusal of a defence of consent to them in the United Kingdom. For a more liberal approach towards sado-masochistic role play, see *Pay v United Kingdom*, (App. 32792/05), Decision of 16 September 2008.

[80] *ADT v United Kingdom* (App. 35765/97), 31 July 2000, (2001) 31 EHRR 33, ECHR 2000-IX.

[81] As part of the phrase 'for the reputation or rights of others'.

[82] See further ch.18 below.

[83] *Lindon, Otchakovsky-Laurens and July v France*, (Apps. 21279/02 and 36448/02), 22 October 2007 [GC], (2008) 46 EHRR 761, ECHR 2007-XI.

[84] Leader of the *Front National*, a far-right nationalist party in France, which campaigns against immigration, particularly from North Africa.

[85] Jean-Marie Le Pen and the *Front National* party.

[86] See, for example, *Schmidt v Austria*, (App. 513/05), 17 July 2008, where it was the reputation of the Vienna Food Inspection Agency which was in issue.

This ground was used, somewhat controversially, as the basis for upholding the German Unfair Competition Act in the *Jacubowski* case.[87] A provision seeking to protect the reputation of others does not at first sight appear to have anything to do with protecting commercial interests.

THE PROTECTION OF THE RIGHTS OR FREEDOMS OF OTHERS

This too is a frequently raised limitation, which covers a wide range of matters. There can often be an overlap between this aim and other specified aims.

The limitation was used in the *Otto-Preminger Institute* case[88] where the showing of the offending film was considered to breach the right to respect for religious feelings when the rights in Articles 9 and 10 were read together.[89]

This limitation has also been applied frequently in child-care cases, where it is readily accepted that national legislation for placing children in care serves the purpose of 'protecting the rights and freedoms of others': in this case the child.[90]

The existence of this ground shows just how open-ended the limitations can be. The range of rights which might be protected is not limited. This may be useful. For example, it enabled the Strasbourg Court in the *Chappell* case[91] to regard search warrants,[92] designed to discover items produced in breach of intellectual property rights which could then be seized, as falling within the limitations to Article 8.[93]

THE PREVENTION OF THE DISCLOSURE OF INFORMATION RECEIVED IN CONFIDENCE

Article 10(2) contains two additional limitations. The first relates to measures for preventing the disclosure of information received in confidence. Interestingly in the *Weber* case,[94] where the applicant had been fined for breaching the confidentiality of the judicial investigation, the Strasbourg Court regarded the limitation as designed to protect the authority and impartiality of the judiciary, rather than on this ground. This suggests that this limitation is seen as rather more concerned with material received in confidence outside the courtroom.

---

[87] *Jacubowski v Germany*, (App. 15088/89), 23 June 1994, Series A No 291, (1995) 19 EHRR 64. See also *Barthold v Germany*, (App. 8734/79), 23 March 1985, Series A No 90, (1985) 7 EHRR 383, and *Markt Intern Verlag GmbH and Klaus Beermann v Germany*, (App. 10572/83), 20 November 1989, Series A No 165, (1990) 12 EHRR 161. See discussion of these cases in ch.18 below.

[88] *Otto-Preminger Institute v Germany*, (App. 13470/87), 20 September 1994, Series A No 295-A, (1995) 19 EHRR 34.

[89] §§46–8.

[90] See, for example, *Johansen v Norway*, (App. 17383/90), 7 August 1996, (1997) 23 EHRR 33, ECHR 1996-III.

[91] *Chappell v United Kingdom*, (App. 10461/83), 30 March 1989, Series A No 152, (1990) 12 EHRR 1.

[92] Anton Piller orders.

[93] Further examples of the use of this ground can be found in the *Spycatcher* cases: *Observer and Guardian v United Kingdom*, (App. 13585/88), 26 November 1991, Series A No 216, (1992) 14 EHRR 153; and *Sunday Times v United Kingdom (No. 2)*, (App. 13166/87), 26 November 1991, Series A No 217, (1992) 14 EHRR 229. See ch.18 below.

[94] *Weber v Switzerland*, (App. 11034/84), 22 May 1990, Series A No 177, (1990) 12 EHRR 508.

There is only one clear example of the use of this legitimate aim. In the *Autronic* case,[95] which concerned the reception and re-transmission of televised material from the Soviet Union which was intended for reception only within the Soviet Union, the Strasbourg Court regarded the Swiss measure as serving the aim of preventing the disclosure of confidential information.[96]

MAINTAINING THE AUTHORITY AND IMPARTIALITY OF THE JUDICIARY

Article 10(2) also permits limitations justified as maintaining the authority and impartiality of the judiciary. Resort to this ground for interferences with the rights contained in Article 10 is relatively rare. Where the interests of the judiciary are concerned it is more usual to rely upon the protection of the reputation or rights of others. In one case,[97] the applicant company complained that the grant of injunctions by the Austrian authorities prohibiting the publication of a photograph of a suspect violated the rights in Article 10. The injunctions were granted on the basis that they were intended to protect the suspect against insult and defamation and against violations of the presumption of innocence. The Strasbourg Court concluded that this met the aim of protecting the reputation of others and also served to maintain the authority and impartiality of the judiciary.[98] In the *Schöpfer* case,[99] the Court accepted that a penalty imposed upon a lawyer by a professional body in respect of a lawyer's inflammatory criticisms of the judiciary pursued the legitimate aim of maintaining the authority and impartiality of the judiciary. But in the *Wille* case,[100] the Strasbourg Court appears to have been uncertain. The case concerned a complaint by a former politician that, following a lecture he had given on constitutional law, the monarch of Liechtenstein had written to him announcing his intention not to appoint the applicant to political office again. The applicant complained that this was a violation of Article 10. The Strasbourg Court appears somewhat hesitant both over whether the measure was prescribed by law and over the underlying objective of the measure. It was argued that the measure was required to maintain public order and to promote civil stability, and to preserve judicial independence and impartiality. The Court did not find it necessary to consider these issues but proceeded on the assumption that the measure was prescribed by law and pursued a legitimate aim in deciding that such a measure was not necessary in a democratic society.[101]

---

[95] *Autronic Ag v Switzerland*, (App. 12726/87), 22 May 1990, Series A No 178, (1990) 12 EHRR 485.
[96] §59.
[97] *News Verlags GmbH and CoKG v Austria* (App. 31457/96), 11 April 2000, (2001) 31 EHRR 246, ECHR 2000-I.
[98] §§44–5.
[99] *Schöpfer v Switzerland* (App. 25054/94), 20 May 1998, (2001) 33 EHRR 845, ECHR 1998-III.
[100] *Wille v Liechtenstein* (App. 28396/95), 28 October 1999, (2000) 30 EHRR 558, ECHR 1999-VII.
[101] §§53–6.

THE LIMITATION MUST BE NECESSARY IN A DEMOCRATIC SOCIETY

THE BASIC TEST

In addition to being lawful and serving a legitimate purpose, the restriction must be 'necessary in a democratic society'[102] for serving that purpose. Establishing that the measure is necessary in a democratic society involves showing that the action taken is in response to a pressing social need, and that the interference with the rights protected is no greater than is necessary to address that pressing social need. The latter requirement is referred to as the test of proportionality. This test requires the Strasbourg Court to balance the severity of the restriction placed on the individual against the importance of the public interest. The classic formulation of the test is to be found in the *Silver* case:

   (a) the adjective 'necessary' is not synonymous with 'indispensable', neither has it the flexibility of such expressions as 'admissible', 'ordinary' 'reasonable' or 'desirable';

   (b) the Contracting States enjoy a certain but not unlimited margin of appreciation in the matter of the imposition of restrictions, but it is for the Court to give the final ruling on whether they are compatible with the Convention;

   (c) the phrase 'necessary in a democratic society' means that, to be compatible with the Convention, the interference must, *inter alia*, correspond to a 'pressing social need' and be 'proportionate to the legitimate aim pursued';

   (d) those paragraphs of Articles of the Convention which provide for an exception to a right guaranteed are to be narrowly construed.[103]

THE MARGIN OF APPRECIATION AND PROPORTIONALITY

In deciding whether action is necessary in a democratic society, the notion of the State's margin of appreciation has arisen and can often be troublesome.[104] To what extent should the Strasbourg organs defer to a Contracting Party's interpretation of the situation it faces in allowing a limitation on the rights guaranteed by the Convention?[105]

---

[102] Articles 8(2), 9(2), 10(2) and 11(2).

[103] *Silver v United Kingdom*, (Apps 5947/72, 6205/73, 7052/75, 7061/75, 7107/75, 7113/75, and 7136/75), 25 March 1983, Series A No 61, (1983) 5 EHRR 347, §97.

[104] See, especially, Y. Arai-Takahashi, *The Margin of Appreciation Doctrine and the Principle of Proportionality in the Jurisprudence of the ECHR* (Intersentia, Antwerp 2002); A. McHarg, 'Reconciling Human Rights and the Public Interest: Conceptual Problems and Doctrinal Uncertainty in the Jurisprudence of the European Court of Human Rights' (1999) 62 MLR 671; and G. Letsas, *A Theory of Interpretation of the European Convention on Human Rights* (OUP, Oxford 2007), ch.4.

[105] The doctrine is also relevant when consideration is given to the validity of derogations under Article 15. See ch.6 above, and *A and others v United Kingdom*, (App. 3455/05), 19 February 2009 [GC], (2009) 49 EHRR 29, ECHR 2009-nyr, §§173–4.

The scope of the margin of appreciation will sometimes be broad and sometimes narrow depending on the nature of the rights in issue, or on the balancing of competing rights. The doctrine is of relevance both in considering the scope of a Contracting Party's choices when interfering with a right protected by Articles 8–11,[106] and in considering the steps which a Contracting Party must take to guarantee the rights protected for individuals within their jurisdiction.[107] It is not easy to provide a definition of the doctrine which applies in every case, and the concept has been regarded as indeterminate and its application difficult to predict. The concept would appear to be a sliding scale whose application will depend on its context. One commentator has observed:

...the margin of appreciation varies not only in relation to different exceptions, but in relation to the *same* exceptions in different contexts.

A final layer of uncertainty arises from inconsistency as to the order in which the various elements of the *Handyside/Silver/Lingens* framework are addressed, if indeed they are addressed at all. Thus, is the nature of democratic necessity distinct from or part of the assessment of proportionality? Does the margin of appreciation apply to states' assessment of what the public interest requires, or to the balance to be struck between individuals and the collective, or both?...Rather than being a 'test' in the conventional dispositive sense, therefore, the *Handyside/Silver/Lingens* framework provides a set of highly imprecise justificatory strategies which can be used to support a number of approaches to the issue.[108]

In the *Handyside* case[109] the Strasbourg Court said:

By reason of their direct and continuous contact with the vital forces of their countries, State authorities are in principle in a better position than the international judge to give an opinion on the exact content of these requirements as well as on the 'necessity' of a 'restriction' or 'penalty' intended to meet them.[110]

In considering whether a Contracting Party has gone beyond what the situation requires:

The Court's supervisory functions oblige it to pay the utmost attention to the principles characterizing a 'democratic society'.[111]

In the *Refah Partisi* case,[112] the Strasbourg Court explored the characteristics of a democratic society in the light of its earlier case-law.[113] From this discussion it is

---

[106] Negative obligations.

[107] Positive obligations.

[108] A. McHarg, 'Reconciling Human Rights and the Public Interest: Conceptual Problems and Doctrinal Uncertainty in the Jurisprudence of the European Court of Human Rights' (1999) 62 MLR 671, 688.

[109] *Handyside v United Kingdom*, (App. 5493/72), 7 December 1976, Series A No 24, (1979–80) 1 EHRR 737.

[110] §48.   [111] §26.

[112] See J. Merrills, *The Development of International Law by the European Court of Human Rights* (MUP, Manchester 1993), ch.8, 'Human rights and democratic values' at 125–50. For a detailed discussion of the qualities of a democratic society by the Court, see *Refah Partisi (the Welfare Party) v Turkey*, (Apps. 41340/98, 41342/98, and 41344/98), 13 February 2003 [GC], (2003) 37 EHRR 1, ECHR 2003-II.

[113] §§86–95.

possible to discern that the Court regards the qualities of pluralism, tolerance, broad-mindedness, equality, liberty, and encouraging self-fulfilment as important ingredients of any democracy, together with freedom of religion, expression and assembly, and the right to a fair trial.

A few general principles relating to the breadth of the margin of appreciation to be applied have been established.

Where a particularly important facet of an individual's existence or identity is in issue under Article 8, the Strasbourg Court will be less likely to accept that a Contracting Party should be afforded a broad discretion.

One example is the *X and Y* case,[114] which concerned a young mentally handicapped girl who had been seriously sexually assaulted. Because of a lacuna in Dutch law, it was not possible for criminal proceedings to be instituted, although she could have brought a civil claim for damages. While recognizing that in principle Contracting Parties enjoyed a margin of appreciation when it came to the choice of means calculated to secure respect for private life between individuals, the Court ruled that the precise nature of the Contracting Party's obligation would depend on the particular aspect of private life in issue. This was a case where 'fundamental values and essential aspects of private life' (that is, a woman's right to physical integrity and freedom from sexual assault) were at stake. Since it was of vital importance to protect women from interference of this kind, the Contracting Party could not be allowed a great deal of discretion: effective deterrence, in the form of criminal sanctions, was indispensable.[115]

Similarly, in *Z v Finland*,[116] while accepting that individual interests could sometimes be outweighed by the public interest in the investigation and prosecution of crime, the Strasbourg Court emphasized the fundamental importance of protecting the confidentiality of medical data, for the sake of personal privacy and to preserve confidence in the medical profession and health services. It found that measures including the disclosure of the applicant's medical records without her consent in the course of criminal proceedings against her husband amounted to a violation of Article 8.

A similar balancing exercise was undertaken in the *Dudgeon* case,[117] where the complaint was that certain forms of homosexual activity were prohibited by the criminal law. Although the tendency is to allow a wide margin to a Contracting Party where questions of morality are in issue, the applicable criminal law inhibited the applicant from enjoying 'a most intimate aspect of private life' and the Strasbourg Court therefore required particularly serious reasons to be shown before it would accept that this interference was 'necessary'.

In some cases, the interests of two private parties will be in issue, as in the *Evans* case,[118] which concerned a conflict between the wish of a woman to become pregnant

---

[114] *X and Y v Netherlands*, (App. 8978/80), 26 March 1985, Series A No 91, (1986) 8 EHRR 235.

[115] §§24 and 27.

[116] *Z v Finland* (App. 22009/93), 25 February 1997, (1998) 25 EHRR 371, ECHR 1997-I.

[117] *Dudgeon v United Kingdom*, (App. 7525/76), 22 October 1981, Series A No 45, (1982) 4 EHRR 149.

[118] *Evans v United Kingdom*, (App. 6339/05), 10 April 2007 [GC], (2008) 46 EHRR 728, ECHR 2007-IV, §§77–82.

using embryos frozen at an earlier date, and the wish of her former partner that the embryos not be used. United Kingdom law requires the consent of both man and woman for the use of such embryos. The Grand Chamber could find no uniform European approach to the new moral and ethical issues presented by the case, and considered that the legislative scheme in the United Kingdom had been the product of much consideration, consultation, and debate. In such circumstances it was appropriate to afford the respondent State a wide margin of appreciation.

The *Evans* case can be contrasted with the *S and Marper* case,[119] concerning the retaining of DNA data. Here the United Kingdom was alone in adopting such an extensive scheme for the retention of such data, and so could not enjoy the wide margin of appreciation it was seeking.[120]

In areas of morality,[121] the scope of the margin is likely to be wide, since there is among the Contracting States no uniform conception of morals. This is illustrated by the *Handyside* case concerning *The Little Red Schoolbook*,[122] and also explains how its publication could be accepted in some Contracting States but not others. It may also explain the decision in the *Otto-Preminger Institute* case.[123] The location of the cinema in a predominantly Roman Catholic area, where a film was shown that would be deeply offensive to devout Roman Catholics, appears to have been an important factor in the Strasbourg Court's decision that the interference with the rights in Article 10 was justified.

Though at first sight the Strasbourg Court may appear to grant a wider margin of appreciation where positive obligations are in issue, this is often more apparent than real, since it will often be the case that the nature of the right in respect of which positive obligations are argued is finely balanced against the wider interests of the whole community.[124] In some of the earlier cases involving transsexuals which have come before it, the Strasbourg Court had allowed Contracting Parties a wide margin of appreciation, despite the fact that the same 'intimate aspect of private life' (an individual's sexual identity) was in issue here as in *Dudgeon*.

In the *Rees* case,[125] for example, the Strasbourg Court was asked to decide whether the respondent State was under a positive obligation to allow the entry in the register of births relating to the applicant and his birth certificate to be altered to reflect his change of sex from female to male. In the view of the Court, since the 'particular

---

[119] *S and Marper v United Kingdom*, (Apps. 30562/04 and 30566/04), 4 December 2008 [GC], (2009) 48 EHRR 1169; ECHR 2008-nyr.

[120] §§105–26.

[121] As noted above, much of the case-law is concerned with sexual morality.

[122] *Handyside v United Kingdom*, (App. 5493/72), 7 December 1976, Series A No 24, (1979–80) 1 EHRR 737.

[123] *Otto-Preminger Institute v Austria*, (App. 13470/87), 20 September 1994, Series A No 295-A, (1995) 19 EHRR 34.

[124] See *Monory v Romania and Hungary* (App. 71099/01), 5 April 2005, (2005) 41 EHRR 771, §72.

[125] *Rees v United Kingdom*, (App. 9532/81), 17 October 1986, Series A No 106, (1987) 9 EHRR 56, §§37–8; and see also the *Cossey v United Kingdom*, (App. 10843/84), 27 September 1990, Series A No 184, (1991) 13 EHRR 622.

features [of transsexualism] [had] been identified and examined only fairly recently'
and there was no European consensus to how such individuals should be treated, a
wide margin of appreciation was permitted. In contrast, as the Strasbourg Court had
observed in the *Dudgeon* case:

> [I]n the great majority of the member States of the Council of Europe it is no longer consid-
> ered necessary or appropriate to treat homosexual practices of the kind now in question as in
> themselves a matter to which the sanctions of the criminal law should be applied; the Court
> cannot overlook the marked changes which have occurred in this regard in the domestic law
> of the member States.[126]

In the *X, Y and Z* case,[127] the Strasbourg Court again pointed to the lack of any common European standard, when it ruled that a failure to allow a female-to-male transsexual to be registered as the father of a child born by artificial insemination to his
female partner did not violate Article 8. Although in the past it had held that Article 8
required Contracting Parties to establish legal mechanisms to reinforce a child's stability within the family, these earlier cases had been concerned with family ties between
biological parents and their children. Since there was no generally shared approach
among the Contracting Parties with regard to either the granting of parental rights to
transsexuals or the manner in which the social relationship between a child conceived
by artificial insemination by donor and the 'social father' should be reflected in law,
and since the law in these fields at national level appeared to be in a transitional stage,
it was not for the Court to adopt or impose any single viewpoint; in other words, the
respondent State had to be afforded a wide margin of appreciation.

These cases, where a wide margin of appreciation is allowed because of a lack of
common ground in Europe, can be seen as further examples of the principle that the
nature of the individual right determines the breadth of the margin, since a divergence
in national law may indicate that the nature and degree of importance of the individual interest is still in the process of being understood, recognized, and accepted.

In some cases, the width of the margin allowed to Contracting Parties depends not
so much on the importance to the individual of the rights concerned, but rather on
the nature of the general interest with which they conflict. As the Strasbourg Court
remarked in the *Dudgeon* case, 'the scope of the margin of appreciation is not identical
in respect of each of the aims [set out in the second paragraph of Article 8] justifying
restrictions on a right.'[128]

Thus, in the *Laskey, Jaggard and Brown* case,[129] where the applicants complained
of having been prosecuted and convicted for offences of assault and wounding arising from consensual sado-masochistic activities, the Strasbourg Court judgment

---

[126] *Dudgeon v United Kingdom*, (App. 7525/76), 22 October 1981, Series A No 45, (1982) 4 EHRR 149,
§60.

[127] *X, Y and Z v United Kingdom* (App. 21830/93), 22 April 1997, (1997) 24 EHRR 143, ECHR 1997-II.

[128] *Dudgeon v United Kingdom*, (App. 7525/76), 22 October 1981, Series A No 45, (1982) 4 EHRR 149,
§52.

[129] *Laskey, Jaggard and Brown v United Kingdom* (Apps. 21627/93, 21826/93, and 21974/93), 19 February
1997, (1997) 24 EHRR 39, ECHR 1997-I.

means that Contracting Parties are entitled to seek to regulate practices involving the infliction of physical harm:

The determination of the level of harm that should be tolerated by the law in situations where the victim consents is in the first instance a matter for the State concerned since what is at stake is related, on the one hand, to public health considerations and to the general deterrent effect of the criminal law, and, on the other, to the personal autonomy of the individual.

National security is another area where Contracting Parties are allowed a wide margin, since the protection of large numbers of people is in issue and the information on which such decisions are based is frequently highly sensitive. Thus, in the *Klass* case,[130] the Strasbourg Court, which accepted that the sophistication of modern terrorism entailed that some system of secret surveillance over post and telecommunications might in exceptional circumstances be necessary, allowed a certain discretion to the national legislature as to how such a system should be organized and controlled: it was 'certainly not for the Court to substitute for the assessment of the national authorities any other assessment of what might be the best policy in this field.' Nonetheless, in view of the encroachment on individual rights inherent in such a system, Contracting Parties could not be afforded an unlimited licence but had to satisfy the Court that adequate and effective safeguards were in place.

In the *Leander* case,[131] the applicant complained that he had been excluded from employment in the civil service because he had been registered as a security risk by the police. Since it was undoubtedly necessary, for security reasons, for Contracting Parties to have laws enabling the secret collection and storage of information and to use it when assessing the suitability of candidates for employment in sensitive posts, and since Leander's private life was not affected except in so far as he was prevented from gaining employment as a civil servant (a right which was not as such enshrined in the Convention), the Strasbourg Court accepted that the respondent State should enjoy a wide margin of appreciation, both in assessing the existence of a pressing social need and in choosing the means for achieving the legitimate aim of protecting national security.[132]

It is not only in cases involving national security that the Strasbourg Court allows a wide margin in recognition of the practical realities of certain types of State activity. In child-care cases, for example, the national authorities may frequently be called upon to make extremely difficult and delicate decisions rapidly, for the benefit of the child. In these circumstances, the scope of the discretion allowed to the Contracting Party will vary, depending both on the urgency of the case and the competing interests at stake. Thus, the Strasbourg Court recognizes that the authorities enjoy a wide margin of appreciation in assessing the necessity of taking a child into care. In such cases it considers that it would not be appropriate for it to substitute its own judgment,

---

[130] *Klass v Germany*, (App. 5029/71), 6 September 1978, Series A No 28, (1979–80) 2 EHRR 214, §§48–50.

[131] *Leander v Sweden*, (App. 9248/81), 26 March 1987, Series A No 116, (1987) 9 EHRR 433.

[132] §59.

reached with the benefit of hindsight but without direct contact with the individuals concerned or the prevailing social and cultural conditions.[133] On the other hand, decisions taken in this area often prove to be irreversible: children who have been taken away from their parents may in the course of time establish new bonds which should not be disrupted by renewed parental contact. There is, accordingly, an even greater call than usual for protection against arbitrary interferences.[134] The Strasbourg Court therefore sees its role predominantly as one of reviewing the quality of the decision-making process, including whether relevant and sufficient reasons were given[135] and the parents were consulted if possible.[136] A stricter scrutiny is, however, called for in relation to any further measures such as restrictions on access, not only because these could eradicate the family life shared between parent and child,[137] but also because the public interest in protecting the child carries less weight once the child is in a safe place.

Another area where the Strasbourg Court in principle allows a wide margin to the national authorities is town and country planning. As with the national security and child-care cases, the reasons for this are twofold. First, the public interest, in safeguarding a pleasant environment, is weighty. Secondly, such measures require an appreciation of local, social, economic, and environmental conditions, which the national authorities are best placed to assess.[138] Thus, in the *Gillow* case,[139] the Strasbourg Court took the view that 'the Guernsey legislature is better placed than the international judge to assess the effects of any relaxation of the housing controls.' However, the discretion of a Contracting Party in this field is not unlimited, particularly where important Convention rights, such as the right to respect for a 'home', are in issue. As in the child-care cases referred to above, the Strasbourg Court will pay particular attention to the procedural safeguards in the decision-making process in determining whether the impugned measure falls within the margin of appreciation.[140]

The *Hatton* case[141] concerned an alleged breach of Article 8 arising from exposure to aircraft noise. The Grand Chamber, reversing the decision of the Chamber,[142]

---

[133] *Olsson v Sweden (No. 2)*, (App. 13441/87), 27 November 1992, Series A No 250, (1994) 17 EHRR 134, §90.

[134] *W v United Kingdom*, (App. 9749/82), 8 July 1987, Series A No 121, (1988) 10 EHRR 29.

[135] *Hokkanen v Finland*, (App. 19823/92), 23 September 1994, Series A No 299-A, (1994) 19 EHRR 139, §55.

[136] *W v United Kingdom*, (App. 9749/82), 8 July 1987, Series A No 121, (1988) 10 EHRR 29.

[137] *Johansen v Norway*, (App. 17383/90), 7 August 1996, (1997) 23 EHRR 33, ECHR 1996-III, §64.

[138] And see also *Powell and Rayner v United Kingdom*, (App. 9310/81), 21 February 1990, Series A No 172, (1990) 12 EHRR 355, §44, where the Court ruled that it should not 'substitute for the assessment of the national authorities any other assessment of what might be the best policy in this difficult social and technical sphere [the regulation of aircraft noise]. This is an area where the Contracting States are to be recognized as enjoying a wide margin of appreciation.'

[139] *Gillow v United Kingdom*, (App. 9063/80), 24 November 1986, Series A No 109, (1986) 11 EHRR 355, §56.

[140] *Buckley v United Kingdom* (App. 20348/92), 25 September 1996, (1997) 23 EHRR 101, ECHR 1996-IV, §76.

[141] *Hatton v United Kingdom* (App. 36022/97), 8 July 2003 [GC], (2003) 37 EHRR 611, ECHR 2003-VIII; see also J. Hyam, '*Hatton v United Kingdom* in the Grand Chamber: One Step Forward, Two Steps Back?' [2003] EHRLR 631.

[142] *Hatton v United Kingdom* (App. 36022/97), 2 October 2001, (2001) 34 EHRR 1.

concluded that there was no breach of Article 8. The Grand Chamber was faced with conflicting arguments on the margin of appreciation. The applicants argued that there was a narrow margin of appreciation since rights under Article 8 were in issue, whereas the United Kingdom argued that the margin was wide since the case concerned matters of general policy. The Grand Chamber's answer was as follows:

The Court must consider whether the Government can be said to have struck a fair balance between [the economic interests of the country as a whole] and the conflicting interests of the persons affected by noise disturbances, including the applicants. Environmental protection should be taken into consideration by Governments in acting within their margin of appreciation and by the Court in its review of that margin, but it would not be appropriate for the Court to adopt a special approach in this respect by reference to a special status of environmental human rights. In this context the Court must revert to the question of the scope of the margin of appreciation available to the State when taking policy decisions of the kind at issue.[143]

This approach has been criticized by one commentator for focusing on the circumstances in which the infringement had arisen rather than by reference to the nature of the infringement.[144] However, it should be noted that the Strasbourg Court does not always focus on the effect of the interference on the right in issue, but sometimes focuses on the exception which has been invoked.

Letsas[145] helpfully draws a distinction between two uses of the term 'margin of appreciation. The first, which he labels the substantive concept, addresses the relationship between individual freedoms and collective goals.[146] The second, which he labels the structural concept, addresses the intensity of review by the Strasbourg Court.[147] Letsas observes:

It is my view that much of the confusion and controversy surrounding the margin of appreciation is due to the Court's failure to distinguish between these two ideas in its case-law. The Court uses the same term…both for saying that the applicant did not, as a matter of human rights, have the right he or she claimed, and for saying that it will not substantively review the decision of national authorities as to whether there has been a violation.[148]

The significance of the margin of appreciation in examining the requirement that any restriction be necessary in a democratic society cannot be underestimated. It will be at the heart of nearly all the cases coming before the Strasbourg Court.[149]

---

[143] *Hatton v United Kingdom* (App. 36022/97), 8 July 2003 [GC], (2003) 37 EHRR 611, ECHR 2003-VIII, §122.

[144] J. Hyam, '*Hatton v United Kingdom* in the Grand Chamber: One Step Forward, Two Steps Back?' [2003] EHRLR 631, 638.

[145] G. Letsas, *A Theory of Interpretation of the European Convention on Human Rights* (OUP, Oxford 2007), ch.4.

[146] 85; typified by the limitation clauses in Articles 8–11.

[147] 91; typified by those cases where the Strasbourg Court refuses to intervene because there is no European consensus.

[148] 81.

[149] R. MacDonald, 'The margin of appreciation in the jurisprudence of the European Court of Human Rights' in *Le Droit International à l'heure de sa Codification: études en l'honneur de Roberto Ago* (Giuffré, Milan 1987), 187.

THE POLITICAL ACTIVITIES OF ALIENS

Article 16 provides:

Nothing in Articles 10, 11 and 14 shall be regarded as preventing the High Contracting Parties from imposing restrictions on the political activity of aliens.

This is potentially a very restrictive provision, which could be used to exclude from the application of the Convention those within the jurisdiction of the Contracting States who otherwise enjoy the protection of the Convention. It is not a blanket derogation from the requirements of Articles 10, 11, and 14, but merely permits derogation from the rights contained in those articles which relate to political activity. It is not easy to see how objectionable conduct by those who are not nationals of the State might fall outside the widely drafted limitations discussed earlier in this chapter. This may explain why the provision does not appear to have been used. It has certainly never been considered by the Strasbourg Court.

The Parliamentary Assembly has recommended that the permitted derogation be removed from the Convention.[150]

CONCLUDING REMARKS

The application of the limitations to be found in Articles 8 to 11 (and elsewhere in the Convention) arises with great frequency. Since the majority of cases turn on whether the limitation is 'necessary in a democratic society', the margin of appreciation doctrine is at the heart of the review by the Strasbourg Court of decisions made by Contracting Parties. This brings into play the doctrine of proportionality. It would seem that the margin of appreciation goes to the legitimacy of the aim of the interference in meeting a pressing social need, whereas the doctrine of proportionality concerns the means used to achieve that aim. The two doctrines are, however, intertwined, and many cases illustrate how the principle of proportionality has been used to show that a Contracting Party has gone beyond its margin of appreciation. As a device to protect the value pluralism that is central to the European Convention system, the doctrine has served its purpose well. As a device for providing predictability of outcome in any given case, it remains an indeterminate and elusive doctrine full of complexity in its operation.

---

[150] Recommendation 799 (1977) on the political rights and positions of aliens, 25 January 1977. Council of Europe, Parliamentary Assembly, texts adopted at the 28th ordinary session.

15

PROTECTING FAMILY LIFE

INTRODUCTION

This and the following chapter consider the development of the rights protected by Article 8, which is one of the most open-ended provisions of the Convention.[1] Article 8 provides:

1. Everyone has the right to respect for his private and family life, his home and his correspondence.

2. There shall be no interference by a public authority with the exercise of this right except such as is in accordance with the law and is necessary in a democratic society in the interests of national security, public safety or the economic well-being of the country, for the prevention of disorder or crime, for the protection of health or morals, or for the protection of the rights and freedoms of others.

The protection of the family, as the fundamental unit of society, figures at more than one place in the Convention. Article 12 guarantees the right to marry and to found a family, while Article 8 prohibits, in principle, and subject to the provisions of paragraph (2), interference with an existing family unit. Article 2 of the First Protocol deals with an important aspect of the rights of parents in relation to their children's education. It provides for the right of parents to ensure such education in conformity with their own religious and philosophical convictions.[2]

The right to marry and found a family may be considered as a particular form of family life, but it is separately protected in Article 12, which provides:

Men and women of marriageable age have the right to marry and found a family, according to the national laws governing the exercise of this right.

Article 5 of Protocol 7 adds to the rights in Article 12 by providing for equality of rights and responsibilities of a private law character between spouses, and in their relations with their children.

---

[1] See generally D. Feldman, 'The developing scope of Article 8 of the European Convention on Human Rights' [1997] EHRLR 265; C. Warbrick, 'The structure of Article 8' [1998] EHRLR 32; and U. Kilkelly, *The right to respect for private and family life: a Guide to the implementation of Article 8 of the European Convention on Human Rights,* Human Rights Handbook No. 1 (Council of Europe Publishing, Strasbourg 2003).

[2] See ch.21 below.

The rights protected by Articles 8 and 12, and Article 5 of Protocol 7, are some-what disparate. However, the fact that the rights in Article 8 are grouped together in the same article strengthens the protection given by that article, since each right is reinforced by its context. Thus, the right to respect for family life, the right to respect for private life, and the right to respect for the home and correspondence may be read together as guaranteeing collectively more than the sum of their parts. Subject to that important point, it is now possible to categorize the rights protected by Article 8 in providing a synthesis of the case-law of the Strasbourg Court. This chapter considers matters related to family life, while the following chapter focuses on the protection of private life, as well as respect for the home and correspondence. As with a number of articles, the rights contained in the first paragraph are subject to the limitations set out in the second paragraph. In many cases, the interference will be justifiable on the basis of these limitations.[3]

DEFINING FAMILY LIFE

Respect for family life requires identification of what constitutes a family.[4] The exist-ence, or absence, of family life is essentially a question of fact.[5] A mother and father and children who are dependent on them, including illegitimate and adopted children, constitute a family. Indeed, the Strasbourg Court has said that 'the mutual enjoyment by parent and child of each other's company constitutes a fundamental element of family life.'[6] De facto family ties can arise where parties are living together outside marriage.[7]

It is implicit in the Strasbourg Court's judgment in the *Marckx* case that mar-riage gives rise to a presumption of family life between the husband and wife,[8] even if the couple have not set up home together.[9] In relation to children, family life exists between children and their parents (whether married or not) from the moment of the child's birth. The family ties exist even where the parents are not living together at the time of the child's birth.[10] Only in exceptional circumstances will this bond between

---

[3] For a discussion of the limitations in Articles 8–11, see ch.14 above.

[4] See J. Liddy, 'The concept of family life under the ECHR' [1998] EHRLR 15; and U. Kilkelly, *The Child and the European Convention on Human Rights* (Ashgate, Dartmouth 1999), ch.7.

[5] *K & T v Finland*, (App. 25702/94), 12 July 2001, (2003) 36 EHRR 255, ECHR 2001-VII, §150.

[6] *B v United Kingdom*, (App. 9840/82), 8 July 1987, Series A No 121, (1988) 10 EHRR 87, §60.

[7] *Johnston and others v Ireland*, (App. 9697/82), 18 December 1986, Series A No 112; (1987) 9 EHRR 203, §25.

[8] *Marckx v Belgium*, (App. 6833/74), 13 June 1979, Series A No 31, (1979–80) 2 EHRR 330.

[9] But note the somewhat odd decision in *Şerife Yiğit v Turkey*, (App. 3976/05), 20 January 2009, where a religious marriage was not recognized for certain purposes because Turkish law provided that a religious ceremony performed by an imam did not give rise to any commitments towards third parties or the State.

[10] *Berrehab v Netherlands*, (App. 10730/84), 21 June 1988, Series A No 138, (1989) 11 EHRR 322, §21, and *Keegan v Ireland*, (App. 16969/90), 26 May 1994, Series A No 290, (1994) 18 EHRR 342, §44.

parent and child be broken and family life cease to exist.[11] It is a violation of Article 8 to deny a mother the opportunity to enable recognition of the biological father of her child; a legal presumption that the husband is the father of a child born in wedlock which cannot be denied by the mother may violate Article 8.[12] Relationships between brothers and sisters, taken together with those between parents and children are also covered.[13]

Adoption places the adoptive parents in the same position as biological parents for the purposes of the protection of family life, even where there has been little contact with the adopted child and where the adoption is contested.[14]

The *Emonet* case[15] involved the loss, on adoption, of the parental tie between a mother and daughter under provisions of Swiss law. The applicants were the child, the biological mother, and her cohabitee. Isabelle's mother was living with Roland Emonet, but he was not the father of Isabelle. Her mother had divorced Isabelle's father in 1985. The father had died in 1994. Isabelle came to regard Roland as her father, and Isabelle, her mother and Roland Emonet wished to be a family in the eyes of the law. But the effect of the adoption of Isabelle by Roland was that the parental tie between Isabelle and her mother came to an end. Despite their objections, the Swiss courts refused to make any accommodations to the situation. The position would have been different if Roland and Isabelle's mother had married, but they were cohabiting. The Strasbourg Court noted that the European Convention on the Adoption of Children 1967[16] provided that the rights and obligations between adopted children and their parents should cease on adoption. But the Court also noted the limited number of ratifications to this Convention, and the existence of a draft revised Convention[17] which provided that there would be no loss of parental ties where the adoption was by a spouse or registered partner of the child's parent. According to the Court, respect for the applicants' family life required both the biological and social realities to be taken into account. The automatic and permanent loss of parental rights by the mother in the circumstances of this case served no one's interests, and this situation had not been foreseen in the law. There was a violation of Article 8.

In some circumstances, relations with grandparents may be protected under Article 8.[18] More remote relationships are generally not close enough to constitute

---

[11] *Gül v Switzerland*, (App. 23218/94), 19 February 1996, (1996) 22 EHRR 93, ECHR 1996-I, §32.

[12] *Kroon and others v Netherlands*, (App. 18535/91), 27 October 1994, Series A No 297-C, (1995) 19 EHRR 263, and see further ch.16 below.

[13] *Moustaquim v Belgium*, (App. 12313/86), 18 February 1991, Series A No 193; (1991) 13 EHRR 802, §36.

[14] *Pini and others v Romania*, (Apps. 78028/01 and 78030/01), 22 June 2004, (2005) 40 EHRR 312, ECHR 2004-V, §§136–48.

[15] *Emonet and others v Switzerland*, (App. 39051/03), 13 December 2007, (2009) 49 EHRR 234, ECHR 2007-XIV.

[16] ETS 58, which has been ratified by 18 Contracting Parties.

[17] *Emonet and others v Switzerland*, (App. 39051/03), 13 December 2007), (2009) 49 EHRR 234, ECHR 2007-XIV, §25.

[18] See *Vermeire v Belgium*, (App. 12849/87), 29 November 1991, Series A No 214-C, (1993) 15 EHRR 488, which concerned exclusion of a granddaughter from the estate of a grandparent because of the illegitimate nature of the kinship.

family relationships protected by Article 8, though they might nevertheless fall within the sphere of private life.

In deciding whether a relationship between unmarried adults constitutes family life, the Strasbourg Court has identified a number of factors which should be taken into account:

…whether the couple live together, the length of their relationship and whether they have demonstrated their commitment to each other by having children together or by any other means….[19]

Engagement to marry does not in itself constitute family life, but the Commission has held that the relationship between a prisoner and his fiancée falls within private life.[20] The relationship between homosexual couples falls within the ambit of private life.[21]

The relationship of adult children with their parents concerns their private life, and does not give rise to any positive obligations on the part of a Contracting Party. The question has been left open whether Article 8 guarantees the right of parents to receive support and care from their children as they grow old and in the event of sickness and infirmity.[22]

The *Poluhas Dödsbo* case[23] concerned a complaint that a refusal to permit the removal by the widow of an urn containing the ashes of her husband from one town in Sweden to another. The Strasbourg Court did not consider it necessary to classify whether this constituted an aspect of family life or private life, although it did regard Article 8 as applying to the situation.

The Strasbourg Court's pronouncements on the nature of the family suggest that there is a hierarchy of relationships. At the top of the hierarchy is the traditional heterosexual relationship of married couples, moving through parenting between non-married heterosexual couples down to more removed family relationships at the bottom of the hierarchy. The core family within the case-law of the Strasburg Court is very much a man and a woman with children of whom they are the parents.

POSITIVE OBLIGATIONS AND FAMILY LIFE

The wording of Article 8(1) differs from the wording of Articles 2 to 7. It refers to a right to respect for private and family life, home, and correspondence. The notion of 'respect' is a relatively imprecise one, but the Commission and the Strasbourg Court

---

[19] *Al-Nashif v Bulgaria*, (App. 50963/99), 20 June 2002, (2003) 36 EHRR 655, §112. See also *Kroon and others v Netherlands*, (App. 18535/91), 27 October 1994, Series A No 297-C, (1995) 19 EHRR 263, §30; and *X, Y and Z v United Kingdom*, (App. 21830/93), 22 April 1997, (1997) 24 EHRR 143, ECHR 1997-II, §§36–7.

[20] App. 15817/89, *Wakeford v United Kingdom*, Decision of 1 October 1990; (1990) 66 DR 251.

[21] App. 11716/85, *X v United Kingdom*, Decision of 14 May 1986; (1986) 47 DR 274.

[22] *Şijakova and others v Former Yugoslav Republic of Macedonia*, (App. 67914/01), Decision of 6 March 2003.

[23] *Elli Poluhas Dödsbo v Sweden*, (App.61564/00), 17 January 2006, ECHR 2006-I.

have applied an interpretation which serves to give effect to the continuing evolution of concepts of privacy and family life.[24] Article 8 prohibits arbitrary interferences by a Contracting Party into respect for family and private life, the home, and correspondence.

Positive obligations under Article 8 can arise in two types of situations. The first is where a Contracting Party must take some action to secure respect for the rights included in the article, as distinct from simply refraining from interfering with the rights protected. Examples of this type of case are the immigration cases where a Contracting Party must allow a person to enter or remain in the country. The second type of situation is where a duty arises for a Contracting Party to protect an individual from interferences by other individuals.

An increasing number of cases in which violations of Article 8 are raised concerns positive obligations, although these arise more frequently in the context of the protection of private life. There are many illustrations of such cases appearing in this and the following chapter.

CUSTODY, ACCESS, AND CARE PROCEEDINGS

Many applications under Article 8 concern the relationships of parents and children after marriage breakdown or other family crisis. The issue may arise after the separation or divorce of the parents, when the courts make an order concerning the custody of, or access to, the children. Or it may arise when children are taken into the care of the public authorities.

In these situations, the State authorities are required to balance a number of rights, which may compete or conflict with each other. Each parent, and to a lesser degree other family members such as grandparents,[25] has a right to respect for his or her family ties with the child under Article 8. The child, similarly, has a right to respect for his or her family life. But the best interests of the child may not be in staying with the birth parents. The State also has duties under Articles 8 and 3 to protect the child from emotional, sexual, and physical abuse, and this may mean removing the child quickly from a bad home environment.[26] In all such cases, the overriding interest is the child's safety and well-being.[27]

Unlike the Strasbourg judges, the national social workers and courts will usually have had direct contact with all the people concerned, often at the stage when care measures are being envisaged or immediately after their implementation. The

---

[24] See G. Cohen-Jonathan, 'Respect for private and family life' in R. Macdonald, F. Matscher, and H. Petzold, *The European System for the Protection of Human Rights* (Martinus Nijhoff, Dordrecht 1993), 405.

[25] *Bronda v Italy*, (App. 22430/93), 9 June 1998, (2001) 33 EHRR 81, ECHR 1998-IV, §59.

[26] *Z and others v United Kingdom*, (App. 29392/95), 10 May 2001 [GC], (2002) 34 EHRR 97, ECHR 2001-V.

[27] *K & T v Finland*, (App. 25702/94), 12 July 2001 [GC], (2003) 36 EHRR 255, ECHR 2001-VII, §173.

Strasbourg Court will not be so well placed to assess the personalities, needs, and capacities of the parents and children, and in any event, by the time the case gets to Strasbourg, irreversible decisions may have been made. In assessing the 'necessity' of the measures, the Court does not, therefore, attempt to substitute itself for the domestic authorities but instead reviews their decisions, looking particularly to see whether the reasons given were relevant and sufficient and that the procedure was fair, to ensure that the authorities have not exceeded their margin of appreciation.[28]

This margin of appreciation varies from case to case, depending on the nature of the issues and the seriousness of the interests at stake. The State authorities enjoy a broad margin when it comes to assessing the necessity of taking a child into care, although the fact that a child could be placed in a more beneficial environment for his or her upbringing will not on its own justify a compulsory measure of removal.[29] The margin is, however, narrower in respect of any further limitations which carry the risk of entirely destroying the relationship between parent and child, such as restrictions on access visits or other forms of contact.[30]

The applicants in the *K & T* case[31] were a mother and her male partner. The mother had a history of severe psychotic mental illness and had been hospitalized on a number of occasions. She had two young children from previous relationships and became pregnant again by the second applicant. In the light of expert reports which indicated that the older child's mental health would be damaged by continued contact with her mother, a court order was made placing the older child in her father's care and allowing only very limited, supervised, access to the mother. The applicants subsequently voluntarily placed the younger child, who was showing behavioural problems, in a children's home. There was evidence that the mother behaved inappropriately during visits to the children's home and that the child was disturbed following her visits. Immediately after the third child was born, emergency care orders were made in respect of the baby and the second child. The baby was taken to a children's home within hours of birth and the other child's placement in the home became compulsory. The father was allowed to visit and care for the baby in the home without restriction. The mother, who was again hospitalized for mental health reasons, was allowed to visit the baby if accompanied by a psychiatric nurse. Subsequently a care plan was drawn up placing both the younger children together with foster parents. The father applied for custody of the baby, but his application was refused because, in the light of his continuing relationship with the mother, it was not considered that he would be able properly to care for the baby or guarantee her safety. The applicants were allowed only monthly supervised access visits, to allow the children to settle down with their new family. By the time the children had been in their foster home for a little over a

---

[28] *Olsson v Sweden (No.2)*, (App. 13441/87), 27 November 1992, Series A No 250, §90; and *K & T v Finland*, (App. 25702/94), 12 July 2001 [GC], (2003) 36 EHRR 255, ECHR 2001-VII, §154.

[29] *K & T v Finland*, (App. 25702/94), 12 July 2001 [GC], (2003) 36 EHRR 255, ECHR 2001-VII, §173.

[30] *Johansen v Norway*, (App. 17383/90), 7 August 1996; (1997) 23 EHRR 33, ECHR 1996-III; and *K & T v Finland*, (App. 25702/94), 12 July 2001 [GC], (2003) 36 EHRR 255, ECHR 2001-VII, §155.

[31] *K & T v Finland*, (App. 25702/94), 12 July 2001 [GC], (2003) 36 EHRR 255, ECHR 2001-VII.

year, the mother's health improved and she had a fourth child, whom she was allowed to keep, and she and her partner applied to have the other children returned to their care. The application was refused.

The Grand Chamber examined all of the above compulsory measures separately and the case therefore provides useful guidance as regards a range of restrictions on parental rights. In respect of the emergency care orders, it accepted that it might not always be possible, because of the urgency of the situation or fears about the parents' reactions, to associate them in the decision-making process or give them prior warning. However, the State authorities had to show that a careful assessment of the impact of the proposed care measure on the parents and the children, as well as of the possible alternatives to taking the children into public care, was carried out prior to the implementation of such a measure. The Court emphasized that the taking of a newborn baby into public care at the moment of its birth is an extremely harsh measure, likely to cause great distress to any mother, and requiring extraordinarily compelling reasons in justification. It was not satisfied that such reasons had been shown to exist in the instant case. Both the mother and the baby were in hospital care at the time. The authorities had known about the forthcoming birth for months in advance and were well aware of the mother's mental problems, so that the situation was not an emergency in the sense of being unforeseen. When such a drastic measure was contemplated, it was incumbent on the national authorities first to examine whether alternative methods of protecting the baby would be feasible. There was no evidence that alternatives to removal had been considered.

The Court also criticized the State authorities for failing to take sufficient steps to reunite the family despite evidence of an improvement in the mother's health. In this connection it placed emphasis on 'the guiding principle whereby a care order should be regarded as a temporary measure, to be discontinued as soon as circumstances permit'.[32] It continued by observing that:

> 178. ... The positive duty to take measures to facilitate family reunification as soon as reasonably feasible will begin to weigh on the competent authorities with progressively increasing force as from the commencement of the period of care, subject always to its being balanced against the duty to consider the best interests of the child.

> 179. In the instant case, the Court notes that enquiries were made in order to ascertain whether the applicants would be able to bond with the children.... They did not, however, amount to a serious or sustained effort directed towards facilitating family reunification such as could reasonably be expected for the purposes of Article 8 § 2—especially since they constituted the sole effort on the authorities' part to that effect in the seven years during which the children have been in care. The minimum to be expected of the authorities is to examine the situation anew from time to time to see whether there has been any improvement in the family's situation. The possibilities of reunification will be progressively diminished and

---

[32] *K & T*, §178.

eventually destroyed if the biological parents and the children are not allowed to meet each other at all, or only so rarely that no natural bonding between them is likely to occur. The restrictions and prohibitions imposed on the applicants' access to their children, far from preparing a possible reunification of the family, rather contributed to hindering it. What is striking in the present case is the exceptionally firm negative attitude of the authorities. . . .[33]

Where a care order is implemented in an inappropriate manner, as, for example, where children are dispersed over some distance which renders the objective of reuniting the family difficult to achieve, there may be a violation of respect for family life by such action.[34] A similar conclusion was reached where, for a period of six years, a mother's access to her daughter was restricted and she had no enforceable visiting rights under a regime designed ultimately to reunite the family.[35]

In the *RK and AK* case,[36] the applicants, who were Pushto speakers and had difficulties in speaking and understanding English, brought their two-month-old daughter to the hospital with a fracture to her arm. The parents were interviewed without an interpreter by a consultant paediatrician, who concluded that it was a non-accidental injury. When the child was ready to be discharged from hospital, a care order was made placing her in the care of her aunt, who lived near the parents. The parents were permitted supervised access. They contested the care order but, following a hearing where they gave evidence through an interpreter, the judge concluded that they were lying and were concealing information about how the child had come by the injury. Some months later the child sustained another fracture while in her aunt's care. Further tests were carried out and she was diagnosed with brittle bone disease. Further expert reports confirmed that this was likely to have been the cause of the first injury and the care order was discharged. The applicants complained about the care order under Article 8. The Court found no violation, commenting that:

. . . mistaken judgments or assessments by professionals do not *per se* render child-care measures incompatible with the requirements of Article 8. The authorities, medical and social, have duties to protect children and cannot be held liable every time genuine and reasonably-held concerns about the safety of children *vis-à-vis* members of their families are proved, retrospectively, to have been misguided.[37]

There may also be a violation of Article 8 if no adequate steps are taken to enable a non-custodial parent to have access to a child.[38] Where paternal access is sought to a child

[33] §§178–9.

[34] *Olsson v Sweden (No. 1)*, (App. 10465/83), 24 March 1988, Series A No 130, (1989) 11 EHRR 259.

[35] *Eriksson v Sweden*, (App. 11373/85), 22 June 1989, Series A No 156, (1990) 12 EHRR 183. See also *Margareta and Roger Andersson v Sweden*, (App. 12963/87), 25 February 1992, Series A No 226-A, (1992) 14 EHRR 615. Contrast *Rieme v Sweden*, (App. 12366/86), 22 April 1992, Series A No 226-B, (1992) 16 EHRR 155, and *Olsson v Sweden (No.2)*, (App. 13441/87), 27 November 1992, Series A No 250. See also *Johansen v Norway*, (App. 17383/90), 7 August 1996; (1997) 23 EHRR 33, ECHR 1996-III; and *L v Finland*, (App. 25651/94), 27 April 2000; (2001) 31 EHRR 737.

[36] *RK and AK v United Kingdom*, (App. 38000/05), 30 September 2008.   [37] §36.

[38] *Nuutinen v Finland*, (App. 32842/96), 27 June 2000; (2002) 34 EHRR 358, ECHR 2000-VIII.

born outside marriage, securing family life for the father can involve competing interests with the mother and with the child. In the *Elsholz* case,[39] the Strasbourg Court
stressed the wide margin of appreciation to be accorded to the national authorities
in assessing the necessity to take a child into care, but that a narrower margin would
apply where access by the absent parent following a family breakdown was involved.
The views of the child will be particularly important, but expert psychological evidence should be available to evaluate such views. If such safeguards are not present,
then the involvement of the father in crucial decisions relating to his access to his
child will not alone be sufficient to meet the requirements of respect for the family
life of himself and his child. This approach has been approved by a majority judgment
of the Grand Chamber.[40] Whether the decision-making process sufficiently protects
the interests of a parent will depend upon the circumstances of each case. The Grand
Chamber in the *Sommerfield* case[41] did not regard it as necessary to obtain an expert
psychological report where views had been expressed by a daughter at the ages of 10,
11, and 13. Three dissenting judges considered that the Convention did require such
evidence even in the case of a child of this age.

The applicant in the *Keegan* case[42] was the father of a daughter by his unmarried
partner. The case concerned the adoption of the daughter against the wishes of the
natural father, who complained that this violated his rights under Article 8. The relationship between the mother and father had broken down shortly after the mother had
become pregnant. The father visited the newborn baby at the nursing home where she
was born, but was subsequently denied access when he tried to visit the child at the
home of his former partner's parents. The mother made arrangements for the child
to be adopted, and the child was subsequently placed by a registered adoption society
with prospective adoptive parents. The applicant was advised of these actions by letter
from his former partner after the child had been placed with the prospective adoptive
parents. The applicant sought appointment from the courts as guardian of the child,
and to be granted custody of the child. A decision by the courts to appoint the applicant guardian and to award him custody of the child was appealed by the mother and
the prospective adoptive parents. In the meantime the child remained with the adoptive parents. Following a decision in favour of the father, a case was stated for the opinion of the Irish Supreme Court. The majority decision of the Supreme Court was that
only married fathers were entitled to apply to be appointed as guardian, and the matter
was referred back to the High Court. The decision was that the child should remain
with the adoptive parents. An adoption order was subsequently made in respect of the
child.

Noting that the birth of the child was not the result of casual sex but 'was the fruit of
a planned decision taken in the context of a loving relationship', the Strasbourg Court

---

[39] *Elsholz v Germany*, (App. 25735/94), 13 July 2000 [GC], (2002) 34 EHRR 1412, ECHR 2000-VIII.
[40] *Sahin v Germany*, (App. 30943/96), 8 July 2003 [GC], ECHR 2003-VIII.
[41] *Sommerfield v Germany*, (App. 31871/96), 8 July 2003 [GC], (2004) 38 EHRR 756, ECHR 2003-VIII.
[42] *Keegan v Ireland*, (App. 16969/90), 26 May 1994, Series A No 290, (1994) 18 EHRR 342.

concluded that there was family life in this case.[43] The question was whether a process of adoption which allowed no involvement by the father could be justified.

The Strasbourg Court found that the procedure could not be justified by the limitations in paragraph (2). The Court was clearly influenced by the existence of a sequence of events the outcome of which 'was likely to prove to be irreversible'.[44] The Strasbourg Court places great stress on the quality of the procedure by which adoption decisions are taken, because decisions on adoption are generally irreversible. The procedure must involve participation by the biological parent even where that parent has a severe mental illness.[45]

THE RIGHT TO ADOPT

The Strasbourg Court has held that the Convention does not include a right to adopt a child.[46] Adoption means 'providing a child with a family, not a family with a child'[47] Where there are competing interests between those of the child and of those seeking to adopt, then the best interests of the child will be key in determining how those competing interests are to be resolved.

The circumstances of the *Pini* case[48] are rather sad. Two Italian couples had agreed to adopt Romanian children who had been placed for adoption following their abandonment by their parents. Adoption orders were made when the children were nine years old; they had had very little contact with their adoptive parents and the adoption orders were challenged in the Romanian courts by the CEPSB,[49] and by the children. It seems that the adoption was not the wish of the children (who by this time were more than ten years old). This was to have a decisive impact upon the Strasbourg Court's conclusions on compliance with Article 8. The Court said:

The Court has consistently held that particular importance must be attached to the best interests of the child in ascertaining whether the national authorities have taken all the necessary steps that can reasonably be demanded to facilitate the reunion of the child and his or her parents. In particular, it has held in such matters that the child's interests may, depending on their nature and seriousness, override those of the parent. . . . The Court considers that it is even more important that the child's interests should prevail over those of the parents in

---

[43] §§44–5.   [44] §55. See also *Todorova v Italy*, (App. 33932/06), 13 January 2009.

[45] *X v Croatia*, (App. 11223/04), 17 July 2008.

[46] *Fretté v France*, (App. 36515/97), 26 February 2002, (2004) 38 EHRR 438, ECHR 2002-I. This case concerned a situation where an application to adopt had been rejected solely on the basis of the applicant's sexual orientation; the complaint was raised under Art. 14 read in conjunction with Art. 8.

[47] §42.

[48] *Pini and others v Romania*, (Apps. 78028/01 and 78030/01), 22 June 2004, (2005) 40 EHRR 312, ECHR 2004-V.

[49] Poiana Soarelui Educational Centre in Braşov, which was an agency with whom the Child Welfare Board had placed the children when they were abandoned. See §130 for a brief description of the role of CEPSB. There is a suggestion that the Centre was opposed to the adoption of Romanian children by non-nationals.

the case of a relationship based on adoption, since, as it has previously held, adoption means 'providing a child with a family, not a family with a child'.[50]

The Strasbourg Court concluded that the Romanian authorities had not violated Article 8 in the manner in which it dealt with the applicants' efforts to secure the delivery of the children to them.

INHERITANCE RIGHTS

In the *Marckx* case[51] the Strasbourg Court accepted that rights of succession between near relatives came within the sphere of family life.

In the *Pla and Puncernau* case,[52] the Strasbourg Court faced, for the first time, a case involving inheritance rights in the private sphere, that is, in the context of the freedom to leave property to persons of your choice. The dispute arose in the context of a will made in Andorra which, as interpreted by the courts of Andorra, operated to exclude adopted children from succession. It was argued that the sole purpose of the contested clause in the will was to exclude only illegitimate children from entitlement to inherit the testatrix's property. Though the applicants claimed a violation of Article 8 taken alone, as well as of Article 8 when read in conjunction with Article 14, the Court begins by dealing with the second complaint first 'since the issue of alleged discriminatory treatment ... is at the heart of the applicants' complaint'.[53] The Strasbourg Court is at pains to stress that it bases its decision on the interpretation by the Andorran courts of the will in issue, and not with the freedom of the testatrix to dispose of her property as she wished. The Court, by five votes to two, concluded that there had been a violation of Article 8 when read with Article 14. The national court's interpretation amounted to a judicial deprivation of an adopted child's inheritance rights; it was 'blatantly inconsistent with the prohibition of discrimination established by Article 14'. It was not therefore necessary to consider separately the question of whether there had been a violation of Article 8 taken alone.

Many cases involving rights of inheritance are pleaded under Article 1 of Protocol 1 and Article 14.[54]

THE FAMILY LIFE OF NON-NATIONALS

Action by the authorities, such as expelling a person from a country, or refusing to admit someone, may result in separation of husband and wife, or of parents and children. When expulsion or refusal of admission is the source of the complaint,

---

[50] *Pini and others v Romania*, (Apps. 78028/01 and 78030/01), 22 June 2004, (2005) 40 EHRR 312, ECHR 2004-V, §§155–6.
[51] *Marckx v Belgium*, (App. 6833/74), 13 June 1979, Series A No 31, (1979–80) 2 EHRR 330.
[52] *Pla and Puncernau v Andorra*, (App. 69498/01), 13 July 2004, (2006) 42 EHRR 522, ECHR 2004-VIII.
[53] §42.   [54] See ch.24 below on Art.14.

that action of itself cannot constitute a breach of the Convention. The Convention does not guarantee, at any rate outside the Fourth Protocol, any right to reside in a particular country. The Strasbourg Court has repeatedly stated that 'no right of an alien to enter or reside in a particular country is as such guaranteed by the Convention.'[55] But, as in the *East African Asians* cases,[56] the question may arise whether, for example, a refusal of admission does not infringe some other right which is guaranteed. Thus, while the right to reside in a particular country is not, as such, guaranteed by the Convention, it is necessary to examine complaints of expulsion or of refusal of admission in relation to Article 8 where such a measure might disrupt the family unit. The interests of preserving family life may also be relevant when decisions to deport someone arise. Such questions can involve the protection of private life as well as of family life.[57]

Where there has been an interference with family life by reason of an exclusion or deportation, that decision must be made 'in accordance with law', which requires a legal basis that is accessible and foreseeable. There must be some measures of legal protection in domestic law against arbitrary action by the authorities. The Strasbourg Court refers to this as the 'quality of law criterion'.[58] The level of protection provided within the national legal order will depend on the nature and extent of the interference with family life.[59] Safeguards will be required even in cases involving national security, since the individual must be able to challenge the executive's assertion that national security is at stake.[60]

In the *CG* case[61] a Turkish national living in Bulgaria with his wife and daughter was made the subject of a deportation order and summarily deported to Turkey. It was said that his residence permit was withdrawn because he was a threat to national security; he was, in fact, believed to be involved in drug dealing. The Strasbourg Court considered that, in this context, Article 8 required that deportation measures should be subject to some form of adversarial proceedings before an independent authority competent to scrutinize the reasons put forward for the deportation. The information in that case was the result of secret surveillance procedures which may themselves have been in breach of Article 8. In finding a violation of Article 8, the Strasbourg Court said:

---

[55] For example, *Al-Nashif v Bulgaria*, (App. 50963/99), 20 June 2002, (2003) 36 EHRR 655, §114.

[56] Apps. 4403–19/70, 4422/70, 4434/70, 4476–8/70, 4486/70, 4501/70, 4526–30/70, *East African Asians v United Kingdom*, Decision of the Commission, 10 and 18 October 1970, (1970) 13 *Yearbook* 928; Report of the Commission, 14 December 1973, (1994) 78-A DR 5; Committee of Ministers' Resolution DH (77) 2 of 21 October 1977, (1977) 20 *Yearbook* 642; and Committee of Ministers' Resolution DH (94) 30 of 21 March 1994, (1994) 78-A DR 70, deciding to make the Report of the Commission public at the request of the United Kingdom Government.

[57] *Dalia v France*, (App. 26102/95), 19 February 1998, (2001) 33 EHRR 26, ECHR 1998-I, §§43–5; and *Slivenko v Latvia*, (App. 48321/99), 9 October 2003 [GC], (2004) 39 EHRR 490, ECHR 2003-X, §95; and see discussion in ch.16 below.

[58] *Al-Nashif v Bulgaria*, (App. 50963/99), 20 June 2002, (2003) 36 EHRR 655, §121.

[59] *PG and JH v United Kingdom*, (App. 44787/98), 25 September 2001, ECHR 2001-IX, §46.

[60] *Al-Nashif v Bulgaria*, (App. 50963/99), 20 June 2002, (2003) 36 EHRR 655, §§123–4.

[61] *CG and others v Bulgaria*, (App. 1365/07), 24 April 2008. See also *Lupsa v Romania*, (App. 10337/04), 8 June 2006, ECHR 2006-VII; and *Liu v Russia*, (App. 42086/05), 6 December 2007.

While actions taken in the interests of national security may, in view of the sensitivity of the subject-matter, attract considerably less in terms of guarantees than might otherwise be the case, an expulsion designed to forestall lesser evils such as run-of-the-mill criminal activities may have to be reviewed in proceedings providing a higher degree of protection of the individual.[62]

There was patently in this case an absence of protection from arbitrary action by the State.

The *Al-Nashif* case[63] concerned a stateless man of Palestinian origin who was living in Bulgaria with his wife and children. He was prosecuted and subsequently deported seemingly for engaging in certain religious activities: teaching the Muslim religion without authority and being linked to a fundamentalist organization. The basis of the decision to deport was not made known to the applicant or his lawyers, and the decisions could be taken without following any form of adversarial process. The Strasbourg Court by four votes to three determined that there was a lack of required safeguards against arbitrary action. The dissenting judges were concerned at the elevation of the procedural requirements to a separate issue, noting that earlier case-law had regarded the quality of the decision-making process as a matter going to the question of the proportionality of the decision to deport.

If the quality of law criterion is satisfied, the Strasbourg Court will go on to consider whether the deportation or exclusion serves a legitimate aim. This has not generally proved problematic. In the most commonly met cases in which the applicant has become involved in some criminal activity, the measure will serve the purpose of being for the prevention of disorder or crime.

Finally, the Strasbourg Court will decide whether the deportation or exclusion is necessary in a democratic society, which requires the Contracting Party to show that the action is justified by a pressing social need and is proportionate to the aim pursued.[64] In the *Boultif* case,[65] the Strasbourg Court laid down guiding principles in order to examine whether a measure of expulsion was necessary in a democratic society:

In assessing the relevant criteria in such a case, the Court will consider the nature and seriousness of the offence committed by the applicant; the duration of the applicant's stay in the country from which he is going to be expelled; the time which has elapsed since the commission of the offence and the applicant's conduct during that period; the nationalities of the various persons concerned; the applicant's family situation, such as the length of the marriage; other factors revealing whether the couple lead a real and genuine family life; whether the spouse knew about the offence at the time when he or she entered into a family relationship; and whether there are children in the marriage and, if so, their age. Not least, the Court will also consider the seriousness of the difficulties which the spouse would be

---

[62] *CG*, §45.

[63] *Al-Nashif v Bulgaria*, (App. 50963/99), 20 June 2002, (2003) 36 EHRR 655.

[64] *Mehemi v France*, (App. 25017/94), 26 September 1997, (2000) 30 EHRR 739, ECHR 1997-VI, §34; and *Dalia v France* (App. 26102/95), 19 February 1998, (2001) 33 EHRR 26, ECHR 1998-I, §52.

[65] *Boultif v Switzerland*, (App. 54273/00), 2 August 2001, (2001) 33 EHRR 1179, ECHR 2001-IX.

likely to encounter in the applicant's country of origin, although the mere fact that a person might face certain difficulties in accompanying her or his spouse cannot in itself preclude expulsion.[66]

Boultif was an Algerian national living in Switzerland with his Swiss wife. He was prosecuted, convicted and imprisoned for the offences of robbery and damage to property (committed sixteen months after his entry into Switzerland) which are described as 'particularly ruthless and brutal'. His behaviour in prison appears to have been exemplary, and he was in work following his release from prison. His residence permit was then withdrawn; he moved to Italy. The Strasbourg Court considered that the seriousness of his offence in terms of his being a continuing danger was mitigated by his conduct in prison and on his release. The Court then considered whether the family could establish their family life elsewhere. Algeria was considered but rejected: the wife had never lived there, and though she speaks French did not speak Arabic. It could not be expected that she would follow her husband to Algeria. The establishment of family life in Italy was also considered, but the applicant's current residence in Italy was unlawful and the Court did not consider that family life could be established there. The Court concluded, unanimously, that there had been a serious impediment to family life, since it was practically impossible for the applicant to live his family life outside Switzerland. The interference was accordingly not proportionate to the aim of the prevention of disorder and crime.[67]

The question of the nature and extent of a person's family life will be determined in the light of the position obtaining at the time when any exclusion order becomes final.[68] The *Maslov* case[69] concerned the deportation of a seventeen-year-old who had lived in Austria since the age of six and had been convicted of a string of burglaries. The Grand Chamber ruled that, although Article 8 provides no absolute protection against expulsion for any category of non-national, including those where were born in the host country or moved there in their early childhood, very serious reasons would be required for the removal of a settled migrant who has lawfully spent all or the major part of his or her childhood and youth in the host country.[70]

In the *Moustaquim* case[71] the applicant, a Moroccan national, who had lived in Belgium since the age of two, was successful in arguing that deportation would interfere

---

[66] §48. See also *Amrollahi v Denmark* (App. 56811/00), 11 July 2002, §35.

[67] For an example of a case where consideration of these factors resulted in a decision that there was no violation of Article 8, see *Üner v Netherlands*, (App. 46410/99), 18 October 2006 [GC], (2007) 45 EHRR 421, ECHR 2006-XII.

[68] *Maslov v Austria*, (App. 1638/03), 23 June 2008 [GC], ECHR 2008-nyr, §61.

[69] *Maslov v Austria*, (App. 1638/03), 23 June 2008 [GC], ECHR 2008-nyr. See also R. Cholewinski, 'Strasbourg's "Hidden Agenda"? The Protection of Second-Generation Migrants from Expulsion under Art. 8 of the ECHR' (1994) 3 NQHR 287.

[70] §75; the Strasbourg Court joins consideration of rights flowing from family life and private life in this judgment.

[71] *Moustaquim v Belgium*, (App. 12313/86), 18 February 1991, Series A No 193, (1991) 13 EHRR 802.

with his family life by depriving him of contact with his parents and brothers and sisters.[72]

In the *Nasri* case,[73] the Strasbourg Court ruled that execution of a deportation order against an Algerian national violated his right to family life, because it would be disproportionate in the exceptional circumstances of the particular case. The applicant was deaf and without speech from birth, had lived virtually all his life in France with his parents and eight siblings, was illiterate, could not read, and did not know a recognized sign language, but had been convicted of gang rape.

In the *Al-Nashif* case, the Strasbourg Court said:

Where immigration is concerned, Article 8 cannot be considered to impose on a State a general obligation to respect the choice by married couples of the country of their matrimonial residence and to authorize family reunion in its territory.

However, the removal of a person from a country where close members of his family are living may amount to an infringement of the right to respect for family life as guaranteed by Article 8(1) of the Convention.[74]

The Strasbourg Court has recognized the State's margin of appreciation in such cases, but has increasingly subjected this to supervision at the European level. This will involve a consideration of whether the exclusion measure strikes a fair balance between the individual's rights under the Convention and the wider interests of the community.[75]

There have, for example, been many cases where the applicant complains of being separated from his wife as a result of his expulsion from the country where they lived together, or as a result of his not being allowed entry or permanent admission to the country in which she lives. In such cases the Strasbourg Court (and, in its time, the Commission) has first examined whether there existed an effective family life between the members of the family concerned. This normally requires two elements: a close relationship; and one between persons who have been living together at the time of, or shortly before, the alleged interference. Over time the Strasbourg Court has developed a notion of the core or nuclear family whose unity is protected under Article 8 independently of the length of its existence.[76] By contrast, wider family ties have been recognized as forming part of private life, but such ties only come into existence after the passage of time and tend to become more significant the longer a person has lived in a country and developed the wider network of family ties.[77]

---

[72] See also *Beldjoudi v France*, (App. 12083/86), 26 March 1992, Series A No 234-A, (1992) 14 EHRR 801; *Djeroud v France*, (App. 13446/87), 23 January 1991, Series A No 191-B, (1992) 14 EHRR 68; *Boughanemi v France* (App. 22070/93) 24 April 1996, (1996) 22 EHRR 228, ECHR 1996-II; and *Gül v Switzerland*, (App. 23218/94), 19 February 1996; (1996) 22 EHRR 93, ECHR 1996-I.

[73] *Nasri v France*, (App. 19465/92), 13 July 1995, Series A No 324, (1996) 21 EHRR 458. See also *Ezzouhdi v France*, (App. 47160/99), 6 February 2001; and *Boultif v Switzerland*, (App. 54273/00), 2 August 2001, (2001) 33 EHRR 1179, ECHR 2001-IX.

[74] *Al-Nashif v Bulgaria*, (App. 50963/99), 20 June 2002, (2003) 36 EHRR 655, §114.

[75] *Maslov v Austria*, (App. 1638/03), 23 June 2008 [GC], ECHR 2008-nyr, §76.

[76] *X v Croatia*, (App. 11223/04), 17 July 2008, §37.

[77] See D. Thym, 'Respect for Private and Family Life under Article 8 ECHR in Immigration Cases: a Human Right to Regularize Illegal Stay?' (2008) 57 ICLQ 87. See also discussion in relation to the protection of private life and immigration issues in ch.16 below.

Similar considerations may apply to decisions on entry. If it is doubtful whether the family could establish itself elsewhere, and members of the family are seeking to join other members of the family in the territory of a Contracting Party, then the complaint must be examined on the merits. This was the situation in two applications in the first group of *East African Asians* cases.[78] In each of the two, the applicant had been refused permission to enter the United Kingdom from Uganda to join his wife, who had lawfully entered the United Kingdom, in one case with six children, some time previously. The complaints were declared admissible, but shortly afterwards all the applicants in this group of cases were admitted for permanent residence.

The conclusion seems to be that the Convention does not *guarantee* the right to family life in a particular country, but only an effective family life as such, no matter where. This principle, however, appears to be modified in the case of the relationships between parents and their children if the latter are not admitted to the country where the former have their residence.

It would seem to follow that, while the admission of a person to permanent residence may not imply any obligation to admit the spouse (present or future), it may imply an obligation to admit any dependent children. The issue of the admission of spouses of those permanently settled was raised by the Strasbourg Court in the *Abdulaziz, Cabales and Balkandali* cases[79] where three women applicants lawfully and permanently settled in the United Kingdom who had subsequently married husbands from their countries of origin complained that the refusal of the British authorities to permit their husbands to join them in the United Kingdom constituted a violation of Article 8. In the face of a submission from the United Kingdom that the issue raised concerned immigration control for which Protocol 4 (to which the United Kingdom is not a party) alone made provision, the Court stated that the Convention and its Protocols must be read as a whole; it did not follow that because a Contracting Party had not ratified a part of the Convention concerned with immigration that those parts of the Convention to which they were a party and which touched on measures taken in that field would not be applicable. The Court noted that the nature of the application was that the wives (who were settled in the United Kingdom) were complaining that they were threatened with deprivation of the society of their spouses.

The United Kingdom advanced two further arguments. First, there was no family life to protect, since the couples had never established homes together; and, secondly, there was no obstacle to the couples living together in the countries of their husband's residence and the claim was, in effect, a claim to choose their country of residence.

---

[78] Apps. 4403–19/70, 4422/70, 4434/70, 4476–8/70, 4486/70, 4501/70, 4526–30/70, *East African Asians v United Kingdom*, Decision of the Commission, 10 and 18 October 1970, (1970) 13 *Yearbook* 928, at 1004; see also Report of the Commission, 14 December 1973, (1994) 78-A DR 5; Committee of Ministers Resolution DH (77) 2 of 21 October 1977, (1977) 20 *Yearbook* 642; and Committee of Ministers Resolution DH (94) 30 of 21 March 1994, (1994) 78-A DR 70.

[79] *Abdulaziz, Cabales and Balkandali v United Kingdom*, (Apps. 9214/80, 9473/81, and 9474/81), 28 May 1985, Series A No 94, (1985) 7 EHRR 471.

The Court recalled that it had said in the *Marckx* case[80] that Article 8 presupposes the existence of a family, but considered that marriage established a family life between husband and wife that was protected by the Convention even if the couple had not yet set up home together. Cohabitation was seen as a normal incident of marriage; all three couples had cohabited, and one had a son. This was sufficient to establish the family life protected by the article. The Strasbourg Court, differing from the Commission, went on to consider whether there was a violation of Article 8 taken alone in these circumstances. The Court confirmed that in the circumstances presented by the applicants, there was no violation of Article 8 taken alone:

The duty imposed by Article 8 cannot be considered as extending to a general obligation on the part of a Contracting State to respect the choice by married couples of the country of their matrimonial residence and to accept the non-national spouses for settlement in that country.[81]

A final point that has arisen in some of these cases is whether the immigration laws involve an element of discrimination based on sex which might raise an issue under Article 14 taken together with Article 8. In the United Kingdom, as in other European countries, the rule is frequently applied that a woman may normally be admitted to join her husband, but that only exceptionally may a man be admitted to join his wife. In the *East African Asians* cases, the Government submitted that the place of residence of a family is normally the place of residence of the husband, and that Article 8 does not safeguard any right for husband and wife to live together permanently in any other place than the place of residence of the husband, or at a place where he is entitled to be.[82] The question is whether such differential treatment of men and women in this field is justifiable under Article 14, or whether it constitutes discrimination under that article.

The question of discrimination on grounds of sex was also raised in the *Abdulaziz, Cabales and Balkandali* cases[83] since it was easier for a man settled in the United Kingdom to be joined by his wife than for a woman to be joined by her husband. The Court found a violation of Article 8 taken together with Article 14.

Where a marriage ends, immigration issues can also arise. In the *Berrehab* case[84] a Moroccan national became divorced from his Dutch wife; the couple had a daughter who was born after the couple had ceased living together, though Mr Berrehab saw her regularly over a number of years. Following the divorce, he was then refused a residence permit and complained that this violated his family life under Article 8. The Strasbourg Court held that Article 8 was applicable and rejected an argument that Berrehab could travel from Morocco to the Netherlands to see his daughter. The Dutch

---

[80] *Marckx v Belgium*, (App. 6833/74), 13 June 1979, Series A No 31, (1979–80) 2 EHRR 330.

[81] *Abdulaziz, Cabales and Balkandali v United Kingdom*, (Apps. 9214/80, 9473/81, and 9474/81), 28 May 1985, Series A No 94, (1985) 7 EHRR 471, §68.

[82] (1970) 13 *Yearbook* 928, 978, cf. 1004.

[83] *Abdulaziz, Cabales and Balkandali v United Kingdom*, (Apps. 9214/80, 9473/81, and 9474/81), 28 May 1985, Series A No 94, (1985) 7 EHRR 471.

[84] *Berrehab v Netherlands*, (App. 10730/84), 21 June 1988, Series A No 138, (1989) 11 EHRR 322.

authorities relied on the exception in paragraph (2) in the interests of public order. The Court concluded that the exclusion of Berrehab in these circumstances was excessive in protecting public order and so constituted a violation of Article 8.

THE FAMILY LIFE OF PRISONERS

Applicants detained in prison have frequently complained of interference with the right to respect for family life. Some have complained that they have been refused permission to have visits from their children.[85] The Commission frequently rejected such complaints under paragraph (2), for example on the ground that such interference with family life was necessary for the prevention of crime.[86]

The issue was raised before the Strasbourg Court in the *Boyle and Rice* case in the context of a complaint of a violation of Article 13.[87] The Court said:

When assessing the obligations imposed on the Contracting Parties by Article 8 in relation to prison visits, regard must be had to the ordinary and reasonable requirements of imprisonment and to the resultant degree of discretion which the national authorities must be allowed in regulating a prisoner's contact with his family.[88]

The Court found that there was no arguable complaint where a prisoner in the lowest security category was allowed twelve visits a year of one hour's duration.[89]

The *Moiseyev* case[90] concerned an applicant convicted and sentenced to four years and six months' imprisonment in a strict security correctional colony. Initially no visits from his family were permitted during the first nine months following his arrest. Thereafter two visits per month of one hour each were allowed. During these visits, he was separated from his wife and daughter by a glass partition and a prison warden was present. For periods totalling seven months while his appeals were being examined, visits were suspended altogether. The Strasbourg Court found that the refusal of family visits had not been determined by reference to a law whose application was foreseeable, since the law conferred an unfettered discretion on the investigator without defining in any way the circumstances in which visits could be refused.

The Strasbourg Court next considered the limitations on the frequency and duration of visits. Such limitations were, in the circumstances of this case, not proportionate to the aim of preventing disorder or crime. The applicant's circumstances could be

---

[85] See, for example, *Ostrovar v Moldova*, (App. 35207/03), 13 September 2005.

[86] App. 1983/63, *X v Netherlands*, Decision of 13 December 1965, (1966) 18 CD 19; cf. App. 2515/65, *X v Federal Republic of Germany*, Decision of 23 May 1966, (1966) 20 CD 28.

[87] *Boyle and Rice v United Kingdom*, (Apps. 9659/82 and 9658/82), 27 April 1988, Series A No 131, (1988) 10 EHRR 425.

[88] §74.

[89] See also *Messina v Italy (No. 2)* (App. 25498/94), 28 September 2000, ECHR 2000-X.

[90] *Moiseyev v Russia*, (App. 62936/00), 9 October 2008.

distinguished from certain Italian cases which involved imprisoned Mafia members.[91] Finally, the Court ruled that separation of visitors by a glass screen could only be justified if there was an established security risk.[92] The imposition of such a measure was disproportionate and constituted a violation of Article 8.

However, a refusal to grant compassionate leave to attend the funeral of the prisoner's father may breach respect for family life in Article 8.[93]

The Grand Chamber has given further consideration to the family life of prisoners in the *Dickson* case.[94] The applicants were a married couple. Kirk Dickson had been convicted of murder in 1994 and sentenced to life imprisonment with a direction that the minimum term to be served was fifteen years. He met Lorraine through a prison pen-pal network while he was in prison, and in 2001, they married. The couple requested artificial insemination facilities to enable them to have a child together, arguing that a combination of the length of his sentence and her age meant that this was the only way in which they could have a child. The Secretary of State has a discretion in such matters, but did not consider that there were exceptional circumstances which would warrant granting the application. It was refused. The applicants complained of a violation of Article 8 and 12.[95] The Grand Chamber ruled, citing its judgment in the *Hirst* case,[96] that automatic forfeiture of rights should not attend imprisonment purely on the ground that public opinion might be offended by accommodations made for prisoners, although it did accept that maintaining public confidence in the penal system had a role to play in the establishment of penal policy. Equally, the Grand Chamber acknowledged that consideration of the welfare of any child conceived in the circumstances of this case was relevant. The Grand Chamber was, however, clearly influenced by the fact that 30 Contracting Parties permitted conjugal visits,[97] although it did not consider that Contracting Parties were under any obligation to make provision for such visits. In concluding by twelve votes to five that there had been a violation of Article 8, the Grand Chamber felt that the exceptional circumstances threshold had been set too high, and that there had not been any proper consideration of the balance to be struck. Furthermore the policy was not embodied in primary legislation, which meant that the various competing interests had never been fully weighed, nor proportionality assessed, by Parliament.

---

[91] Such as *Messina v Italy (No. 2)*, (App. 25498/94), 28 September 2000, ECHR 2000-X.

[92] *Ciorap v Moldova*, (App. 12066/02), 19 June 2007, §117.

[93] *Czarnowski v Poland*, (App. 28586/03), 20 January 2009.

[94] *Dickson v United Kingdom*, (App. 44362/04), 4 December 2007 [GC], (2008) 46 EHRR 927, ECHR 2007-XIII.

[95] The Grand Chamber ruled that no separate issue under Article 12 arose.

[96] *Hirst v United Kingdom (No. 2)*, (App. 74025/01), 6 October 2005 [GC], (2006) 42 EHRR 849, ECHR 2005-IX; discussed in ch.16 below.

[97] Which, of course, obviated the need to making artificial insemination facilities available.

THE RIGHT TO MARRY AND FOUND A FAMILY

Article 12 guarantees the right to marry and to found a family. These rights are not subject to limitations of the kind set out in paragraph (2) of Articles 8 to 11. Instead, limitations are to be found in the provision that men and women of marriageable age have the right to marry and to found a family, 'according to the national laws governing the exercise of this right'.

The scope of this qualification is not clear. It is evident that the exercise of the rights guaranteed cannot be wholly governed by national law. In that case, the protection of Article 12 would extend only to cases where there was a breach of national law. But the purpose of the Convention, here as elsewhere, is to guarantee certain human rights irrespective of the provisions of national law.[98] The correct view, therefore, is that Article 12 imposes an obligation to recognize, both in principle and in practice, the right to marry and to found a family. This obligation implies that the restrictions placed on these rights by national law must be imposed for a legitimate purpose, for example, to prevent polygamy or incest, and must not go beyond a reasonable limit to attain that purpose. On the other hand, the precise scope of the restrictions may vary among the Contracting Parties, as does, for example, marriageable age.

In the *B and L* case[99] the Strasbourg Court was asked to consider the rules in the United Kingdom which prohibited a marriage between a father-in-law and a daughter-in-law unless the former husband and the mother of the former husband had died. The purpose of the restriction was to protect the integrity of the family by preventing sexual rivalry between parents and children. There had already been proposals in the United Kingdom for amending the law to lift the prohibition, since it was considered that the ban served no useful purpose of public policy. The Strasbourg Court concluded that there had been a violation of Article 12.

Article 14 is also of special importance in relation to Article 12, since it prohibits discrimination not only, for example, on racial or religious grounds, but also on grounds of sex. Thus, in relation to marriage and the founding of a family, there must be no discrimination between men and women. Not all forms of differential treatment constitute discrimination so that there is no requirement that marriageable age, for example, should be the same for both men and women but all differential treatment must be examined by reference to its purpose and justification to ensure that it is not unlawful.

---

[98] See Opsahl, 'The Convention and the right to respect for family life, particularly as regards the unity of the family and the protection of the rights of parents and guardians in the education of children' in A. H. Robertson, *Privacy and Human Rights* (MUP, Manchester 1973), 182.

[99] *B and L v United Kingdom*, (App. 36536/02), 13 September 2005, (2006) 42 EHRR 195.

In two cases against the United Kingdom,[100] the Strasbourg Court concluded that the provisions of national law under which the allocation of sex to that registered at birth was fixed and determined the sex of the partner a person could marry impaired the essence of the right to marry in the case of transsexuals. Such provisions accordingly constituted a breach of Article 12.[101]

While the right to marry and the right to found a family are two separate rights, it seems from the wording of the article that only married heterosexual couples can claim the right to found a family. If the article had been worded 'Everyone has the right to marry and to found a family', it might have been easier to infer that unmarried people or same sex couples also had the right to found a family. It may be significant, also, that the article ends with a reference to 'this right', rather than 'these rights', thus apparently envisaging a close connection between the two.[102]

But while unmarried persons may have no right under Article 12 to found a family, the term 'family' in Article 8 has a wider meaning, and the relations of a parent with an illegitimate child are protected under that article. It cannot be argued that the meaning of 'family' in Article 8 is as restricted as in Article 12, for it is necessary to give it a wider interpretation in other respects also. 'Family' in Article 8 must include the family into which a person is born, as well as the family which he or she founds. Otherwise the absurd conclusion would follow that only parents, and not children, could claim the right to respect for family life. It is therefore reasonable to interpret Article 8, as the Commission and the Court have done, as extending in principle to any close relationship, whether by blood or marriage, and whether legitimate or not.

The right of men and women, once married, to found a family may be subject to increasing strain in a society preoccupied with the dangers of overpopulation. Article 12 plainly does not preclude the provision of family planning services; at the other extreme, sterilization carried out in dubious circumstances may well involve a violation of Articles 8 and 12 of the Convention.[103] Fiscal incentives for marriage have been held to be acceptable under Article 14 when read with Article 1 of Protocol 1.[104] A temporary prohibition on remarriage within three years after divorce imposed under Swiss law applicable at the time on the spouse held responsible for the breakdown of the marriage was held to violate Article 12 as being disproportionate to the legitimate

---

[100] *Goodwin v United Kingdom*, (App. 28957/95), 11 July 2002 [GC], (2002) 35 EHRR 447, ECHR 2002-VI, and *I. v United Kingdom*, (App. 25680/94), 11 July 2002 [GC], (2003) 36 EHRR 967.

[101] For earlier case-law, see *Rees v United Kingdom*, (App. 9532/81), 17 October 1986, Series A No 106, (1987) 9 EHRR 56; *Cossey v United Kingdom*, (App. 10843/84), 27 September 1990, Series A No 184, (1991) 13 EHRR 622; and *Sheffield and Horsham v United Kingdom* (Apps. 22885/93 and 23390/94), 30 July 1998, (1999) 27 EHRR 163, ECHR 1998-V.

[102] Contrast the wording of the European Union Charter of Fundamental Rights which provides in Article 9, 'The right to marry and the right to found a family shall be guaranteed in accordance with the national laws governing the exercise of these rights.' See also C. McGlynn, 'Families and the European Union Charter of Fundamental Rights: progressive change or entrenching the status quo?' (2001) 26 ELRev 582.

[103] *KH and others v Slovakia*, (App. 32881/04), 28 April 2009, (2009) 49 EHRR 857 and *VC v Slovakia*, (App. 18968/07), Decision of 16 June 2009.

[104] *Burden v United Kingdom*, (App. 13378/05), 29 April 2008 [GC], (2008) 47 EHRR 857, ECHR 2008-nyr.

aim being pursued, namely protecting the institution of marriage and the rights of others.[105]

Several applications have sought to read into the provisions of Articles 8 and 12 a right to divorce. In the *Johnston* case[106] the Strasbourg Court concluded that the right to divorce cannot be derived from the provisions of Article 12, and it would accordingly be inconsistent to interpret the extent of the positive obligations flowing from Article 8 to include a right to divorce.

EQUALITY BETWEEN SPOUSES

Article 5 of Protocol 7 provides:

Spouses shall enjoy equality of rights and responsibilities of a private law character between them, and in their relations with their children, as to marriage, during marriage and in the event of its dissolution. This article shall not prevent States from taking such measures as are necessary in the interests of children.

The rights protected under this article are of a private law character, and the articles have no application to public law areas, such as tax, social security, labour laws, or the criminal law. It is only spouses who are protected, so the position of those about to marry remains governed wholly by Article 12. The article should not be regarded as having any application to the disposition of property in the event of a dissolution of the marriage, nor does it imply any obligation on a Contracting Party to provide for dissolution of the marriage.[107]

CONCLUDING REMARKS

This chapter has mainly considered those cases where the Strasbourg Court has rooted its judgment in the protection of family life. Though the Court does not always make a clear distinction between the protection of private life and family life, and rightly views the protection of the article taken as a whole as potentially providing broader protection than its individual elements might if taken alone, it is now possible to divide the Strasbourg Court's case-law into those cases primarily concerned with family life and those primarily concerned with private life. The following chapter considers the Strasbourg Court's case-law on private life, home, and correspondence.

---

[105] *F v Switzerland*, (App. 11329/85), 18 December 1987, Series A No 128, (1988) 10 EHRR 411.

[106] *Johnston and others v Ireland*, (App. 9697/82), 18 December 1986, Series A No 112, (1987) 9 EHRR 203.

[107] Explanatory memorandum to Protocol 7, Council of Europe Document H(84)5, at 12.

In this chapter, we have seen that the Strasbourg Court has added a procedural superstructure to Article 8 which provides safeguards for individuals in relation to interferences with their family life. These procedural safeguards must enable national decision-makers to consider the competing interests that will frequently be at the heart of interferences with family life. Decision-making which is sensitive to the protection of family life is unlikely to result in the finding of a violation of Article 8, but it remains surprising how often Contracting Parties have given insufficient consideration to the balancing of the right to respect for family life with their internal policy preferences.

16

PROTECTING PRIVATE LIFE, THE HOME, AND CORRESPONDENCE

INTRODUCTORY REMARKS

The scope of the protection of private life under the Convention is being increasingly explored in the Strasbourg Court's case-law. It was suggested some years ago that the Convention protects the individual, under this head, against attacks on physical or mental integrity or moral or intellectual freedom, attacks on honour and reputation, the use of a person's name, identity, or likeness, being spied upon, watched, or harassed, and the disclosure of information protected by the duty of professional secrecy.[1] This has proved to be the case.

In a more recent, and both penetrating and compelling, analysis, Moreham has proposed that the Strasbourg Court's case-law on private life can be synthesized into five categories: freedom from interference with physical and psychological integrity; freedom from unwanted access to and collection of information; freedom from serious environmental pollution; the right to be free to develop one's identity; and the right to live one's life in the manner of one's choosing.[2] This analysis, with slight modification, is adopted in this chapter in presenting an exposition of the way in which the Strasbourg Court has developed the right to private life. Moreham's analysis also largely incorporates the concept of the right to respect for the home and correspondence into the protection of private life, since where you live and your communications with others and theirs with you are essential ingredients of a social life in a community. Nevertheless, there remain one or two aspects of respect for the home and correspondence which are more conveniently addressed separately from the five areas in Moreham's synthesis.

---

[1] C. Velu, 'The European Convention on Human Rights and the Right to Respect for Private Life, the Home and Communications' in A. H. Robertson, *Privacy and Human Rights* (MUP, Manchester 1973), 12.

[2] N. Moreham, 'The right to respect for private life in the European Convention on Human Rights: a re-examination' [2008] EHRLR 44, 45. See also J. Marshall, 'A right to personal autonomy at the European Court of Human Rights' [2008] EHRLR 337.

DEFINITIONS

PRIVATE LIFE

In 1976, the Commission defined private life as follows:

For numerous Anglo-Saxon and French authors the right to respect for 'private life' is the right to privacy, the right to live as far as one wishes, protected from publicity.... In the opinion of the Commission however, the right to respect for private life does not end there. It comprises also, to a certain degree, the right to establish and develop relationships with other human beings especially in the emotional field, for the development and fulfilment of one's own personality.[3]

Cohen-Jonathan observes:

One can consider anything having to do with personal health, philosophical, religious or moral beliefs, family and emotional life, friendships and, subject to reservations, professional and material life as part of private life.[4]

The Strasbourg Court had occasion to comment on the meaning of 'private life' in the *Niemietz* case,[5] which concerned the question of whether a search of law offices violated Article 8, and has always resisted providing an exhaustive definition. The Court observed:

The Court does not consider it possible or necessary to attempt an exhaustive definition of the notion of 'private life.' However, it would be too restrictive to limit the notion to an 'inner circle' in which the individual may live his own personal life as he chooses and to exclude therefrom entirely the outside world not encompassed within that circle. Respect for private life must also comprise to a certain degree the right to establish and develop relationships with other human beings. There appears, furthermore, to be no reason of principle why this understanding of the notion of 'private life' should be taken to exclude activities of a professional or business nature since it is, after all, in the course of their working lives that the majority of people have a significant, if not the greatest, opportunity of developing relationships with the outside world.... Thus, especially in the case of a person exercising a liberal profession, his work in that context may form part and parcel of his life to such a degree that it becomes impossible to know in what capacity he is acting at a given moment of time.[6]

In the *Peck* case, the Strasbourg Court recapitulated its approach to the scope of private life:

---

[3] App. 6825/74, *X v Iceland*, Decision of 18 May 1976, (1976) 5 DR 86. See also L. Doswald-Beck, 'The Meaning of the "Right to respect for Private Life" under the European Convention on Human Rights' (1983) 4 HRLJ 283, and L. Loucaides, 'Personality and Privacy under the European Convention on Human Rights' (1990) 61 BYIL 175.

[4] G. Cohen-Jonathan, 'Respect for private and family life' in Macdonald, Matscher, and Petzold, *The European System for the Protection of Human Rights* (Martinus Nijhoff, Dordrecht 1993), 405, 407. See also H. Tomás Gómez-Arostegui, 'Defining Private Life under the European Convention on Human Rights by Referring to Reasonable Expectations' (2005) 35 *California Western International Law Journal* 153.

[5] *Niemietz v Germany*, (App. 13710/88), 16 December 1992, Series A No 251-B, (1993) 16 EHRR 97.

[6] §29. See also *Bigaeva v Greece*, (App. 26713/05), 28 May 2009, §23.

Private life is a broad term not susceptible to exhaustive definition. The Court has already held that elements such as gender identification, name, sexual orientation and sexual life are important elements of the personal sphere protected by Article 8. That Article also protects a right to identity and personal development, and the right to establish and develop relationships with other human beings and the outside world and it may include activities of a professional or business nature. There is, therefore, a zone of interaction of a person with others, even in a public context, which may fall within the scope of 'private life'....[7]

In concluding that mental health must also be regarded as a crucial part of private life associated with the aspect of moral identity, the Strasbourg Court again stated that private life is a broad term 'not susceptible to exhaustive definition' but will protect such important elements of the personal sphere as 'gender identification, name and sexual orientation and sexual life'.[8]

The Strasbourg Court uses the term 'physical and moral integrity of the person' as within the concept of private life.[9] Where conduct, such as child sexual abuse, is in issue, there is a positive obligation on the State to provide protection from such grave interferences with private life. This will not, however, require unlimited civil actions where the conduct is adequately covered by criminal law sanctions. The Court has stated on a number of occasions that private life includes a right to identity and personal development, and to establish personal relationships. In the *Odièvre* case, the Grand Chamber said:

Matters of relevance to personal development include details of a person's identity as a human being and the vital interest protected by the Convention in obtaining information necessary to discover the truth concerning important aspects of one's personal identity, such as the identity of one's parents, birth, and in particular the circumstances in which a child is born, forms part of a child's, and subsequently the adult's, private life guaranteed by Article 8 of the Convention.[10]

Although the increasingly broad concept of private life has in many cases been taken to include issues relating to the home and correspondence, the right to respect for home and correspondence remain specified features in the text of Article 8. Consideration of the definitions of these terms in the case-law of the Strasbourg Court continues to be warranted.

HOME

Applications relating specifically to this aspect of Article 8 have not been numerous; many issues have involved a combination of private life and home. Also, many issues which might otherwise have fallen within its provisions have been considered under

---

[7] *Peck v United Kingdom*, (App. 44647/98), 28 January 2003, (2003) 36 EHRR 719; ECHR 2003-I, §57.

[8] *Bensaid v United Kingdom*, (App. 44599/98), 6 February 2001, (2001) 33 EHRR 205; ECHR 2001-I, §47.

[9] *Stubbings and others v United Kingdom*, (Apps. 22083/93 and 22095/93), 22 October 1996, (1997) 23 EHRR 213, ECHR 1996-IV, §59.

[10] *Odièvre v France*, (App. 42326/98), 13 February 2003 [GC], (2004) 38 EHRR 871; ECHR 2003-III, §29.

Article 1 of Protocol 1.[11] In the *Greek* case,[12] Article 8 was violated by the suspension of the right to respect for the home in the Greek Constitution, and by 'the consequent disregard of this right, in particular by the practice of the Greek authorities of carrying out arrests at night.'[13]

Article 8 requires Contracting Parties to guarantee respect for the home.[14] This does not appear to include a right to a home,[15] nor to a particular home.[16] But it does cover a requirement that Contracting Parties protect the physical security of a person's actual home and belongings there.[17] So deliberate destruction of homes by the security forces is a particularly grave and unjustified interference with the rights in Article 8.[18] In *Cyprus v Turkey*,[19] the refusal of the authorities in the occupied part of northern Cyprus to allow displaced Greek Cypriots to return to their homes there constituted a continuing violation by Turkey of Article 8.[20] The 'multitude of adverse circumstances' which attended the daily lives of Greek Cypriots living in the Karpas region[21] of northern Cyprus violated their right to respect for their private and family life and home under Article 8.[22]

A broad view is taken of what is a person's home. It can include the business premises of a professional person,[23] or a caravan site used as a home in breach of planning permission.[24]

CORRESPONDENCE

Correspondence covers written materials including materials sent through the post, as well as telephonic communications and email.[25] What appears to

---

[11] See ch.20 below.

[12] App. 3321/67, *Denmark v Greece*, App. 3322/67, *Norway v Greece*, App. 3323/67, *Sweden v Greece*, and App. 3344/67, *Netherlands v Greece*, ('the *Greek* case'), Report of 18 November 1969, (1969) 12 *Yearbook* 1.

[13] (1969) 12 *Yearbook* 152–3.

[14] For the substantive nature of the guarantee, see below in this chapter.

[15] See Commission's decision in App. 159/56, *X v Germany*, (1955–7) 1 *Yearbook* 202, concerning a claim that the article required a State to provide a home for a refugee.

[16] See Commission's decision in App. 31600/96, *Burton v United Kingdom*, 15 September 1996, (1996) 22 EHRR CD135 concerning a claim by a gypsy to be permitted to live her last days in a caravan according to gypsy tradition.

[17] *Novoseletskiy v Ukraine*, (App. 47148/99), 22 February 2005, (2006) 43 EHGRR 1139, ECHR 2005-II.

[18] *Selçuk and Asker v Turkey*, (Apps. 23184/94 and 23185/94), 24 April 1998, (1998) 26 EHRR 477, ECHR 1998-II, §86.

[19] *Cyprus v Turkey*, (App. 25781/94), 10 May 2001 [GC], (2002) 35 EHRR 731; ECHR 2001-IV. See also *Xenides-Arestis v Turkey*, (App. 46347/99), 22 December 2005.

[20] §175.

[21] This perhaps should, more appropriately, have been referred to by the Strasbourg Court as the 'Karpasi region' of Cyprus, since this is the way in which the region is described by Greek Cypriots.

[22] *Cyprus v Turkey*, (App. 25781/94), 10 May 2001 [GC], (2002) 35 EHRR 731; ECHR 2001-IV, §296.

[23] *Niemietz v Germany*, (App. 13710/88), 16 December 1992, Series A No 251-B, (1993) 16 EHRR 97, §§30–1.

[24] *Buckley v United Kingdom*, (App. 20348/92), 25 September 1996, (1997) 23 EHRR 101, ECHR 1996-IV, §54. See also *Gillow v United Kingdom*, 24 November 1986, Series A No 109. (1989) 11 EHRR 335, §46.

[25] *Copland v United Kingdom*, (App. 62617/00), 3 April 2007, (2007) 45 EHRR 858, ECHR 2007-IV.

characterize 'correspondence' as distinct from materials constituting 'expression' within Article 10 is direct communication to another. Applications concerning interference with correspondence have mainly been brought by those in prison,[26] and in relation to various surveillance techniques, most notably telephone tapping,[27] but in the latter case the right to respect for correspondence is almost always taken together with private life. Interference with correspondence has also arisen in the context of bankruptcy proceedings.[28] The application of a rule in Italian bankruptcy law that all correspondence had to be handed over to the trustee in bankruptcy, which lasted for a period of over fourteen years, was found in the circumstances of this case to constitute an interference with the applicant's correspondence which violated Article 8.

POSITIVE OBLIGATIONS AND PRIVATE LIFE

The Strasbourg Court has frequently referred to positive obligations in the context of respect for private life within Article 8. However, where positive obligations are in issue, there is a considerable margin of appreciation for a Contracting Party as to how it regulates a particular area.[29] In the *Hatton* case in 2003, the Grand Chamber indicated that the approach to positive obligations was essentially the same as where there were interferences:

Article 8 may apply in environmental cases whether the pollution is directly caused by the State or whether State responsibility arises from the failure properly to regulate private industry. Whether the case is analysed in terms of a positive duty on the State to take reasonable and appropriate measures to secure the applicants' rights under paragraph 1 of Article 8 or in terms of an interference by a public authority to be justified in accordance with paragraph 2, the applicable principles are broadly similar. In both contexts regard must be had to the fair balance that has to be struck between the competing interests of the individual and of the community as a whole; and in both contexts the State enjoys a certain margin of appreciation in determining the steps to be taken to ensure compliance with the Convention. Furthermore, even in relation to the positive obligations flowing from the first paragraph of Article 8, in striking the required balance the aims mentioned in the second paragraph may be of a certain relevance.[30]

---

[26] See below in this chapter.

[27] See below in this chapter.

[28] *Luordo v Italy*, (App. 32190/96), 17 July 2003, (2005) 41 EHRR 547; ECHR 2003-IX. See also *Campagnano v Italy*, (App. 77955/01), 23 March 2006, ECHR 2006-IV.

[29] See *Rees v United Kingdom*, (App. 9532/81), Series A No 106, (1987) 9 EHRR 56, §§37 and 44, and the discussion of this issue in ch.16 above.

[30] *Hatton and others v United Kingdom* (App. 36022/97), 8 July 2003 [GC], (2003) 37 EHRR 611, ECHR 2003-VIII, §98. See also *Dickson v United Kingdom*, (App. 44362/04), 4 December 2007 [GC], (2008) 46 EHRR 927, ECHR 2007-XIII.

It follows that the dividing line between negative and positive obligations under Article 8 is a fine one. The current position of the Strasbourg Court is summarized by the Grand Chamber as follows:

> 70. The Court recalls that, although the object of Article 8 is essentially that of protecting the individual against arbitrary interference by the public authorities, it does not merely compel the State to abstain from such interference. In addition to this primarily negative undertaking, there may be positive obligations inherent in an effective respect for private and family life. These obligations may involve the adoption of measures designed to secure respect for private and family life even in the sphere of the relations of individuals between themselves. The boundaries between the State's positive and negative obligations under Article 8 do not lend themselves to precise definition. The applicable principles are nonetheless similar. In particular, in both instances regard must be had to the fair balance to be struck between the competing interests....[31]

The Strasbourg Court went on to indicate that, in some cases, the analysis of a situation as involving positive or negative obligations would be very similar, since the essential question is whether a fair balance has been struck.[32] The similarity of the approach to positive and negative obligations has arisen because the Strasbourg Court has indicated that, in determining the balance to be struck between the interests of the community and the interests of the individual, the aims referred to in Article 8(2) 'may be of a certain relevance.'[33] The *Babylonová* case[34] illustrates the application of this approach in relation to the requirement to adopt measure to protect Article 8 rights in the sphere of relations between individuals. The applicant was unable to secure the cancellation of the registration of a former occupier of her home as permanently resident at that address. There was a lacuna in the national law which prevented the former occupier from securing cancellation of the registration where he had not established an alternative permanent residence, even though it was accepted that he had ceased to be permanently resident at the property in question. The Strasbourg Court found that the national law did not strike a fair balance between the interests of the applicant and those of the community, and there was a violation of the applicant's right to respect for her private life and home.

Because of the way in which the Strasbourg Court has brought together the questions to be considered in relation to positive and negative obligations, cases involving positive obligations are not treated separately, but are considered within the headings which follow.

---

[31] *Dickson v United Kingdom*, (App. 44362/04), 4 December 2007 [GC], (2008) 46 EHRR 927, ECHR 2007-XIII, §70. See also *Codarcea v Romania*, (App. 31675/04), 2 June 2009.

[32] §71.

[33] *Babylonová v Slovakia*, (App. 69146/01), 20 June 2006, (2008) 46 EHRR 183, ECHR 2006-VIII.

[34] Ibid.

FREEDOM FROM INTERFERENCE WITH PHYSICAL AND PSYCHOLOGICAL INTEGRITY

INTERFERENCE WITH THE PERSON

In the *YF* case, which concerned, in part, a gynaecological examination against the will of the woman concerned, the Strasbourg Court said:

The Court observes that Article 8 is clearly applicable to these complaints, which concern a matter of 'private life', a concept which covers the physical and psychological integrity of a person.... It reiterates in this connection that a person's body concerns the most intimate aspect of private life. Thus, a compulsory medical intervention, even if it is of minor importance, constitutes an interference with this right....[35]

Inappropriate strip searching of persons visiting someone in prison will also constitute a violation of Article 8, even though the treatment falls short of that within the scope of Article 3.[36]

In a case against the Netherlands,[37] the Strasbourg Court considered an application made on behalf of a mentally disabled girl aged 16, who had been raped while in a privately run home for the those with special needs. The law of the Netherlands did not recognize a complaint unless made by the victim in person. If she lacked capacity, the criminal law could take no cognizance of the alleged offence. It appeared that there was no similar bar on the use of the civil law. The family argued that this violated respect for the private life of their daughter, and there was no dispute as to the applicability of the article, since the concept of private life covers the physical and moral integrity of the person, including their sexual life.[38] The absence of protection by the criminal law in so serious a case was found to be a violation of Article 8. A similar issue arose in the *MC* case.[39] The applicant complained that the law in Bulgaria did not provide effective protection against rape and sexual abuse, since only cases where the victim had resisted actively were prosecuted. The Strasbourg Court considered that the Contracting Parties have positive obligations inherent in Articles 3 and 8 to enact legislation effectively punishing rape and to apply them in practice through effective investigation and prosecution.[40]

The use of corporal punishment in schools has been examined by the Strasbourg Court in a number of complaints of violations of Article 3.[41] Comments in the

---

[35] *YF v Turkey*, (App. 24209/94), 22 July 2003, (2004) 39 EHRR 715; ECHR 2003-IX, §33.

[36] *Wainwright v United Kingdom*, (App. 12350/04), 26 September 2006, (2007) 44 EHRR 809; ECHR 2006-X, §§41–9.

[37] *X and Y v Netherlands*, (App. 8978/80), 26 March 1985, Series A No 91; (1986) 8 EHRR 235.

[38] §22.

[39] *MC v Bulgaria*, (App. 39272/98), 4 December 2003, (2005) 40 EHRR 459, ECHR 2003-XII.

[40] §§148–53.   [41] See ch.9, above.

Costello-Roberts case[42] suggest that certain aspects of schooling and school discipline might attract protection under Article 8 additional to that afforded by Article 3. The Court recognized that even the act of 'sending a child to school necessarily involved some degree of interference with his or her private life', though it is not clear that such interference would entail adverse effects for the person's physical or moral integrity. Indeed, in this case the Court concluded that the disciplinary regime at the independent preparatory boarding school, which included the possibility of being beaten on the bottom with a rubber-soled gym shoe, did not come within the scope of the prohibition in Article 8. But the Strasbourg Court did not exclude 'the possibility that there might be circumstances in which Article 8 could be regarded as affording in relation to disciplinary measures a protection which goes beyond that given by Article 3.[43]

SEARCHES OF PROPERTY

A number of Article 8 cases concern respect for private life and the home in the context of the legitimacy of searches of either the home or business premises.

The *Chappell* case[44] challenged the use of Anton Piller orders under English law. Anton Piller orders represent a common law development of interlocutory measures in civil proceedings, *inter alia*, enabling a search of premises to take place often with the object of seizing material produced in breach of a copyright or trademark. The Strasbourg Court concluded that the search of the applicant's home authorized by the order constituted an interference with respect for his home. The aim, namely, to protect the rights of others, was legitimate and the order met the requirements of Article 8 as being in accordance with law. The necessary safeguards existed to ensure that action was only taken where it was necessary in a democratic society. The undertaking given by solicitors for plaintiffs seeking such an order was sufficient to ensure the proper supervision of the implementation of any order granted by the court.

The *Niemietz* case[45] concerned a search of a lawyer's office under warrant from the court in order to establish the true identity of a person who had signed himself Klaus Wegner which was believed to be a pseudonym. The Strasbourg Court concluded that the interference was in accordance with law and pursued the legitimate aim of being for the prevention of crime and the protection of the rights of others, but went on to consider whether it was necessary in a democratic society. The Court found that the interference was out of all proportion to the aim pursued, in that it impinged on professional secrecy and that searches of lawyer's offices in Germany had not been surrounded by any special procedural safeguards.[46]

---

[42] *Costello-Roberts v United Kingdom*, (App. 13134/87), 25 March 1993, Series A No 247-C, (1994) 19 EHRR 112.

[43] §36. That view is supported by the approach of the Court in *Wainwright v United Kingdom*, (App. 12350/04), 26 September 2006, (2007) 44 EHRR 809; ECHR 2006-X, §§41–9.

[44] *Chappell v United Kingdom*, (App. 10461/83), 30 March 1989, Series A No 152, (1990) 12 EHRR 1.

[45] *Niemietz v Germany*, (App. 13710/88), 16 December 1992, Series A No 251-B, (1993) 16 EHRR 97.

[46] See also *Buck v Germany*, (App. 41604/98), 28 April 2005, (2006) 42 EHRR 440; ECHR 2005-IV, for an example of a 4:3 decision of a Chamber finding a violation of Art. 8 in the context of the search of business premises in order to ascertain the identity of the driver of car caught speeding in a radar trap.

The *Funke* case[47] involved consideration of the legitimacy of search of the applicants' homes by customs officers in France in connection with alleged exchange control irregularities. The aim was legitimate in that it could be said to be for the economic well-being of the country and the prevention of crime. Once again the issue came down to determination of whether the interferences were necessary in a democratic society. There must always be adequate safeguards against abuse, but this was not so in the present case. The customs authorities had very wide powers, including exclusive competence to assess the expediency, number, length, and scale of searches. There was no requirement to obtain a judicial warrant. This resulted in a situation in which the restrictions and limitations provided for in the law were too lax and full of loopholes for the interferences to be strictly proportionate to the legitimate aim pursued. The situation in the case of Funke was made worse in that the customs authorities never lodged any complaint against him alleging an offence against the exchange control regulations.

A search which is authorized under national law where there are special procedural safeguards will violate Article 8 if it can be shown that the underlying purpose is to find out a journalist's sources through his lawyer, since this will have repercussions on rights under Article 10 of the Convention.[48] The Strasbourg Court will expect that search warrants are not drafted in terms which are too wide and do not give any indication of the reasons for the search. This is particularly so where the search is of premises of those who have not been accused of any offence.[49] Equally the Court will expect the national authorities to have shown reasonable care in ensuring that the target of a forcible entry to property remains at that property. In the *Keegan* case,[50] the applicants (in whom the police had no interest at all) had been living at the address for about six months prior to the forcible and dramatic search which took place of their home. Once their error was discovered, the police were duly apologetic and repairs were carried out to the applicants' home. There was nevertheless a breach of Article 8; basic steps to check the connection between the address and the offence as at the time of the search had not been effectively carried out, and the entry and search had caused significant fear and alarm to innocent people. There was a violation of Article 8.

Entries and searches, including recording and retaining personal details and photographing individuals which are properly applied under anti-terrorist legislation are unlikely to give rise to successful complaints under Article 8, since they will normally be easily justified as measures for the prevention of crime.[51]

SURVEILLANCE AND INTERCEPTION OF COMMUNICATIONS

A group of cases has concerned the extent to which Article 8 protects the citizen from various forms of surveillance, which might include the opening of correspondence or

---

[47] *Funke and others v France*, (App. 10828/84), 25 February 1993, Series A No 256-A, (1993) 16 EHRR 297.
[48] *Roemen and Schmit v Luxembourg*, (App. 51772/99), 25 February 2003, ECHR 2003-IV, §§64–71.
[49] See, for example, *Ernst and others v Belgium*, (App. 33400/96), 15 July 2003.
[50] *Keegan v United Kingdom*, (App. 28867/03), 18 July 2006, (2007) 44 EHRR 716; ECHR 2006-X.
[51] *Murray v United Kingdom*, (App. 14310/88), 28 October 1994, Series A No 300-A, (1995) 19 EHRR 193.

listening to telephone communications. The whole area of covert surveillance is one where advances in technology present increasing threats to the private life of the individual. The Strasbourg Court is not unaware of the need for vigilance in the light of an increasingly sophisticated technology.[52] The Court has decided that it is not only the party whose telephone line is tapped who has standing to complain, but also third parties whose conversations are intercepted.[53] Although the existence of intelligence services with powers of secret surveillance is tolerated under Convention principles, the practices of such services must be shown to be necessary for safeguarding democratic institutions, and any interference must be supported by relevant and sufficient reasons and be proportionate to the aims pursued.[54]

The *Klass* case[55] raised the question of the compatibility of German law with Article 8. The applicants objected that the German law on surveillance did not oblige the authorities to notify the persons subject to the surveillance after the event and did not provide any system of remedies for the ordering and execution of such measures. The Court agreed with the Commission that the applicants could claim to be victims of a violation of the Convention as required under former Article 25.[56] On the substantive complaint, the Strasbourg Court considered that telephone conversations came within the ambit of 'private life' and the concept of 'correspondence'. As in so many cases under Article 8, the Court concluded that surveillance could constitute an interference, that it was in accordance with law, and that it could serve a legitimate aim, but the key question was whether the interference was necessary in a democratic society. The answer to this question turned on the existence and adequacy of safeguards against possible abuse; this is a theme which constantly appears in such cases. The German conditions were considered to be appropriately restrictive and to be within the State's margin of appreciation. The test laid down by the Strasbourg Court was as follows:

The Court must be satisfied that, whatever system of surveillance is adopted, there exist adequate and effective guarantees against abuse. This assessment has only a relative character: it depends on all the circumstances of the case, such as the nature, scope and duration of the possible measures, the grounds required for ordering such measures, the authorities competent to permit, carry out and supervise such measures, and the kind of remedy provided by the national law.[57]

---

[52] *Kopp v Switzerland* (App. 23224/94), 25 March 1998, (1999) 27 EHRR 91, §72. See also *PG and JH v United Kingdom*, (App. 44787/98), 25 September 2001, ECHR 2001-IX; and *Copland v United Kingdom*, (App. 62617/00), 3 April 2007, (2007) 45 EHRR 858, ECHR 2007-IV.

[53] *Lambert v France*, (App. 23618/94), 24 August 1998, (2000) 30 EHRR 346, ECHR 1998-V.

[54] *Segerstedt-Wiberg and others v Sweden*, (App. 62332/00), 6 June 2006, (2007) 44 EHRR 14, ECHR 2006-VII, §88; see also *Rotaru v Romania*, (App. 28341/95), 4 May 2000 [GC], ECHR 2000-V.

[55] *Klass and others v Germany*, 6 September 1978, Series A No 28, (1979–80) 2 EHRR 214.

[56] See ch.2 above.

[57] *Klass and others v Germany*, (App. 5029/71), 6 September 1978, Series A No 28, (1979–80) 2 EHRR 214, §50.

The Strasbourg Court expressed mild concern that supervisory control was not exercised by a judge, but noted that initial control under the German legislation was effected by an 'official qualified for judicial office and by the control provided by the Parliamentary Board and the G 10 Commission'.[58] The Court concluded that, taking judicial notice of technical advances in the means of espionage and surveillance, and of the development of terrorism in Europe, the German system for controlling covert surveillance met the requirements of Article 8 of the Convention.

In subsequent cases, the Court has tended to consider the adequacy of safeguards as a matter going to the 'lawfulness' of the measure in question rather than its proportionality. It would defeat the purpose of secret surveillance if individuals were able to pinpoint exactly when the police were likely to be listening in on their conversations and adapt their behaviour accordingly, and the Court has not interpreted Article 8 to require that this information should be provided to individuals, either before, during, or after they have been the subject of surveillance measures. On the other hand, however, secret powers of surveillance are open to abuse by the State authorities.[59] The Court has therefore held that, to comply with Article 8, national law should provide fairly detailed guidelines as to the circumstances when surveillance is allowed and any individual measure of surveillance must comply with national law. While national law need not be entirely clear in all its detail, it must not give the executive an unfettered or excessively broad discretion. The law must indicate the scope of any discretion conferred on the competent authorities and the manner of its exercise with sufficient clarity to give the individual adequate protection against arbitrary interference. In relation to secret measures of surveillance, the Court has developed the following minimum safeguards that should be set out in statute law in order to avoid abuses of power: the nature of the offences which may give rise to an interception order; a definition of the categories of people liable to have their telephones tapped; a limit on the duration of telephone tapping; the procedure to be followed for examining, using, and storing the data obtained; the precautions to be taken when communicating the data to other parties; and the circumstances in which recordings may or must be erased or the tapes destroyed.[60]

The *Malone* case[61] concerned the law of England and Wales on the interception of communications on behalf of the police for the purposes of the prevention and detection of crime. Interception involved both postal and telephonic communication. The practice of 'metering' also came under scrutiny. Metering involves the use of a meter check printer which registers the number dialled on a particular telephone and

---

[58] §56. A revised version of the German G10 law was considered in *Weber and Saravia v Germany*, (App. 54934/00), Decision of 29 June 2006, and found to contain sufficient safeguards.

[59] *Rotaru v Romania*, (App. 28341/95), 4 May 2000 [GC], ECHR 2000-V.

[60] *Rotaru v Romania*, (App. 28341/95), 4 May 2000 [GC], ECHR 2000-V; *Weber and Saravia v Germany*, (App. 54934/00), Decision of 29 June 2006; and *Liberty and others v United Kingdom*, (App. 58243/00), 1 July 2008, (2009) 48 EHRR 1.

[61] *Malone v United Kingdom*, (App. 8691/79), 2 August 1984, Series A No 82, (1985) 7 EHRR 14.

the time and duration of each call. It does not record speech. James Malone was an antiques dealer, who was charged and convicted of handling stolen goods. The investigation had involved the interception of Malone's telephone calls. He also complained that his telephone line had been metered. At the time there was no overall statutory code governing the interception of postal and telephone communications. Metering was essentially a system by which the Post Office checked that customers were correctly charged, though it was admitted in the proceedings that the Post Office did on occasion cooperate with the police in metering a telephone line if 'the information is essential to police enquiries in relation to serious crime and cannot be obtained from other sources.'[62] The absence of a proper statutory code governing interception of communications proved fatal to the respondent State's defence of the case. The Court said:

[I]t cannot be said with any reasonable certainty what elements of the powers to intercept are incorporated in legal rules and what elements remain within the discretion of the executive. In view of the attendant obscurity and uncertainty as to the state of the law in this essential respect, ... the law of England and Wales does not indicate with reasonable clarity the scope and manner of exercise of the relevant discretion conferred on the public authorities. To that extent, the minimum degree of legal protection to which citizens are entitled under the rule of law in a democratic society is lacking.[63]

The interferences with James Malone's communications were therefore in breach of Article 8 in that they were not 'in accordance with the law'. The Strasbourg Court came to a similar conclusion in relation to the practice of metering.

The examination of the French system for authorizing telephone-tapping in the *Huvig* and *Kruslin* cases[64] revealed a system midway between that of Germany and the United Kingdom in the two cases already examined. Since the French Courts had consistently viewed various provisions of the Code of Criminal Procedure as authorizing the carrying out of telephone-tapping by a senior police officer on a warrant issued by an investigating judge, the Strasbourg Court regarded the practice as being in accordance with law. But the Court went on to say that to be fully in accordance with the law, the quality of the law must be such as to provide safeguards against what is a serious interference with private life. The French system was very short on processes to prevent abuse, with key aspects of the process not adequately defined, such as the categories of person liable to have their telephones tapped or the nature of the offences which warranted such measures. There was consequently a violation of Article 8.[65]

---

[62] *Malone*, §56.   [63] §79.

[64] *Huvig v France*, (App. 11105/84), 24 April 1990, Series A No 176-B, (1990) 12 EHRR 528; *Kruslin v France*, (App. 11801/850), 24 April 1990, Series A No 176-B, (1990) 12 EHRR 547; *Valenzuela Contreras v Spain*, (App. 27671/95), 30 July 1998, (1999) 28 EHRR 483; ECHR 1998-V; *Liberty and others v United Kingdom*, (App. 58243/00), 1 July 2008, (2009) 48 EHRR 1; and *Bykov v Russia*, (App. 4378/02), 10 March 2009 [GC], ECHR 2009-nyr.

[65] See also *Herczegfalvy v Austria*, (App. 10533/83), 24 September 1992, Series A No 242-B, (1993) 15 EHRR 437, §91.

Obviously a telephone tap without obtaining legal authority where such a procedure is provided for will amount to a violation of Article 8, as in one case, where a senior police officer colluded in obtaining a recording of a telephone conversation in a manner inconsistent with the requirements of French law.[66]

The *Halford* case[67] concerned the interception of telephone calls made by Alison Halford, Assistant Chief Constable of the Merseyside Police, both in her office and at home. The Strasbourg Court rejected an argument by the British Government that Article 8 did not apply because the applicant could have no reasonable expectation of privacy in relation to calls made from her office, recalling its earlier case-law as set out above. The Court concluded that telephone conversations came within the scope of 'private life' and 'correspondence' in Article 8. The interception of office telephone calls was not in accordance with law since there was no regulation of interception of calls outside the public network; and there was a violation in relation to telephone calls from her office. However, the Court was not satisfied that the applicant had proved on the balance of probabilities that there was interception of calls made from her home. Accordingly there was no violation in this regard. The Court noted that the applicant was complaining of measures of surveillance actually applied to her, and not, as in *Klass*, that the very possibility of telephone interceptions violated her Article 8 rights.

The storing of information concerning a person's private life in a secret police register interferes with the right to respect for private life guaranteed by Article 8.[68] The potentially pervasive extent of telephone surveillance and data collection by the State is illustrated by the facts and judgment in the *Copland* case,[69] which concerned the monitoring of telephone, email, and internet usage of an employee of a further education college in order to determine whether she was making excessive use of the facilities for personal purposes. The respondent State argued that the college's powers to do 'anything necessary or expedient' for the purposes of providing further education included the monitoring activities. The Strasbourg Court did not find this at all persuasive: all the more so since subsequent legislation did make provision for monitoring of employee communications by employers. The monitoring was not in accordance with law and there was a violation of Article 8. The *Kahn* case[70] concerned another lacuna at the time in the national law of the United Kingdom. The applicant was convicted of a serious drugs offence after the police had used secret listening devices to obtain evidence against him. At the time the only regulatory measures were non-binding Home Office guidelines which were not directly accessible to members of the public.

The *Foxley* case[71] concerned a rather different set of circumstances. Foxley had been convicted of serious offences of corruption committed while he worked as an

---

[66] *A v France*, (App. 14838/89), 23 November 1993, Series A No 277-B, (1994) 17 EHRR 462. See also *MM v The Netherlands* (App. 39339/98), 8 April 2003, (2004) 39 EHRR 414.

[67] *Halford v United Kingdom*, (App. 20605/92), 25 June 1997, (1997) 24 EHRR 523, ECHR 1997-III.

[68] *Hewitt and Harman v United Kingdom*, (App. 12175/86), 9 May 1989, (1992) 14 EHRR 657.

[69] *Copland v United Kingdom*, (App. 62617/00), 3 April 2007, (2007) 45 EHRR 858, ECHR 2007-IV.

[70] *Khan v United Kingdom*, (App. 39394/97), 12 May 2000, (2001) 31 EHRR 1016, ECHR 2000-V.

[71] *Foxley v United Kingdom*, (App. 33274/96), 20 June 2000, (2001) 31 EHRR 25.

ammunition procurement officer for the Ministry of Defence. A confiscation order for £1.5 million was made against him as his total assessed realizable assets in respect of his having benefited in the sum of £2 million from the offences. The applicant did not pay. Subsequently a Receiver and Trustee in Bankruptcy were appointed, and an order was obtained from the court for the interception of all postal packets for a three-month period. The applicant's mail was intercepted under the order for a period of nearly four months. Among the intercepted mail were communications by the applicant with his legal advisers; these letters were read and copied to the file before being forwarded to the applicant. He complained that the interception of his mail violated Article 8.

Unsurprisingly, the Strasbourg Court found that there was a proper legal base for the interception until the expiry of the order but not for the period of nearly one month thereafter when the applicant's mail continued to be intercepted. The applicant accepted that the interception of his mail was for a legitimate reason: the protection of the rights of others. But the applicant argued strongly that the interception and retention of copies of his correspondence with his legal advisers was not necessary in a democratic society. Even where the State is facing a situation where a person may be concealing assets to the detriment of his creditors:

the implementation of the measures must be accompanied by adequate and effective safeguards which ensure minimum impairment of the right to respect for his correspondence. This is particularly so where…correspondence with the bankrupt's legal advisers may be intercepted. The Court notes in this connection that the lawyer–client relationship is, in principle, privileged and correspondence in that context, whatever its purpose, concerns matters of a private and confidential nature.[72]

The *Liberty* case[73] concerned legislation which allowed the executive to intercept communications passing between the United Kingdom and any individual or transmitter located outside the United Kingdom. The law was drafted in very broad terms: there was no limitation on the type of communications which could be intercepted.[74] Once captured, the applicants claimed that the data were filtered using an electronic search engine. Search terms were devised by officials. The only legal requirement was that material could only be searched for, listened to, or read, if it fell within very broad categories, such as material helpful for the detection of crime or the prevention of terrorism. The law required the Government Minister to 'make such arrangements as he consider[ed] necessary' to ensure that material which did not fall within one of these broad categories was not examined and that any data which were examined were disclosed and reproduced only to the extent necessary, but these 'arrangements' were not made public. Although the respondent State maintained that there was a Code of Practice, it was secret, and there were no statutory limitations on the type of information collected or the way in which it could be used, shared, or stored. There was therefore a violation of Article 8.

---

[72] *Foxley*, §43.   [73] *Liberty and others v United Kingdom*, (App. 58243/00), 1 July 2008, (2009) 48 EHRR 1.
[74] For example, all communications passing through cables under the sea between the United Kingdom and mainland Europe.

The respondent State had argued that the publication of information regarding the arrangements made for the examination, use, storage, communication and destruction of intercepted material during the period in question might have damaged the efficacy of the intelligence-gathering system or given rise to a security risk. However, the Court referred to the German G10 Act, which it had examined in an earlier case and found to be compliant with the Convention.[75] The G10 law contained express provisions about a similar scheme for the strategic interception of external communications. In particular, the G10 law stated that the Federal Intelligence Service was authorized to carry out monitoring of communications only with the aid of search terms which served, and were suitable for, the investigation of the dangers described in the monitoring order. The search terms had to be listed in the monitoring order, which also set out detailed rules on storing and destroying data obtained through strategic monitoring. The authorities storing the data had to verify every six months whether those data were still necessary to achieve the purposes for which they had been obtained by or transmitted to them. If that was not the case, they had to be destroyed and deleted from the files or, at the very least, access to them had to be blocked; the destruction had to be recorded in minutes, and in certain cases had to be supervised by a staff member qualified to hold judicial office. The G10 law further set out detailed provisions governing the transmission, retention and use of data obtained through the interception of external communications.

RECORDING AND DISSEMINATING IMAGES

In the *Von Hannover* case,[76] the Strasbourg Court recapitulated its views on the use of photographs:

> 50. The Court reiterates that the concept of private life extends to aspects relating to personal identity, such as a person's name…, or a person's picture…. Furthermore, private life, in the Court's view, includes a person's physical and psychological integrity; the guarantee afforded by Article 8 of the Convention is primarily intended to ensure the development, without outside interference, of the personality of each individual in his relations with other human beings…. There is therefore a zone of interaction of a person with others, even in a public context, which may fall within the scope of 'private life'….
>
> …
>
> 52. As regards photos, with a view to defining the scope of the protection afforded by Article 8 against arbitrary interference by public authorities, the European Commission of Human Rights had regard to whether the photographs related to private or public matters and whether the material thus obtained was envisaged for a limited use or was likely to be made available to the general public….[77]

---

[75] See *Weber and Saravia v Germany*, (App. 54934/00), Decision of 29 June 2006.

[76] *Von Hannover v Germany*, (App. 59320/00), 24 June 2004, (2005) 40 EHRR 1, ECHR 2004-VI. See also *Reklos and Davourlis v Greece*, (App. 1234/05), 15 January 2009.

[77] §§50 and 52.

The applicant in this case was Princess Caroline of Monaco who complained that failed attempts in judicial proceedings in Germany to control the publication there of photographs of herself constituted a violation of her right to respect for her private life. The Strasbourg Court grappled with the tension between the right to privacy and freedom of expression in Article 10 of the Convention, but noted that both articles permit limitations for the protection of the rights and reputation of others, which they considered took on particular importance in this context. The touchstone was whether publication was justified by considerations of public concern:

> The Court considers that a fundamental distinction needs to be made between reporting facts—even controversial ones—capable of contributing to a debate in a democratic society relating to politicians in the exercise of their functions, for example, and reporting details of the private life of an individual who, moreover, as in this case, does not exercise official functions. While in the former case the press exercises its vital role of 'watchdog' in a democracy by contributing to 'impart[ing] information and ideas on matters of public interest', it does not do so in the latter case.[78]

This test is certainly not, in the view of the Strasbourg Court, satisfied where the sole purpose of publication of the photographs is to satisfy the curiosity of readers about the private life of a particular person. This does not contribute to any debate of general interest to society. The conditions under which the applicant could secure protection of her right to privacy in the German courts did not strike a fair balance between the competing interests in this case. There was a violation of Article 8.

The *Sciacca* case[79] explains this approach in relation to the ordinary person, as distinct from someone in the public eye. This aspect 'enlarges the zone of interaction which may fall within the scope of private life... .'[80] It did not matter that the applicant was at the time the subject of criminal proceedings. Photographs of the applicant, which had apparently been provided by a State agency, were reproduced in newspapers. The Strasbourg Court found a violation because the use of the photographs for this purpose was not in accordance with law; the supply of the photographs in the case before the Strasbourg Court was not within such provisions as existed in Italy. In the *Khuzhin* case,[81] the use on a television programme of photographs of three brothers charged with serious offences was held to have no information value in itself, and, in such cases, there had to be compelling reasons for interfering with the applicants' right to respect for their private life. No such justification could be found; the brothers were in custody and not fugitives, and the use of the photograph added nothing the forthcoming trial. There was a violation of Article 8.

---

[78] *Von Hannover*, §63.
[79] *Sciacca v Italy*, (App. 50774/99), 11 January 2005, (2006) 43 EHRR 400, ECHR 2005-I.
[80] §29.   [81] *Khuzhin and others v Russia*, (App. 13470/02), 23 October 2008.

Disseminating the photograph of a person the police wished to interview as a witness but describing him as a 'wanted person' will violate Article 8.[82]

The Strasbourg Court has begun to comment on the impact of closed-circuit television (CCTV) in public places. In the *Peck* case,[83] the Court noted that the monitoring of the actions of an individual in a public place by the use of photographic equipment does not give rise to an interference with a person's private life.[84] However, most CCTV cameras are linked to video recording facilities. The Court acknowledged that such recordings, and the systematic or permanent nature of the record, may give rise to interferences with private life. But in this case, the applicant was not complaining about the CCTV recording itself, but about its release to the local press as an example of the success of CCTV monitoring. The applicant had at the time been severely depressed, and was identifiable on the CCTV recording carrying a kitchen knife with which he subsequently attempted to slit his wrists. He accepted that being seen on the CCTV system, which led to police intervention, may have saved his life.

There was a violation of Article 8 in this case, since there had been no attempt to obtain Peck's consent to the showing of the recording, and the local authority did not appear to have considered disguising the applicant's identity. The violation was not mitigated in any way by the subsequent media appearances of Peck as a means of raising his concerns about the use of the video recording.

The circumstances of the *Perry* case were somewhat different, but also unusual.[85] The applicant was suspected of committing armed robberies. He refused to participate in identification parades. He was then covertly filmed in the police station using the custody suite cameras which had been especially adjusted for this purpose. The video footage was used for identification purposes, and contributed to securing his conviction. In the course of its judgment, the Court said:

…the normal use of security cameras *per se* whether in the public street or on premises, such as shopping centres or police stations where they serve a legitimate and foreseeable purpose, do not raise issues under Article 8(1) of the Convention.[86]

But the unusual and irregular manner of using these facilities in this case (which breached national rules of criminal procedure on identification evidence in a number of respects) meant that there had been a violation of Article 8.

So, it is clear that the use of CCTV cameras in public places, or places to which the public have ready access such as shopping centres and police stations, and the recording of the images they see, do not engage Article 8. However, the use to which the recordings are put may, in the particular circumstances of each case, constitute an interference with the rights protected by Article 8. Such actions will need to have a proper legal base, a legitimate aim, and be necessary in a democratic society.

---

[82] *Nikolaishvili v Georgia*, (App. 37048/04), 13 January 2009.

[83] *Peck v United Kingdom*, (App. 44647/98), 28 January 2003, (2003) 36 EHRR 41; ECHR 2003-I.

[84] §59.

[85] *Perry v United Kingdom*, (App. 63737/00), 17 July 2003, (2004) 39 EHRR 76, ECHR 2003-IX.

[86] §40.

THE COLLECTION, STORAGE, AND USE OF PERSONAL INFORMATION

The collection of information by officials of the State about individuals without their consent will interfere with their private life, as will its use, for example, in court proceedings. Examples include covert measures, such as the keeping of secret files. There may be an interference with private life even when the information kept on file relates to 'public' activities such as membership of organizations or participation in politics. This is because, as previously mentioned, it is not always easy to draw a clear line between 'private' and 'public' activities. However, the Strasbourg Court has also said that 'public information can fall within the scope of private life where it is systematically collected and stored in files held by the authorities'.[87] An interference with private life can also arise from overt measures, such as official censuses and the collection and retention of fingerprints, photographs, or genetic material by the police.[88]

The *Leander* case[89] established that the storage of information is capable of resulting in a breach of the right to respect for private life, although in the particular circumstances of that case, it did not because there were appropriate safeguards. The case concerned the 'personnel control procedure' applicable to navy employees in Sweden. This had resulted in the applicant's being found unsuitable for particular employment, and he complained of an interference in his private life. The procedure involved the maintenance of a secret police register containing information concerning his private life. The Strasbourg Court found the Swedish law setting up the system sufficiently clear and precise as to its ambit to meet the requirements of the Convention that interferences with private life be in accordance with law. This left the question of whether the system was necessary in a democratic society in the interests of national security. Where national security is involved the margin of appreciation allowed to the Contracting Party is a wide one, but there must nevertheless be safeguards for the citizen. There was, in fact, in this case an elaborate system of safeguards, which met the requirements of the Convention.

Safeguards were, however, found to be lacking in the *Turek* case.[90] The applicant had lost his job when a negative security clearance was issued under lustration legislation[91] and his legal challenge to the issue of that negative security clearance were frustrated because key evidence was kept secret. There was a breach of Article 8 because there

---

[87] *Rotaru v Romania*, (App. 28341/95), 4 May 2000 [GC], ECHR 2000-V, §43.

[88] *S and Marper v United Kingdom*, (App. 30562/04), 4 December 2008 [GC], (2009) 48 EHRR 1169; ECHR 2008-nyr.

[89] *Leander v Sweden*, 26 March 1987, Series A No 116, (1987) 9 EHRR 433; see also *Rotaru v Romania*, (App. 28341/95), 4 May 2000 [GC], ECHR 2000-V; and *Amman v Switzerland*, (App. 27798/95), 16 February 2000 [GC], (2000) 30 EHRR 843, ECHR 2000-II.

[90] *Turek v Slovakia*, (App. 57986/00), 14 February 2006, (2007) 44 EHRR 861, ECHR 2006-II.

[91] Legislation concerned with declarations by people who had been involved with State security agencies under communist regimes.

were insufficient safeguards to enable the applicant to secure effective protection of his right to respect for his private life.

The *Rotaru* case[92] concerned complaints by a Romanian lawyer that information going back more than fifty years had been held concerning him by the intelligence services, and that there were no procedures by which he could seek to refute some of that information. The Romanian system had some basis in law, but the requirement of foreseeability was not satisfied. There were no apparent limits on the exercise of the powers by the State to collect and store the information; there was no procedure under which the subject of the information could consult it, find out its nature, or seek to correct it. The failure of the national law to indicate with reasonable clarity the scope and manner of the exercise of the State's powers, and the interference with the applicant's private life was not 'in accordance with law' resulting in a violation of Article 8.

The retention without limit of time of DNA samples and fingerprints in part of the United Kingdom was at issue in the *S and Marper* case.[93] S, a juvenile, and Marper had both had DNA samples and fingerprints taken. In S's case, he was acquitted of all charges against him, and in Marper's case, the case against him was formally discontinued. However, under English law, the DNA samples and fingerprints were kept on record despite their requests that they be destroyed. Both complained that this constituted a violation of their right to private life under Article 8. The Strasbourg Court regarded the retention of DNA samples as having a more important impact on private life than fingerprints, but nevertheless the retention of each constituted an interference with private life. The Strasbourg Court had some reservations about the quality of law requirements in relation to the statutory provision permitting retention of this material, but drew no formal conclusion on this issue. The Strasbourg Court accepted that the retention of these personal data could be said to be for the prevention of crime, and so the compatibility of the scheme fell to be determined on an analysis of whether retention of the personal data in the circumstances of this case was necessary in a democratic society. The Court looked for something approaching a European consensus, and noted that the great majority of Contracting Parties required samples to be removed or destroyed within a certain period following acquittal or discharge of those from whom the samples had been taken. The system in England, Wales, and Northern Ireland[94] appeared to be the only one among the Contracting Parties which allowed the indefinite retention of such material in relation to a person of any age suspected of any recordable offence. The Court was not persuaded by an argument that the United Kingdom was more advanced than other countries in its use of DNA profiling. There was a risk of stigmatization, and feelings of stigmatization, in such a system, which was particularly acute in the case of juveniles. A fair balance of competing interests

---

[92] *Rotaru v Romania*, (App. 28341/95), 4 May 2000 [GC], ECHR 2000-V.

[93] *S and Marper v United Kingdom*, (App. 30562/04), 4 December 2008 [GC], (2009) 48 EHRR 1169; ECHR 2008-nyr.

[94] The position in Scotland permits retention, initially for three years, of such data only in the case of adults charged with violent or sexual offences.

had not been struck and there was a unanimous finding by the Grand Chamber of a breach of Article 8.

The *Craxi* case[95] shows that dissemination by newspapers of information collected by a public authority in circumstances where those newspapers must have obtained the information from the public authority without any procedural safeguards constitutes a breach of Article 8.

The circumstances in the *LL* case[96] were rather different. In contested divorce proceedings in France, the wife adduced medical reports concerning the husband which indicated that he was an alcoholic and prone to domestic violence. The husband denied this. Somewhat earlier in *Z v Finland*[97] the Strasbourg Court had ruled that the protection of medical data is of fundamental importance to a person's enjoyment of private life, and that respecting the confidentiality of such information was of paramount importance.[98] Though the Court accepted that the interests of the community in disclosure of such information might outweigh the right to confidentiality, the context will determine the extent of a Contracting Party's margin of appreciation in authorizing disclosure. In the *LL* case, the Court found that the use of the disputed medical report was not proportionate to the legitimate aim of protecting the rights and freedoms of others.

In serious cases, the Contracting Parties will have a positive obligation to compel disclosure of a person's identity which might otherwise be regarded as a confidential matter. So, in the *KU* case,[99] the respondent State was found to be in breach of Article 8 when it had no framework for compelling an internet service provider to disclose the identity of a customer who had posted an advertisement of a sexual nature on an internet dating site pretending to be the applicant, a twelve-year-old boy, and soliciting an intimate relationship with a male.

The duty of confidentiality in relation to records lawfully held has also been the subject of proceedings before the Strasbourg Court.[100] Though the disclosure of which the applicant complained (of her health records in connection with a social security claim) was found not to be a violation of Article 8, the Court noted:

The Court reiterates that the protection of personal data, particularly medical data, is of fundamental importance to a person's enjoyment of his or her right to respect for private and family life as guaranteed by Article 8 of the Convention. Respecting the confidentiality of health data is a vital principle in the legal systems of all the Contracting Parties to the Convention. It is crucial not only to respect the sense of privacy of a patient but also to preserve his or her confidence in the medical profession and in the health services in general. The domestic law must afford appropriate safeguards to prevent any such communication

---

[95] *Craxi v Italy (No. 2)*, (App. 25337/94), 17 July 2003, (2004) 38 EHRR 995.

[96] *LL v France*, (App. 7508/02), 10 October 2006, ECHR 2006-XI.

[97] *Z v Finland*, (App. 22009/93), 25 February 1997, (1998) 25 EHRR 371, ECHR 1997-I.

[98] §95.

[99] *KU v Finland*, (App. 2872/02), 2 December 2008, (2009) 48 EHRR 1237.

[100] *MS v Sweden*, (App. 20837/92), 27 August 1997, (1999) 28 EHRR 313, ECHR 1997-IV. See also *Z v Finland*, (App. 22009/93), 25 February 1997, (1998) 25 EHRR 371, ECHR 1997-I.

or disclosure of personal health data as may be inconsistent with the guarantees in Article 8 of the Convention.[101]

FREEDOM TO DEVELOP ONE'S IDENTITY

PARENTAL LINKS AND CHILDHOOD

Article 8 may assist children to know and understand their childhood. Though there is no right of access to case records and a refusal of complete access does not amount to an interference with family life, nevertheless a system which allows disclosure of care records to children formerly in care only with the consent of contributors but makes no provision for considering the reasonableness of any refusal of consent will go beyond the margin of appreciation permitted by the article.[102] The Strasbourg Court has sometimes classified these issues as relating to family life, and sometimes to private life. All the cases are, however, considered in this chapter since they adopt a common approach both for children seeking to establish who their biological parents are, as well as cases in which fathers have sought to establish or contest paternity.

The Grand Chamber revisited the question of resolving competing interests of confidentiality and openness in the context of the provision of information for adopted children about their biological family in the *Odièvre* case.[103] The factual situation was very simple. An adopted child, who had attained the age of majority, was seeking information about her biological family. She had been abandoned by her natural mother who had requested that the birth be kept secret. In France, the effect of a declaration like that signed by the mother at birth resulted in a permanent inability of the child to learn the identity of her biological mother.[104] The applicant was only able to obtain non-identifying information about her biological family, from which she learned that she had three brothers. The Court considered that access to such information fell within the ambit of private life in Article 8. The Strasbourg Court recognized that the two competing interests of the mother for confidentiality and of the grown-up child for information are not easily reconciled. The Court, after rather slender reasoning, concluded that the respondent State had not breached Article 8 and had not overstepped its margin of appreciation in dealing with the competing interests which it faced. This was a majority decision by ten judges from which seven judges dissented in a powerfully argued joint dissenting opinion. They agreed that a balance had to be struck, but considered that the majority had not had proper regard

---

[101] *MS v Sweden*, §41.

[102] *Gaskin v United Kingdom*, (App. 10454/83), 7 July 1989, Series A No 160, (1990) 12 EHRR 36; *MG v United Kingdom*, (App. 39393/98), 24 September 2002, (2003) 36 EHRR 22.

[103] *Odièvre v France*, (App. 42326/98), 13 February 2003 [GC], (2004) 38 EHRR 871; ECHR 2003-III.

[104] The Joint Dissenting Opinion records that 'no other legislative system is so weighted in favour of maternal anonymity' (§13).

to developments in understanding the needs of adopted children to trace their natural parents. Furthermore, the French legislation effectively gave the natural mother a 'right of veto' 'condemning the child to lifelong ignorance'.[105] The dissenting judges concluded that, if a system of anonymous births is to be retained, a Contracting Party has a positive obligation to establish an independent authority with the power to decide whether or not to grant access.

The *Jäggi* case[106] shows the Strasbourg Court in rather more sympathetic mood towards a person seeking to establish who his father was. In this case it was a 67-year-old man who was seeking authorization for a DNA test to be carried out on the remains of the person he claimed to be his father. The refusal of the authorities to permit this was a violation of respect for his private life; the Court observed that 'an individual's interest in discovering his parentage does not disappear with age, quite the reverse.'[107]

A procedural barrier to establishment of paternity was found to be a violation of Article 8 in the *Phinikaridou* case.[108] There had been a deathbed confession to the applicant, then aged 52, by her mother telling her the name of her biological father. An absolute limitation period in the national legal order resulted in the rejection of efforts by the applicant to secure judicial recognition of paternity. The application of so rigid a time limit, without any exceptions and regardless of the circumstances, impaired the very essence of the right to respect for private life.

The *Shofman* case[109] concerned a father's action contesting paternity. Some two years after a child was born, of whom the applicant believed he was the father, it was established through DNA tests that he was not. He immediately began divorce proceedings and proceedings to contest the paternity of the child. The paternity suit was dismissed because the national law set a one-year time limit from the date on which the putative father was informed that he had been registered as the father. This time limit had passed by the time the applicant discovered that he was not the child's father. The Strasbourg Court found a violation of respect for the private life of the applicant, since it was not necessary in a democratic society to establish an inflexible time limit. Although practice in other Contracting Parties was not uniform, it was possible in some States in exceptional circumstances to bring paternity challenge proceedings out of time. The existence of such exceptions did not defeat what was accepted as a legitimate aim of time limits to balance legal certainty in family relations and the interests of the child.

The facts of the *Paulík* case[110] are rather sad. The appellant had a sexual relationship with a woman in 1966; she subsequently gave birth to a daughter. Under provisions of national law at the time, he was presumed to be the father and was so regarded. An order to pay maintenance for the child was made, with which the applicant complied.

---

[105] §7 of the Joint Dissenting Opinion.
[106] *Jäggi v Switzerland*, (App. 58757/00), 13 July 2006, (2008) 47 EHRR 702, ECHR 2006-X.
[107] §40.
[108] *Phinikaridou v Cyprus*, (App. 23890/02), 20 December 2007, ECHR 2007-XIV.
[109] *Shofman v Russia*, (App. 74826/01), 24 November 2005, (2007) 44 EHRR 741.
[110] *Paulík v Slovakia*, (App. 10699/05), 10 October 2006, (2008) 46 EHRR 142, ECHR 2006-XI.

The applicant maintained contact with her. In 2004, the applicant's 'daughter (who was by now married and had a family of her own which was financially supported by the applicant) had an argument with him over his financial contribution, and proposed that paternity be re-tested. A DNA test established that the applicant was not the father. The applicant then sought to initiate proceedings in the national courts to challenge his paternity of the 'daughter'. The 'daughter' indicated that she had no objection to his denial of paternity. The national authorities nevertheless regarded the establishment of paternity which had occurred many years earlier to be irreversible. The Strasbourg Court found a violation of Article 8 in that there was no procedure 'for bringing the legal position into line with the biological reality' and this did not benefit anyone.[111]

The circumstances of the *Różański* case[112] were the reverse; the applicant was seeking to establish that he was the father of a child. The circumstances involved a number of changes of mind by both the applicant and the mother of the child, and ultimately the applicant got nowhere in his attempts to get proceedings under way (partly because the proceedings required the consent of the mother) which would determine the paternity of the child in question. The Strasbourg Court characterized the issue as one concerning the applicant's right to family life. There was a violation of Article 8 in that there was no proper investigation by the national authorities of the applicant's assertion that he was the biological father of the child.

Issues of recognition of parenthood have also afflicted transsexuals. The *X, Y and Z* case[113] concerned X, a female-to-male transsexual, who lived in a permanent stable relationship with Y. Y underwent artificial insemination by an anonymous donor and gave birth to a child, Z. X sought registration as the father of the child. The Registrar-General advised that only a biological man could be regarded as the father for the purposes of registration, though the child could bear X's last name and that X would be entitled to a personal tax allowance in respect of the child provided he could show that he maintained the child. X went ahead and sought to register himself as the father of the child but was not permitted to do so. In considering the complaint of a violation of Article 8, the Strasbourg Court considered that de facto family ties linked the three applicants and so Article 8 was applicable. The Court noted that the issues raised in this case were different from those raised in the earlier transsexual cases, and concerned recognition of parenthood in cases where there had been artificial insemination by donor. Since there was no common ground on these issues among the Contracting Parties, a wide margin of appreciation should be accorded to individual States. Had a fair balance been struck between the competing interests of the individual and those of the community as a whole? After considering the arguments on both sides, the Court concluded that there was no obligation falling on the United Kingdom formally to recognize X as the father of Z, and there was no violation of

---

[111] §46.

[112] *Różański v Poland*, (App. 55339/00), 18 May 2006, (2007) 45 EHRR 625. See also *Mizzi v Malta*, (App. 26111/02), 12 January 2006, (2008) 46 EHRR 529, ECHR 2006-I.

[113] *X, Y and Z v United Kingdom*, (App. 21830/93), 22 April 1997, (1997) 24 EHRR 143, ECHR 1997-II.

Article 8. Four dissenting judges would have found a violation of Article 8, while one further judge would have found a violation of Article 14 taken in conjunction with Article 8, and one further judge would have found violations of Article 8 and Article 14.

CULTURAL IDENTITY

A series of cases has concerned the rights of gypsies. The *Buckley* case[114] concerned the refusal of planning permission to enable a gypsy to live in a caravan on her own land. The Strasbourg Court rejected a suggestion that respect for the home was only engaged where the home had been established lawfully. A refusal of planning permission constituted an interference which was in accordance with law, and planning legislation was accepted to serve the interests of the economic well-being of the country, the protection of health, and the protection of the rights of others. In considering whether the interference is necessary in a democratic society, the Court noted, in concluding that there was no violation of Article 8, that the process by which decisions were made had to be fair:

> Whenever discretion capable of interfering with the enjoyment of a Convention right such as the one at issue in the present case is conferred on national authorities, the procedural safeguards available to the individual will be especially material in determining whether the respondent State has, when fixing the regulatory framework, remained within the margin of its appreciation. Indeed, it is settled case-law that, whilst Article 8 contains no explicit procedural requirements, the decision-making process leading to measures of interference must be fair and such as to afford due respect to the interests safeguarded to the individual by Article 8.[115]

Judgment was given in January 2001 in five further cases against the United Kingdom concerning planning and enforcement measures taken against gypsies in respect of their occupation on their own land of caravans as their homes.[116] The cases contain a wealth of information on domestic and international texts on gypsies. The facts of these cases were broadly similar. The applicants were gypsies by birth and had lived a travelling lifestyle. They bought land with the intention of living on it in caravans; they moved onto the land and applied for planning permission, which was refused. Enforcement notices were served requiring the use of the land for residential purposes to cease. The Grand Chamber referred to its decision in the *Buckley* case, and noted that it was 'in the interests of legal certainty, foreseeability and equality before the law that it should not depart, without good reason, from precedents laid down

---

[114] *Buckley v United Kingdom*, (App. 20348/92), 25 September 1996, (1997) 23 EHRR 101.

[115] §76.

[116] *Chapman v United Kingdom*, (App. 27238/95), (2001) 33 EHRR 399; ECHR 2001-I; *Beard v United Kingdom*, (App. 24882/94), (2001) 33 EHRR 442; *Coster v United Kingdom*, (App. 24876/94), (2001) 33 EHRR 479; *Lee v United Kingdom*, (App. 25289/94), (2001) 33 EHRR 677; and *Smith (Jane) v United Kingdom*, (App. 25154/94), (2001) 33 EHRR 712; all 18 January 2001 [GC].

in previous cases' though due regard should be had to changing conditions and any emerging consensus among the Contracting Parties.[117] The Court considered the measures in issue to affect the applicants' private and family life, and home. There had been an interference with those rights which was in accordance with law, and in the interests of protecting the rights of others. The question was therefore whether the interference was necessary in a democratic society. The applicants relied heavily on the growing international consensus about the importance of providing legal protection of the rights of minorities, and an obligation to protect their security, identity, and lifestyle. The respondent State stressed the importance of planning controls in balancing the needs of the individual and the community, and that national authorities were better placed to make the necessary judgments on these issues. The Court came down in favour of the respondent State; the decisions on planning matters had been taken after weighing the various competing interests, and there were adequate procedural safeguards for the applicants. The Court was influenced by the fact that the homes were initially established unlawfully, that is, without the required planning permission.[118] A dissenting opinion of seven judges would have found a violation of Article 8 on the grounds that there is an international consensus which is sufficiently concrete that gypsies require special protection in respect of their right to respect for home, private and family life, which has a dimension beyond environmental concerns. Such concerns when weighed against the interference in the applicants' rights did not disclose a pressing social need. The dissenting judges denied that their decision was tantamount to excluding gypsies from the system of planning control.

In the *Connors* case,[119] the Strasbourg Court found that the lack of procedural safeguards surrounding the summary eviction of gypsies from a local authority gypsy site breached Article 8 of the Convention. The only basis for the eviction appeared to be some concern that a member of the family was a 'magnet for trouble'. In the course of its judgment, the Strasbourg Court noted:

The vulnerable position of gypsies as a minority means that some special consideration should be given to their needs and their different lifestyle both in the relevant regulatory framework and in reaching decisions in particular cases.....[120]

A statutory scheme permitting the summary eviction of gypsies was a disproportionate response to the problems local authorities faced. It could not be shown that the scheme was used to ensure a turnover of vacant pitches (so sustaining a nomadic lifestyle) nor to prevent families from becoming long-term residents.[121]

---

[117] *Chapman*, §70.   [118] *Chapman*, §102.
[119] *Connors v United Kingdom*, (App. 66746/01), 27 May 2004, (2005) 40 EHRR 189.   [120] §84.
[121] For a wide-ranging article on the human rights of travellers, see R. Sandland, 'Developing a Jurisprudence of Difference: The Protection of the Human Rights of Travelling Peoples by the European Court of Human Rights' (2008) 8 HRLRev 475.

NAMES

Some international conventions make explicit reference to names.[122] The European Convention is silent on this issue, but both the Commission and the Court have held that regulation of names falls within the ambit of private life. This includes the choice of a children's forenames by their parents.[123]

In the *Burghartz* case,[124] the applicants were Swiss nationals who had married in Germany. They chose the wife's last name, Burghartz, as their family name under the provisions of the German Civil Code. On returning to Switzerland, they applied to use Burghartz as their family name, and Mr Burghartz sought to use the name Schnyder Burghartz. The applications were turned down. Under Swiss law, the wife was permitted to use her family name before that of her husband. An appeal in respect of the use of the name Burghartz as the family name succeeded, but Mr Burghartz was denied the use of his family name before Burghartz.

The Strasbourg Court ruled that a person's name as a means of personal identification and of linking to a family concerns family and private life under Article 8. Nevertheless the State has an interest in regulating the use of names. In this case, the different treatment accorded to men and women in the use of names constituted a violation of Article 8 taken in conjunction with the non-discrimination provision in Article 14.[125]

In another case[126] a Finnish national challenged the refusal of the Finnish authorities to permit him to change his last name. The Strasbourg Court considered whether there was an interference in this case, and noted that there is a distinction between a situation in which the State refuses to permit a name to be changed and in which the State requires a name to be changed. The distinction is between the positive and negative obligations of States under the Convention. The Court went on:

Despite the increased use of personal identity numbers in Finland and in other Contracting States, names retain a crucial role in the identification of people. Whilst therefore recognizing that there may exist genuine reasons prompting an individual to wish to change his or her name, the Court accepts that legal restrictions on such a possibility may be justified in the public interest; for example in order to ensure accurate population registration or to safeguard the means of personal identification and of linking the bearers of a given name to a family.[127]

In the absence of common ground among the Contracting Parties, the Strasbourg Court allowed Finland a wide margin of appreciation. There was no interference with

---

[122] Art. 24(2) of the International Covenant on Civil and Political Rights, Arts. 7 and 8 of the Convention on the Rights of the Child, and Art. 18 of the American Convention on Human Rights. For a Community law case concerning names, see Case C-168/91, *Konstantinidis v Altensteig-Standesamt*, [1993] ECR-I 2755. See generally H. Greve, '"What's in a Name?" The Human Right to a Recognized Individual Identity' in S. Breitenmoser and others, *Human Rights, Democracy and the Rule of Law. Liber Amicorum Luzius Wildhaber* (Nomos, Baden Baden 2007), 295.

[123] *Guillot v France*, (App. 22500/93), 24 October 1996, ECHR 1996-V.

[124] *Burghartz v Switzerland*, (App. 16213/90), 22 February 1994, Series A No 280-B, (1994) 18 EHRR 101.

[125] See ch.24 below.

[126] *Stjerna v Finland*, (App. 18131/91), 25 November 1994, Series A No 299-B, (1997) 24 EHRR 195.

[127] §39.

the rights in Article 8(1) in this case because the sources of inconvenience to the applicant were not sufficient to raise an issue of failure to respect his private life; there were also alternative names which the authorities would have permitted him to use.

A violation was, however, found in the *Johansson* case.[128] The applicants wished to name their son 'Axl' in a manner which did not comply, in relation to the form of spelling, with the Finnish legislation on names. While the Strasbourg Court accepted that the protection of children from being given an unsuitable name, which might open them to ridicule, or be a mere expression of parental whimsy, and the preservation of national naming practices are in the public interest, the broad discretion accorded to the Contracting Parties was not without limit. In the absence of compelling evidence that a name would have negative consequences for the preservation of the cultural and linguistic identity of Finland, there was a violation of Article 8 in the interference with the choice of name by the parents.

TRANSSEXUALS

Transsexuals[129] have long been assertive in using Article 8 to secure recognition of their gender identity in some of the Contracting States. This line of cases provides an excellent case study of both the interpretation of the Convention as a living instrument and the development of positive obligations for Contracting Parties under the European Convention, though the law now appears well settled following the Strasbourg Court's judgments in two cases against the United Kingdom in 2002.[130]

The tide turned with the unanimous judgments of the Grand Chamber in the *Goodwin* and *I* cases,[131] which concerned post-operative male-to-female transsexuals. The *Goodwin* case raised the inability of Goodwin to change her gender as recorded in a number of official government records, while the *I* case raised the issue of change to a birth certificate. Though there was not yet evidence of a common European approach, the Court concluded that there was:

the clear and uncontested evidence of a continuing international trend in favour not only of increased social acceptance of transsexuals but of legal recognition of the new sexuality of post-operative transsexuals.[132]

---

[128] *Johansson v Finland*, (App. 10163/02), 6 September 2007, (2008) 47 EHRR 369, ECHR 2007-X.

[129] See Council of Europe and the International Commission on Civil Status, *Transsexualism in Europe* (Council of Europe Publishing, Strasbourg 2000). See also A. Campbell and H. Lardy, 'Transsexuals—the ECHR in Transition' (2003) 54 NILQ 209.

[130] *Goodwin v United Kingdom*, (App. 28957/95), 11 July 2002 [GC], (2002) 35 EHRR 447; ECHR 2002-VI; and *I v United Kingdom*, (App. 25680/94), 11 July 2002 [GC], (2003) 36 EHRR 967. For the earlier case-law, see *Van Oosterwijck v Belgium*, (App. 7654/76), 6 November 1980, Series A No 40, (1981) 3 EHRR 557; *Rees v United Kingdom*, (App. 9532/81), 17 October 1986, Series A No 106, (1987) 9 EHRR 56; *Cossey v United Kingdom*, (App. 10843/84), 27 September 1990, Series A No 184, (1991) 13 EHRR 622; *B. v France*, (App. 13343/87), 25 March 1992, Series A No 232-C, (1994) 16 EHRR 1; and *Sheffield and Horsham v United Kingdom* (Apps. 22885/93 and 23390/94), 30 July 1998, (1999) 27 EHRR 163, ECHR 1998-V.

[131] *Goodwin v United Kingdom*, (App. 28957/95), 11 July 2002 [GC], (2002) 35 EHRR 447; ECHR 2002-VI; and *I v United Kingdom*, (App. 25680/94), 11 July 2002 [GC], (2003) 36 EHRR 967.

[132] *Goodwin*, §85; and *I*, §65.

It was significant that the Strasbourg Court had, in earlier cases, 'signalled its consciousness of the serious problems facing transsexuals and stressed the importance of keeping the need for appropriate legal measures in the area under review.'[133] Goodwin is a male-to-female transsexual who had undergone gender re-assignment surgery, and lived as a woman. But for legal purposes in the United Kingdom, she remained classified as a man. The situation was far from a minor inconvenience; it resulted in feelings of vulnerability, humiliation, and anxiety. The Strasbourg Court considered that, where medical services in a Contracting Party provided for gender re-assignment surgery with a view to creating a biological identity of the gender the person perceives that he or she has, it was illogical to refuse to recognize the legal implications of such treatment. The Court undertook a detailed analysis of current knowledge of the phenomenon of gender dysphoria, and noted that there was not yet a universal approach to the disorder. This meant that Contracting Parties would enjoy a wide margin of appreciation, but that margin is not without its limits. The Grand Chamber observed:

Nonetheless, the very essence of the Convention is respect for human dignity and human freedom. Under Article 8 of the Convention in particular, where the notion of personal autonomy is an important principle underlying the interpretation of its guarantees, protection is given to the personal sphere of each individual, including the right to establish details of their identity as individual human beings.... In the twenty first century the right of transsexuals to personal development and to physical and moral security in the full sense enjoyed by others in society cannot be regarded as a matter of controversy requiring the lapse of time to cast clearer light on the issues involved. In short, the unsatisfactory situation in which post-operative transsexuals live in an intermediate zone as not quite one gender or the other is no longer sustainable.[134]

Once the Strasbourg Court had reached that position, it was inevitable, in the light of the earlier cases, that it would find that there was a violation of Article 8.[135]

Despite the significant development in the Strasbourg Court's position as reflected in these cases, new issues relating to the rights of transsexuals under Article 8 nevertheless continue to emerge. Under the legislation in the United Kingdom following these cases, a system of certification of gender has been introduced, but married parties can only obtain a full certificate where annulment of the marriage is obtained. In the *Parry* case,[136] following gender re-assignment of one of the parties to a marriage, neither party wished to seek annulment of the marriage, and complained that their failure to be eligible for a full certificate constituted a violation of Article 8. The Court ruled the application inadmissible on the grounds that it was not disproportionate. It was noted that the parties could continue their relationship as a civil partnership.

---

[133] *Goodwin*, §75.   [134] *Goodwin*, §90.

[135] The United Kingdom has responded by passing the Gender Recognition Act 2004.

[136] *Parry v United Kingdom*, (App. 42971/05), 28 November 2006, ECHR 2006-XV.

In the *Van Kück* case,[137] the applicant argued that court decisions in Germany which confirmed decisions that the costs of hormone treatment and gender re-assignment surgery were not reimbursable by her health insurance company violated her rights under Article 8. The Strasbourg Court considered the applicant's complaints both under Article 6 and under Article 8. Violations of both articles were found by a majority of four votes to three. The case is not authority for the proposition that all medical costs connected with hormone treatment and surgery are to be met by public health systems, since the decision turns on the manner in which the Court of Appeal in Germany characterized the applicant's condition as one of her own making, and required her to show, beyond a level that was proportionate in the case, the genuineness of her medical condition and the need for treatment for it.

In the *Grant* case[138] the Strasbourg Court found a violation of Article 8 where the national authorities refused to recognize the applicant's status as a woman for the purpose of entitlement at the age of 60 to a State retirement pension, whereas the pensionable age for a man was 65.[139]

HOMOSEXUALITY

In the *Dudgeon* case[140] the applicant complained that, under the law in force in Northern Ireland, he was liable to criminal prosecution on account of his homosexual conduct and that he had experienced fear, suffering, and psychological distress directly caused by the very existence of the laws in question, including fear of harassment and blackmail. He further complained that, following a search of his house, he was questioned by the police about certain homosexual activities and that personal papers belonging to him were seized during the search and not returned until more than a year later. Dudgeon alleged that, in breach of Article 8, he had suffered, and continued to suffer, an unjustified interference with his right to respect for his private life. In Northern Ireland, but not, as a result of changes in the law, elsewhere in the United Kingdom, the offences were committed whether the act took place in public or in private, whatever the age or relationship of the participants involved, and whether or not the participants consented. The Strasbourg Court said:

[T]he maintenance in force of the impugned legislation constitutes a continuing interference with the applicant's right to respect for his private life (which includes his sexual life) within the meaning of Article 8, paragraph (1). In the personal circumstances of the applicant, the very existence of this legislation continuously and directly affects his private life…either he respects the law and refrains from engaging—even in private with consenting male

---

[137] *Van Kück v Germany*, (App. 35968/97), 12 June 2003, (2003) 37 EHRR 973; ECHR 2003-VII. See also *Schlumpf v Switzerland*, (App. 29002/06), 9 January 2009.

[138] *Grant v United Kingdom*, (App. 32570/03), 23 May 2006, (2007) 44 EHRR 1, ECHR 2006-VII.

[139] But the entitlement to such recognition only arose from 5 September 2002, the date of the Court's judgment in the *Goodwin* case.

[140] *Dudgeon v United Kingdom*, (App. 7525/76), 22 October 1981, Series A No 45, (1982) 4 EHRR 149.

partners—in prohibited sexual acts to which he is disposed by reason of his homosexual tendencies, or he commits such acts and thereby become liable to criminal prosecution.[141]

The question was whether the interference was justified under paragraph (2). There was no doubt that the limitation was in accordance with the law, but a more contentious issue was whether the prohibition in the law of Northern Ireland was 'necessary in a democratic society' for 'the protection of morals' or the 'protection of the rights and freedoms of others'. The Court accepted that some degree of regulation of male homosexual conduct, as indeed of other forms of sexual conduct, by means of the criminal law can be justified as 'necessary in a democratic society', and recalled that the national authorities have a margin of appreciation in assessing this necessity. Nevertheless, any restriction must be proportionate to the legitimate aim pursued. This was particularly striking in a situation where the law of Great Britain and Northern Ireland differed, even though they were constituent parts of the same State. Despite the acknowledged conservatism of society in Northern Ireland, as compared to other parts of the United Kingdom, the Court did not consider that there remained any justification for keeping the prohibitory law on the statute book. The Court did not consider that decriminalization implied approval of the conduct regulated previously by the criminal law. Taking all the circumstances into account, the maintenance in force of the criminal sanctions for homosexual conduct between adult males in private was disproportionate to the aims sought to be achieved and violated Article 8 of the Convention.[142]

A similar approach was taken in the *Norris* case[143] which concerned legislation in effect in Ireland, and in the *Modinos* case,[144] which concerned the law of Cyprus.[145]

Two cases decided in 1999 addressed the issue of whether a discharge from the Royal Navy solely on the grounds of the applicants' homosexuality and in pursuance of the Ministry of Defence policy to exclude homosexuals from the armed forces violated their right to a private life.[146] The Strasbourg Court found that the exclusion of homosexuals from the armed forces was in accordance with law, and could be said to be in the interests of national security and for the prevention of disorder, but concluded that the exclusion in the case of the applicants was not necessary in a democratic society. A detailed consideration of the issue had been conducted by the British Government by its Homosexuality Assessment Policy Team (HAPT) which concluded that the policy should be maintained. The Court was clearly influenced by the policies

---

[141] *Dudgeon*, §41.   [142] §§60–1.

[143] *Norris v Ireland*, (App. 10581/83), 26 October 1988, Series A No 142, (1991) 13 EHRR 186.

[144] *Modinos v Cyprus*, (App. 10570/89), 22 April 1993, Series A No 259, (1994) 16 EHRR 485.

[145] See also P. van Dijk, 'The Treatment of Homosexuals under the European Convention on Human Rights' in K. Waaldijk and A. Clapham, *Homosexuality: A European Community Issue* (Martinus Nijhoff, Dordrecht 1993), 179.

[146] *Smith and Grady v United Kingdom*, (Apps. 33985/96 and 33986/96), 27 September 1999, (2000) 29 EHRR 493; ECHR 1999-VI; and *Lustig-Prean and Beckett v United Kingdom*, (Apps. 31417/96 and 32377/96), 27 September 1999, (2000) 29 EHRR 548. See also *Perkins and R v United Kingdom*, (Apps. 43208/98 and 44875/98), 22 October 2002; and *Beck, Copp and Bazeley v United Kingdom*, (Apps. 48535/99, 48536/99, and 48537/99), 22 October 2002.

of other Contracting Parties. Although the margin of appreciation to the State was acknowledged, the Court considered that, where the restrictions concerned 'a most intimate part of an individual's private life', particularly serious reasons would be required before such interferences would fall within the limitations in Article 8(2).[147] These decisions are to be welcomed and show that the Court's assessment of a State's margin of appreciation requires substantiated specific examples of the risks asserted by the State which are claimed to justify an interference with private life.

In the *Sutherland* case[148] the applicant successfully argued before the Commission that United Kingdom legislation which fixed the minimum age of consent for homo-sexual conduct by men at the age of 18 rather than at the age of 16 which was the age of consent applicable to a woman constituted a violation of Article 8 when read with Article 14 prohibiting discrimination.[149] The Commission concluded that this was so. The case was subsequently struck out of the list following amendment of the United Kingdom legislation on the age of consent for homosexuals.[150]

SADO-MASOCHISM

The issue of the criminalization of specific sexual practices of some homosexual men was considered in the *Laskey, Jaggard and Brown* case.[151] Three men were convicted of assault and wounding arising from sado-masochistic practices between consent-ing adults and taking place wholly in private. The men argued that the decision of the House of Lords refusing a defence of consent to the practices in which they had engaged constituted violations of their right to respect for their private life. No justification for the interference could be sustained under the Convention. They also argued that there was discrimination in comparison to other acts likely to cause greater harm and cited the availability of the defence of consent in the sport of boxing as an example.

The Strasbourg Court accepted that the regulation of the conduct in question was in accordance with law, and that it could be said to be for the protection of health or morals. Some hesitation can be detected in the decision of the majority, which noted that, although sexual orientation and activity concern an intimate aspect of private life, 'not every sexual activity carried out behind closed doors necessarily falls within the scope of private life'.[152] However, the Court proceeded on the assumption that the activities in issue formed part of private life. Given the nature of the activities, the Court allowed the State a wide margin of appreciation since the activities involved the infliction of physical harm; it did not matter that the context was in the course

---

[147] *Smith and Grady*, §89; *Lustig-Prean*, §82.

[148] *Sutherland v United Kingdom*, (App. 25186/94), Decision of the Commission of 21 May 1996; Judgment of the Court of 27 March 2001 [GC].

[149] On Article 14, see ch.24 below.

[150] Sexual Offences (Amendment) Act 2000 which entered into force on 8 January 2001.

[151] *Laskey, Jaggard and Brown v United Kingdom*, (Apps. 21627/93, 21826/93, and 21974/93), 19 February 1997, (1997) 24 EHRR 39, ECHR 1997-I.

[152] §36. In a short and trenchant concurring opinion, Judge Pettiti concludes that Article 8 was not applicable in this case.

of sexual conduct. The Court rejected the suggestion by the applicants that they had been singled out because they were homosexuals, noting the comment of the trial judge that the unlawful conduct would be dealt with equally whether it arose between homosexuals, heterosexuals, or bisexuals.[153] The Strasbourg Court concluded that the measures were necessary in a democratic society for the protection of health, and did not find it necessary to address the issue of whether the interference could also be justified for the protection of morals.

The case may usefully be contrasted with the *ADT* case,[154] which involved the prosecution for gross indecency of a male homosexual arising from sexual conduct[155] involving up to four other men which had been recorded on videotape for the private use of the applicant. Here the Court readily characterized the activity as falling within the private life of those involved. It was appropriate to apply a narrow margin of appreciation; 'the absence of any public health considerations and the purely private nature of the behaviour'[156] did not justify the application of criminal sanctions. The Court was unanimous in finding that there had been a violation of Article 8.

Whereas the Strasbourg Court has found it relatively easy to require the decriminalization of homosexual conduct between consenting adults in private because of the general consensus on this issue among the Contracting Parties, the Court appears less comfortable when dealing with the extreme forms of sexual gratification in issue in the *Laskey* case, and can be criticized for responding with extreme caution.[157] In so far as the fact that the conduct was recorded on videotape may have been relevant, that seems not now to be significant in the light of the decision in *ADT*. That must be right.

The *Pay* case[158] concerned the dismissal of a probation officer whose sexual preferences included bondage, domination, and sado-masochism. He had some business interests connected with these preferences, which included a website. He also engaged in sexual activities in a private members' club which involved male domination over submissive women. This public performance aspect of his sexual activities was claimed by the applicant to be a fundamental part of his sexual expression rather than a mere adjunct to it. He argued that his dismissal violated his right to respect for his private life. An issue arose as to whether the applicant had, by his performances in the private club (which had been video-recorded) resulted in his having waived his Article 8 rights. The Strasbourg Court did not find it necessary to determine this point, but went on to find the application to be manifestly ill-founded. The applicant's unwillingness to accept that his sexual activities, coupled with his business interests, might compromise his work as a probation officer whose work included work with sexual offenders, led the Court to conclude that his dismissal was not a disproportionate response on the part of the authorities.

---

[153] §47.
[154] *ADT v United Kingdom*, (App. 35765/97), 31 July 2000, (2001) 31 EHRR 33; ECHR 2000-IX.
[155] Oral sex and mutual masturbation.   [156] *ADT*, §38.
[157] See L. Moran, '*Laskey v The United Kingdom*: Learning the Limits of Privacy' (1998) 61 MLR 77.
[158] *Pay v United Kingdom*, (App.32792/05), Decision of 16 September 2008.

IMMIGRATION ISSUES AND PRIVATE LIFE

A comparatively recent development has been the extension of the Strasbourg Court's case-law on private life within Article 8 to offer a degree of protection to certain migrants.[159] The previous chapter has considered how the Court's case-law on family life provides a degree of protection against adverse immigration decisions where family life would be affected; it noted that in immigration questions, the notion of the core family has been introduced. In the *Slivenko* case,[160] the Grand Chamber acknowledged that removal of persons from a country had the capacity to adversely affect 'the network of personal, social and economic relations that make up the private life of every human being.'[161] The applicants were the wife and daughter of a former Soviet army officer of Russian origin who wished to remain in Latvia. The wife, Tatjana Slivenko, was born in 1959 in Estonia, and moved to Latvia at the age of one month; the daughter, Karina, was born in 1981 in Latvia. The husband served in the Russian army until 1994; he moved to Russia in 1996, but his wife and daughter remained in Latvia. The attempts of the wife and daughter to contest a deportation order were unsuccessful, and Tatjana and Karina moved to Russia in 1999 to join the father. Tatjana's parents remained in Latvia, and became seriously ill; the terms of the deportation order prevented Tatjana and Karina from entering Latvia for five years from 1996.

Tatjana Slivenko could not rely on family life (in relation to her relationship as an adult child with her parents), and so the case turned on the long-term residence with its establishment of a network of personal, social, and economic relations as the basis of the Court's decision that there had been a violation of Article 8. The Latvian authorities had overstepped the margin of appreciation, and the removal of Tatjana and Karina was not proportionate.

The *Sisojeva* case[162] also concerned Russian nationals living in Latvia.[163] The case was, however, not directly about deportation, since the Latvian authorities had given assurances that they would not proceed with deportation. The residence status of the applicants rested on a series of temporary residence permits; this, they argued, placed them in a position of insecurity and legal uncertainty which interfered with their private life. The Grand Chamber's decision was to strike the case out of the list in so far as it related to Article 8. The respondent State had offered to regularize the residence of the applicants by the time the Court came to consider the issue, but the Court's

---

[159] This section draws on an analysis of this case-law in D. Thym, 'Respect for Private and Family Life under Article 8 ECHR in Immigration Cases: a Human Right to Regularize Illegal Stay?' (2008) 57 ICLQ 87.

[160] *Slivenko v Latvia*, (App. 48321/99), 9 October 2003 [GC], (2004) 39 EHRR 490, ECHR 2003-X. See generally G. Guliyeva, 'Lost in transition: Russian-speaking non-citizens in Latvia and the protection of minority rights in the European Union' (2008) 33 ELRev 843.

[161] §96.

[162] *Sisojeva and others v Latvia*, (App. 60654/00), 15 January 2007 [GC], (2007) 45 EHRR 753, ECHR 2007-II.

[163] Though one of the applicants was stateless.

judgment makes it clear that the effects of uncertainty in relation to immigration status can interfere with private life, but went on to observe that the Convention did not guarantee any right to a particular type of residence permit. That was a matter for the discretion of the Contracting Parties.[164]

Thym argues convincingly that these cases signal the Court's 'new readiness to extend the protective reach of Article 8 ECHR in the field of immigration'[165] and are not limited to the particular facts of Russian minorities in the Baltic States.

Article 8 may also be engaged when steps are taken to prevent someone from leaving a country. In the *Iletmiş* case[166] the applicant, who lived in Germany, was arrested in Turkey on a visit to his family members there. On his release, his passport was not returned to him. His wife and children were at the time in Germany; they left Germany to join him in Turkey. He was subsequently acquitted of the offences with which he had been charged. He complained that the retention of his passport which prevented him from leaving the country amounted to a violation of his private and family life under Article 8. The Strasbourg Court considered that this was a case concerning private life. Although preventive measures such as confiscation of a passport can constitute measures permitted by Article 8(2), there is always the requirement that the confiscation, and its continuation, are necessary in a democratic society. The confiscation in this case went on for far too long. The Court observed:

At a time when freedom of movement, particularly across borders, is considered essential to the full development of a person's private life, especially when, like the applicant, the person has family, professional and economic ties in several countries, for a State to deprive a person under its jurisdiction of that freedom for no reason is a serious breach of its obligations.[167]

HEALTH AND MEDICAL PROCEDURES

The right to respect for private life also encompasses a right to be informed about health risks to which persons have been exposed, and issues relating to access to particular medical procedures. It will also cover the use of medical procedures to which the person has not consented, but this generally falls under the heading of freedom from interference with the person discussed earlier in this chapter. Issues can also arise in relation to consent by a parent to the medical treatment of a child.

The *Glass* case[168] concerned disputes which arose between doctors and the mother of a severely mentally and physically disabled child. The mother had made it clear that

---

[164] §91. See also *Kaftailova v Latvia*, (App. 59643/00), 7 December 2007 [GC]; and *Shevanova v Latvia*, (App. 58822/00), 7 December 2007 [GC].

[165] D. Thym, 'Respect for Private and Family Life under Article 8 ECHR in Immigration Cases: a Human Right to Regularize Illegal Stay?' (2008) 57 ICLQ 87, 111.

[166] *Iletmiş v Turkey*, (App. 29871/96), 6 December 2005, ECHR 2005-XII.

[167] §50.

[168] *Glass v United Kingdom*, (App. 61827/00), 9 June 2004, (2004) 39 EHRR 341; ECHR 2004-II.

she was opposed to the admission of morphine or diamorphine to her son, which the doctors considered necessary to relieve distress when they considered that he was in the terminal phase of respiratory failure. Such medication was administered despite her opposition. The Strasbourg Court concluded that the decision to impose treatment in the face of the mother's objections constituted an interference with respect for the child's private life, and, in particular, his right to physical integrity. The interference had not been necessary in a democratic society since the hospital could have made, but failed to make, an early application to the courts for their determination of whether the administration of such powerful medication was in the best interests of the child.

Even more disturbing are cases involving the sterilization of women of Roma origin, where doubts exist in the circumstances of the case whether the consent to sterilization was properly given. Cases where consent has been given in dubious circumstances such that there may have been no consent at all will clearly involve violations of Article 8.[169]

Abuse of mental health procedures will also engage Article 8. In a case with unedifying facts involving the use of mental health procedures to remove a person's legal capacity so that the mother could claim possession of property the applicant had inherited from his grandmother,[170] the Strasbourg Court found a violation of the right to respect for private life arising from the failure of the proceedings in which the applicant's mental capacity was considered to afford him protection.

In the *Guerra* case,[171] the Strasbourg Court found a violation of a positive obligation to provide information to local residents of the dangers to those living about one kilometre away from a factory producing fertilizers which had been classified as presenting a high risk of causing severe environmental pollution with attendant health hazards. There is, in such circumstances, a positive obligation of the State to provide essential information which would enable individuals to assess the risks they and their families might face if they continued to live so close to the source of the risk. This principle of entitlement of access to information has been extended to a general entitlement of access to medical records, which may only be curtailed in clearly defined and justifiable circumstances.[172]

Access to records and to personal information may well prove to be an area where the requirements of Article 8 increasingly impose positive obligations on a Contracting Party. An interesting set of circumstances was presented to the Court in the *McGinley and Egan* case.[173] The applicants had been stationed on or near Christmas Island and took part in the line-up procedure during atmospheric nuclear tests.[174] They sought

---

[169] *KH and others v Slovakia*, (App. 32881/04), 28 April 2009, (2009) 49 EHRR 857, and *VC v Slovakia*, (App. 18968/07), Decision of 16 June 2009.

[170] *Shtukaturov v Russia*, (App. 44009/05), 27 March 2008.

[171] *Guerra and others v Italy*, (App. 14967/89), 19 February 1998, (1998) 26 EHRR 357, ECHR 1998-I.

[172] *KH and others v Slovakia*, (App. 32881/04), 28 April 2009, (2009) 49 EHRR 857.

[173] *McGinley and Egan v United Kingdom*, (Apps. 21825/93 and 23414/94), 9 June 1998, (1999) 27 EHRR 1, ECHR 1998-III; ECHR 2000-I (revision).

[174] Service personnel were ordered to line up in the open and to face away from the explosions with their eyes closed and covered until twenty seconds after the blast.

increases of their war pensions on the basis that they had developed medical conditions caused by their exposure to radiation. They believed that documents in the possession of the Government would assist them, but were refused access to them. They claimed that non-disclosure of records constituted an unjustifiable interference with their private lives. The Court concluded that Article 8 did apply:

Where a Government engages in hazardous activities, such as those in issue in the present case, which might have hidden adverse consequences on the health of those involved in such activities, respect for private and family life under Article 8 requires that an effective and accessible procedure be established which enables such persons to seek all relevant and appropriate information.[175]

There was, however, in this case no violation, since there was a procedure under the Pensions Appeal Tribunal Rules of Procedure under which the applicants could have requested the documents which had not been used.[176]

The *Roche* case[177] concerned a former soldier who developed health problems which he believed to be related to his participation in 1962 and 1963 in tests at a military defence establishment working on chemical weapons of various kinds. He complained that his difficulties in getting access to information about the tests raised issues under Article 8. In the particular circumstances of this case, the Grand Chamber was unanimous in concluding that there had not been:

an effective and accessible procedure enabling the applicant to have access to all relevant and appropriate information that would allow him to assess any risk to which he had been exposed....[178]

Since little progress has been made in claims that Article 2 has been violated when there is a medical termination of a pregnancy, there are a number of cases in which applicants seek to rely on Article 8 in this context. In the *Tysiąc* case,[179] the Strasbourg Court, echoing a decision of the Commission in *Brüggeman and Scheuten*,[180] said:

[The Court] re-iterates that legislation regulating the interruption of pregnancy touches upon the sphere of private life, since whenever a woman is pregnant her private life becomes closely connected with the developing foetus.[181]

The applicant in this case was challenging the availability in Poland of medical termination of pregnancy in the circumstances she had faced. She had health

---

[175] *McGinley and Egan v United Kingdom*, (Apps. 21825/93 and 23414/94), 9 June 1998, (1999) 27 EHRR 1, ECHR 1998-III; ECHR 2000-I (revision), §101.

[176] A subsequent request for revision on the basis that the procedure under the Pensions Appeal Tribunal rules would not have secured the relevant documents failed by 5 votes to 2: see *McGinley and Egan v United Kingdom*, (Apps. 21825/93 and 23414/94) (Revision request), 28 January 2000; ECHR 2000-I.

[177] *Roche v United Kingdom*, (App. 32555/96), 19 October 2005 [GC], (2006) 42 EHRR 599, ECHR 2005-X.

[178] §167.

[179] *Tysiąc v Poland*, (App. 5410/03), 20 March 2007, (2007) 45 EHRR 947, ECHR 2007-IV.

[180] App. 6959/75, *Brüggeman and Scheuten v Germany*, Report of 12 July 1977, (1977) 10 DR100.

[181] *Tysiąc v Poland*, (App. 5410/03), 20 March 2007, (2007) 45 EHRR 947, ECHR 2007-IV, §106. Contrast *D v Ireland*, (App. 26499/02), Decision of 27 June 2006.

problems, and the pregnancy (her third) and delivery constituted a risk to her eyesight. She wished to have the pregnancy terminated for this reason, but she was unable to persuade doctors to approve this. In Poland, medical terminations of pregnancy remain a criminal offence save for certain exceptions which include danger to the mother's life or health. She had the child and her eyesight deteriorated badly after the delivery. The Strasbourg Court found that the operation of the national legislation failed to distinguish between cases where there is full agreement between the woman and the doctors, and cases where there is no agreement; there was no particular and timely procedural framework for resolving differences of opinion. This created for the applicant a situation of prolonged uncertainty. A violation of Article 8 was found by six votes to one. It is important not to read too much into this case. As Judge Bonello pointed out in a separate opinion, there is in Poland a system under which medical termination of pregnancy is legally available, and the issues in the case related to the procedures for determining, where there was a difference of opinion among doctors, whether the conditions to obtain a lawful termination of a pregnancy were satisfied.

In the *Evans* case,[182] the Grand Chamber acknowledged that respect for private life 'incorporates the right to respect for both the decisions to become and not to become a parent.'[183] Natallie Evans wished to have children; her partner at the time also wished to have children by her. It was discovered that she had ovarian tumours for which the treatment was the removal of her ovaries with the consequence that she would be unable to have children. The couple decided to create and freeze embryos for later use. The relationship subsequently broke down, and the partner decided that he no longer wished the embryos to be used. Where consent is withdrawn, the embryos must be destroyed. Natallie Evans sought to have the embryos preserved, since this was her only opportunity of becoming a biological parent.[184] She argued that there was a breach of her Article 8 rights to respect for her private life in the requirement for continuing consent by the man for the use of the embryos.

The Grand Chamber by thirteen votes to four concluded that there was no violation of Article 8. The position under national law was clear; both parties had been made aware of the regime when they undertook the creation of the embryos. There was a clash of rights here: between respect for the private life of the woman to choose to become pregnant, and the private life of the man to choose not to become a parent with a woman with whom his relationship had ended. The Strasbourg Court was clearly aware of the dilemma, but, in the absence of a uniform approach among the Contracting Parties, and in the face of a clear scheme which had been put to both the man and the woman, concluded that the national legislation (which had been the

---

[182] *Evans v United Kingdom*, (App. 6339/05), 10 April 2007 [GC], (2008) 46 EHRR 728, ECHR 2007-IV; see also M. Ford, 'Evans v United Kingdom: what implications for the jurisprudence of pregnancy?' (2008) 8 HRLRev 171.

[183] §71.

[184] As noted in ch.2 above, the Strasbourg Court ordered interim measures to preserve the embryos pending the determination of the case before the Strasbourg Court.

product of much reflection, consultation, and debate) struck a reasonable balance between the competing interests at stake.

Issues relating to euthanasia have also been argued under Article 8, as well as Article 2. In the *Pretty* case,[185] the applicant was concerned that her husband should be immune from prosecution if he were to assist her suicide, and sought to challenge the blanket ban on assisted suicide in the United Kingdom. Although the Strasbourg Court found no violation of respect for the right to private life having regard to the limitations set out in Article 8(2),[186] it did observe:

> The applicant in this case is prevented by law from exercising her choice to avoid what she considers will be an undignified and distressing end to her life. The Court is not prepared to exclude that this constitutes an interference with her right to respect for her private life as guaranteed under Article 8(1) of the Convention.

PROTECTION OF ONE'S LIVING ENVIRONMENT

It seems that the use of Article 8 as a means of generating environmental rights is heavily circumscribed. The current position is perhaps best summed up in the words of the Strasbourg Court itself in the *Kyrtatos* case:

> ...according to its established case-law, severe environmental pollution may affect individuals' well-being and prevent them from enjoying their homes in such a way as to affect their private and family life adversely, without, however, seriously endangering their health.... . Yet the crucial element which must be present in determining whether, in the circumstances of a case, environmental pollution has adversely affected one of the rights safeguarded by paragraph 1 of Article 8 is the existence of a harmful effect on a person's private or family sphere and not simply the general deterioration of the environment. Neither Article 8 nor any of the other Articles of the Convention are specifically designed to provide general protection of the environment as such; to that effect, other international instruments and domestic legislation are more pertinent in dealing with this particular aspect.[187]

A number of complaints arising from nuisance caused by adjacent commercial activity have been made under Article 1 of Protocol 1,[188] but a better basis for complaint may be Article 8.[189] In the *López Ostra* case[190] the applicant complained that the operations

---

[185] *Pretty v United Kingdom*, (App. 2346/02), 29 April; 2002, (2002) 35 EHRR 1, ECHR 2002-III.

[186] Relying heavily on a State's margin of appreciation: see §§68–78.

[187] *Kyrtatos v Greece*, (App. 41666/98), 22 May 2003, (2005) 40 EHRR 390; ECHR 2003-VI, §52.

[188] See ch.20 below.

[189] See Council of Europe, *Environmental Protection and the European Convention on Human Rights*, Human Rights File No. 21 (Council of Europe Publishing, Strasbourg 2005). See also Council of Europe, *Overview of the case-law of the European Court of Human Rights in environmental matters*, DH–DEV(2004)002rev; and Council of Europe, *Elements on the Protection of Human Rights and the Environment*, DH–DEV(2005)001.

[190] *López Ostra v Spain*, (App. 16798/90), 9 December 1994, Series A No 303-C, (1995) 20 EHRR 277. See also *Branduse v Romania*, (App. 6586/03), 7 April 2009 (smells from a tip).

of a liquid and solid waste management plant operated by a group of tanneries twelve metres from her home which released 'gas fumes, pestilential smells and contamination' harmful to health violated respect for her home guaranteed by Article 8. The Strasbourg Court found that Article 8 was applicable and stressed the need to strike a fair balance between the competing interests of the individual and of the community as a whole. Despite the relatively wide margin of appreciation enjoyed by the State, this was a case where the level of nuisance borne by the applicant exceeded that which would be viewed as reasonable when weighing the competing interests.

The *Guerra* case[191] concerned the risks associated with the operation of a chemical factory producing fertilizer and other chemical compounds. The applicants all lived about a kilometre from the factory. The Court concluded that the direct effect of emissions from the factory was that the applicants' private and family life was involved. This was, however, a case where a State's positive obligations were engaged; the question was whether the national authorities had taken the necessary steps to ensure effective protection of the applicants' rights under Article 8. The Court concluded that the failure of the authorities to provide timely information concerning the nature of the risks associated with the factory's activities denied the applicants the opportunity to assess the risks to themselves and their families if they continued to live close to the factory. There was accordingly a violation of Article 8.

In the *Fadeyeva* case[192] the Court concluded that the positive obligations under Article 8 might require a State to re-house those living close to industrial plants where the level of toxic emissions was shown to be hazardous to health.

Where an activity presents risks to the environment which might impact upon the personal lives of those living nearby, there must be a genuine and procedurally fair environmental impact assessment, otherwise there will be a failure to respect the private life of those persons.[193] Though the Strasbourg Court commonly states that Article 8 contains no explicit procedural requirements, it has read in a requirement for proper procedures in environmental cases. In the *Taşkin* case, it said:

Where a State must determine complex issues of environmental and economic policy, the decision-making process must firstly involve appropriate investigations and studies in order to allow them to predict and evaluate in advance the effects of those activities which might damage the environment and infringe individuals' rights and to enable them to strike a fair balance between the various conflicting interests at stake.... The importance of public access to the conclusions of such studies and to information which would enable members of the public to assess the danger to which they are exposed is beyond question.... Lastly, the individuals concerned must also be able to appeal to the courts against any decision, act or omission where they consider that their interests or their comments have not been given sufficient weight in the decision-making process....[194]

---

[191] *Guerra and others v Italy*, (App. 14967/89), 19 February 1998, (1998) 26 EHRR 357, ECHR 1998-I.
[192] *Fadeyeva v Russia*, (App. 55723/00), 9 June 2005, (2007) 45 EHRR 295, ECHR 2005-IV.
[193] *Taşkin v Turkey*, (App. 46117/99), 10 November 2004, (2006) 42 EHRR 1127, ECHR 2004-X.
[194] §119. See also *Giacomelli v Italy*, (App. 59909/00), 2 November 2006, (2007) 45 EHRR 871, ECHR 2006-XII.

The problems of aircraft noise were first raised before the Strasbourg Court under Article 8 in the *Powell and Rayner* case as possible violations of the right to respect for their private life and homes.[195] The Court noted that any violation of the article would arise as a breach of the State's positive obligations since Heathrow Airport is not owned or operated by the State. Having regard to the measures taken to control night flights and noise from the airport, the Court concluded that there was no serious ground on which a violation of the United Kingdom's positive obligations could be maintained.

The *Hatton* case[196] also concerned complaints that the noise from night flights for those living in the vicinity of Heathrow Airport constituted a violation of their rights under Article 8, and was ultimately considered by a Grand Chamber. The Court considered that this was a case in which they had to consider whether the United Kingdom Government had met its positive obligations to take reasonable and appropriate measures to secure the applicants' rights under Article 8. The Court noted that the earlier cases in which environmental rights had been in issue turned on the failure of the State to comply with some aspect of the regime operating in the national legal order:

...in *López Ostra* the waste treatment plant at issue was illegal in that it operated without the necessary licence, and it was eventually closed down. In *Guerra*, too, the violation was founded on an irregular position at the domestic level, as the applicants had been unable to obtain information that the State was under a statutory obligation to provide.[197]

A distinguishing feature in the *Hatton* case was that the domestic regime had been tested in the national legal order and found to be compatible with it. The Strasbourg Court accepted that night flying would be in the interests of the economic well-being of the country as a whole, and rejected an approach in the context of environmental rights which would accord them a special status. Having regard to the balance of competing interests, the national authorities could not be said to have overstepped their margin of appreciation. No violation of Article 8 was found, reversing the decision of the Chamber. Five dissenting judges felt that the interpretation of the Convention as a living instrument required greater weight to be given to environmental protection in balancing the interests of the State and those of the individual:

After all, as in this case, what do human rights pertaining to the privacy of the home mean if day and night, constantly or intermittently, it reverberates with the roar of aircraft engines?[198]

However, a failure by the authorities to police effectively noise nuisance caused by night clubs and bars in breach of the conditions under which they were permitted to

---

[195] *Powell and Rayner v United Kingdom*, (App. 9310/81), 21 February 1990, Series A No 172, (1990) 12 EHRR 355.

[196] *Hatton and others v United Kingdom*, (App. 36022/97), 8 July 2003 [GC], (2003) 37 EHRR 611; ECHR 2003-VIII. See also J. Hyam, '*Hatton v United Kingdom* in the Grand Chamber: One Step Forward, Two Steps Back?' [2003] EHRLR 632.

[197] §120.

[198] Joint Dissenting Opinion of Judges Costa, Ress, Türmen, Zupančič, and Steiner, §12.

operate, which prevents a person from sleeping and causes insomnia, will constitute a breach of Article 8.[199]

PROTECTION OF THE HOME

Many cases involving housing and the home will fall to be considered under Article 1 of Protocol 1.[200] But it is clear that aspects of security of tenure under landlord and tenant laws can involve issues touching on respect for the home.[201] The *McCann* case[202] illustrates the protection afforded. The applicant and his wife were tenants of a home rented to them by a local authority. The marriage broke down in circumstances where the husband was allegedly guilty of domestic violence. The wife and the children were re-housed, and the husband moved back into the home. The wife was then asked to end the joint tenancy by signing a notice to quit. She did this, but a week later sought to retract it; she had not appreciated that the effect would be to remove her former husband's right to live in the property. He said he needed the space to enable his children to visit. The local authority were reluctant to let him remain because of their policy not to assist those who had been involved in domestic violence. In possession proceedings, it was ruled that the applicant had no defence because of the termination of his tenancy as a result of the wife's notice to quit. The Strasbourg Court found a violation of Article 8 because, under the summary eviction procedure, the applicant had lost his home in circumstances when he had no opportunity to have the proportionality of the measure determined by an independent tribunal. Where a person lacks legal capacity and her home is at risk, Contracting Parties must ensure that procedures affecting a person's home reflect the need to protect their interests. Specific justification would be required where a time limit operated to prevent a vulnerable person from participating effectively in proceedings under which she was deprived of her home. The principle of legal certainty would not be violated by very limited exceptions to the operation of time limits designed to serve the interests of legal certainty.[203]

The leading case on housing rights under Article 8 is the *Gillow* case.[204] Mr and Mrs Gillow sought to challenge under Article 8 the restrictive system of licences for the occupation of housing on Guernsey. The couple had acquired a house on Guernsey during a period of employment there, which had subsequently been let while the couple were working elsewhere than Guernsey. They returned to occupy it, but were refused the requisite licence and were prosecuted and convicted for unlawful occupation

---

[199] *Moreno Gómez v Spain*, (App. 4143/02), 16 November 2004, (2005) 41 EHRR 899, ECHR 2004-X. It is significant that the conduct which caused the difficulties was a breach of the conditions under which the night clubs and bars were permitted to operate.

[200] See ch.20 below.

[201] See *Larkos v Cyprus*, (App. 29515/95), 18 February 1999 [GC], (2000) 30 EHRR 597; ECHR 1999-I.

[202] *McCann v United Kingdom*, (App. 19009/04), 13 May 2008, (2008) 47 EHRR 913.

[203] *Zehetner v Austria*, (App. 20082/02), 16 July 2009.

[204] *Gillow v United Kingdom*, (App. 9063/80), 24 November 1986, Series A No 109, (1989) 11 EHRR 335.

under Guernsey law. The Strasbourg Court considered that there was an interference with respect for the home, which was in accordance with law. The legislation restricting who could live on the island was accepted as having a legitimate aim. Was the interference necessary in a democratic society? The Strasbourg Court concluded that on its terms, there was no violation of Article 8 as far as the contested legislation *per se* was concerned. But the Court went on to consider whether the manner of its application to Mr and Mrs Gillow violated Article 8. On the particular facts of the case, the Court concluded that the refusal of both temporary and permanent licences to occupy their home and the conviction and fine imposed were disproportionate to the legitimate aim of the legislation and so constituted a violation of Article 8.

PROTECTION OF PRISONERS' CORRESPONDENCE

Article 8 has been used as a vehicle for addressing a number of prisoners' rights, particularly the rights of correspondence of those detained in prison.[205] 'Correspondence' refers primarily, but not exclusively, to communication in writing. Article 8 prohibits, subject to the exceptions in paragraph (2), any form of interference with correspondence, whether by censorship or otherwise. Prisoners' letters may be stopped or intercepted. There may be censorship of incoming and of outgoing letters. Or there may be a restriction on the number of letters that may be written. The subject may be treated in two parts: restrictions on the correspondence of prisoners, and other detained persons; and restrictions on correspondence with defence counsel. Often, of course, interference with prisoners' letters can be justified on one of the grounds stated in paragraph (2), as being necessary, for example, for the prevention of crime, or for the protection of the rights of others.[206]

The leading case is the *Golder* case.[207] Golder was serving a term of imprisonment for robbery. There was a riot in Parkhurst Prison and Golder was wrongly accused of being involved in it. Certain letters he wrote concerning the consequences of the allegation were stopped by the prison governor because he had not raised his complaints internally first; his petition to the Home Secretary asking for a transfer and requesting permission to consult a lawyer with a view to bringing civil proceedings in respect of the allegations against him were rejected. The effect of this was to bar him from communicating with a lawyer about his complaints. The Strasbourg Court concluded that there was an interference with the applicant's correspondence, and went on to consider whether the interference could be justified under the second paragraph of Article 8.

---

[205] See also European Prison Rules 1987; see generally N. Loucks, *Prison Rules: A Working Guide. The Millenium* [sic] *Edition* (Prison Reform Trust, London 2000).

[206] App. 3717/68, *X v Ireland*, 6 February 1970, (1970) 31 CD 96.

[207] *Golder v United Kingdom*, (App. 4451/70), 21 February 1975, Series A No 18, (1979–80) 1 EHRR 524.

The issue was whether the interference was 'necessary' for one of the grounds set out in the paragraph. This must, said the Court, be considered 'having regard to the ordinary and reasonable requirements of imprisonment'.[208] The Court concluded that there was no justification for a restriction on Golder's right to communicate with a lawyer with a view to seeking advice in connection with possible civil proceedings.[209]

The position which appears to have emerged from the case-law is that freedom of correspondence for prisoners will be protected to a high degree. The Strasbourg Court requires the national law authorizing the interference to be drafted with precision in order to meet the requirement that the interference is in accordance with law.[210] The Court will also require the clearest evidence that the action taken is proportionate to the aim of the limitation of freedom of correspondence. Exceptional circumstances will need to be present before control can be exercised over correspondence between prisoners with serious medical conditions and their doctors.[211] Stopping or censoring letters containing what are regarded as derogatory remarks about the prison authorities will not be justified.[212] The position is neatly summarized in the words of the Court:

The Court recognizes that some measures of control over prisoners' correspondence is not of itself incompatible with the Convention, but the resulting interference must not exceed what is required by the legitimate aim pursued.[213]

In the *Campbell* case[214] Campbell, who had been convicted of assault and murder and sentenced to life imprisonment with a recommendation that he serve not less than twenty years in prison, complained that his correspondence with his lawyer concerning a number of civil matters was opened and read by the prison authorities. The Strasbourg Court concluded that there had been an interference which was in accordance with law with the aim of preventing disorder or crime. Once again the consideration came down to determining whether the interference was necessary in a democratic society. The Court saw:

no reason to distinguish between the different categories of correspondence with lawyers which, whatever their purpose, concern matters of a private and confidential character. In principle, such letters are privileged under Article 8.[215]

---

[208] §45. See also *Campbell and Fell v United Kingdom*, (Apps. 7819/77 and 7878/77), 28 June 1984, Series A No 80, (1985) 7 EHRR 165.

[209] See also *Silver and others v United Kingdom*, (Apps. 5947/72, 6205/73, 7052/75, 7061/75, 7107/75, 7113/75, and 7136/75), 25 March 1983, Series A No 61, (1983) 5 EHRR 347.

[210] For examples of cases where the national law left the authorities too much latitude and so did not meet the requirement, see *Domenichini v Italy* (App. 15943/90), 21 October 1996; *Petra v Romania* (App. 27273/95), 24 August 1998; and *Moiseyev v Russia*, (App.62936/00), 9 October 2008.

[211] *Szuluk v United Kingdom*, (App. 36936/05), 2 June 2009.

[212] *Pfeifer and Plankl v Austria*, (App. 10802/84), 25 February 1992, Series A No 227, (1992) 14 EHRR 692.

[213] §46.

[214] *Campbell v United Kingdom*, (App. 13590/88), 25 March 1992, Series A No 223, (1993) 15 EHRR 137.

[215] §48.

The opening of mail might be justified to determine whether it contained any illicit enclosure, but that would not extend to reading the letter. This could be guaranteed by opening the letter in the presence of the prisoner. The reading of any letters between lawyer and prisoner could only be justified where the authorities have reasonable cause to believe that the privilege is being abused. In the *Campbell* case, the Court concluded that there was no pressing social need for the opening and reading of Campbell's correspondence with his solicitor.

It is vital to distinguish the different elements involved in 'control' of correspondence, and to differentiate quite clearly the grounds of exception permitted under Article 8(2).

Some aspects of the control of prisoners' correspondence would present no difficulties on this analysis. The stopping of a particular letter could obviously be justified in a particular case on one of the grounds mentioned in paragraph (2) (for example, 'for the prevention of crime') if the object of the letter were for example to effect an escape from prison. This in turn would justify, on the same ground, the reading by prison authorities of all letters, both incoming and outgoing. Finally, the fact that all letters may have to be read by prison authorities, who are responsible for good order in prisons, might in turn be said to justify the imposition of a limit to the number of letters which a prisoner may send or receive. In each case, however, the interference would have to be properly justified on one of the grounds stated in paragraph (2), and the reasons given by the authorities ascertained and assessed on this basis.

The correspondence of detained persons with their defence counsel is specially privileged. This follows from Article 6(3)(b) of the Convention which guarantees to everyone charged with a criminal offence the right to have adequate time and facilities for the preparation of his defence. This provision applies equally to proceedings on appeal.

The *Schönenberger and Durmaz* case[216] concerned the stopping of a letter from a lawyer instructed by the wife of Durmaz, who had been arrested and was being held in custody. Despite the letter's having been received, the district prosecutor kept it from Durmaz, who then had a lawyer assigned to him as an indigent. The lawyer's letter had urged Durmaz to make no statement to the authorities. The issue before the Court was whether the interference which had taken place was necessary in a democratic society. The respondent State argued that the stopping of the letter was necessary because the advice jeopardized the proper conduct of pending criminal proceedings by inviting the suspect not to make a statement. The Strasbourg Court noted that the advice contained in the letter did not amount to any exhortation to act unlawfully; it did not pose a threat to the normal conduct of the prosecution. Nor was it relevant that the lawyer had at the time of sending the letter been instructed by Durmaz's wife. The Court was unanimous in finding that there was a violation of Article 8.

---

[216] *Schönenberger and Durmaz v Switzerland*, (App. 11368/85), 20 June 1988, Series A No 137, (1989) 11 EHRR 202.

CONCLUDING REMARKS

The range of rights protected under the umbrella of private life under Article 8 is now very wide indeed, and the range of rights may not yet be fully explored. The analysis offered in this chapter seeks to bring some coherence to a large body of case-law in a context where the Strasbourg Court continues to indicate that private life is not susceptible of an exhaustive definition. It is now abundantly clear that private life is not just about notions of privacy in its traditional sense. What does emerge is that the distinction between negative and positive obligations in this context is becoming increasingly blurred, and that the procedural dimension to decision-making affecting rights within the ambit of private life is taking on greater importance. Procedures in this context must offer an effective means for national authorities to consider and reflect upon the private life dimension to situations ranging from artificial insemination to permits for large-scale projects with the capacity to harm the environment.

17

FREEDOM OF THOUGHT, CONSCIENCE, AND RELIGION

INTRODUCTION

In the first case under Article 9 to come before it,[1] the Strasbourg Court underlined the importance of the rights protected:

...freedom of thought, conscience and religion is one of the foundations of a 'democratic society' within the meaning of the Convention. It is, in its religious dimension, one of the most vital elements that go to make up the identity of believers and their conception of life, but it is also a precious asset for atheists, agnostics, sceptics and the unconcerned. The pluralism indissociable from a democratic society, which has been dearly won over the centuries, depends on it.

After a rather slow start to its case-law on freedom of thought, conscience, and religion, the Strasbourg Court has now established some rather loose guidelines, seemingly following earlier decisions of the Commission, on what constitutes religious or other beliefs, and has begun to fashion a concept of institutional freedom of religion free from unnecessary regulation by the State.[2] Despite this, some of the Court's judgments can be criticized for their minimalist reasoning, and there are a number of areas, such as the regulation of the wearing of religious insignia, which remain controversial. The Convention organs have also allowed Contracting Parties a wide margin of appreciation when it comes to placing limitations on the manifestation of religion and belief.

Article 9 provides:

1. Everyone has the right to freedom of thought, conscience and religion; this right includes freedom to change his religion or belief and freedom, either alone or in

---

[1] *Kokkinakis v Greece*, (App. 14307/88), 25 May 1993, Series A No 260-A, (1994) 17 EHRR 397, §31.

[2] See generally J-F. Renucci, *Article 9 of the European Convention on Human Rights. Freedom of thought, conscience and religion*, Human Rights Files No. 20 (Council of Europe Publishing, Strasbourg 2005); J. Murdoch, *Freedom of thought, conscience and religion: a guide to the implementation of Article 9 of the European Convention on* Human Rights, Human Rights Handbooks, No. 9 (Council of Europe Publishing, Strasbourg 2007); M. Evans, *Religious Liberty and International Law in Europe* (CUP, Cambridge 1998); and C. Evans, *Freedom of Religion under the European Convention on Human Rights* (OUP, Oxford 2001).

    community with others and in public or private, to manifest his religion or belief, in worship, teaching, practice and observance.

2. Freedom to manifest one's religion or beliefs shall be subject only to such limitations as are prescribed by law and are necessary in a democratic society in the interests of public safety, for the protection of public order, health or morals, or for the protection of the rights and freedoms of others.

The freedoms guaranteed are closely related to the freedom of expression guaranteed by Article 10,[3] and to Article 11 since many religions and belief systems expect some form of community worship or association. Religious education, which is a subject of special difficulty, is dealt with by Article 2 of the Protocol 1.[4]

THE SCOPE OF ARTICLE 9

DEFINING RELIGION OR BELIEF

The protection of Article 9 extends to a wide range of convictions and philosophies, not limited to, for example, religious belief. However, for the article to apply, a belief must 'attain a certain level of cogency, seriousness, cohesion and importance'.[5] This means that mere ideas or opinions will not constitute a belief. The borderline can frequently be difficult to draw, since belief is, of course, inherently subjective. The approach has resulted in a rather loose and ill-defined notion of religion or belief, and many of the authorities are somewhat dated admissibility decisions of the Commission. The Strasbourg Court, in the *Pretty* case,[6] rejected Diane Pretty's argument that the threatened prosecution of her husband for assisting her suicide was an interference with her ability to manifest her belief in the notion of assisted suicide for herself. But the Court did not offer a definition of religion or belief; it merely said that not all opinions or convictions constitute beliefs in the sense protected by Article 9(1), and that her claims did not involve a form of manifestation of a religion or belief.[7]

    Both the Commission and the Strasbourg Court have adopted a broad approach to what amounts to religions or beliefs. So the following have been accepted as religions or beliefs: Christian denominations of many kinds[8] including Jehovah's Witnesses[9] and

---

[3] See *Otto-Preminger Institute v Austria*, (App. 13470/87), 20 September 1994, Series A No 295-A, (1994) 19 EHRR 34, §47; and *Wingrove v United Kingdom*, (App. 17419/90), 25 November 1996, (1997) 24 EHRR 1, ECHR 1996-V, §§47–8.

[4] See ch.21 below.

[5] *Campbell and Cosans v United Kingdom*, (Apps. 7511/76, and 7743/76), 25 February 1982, Series A No 48, (1982) 4 EHRR 293, §36.

[6] *Pretty v United Kingdom* (App. 2346/02), 29 April 2002, (2002) 35 EHRR 1, ECHR 2002-III.

[7] §82.

[8] App. 11045/84, *Knudsen v Norway*, Decision of 8 March 1985, (1985) 42 DR 247.

[9] *Kokkinakis v Greece*, (App. 14307/88), 25 May 1993, Series A No 260-A, (1994) 17 EHRR 397; and *Manoussakis and others v Greece* (App. 18748/91), 26 September 1996, (1997) 23 EHRR 387, ECHR 1996-IV.

the Salvation Army,[10] Judaism,[11] Islam,[12] Hinduism,[13] Sikhism,[14] and Buddhism.[15] Less mainstream belief systems have also been recognized, such as atheism,[16] Druidism,[17] the Divine Light Zentrum,[18] and the Osho movement.[19] Even the controversial Church of Scientology has been accepted as falling within the scope of the article.[20]

In one case involving a prisoner,[21] the Commission held that it did not have sufficient evidence to substantiate the applicant's claim to being a 'light worshipper' whose rights under Article 9 had been violated.[22] In another case where a prisoner applicant claimed that he was being denied the practice of the Wicca religion in prison, the question of the recognition of Wicca as a religion did not arise since the applicant had not mentioned any facts, making it possible to establish the existence of the religion.[23] Evans comments on this case that it raises questions about when applicants can be expected to adduce evidence to establish that their claimed religion is a known religion, and what evidence the Commission (and now the Strasbourg Court) would find acceptable to sustain such a conclusion.[24]

The rather loose definition of religion inevitably raises the question of the borderline between a religion and a sect, which the Strasbourg organs may view with some distrust even though any issues arising under Article 9 are likely to relate to the manifestation of the belief, which are subject to the limitations set out in Article 9(2). Interestingly, as Renucci notes, the Commission has never used the word 'sect'.[25] The Strasbourg Court has, however, in its judgments in the *Manoussakis* case[26] and in the *Kalaç* case,[27] used the word 'sect' and 'sects', but very much in passing (though also in a pejorative sense). The question was presented more squarely in a case against France, though ultimately it was not necessary to provide an answer to the question

---

[10] *Moscow Branch of the Salvation Army v Russia*, (App. 72881/01), 5 October 2006, (2007) 44 EHRR 912, ECHR 2006-XI.

[11] App.10180/82, *D v France*, Decision of 6 December 1983, (1983) 35 DR 199.

[12] App. 16278/90, *Karaduman v Turkey*, Decision of 3 May 1993, (1993) 74 DR 93.

[13] App. 20490/92, *ISKCON and others v United Kingdom*, Decision of 8 March 1994, (1994) 76-A DR 41.

[14] App. 8121/78, *X v United Kingdom*, Decision of 6 March 1982, (1982) 28 DR 5, 38.

[15] App. 5442/72, *X v United Kingdom*, Decision of 20 December 1974, (1974) 1 DR 41.

[16] App. 10491/83, *Angelini v Sweden*, Decision of 3 December 1986, (1986) 51 DR 41.

[17] App. 12587/86, *Chappell v United Kingdom*, Decision of 14 July 1987, (1987) 53 DR 241.

[18] App. 8118/77, *Omkarananda and the Divine Light Zentrum v Switzerland*, Decision of 19 March 1981, (1981) 25 DR 105.

[19] *Leela Förderkreis E.V and others v Germany*, (App. 58911/00), 6 November 2008, (2009) 49 EHRR 117.

[20] App. 7805/77, *Pastor X and the Church of Scientology v Sweden*, Decision of 5 May 1979, (1979) 22 *Yearbook* 244; and *Church of Scientology Moscow v Russia*, (App. 18147/02), 5 April 2007.

[21] See below in this chapter for specific comment on prisoners and Article 9.

[22] App. 4445/70, *X v Germany*, Decision of 1 April 1970, (1970) 37 CD 119.

[23] App. 7291/75, *X v United Kingdom*, Decision of 4 October 1977, (1977) 11 DR 55.

[24] C. Evans, *Freedom of Religion under the European Convention on Human Rights* (OUP, Oxford 2001), 58.

[25] J-F. Renucci, *Article 9 of the European Convention on Human Rights. Freedom of thought, conscience and religion*, Human Rights Files No. 20 (Council of Europe Publishing, Strasbourg 2005), 17.

[26] *Manoussakis and others v Greece* (App. 18748/91), 26 September 1996, (1997) 23 EHRR 387, ECHR 1996-IV, §39.

[27] *Kalaç v Turkey* (App. 20704/92), 1 July 1997, (1999) 27 EHRR 552, ECHR 1997-V, §26.

of what constitutes a sect which is outside the scope of the protection of Article 9.[28] Jehovah's Witnesses in France complained that the publication of two reports of a parliamentary commission, and a legislative bill to strengthen preventive and punitive actions against sectarian groups, had seriously jeopardized the exercise of its freedom of religion. A law had been passed in June 2001 in this area. Jehovah's Witnesses had been named in one of the reports as a dangerous sect. The Strasbourg Court concluded that the application was an attempt to call into question the compatibility, in the abstract, of French proposals (which were devoid of any legal effect), and the applicants could not establish that they were a victim, or even a potential victim of a violation of Article 9.

The notion that sects are bad was at the heart of the *Leela Förderkreis E.V* case.[29] The case concerned associations in Germany which belonged to the Osho movement, better known to many under its former label, the Bhagwan movement. The German authorities became concerned about the potential danger these associations could be to the personal development and social relations of young people. An information campaign was undertaken which described the Osho movement in pejorative terms.[30] The complaints of the associations wound their way to the Bundesverwassungsgericht, which upheld the legality of the information campaign, including its use of language. The associations complained that the campaign constituted an interference with their right to manifest their religion. The Strasbourg Court accepted that the activities of the associations constituted a manifestation of the associations' beliefs, and proceeded, without determining the issue one way or another, on the basis that the information campaign constituted an interference with that right. The Court accepted that the German Basic Law, which included a duty to impart information on subjects of public concern, was wide enough to provide a legal base for its actions. It was clear that the German authorities were acting for a legitimate aim.[31] The majority of five concluded that the information campaign had not gone beyond what was necessary in a democratic society in the circumstances in which there was some conflict and tension in German society about the increasing number of new religions and ideological movements. Somewhat controversially, the Strasbourg Court added:

…such a power of preventive intervention on the State's part is also consistent with the Contracting Parties' positive obligations under Article 1 of the Convention to secure the rights and freedoms of persons within their jurisdiction. Those obligations relate not only to any interference that may result from acts or omissions imputable to agents of the State or occurring in public establishments, but also to interference imputable to private individuals within non-State entities….[32]

---

[28] *The Christian Federation of Jehovah's Witnesses in France v France* (App. 53430/99), Decision of 6 November 2001, ECHR 2001-XI.

[29] *Leela Förderkreis E.V and others v Germany*, (App. 58911/00), 6 November 2008, (2009) 49 EHRR 117.

[30] Describing them as 'sects', 'youth sects', 'psycho-sects' and 'psycho-groups'.

[31] For the protection of public safety, public order, and the protection of the rights and freedoms of others: §94.

[32] §99.

Two judges attached partly dissenting opinions. Judge Trajkovska emphasized the role of the authorities to ensure that competing groups tolerate each other, and could not find any indication that the teachings of the Osho movement threatened public safety, public order, or the rights or freedoms of others. Judge Kalaydjieva also emphasized this point, but took issue with the majority's view on positive obligations; the positive duty to impart information on subjects of public concern related to matters which were urgent or objective risks 'such as imminent calamities and the like, which beliefs as such may hardly be considered to constitute'. Judge Kalaydjieva considered that there was a breach of Article 9 read with Article 14 of the Convention, because the applicant associations had endured treatment to which the mainstream religion was not subjected, and for which the respondent State could provide no justification.

A distinction must be drawn between the holding and communication of a belief, and acts motivated by the belief but not central to its expression. Thus, although pacifism has been held to fall within the scope of Article 9 as a belief, the Commission did not consider that an applicant was able to challenge her conviction and sentence resulting from the distribution of leaflets indicating opposition to the policy of the United Kingdom Government in Northern Ireland, since the leafleting 'did not manifest her belief in the sense of Article 9(1).'[33] In another case, the Commission received a complaint that a decision of the Market Court in Sweden, restricting the terms used in advertisements for the sale by the Church of Scientology of the Hubbard Electrometer, violated Article 9. The Hubbard Electrometer was described by the applicants as a religious artefact used to measure the electrical characteristics of the 'static field' surrounding the body. The Commission distinguished between words in publicity material related to the beliefs of the Church and words aimed at selling, which were not within Article 9(1) since they were 'more a manifestation of a desire to market goods for profit than the manifestation of a belief in practice'.[34]

MATTERS FALLING OUTSIDE ARTICLE 9

In the *Refah Partisi* case, in the context of a Contracting Party's obligation to ensure mutual tolerance between opposing groups, the Grand Chamber observed:[35]

> 92. The Court's established case-law confirms this function of the State. It was held that in a democratic society the State may limit the freedom to manifest a religion, for example by wearing an Islamic headscarf, if the exercise of that freedom clashes with the aim of protecting the rights and freedoms of others, public order and public safety.... . While freedom of religion is in the first place a matter of individual conscience, it also implies freedom to manifest one's religion alone and in private or in community

---

[33] App. 7050/75, *Arrowsmith v United Kingdom*, Decision of 12 October 1978 (1980) 19 DR 5.

[34] App. 7805/77, *Pastor X and the Church of Scientology v Sweden*, Decision of 5 May 1979, (1979) 22 *Yearbook* 244, 250.

[35] *Refah Partisi (The Welfare Party) v Turkey*, (Apps. 41340/98, 41342/98, and 41344/98), 13 February 2003 [GC], (2003) 37 EHRR 1, ECHR 2003- II, §§92–3. See K Boyle, "Human Rights, Religion and Democracy: The Refah Party Case' (2004) 1 *Essex Human Rights Review* 1.

with others, in public and within the circle of those whose faith one shares. Article 9 lists a number of forms which manifestation of a religion or belief may take, namely worship, teaching, practice and observance. Nevertheless, it does not protect every act motivated or influenced by a religion or belief.... The obligation for a teacher to observe normal working hours which, he asserts, clash with his attendance at prayers, may be compatible with the freedom of religion, ... as may the obligation requiring a motorcyclist to wear a crash helmet, which in his view is incompatible with his religious duties....

93. In applying the above principles to Turkey, the Convention institutions have expressed the view that the principle of secularism is certainly one of the fundamental principles of the State which are in harmony with the rule of law and respect for human rights and democracy. An attitude which fails to respect that principle will not necessarily be accepted as being covered by the freedom to manifest one's religion and will not enjoy the protection of Article 9 of the Convention....

It follows that religions or belief systems which do not respect the rule of law, human rights, and democracy will not fall within the protection of Article 9. To date, no religion or belief system has been so excluded, but aspects of the observance of the Muslim faith in secular countries have been excluded from legitimate expressions of that faith.[36]

An interesting issue was raised in the *El Majjaoui* case.[37] A mosque in The Netherlands, which served Muslims from the local Moroccan community, had recruited an imam from abroad, but failed to secure a work permit for him. The individual and the mosque argued that there was a breach of Article 9 in the refusal to provide a work permit for the imam. The Chamber had relinquished the case to the Grand Chamber, but, by the time the case came before the Grand Chamber, a subsequent application for a work permit had been successful. The Grand Chamber struck the case out of its list. In so doing, the Grand Chamber expressed its agreement with a Commission decision[38] that Article 9 does not guarantee foreign nationals a right to obtain a residence permit for work, even if the employer is a religious association.

Article 9 is unlikely to be of assistance where immigration questions are linked to freedom of religion. The *Z and T* case[39] concerned a couple who had left Pakistan in October 2001 in the face of attacks on Christian churches in Bahwalpur, and travelled to the United Kingdom where they claimed asylum. When their applications were unsuccessful, they argued that they would be unable to live openly and freely as Christians if they were returned to Pakistan, and that this violated Article 9. In deciding that the application was inadmissible, the Strasbourg Court ruled that it was highly unlikely that Article 9 could ever be used for this purpose, since the sort of

---

[36] See below in this chapter.
[37] *El Majjaoui & Stichting Touba Moskee v The Netherlands*, (App. 25525/03), 20 December 2007 [GC].
[38] App. 32168/96, *Hüsnü Öz v Germany*, Decision of 3 December 1996.
[39] *Z and T v United Kingdom*, (App. 27034/05), Decision of 28 February 2006, ECHR 2006-III.

risk in relation to the exercise of religious beliefs which might justify a prohibition on removal would almost certainly fall within Articles 2 or 3. The Court observed:

...protection is offered to those who have a substantiated claim that they will either suffer persecution for, inter alia, religious reasons or will be at real risk of death or serious ill-treatment, and possibly flagrant denial of a fair trial or arbitrary detention because of their religious affiliation (as for any other reason). Where...an individual claims that on return to his own country he would be impeded in his religious worship in a manner which falls short of those proscribed levels, the Court considers that very limited assistance, if any, can be derived from Article 9 by itself. Otherwise it would be imposing an obligation on Contracting States effectively to act as indirect guarantors of freedom of worship for the rest of the world.

Nor will Article 9 assist where the beliefs relate to the regulation of marriage. The husband in a married couple had undergone gender re-assignment surgery and lived as a woman. She then sought to obtain a Gender Recognition Certificate under United Kingdom law. An interim certificate was granted, the only purpose of which was to enable the applicant to seek annulment of the marriage following which a full certificate would be issued. The applicant complained, among other things, that there was a breach of Article 9 in that the requirement to seek annulment of the marriage interfered with the strongly held beliefs of the couple who did not want to end their marriage. The Strasbourg Court ruled the complaint inadmissible. Article 9 does not regulate marriage in any religious sense, and it is for each Contracting Party to determine the conditions on which it grants recognition of gender changes for transsexuals.[40]

DOES ARTICLE 9 COVER INSTITUTIONS AS WELL AS INDIVIDUALS?

For some time it was uncertain whether a church was itself capable of exercising the right contained in Article 9. An apparently serious interference with religious freedom was brought before the Commission in an early application against the United Kingdom by the Church of Scientology of California.[41] The authorities considered that the applicant church was a dangerous sect and accordingly took certain measures, including the denial or withdrawal of visas, to prevent its members from entering and remaining in the country. Rejecting the application under Article 9, the Commission held that a legal, as opposed to a natural, person was incapable of having or exercising the rights mentioned in Article 9(1). In any event, it considered that the impugned measures did not prevent adherents of the Church of Scientology, whether resident or coming from abroad, from attending the college of the church or its other branches in the United Kingdom, or otherwise manifesting their religious beliefs—despite the fact that this was precisely what the restrictions were designed to prevent.

---

[40] *Parry v United Kingdom*, (App. 42971/05), 28 November 2006, ECHR 2006-XV.
[41] App. 3798/68, *Church of X v United Kingdom*, Decision of 17 December 1968, (1969) 12 *Yearbook* 306.

In 1979 the Commission reversed this case-law, holding that a church or association with religious or philosophical objects could exercise the right to manifest religion under Article 9, since it was really no more than the collection of its members.[42] By contrast, it seems to be established that an association is not capable of exercising the right of freedom of conscience,[43] since this would be a metaphysical impossibility.

Whether the application is brought by the church or one or more of its members, the Strasbourg Court treats attempts by a Contracting Party to interfere in the running of mainstream religious organizations very seriously:

Where the organization of the religious community is at issue, Article 9 must be interpreted in the light of Article 11 of the Convention which safeguards associative life against unjustified State interference. Seen in this perspective, the believer's right to freedom of religion encompasses the expectation that the community will be allowed to function peacefully free from arbitrary State intervention. Indeed, the autonomous existence of religious communities is indispensable for pluralism in democratic society and is thus an issue at the very heart of the protection which Article 9 affords.[44]

THE MANIFESTATION OF RELIGION OR BELIEF

Freedom of thought, conscience, and religion includes freedom to manifest one's religion or belief.[45] The general right to freedom of thought, conscience, and religion protected by Article 9(1) is absolute. The manifestation of religion or belief is, however, subject to the limitations set out in paragraph (2), where 'necessary in a democratic society in the interests of public safety, for the protection of public order, health or morals, or for the protection of the rights and freedoms of others'. The dividing line between interferences with freedom of religion or belief and its manifestation is a fine one in some cases. All measures taken to impose restrictions on the manifestation of religion or belief must be in accordance with law, that is, have an identifiable legal basis and be sufficiently clear that persons will know how to regulate their behaviour.[46] The Strasbourg Court says that it affords a limited margin of appreciation to Contracting

---

[42] App. 7805/77, *Pastor X and the Church of Scientology v Sweden*, Decision of 5 May 1979 (1979), 22 *Yearbook* 244; see also App. 12587/86, *Chappell v United Kingdom*, Decision of 14 July 1987, (1987) 53 DR 241. The Strasbourg Court has followed this approach: *Religionsgemeinschaft der Zuegen Jehovas and others v Austria*, (App. 40825/98), 31 July 2008; and *Leela Förderkreis E.V and others v Germany*, (App. 58911/00), 6 November 2008, (2009) 49 EHRR 117, §79.

[43] App. 11308/84, *Vereniging Rechtswinkels Utrecht v Netherlands*, Decision of 13 March 1986, (1986) 46 DR 200. See also App. 11921/86, *Kontakt-Information-Therapie and Hagen v Austria*, Decision of 12 October 1988, (1988) 57 DR 81.

[44] *Hasan and Chaush v Bulgaria* (App. 30985/96), 26 October 2000 [GC], (2002) 34 EHRR 1339, ECHR 2000-XI, §62.

[45] See P. Cumper, 'The public manifestation of religion or belief: challenges for a multi-faith society in the twenty-first century' in A. Lewis and R. O'Dair, *Law and Religion* (OUP, Oxford 2001), 311.

[46] For example of cases, where the Strasbourg Court decided that there was no foundation in law, see *Kuznetsov and others v Russia*, (App. 184/02), 11 January 2007, (2009) 49 EHRR 355 (interfering with a

Parties in this area, but that is rather contradicted by a narrow view of the manifestation of religion or beliefs, where the Court tends to protect only those manifestations which are the objectively necessary outward displays of the religion or beliefs.[47]

In the *Kokkinakis* case, the Strasbourg Court said:

While religious freedom is primarily a matter of individual conscience, it also implies, inter alia, freedom to 'manifest [one's] religion'. Bearing witness in words and deeds is bound up with the existence of religious convictions.[48]

In its judgment in the *Cyprus v Turkey* case, the Strasbourg Court found a violation of Article 9 arising from the limitations on the movement of Greek Cypriots in the occupied north of the island which prevented them from being able to manifest their religion.[49]

Clearly, dismissing someone from employment[50] solely because of their religious beliefs will violate Article 9.[51] This will be an infringement of freedom of religion, rather than its manifestation. But Article 9 does not, of itself, give any entitlement to time off work for religious festivals. In the *Kosteski* case,[52] the applicant complained of a breach of Article 9 when he was fined for taking time of work to observe Muslim religious festivals. The accommodations at his place of work required him to substantiate his claims that he was a practising Muslim, and he had declined to do so. It was not disproportionate to make this requirement of him. Nor was it a breach of Article 9 when read with Article 14 (prohibiting discrimination), since it was not unreasonable to require him to substantiate his claim to be a practising Muslim.

According to Article 9, freedom to manifest one's religion is not only exercisable in community with others, 'in public' and within the circle of those whose faith one shares, but can also be asserted 'alone' and 'in private'; furthermore, it includes in principle the right to try to convince one's neighbour, for example through 'teaching', failing which, moreover, 'freedom to change [one's] religion or belief', enshrined in Article 9, would be likely to remain a dead letter.[53] Note that there is no right to manifest conscience,[54] though most such claims could almost certainly be framed in terms of manifestation of beliefs. The case-law, discussed later in this chapter, concerning conscientious objection to military service may be classified in this way.

---

religious assembly of Jehovah's Witnesses); and *Igor Dmitrijevs v Latvia*, (App. 61638/00), 30 November 2006 (refusal to allow a prisoner applicant to attend the prison's religious services).

[47] This is most noticeable in the case-law relating to the religious freedom of prisoners, which is discussed later in this chapter.

[48] *Kokkinakis v Greece*, (App. 14307/88), 25 May 1993, Series A No 260-A, (1994) 17 EHRR 397, §31.

[49] *Cyprus v Turkey*, (App. 25781/94), 10 May 2001, (2002) 35 EHRR 731, ECHR 2001-IV, §§241–7.

[50] Where that employment has no special characteristics which might be considered to warrant a narrower view.

[51] *Ivanova v Bulgaria*, (App. 52435/99), 12 April 2007, (2008) 47 EHRR 1173, ECHR 2007-IV.

[52] *Kosteski v the Former Yugoslav Republic of Macedonia*, (App. 55170/00), 13 April 2006, (2007) 45 EHRR 712.

[53] Ibid.

[54] But see P. Edge, 'Current Problems in Article 9 of the European Convention on Human Rights' [1996] *Juridical Review* 42 which might be taken to suggest to the contrary.

The applicants in the *Kokkinakis* case[55] were Jehovah's Witnesses engaged in evangelical activity, including calling at houses to persuade the occupiers to join them. They had the misfortune to call upon the wife of an Orthodox priest, who reported them to the police, since in Greece proselytism (defined as attempting to convert believers away from the Orthodox religion)[56] is a criminal offence. The applicants were arrested, charged, and subsequently convicted and fined.

The Strasbourg Court concluded that the Greek law against proselytism was sufficiently clearly drafted for the purposes of Article 9(2) and that it pursued the legitimate aim of protecting the rights and freedoms of others. This left consideration of whether the limitation was necessary in a democratic society. A fine distinction is made in this part of the majority's judgment. Bearing Christian witness—an interesting phrase—is described as true evangelism, and is contrasted with 'improper proselytism', described as 'a corruption or deformation of it which was not compatible with respect for freedom of thought, conscience and religion'. The Greek action violated Article 9 because there was no evidence that the applicants had attempted to convince the householder by improper means. The conviction was accordingly not justified by a pressing social need.

An example of what the Strasbourg Court considers 'improper proselytism' was provided by the *Larissis and others* case.[57] The applicants were officers in the Greek air force who were convicted of proselytism after complaints from soldiers under their command that they had attempted to persuade the soldiers to become Jehovah's Witnesses. The Court decided that the Greek authorities had been justified in taking measures to protect the junior airmen from the applicants, in view of the fact that the hierarchical and claustrophobic nature of life within the armed forces might make it difficult for a subordinate to rebuff the approaches of an individual of superior rank or to withdraw from a conversation initiated by him. There was a risk of indoctrination.

The Strasbourg Court emphasized that not every discussion about religion or other sensitive matters between individuals of unequal rank would justify a Contracting Party in taking repressive measures under Article 9(2). However, such justification would arise wherever there was evidence of harassment or the application of undue pressure in abuse of power.

Similar issues had arisen in the *Kalaç* case.[58] The applicant was a judge advocate in the Turkish air force. He was compulsorily retired partly on the grounds that his conduct and attitude 'revealed that he had adopted unlawful fundamentalist opinions.' The respondent State argued that his retirement did not constitute an interference with the applicant's freedom to practise his religion, but that his manifestation of his religious beliefs was, as a member of the armed forces, incompatible with the requirement for loyalty to the secular foundation of the Turkish State. The Strasbourg Court

[55] *Kokkinakis v Greece*, (App. 14307/88), 25 May 1993, Series A No 260-A; (1994) 17 EHRR 397.

[56] Ibid.

[57] *Larissis and others v Greece*, (Apps. 23772/94, 26377/94, and 23678/94), 24 February 1998, (1999) 27 EHRR 329, ECHR 1998-I.

[58] *Kalaç v Turkey*, (App. 20704/92), 1 July 1997, (1999) 27 EHRR 552, ECHR 1997-V.

found no violation of Article 9. As a member of the armed forces, there were no limitations on his ability to 'fulfil the obligations which constitute the normal forms through
which a Muslim practises his religion.'[59] A Contracting Party, however, remained free
to regulate certain conduct which would not be objectionable outside the context of
the hierarchy of the armed forces.

Similar considerations may apply in the professional sphere. The Strasbourg
Court ruled as manifestly ill-founded a complaint that prosecution of pharmacists
for refusing to supply contraceptives breached their right to manifest their religious
beliefs. It was legitimate to limit the manifestation of religious beliefs in the professional sphere, and there was no evidence that the applicants could not manifest their
religious beliefs without interference outside that sphere.[60]

Schools are also hierarchical structures, and teachers are in a powerful position
to influence the children in their charge. The applicant in the *Dahlab* case[61] was a
teacher in a Swiss state school for four- to eight-year-olds. She converted to Islam and
began wearing the Islamic headscarf to school. Although there was no evidence that
she had spoken about religion to her pupils, the Strasbourg Court considered that the
Swiss authorities were justified in forbidding her from wearing the Islamic headscarf
at work, consistent with their policy of maintaining religious neutrality in schools.
The Court held that seeing their teacher wearing the Islamic headscarf might have a
'proselytizing effect' on children at a young and impressionable age, and would transmit negative messages to them about lack of equality between the sexes. It does not
appear to have given much weight to the argument that the experience of being taught
by a woman in traditional Islamic dress might have passed on to the children positive
messages about the equality of different religious and cultural groups. The Court did
not attempt to determine what it meant to the applicant to wear the headscarf or, for
example, whether she would consider herself obliged to retire from her teaching post
in the public sector if required to remove it. The balancing exercise for the proportionality test was, therefore, too one-sided.

The prohibition of wearing the Islamic headscarf in Turkish universities was
raised in the *Leyla Şahin* case.[62] The applicant had been a medical student at Istanbul
University. The Grand Chamber recognized the significance of secularism in Turkey,
and recalled that, in countries where several religions coexist, it may be necessary to
place restrictions on the manifestation of religious beliefs in order to reconcile the
interests of different groups and to ensure that everyone's beliefs are respected. There
was, accordingly, a need for a margin of appreciation in the regulation of the wearing

---

[59] §29.

[60] *Pichon and Sajous v France*, (App. 49853/99), Decision of 2 October 2001, ECHR 2001-X.

[61] *Dahlab v Switzerland* (App. 42393/98), Decision of 15 February 2001, ECHR 2001-V.

[62] *Leyla Şahin v Turkey* (App. 44774/98), 10 November 2005 [GC], (2007) 44 EHRR 99, ECHR 2005-IX.
See also M. Evans, *Manual on the Wearing of Religious Symbols in Public Areas* (Strasbourg, 2009); A.
Vakulenko, 'Islamic Dress in Human Rights Jurisprudence: A Critique of Current Trends' (2007) 4 HRLRev
717; and J. Marshall, 'Conditions for Freedom? European Humans Law and the Islamic Headscarf Debate'
(2008) 30 HRQ 631. See also *Dogru v France*, (App. 27058/05), 4 December 2008, (2009) 49 EHRR 179; and
Kervanci v France, (App. 31645/04), 4 December 2008.

of religious dress or symbols in teaching institutions. The Grand Chamber, in concluding that there was no violation of Article 9, said:

...it is the principle of secularism, as elucidated by the [Turkish] Constitutional Court..., which is the paramount consideration underlying the ban on the wearing of religious symbols in universities. In such a context, where the values of pluralism, respect for the rights of others and, in particular, equality before the law of men and women are being taught and applied in practice, it is understandable that the relevant authorities should wish to preserve the secular nature of the institution concerned and so consider it contrary to such value to allow religious attire, including, as in the present case, the Islamic headscarf, to be worn.[63]

It is trite to observe that different Contracting Parties adopt different approaches to the wearing of the Islamic headscarf.[64] But it can be argued that this decision is limited to the special circumstances in Turkey. That is not to be uncritical of the Strasbourg Court, which has failed to spell out exactly what the requirements of secularism are, and how the collective commitment to secularism can be balanced against the wish of some Muslim women to wear the headscarf as a symbol of their religious beliefs. The judgment of the Court in the *Leyla Şahin* case can be criticized for concluding that the wearing of the headscarf by an individual constitutes a form of indoctrinating others. These different views are taken up in the sole dissenting opinion in this case. Judge Tulkens considers that the judgment of the Court displays a lack of European supervision here, in the face of arguments by the applicant that she supported the principle of secularism and had no intention to challenge it by wearing a headscarf. The dissenting judge also observes that no other Contracting Party has a ban on wearing religious symbols which extends to higher education. Judge Tulkens is critical of the reasoning of the majority in linking the issue to one of sexual equality and notes that a decision of the German Constitutional Court had indicated that wearing the headscarf had no single meaning. It would be logical to argue (as Judge Tulkens observes) that, if sexual equality was at issue here, and if the wearing of the headscarf indicated the subordination of women, there would be a violation of equality principles by those Contracting Parties which did *not* ban the headscarf.

Compliance with dietary laws is another aspect of the manifestation of religious belief, and was considered by the Strasbourg Court in the case of *Cha'are Shalom Ve Tsedek v France*.[65] The applicant association represented a group of ultra-orthodox Jews who refused to eat any meat which was not certified as '*glatt*', meaning that the animal had been ritually slaughtered and that the lungs had been examined for impurities. The French authorities authorized a number of slaughterhouses administered

---

[63] §116. See also *Aktas ve France*, (App. 43563/08); *Bayrak v France*, (App. 14308/08); *Gamaleddyn v France*, (App. 18527/08); *Ghazal v France*, (App. 29134/08); *J Singh v France*, (App. 25463/08); and *R Singh v France*, (App. 27561/08); Decisions of 17 July 2009, all declaring applications concerning the wearing of conspicuous religious symbols to be manifestly ill-founded.

[64] See generally I. Gallala, 'The Islamic Headscarf: An Example of Surmountable Conflict between *Shari'a* and the Fundamental Principles of Europe' (2006) 12 ELJ 593; and S. Langlaude, 'Indoctrination, Secularism, Religious Liberty and the ECHR' (2006) 55 ICLQ 929.

[65] *Cha'are Shalom Ve Tsedek v France*, (App. 27417/95), 27 June 2000, ECHR 2000-VII.

by a body representing the majority of Jews in France, which ensured that meat was prepared in such a way as to be kosher, but not '*glatt*', but the respondent State refused to allow the applicant to set up its own slaughterhouses. In the event, the Strasbourg Court was not required to examine the question whether the respondent State's refusal was necessary in a democratic society, because it found that, since '*glatt*' meat imported from Belgium was available in France, there had been no interference with the applicant association's members' right to freedom to manifest their religion.

MANIFESTATION OF RELIGION AND BELIEF BY PRISONERS

There have been a number of complaints by prisoners of interference with religious liberty. It remains doubtful how far a prisoner can claim under Article 9 facilities to practise a religion which is not generally practised in that Contracting Party. Where a British prisoner complained of the absence of the services of a Church of England priest in a German jail, the Commission appears to have considered that a German Protestant pastor might have been sufficient to comply with Article 9 in such a case.[66] The Commission has stated that a refusal by the prison authorities to provide special food required by a religion which was not a religion usually practised in that State was permitted under Article 9(2).[67] Nor, in the Commission's opinion, does Article 9 impose any obligation to put at the disposal of prisoners books which they consider necessary for the exercise of their religion or for the development of their philosophy of life.[68] The Commission might, however, have considered this complaint under Article 10 of the Convention, or even under Article 2 of Protocol 1. In the same case, the applicant's complaint that the prison authorities had refused him permission to grow a beard, as prescribed by his religion, was rejected under Article 9(2). The respondent State had submitted, somewhat curiously, that the refusal was justified as being necessary in order to be able to identify the prisoner. The decision is not satisfactory.

One application[69] concerned a Buddhist prisoner who was refused permission to send out articles for publication in a Buddhist magazine. He claimed that the exchange of ideas with his fellow Buddhists was an element in the exercise of his religion, and alleged a violation of Article 9. The Commission noted that the prison authorities had tried to find a Buddhist minister for him and, when they had been unable to do so, allowed him an extra letter each week to communicate with a fellow Buddhist. The Commission found that the applicant had failed to prove that communication with other Buddhists was a necessary, as distinct from important, part of the practice of his religion. Consequently the application was manifestly ill-founded.

---

[66] App. 2413/65, *X v Federal Republic of Germany*, Decision of 16 December 1966, (1967) 23 CD 1, 8.
[67] Not published. See Case Law Topics No. 1, *Human Rights in Prison*, 31.
[68] App. 1753/63, *X v Austria*, Decision of 15 February 1965, (1965) 8 *Yearbook* 174, 184.
[69] App. 5442/72, *X v United Kingdom*, Decision of 20 December 1974, (1975) 1 DR 41.

In another application[70] the prison authorities refused to allow a prisoner to retain a copy of *Tai Chi Ch'ua and I Ching (A Choreography of Body and Mind)* because it contained an illustrated section on the martial arts and self-defence, which they considered would be dangerous if used against others. The Commission concluded that there had been an interference with the applicant's freedom of religion, but that it was justified under the limitations in Article 9(2). Again the application was manifestly ill-founded.

In one extraordinary case, an Indian, of Sikh ethnic origin and religion, found himself imprisoned for breaking nine windows in a University Senate House during a degree ceremony. He refused to wear prison clothes and spent twenty-three months dressed only in a towel or a blanket. His refusal to wear clothes led to his isolation from other prisoners and he refused to clean out his cell. He complained, *inter alia*, of violations of Article 9. The Commission ruled that Article 9 does not imply any right for prisoners to wear their own clothes and that the applicant had failed to show any reason within Article 9 why he should not wear prison clothes. The Commission was prepared to accept that his religion might require a practice of high-class Sikhs of not cleaning floors and that an interference with his rights under Article 9 in this respect might have arisen. However, the Commission went on to hold that any such interference would be justified as necessary in a democratic society under the limitations recognized by Article 9(2).[71] Accordingly the application was in this respect manifestly ill-founded.

The reported cases taken together give the impression that the Commission was somewhat unsympathetic to complaints of interference with religious freedom by prisoners. As Evans notes,[72] there is a hint in some of the cases involving prisoners that they may be using personal beliefs as a means of seeking privileges which would not otherwise be available. She argues that such doubts should perhaps be tackled more directly. This would avoid a situation in which an unreasonable threshold for establishing the requirements of a particular set of beliefs might arise for those sincerely holding them, while recognizing that in some circumstances, a more searching enquiry is appropriate. She says:

In cases where fraud may be suspected the precise nature of the evidence that would be required to demonstrate insincerity would differ from case to case, but the burden of proof should be on the State to show some reason to think that the person is using religious or other belief fraudulently in order to obtain an advantage to which he or she would not otherwise be entitled.[73]

The Strasbourg Court has not yet been called upon to decide any such case since, as has been seen, under the old system most were declared inadmissible by the Commission. It will be interesting to see whether the Strasbourg Court takes a less pragmatic stand when such questions do come before it.

---

[70] App. 6886/75, *X v United Kingdom*, Decision of 18 May 1976, (1976) 5 DR 100.

[71] App. 8121/78, *X v United Kingdom*, Decision of 6 March 1982 (1982) 28 DR 5, 38.

[72] C. Evans, *Freedom of Religion under the European Convention on Human Rights* (OUP, Oxford 2001), 57–9.

[73] Ibid., 59.

CONSCIENTIOUS OBJECTION
TO MILITARY SERVICE

Considerable problems arise in balancing the competing interests where a Contracting Party requires a citizen to behave in a manner contrary to his beliefs in pursuit of a more obviously useful social aim. Compulsory military service is a prime example, since in a number of Contracting Parties[74] it is still considered necessary to safeguard national security even in peacetime, while many pacifists find it objectionable in the extreme. Moreover, Article 4(3)(b) expressly excludes from the prohibition on forced or compulsory labour, 'any service of a military character or, in the case of conscientious objectors where they are recognized, service exacted instead of compulsory military service'.

Two conclusions seem to follow from the wording of Article 4(3)(b). First, since it speaks of conscientious objectors 'in countries where they are recognized', it seems that Contracting Parties are not obliged, under Article 9, to recognize a right to conscientious objection. Secondly, since it makes express provision for substitute service, it follows that where conscientious objectors are permitted to perform substitute service in lieu of military service, they cannot claim, under Article 9, exemption from substitute service. Hence no one is entitled under Article 9 to exemption on grounds of conscience either from military service or from substitute service.[75] The issue was examined by the Commission in the *Grandrath* case.[76] The applicant was a Jehovah's Witness and was a Bible study leader. Like other Jehovah's Witnesses he objected, for reasons of conscience and religion, not only to performing military service but also to any kind of substitute service. The German authorities recognized him as a conscientious objector but required him to perform substitute civilian service. When he refused to do so, criminal proceedings were instituted and he was convicted and sentenced to eight months' imprisonment, a sentence which was reduced on appeal to six months. In addition to the applicant's complaint under Article 9, the Commission considered of its own motion the question whether, under Article 14 in conjunction with Article 9 or Article 4, he had been subject to discrimination as compared with Roman Catholic or Protestant ministers.[77]

In the Commission's opinion, there were two aspects to be considered under Article 9.[78] First, the question whether civilian service would have restricted the

---

[74] For example, Albania, Austria, Bulgaria, Cyprus, Denmark, Estonia, Finland, Germany, Greece, Norway, Poland, Romania, Russia, Sweden, Switzerland, Turkey, and Ukraine are understood to require military service, though many permit substitute service.

[75] App. 17086/90, *Autio v Finland*, Decision of 6 December 1991, (1992) 72 DR 245.

[76] App. 2299/64, *Grandrath v Federal Republic of Germany*, Report of Commission, 12 December 1966, Decision of Committee of Ministers, 29 June 1967, (1967) 10 *Yearbook* 626; see also App. 5591/72, *X v Austria*, Decision of 2 April 1973 (1973) 43 CD 161, and App. 7705/76, *X v Federal Republic of Germany*, Decision of 5 July 1977, (1978) 9 DR 196.

[77] See also *Gutl v Austria*, (App. 49686/99), 12 March 2009.

[78] App. 2299/64, *Grandrath v Federal Republic of Germany*, Report of Commission, 12 December 1966, Decision of Committee of Ministers, 29 June 1967, (1967) 10 *Yearbook* 626, 672.

applicant's right to manifest his religion. The Commission considered that, given the nature of the service in question, it would not in fact have interfered either with the private and personal practice of his religion or with his duties to his religious community, which were in any case a spare-time activity. Secondly, the Commission examined whether Article 9 had been violated by the mere fact that the applicant had been required to perform a service which was contrary to his conscience or religion. It concluded that, having regard to the provisions of Article 4, objections of conscience did not, under the Convention, entitle a person to exemption from substitute service.

Under the German legislation, an ordained Evangelical or Roman Catholic minister was exempt from military service, and therefore also from substitute service, while a minister of another religion was exempt if the ministry was his principal occupation and if his functions were equivalent to those of an ordained Evangelical or Roman Catholic Minister. The Commission, finding that this difference in treatment did not amount to discrimination in violation of Article 14 taken in conjunction with Article 9, noted that the legislation had been drafted in such a way in order to prevent a large-scale evasion of the general duty to perform military service. If the limitation were abandoned, the result might well be to exempt an entire religious community.

While the Commission's analysis of Article 14 is persuasive, its application of the article to the facts of this case is more questionable. It would have been acceptable if exemption from compulsory service had been based solely on the criterion of the minister's function; but it was not. There was the additional requirement in the case of a minister who was neither Roman Catholic nor Evangelical that his ministry must be his principal occupation. The Commission's finding with regard to the reason for the distinction made by German law also raises some doubts. Even if this were in fact the reason, and even if differential treatment can be justified in some cases by the objects of the legislation, as the Strasbourg Court held in the *Belgian Linguistic* case,[79] it seems doubtful whether this would be adequate justification for this distinction. For it would have been open to the legislature simply to provide that any minister of religion should be exempt whose ministry was his principal occupation.[80]

While the Strasbourg Court has not, to date, found that the obligation to perform military service breaches Article 9,[81] it has been prepared to examine the proportionality of sanctions imposed against conscientious objectors, and to find violations of Article 9 if they are excessive.

---

[79] *Case relating to certain aspects of the laws on the use of languages in education in Belgium (Belgian Linguistic Case (No. 2)*, (Apps. 1474/62, 1677/62, 1691/62, 1769/63, 1994/63, and 2126/64), 23 July 1968, Series A No 6, (1979–80) 1 EHRR 252.

[80] See also Committee of Ministers Recommendation No. R(87)8 of 9 April 1987, reproduced in Council of Europe *Information Sheet No. 21*, H/INF(87)1, 160.

[81] See *Tsirlis and Kouloumpas v Greece*, (Apps. 19233/91 and 19234/91), 29 May 1997, (1998) 25 EHRR 198, where the Strasbourg Court found a violation of Art. 5(1) arising from the imprisonment of two Jehovah's Witnesses' ministers for refusing to do military service, on the basis that the detention was 'unlawful' under Greek law. It did not find it necessary to examine the complaint under Arts. 9 and 14 of the Convention. See also *Valsamis v Greece*, (App. 21787/93), 18 December 1996, (1997) 24 EHRR 294, ECHR 1996-VI, where the Court decided that requiring the children of Jehovah's Witnesses to attend a military parade did not offend against their pacifist beliefs.

In the *Thlimmenos* case[82] the applicant, another Greek Jehovah's Witness, had been convicted of the criminal offence of 'insubordination' as a result of his refusal to wear a military uniform. He was subsequently refused permission to practise as an accountant, in accordance with a law excluding anyone with a criminal record from the profession. The Court did not examine the proportionality of the criminal measures—since the applicant did not complain about them—but it did find that the accountancy ban amounted to a violation of Articles 9 and 14 taken together.

PARTICIPATION IN NATIONAL LIFE

Article 9 also prevents a Contracting Party from imposing obligations on citizens in relation to participation in national life which offend their religious beliefs, unless these obligations are necessary in a democratic society.

A State-imposed obligation found not to serve a pressing social need was examined in the case of *Buscarini and others*.[83] The applicants had been elected as Members of the San Marino Parliament. Before taking office they were required to swear an oath 'on the Holy Gospels' to uphold the Constitution. The Strasbourg Court held that this was tantamount to requiring elected representatives of the people to swear allegiance to a particular religion, and was not, therefore, compatible with Article 9. In many Contracting Parties an affirmation is accepted in place of an oath where there is a requirement to take an oath in connection with some public office.[84]

THE RECOGNITION AND AUTHORIZATION OF RELIGIOUS ORGANIZATIONS

The status of religion within the Contracting Parties varies considerably.[85] Some States have established religions,[86] while others have de facto State religions.[87] By contrast some States are explicitly secular.[88] The German Constitution provides that there shall be no State church. In a number of Contracting Parties,[89] there are provisions for official recognition of religious organizations. The most obvious policy

---

[82] *Thlimmenos v Greece*, (App. 34369/97), 6 April 2000, (2001) 31 EHRR 411, ECHR 2000-IV.

[83] *Buscarini and others v San Marino*, (App. 24645/94), 18 February 1999, (2000) 30 EHRR 208, ECHR 1999-I.

[84] As, for example, in the case of the judicial oath in the United Kingdom.

[85] See C. Evans, *Freedom of Religion under the European Convention on Human Rights* (OUP, Oxford 2001), ch.2, section 2.2.

[86] For example, the United Kingdom, Iceland, and Norway.

[87] For example, the Orthodox Church in Greece.

[88] The constitutions of both France and Turkey contain explicit commitments to secularism.

[89] Predominantly but not exclusively the new democracies of central and eastern Europe.

obstructing the manifestation of religion or belief is action by a Contracting Party refusing to recognize a religious grouping. Serious and unexplained delays in granting recognition to a religious association under national law will constitute a violation of Article 9.[90] The application of such laws is coming under challenge in the context of Articles 9 and 11.

Where issues relating to the recognition of a religion are raised, the Strasbourg Court has adopted a policy of reading Articles 9 and 11 as closely interlinked. The starting point is freedom of association with others, but the context is freedom of religion.

This approach is most clearly spelled out in the *Moscow Branch of the Salvation Army* case.[91] The Salvation Army had been registered in Russia as a religious organization with status as a legal entity since May 1992. In 1997 a new law entered into force which required religious organizations to re-register and to ensure that their articles of association conformed to the new law. Despite litigation in the Russian courts, the Salvation Army failed to secure re-registration, and the Russian authorities then took action for dissolution of the Moscow Branch. The applicant complained of a violation of Articles 9 and 11. The Strasbourg Court reiterated the centrality of religious freedom in a democratic society and continued:

…the autonomous existence of religious communities is indispensable for pluralism in a democratic society, and is thus an issue at the very heart of the protection which Article 9 affords. The State's duty of neutrality and impartiality, as defined in the Court's case-law, is incompatible with any power on the State's part to assess the legitimacy of religious beliefs (see Metropolitan Church of Bessarabia…, and Hasan and Chaush v Bulgaria [GC], no. 30985/96, §62, ECHR 2000-XI).[92]

The Strasbourg Court then reiterates that the right to form an association is an inherent part of the rights protected by Article 11, and observes:

While in the context of Article 11 the Court has often referred to the essential role played by political parties in ensuring pluralism and democracy, associations formed for other purposes, including those proclaiming or teaching religion, are also important to the proper functioning of democracy.[93]

The Court stressed that the need for any regulation of associations in order to protect the State's institutions and citizens must be used sparingly in the context of a strict interpretation of the limitations to freedom of association. The Strasbourg Court considered that there had been an interference with the applicant's rights under Article 11 when read in the light of Article 9. In this context there was only a limited margin of appreciation for the respondent State. The Court then examined the two main grounds put forward for the refusals of recognition: that the branch was subordinate

---

[90] *Religionsgemeinschaft der Zuegen Jehovas and others v Austria*, (App. 40825/98), 31 July 2008.

[91] *Moscow Branch of the Salvation Army v Russia*, (App. 72881/01), 5 October 2006, (2007) 44 EHRR 912, ECHR 2006-XI. See also *Verein der Freunde der Christengemeinschaft and others v Austria*, (App. 76581/01), 26 February 2009.

[92] §58.   [93] §61.

to a foreign national. While the Russian law prohibited foreign nationals from being founders of Russian religious organizations, it did not extend to prohibition of local branches of such religions. Where there was a situation in which a church's head-quarters were abroad, there was simply an additional requirement that the articles of association of the foreign governing body were also filed. The Court concluded that the foreign origins of the local branch could not constitute a relevant and sufficient ground for refusing registration under the Russian law. The second objection was that the Salvation Army was organized on hierarchical grounds; indeed it had been described by the Moscow Justice Department as a 'paramilitary organization'. The Court found no basis from the lawful activities of the Salvation Army over a period of seven years, nor in its religious organization, to suggest that it advocated a violent change in the respondent State's constitutional foundations and so undermined State security or integrity. The findings to this effect by Russian authorities were without any evidentiary basis and so were an arbitrary ground of interference. The Strasbourg Court concluded that the Russian authorities had not acted in good faith and had neglected their duty of neutrality and impartiality towards the Salvation Army. The unanimous decision of the Chamber was that there was a violation of Article 11 when read in the light of Article 9.[94]

The *Metropolitan Church of Bessarabia* case also concerned recognition of a church.[95] Moldova refused to recognize the Metropolitan Church of Bessarabia in circumstances where only religions recognized by the respondent State may be prac-tised in Moldova. In finding a violation of Article 9, the Strasbourg Court took the opportunity to restate both the role of the State in the regulation of religious activ-ities, and the relationship of the freedom protected by Article 9 with certain other freedoms:

> 117. The Court further observes that in principle the right to freedom of religion for the purposes of the Convention excludes assessment by the State of the legitimacy of religious beliefs or the ways in which those beliefs are expressed. State measures favouring a particular leader or specific organs of a divided religious community or seeking to compel the community or part of it to place itself, against its will, under a single leadership, would also constitute an infringement of the freedom of religion. In democratic societies the State does not need to take

---

[94] See also *Church of Scientology Moscow v Russia*, (App. 18147/02), 5 April 2007, (2008) 46 EHRR 304.

[95] *Metropolitan Church of Bessarabia v Moldova* (App. 45701/99), 14 December 2001; (2002) 35 EHRR 306, ECHR 2001-XII. See also *Biserica Adevărat Ortodoxă din Moldova and others v Modlova*, (App. 952/03), 27 February 2007. For an example of a dispute in which Article 9 was pleaded but where the Strasbourg Court determined the case by reference to rights arising under Article 6, see *Canea Catholic Church v Greece*, (App. 25528/94), 16 September 1997, (1999) 27 EHRR 521. Renucci suggests that the Court has displayed a tendency to sidestep some questions arising under Article 9 by preferring to decide cases under other articles to the detriment of Article 9: see J-F. Renucci, *Article 9 of the European Convention on Human Rights. Freedom of thought, conscience and religion*, Human Rights Files No. 20 (Council of Europe Publishing, Strasbourg 2005), 36–41.

measures to ensure that religious communities remain or are brought under a unified leadership.... . Similarly, where the exercise of the right to freedom of religion or of one of its aspects is subject under domestic law to a system of prior authorisation, involvement in the procedure for granting authorisation of a recognised ecclesiastical authority cannot be reconciled with the requirements of paragraph 2 of Article 9....

The earlier *Manoussakis* case[96] had concerned Jehovah's Witnesses living in Crete. They rented a room for the purpose of conducting activities, such as meetings and weddings, connected with their beliefs as Jehovah's Witnesses. They were subsequently prosecuted and convicted for having established and operated a place of worship without the authorizations required by law. Though the Strasbourg Court is at pains to indicate that it will not pass judgment on a generalized complaint by the applicants about policies of the respondent State which might affect the practice of their religion by Jehovah's Witnesses, on the specific issues it did consider there was some doubt about whether the interference with their rights under Article 9 was prescribed by law. The Court reviewed the national legislation on the granting of authorization for the use of premises for the practice of religious beliefs, and noted that the State had tended to use the system of authorization 'to impose rigid, or indeed prohibitive, conditions on practice of religious beliefs by certain non-orthodox movements, in particular Jehovah's Witnesses'.[97] The Court, like the Commission, concluded that the conviction of which the applicants complained had such a direct effect on their freedom of religion that it could not be regarded as proportionate to the aim pursued and so was not necessary in a democratic society. The Court also indicated that intervention in the procedure for authorization of the established church—in this case the Greek Orthodox Church—could not be reconciled with the provisions in Article 9(2).[98]

However, a specific system for authorization of the use of premises for religious purposes must be distinguished from the application of generally applicable legal provisions concerning planning consent. In the latter case, it will be rather easier to justify the application of planning requirements which affects the use of premises for religious purposes.[99]

Non-recognition of a religion by the State does not, however, deprive adherents of that religion from the protection of Article 9, since such an approach would mean that the State could exclude certain beliefs by withholding recognition. Punishing those who manifest religious beliefs which have not been recognized by the State constitutes a violation of Article 9.[100]

---

[96] *Manoussakis and others v Greece*, (App. 18748/91), 26 September 1996, (1997) 23 EHRR 387, ECHR 1996-IV.

[97] §48.   [98] §§51–3.

[99] *Vergos v Greece*, (App. 65501/01), 24 June 2004, (2005) 41 EHRR 913.

[100] *Masaev v Moldova*, (App. 6303/05), 12 May 2009.

POSITIVE OBLIGATIONS

In the *Hasan and Chaush* case[101] the Strasbourg Court observed that:

[w]ere the organizational life of the [religious] community not protected by Article 9 of the Convention, all other aspects of the individual's freedom of religion would become vulnerable.

In the *Father Basil* case,[102] the Strasbourg Court condemned as a violation of Article 9 the failure of the Georgian authorities to ensure tolerance of the exercise by the applicants (a group of Jehovah's Witnesses) of their right to freedom of religion in the face of a violent and outrageous attack on worshippers and their place of worship by Father Basil (a defrocked Orthodox priest) and a group of extremists.

In its judgment in the *Otto-Preminger Institute* case, the Strasbourg Court ruled that Contracting Parties have positive obligations under Article 9 to 'ensure the peaceful enjoyment of the rights guaranteed under Article 9 to the holders of those beliefs and doctrines', though it also recognized that the pluralism inherent in the Convention values meant that those holding religious beliefs 'cannot reasonably expect to be exempt from all criticism' and must 'tolerate and accept the denial by others of their religious beliefs and even the propagation by others of doctrines hostile to their faith.'[103]

This means that Contracting Parties have a responsibility to ensure tolerance between the rival factions between and within religious and belief groups.[104] In the *Leela Förderkreis E.V* case,[105] the Strasbourg Court, in a case where the authorities had run an information campaign using pejorative terms about associations belong to the Osho movement, somewhat controversially based its decision to find no violation of Article 9 on the positive duty of Contracting Parties to provide information about matters of concern to its people.

The applicant in the *Serif* case[106] enjoyed the support of part of the Muslim community in Thrace, and was elected Mufti (religious leader), despite the fact that another Mufti had already been appointed by the respondent State. The applicant was subsequently convicted of the criminal offences of having usurped the functions of a minister of a 'known religion' and having publicly worn the uniform of such a minister without having the right to do so. The respondent State argued before the Strasbourg

---

[101] *Hasan and Chaush v Bulgaria*, (App. 30985/96), 26 October 2000 [GC], (2002) 34 EHRR 1339, ECHR 2000-XI.

[102] *97 members of the Gldani Congregation of Jehovah's Witnesses and 4 others v Georgia*, (App. 71156/01), 3 May 2007, (2008) 46 EHRR 613, ECHR 2007-nyr.

[103] *Otto-Preminger Institute v Austria*, (App. 13470/87), 20 September 1994, Series A No 295-A, (1994) 19 EHRR 34.

[104] *Serif v Greece*, (App. 38178/97), 4 December 1999, (2001) 31 EHRR 561, ECHR 1999-IX, §53. See also *Metropolitan Church of Bessarabia v Moldova*, (App. 45701/99), 14 December 2001, (2002) 35 EHRR 306, ECHR 2001-XII.

[105] *Leela Förderkreis E.V and others v Germany*, (App. 58911/00), 6 November 2008, (2009) 49 EHRR 117; and see further later in this chapter.

[106] *Serif v Greece*, (App. 38178/97), 4 December 1999, (2001) 31 EHRR 561, ECHR 1999-IX.

Court that the authorities had had to intervene in order to avoid the creation of tension between different religious groups in the area. The Court, finding a violation of Article 9, observed that tension between competing religious groups was an unavoidable consequence of pluralism, but that the role of the authorities in such a situation was not to remove the cause of the tension, thereby eliminating pluralism, but instead to ensure tolerance between the rival factions.[107] In a democratic society, it commented, there was no need for the State to take measures to ensure that religious communities remained or were brought under a unified leadership. In the *Hasan and Chaush* case,[108] where the Bulgarian authorities were found to have similarly interfered in the affairs of the Muslim community, the Court declared a violation of Article 9 based on the arbitrary nature of the relevant legislation, which gave an almost unfettered power to the executive to appoint the person of its choice as Chief Mufti.[109]

CONCLUDING REMARKS

The pursuit of multiculturalism and peaceful co-habitation of different religious groups within society has frequently proved challenging. The history of Europe is littered with examples of extreme religious intolerance and, indeed, the European Convention was conceived in the immediate aftermath of the persecution and genocide of the adherents of one religion, Judaism, in the hope that it would help to prevent such an atrocity ever taking place again. For many believers, religious faith is central to their existence and their most important defining characteristic. The Court is correct, therefore, to stress in its case-law the duty of the State as a guarantor of pluralism and the fundamental nature of the rights to freedom of belief and freedom to manifest religion. The case-law can, however, be criticized as lacking in any detailed formulation of principles and concepts. The Strasbourg Court has yet to define 'religion' or to elaborate any guidelines as to how mainstream or established a religion has to be before it requires recognition by the State. While the Court has accepted that restrictions might be permissible to prevent religious pressure being placed on individuals by their superiors in hierarchical structures, it has not attempted to elaborate any general guidelines as to when attempts at conversion become abusive, what constitutes a 'cult' or when the State should step in to protect children or other vulnerable individuals from violations of human rights carried out in the name of religion. In addition, the case-law regarding the extent to which restrictions can be placed on the manifestation

---

[107] See also *Metropolitan Church of Bessarabia v Moldova*, (App. 45701/99), 14 December 2001, (2002) 35 EHRR 306, ECHR 2001-XII; and *Holy Synod of the Bulgarian Orthodox Church (Metropolitan Inokentiy) v Bulgaria*, (Apps. 412/03 and 35677/04), 22 January 2009.

[108] *Hasan and Chaush v Bulgaria*, (App. 30985/96), 26 October 2000 [GC], (2002) 34 EHRR 1339, ECHR 2000-XI.

[109] See also *Svyato-Mykhaylivska Parafiya v Ukraine*, (App. 77703/01), 14 June 2007, which concerned registration issues where a religious organization wished to changed the leadership of the church to which it is affiliated, and arbitrary action by the authorities.

of religious belief is not consistent. These are all difficult questions, but that is why the Court's guidance is needed. Following the attack on the United States of 11 September 2001 and the ensuing 'war on terror' which has been joined by America's European allies, many of the 100 million Muslims living within the Convention States have felt themselves to be the targets of prejudice and suspicion. It is therefore extremely regrettable that the Court has, in its judgments on the Islamic headscarf, shown a lack of understanding of the meaning of this symbol and has left itself open to the charge of perpetuating, rather than dispelling, prejudices and misunderstandings about Islam. It is noteworthy that there was no third party intervention in any of the key 'Islamic' cases to date. It is to be hoped that, the next time such a question comes before the Court, it actively seeks expert advice from one or more Muslim organizations to prevent it making the same mistakes again.

18

FREEDOM OF EXPRESSION

INTRODUCTION

In its seminal judgment in the *Handyside* case, the Strasbourg Court emphasized the importance of the rights protected by Article 10, which, it said, 'constitutes one of the essential foundations of a democratic society, one of the basic conditions for its progress and for the development of every man.'[1] Since then, the Court has repeatedly stressed this fundamental importance of freedom of expression as 'one of the essential foundations of a democratic society and one of the basic conditions for its progress and for each individual's self-fulfilment.'[2] There is a link with Article 9 on freedom of thought, conscience, and religion, since expression of personal beliefs and ideas is for many an inherent part of the holding of those beliefs and ideas. Article 11 also has relevance, since individuals may wish to come together to express their ideas either in private or in public, as does Article 8 where issues of privacy overlap with the rights protected by Article 10. Given its foundational aspect, it is, therefore, perhaps surprising that the list of restrictions is longer than for other articles of the Convention. The article also, uniquely, makes specific reference to duties and responsibilities in the exercise of the rights the article protects.[3]

Article 10 provides,

1. Everyone has the right to freedom of expression. This right shall include freedom to hold opinions and to receive and impart information and ideas without interference by public authority and regardless of frontiers. This article shall not prevent States from requiring the licensing of broadcasting, television or cinema enterprises.

2. The exercise of these freedoms, since it carries with it duties and responsibilities, may be subject to such formalities, conditions, restrictions or penalties as are prescribed

---

[1] *Handyside v United Kingdom*, (App. 5493/72), 7 December 1976, Series A No 24, (1979–80) 1 EHRR 737, §48.

[2] See, for modern examples, *Lindon, Otchakovsky-Laurens and July v France*, (Apps. 21279/02 and 36448/02), 22 October 2007 [GC], (2008) 46 EHRR 761, ECHR 2007-XI, §45; *Guja v Moldova*, (App. 14277/04), 12 February 2008 [GC], ECHR 2008-nyr, §69; and *Frankowicz v Poland*, (App. 53025/99), 16 December 2008, §38.

[3] See generally, M. Macovei, *Freedom of expression: a guide to the implementation of Article 10 of the European Convention on Human Rights*, Human Rights Handbooks No. 2 (Council of Europe Publishing, Strasbourg 2004).

by law and are necessary in a democratic society, in the interests of national security, territorial integrity or public safety, for the prevention of disorder or crime, for the protection of health or morals, for the protection of the reputation or rights of others, for preventing the disclosure of information received in confidence, or for maintaining the authority and impartiality of the judiciary.

The right to freedom of expression set out in the article's first paragraph, including freedom to hold opinions and to receive and impart information and ideas[4] without interference by the State, is extremely broad. All forms of expression are included, through any medium: this includes paintings,[5] books,[6] cartoons,[7] films,[8] video-recordings,[9] statements in radio interviews,[10] information pamphlets,[11] and the internet;[12] and with any content, including racist hate speech,[13] and pornography.[14]

To quote again from the *Handyside* case:

[Article 10] is applicable not only to 'information' or 'ideas' that are favourably received or regarded as inoffensive or as a matter of indifference, but also those that offend, shock or disturb the State or any sector of the population. Such are the demands of that pluralism, tolerance and broadmindedness without which there is no 'democratic' society.[15]

However, as is explicitly recognized in the text of Article 10(2), and by the Strasbourg Court in its case-law, free expression, particularly by way of the mass media, is a powerful tool, carrying special duties and responsibilities. If it is vital to protect the right to free speech because of its power to promote democracy, uncover abuses, and advance political, artistic, scientific, and commercial development, it is also important to recognize that free speech can equally be used to incite violence, spread hatred, and impinge on individual privacy and safety. The Court's case-law is an attempt to strike the proper balance between these competing interests.[16]

The majority of cases concerning Article 10 are brought by persons who have received some penalty for defaming or insulting other people. When considering whether such a penalty constitutes a violation of Article 10 the Strasbourg Court will

---

[4] *Autronic AG v Switzerland*, (App. 12726/87), 22 May 1990, Series A No 178, (1990) 12 EHRR 485.

[5] *Müller v Switzerland*, (App. 10737/84), 24 May 1988, Series A No 133, (1991) 13 EHRR 212.

[6] *Handyside v United Kingdom*, (App. 5493/72), 7 December 1976, Series A No 24, (1979–80) 1 EHRR 737.

[7] *Leroy v France*, (App. 36109/03), 2 October 2008.

[8] *Otto-Preminger Institute v Austria*, (App. 13470/87), 20 September 1994, Series A No 295-A, (1994) 19 EHRR 34.

[9] *Monnat v Switzerland*, (App. 73604/01), 21 September 2006, ECHR 2006-X.

[10] *Barthold v Germany*, (App. 8734/79), 23 March 1985, Series A No 90, (1985) 7 EHRR 383.

[11] *Open Door Counselling and Dublin Well Woman v Ireland*, (Apps. 14234/88 and 14235/88), 29 October 1992, Series A No 246, (1993) 15 EHRR 244.

[12] *Perrin v United Kingdom*, (App. 5446/03), Decision of 18 October 2005, ECHR 2005-XI. See also *Times Newspapers Ltd (Nos. 1 and 2) v United Kingdom*, (Apps 3002/03 and 23676/03), 10 March 2009.

[13] *Jersild v Denmark*, (App. 15890/89), 24 September 1994, Series A No 298, (1994) 19 EHRR 1.

[14] *Wingrove v United Kingdom*, (App. 17419/90), 25 November 1996, (1997) 24 EHRR 1.

[15] *Handyside v United Kingdom*, (App. 5493/72), 7 December 1976, Series A No 24, (1979–80) 1 EHRR 737, §48.

[16] See E. Barendt, *Freedom of Speech* (OUP, Oxford 2005).

take into account a number of factors, including the function fulfilled by the author and the subject, whether the impugned expression consists of a statement of fact or a value judgment, and the severity of the penalty.[17]

WHAT CONSTITUTES AN INTERFERENCE WITH FREE EXPRESSION?

The Strasbourg Court takes a broad view of what constitutes an interference with free expression. At its most obvious this includes executive orders preventing publication[18] or the confiscation of published material.[19] Article 10(2) makes clear that 'penalties' as well as 'restrictions', 'conditions', and 'formalities' must be justified. The 'penalties' referred to can include criminal sanctions,[20] damages in a civil action,[21] reprimands in disciplinary proceedings,[22] or dismissals, at least when the person in question is a public sector employee.[23] Other forms of post-publication measures can also constitute interferences if they have a chilling effect on future speech. For example, the Strasbourg Court has held that attempts to uncover journalistic sources, either by search order[24] or by disclosure order,[25] are interferences requiring justification under Article 10(2). Refusal to authorize the performance of a play constitutes a restriction on freedom of expression,[26] as can confiscation of written materials intended to be given to others in order to impart information and ideas.[27] A prohibition on wearing the five-pointed red star, as the symbol of the international workers' movement falls

---

[17] For a critical comment on the development of the case-law in this area, see G. Millar, 'Whither the spirit of Lingens?' [2009] EHRLR 277.

[18] See the 'Spycatcher' cases: *The Observer and Guardian Newspapers Ltd v United Kingdom*, (App. 13585/88), 26 November 1991, Series A No 216, (1992) 14 EHRR 153 and *Sunday Times v United Kingdom (No 2)*, (App. 13166/87), 26 November 1991, Series A No 217, (1992) 14 EHRR 229.

[19] *Vereniging Weekblad Bluf! v Netherlands*, (App. 16616/90), 9 February 1995, Series A No 306-A, (1995) 20 EHRR 189.

[20] *Zana v Turkey*, (App. 18954/91), 25 November 1997, (1999) 27 EHRR 667, ECHR 1997-VII.

[21] *Tolstoy Miloslavsky v United Kingdom*, (App. 18139/91), 13 July 1995, Series A No 316-B, (1995) 20 EHRR 442.

[22] *Steur v Netherlands*, (App. 39657/98), 28 October 2003, (2004) 39 EHRR 706, ECHR 2003-XI; *Frankowicz v Poland*, (App. 53025/99), 16 December 2008; and *Wojtas-Kaleta v Poland*, (app. 20436/02), 16 July 2009.

[23] *Vogt v Germany*, (App. 17851/91), 26 September 1995, Series A No 323, (1996) 21 EHRR 205; *Fuentes Bobo v Spain*, (App. 39293/98), 29 February 2000; and *Guja v Moldova*, (App. 14277/04), 12 February 2008 [GC], ECHR 2008-nyr.

[24] *Roemen and Schmit v Luxembourg*, (App. 51772/99), 25 February 2003, ECHR 2003-IV, §§47 and 57.

[25] *Goodwin v United Kingdom*, (App. 17488/90), 27 March 1996, (1996) 22 EHRR 123, ECHR 1996-II, §28. See also *Nordisk Film & TV A/S v Denmark*, (App. 40485/02), Decision of 8 December 2005, ECHR 2005-XIII.

[26] *Ulusoy and others v Turkey*, (App. 34797/03), 3 May 2007.

[27] *Foka v Turkey*, (App. 28940/95), 24 June 2008, §§102–9.

within the ambit of Article 10.[28] Revocation of a call-up for military service can be an interference with freedom of expression.[29]

LIMITATIONS ON FREEDOM OF EXPRESSION

Certain restrictions are expressly allowed. Article 10(1) itself provides that Contracting Parties may require the licensing of broadcasting, television or cinema enterprises. Moreover, in common with Articles 8, 9, and 11, Article 10 includes a second paragraph which permits a Contracting Party to limit the right set out in the first paragraph, provided that such limitations are 'prescribed by law', and 'necessary in a democratic society' in pursuit of one of the specified aims.[30]

The situations in which a restriction may be justifiable include the need to protect important public interests—such as national security, territorial integrity, freedom from crime and disorder, health and morality, and the authority and impartiality of the judiciary—and also other individual rights, such as a person's right to privacy or reputation. The margin of appreciation allowed to Contracting Parties in restricting freedom of expression will vary depending on the purpose and nature of the limitation and of the expression in question. As the Strasbourg Court made clear in its *Handyside* judgment, 'every "formality", "condition", "restriction" or "penalty" imposed in this sphere must be proportionate to the legitimate aim pursued.'[31]

On the other side of the balance, to be weighed against the importance of the aim pursued by the restriction, is the nature of the expression restricted. The Strasbourg Court takes into account the fact that, in the context of effective political democracy and respect for human rights mentioned in the Preamble to the Convention, freedom of expression not only is important in itself, but also plays a central role in the protection of the other rights under the Convention. Thus the Court consistently gives a higher level of protection to publications and speech which contribute towards social and political debate, criticism, and information—in the broadest sense. Artistic and commercial expression,[32] in contrast, receive a lower level of protection.

Other important factors to take into account include the extent of the restriction and the form of the expression. The Court will scrutinize prior restraints on expression more closely, because of their inherent dangers. Such restraints will require safeguards against their misuse. A ban on the publication and distribution of a newspaper, for example, will be compatible with the Convention only if there is a particularly

---

[28] *Vajnai v Hungary*, (App. 33629/06), 8 July 2008. No issue appears to have been raised in this case that this was the manifestation of a personal belief, which would, of course, fall within Article 9. So it seems that secular insignia will be treated differently from religious insignia.

[29] *Erdel v Germany*, (App. 30067/04), Decision of 13 February 2007, ECHR 2007-II.

[30] See ch.14 above.

[31] *Handyside v United Kingdom*, (App. 5493/72), 7 December 1976, Series A No 24, (1979–80) 1 EHRR 737, §48.

[32] *Vgt Verein gegen Tierfabriken v Switzerland*, (App. 24699/94), 28 June 2001, (2002) 34 EHRR 159, ECHR 2001-VI, §71.

strict framework of legal rules regulating the scope of the ban and ensuring the effectiveness of judicial review to prevent the possibility of abuse.[33]

As for the form of the expression, the Strasbourg Court has acknowledged that
account must be taken of the fact that audio-visual media have a more immediate and
powerful effect than print media.[34] In general, more restrictive measures will be permissible in relation to the audio and visual media, because the potential for damage
is greater.[35]

The Strasbourg Court now adopts a formulaic description of its role in assessing
whether a Contracting Party's reliance on the restrictions in the second paragraph of
the article is compatible with Article 10:

> 45. … The Court's task, in exercising its supervisory jurisdiction, is not to take the
> place of the competent national authorities but rather to review under Article 10 the
> decisions they delivered pursuant to their power of appreciation. This does not mean
> that the supervision is limited to ascertaining whether the respondent State exercised
> its discretion reasonably, carefully and in good faith; what the Court has to do is to
> look at the interference complained of in the light of the case as a whole and determine
> whether the reasons adduced by the national authorities to justify it are 'relevant and
> sufficient' and whether it was 'proportionate to the legitimate aim pursued'. In doing so,
> the Court has to satisfy itself that the national authorities applied standards which were
> in conformity with the principles embodied in Article 10 and, moreover, that they relied
> on an acceptable assessment of the relevant facts.…

> 46. There is little scope under Article 10 §2 of the Convention for restrictions on freedom
> of expression in the area of political speech or debate—where freedom of expression
> is of the utmost importance.…
>
>   Furthermore, the limits of acceptable criticism are wider as regards a politician
> as such than as regards a private individual. Unlike the latter, the former inevitably
> and knowingly lays himself open to close scrutiny of his every word and deed by both
> journalists and the public at large, and he must consequently display a greater degree
> of tolerance.…[36]

INCITEMENT TO VIOLENCE AND HATE SPEECH

In the *Gündüz* case, the Court said:

…tolerance and respect for the equal dignity of all human beings constitute the foundations of a democratic, pluralistic society. That being so, as a matter of principle it may be

[33] *Çetin and Others v Turkey*, (Apps. 40153/98 and 40160/98), 13 February 2003, ECHR 2003-III; see also
Gawęda v Poland, (App. 26229/95), 14 March 2002, (2004) 39 EHRR 90, ECHR 2002-II.

[34] *Pedersen and Baadsgaard v Denmark*, (App. 49017/99), 17 December 2004 [GC], (2006) 42 EHRR 486,
ECHR 2004-XI, §79.

[35] *Murphy v Ireland*, (App. 44179/98), 10 July 2003, (2004) 38 EHRR 212, ECHR 203-IX, §74.

[36] *Lindon, Otchakovsky-Laurens and July v France*, (Apps. 21279/02 and 36448/02), 22 October 2007
[GC], (2008) 46 EHRR 761, ECHR 2007-XI, §§45–6.

considered necessary in certain democratic societies to sanction or even prevent all forms of
expression which spread, incite, promote or justify hatred based on intolerance (including
religious intolerance), provided that any 'formalities', 'conditions', 'restrictions' or 'penalties' imposed are proportionate to the legitimate aim pursued.

Furthermore...there can be no doubt that concrete expressions constituting hate speech,
which may be insulting to particular individuals or groups, are not protected by Article 10
of the Convention.[37]

In practice the Strasbourg Court has not maintained any clear distinction between
statements that 'spread, incite, promote or justify hatred based on intolerance' and
'concrete expressions constituting hate speech'. The Court, and the Commission in its
time, have relied on Article 17 of the Convention,[38] and on the limitations set out in
Article 10(2), as interchangeable justifications for declaring inadmissible complaints
where the expression in question incites violence or hatred based on intolerance.[39]

In determining whether or not a statement constitutes such an incitement, context is very important. A statement is less likely to be interpreted as an incitement to
violence if it is reported to a well-informed audience as part of a pluralistic debate.
So, for example, the *Jersild* case[40] concerned the broadcast on Danish television of a
programme in which a group of self-confessed racist youths made extremely offensive
remarks about black people. The presenter and the head of the news section were prosecuted and convicted. They complained to the Commission of a breach of Article 10.
The Strasbourg Court was satisfied that the presentation of the item was not intended
to propagate racist views, but to address an issue of some public interest. The broadcast
was part of a serious Danish news programme and was intended for a well-informed
audience. Taking account of all these factors, the penalties imposed on the presenter
and the head of the news section were not necessary in a democratic society for the
protection of the rights of others.

If the context is one of conflict and tension, on the other hand, particular caution
will be required of the media. In such situations journalists bear special responsibilities and duties, because they can become 'a vehicle for the dissemination of hate
speech and violence'.[41] The majority of the Grand Chamber considered that the *Surek
(No. 1)* case was an example of this. The applicant was the owner of a newspaper who

---

[37] *Gündüz v Turkey*, (App. 35071/97), 4 December 2003, (2005) 41 EHRR 59, ECHR 2003-XI, §40.

[38] See ch.6 above.

[39] See, for example, App. 21128/92, *Walendy v Germany*, Decision of 11 January 1995, (1995) 80 DR 94;
App. 25096/94, *Remer v Germany*, Decision of 6 September 1995, (1995) 82 DR 117; App. 25062/94, *Honsik
v Austria*, Decision of 18 October 1995, (1995) 83 DR 77; App. 31159/96, *Marais v France*, Decision of 24
June 1996, (1996) 86 DR 184; *Witzsch v Germany*, (App. 32307/96), Decision of 20 April 1999; *Schimanek v
Austria*, (App. 41448/98), Decision of 1 February 2000.

[40] *Jersild v Denmark*, (App. 15890/89), September 24, 1994, Series A No 298; (1994) 19 EHRR 1.

[41] *Erdogdeu and Ince v Turkey*, (Apps. 25067/94 and 25068/94), 8 July 1999 [GC], ECHR 1999-IV, §54;
and see the series of judgments of the Grand Chamber on the same day: *Sürek and Özdemir v Turkey*, (Apps.
23927/94 and 24277/94), 8 July 1999 [GC]; *Sürek v Turkey (No. 1)*, (App. 26682/95), 8 July 1999 [GC], ECHR
1999-IV; *Sürek v Turkey (No. 2)*, (App. 24122/94), 8 July 1999 [GC]; *Sürek v Turkey (No. 4)*, (App. 24762/94), 8
July 1999 [GC]; and see also *Ceylan v Turkey*, (App. 23556/94), 8 July 1999 [GC], (2000) 30 EHRR 73, ECHR
1999-IV and *Okçuoglu v Turkey*, (App. 24246/94), 8 July 1999 [GC]. Politicians and other public figures must

was prosecuted and fined for publishing readers' letters about the Kurdish conflict. These letters condemned the military actions of the authorities in south-east Turkey and accused them of brutal suppression of the Kurdish people in their struggle for independence and freedom. One of the letters alleged that the State had connived in imprisonment, torture, and killing of dissidents in the name of the protection of democracy and the Republic. The other letter referred to two massacres which the writer claimed were intentionally committed by the authorities as part of a strategic campaign to eradicate the Kurds, and concluded:

[T]he struggle of our people for national freedom in Kurdistan has reached a point where it can no longer be thwarted by bloodshed, tanks and shells. Every attack launched by the Turkish Republic to wipe out the Kurds intensifies the struggle for freedom. The bourgeoisie and its toadying press, which draw attention every day to the brutalities in Bosnia-Herzegovina, fail to see the brutalities committed in Kurdistan. Of course, one can hardly expect reactionary fascists who call for a halt in the brutalities in Bosnia-Herzegovina to call for a halt in the brutalities in Kurdistan.

The Kurdish people, who are being torn from their homes and their fatherland, have nothing to lose. But they have much to gain.

The Strasbourg Court emphasized that there was limited scope under Article 10(2) for restrictions on political speech or on debate on matters of public interest, and that the boundaries of permissible criticism were wider with regard to the government than in relation to a private citizen or even a politician. The Contracting Parties should display restraint in resorting to criminal proceedings, particularly where other means were available for replying to unjustified criticism. Nevertheless, in the Court's view, the letters amounted to 'an appeal to bloody revenge by stirring up base emotions and hardening already embedded prejudices which have manifested themselves in deadly violence'. In view of the tense security situation in south-east Turkey, the authorities were justified in penalizing the publisher. The case was by no means clear-cut. Six of the seventeen judges in the Grand Chamber dissented, on the ground, broadly, that it had not been established that there was a real risk of the letters, inciting hatred or violence.

There are some historical facts which are still so sensitive that attempts to deny or revise them would be considered hate speech and removed from the protection of Article 10 by Article 17. The applicant in the *Garaudy* case,[42] for example, was an historian who wrote a book which denied various aspects of the Holocaust. The Strasbourg Court observed:

There can be no doubt that denying the reality of clearly established historical facts, such as the Holocaust, as the applicant does in his book, does not constitute historical research akin to a quest for the truth. The aim and the result of that approach are completely different, the real purpose being to rehabilitate the National-Socialist regime and, as a consequence,

also act responsibly, because of their power to influence the public mood: *Zana v Turkey*, (App. 18954/91), 25 November 1997, (1999) 27 EHRR 667, ECHR 1997-VII.

 [42] *Garaudy v France*, (App. 65831/01), Decision of 24 June 2003, ECHR 2003-IX.

accuse the victims themselves of falsifying history. Denying crimes against humanity is therefore one of the most serious forms of racial defamation of Jews and of incitement to hatred of them. The denial or rewriting of this type of historical fact undermines the values on which the fight against racism and anti-Semitism are based and constitutes a serious threat to public order. Such acts are incompatible with democracy and human rights because they infringe the rights of others. Its proponents indisputably have designs that fall into the category of aims prohibited by Article 17 of the Convention.[43]

The Strasbourg Court has so far declined to extend this category of clearly established historical facts beyond the Holocaust.[44] Hence, it has held that articles that exculpated Marshal Pétain[45] from any wrongdoing in the Second World War and a book that cast doubt on the account of heroes of the Resistance[46] were not removed from the protection of Article 10 by Article 17. Nor, in a very different context, was the publication of a book which appeared to advocate the use of prohibited drugs.[47]

The dividing line between material which incites violence and that which merely offends is a fine one to be determined in all the circumstances of the case. So a cartoon published in a Basque newspaper two days after the devastating attacks on the United States on 11 September 2001, which seemed to glorify the conduct of the attackers, and which attracted a fine and a requirement to publish the court's judgment gave rise to no violation of Article 10.[48] The Strasbourg Court considered that the drawing assumed a special significance both by reason of the proximity in time to the terrorist attacks in the United States, and its publication in the Basque region. Taken together this increased the propensity of the drawing to stir up violence and public disorder. The nature of the penalty had been modest, and the action of the French authorities was not disproportionate.[49]

THE PRESS AS THE 'WATCHDOG' OF DEMOCRACY

The Strasbourg Court has repeatedly emphasized that the press act as a 'public watchdog' in a democratic society.[50] Although they must not overstep certain bounds, they have a duty nevertheless to impart information and ideas on all matters of public

---

[43] *Garaudy*, p.23.

[44] Although in *Ivanov v Russia*, (App. 35222/04), Decision of 20 February 2007, the Court did rule that 'a general vehement attack on one ethnic group [Jews]' was so at odds with the requirements of tolerance that Article 17 deprived the applicant of the benefit of the protection afforded by Article 10.

[45] *Lehideux and Isorni v France*, (App. 24662/94), 23 September 1998, (2000) 30 EHRR 665.

[46] *Chauvy and others v France*, (App. 64915/01), 29 June 2004, (2005) 41 EHRR 610, ECHR 2004-VI.

[47] *Palusiński v Poland*, (App. 62414/00), Decision of 3 October 2006, ECHR 2006-XIV, 9.

[48] *Leroy v France*, (App. 36109/03), 2 October 2008.

[49] For an example of a case where the reverse was true, see *Orban and others v France*, (App. 20985/05), 15 January 2009.

[50] *Goodwin v United Kingdom*, (App. 17488/90), 27 March 1996, (1996) 22 EHRR 123, ECHR 1996-II, §39.

interest.[51] Not only does the press have the task of imparting such information and ideas, the public also has a right to receive them. As a result, the national margin of appreciation is limited when the author of the expression in question is a journalist, fulfilling his social duty to impart information and ideas on matters of public concern. Journalists should even be free to use a degree of exaggeration and provocation.[52]

More recently the Strasbourg Court has recognized that other associations, such as environmental campaign groups, fulfil a role, similar to that of the press, in stimulating public discussion.[53] As a result, the Court will be careful to ensure that any penalty imposed on them does not have a disproportionate 'chilling effect' on their ability to contribute to the public debate.

Lawyers, however, are expected to be circumspect in their expression, especially when they are acting in litigation:

45. The Court reiterates that the special status of lawyers gives them a central position in the administration of justice as intermediaries between the public and the courts. Such a position explains the usual restrictions on the conduct of members of the Bar. Moreover, the courts—the guarantors of justice, whose role is fundamental in a State based on the rule of law—must enjoy public confidence. Regard being had to the key role of lawyers in this field, it is legitimate to expect them to contribute to the proper administration of justice, and thus to maintain public confidence therein....

46. ...While lawyers too are certainly entitled to comment in public on the administration of justice, their criticism must not overstep certain bounds. In that connection, account must be taken of the need to strike the right balance between the various interests involved, which include the public's right to receive information about questions arising from judicial decisions, the requirements of the proper administration of justice and the dignity of the legal profession....[54]

The function of the subject in society is also important. Penalties imposed for criticizing the government of a State will require extremely strong justification. As the Strasbourg Court said in the *Castells* case:[55]

The limits of permissible criticism are wider with regard to the Government than in relation to a private citizen, or even a politician. In a democratic system the actions or omissions of the Government must be subject to the close scrutiny not only of the legislative and judicial authorities but also of the press and public opinion. Furthermore, the dominant position which the Government occupies makes it necessary for it to display restraint in resorting

---

[51] *Thorgeir Thorgeirson v Iceland*, (App. 13778/88), 25 June 1992, Series A No 239, (1992) 14 EHRR 843, §63; *Jersild v Denmark*, (App. 15890/89), 23 September 1994, Series A No 298, (1994) 19 EHRR 1, §31; and *De Haes and Gijsels v Belgium*, (App. 19983/92), 24 February 1997, (1997) 25 EHRR 1, ECHR 1997-I, §37.

[52] *Prager and Oberschlick v Austria*, (App. 15974/90), 26 April 1995, Series A No 313, (1996) 21 EHRR 1, §38.

[53] *Steel and Morris v United Kingdom*, (App. 68416/01), 15 February 2005, (2005) 41 EHRR 403, ECHR 2005-II, §95.

[54] *Nikula v Finland*, (App. 31611/96), 21 March 2002, (2004) 38 EHRR 944, ECHR 2002-II, §§45–6.

[55] *Castells v Spain*, (App. 11798/85), 23 April 1992, Series A No 236, (1992) 14 EHRR 445, §46.

to criminal proceedings, particularly where other means are available for replying to the unjustified attacks and criticisms of its adversaries or the media.

It is not just the State that has to be tolerant. The limits of acceptable criticism are wide in regard to all politicians, whether or not they are in the government, because they knowingly lay themselves open to the scrutiny of the press and public.[56] The same holds for criticism of civil servants acting in an official capacity;[57] and similar principles apply to other persons who have voluntarily entered the public arena: for example prominent businesspeople, who are actively involved in the affairs of large public companies,[58] or persons and associations that participate in a public debate.[59]

Of course, even public figures are entitled to some privacy, however, and since there is little public benefit to be derived from exposing certain aspects of a politician's private life, the national authorities may be justified in taking preventive measures.[60]

The scope for attacking public servants is narrower than politicians because they do not knowingly lay themselves open to close scrutiny of their every word and deed to the extent to which politicians do and because they must enjoy public confidence in conditions free of undue perturbation if they are to be successful in performing their tasks.[61] The Strasbourg Court is particularly protective of judges. Article 10(2) expressly authorizes limitations for maintaining the authority and impartiality of the judiciary, and the Court has frequently held that, in order to maintain public confidence in the judiciary, judges should be protected from unjustified, destructive, and untrue attacks.[62] However, judges will lose this protection if they enter political life.[63]

If the person attacked is a public servant, the Strasbourg Court will pay particular attention to whether the attacks were professional or personal. Public servants and judges should be expected to endure criticism but not insult. So, for example, the Court found a violation in a case[64] where the applicant journalists had criticized in virulent terms the Court of Appeal judges who had awarded custody of two children to their father, a notary who had been accused by his ex-wife of child abuse. The journalists had been sued in defamation by the judges and ordered to pay nominal damages. The Strasbourg Court placed reliance on the fact that the articles had been well researched and had formed part of a public debate which had been taking place in Belgium at the time on incest, child abuse, and judicial reactions to these problems. By contrast, the

---

[56] *Dichand and others v Austria*, (App. 29271/95), 26 February 2002, §39. See also *Scharsach and News Verlagsgesellschaft mbH v Austria*, (App. 39394/98), 13 November 2003, (2005) 40 EHRR 569, ECHR 2003-XI; and *Kuliş v Poland*, (App. 15601/02), 18 March 2008.

[57] *July and SARL Libération v France*, (App. 20893/03), 14 February 2008.

[58] *Fayed v United Kingdom*, (App. 17101/90), 21 September 1994, Series A No 294-B, (1994) 18 EHRR 393. See also *Verlagsgruppe News GmbH v Austria (No. 2)*, (App. 10520/02), 14 December 2006.

[59] *Nilsen and Johnsen v Norway*, (App. 23118/93), 25 November 1999 [GC], ECHR 1999-VIII, §52; and *Jerusalem v Austria*, (App. 26958/95), 27 February 2001, (2003) 37 EHRR 567, ECHR 2001-II, §39.

[60] *Tammer v Estonia*, (App. 41205/98), 6 February 2001, (2003) 37 EHRR 857, ECHR 2001-I. See also *Standard Verlags GmbH v Austria (No. 2)*, (App. 21277/05), 4 June 2009.

[61] *Lešník v Slovakia*, (App. 35640/97), 11 March 2003, ECHR 2003-IV, §53.

[62] *Skalka v Poland*, (App. 43425/98), 27 May 2003, §40. See also *Perna v Italy* (App. 48898/99), 6 May 2003 [GC], (2004) 39 EHRR 563, ECHR 2003-V.

[63] *Hrico v Slovakia*, (App. 49418/99), 20 July 2004, §46.

[64] *De Haes and Gijsels v Belgium*, (App.19983/92), 24 February 1997; (1997) 25 EHRR 1, ECHR 1997-I.

Court found no violation in the *Barfod* case,[65] where the applicant had been convicted of criminal defamation following his publication of an article questioning the impartiality of two lay judges. The attack on the judges in this case had been personal and destructive, and the applicant had not been prevented from voicing criticism of the judgment, rather than of the judges themselves.

In the *Steel and Morris* case, the subject of the defamation was the fast-food chain, McDonald's. The applicants sought to argue that large multi-national companies, like McDonald's, should never be able to bring defamation proceedings. However, the Strasbourg Court rejected this argument. It held that, although the limits of acceptable criticism are wide in the case of such companies (because they inevitably and knowingly lay themselves open to close scrutiny of their acts), national authorities were entitled to afford companies some protection from defamation because there is a public interest in protecting the commercial success and viability of companies, not only for the benefit of shareholders and employees, but also for the wider economic good.[66]

The Strasbourg Court makes a critical distinction between value judgments and statements of fact. Value judgments cannot be proved. A requirement, in defamation proceedings, that a defendant prove the truth of a value judgment will violate his right to freedom of expression, protected by Article 10.[67] However, that does not mean that defendants can express any opinions, no matter how damaging, without any evidence to support them. Even value judgments will require, at the very least, some basis in fact.[68] Factual statements, on the other hand, are susceptible of proof. In general, it will be reasonable, in the interests of protecting the rights and reputations of others, to require defendants in defamation proceedings to prove the truth of factual statements that they have made.[69] However, they should be given the chance to do so. The protection of the rights and reputation of others will not normally justify a rule that prevents defendants from pleading justification in their defence.[70]

There are some statements of fact which it is in the interest of the public to hear but which are impossible to prove. For example, many important newspaper stories come from sources that would not be prepared to give evidence in defamation proceedings. As a result, the Strasbourg Court has recognized that there are some circumstances where the interests of society require that defendants in defamation proceedings be exempted from their ordinary duty to verify statements of fact. In considering whether those circumstances exist, the Court will have regard to the nature and degree of the

---

[65] *Barfod v Denmark*, (App. 11508/85), 22 February 1989, Series A No 149, (1991) 13 EHRR 493.

[66] *Steel and Morris v United Kingdom*, (App. 68416/01), 15 February 2005, (2005) 41 EHRR 403, ECHR 2005-II, §94.

[67] *Lingens v Austria*, (App. 9815/82), 8 July 1986, Series A No 103, (1986) 8 EHRR 407, §46; *Oberschlick v Austria*, (App. 11662/85), 23 May 1991, Series A No 204, (1994) 19 EHRR 389, §63; and *Ukrainian Media Group v Ukraine*, (App. 72713/01), 29 March 2005, (2006) 43 EHRR 499.

[68] *Dichand and Others v Austria*, (App. 29271/95), 26 February 2002, §52.

[69] *McVicar v United Kingdom*, (App. 46311/99), 7 May 2002, (2002) 35 EHRR 566, ECHR 2002-III, §87.

[70] *Colombani and others v France*, (App. 51279/99), 25 June 2002, ECHR 2002-V, §66. See also *Sorguç v Turkey*, (App. 17089/03), 23 June 2009, §33.

defamation and the reliability of any sources.[71] The conduct of the defendant will be important. The Court will examine, *inter alia*, whether the defendant conducted a reasonable amount of research before making the defamatory statement,[72] whether it presented the allegations in a reasonably balanced manner,[73] and whether it gave the person defamed the opportunity to defend himself or herself.[74]

The Strasbourg Court will judge for itself whether the statement was a value judgment or a statement of fact. That determination can be very controversial.[75] In the *Pedersen and Baadsgard* case,[76] for example, the applicants produced two television programmes concerning the conviction of a person for murder. The programme strongly criticized the conduct of the police and, in particular, the Chief Superintendent, who was identified by name. A witness was interviewed, who claimed that she had provided an alibi for the convicted person, which the police had ignored. The applicants then showed a photograph of the Chief Superintendent and asked a series of rhetorical questions, such as:

Was it [the named Chief Superintendent] who decided that the report should not be included in the case? Or did he and the Chief Inspector of the Flying Squad conceal the witness's statement from the defence, the judges and the jury?

Nine out of the seventeen members of the Grand Chamber found that these rhetorical questions amounted to statements of fact, which the applicants had failed to prove. They considered that the nature and degree of the defamation was very serious (as the applicants had identified the Chief Superintendent on national television and accused him of committing a serious criminal offence) and that the applicants had not taken sufficient steps to verify the truth of the witness's story. As a result, they found that there was no violation of Article 10. The remaining eight judges, on the other hand, considered the questions posed by the applicants to be 'value judgments or provocative hypotheses', for which there was a sufficient factual basis.

THE CONFLICT WITH THE RIGHT TO PRIVACY

The Strasbourg Court established some guidelines on the use of photographs in relation to rights protected by Article 8 in the *Von Hannover* case.[77] The test established in that case was whether it was in the public interest to publish the

---

[71] *Bladet Tromsø and Stensaas v Norway*, (App. 21980/93), 20 May 1999 [GC], (2000) 29 EHRR 125, ECHR 1999-III, §66; and *McVicar v United Kingdom*, (App. 46311/99), 7 May 2002, (2002) 35 EHRR 566, ECHR 2002-III, §84.

[72] *Prager and Oberschlick v Austria*, (App. 15974/90), 26 April 1995, Series A No 313, (1996) 21 EHRR 1, §37.

[73] *Bergens Tidende and Others v Norway*, (App. 26132/95), 2 May 2000, (2001) 31 EHRR 430, ECHR 2000-IV, §57.

[74] §58.

[75] For a very odd majority decision by four votes to three which turned on the characterization of the offending material as fact or value judgment, see *Schmidt v Austria*, (App. 513/05), 17 July 2008.

[76] *Pedersen and Baadsgaard v Denmark* (App. 49017/99), 17 December 2004 [GC], (2006) 42 EHRR 486, ECHR 2004-XI.

[77] *Von Hannover v Germany* (App. 59320/00), 24 June 2004, (2005) 40 EHRR 1, ECHR 2004-VI.

photograph, and whether its publication contributes to a debate of general interest to society. The Strasbourg Court has also addressed the question in the context of Article 10, noting the relationship between the two articles. The balancing exercise required is a tricky one for all concerned.[78] When does an expectation of respect for private life get trumped by the right of the general public to be informed, through publication of photographs of the person concerned, of a matter of public interest? When will a photograph in addition to words contribute to a debate of general interest?

The applicant in the *Von Hannover* case[79] was Princess Caroline of Monaco. She complained about the publication in German magazines of paparazzi photographs of her eating in restaurants, playing with her children, and enjoying herself on holiday. She sought an injunction in the German courts to prevent the publication of further photographs. The German Constitutional Court, however, refused an injunction. It attached decisive weight to the freedom of the press, even the entertainment press, and to the public interest in knowing how the applicant behaved outside her representative functions and held that the applicant enjoyed the protection of her private life outside her home but only if she was in a secluded place out of the public eye. The Strasbourg Court observed that:

Although freedom of expression also extends to the publication of photos, this is an area in which the protection of the rights and reputation of others takes on particular importance. The present case does not concern the dissemination of 'ideas', but of images containing very personal or even intimate 'information' about an individual. Furthermore, photos appearing in the tabloid press are often taken in a climate of continual harassment which induces in the person concerned a very strong sense of intrusion into their private life or even of persecution.[80]

The Court drew a 'fundamental distinction' between the reporting of facts capable of contributing to a debate in a democratic society relating to politicians in the exercise of their functions, where the press exercised an important 'watchdog' role, and the reporting of details of an individual's private life, where it did not. Although the public right to be informed could in some extend to aspects of the private life of public figures, particularly politicians, that was not the case here. The Strasbourg Court considered that the sole purpose of the publication of the photographs and articles about the applicant's private life 'was to satisfy the curiosity of a particular readership' and the publication could not be deemed to contribute to any debate of general interest to society despite the applicant being known to the public. In these conditions, freedom of expression called for a narrower interpretation and the Court found that the German law did not strike a fair balance between the competing interests and that the applicant's rights under Article 8 had been violated.[81]

---

[78] As in *Egeland and Hanseid v Norway*, (App. 34438/04), 16 April 2009.

[79] *Von Hannover v Germany* (App. 59320/00), 24 June 2004, (2005) 40 EHRR 1, ECHR 2004-VI.

[80] §59.

[81] Contrast *Hachette Filipacchi Associés 'Ici Paris' v France*, (App. 12268/03), 23 July 2009, where the photographs used in the publication were taken from advertising material, and were not the result of

In the *Armonienė* case,[82] the Strasbourg Court held that, even where the national courts uphold an individual's claim to privacy against the press, there will be a breach of Article 8 if the damages awarded are too low. The applicant was the widow of a man who was not a public figure of any kind. He was, however, named in an article on the front page of the biggest Lithuanian newspaper. The article, which also included his address, claimed that he had AIDs and had fathered a child with an unmarried mother who was also HIV positive. The Lithuanian court found that the newspaper article was unfounded and had damaged the applicant's reputation, health, and relationships, but that it had not been deliberately malicious. It awarded the maximum amount of damages permitted by law in the absence of proof of malice, approximately €3,000. The Strasbourg Court found that there had been an 'outrageous abuse of press freedom' causing substantial harm and found the statutory restriction on the judge's power to award damages to breach Article 8.

The *Hachette Filipacchi Associés* case[83] concerned the publication in *Paris-Match* of the photograph of the body of a murdered politician taken immediately after his assassination. The widow and children of the murdered man sought an order for the seizure of copies of any magazine in which the picture appeared. Their application was not wholly successful. No seizure order was made, but an order was made that the publishers of *Paris-Match* should publish a statement that the family had found the publication of the photograph without their consent deeply distressing. The publishers complained that the order constituted a breach of its rights under Article 10. The Strasbourg Court considers photographs to some extent more powerful than words, noting:

> ...when photographs are published the protection of the rights and reputation of others takes on particular importance, especially when it involves large-scale dissemination of images containing very personal or even intimate 'information' about an individual or his or her family....[84]

In such cases, the Strasbourg Court has to determine whether a fair balance has been struck between freedom of expression in Article 10 and the right to respect for private life in Article 8. The Court decided by five votes to two that the imposition of a requirement to publish a statement was not a disproportionate response to the family's distress at the publication of the picture. The case illustrates just how difficult it is to establish the balance between the conflicting rights. Some will prefer the views of the dissenting judges, who would have found a violation because the assassination was a matter of public interest, the photograph was not prurient in any respect, the victim was shown face down, and the photograph had been widely seen on other media, including the television.

---

contentious or undercover methods of obtaining photographs which had interfered with the privacy of the applicant.

[82] *Armonienė v Lithuania*, (App. 36919/02), 25 November 2008.
[83] *Hachette Filipacchi Associés v France*, (App. 71111/01), 14 June 2007, (2009) 49 EHRR 515, ECHR 2007-VII.
[84] §42.

SEVERITY OF ANY PENALTY

The severity of the penalty imposed will often be important. Large awards of damages in civil proceedings can, in themselves, be enough to violate Article 10, particularly if they are out of proportion to the income of the applicant and there is no evidence of any financial damage to the person defamed.[85] If damages are awarded by juries, the judiciary will be required to exercise a certain amount of control over the level of those damages so as to keep them within reasonable bounds.[86]

Similarly, if applicants are punished for their freedom of expression by way of a criminal sanction, the Strasbourg Court will examine whether that sanction was necessary and appropriate. In so doing, the Court will have regard to the seriousness of the offence and the previous record of the applicant.[87] Sentences of imprisonment will be particularly hard to justify. Indeed the Court has said, in the *Cumpănă* case, that imprisoning a journalist for defamation, when the context is a debate on a matter of legitimate public interest, requires the presence of exceptional circumstances, 'notably where other fundamental rights have been seriously impaired, as, for example, in the case of hate speech or incitement to violence'.[88] Such a sentence creates an unacceptable chilling effect on journalistic freedom of expression.

There are some situations where any penalty, no matter how light, will violate Article 10. In the *Steur* case,[89] the applicant was a lawyer acting on behalf of the defendant in fraud proceedings. In related civil proceedings the applicant accused the social security investigating officer of exerting excessive pressure on his client to obtain an incriminating statement. This officer filed a disciplinary complaint which was upheld by the domestic courts. No sanction was imposed on the applicant. Nonetheless the Strasbourg Court found that the official finding of fault alone was enough to constitute a disproportionate interference with the applicant's right to freedom of expression, because it would have a chilling effect on the applicant's willingness and ability to perform his professional duty to defend the interests of his client with appropriate zeal.

In some cases the conduct of the applicant in adopting 'an exceedingly casual attitude' to national proceedings in which a penalty is imposed may influence the Court in its determination of the proportionality of the measures in issue.[90]

---

[85] *Steel and Morris v United Kingdom*, (App. 68416/01), 15 February 2005, (2005) 41 EHRR 403, ECHR 2005-II, §§96–7.

[86] *Tolstoy Miloslavsky v United Kingdom*, (App. 18139/91), 13 July 1995, Series A No 316-B, (1995) 20 EHRR 442, §50.

[87] *Skalka v Poland*, (App. 43425/98), 27 May 2003, §41.

[88] *Cumpănă and Mazăre v Romania*, (App. 33348/96), 17 December 2004 [GC], (2005) 41 EHRR 200, ECHR 2004-X, §115.

[89] *Steur v Netherlands*, (App. 39657/98), 28 October 2003, (2004) 39 EHRR 706, ECHR 2003-XI.

[90] *Ivanciuc v Romania*, (App. 18624/03), Decision of 8 September 2005, ECHR 2005-XI.

LEGAL AID TO DEFEND
DEFAMATION PROCEEDINGS

The Strasbourg Court has had to consider whether (and when) Article 10 requires the defendants in defamation proceedings to be provided with legal aid. The applicant in the *McVicar* case[91] was a journalist who alleged, in an article for a magazine, that the athlete Linford Christie had used banned performance-enhancing drugs. Christie sued him for defamation. During most of the proceedings the applicant represented himself because he could not afford legal fees and because legal aid was not available for defamation. The jury found that he had not proved the truth of the allegation and he was ordered to pay for the costs of the action and made subject to an injunction forbidding him from publishing the allegation again. McVicar claimed that the lack of legal aid was a violation of his right to a fair trial and his right to freedom of expression. The Court rejected these arguments, noting that he was an experienced and well-educated journalist, that the issues in the case were relatively simple and that he had had the assistance of a specialist defamation lawyer for at least some of the case.

In the *Steel and Morris* case, the applicants were a part-time bar worker and a former postal worker receiving social security benefits. They were associated with London Greenpeace, an environmental group that published a pamphlet that made various defamatory allegations about the fast-food chain McDonald's. The subsequent defamation proceedings brought by McDonald's (dubbed the 'McLibel trial') ran for two and a half years and became the longest in English history. The trial at first instance lasted 313 court days and was preceded by 28 interlocutory proceedings. The appeal hearing lasted twenty-three days. The factual case involved 40,000 pages of documentary evidence and 130 oral witnesses on scientific issues such as nutrition, diet, degenerative disease, and food safety, some of which were considered too complex for a jury to assess. Once again the applicants were not entitled to legal aid and, although they received considerable assistance from lawyers acting *pro bono*, they acted alone for the bulk of the proceedings. The Court relied on the extraordinary length and complexity of the case in finding that, in this particular case, the lack of legal aid did violate the applicants' right to freedom of expression (as well as their right to a fair trial).[92]

CONFIDENTIAL INFORMATION

Article 10 guarantees the freedom to receive as well as impart information, but it does not confer a right of access to information.[93] Although the Strasbourg Court appears

---

[91] *McVicar v United Kingdom*, (App. 46311/99), 7 May 2002, (2002) 35 EHRR 566, ECHR 2002-III.

[92] *Steel and Morris v United Kingdom*, (App. 68416/01), 15 February 2005, (2005) 41 EHRR 403, ECHR 2005-II, §§59–72 and 75.

[93] *Leander v Sweden*, (App. 9248/81), 26 March 1987, Series A No 116, (1987) 9 EHRR 433; and *Gaskin v United Kingdom*, (App. 10454/83), 7 July 1989, Series A No 160, (1990) 12 EHRR 36. Compare Art. 19 of the Covenant on Civil and Political Rights.

increasingly ready to find an obligation on the State to provide information to concerned individuals included in the right to respect for private life under Article 8,[94] Article 10, in contrast, is directed at proscribing interference by a public authority between a willing giver and a willing recipient. But it will be a violation of Article 10 for a Contracting Party to refuse to grant access to documents once a national court has made an order for this to happen.[95]

In the *Hadjianastassiou* case[96] the Strasbourg Court made it clear that the State was to be afforded a very wide margin of appreciation when the protection of national security was in issue. The applicant had been convicted and sentenced for having disclosed military secrets. The leaked information was of very minor importance, but the Court concluded that any disclosure of State secrets was apt to compromise national security and found no violation.

In two cases concerning the publication of Peter Wright's book *Spycatcher*,[97] the newspapers concerned complained of a violation of Article 10 arising from the action by the Attorney General in bringing breach of confidence actions and seeking injunctions restraining publication of extracts of the book. Of particular significance was a decision of the Court of Appeal that the injunctions against *The Observer* and *The Guardian* bound all the media within the jurisdiction of the English courts and that any publication or broadcast of the *Spycatcher* material would constitute a criminal contempt of court. Despite the arrival in the United Kingdom of copies of the book imported from outside the country, the injunctions were kept in force until October 1988. For the first period[98] the Strasbourg Court ruled by 14 to 10 that the risk of material prejudicial to the security services existed and that this justified the imposition of injunctions. For the remaining period, the decision was unanimous that there was a violation of Article 10; the material could no longer be regarded as likely to prejudice the security services since the book was freely circulating in the United States.

WHISTLE-BLOWERS

In a number of cases where civil servants had publicly criticized their employers and suffered disciplinary measures,[99] the Commission accepted that State employees and service personnel have a special 'duty of discretion', meaning that their freedom to criticize government policies in a public manner is curtailed. Nonetheless, restrictive

---

[94] See ch.16 above.

[95] *Kenedi v Hungary*, (App. 31475/05), 26 May 2009.

[96] *Hadjianastassiou v Greece*, (App. 12945/87), 16 December 1992, Series A No 252-A, (1993) 16 EHRR 219, §§38–47.

[97] *Observer and Guardian v United Kingdom*, (App. 13585/88), 26 November 1991, Series A No 216,13585/88), (1992) 14 EHRR 153; and *Sunday Times v United Kingdom (No. 2)*, (App. 13166/87), 26 November 1991, Series A No 217, (1992) 14 EHRR 229. See also *Blake v United Kingdom*, (App. 68890/01), Decision of 25 October 2005, ECHR 2005-XII.

[98] From July 1986 to July 1987.

[99] See, for example, App. 18597/92, *Haseldine v United Kingdom*, Decision of 13 May 1992.

measures must be proportionate, and the motives of the person disclosing the information and the ability to substantiate his or her criticisms are relevant considerations. Criticisms which are made to a more limited audience, for example the commanding officer of military personnel, require a greater degree of tolerance, even if expressed in strong terms.[100]

The *Guja* case[101] is the first to deal explicitly with the practice of whistle-blowing.[102] The applicant was the head of the press office in the Moldovan Prosecutor General's Office. There were concerns about corruption in the practices of law enforcement agencies. Guja saw a letter from a very senior politician which sought to bring pressure on the prosecutor to terminate pending prosecutions against certain police officers. A report concerning two such letters was published in a newspaper, and Guja admitted that he had given copies to the press. He argued that he had acted in good faith, that the letters were not confidential, and that he had acted in line with the President's anti-corruption drive. The applicant was dismissed from his employment, and his legal proceedings seeking reinstatement failed. He complained of a violation of Article 10. The Grand Chamber, in a unanimous judgment finding a violation of Article 10, said:

> 72. ...the Court notes that a civil servant, in the course of his work, may become aware of in-house information, including secret information, whose divulgation or publication corresponds to a strong public interest. The Court thus considers that the signalling by a civil servant or an employee in the public sector of illegal conduct or wrongdoing in the workplace should, in certain circumstances, enjoy protection. This may be called for where the employee or civil servant concerned is the only person, or part of a small category of persons, aware of what is happening at work and is thus best placed to act in the public interest by alerting the employer or the public at large....

> 73. In the light of the duty of discretion [owed by a civil servant], disclosure should be made in the first place to the person's superior or other competent authority or body. It is only where this is clearly impracticable that the information could, as a last resort, be disclosed to the public.... In assessing whether the restriction on freedom of expression was proportionate, therefore, the Court must take into account whether there was available to the applicant any other effective means of remedying the wrongdoing which he intended to uncover.[103]

Two key factors would be considered by the Court in assessing the proportionality of the interference with Article 10 rights. The first is the level of the public interest in the disclosed information, and whether this over-rides the confidentiality of the

---

[100] *Grigoriades v Greece* (App. 24348/94), 25 November 1997, (1999) 27 EHRR 464, ECHR 1997-VII.

[101] *Guja v Moldova*, (App. 14277/04), 12 February 2008 [GC], ECHR 2008-nyr. See also *Juppala v Finland*, (App. 18620/03), 2 December 2008, §42 which concerned a good faith disclosure to a doctor about possible child abuse which resulted in the informant being found guilty of defamation.

[102] The term is derived from the practice of English police officers in times gone by of blowing their whistles to draw attention to criminal activity. Whistle-blowing has typically come to refer to the practice of an insider communicating evidence of misconduct and claiming exemption from sanctions for breaching an employer's confidence.

[103] *Guja v Moldova*, (App. 14277/04), 12 February 2008 [GC], ECHR 2008-nyr, §§72–3.

information. The second factor is the authenticity of the information which is disclosed. There is a heavy burden on the disclosing party to ensure the accuracy and reliability of the information disclosed. Whistle-blowers will also be expected to show that they have acted in good faith, and not from any sense of personal grievance, or expectation of personal advantage. As in other aspects of the application of Article 10, the severity of any penalty imposed upon the whistle-blower will need to be weighed in the balance.

In the *Guja* case, the Court distinguished its judgment in the *Stoll* case.[104] In the latter case, a journalist obtained a confidential document written by the Swiss Ambassador to the United States discussing the strategy which might be adopted by the Swiss authorities in negotiating a settlement of compensation claims for Holocaust victims for unclaimed assets deposited in Swiss bank accounts. It was assumed that the journalist had acquired the document in breach of official secrecy. He then wrote an article in a newspaper critical of the ambassador, which disclosed some of the contents of the confidential document. He was fined 800 Swiss francs for publishing secret official deliberations. The Swiss Press Council found that the publication had been legitimate, but was critical of the content, which made the ambassador's comments appear sensational and shocking. The journalist complained of a violation of Article 10. The Grand Chamber clearly found this a challenging case. They were faced with a conflict not between a private interest and a public interest, but rather between two public interests: 'the interest of readers in being informed on a topical issue and the interest of the authorities in ensuring a positive and satisfactory outcome to the diplomatic negotiations being conducted.'[105] Reversing the Chamber judgment, the Grand Chamber, by twelve votes to five, concluded that there had been no violation of Article 10. In making its assessment, the Grand Chamber considered the issue at stake, namely the dissemination of confidential information on a matter of considerable public interest, the nature of the interests at stake, the review of the sanction on the journalist by the national courts, the conduct of the journalist, and the severity of the penalty. The overwhelming sense in reading the judgment of the Court is that it was very heavily influenced by the interest in protecting the confidentiality of information within the diplomatic service in order to ensure the proper functioning of international relations. In her concurring opinion, Judge Ziemele is critical of the majority in singling out the interests of the respondent State in this way, and their basing their conclusions on the capacity of the disclosure to undermine diplomatic negotiations as distinct from its actual impact. The dissenting judges view the judgment as 'a dangerous and unjustified departure from the Court's well-established case-law' in giving far too great a weight to the confidential nature of the document.

Despite this approach, the Strasbourg Court has made judgments which support journalistic enquiry. In the *Damann* case,[106] a journalist was prosecuted, convicted on

---

[104] *Stoll v Switzzerland*, (App. 69698/01), 10 December 2007 [GC], ECHR 2007-XIV. See also *Kudeshkina v Russia*, (App. 29492/05), 26 February 2009.

[105] §116.

[106] *Damann v Switzerland*, (App. 77551/01), 25 April 2006.

appeal, and fined for inciting another to disclose an official secret. The journalist, as part of his investigation into a spectacular robbery, had obtained information from an administrative assistant in the prosecutor's office about whether certain individuals had any previous criminal convictions. The journalist did not use the information in any published material; he had been prosecuted after he had shown a police officer the information he had received. The Strasbourg Court noted that it was dealing with a journalist's research in investigating a potential story for publication. The Court noted that the provider of the information had not been tricked, threatened or pressurized into providing the information, and the journalist had not published the information (and so there was no interference with the rights of others). In all the circumstances, the conviction and light penalty were such as to have a chilling effect on journalists undertaking research inherent in the task of newspaper reporting; the interference was not necessary in a democratic society. There was a risk that such action would inhibit the role of the press as a public watchdog on matters of public interest.

OBSCENITY AND BLASPHEMY

In the *Handyside* case the Strasbourg Court noted that there was no uniform European concept of 'morality' and made it clear that Contracting Parties would enjoy a wide margin of appreciation in assessing whether measures were required to protect moral standards.[107]

This approach was followed in the *Müller* case,[108] which concerned an exhibition of contemporary art including three paintings depicting sexual acts, seized by the authorities on the grounds that they were obscene. The Strasbourg Court found that it was not unreasonable for the Swiss courts to have found the paintings liable to offend the sense of sexual propriety of persons of ordinary sensitivity. As a result, the imposition of fines did not violate Article 10.

The expression under consideration in the *Wingrove* case[109] was a video made by the applicant portraying a woman, dressed as a nun and described in the credits as 'Saint Teresa' (of Avila), having an erotic fantasy involving the crucified figure of Christ. The video was refused a certificate for distribution by the British Board of Film Classification on the grounds that it appeared to contravene the British blasphemy law, in that the Board considered that its public distribution would outrage and insult the feelings of believing Christians. The Strasbourg Court did not consider that there was yet sufficient common ground in the legal and social orders of the Contracting Parties

---

[107] *Handyside v United Kingdom*, (App. 5493/72), 7 December 1976, Series A No 24, (1979–80) 1 EHRR 737, §43.

[108] *Müller and others v Switzerland*, (App. 10737/84), 24 May 1988, Series A No 133, (1991) 13 EHRR 212. See also *Otto-Preminger Institute v Austria*, (App. 13470/87), 20 September 1994, Series A No 295-A, (1995) 19 EHRR 34.

[109] *Wingrove v United Kingdom*, (App. 17419/90), 25 November 1996, (1997) 24 EHRR 1; ECHR 1996-V.

to conclude that a system allowing a State to impose restrictions on the propagation of material on the basis that it was blasphemous was, in itself, incompatible with the Convention. A wider margin of appreciation was generally available to Contracting Parties when regulating freedom of expression in relation to matters liable to offend intimate personal convictions within the sphere of morals or, especially, religion, since the authorities were in a better position that the international judge to assess what was likely to cause offence to believers in each country. Having viewed the film itself, the Strasbourg Court concluded that the reasons given by the British authorities to justify the measures taken could be considered as both relevant and sufficient for the purposes of Article 10(2).

However, in the *Vereinigung Bildener Künstler* case,[110] the Strasbourg Court, by four votes to three, found a violation of Article 10 where the Austrian authorities had prohibited the continued exhibition of a large collage on display in a public gallery, which depicted public and religious figures engaged in sexual activity.[111] The Court seems to have been influenced by the fact that the art installation was 'some sort of counter-attack against the Austrian Freedom Party'.[112] The dissenting opinions of Judges Spielmann and Jebens took the view that the artwork lost its protection under Article 10 because of its failure to respect the human dignity of certain of those portrayed.[113]

One of the problems of the cases concerned with obscenity and blasphemy (particularly the latter) is that the earlier case-law of the Strasbourg Court came very close to establishing a right not to be insulted by others in relation to religious feelings. This is certainly one conclusion that can be drawn from the Court's approach to the film *Das Liebeskonzil* in the *Otto-Preminger* case,[114] and to the film 'Visions of Ecstasy' in the *Wingrove* case.[115] A preferable way to deal with such cases would be to offer no protection to the advocacy of religious hatred.[116]

There is a line of cases which suggests that the Strasbourg Court is not fully wedded to the notion of protecting a right not to be insulted by others in relation to religious feelings, but is rather concerned with respect for freedom of expression on the one hand while securing the right of others to respect for their freedom of thought, conscience, and religion. Someone writing critically about religion, but without

---

[110] *Vereinigung Bildener Künstler v Austria*, (App. 68354/01), 25 January 2007, (2008) 47 EHRR 189, ECHR 2007-II.

[111] For a graphic description of the artwork, see the dissenting opinion of Judge Loucaides.

[112] *Vereinigung Bildener Künstler*, §34.

[113] On the concept of human dignity, see C. McCrudden, 'Human Dignity and Judicial Interpretation of Human Rights' (2008) 19 EJIL 655.

[114] *Otto-Preminger Institute v Austria*, (App. 13470/87), 20 September 1994, Series A No 295-A, (1994) 19 EHRR 34. See also App. 8710/79, *Gay News Ltd and Lemon v United Kingdom*, Decision of 7 May 1982, (1082) 5 EHRR 123, §11.

[115] *Wingrove v United Kingdom*, (App. 17419/90), 25 November 1996, (1997) 24 EHRR 1.

[116] See J. Temperman, 'Blasphemy, Defamation of Religions and Human Rights Law' (2008) 26 NQHR 517, especially 533–44. See also Art. 20(2) of the International Covenant on Civil and Political Rights which provides: 'Any advocacy of national, racial or religious hatred that constitutes incitement to discrimination, hostility or violence shall be prohibited by law.'

advocating or inciting hatred, does not interfere with the rights protected by Article 9. There is therefore little to balance. The beginnings of this approach can be seen in the *IA* case,[117] in which the Strasbourg Court found by four votes to three no violation of Article 10 where the Turkish authorities had convicted of blasphemy the author of a book which contained critical remarks about aspects of Islam. The Court draws on its judgments in the *Otto-Preminger* and *Wingrove* cases in noting that 'as a matter of principle it may be considered necessary to punish improper attacks on objects of religious veneration.'[118] But the Court does go on to indicate that the judgment of the Court is based not on 'comments that offend or shock, or a "provocative" opinion, but also [constitute] an abusive attack on the Prophet of Islam'.[119] The joint opinion of the dissenting judges invites the Court to reconsider the case-law in this area which 'seems to place too much emphasis on conformism or uniformity of thought and to reflect an overcautious and timid conception of freedom of the press.'[120]

By contrast, in the *Giniewski* case,[121] the Strasbourg Court unanimously found a violation of Article 10 as a result of the prosecution of an author for defamation. The offending material was a critical analysis of Pope John Paul II's encyclical 'The splendour of truth'. The Court characterized the material as not being gratuitously offensive, insulting, or inciting disrespect or hatred.[122] The *Klein* case[123] concerned a response by a journalist and film critic to protests by Archbishop Sokol about the showing of, and publicity for, the film 'The People vs. Larry Flint'. This resulted in complaints. Criminal proceedings were brought against the applicant; he was convicted. His appeals were unsuccessful. The Strasbourg Court unanimously found a violation of Article 10, noting that the applicant's comments 'neither interfered with the right of believers to express and exercise their religion nor did it denigrate the content of their religious faith....'[124]

The Strasbourg Court was spared the difficulty of adjudicating on the twelve cartoons of the prophet Mohammad published in the Danish newspaper *Morgenavisen Jyllands-Posten*,[125] when it ruled that the applicants had no standing to complain about their publication.[126] Had the merits of that controversy come before the Strasbourg Court, it is certainly arguable that the publication of the cartoons did not interfere in any way with freedom of religion, and freedom to manifest religious beliefs. This would have left the Strasbourg Court to elaborate the concept of insult to a religion, and the dividing line between the expression of views, here in art form, which are offensive to many Muslims but legitimate under Article 10, and matters which are likely to incite religious hatred which are not. The case would also have required the

---

[117] *IA v Turkey*, (App. 42571/98), 13 September 2005, (2007) 45 EHRR 703, ECHR 2005-VIII.
[118] §24.   [119] §28.   [120] §8 of joint dissenting opinion.
[121] *Giniewski v France*, (App. 64016/00), 31 January 2006, (2007) 45 EHRR 589, ECHR 2006-I.
[122] §52.   [123] *Klein v Slovakia*, (App. 72208/01), 31 October 2006.   [124] §52.
[125] Which resulted in an international uproar arising from the taboo on representations of the prophet widely held among Muslims, though not apparently spelled out in the Koran.
[126] *Ben el Mahi and others v Denmark*, (App. 5853/06), Decision of 8 February 2006, ECHR 2006-XV. For comment on this saga, see K. Boyle, 'The Danish Cartoons' (2006) 24 NQHR 185; and D. Keane, 'Cartoon Violence and Freedom of Expression' (2008) 30 HRQ 845.

Strasbourg Court to consider positive obligations, since the complaint was that the Danish authorities had not intervened to prevent or punish the publication of the cartoons, when they should have done in order to respect their religious sensitivities.

ADVERTISEMENTS

The Strasbourg Court has recognized that advertising performs a useful function in society, namely to provide individuals with the means of discovering the characteristics of services and goods on offer.[127] Nevertheless, it may sometimes be restricted, especially to prevent unfair competition and untruthful or misleading advertising.[128] National authorities will have a wide margin of appreciation when the advertisements are purely commercial.[129] That margin will be reduced where the advertisements serve a wider public interest.

The cases of *Casado Coca*[130] and *Barthold*[131] illustrate this well. Casado Coca was a member of the Spanish Bar who was disciplined by the Barcelona Bar Council for placing advertisements in newspapers. The Strasbourg Court found that the rules which prevented him advertising fell within the national authorities' margin of appreciation. Barthold, on the other hand, was a veterinary surgeon, who published an article explaining the treatment he had given to a cat outside normal office hours and arguing that a regular night service should be provided in Hamburg. His name and clinic address was given. A private association against unfair competition complained that the article breached the professional rules on advertising of veterinary surgeons. An injunction restraining future similar publications was obtained against him. In finding a violation, the Strasbourg Court relied principally on the fact that the issue raised in the article was one of genuine public interest.

Sometimes the question of whether or not an advertisement serves a wider public interest may be very delicate. In the *Tierfabriken* case,[132] for example, the applicant took out an advert protesting against the treatment of pigs. The advertisement depicted a noisy hall with pigs in small pens, gnawing at the iron bars. The accompanying voice stated, *inter alia*, that the rearing of pigs in such circumstances resembled concentration camps. The association was prevented from broadcasting the

---

[127] See M. Hertig Randall, 'Commercial Speech under the European Convention on Human Rights: Subordinate or Equal?' (2006) 6 HRLRev 53.

[128] *Casado Coca v Spain*, (App. 15450/89), 24 February 1994, Series A No 285-A, (1994) 18 EHRR 1, §51.

[129] *Vgt Verein gegen Tierfabriken v Switzerland*, (App. 24699/94), 28 June 2001, (2002) 34 EHRR 159, ECHR 2001-VI, §71.

[130] *Casado Coca v Spain*, (App. 15450/89), 24 February 1994, Series A No 285-A, (1994) 18 EHRR 1, §51.

[131] *Barthold v Germany*, (App. 8734/79), 25 March 1985, Series A No 90, (1975) 7 EHRR 383.

[132] *Vgt Verein gegen Tierfabriken v Switzerland*, (App. 24699/94), 28 June 2001, (2002) 34 EHRR 159, ECHR 2001-VI. See also *Verein Gegen Tierfabriken Schweiz (VgT) v Switzerland (No. 2)*, (App. 32772/02), 30 June 2009 [GC], ECHR 2009-nyr, in which the Grand Chamber found a violation of Article 10 arising from the continuing failure of the respondent State to permit the broadcasting of the commercial.

advertisement because of a domestic law against political advertising. The Strasbourg Court accepted that a ban on political advertising might be justified in certain circumstances. However, it noted that the applicant was not a powerful financial group and concluded that, in the particular circumstances of the case, the reasons for the ban were not relevant and sufficient.

In the *Murphy* case[133] the applicant was a pastor attached to the Irish Faith Centre who wanted to broadcast an advertisement for the screening of a film on the evidence for the resurrection. However, he was prevented from doing so because of a domestic law against religious advertising. The Strasbourg Court found no violation of Article 10. It distinguished the *Tierfabriken* case on the grounds that national authorities had a wider margin of appreciation in relation to religious matters as they are liable to offend personal convictions.

The two cases are not easy to reconcile. Even taking into account the sensitivity of religion as a topic (especially in Ireland), Murphy's advertisement was unlikely to offend anyone. The Strasbourg Court in *Murphy* relied, instead, on the respondent State's argument that a provision which allowed the filtering, on a case by case basis, of unacceptable or excessive religious advertising would be difficult to apply fairly, objectively, and coherently. Why should it be any easier to filter political advertising on a case by case basis?

In what is certain to be regarded as a controversial decision given the variations in practice among the Contracting Parties, the Strasbourg Court ruled unanimously in the *TV Vest* case[134] that the prohibition in Norway on political advertisements on television breached Article 10. The terms of the judgment do not seem to be limited to the particular facts of that case, which concerned a penalty imposed on the television station and the political party.[135] The judgment emphasizes the permanent and absolute nature of the ban which applied only to television, the importance of political speech, and the lack of any content in the impugned broadcast 'liable to offend intimate personal convictions within the sphere of morals and religion'.[136] This enabled the Court to distinguish its judgment in the *Murphy* case. The judgment is bound to send ripples of concern through those Contracting Parties which ban paid political advertising.[137]

BROADCASTING

Broadcasting is subject to greater regulation than the written word, since Article 10(1) includes the power to license broadcasting, cinema, and television enterprises. The

---

[133] *Murphy v Ireland*, (App. 44179/98), 10 July 2003, (2004) 38 EHRR 212, ECHR 2003-IX.

[134] *TV Vest AS and Rogaland Pensjonistparti v Norway*, (App. 21132/05), 11 December 2008, (2009) 48 EHRR 1206.

[135] The Pensioners Party, which is a small party polling in local and regional elections 1.3 per cent of the votes on a national basis.

[136] §64.

[137] §§24–7 contain a comparative analysis of the position in the Contracting Parties.

purpose of the licensing can be broad,[138] but there is a duty to ensure that the rights under Article 10 remain protected.[139]

In the *Groppera Radio* case,[140] Groppera Radio broadcast radio programmes from Italy to listeners in Switzerland. They failed to comply with a Swiss Ordinance prohibiting cable retransmission of such programmes. The Court ruled that the object, purpose, and scope of the third sentence of Article 10(1) had to be considered in the context of the article as a whole, and in particular the limitations in Article 10(2). No violation was found in the case.

The *Informationsverein Lentia* case[141] concerned five applications for broadcasting licences (one for television and four for radio) which were refused, because the Austrian Broadcasting Corporation held a monopoly. The Austrian Government relied on the third sentence of paragraph (1), or, in the alternative, on the limitations in paragraph (2), and argued that the monopoly enabled the State to regulate the technical aspects of audio-visual activities and to determine their place and role in modern society. The Court found a violation of Article 10, observing that the State is the 'ultimate guarantor' of pluralism, and that a public broadcasting monopoly could be not be justified.

In regulating broadcasting, a Contracting Party must take care not to infringe the right of a person to receive information. In the *Autronic* case,[142] the Swiss Government had refused permission for a company specializing in home electronics to receive programmes from a Soviet satellite. There was a violation of Autronic's rights under Article 10.

In one unusual case,[143] the right to receive information was held to include the right of an Iraqi family living in Stockholm to have a satellite dish in apparent breach of the terms of their tenancy agreement in order to be able to receive television programmes in Arabic and Farsi. There was no other means of their obtaining such media, and they had been evicted from their home. There is a hint in the Court's judgment that the safety reasons put forward by the landlord and accepted by the courts were spurious.

POSITIVE OBLIGATIONS

In the context of Article 10, the Strasbourg Court has been somewhat circumspect about referring to the positive obligations of the Contracting Parties, but it remains clear that positive obligations do arise in relation to securing to all the rights of freedom

---

[138] App. 4515/70, *X and the Association of Z v United Kingdom*, Decision of 12 July 1971, (1971) 14 *Yearbook* 538.

[139] App. 9297/81, *X Association v Sweden*, Decision of 1 March 1982, (1982) 28 DR 204.

[140] *Groppera Radio AG and others v Switzerland*, (App. 10890/84), 28 March 1990, Series A No 173, (1990) 12 EHRR 321.

[141] *Informationsverein Lentia v Austria*, (Apps. 13914/88, 15041/89, 15717/89, 15779/89, and 17207/90), 24 November 1993, Series A No 276, (1994) 17 EHRR 93.

[142] *Autronic AG v Switzerland*, (App. 12726/87), 22 May 1990, Series A No 178, (1990) 12 EHRR 485.

[143] *Khurshid Mustafa and Tarzibachi v Sweden*, (App. 23883/06), 16 December 2008.

of expression enshrined in the provision.[144] As we have seen, in some circumstances, there is an obligation to provide some form of legal assistance to those defending defamation proceedings.[145] Freedom to receive information may also involve positive obligations, but the precise parameters of this obligation are far from clear. There is authority to support the proposition that the freedom to receive information prohibits a Contracting Party from restricting a person from receiving information that others are willing to impart, but that this does not extend to a positive obligation to disseminate information of its own motion.[146]

CONCLUDING REMARKS

The Strasbourg Court has repeatedly emphasized the vital role that freedom of expression, and the free press in particular, have to play in a democratic society. The expansion of the Council of Europe in the last twenty-five years has served to prove the point. The media in central and eastern Europe were instrumental in bringing down totalitarianism, and continue to form a vital safeguard in the new democracies, throughout Europe.

It remains surprising how frequently the criminal law, or the law of defamation, is used to control various forms of expression among the Contracting Parties. This seems to be the key battleground between applicants and the Contracting Parties in many applications made to the Strasbourg Court, despite clear guidance to the Contracting Parties in the judgments of the Court.

[144] See, for example, *Fuentes Bobo v Spain*, (App. 39293/98), 29 February 2000; and *Vgt Verein gegen Tierfabriken v Switzerland*, (App. 24699/94), 28 June 2001, (2002) 34 EHRR 159, ECHR 2001-VI.

[145] *Steel and Morris v United Kingdom*, (App. 68416/01), 15 February 2005, (2005) 41 EHRR 403, ECHR 2005-II.

[146] *Roche v United Kingdom*, (App. 32555/96), 19 October 2005 [GC], (2006) 42 EHRR 599, ECHR 2005-X, §§172–3. But note that access to information has largely been considered to date under Article 8: see ch.16 above.

19

FREEDOM OF ASSEMBLY AND ASSOCIATION

INTRODUCTION

Article 11 includes a somewhat disparate range of rights, and spans the divide between, on the one hand, civil and political rights, and, on the other economic and social rights. The case-law of the Strasbourg Court now ensures that the right to peaceful assembly in Article 11, especially when read with Article 10 of the Convention, provides a right to peaceful protest. The remainder of the article concerns association, but can be divided into three distinct areas: the protection of political parties; the protection of other associations; and a bundle of trade union rights. As noted in chapter 17, Article 11 when read with Article 9 provides protection for religious associations.[1]

The text of Article 11 reads:

1. Everyone has the right to freedom of peaceful assembly and to freedom of association with others, including the right to form and to join trade unions for the protection of his interests.

2. No restrictions shall be placed on the exercise of these rights other than such as are prescribed by law and are necessary in a democratic society in the interests of national security or public safety, for the protection of health or morals or for the protection of the rights and freedoms of others. This article shall not prevent the imposition of lawful restrictions on the exercise of these rights by members of the armed forces, of the police or of the administration of the state.

Assembly and association are clearly interlinked. A group of persons could not form an effective association if they had no right to meet. Freedom of assembly includes the right to meet both in private and in public. In its public aspect, it largely constitutes what this chapter refers to as the right to peaceful protest.

---

[1] See, for example, *Moscow Branch of the Salvation Army v Russia*, (App. 72881/01), 5 October 2006, (2007) 44 EHRR 912, ECHR 2006-XI.

POSITIVE OBLIGATIONS

The Strasbourg organs have long held that there are positive obligations to secure the effective enjoyment of the rights contained in Article 11.[2] In the *Plattform 'Ärzte für das Leben'* case,[3] an association of doctors which campaigned against medical termination of pregnancy with a view to securing changes in the Austrian legislation complained of violations of Article 11 when two demonstrations were disrupted by counter-demonstrations despite a significant police presence. One issue which arose in the case was the extent to which a Contracting Party is required under Article 11 to intervene to secure conditions permitting the exercise of the right. The Strasbourg Court said:

Genuine, effective freedom of peaceful assembly cannot…be reduced to a mere duty on the part of the State not to interfere: a purely negative conception would not be compatible with the object and purpose of Article 11…. Article 11 sometimes requires positive measures to be taken, even in the sphere of relations between individuals, if need be.[4]

In the *Djavit An* case, the Court simply said:

…the Court considers that, although the essential objective of Article 11 is to protect the individual against arbitrary interference by public authorities with the exercise of the rights protected, there may in addition be positive obligations to secure the effective enjoyment of these rights….[5]

It is clear that positive obligations apply in the fields both of the right to peaceful assembly and of freedom of association:

…the Court has often reiterated that the Convention is intended to guarantee rights that are not theoretical or illusory, but practical and effective…. It follows from that finding that a genuine and effective respect for freedom of association cannot be reduced to a mere duty on the part of the State not to interfere; a purely negative conception would not be compatible with the purpose of Article 11 nor with that of the Convention in general. There may thus be positive obligations to secure the effective enjoyment of the right to freedom of association…even in the sphere of relations between individuals…. Accordingly, it is incumbent upon public authorities to guarantee the proper functioning of an association or political party, even when they annoy or give offence to persons opposed to the lawful ideas or claims that they are seeking to promote. Their members must be able to hold meetings without having to fear that they will be subjected to physical violence by their opponents. Such a fear would be liable to deter other associations or political parties from openly expressing their opinions on highly controversial issues affecting the community.

---

[2] App. 8440/78, *Christians against Racism and Fascism v United Kingdom*, Decision of 16 July 1980, (1980) 21 DR 138.

[3] *Plattform 'Ärzte für das Leben' v Austria*, 21 June 1988, Series A No 139, (1991) 13 EHRR 204.

[4] §32.

[5] *Djavit An v Turkey*, (App. 20652/92), 20 February 2003, (2005) 40 EHRR 1002, ECHR 2003-III, §57.

In a democracy the right to counter-demonstrate cannot extend to inhibiting the exercise of the right of association. . . .[6]

PEACEFUL PROTEST

OVERVIEW

Article 11 provides for the right of peaceful assembly. It is questionable whether the word 'peaceful' is really needed, given the limitations for which provision is made in the second paragraph of the article. It is, however, clear that an assembly will not be other than peaceful simply because it is considered likely to, or does, provoke a violent response in others, provided that those complaining of violations of Article 11 remain peaceful in their own intentions and behaviour.[7] Where this is in issue, the Strasbourg Court will determine whether on the evidence before it those involved in the organization of the prohibited meetings had violent intentions.[8] This is one context in which the positive obligations of the Contracting Parties come into play. They will be expected, so far as reasonable and practicable, to police any demonstrations in order to avoid disorder and violence.[9] But there is no immunity from prosecution for unlawful actions during the course of the demonstration, nor for participation in an unauthorized demonstration.[10] The Strasbourg Court has come to read Article 11 with Article 10 in establishing the parameters of the right of peaceful assembly. If the essence of the applicant's complaint relates to participation in a demonstration, the Strasbourg Court will consider the case under Article 11 rather than Article 10;[11] Article 10 is regarded as a *lex generalis*, while Article 11 is regarded as a *lex specialis*.[12] The case-law can legitimately be regarded as now providing a right to peaceful protest.

While recognizing the difficulties of definition, Mead helpfully offers a typology of protest.[13] The distinction between freedom of expression and freedom of assembly

---

[6] *Ouranio Toxo and others v Greece*, (App. 74989/01), 20 October 2005, (2007) 45 EHRR 277, ECHR 2005-X, §37.

[7] *Ziliberberg v Moldova*, (App. 61821/00), 4 May 2004; and *Galstyan v Armenia*, (App. 26986/03), 15 November 2007.

[8] *Stankov and the United Macedonian Organisation Ilinden v Bulgaria*, (Apps. 29221/95 and 29225/95), 2 October 2001, ECHR 2001-IX, §§76–8.

[9] App. 8440/78, *Christians against Racism and Fascism v United Kingdom*, Decision of 16 July 1980, (1980) 21 DR 138; and *Plattform 'Ärzte für das Leben' v Austria*, 21 June 1988, Series A No 139, (1991) 13 EHRR 204, §§34–8.

[10] *Galstyan v Armenia*, (App. 26986/03), 15 November 2007, §115.

[11] But the Court is not wholly consistent in this regard; for an example of cases which seem to relate to protest as much as to expression, see *Açik and others v Turkey*, (App. 31451/03), 13 January 2009.

[12] *Ezelin v France*, (App. 11800/85), 26 April 1991, Series A No 202, (1992) 14 EHRR 362, §§34–5; and *Galstyan v Armenia*, (App. 26986/03), 15 November 2007, §§95–6.

[13] D. Mead, 'The right to peaceful protest under the European Convention on Human Rights—a content study of Strasbourg case-law' [2007] EHRLR 345; see also D. Mead, *The New Law of Peaceful Protest. Rights and Regulation in the Human Rights Act Era* (Hart, Oxford 2009).

is found in the attempt at persuasion in a public context. For Mead there are four criteria which constitute the hallmarks of protest as distinct from simply an expression
of ideas. First, the activity must be politically participative. Secondly, the protest is
directed towards a body that is capable of implementing, or preventing, the change.
Thirdly, the subject matter of the protest must transcend the individual.[14] Finally, protest runs alongside and outside formal political party structures. Against this background, Mead proposes four types of protest: static assemblies, processions, peaceful
persuasion, and obstructive direct action. Mead's conclusions are arguably overstated
in stating that Contracting Parties 'crack down on peaceful demonstrations and
processions',[15] and that, when admissibility decisions are taken into account, 'applications claiming a violation of the right to protest have largely been unsuccessful'.[16]
Typically Contracting Parties succeed in justifying interference with demonstrations
on the grounds of preventing disorder.

AUTHORIZATION AND NOTIFICATION OF DEMONSTRATIONS

There is no prohibition on Contracting Parties requiring authorization for, or notification of, demonstrations. This will not be regarded as encroaching on the right to
peaceful assembly if its purpose is to enable the authorities to take reasonable and
appropriate measures in order to guarantee the smooth running of the demonstration,
whatever its nature.[17] But such systems must operate fairly and in accordance with law;
any penalties for failure to comply with the administrative requirements for obtaining authorization must not be disproportionate. So, in the *Sergey Kuznetsov* case,[18]
the imposition of even a modest fine for submitting a notice eight days in advance of
a small-scale demonstration rather than the ten days required was found to be a violation of Article 11.[19]

There must not be an overreaction to a demonstration for which no notification has been provided; the touchstone is a combination of tolerance and proportionality.[20] A refusal of authorization can itself constitute an interference,

---

[14] Though Mead acknowledges just how difficult the dividing line is to draw in this context, he finds it
helpful to test whether the protest is motivated by self-interest or altruism. Note however that Article 11 does
not exclude the self-interested protest.

[15] D. Mead, 'The right to peaceful protest under the European Convention on Human Rights—a content
study of Strasbourg case-law', [2007] EHRLR 345, 354.

[16] Ibid. There are, however, very many reasons why applications may be declared inadmissible; such decisions do not necessarily involve acceptance that the conduct of the respondent State was justified.

[17] *Sergey Kuznetsov v Russia*, (App. 10877/04), 23 October 2008, §42.

[18] Ibid.

[19] It seems to be significant that this defect was only noticed six weeks after the demonstration had taken
place.

[20] *Oya Ataman v Turkey*, (App. 74552/01), 5 December 2006, ECHR 2006-XV; *Balçik and others v Turkey*,
(App. 25/02), 29 November 2007; and *Saya and others v Turkey*, (App. 4327/02), 7 October 2008. See *Éva
Molnár v Hungary*, (App. 10346/05), 7 October 2008, for a case where the intervention of the authorities did
not fall foul of Article 11.

as can prohibitions on demonstrations,[21] since refusals are capable of having 'a chilling effect on the applicants and other participants in assemblies' and could have discouraged:

> …other persons from participating in the assemblies on the ground that they did not have official authorization and that, therefore, no official protection against possible hostile counter-demonstrations would be ensured by the authorities.[22]

A similar approach will be taken where a demonstration is ordered to disperse; a decision to disperse an assembly must be justified.[23] Ordering a demonstration to disperse simply because there has been a failure to notify the authorities in advance is likely to constitute a violation of Article 11, especially if there is no evidence to suggest that the demonstration presents any real danger to public order.[24] The authorities, usually the police, must not be heavy-handed. The touchstone is always tolerance where demonstrators do not engage in acts of violence. Where the heavy-handed approach of the authorities causes tensions to rise, and violence to break out, that will not usually protect the respondent State from successful complaints that Article 11 has been violated.[25]

In the *Cisse* case,[26] a group of around 300 illegal immigrants, most of African origin, occupied a church in Paris in order to draw attention to the difficulties of securing reviews of their immigration status in France. The occupation went on for two months. Ten occupants went on hunger strike. Concerns arose about the sanitary conditions in the church, although the parish priest made no complaint to the authorities. The church was evacuated in a somewhat heavy-handed manner by the authorities. The applicant, one of the occupants, complained of a violation of Article 11. The Strasbourg Court emphasized that illegal immigrants present in France enjoyed the right to peaceful assembly under Article 11, but, although the judgment of the Court makes critical comments about the heavy-handed evacuation of the church, no violation of Article 11 was found. It was open to the authorities to restrict the protest on the grounds of protecting order after tolerating the occupation for some two months.[27]

Where an issue is particularly sensitive, it may be possible for a Contracting Party to ban all demonstrations relating to a particular issue in particular places.[28] In

---

[21] See *Stankov and the United Macedonian Organisation Ilinden v Bulgaria*, (Apps. 29221/95 and 29225/95), 2 October 2001, ECHR 2001-IX.

[22] *Baczkowski and others v Poland*, (App. 1543/06), 3 May 2007, (2009) 48 EHRR 475, ECHR 2007-VI, §67. See also *Patyi and others v Hungary*, (App. 5529/05), 7 October 2008.

[23] App. 15225/89, *Friedl v Austria*, Decision of 30 November 1992.

[24] *Bukta and others v Hungary*, (App. 25691/04), 17 July 2007, ECHR 2007-IX.

[25] *Nurettin Aldemir and others v Turkey*, (Apps 32124/02, 32126/02, 32129/02, 32132/02, 32133/02, 32137/02, and 32138/02), 18 December 2007.

[26] *Cisse v France*, (App. 51346/99), 9 April 2002, ECHR 2002-III.

[27] For another case where initial tolerance of the situation appears to have been significant, see *Barraco v France*, (App. 31684/05), 5 March 2009.

[28] App. 8191/78, *Rassemblement Jurassien and Unité Jurassienne v Switzerland*, Decision of 10 October 1979, (1979) 17 DR 108.

the *Milan Rai, Gill Allmond and 'Negotiate Now'* case,[29] the applicants complained about a refusal to permit them to hold a demonstration in Trafalgar Square, even though they were offered the opportunity to hold the demonstration in Hyde Park. A policy decision had been taken to refuse all requests for demonstrations relating to Northern Ireland in Trafalgar Square 'founded on the concern to avoid the use of the square by those supporting the use of violence.' It was conceded that this was not the purpose of the proposed demonstration, but the Commission concluded that 'where complex issues arise as to the causes of the conflict and any possible solutions' the policy of the British Government could be considered legitimate in seeking to prevent disorder and in protecting the rights and freedoms of others. A different conclusion might be reached in a case where a proposed alternative venue did not enable those wishing to demonstrate to achieve their objectives in holding the proposed demonstration.

The *Ollinger* case[30] provides guidance on how the authorities in the Contracting Parties should deal with the risks of counter-demonstrations. The applicant, a member of the Green Party, notified the authorities that he would be holding a small meeting at the Salzburg municipal cemetery on All Saints Day in front of the war memorial as a commemoration of the Salzburg Jews killed in the Second World War. He noted that the meeting would coincide with a gathering of *Kameradschaft IV*, who would be commemorating the deaths of SS soldiers killed in the Second World War. The response of the authorities was to prohibit Ollinger's meeting because of the risk of disturbances. An appeal against the decision failed. A complaint to the Constitutional Court also failed, although it was ruled that the approach of the police authorities had been too narrow. However, the wider view was that the prohibition was required by the State's positive obligations under Article 9 of the Convention. All Saints Day was an important religious holiday which was characterized by visits to cemeteries to commemorate the dead, and there had been disturbances in previous years between meetings organized by the applicant and those organized by *Kameradschaft IV*

The question before the Strasbourg Court was whether the authorities had struck a fair balance between the interests of the two groups wishing to hold demonstrations on the same day in the same place. The Strasbourg Court had doubts about whether the competing interests had been fairly weighed, though it agreed that it would be too narrow a view simply to ban the counter-demonstration to protect the initial demonstration. The Court was not convinced that the ban was required to protect ordinary visitors to the cemetery, nor was it convinced that it was unreasonable and impracticable to police the two demonstrations to avoid disorder. The Austrian authorities had failed to strike a fair balance, and there was a violation of Article 11.

---

[29] App. 25522/94, *Milan Rai, Gill Allmond and 'Negotiate Now' v United Kingdom*, Decision of 6 April 1995. See also App. 31416/96, *Arthur Pendragon v United Kingdom*, Decision of 19 October 1998, which concerned a four-day ban on demonstrations within a four mile radius of Stonehenge.

[30] *Ollinger v Austria*, (App. 76900/01), 29 June 2006, (2008) 46 EHRR 849, ECHR 2006-IX.

It would seem that there is no right to hold demonstrations on private property such as a shopping mall. Although the *Appleby* case[31] was decided primarily under Article 10, the Strasbourg Court indicates that a Contracting Party is not obliged to make provision for rights under Articles 10 and 11 to be exercisable in 'quasi-public' places such as shopping malls which are in private ownership. The Strasbourg Court was influenced not only by trends in the case-law of the Supreme Court in the United States, but also by the factual situation in which the applicants were able to seek signatures to their petition and distribute leaflets in the public spaces leading to the shopping mall, and had been able to secure permission to have a stand within a hyper-market in the shopping mall.

Restrictions on movement within a Contracting Party in exercise of the freedom of peaceful assembly may constitute a violation of Article 11. The *Yeşilgöz* case[32] concerned a trip by members of an association to a part of Turkey. They were prevented from entering the region, because there was a state of emergency in effect. While the Strasbourg Court recognized that the political atmosphere was a factor of some weight which could be taken into account, it noted further that no reasons had been given for refusing entry to the members of the association, and there was nothing to indicate that the visit would exacerbate the emergency in the region. The visit was described as a fact-finding visit. Similar issues arose in the *Djavit An* case.[33] The applicant is a Cypriot national of Turkish origin who lives in Nicosia, north of the green line. He is a member of the Movement for an Independent and Federal Cyprus. There is a Turkish Cypriot coordinating committee in the north of the island, and a Greek Cypriot coordinating committee in the south of the island. The applicant was unable to obtain permission to cross the green line in order to participate in bi-communal meetings. He complained of a violation of Article 11. Despite objections that the real issue in the case related to freedom of movement, the Strasbourg Court considered the case under Article 11 as an aspect of freedom of assembly, which includes the right to have private and public meetings. The refusal of permission to cross the green line to attend bi-communal meetings interfered with the Article 11 right. The respondent State could not show how this refusal was prescribed and regulated by law, and there was, accordingly, a violation of Article 11.

UNLAWFUL CONDUCT BY DEMONSTRATORS

Obstructive direct action always runs the risk of involving some unlawful activity on the part of the protesters. This can be illustrated by the facts of the *Drieman* case.[34] The applicants were members of Greenpeace who had been prosecuted and convicted for activities in the Norwegian exclusive economic zone designed to disrupt whaling.

---

[31] *Appleby and others v United Kingdom*, (App. 44306/98), 6 May 2003, (2003) 37 EHRR 783, ECHR 2003-VI.

[32] *Yeşilgöz v Turkey*, (App. 45454/99), 20 September 2005.

[33] *Djavit An v Turkey*, (App. 20652/92), 20 February 2003, (2005) 40 EHRR 1002, ECHR 2003-III.

[34] *Drieman and others v Norway*, (App. 33678/96), Decision of 4 May 2000.

They complained that this constituted a breach of Articles 10 and 11. The Strasbourg Court did not consider it necessary to determine whether the matters complained of fell within Article 10 or Article 11. The complaints were inadmissible. The applicants had been able to protest in general for a period of around one month about the resumption of whaling in Norwegian waters, whereas the convictions related to two specific incidents of conduct which breached Norwegian law; that conduct—seeking to block whaling vessels with manoeuvres in zodiac dinghies—constituted 'a form of coercion forcing the whalers to abandon their lawful activity.'

The *Plattform 'Ärzte für das Leben'* case[35] is somewhat anomalous in that the Strasbourg Court was considering whether Article 13 had been violated, since the Commission had ruled that the complaint based on Article 11 was inadmissible. The only way into Article 11 was accordingly to consider whether it was arguable that Article 11 was engaged. The Strasbourg Court's judgment is not wholly satisfactory, since its reasoning suggests that the case was indeed arguable under Article 11. The Court does examine the nature of the respondent State's conduct in policing the demonstration, and concludes that the police response was reasonable. It then concluded that no 'arguable claim that Article 11 was violated has thus been made out; Article 13 therefore did not apply in the instant case.'[36] The case is, however, frequently cited as authority for the proposition that Article 11 protects a demonstration that may annoy or give offence to persons opposed to the ideas and claims the demonstration seeks to promote.[37]

The *Ezelin* case[38] is rather more helpful. It establishes that exercising the right to peaceful assembly does not protect the demonstrator from sanctions for violence or disorder which ensues but that any sanctions which relate primarily to the fact of demonstrating must be proportionate. The case concerned an application by a lawyer, who was Vice-Chairman of the Trade Union of the Guadeloupe Bar, complaining that the French courts had imposed a disciplinary penalty by way of reprimand on him because he had taken part in a demonstration protesting at the use of the Security and Freedom Act in Guadeloupe, and had failed to express his disapproval of insults uttered by other demonstrators against the judiciary. In assessing the proportionality of the sanction, the Strasbourg Court noted that it was to a certain extent symbolic, because it did not prevent the applicant from practising as a lawyer. However, it observed that:

The proportionality principle demands that a balance be struck between the requirements of the purposes listed in Article 11(2) and those of the free expression of opinions, by word, gesture or even silence by persons assembled on the streets or in other public places. The

---

[35] *Plattform 'Ärzte für das Leben' v Austria*, 21 June 1988, Series A No 139, (1991) 13 EHRR 204.
[36] §39.
[37] As in *Stankov and the United Macedonian Organisation Ilinden v Bulgaria*, (Apps. 29221/95 and 29225/95), 2 October 2001, ECHR 2001-IX, §86.
[38] *Ezelin v France*, 26 April 1991, Series A No 202, (1992) 14 EHRR 362.

pursuit of a just balance must not result in *avocats* being discouraged, for fear of disciplinary sanctions, from making clear their beliefs on such occasions.[39]

The penalty exceeded that which was necessary in a democratic society, since Ezelin had not himself committed any reprehensible act at all during the demonstration.

The *Galstyan* case[40] involved the imposition of a much more severe penalty: three days' detention. The applicant had been present at a large rally protesting about the conduct of recent elections in Armenia. He was arrested for obstructing traffic and behaving in an anti-social way, and subsequently convicted for violating public order by making a loud noise. The Strasbourg Court ruled that the imposition of the sanction for being present and proactive at the demonstration impaired the very essence of the right to freedom of peaceful assembly, and there was a violation of Article 11. It will be particularly difficult for a Contracting Party to show that a penalty imposed essentially for attendance at a demonstration for which authorization has been given can be justified. Respondent States are likely to argue that a public order offence has been committed,[41] but the Strasbourg Court will consider whether such claims are justified and are not simply the direct consequences of participation in the demonstration.[42] Such measures would strike at the 'very essence of the right to freedom of peaceful assembly'.[43]

A particularly strict view will be taken of attempts to restrict demonstrations which can be regarded as the legitimate activities of a political party. The *Christian Democratic People's Party* case[44] concerned demonstrations organized by the applicant political party against Government proposals to make the study of the Russian language compulsory in schools for children aged seven or over. The authorities, on receipt of the notification of the demonstration, changed the proposed venue without giving any reasons for the change of location. Demonstrations went ahead at the original location on several days. As a consequence the authorities suspended some of the political activities[45] of the applicant party for one month. The Strasbourg Court considered the issue of whether this response was necessary in a democratic society without prejudice to the issues of whether the measure was in accordance with law and justified as being for a legitimate reason. The Strasbourg Court said:

In view of the essential role played by political parties in the proper functioning of democracy, the exceptions set out in Article 11 are, where political parties are concerned, to be construed strictly; only convincing and compelling reasons can justify restrictions on such

---

[39] §52. [40] *Galstyan v Armenia*, (App. 26986/03), 15 November 2007.

[41] As in *Ashughyan v Armenia*, (App. 33268/03), 17 July 2008.

[42] See *Çetinkaya v Turkey*, (App. 75569/01), 27 June 2006.

[43] *Ashughyan v Armenia*, (App. 33268/03), 17 July 2008, §93.

[44] *Christian Democratic People's Party v Moldova*, (App. 28793/02), 14 February 2006, (2007) 45 EHRR 392, ECHR 2006-II.

[45] Cited in the separate opinion (partly concurring and partly dissenting) as using the mass media, disseminating propaganda and agitation, carrying out bank transactions or other operations, and participating in elections.

parties' freedom of association. In determining whether a necessity within the meaning of Article 11 §2 exists, the Contracting States have only a limited margin of appreciation, which goes hand in hand with rigorous European supervision.... It therefore follows that the Court must scrutinize very carefully the necessity for imposing a ban on a parliamentary political party's activities, even a ban of fairly short duration.[46]

The respondent State had submitted video recordings of the demonstrations, but these failed to assist its case. They showed that the demonstrations were essentially peaceful affairs, and there was nothing which could be regarded as an incitement to public violence. The Strasbourg Court ruled that 'only very serious breaches such as those which endanger political pluralism or fundamental democratic principles could justify a ban on the activities of a political party.'[47]

There are, however, special responsibilities placed upon elected officials which might be regarded as requiring circumspection in their actions in exercise of their rights under Article 11. This can be illustrated by the admissibility decision in the *Osmani* case.[48] Osmani had been elected mayor of Gostivar. The local council subsequently decided that the Albanian and Turkish flags should fly alongside the Macedonian flag in front of the town hall. Similar provision was made for the flying of flags on other public buildings on public holidays. The Constitutional Court was asked to consider the validity of the decision, and ultimately decided that it was unconstitutional. In the meantime, Osmani had organized a public meeting which was inflammatory in that only the flag of the Republic of Albania was flown and at which Osmani made a speech inciting the crowd not to accept the decision of the Constitutional Court, and promising that Gostivar would become an Albanian town. Two days later, there were violent scenes at the town hall. Osmani organized armed shifts to protect the Albanian flag. Sometime later there were further violent clashes at the town hall when police removed the flags from the town hall. Three people died. Osmani was prosecuted and convicted of a number of offences and sentenced to imprisonment. His appeals failed. He then complained to the Strasbourg Court that there had been a violation of Article 11. In finding the application to be manifestly ill-founded, the Strasbourg Court indicates that freedom of peaceful assembly is of particular importance for an elected representative of the people, but also notes the context and conduct of the applicant in the case before them. The applicant had breached his duties as an elected public official in refusing to uphold decisions of the Constitutional Court, and in becoming actively involved in the planning and setting up of headquarters and armed shifts for the protection of the flag of the Republic of Albania. His conduct was not the expression of personal political opinion, but constituted the stirring up of hatred and intolerance in a very sensitive inter-ethnic situation.

---

[46] *Christian Democratic People's Party*, §68.

[47] §76. See also *Güneri and others v Turkey*, (Apps 42853/98, 43609/98, and 44291/98), 12 July 2005.

[48] *Osmani and others v the Former Yugoslav Republic of Macedonia*, (App. 50841/99), Decision of 11 October 2001, ECHR 2001-X.

CONCLUSION ON PEACEFUL ASSEMBLY

The case-law on peaceful assembly provides a good illustration of the relationship between positive and negative obligations. A Contracting Party is permitted to regulate peaceful assembly in a manner which facilitates it. This includes a positive obligation to police peaceful protests in a manner which enables the protesters to get their message across effectively. In taking action to address disorder which will arise from time to time, the Contracting Parties may be called upon to justify their action as dealing with disorder rather than seeking to impose sanctions simply by reason of the protests having taken place. Some of the case-law does indicate that some Contracting Parties fail to get the balance right between proper regulation and improper repression.

DEFINING ASSOCIATIONS

Article 11 protects the right to 'freedom of association with others'. Put broadly, and subject to the provisos set out in the second paragraph, this constitutes the right to choose whether or not to form and join associations such as political parties and trade unions, and also other organizations, such as lodges of Freemasons.[49]

The case-law on freedom of association addresses three core types of association: (1) political parties; (2) trade unions; and (3) other associations. The essence of freedom of association is that 'citizens should be able to create a legal entity in order to act collectively in a field of mutual interest.'[50] So it is inherent in the concept of freedom of association that there is a right to form associations, and for those associations to be recognized in the national legal orders. If the issue arises, it will be for the Strasbourg Court to decide whether an applicant constitutes an association for the purposes of Article 11:

The term 'association'...possesses an autonomous meaning; the classification in national law has only relative value and constitutes no more than a starting point.[51]

In the *Chassagnou* case, the French Government had argued that *associations communales de chasse agréés*[52] were public law associations with the powers of public authorities and so fell outside the concept of associations in Article 11. But the Strasbourg Court, while accepting the public law aspect of the associations, concluded that they

---

[49] *NF v Italy* (App. 37119/97), 2 August 2001, (2002) 35 EHRR 106, ECHR 2001-IX; and *Grande Oriente d'Italia di Palazzo Giustiniani v Italy* (App. 35972/97), 2 August 2001, (2002) 34 EHRR 629, ECHR 2001-VIII.

[50] *Gorzelik and others v Poland*, (App. 44158/98), Chamber judgment of 20 December 2001, (2004) 38 EHRR 77, §55; the decision was upheld in the Grand Chamber on 17 February 2004, (2005) 40 EHRR 76, ECHR 2004-I.

[51] *Chassagnou and others v France*, (Apps. 25088/94, 28331/95, and 28443/95), 29 April 1999 [GC], (2000) 29 EHRR 615, ECHR 1999-III, §100.

[52] Approved municipal hunters' associations.

were groupings of private individuals who wished to pool their land for the purpose of hunting. They were accordingly associations within the scope of Article 11. However, professional regulatory bodies set up by statute which remain integrated within State structures will not be associations for the purposes of Article 11,[53] particularly where there is no corresponding prohibition on establishing an association of professionals in the private sector.[54]

Where an issue arises as to whether an association is a public law or a private law association, the Strasbourg Court will look to see which characteristics predominate. The issue arose in the *Sigurjónsson* case,[55] which concerned the required membership of '*Frami*' as a precondition to obtaining a licence to operate a taxi. The association had both public law and private law characteristics. It exercised certain functions under the legislation applicable to the provision of taxi services, but was also fully autonomous in determining its own aims and procedures. In particular, it exercised a number of functions designed to protect the interests of its members, and so operated much like a trade union. The Strasbourg Court did not decide that it was a trade union, but concluded that its character was predominantly that of a private law organization and so constituted an association for the purposes of Article 11.[56]

The Strasbourg Court has found no difficulties in regarding political parties as being associations for the purposes of Article 11:

...even more persuasive than the wording of Article 11, in the Court's view, is the fact that political parties are a form of association essential to the proper functioning of democracy. In view of the importance of democracy in the Convention system,...there can be no doubt that political parties come within the scope of Article 11.[57]

REGISTRATION

There is nothing improper in Contracting Parties requiring registration of associations, whatever their purpose, although any decision to refuse registration will be an interference with the freedom of association which will require justification. The *Sidiropoulos* case[58] concerned applicants of Macedonian ethnic origin who were living in Greece; they sought to register an association with broad objectives to promote

---

[53] *Le Compte, Van Leuven and de Meyere v Belgium*, (Apps. 6878/75 and 7238/75), 23 June 1981, Series A No 43, (1982) 4 EHRR 1, §§63–5.

[54] *Albert and Le Compte v Belgium*, (Apps. 7299/75 and 7496/86), 10 February 1983, Series A No 58, (1983) 5 EHRR 533.

[55] *Sigurdur A. Sigurjónsson v Iceland*, (App. 16130/90), 30 June 1993, Series A No. 264, (1993) 16 EHRR 462.

[56] §§31–2.

[57] *United Communist Party of Turkey and others v Turkey*, (App. 19392/92), 30 January 1998, (1998) 26 EHRR 121, ECHR 1998-I, §25.

[58] *Sidiropoulos and others v Greece*, (App. 26695/95), 10 July 1998, (1999) 27 EHRR 633, ECHR 1998-IV. See also *Stankov and the United Macedonian Organisation Ilinden v Bulgaria*, (Apps. 29221/95 and 29225/95), 2 October 2001, ECHR 2001-IX; and *Association of Citizens Radko and Paunkovski v The Former Yugoslav Republic of Macedonia*, (App. 74651/01), 15 January 2009, which concerned dissolution of Macedonian associations.

Macedonian historical and cultural heritage. The refusal was based on a perceived incompatibility between the association's objects and the Greek national interest, in particular suggestions that the association disputed the Greek identity of the region Macedonia. On appeal, the refusal was upheld on the ground that the true intention of the founders of the association was to undermine the territorial integrity of Greece. The Strasbourg Court accepted that the refusal was grounded in law and met one of the legitimate aims set out in Article 11(2), but did not agree that refusal to register (a fundamental interference with freedom of association) was necessary in a democratic society. The Court recognized that the founders of the association regarded themselves as belonging to a minority in Greece, but this could not be regarded as constituting a threat to democratic society. There was a violation of Article 11.

However, the national law regarding registration must be clear in order to comply with the lawfulness requirement under Article 11. In the *Church of Scientology Moscow* case,[59] the applicant Church was repeatedly refused registration on the ground, among other things, that it had submitted an incomplete set of documents. Despite requests, the authorities would never specify which documents were missing. This procedure was repeated until the deadline for registration expired. In the subsequent proceedings brought by the Church, the District Court held that the applicant had not complied with national law in that the application for re-registration only included copies, rather than originals, of the charter and registration certificate. The Strasbourg Court found a breach of Article 11 because the domestic law was not 'formulated with sufficient precision to enable the citizen to foresee the consequences which a given action may entail and to regulate his or her conduct accordingly.'[60] The requirement to submit the original documents did not follow from the text of the national law, and no other regulatory documents which might have set out such a requirement were referred to in the domestic proceedings. It was not mentioned in the grounds for the refusal advanced by the Moscow Justice Department or in the Presidium's decision remitting the matter for a new examination, but appeared for the first time in the District Court's judgment. In these circumstances, the Court was unable to find that the domestic law was formulated with sufficient precision enabling the applicant to foresee the adverse consequences which the submission of copies would entail.

POLITICAL PARTIES

In the case of the *United Communist Party of Turkey*[61] the Strasbourg Court rejected the respondent State's argument that Article 11 applied only to trade-union-type associations, and held that political parties also fell within its scope and were,

---

[59] *Church of Scientology Moscow v Russia*, (App. 18147/02), 5 April 2007, (2008) 46 EHRR 304.

[60] §92.

[61] *United Communist Party of Turkey and others v Turkey* (App. 19392/92), 30 January 1998, (1998) 26 EHRR 121, ECHR 1998-I. See generally H. Cullen, 'Freedom of Association as a Political Right' (1999) 24 ELRev HR/30; and M. Koçak and E. Örücü, 'Dissolution of Political Parties in the Name of Democracy: cases from Turkey and the European Court of Human Rights' (2003) 9 EPL 399.

indeed, entitled to a high level of protection because of their important role in any democracy.

The Party had been dissolved by the Turkish Constitutional Court on the grounds, first, that the word 'Communist' in the title was objectionable and, secondly, because the Party's manifesto had distinguished between the 'Turkish' and the 'Kurdish' nations; in Turkey, the promotion of separatism is unconstitutional. The Strasbourg Court considered that a political party's choice of name could not in principle justify a measure as drastic as dissolution in the absence of other relevant and sufficient circumstances. On the second point, since the Party had advocated a political, rather than a violent, solution to the Kurdish problem, and one of the principal characteristics of democracy was the possibility of resolving a country's problems through dialogue, there could be no justification for hindering a political group solely because it sought to debate in public the situation of part of the State's population and to take part in the nation's political life in order to find, according to democratic rules, solutions capable of satisfying everyone concerned. The dissolution of the Party was, therefore, disproportionate and contrary to Article 11.[62] The Strasbourg Court views pluralism as being at the heart of the concept of democracy which it upholds; political parties are seen as vital participants in the process of debate and dialogue which underpins participatory democracy.

In December 1999, following a survey of the practice among countries which cooperate with the Commission, the Venice Commission[63] adopted a set of guidelines on the dissolution of political parties.[64] The guidelines recognized that:

Prohibition or dissolution of political parties can be envisaged only if it is necessary in a democratic society and if there is concrete evidence that a party is engaged in activities threatening democracy and fundamental freedoms. This could include any party that advocates violence in all forms as part of its political programme or any party aiming to overthrow the existing constitutional order through armed struggle, terrorism or the organisation of any subversive activity.[65]

The guidelines themselves contain seven propositions, which may be summarized as follows:

    (1) States should recognize the right of everyone to form political parties and to hold political opinions without interference by a public authority, although a

---

[62] The Strasbourg Court reached similar conclusions in relation to the dissolution of Turkish political parties in the following cases: *Socialist Party and others v Turkey* (App. 21237/93), 25 May 1998, (1999) 27 EHRR 51, 1998-III; *Freedom and Democracy Party (OZDEP) v Turkey* (App. 23885/94), 8 December 1999, (2001) 31 EHRR 674, ECHR 1999-VIII; and see also *Yazar and others v Turkey*, (Apps. 22723/93, 22724/93 and 22725/93), 9 April 2002, (2003) 36 EHRR 59, ECHR 2002-II; and *Dicle on behalf of the Democratic Party v Turkey*, (App. 25141/94), 10 December 2002. See also *Partidul Comunistilor v Romania*, (App. 46626/99), 3 February 2005, (2007) 44 EHRR 340, ECHR 2005-I.

[63] The European Commission for Democracy through Law (known as the Venice Commission) was established within the framework of the Council of Europe has come to be regarded as an internationally recognized independent legal think tank. See www.venice.coe.int.

[64] Guidelines on the Prohibition and Dissolution of Political Parties and Analogous Measures, adopted by the Venice Commission at its 41st plenary session in Venice, 10–11 December 1999, CDL-INF (2000) 1.

[65] §10 of Explanatory Report attached to the guidelines.

requirement to register political parties will not of itself be considered a violation of this right.[66]

(2) Any limitations on this right should be consistent with the provisions of the European Convention on Human Rights and other international treaties.

(3) Only political parties which advocate the use of violence as a political means to overthrow the democratic constitutional order should be susceptible of prohibition or dissolution. The advocacy of peaceful change is not alone a ground for prohibition or dissolution.

(4) A political party is not to be held responsible for the individual behaviour of its members which have not been sanctioned by the party.

(5) Prohibition or dissolution should be used with utmost restraint; less radical measures to deal with concerns should be explored before resorting to such measures.

(6) Legal measures directed to prohibition or dissolution should be a consequence of a judicial finding of unconstitutionality, be regarded as exceptional measures, be governed by the principle of proportionality, and be based on sufficient evidence of objectionable conduct attributable to the party itself.

(7) Prohibition or dissolution should be decided by the constitutional court or other appropriate judicial body in a procedure offering guarantees of due process.

In the *Refah Partisi* case,[67] the Grand Chamber, in what some regard as a controversial judgment,[68] unanimously took the view that it was compatible with Article 11 to dissolve the applicant political party, which at the time of dissolution had actually been in power for one year as part of a coalition government. The leaders of the *Refah Partisi* had declared their intention to establish a plurality of legal systems in Turkey based on differences in religious belief and to establish Islamic law (Sha'ria), a system of law which was in marked contrast to the values embodied in the Convention. The Grand Chamber held:

...that a political party may promote a change in the law or the legal and constitutional structures of the State on two conditions: firstly, the means used to that end must be legal and democratic; secondly, the change proposed must itself be compatible with fundamental democratic principles. It necessarily follows that a political party whose leaders incite to violence or put forward a policy which fails to respect democracy or which is aimed at

---

[66] For an example of an unjustified refusal to register a political party, see *Linkov v Czech Republic*, (App. 10504/03), 7 December 2006. For a decision relating to funding arrangements for political parties, see *Parti Nationaliste Basque—Organisation Régionale d'Ipparalde v France*, (App. 71251/01), 7 June 2007, (2008) 47 EHRR 1037, ECHR 2007-VII.

[67] *Refah Partisi (Prosperity Party) and others v Turkey*, (Apps. 41340/98, 41342/98, and 41344/98), 13 February 2003 [GC], (2003) 37 EHRR 1, ECHR 2003-II.

[68] K. Boyle, 'Human Rights, Religion and Democracy: The Refah Party Case' (2004) 1 *Essex Human Rights Review* 1. See also P. Macklem, 'Militant Democracy, Legal Pluralism, and the Paradox of Self-Determination' (2006) 4 *International Journal of Constitutional Law* 488.

the destruction of democracy and the flouting of the rights and freedoms recognized in a democracy cannot lay claim to the Convention's protection against penalties imposed on those grounds. . . .

The possibility cannot be excluded that a political party, in pleading the rights enshrined in Article 11 and also in Articles 9 and 10 of the Convention, might attempt to derive therefrom the right to conduct what amounts in practice to activities intended to destroy the rights or freedoms set forth in the Convention and thus bring about the destruction of democracy. . . . In view of the very clear link between the Convention and democracy. . . , no one must be authorized to rely on the Convention's provisions in order to weaken or destroy the ideals and values of a democratic society. Pluralism and democracy are based on a compromise that requires various concessions by individuals or groups of individuals, who must sometimes agree to limit some of the freedoms they enjoy in order to guarantee greater stability of the country as a whole. . . .[69]

Refah Partisi's policies and anti-secular stance could be considered dangerous for the rights and freedoms guaranteed by the Convention, and the real prospect that it would implement its programme after gaining power justified the Constitutional Court's action.

There are a number of startling features of this case. *Refah Partisi* had been in government as part of a coalition for twelve months when it was dissolved. It was a political party of long standing, which had polled the largest share of the votes (22 per cent) in the 1995 general election, and one of its members, Necmettin Erbakan, was Prime Minister. To dissolve such a party in such circumstances was, in the words of one commentator, to take 'the notion of "militant democracy", the measures permissible to defend democracy from being subverted through electoral politics, to a new level.'[70] The Grand Chamber accepted the assessment of the Turkish Constitutional Court that *Refah Partisi* was not committed to peaceful means and the change it advocated by its alleged conduct was such as to be incompatible with fundamental democratic principles. These concerns need to be set in the context of the deep commitment in the Turkish Constitution to secularism. The first constitution of modern Turkey in 1924 was committed to the 'six arrows' of Kemalism: nationalism, secularism, republicanism, populism, statism, and reformism.[71] The 1982 Constitution continues the commitment to secularism, and provides that no protection is to be afforded to activities contrary to the principle of the indivisibility of Turkey, and that there is to be no interference whatsoever by religious sacred feelings in state affairs and politics. Turkey's constitution commits it to be a democratic, secular, and social state governed by the rule of law and respect for human rights. At the heart of the objections to *Refah Partisi* was a concern that its hidden agenda was the conversion of the secular state into a religious state through the promotion of Islam. It is

---

[69] *Refah Partisi*, §§98–99.

[70] K. Boyle, 'Human Rights, Religion and Democracy: The Refah Party Case' (2004) 1 *Essex Human Rights Review* 1, 2.

[71] See M. Koçak and E. Örücü, 'Dissolution of Political Parties in the Name of Democracy: Cases from Turkey and the European Court of Human Rights' (2003) 9 EPL 399, 407–9.

questionable whether there was sufficient evidence before the Court of anti-secular activities. The Strasbourg Court's comments on the tenets of Islam and on Sha'ria and their compatibility with the democratic principles enshrined in the Convention do seem somewhat insensitive.[72] As Boyle notes,[73] the judgment of the Grand Chamber can be read to suggest that peaceful advocacy of the tenets of Islam is unprotected under the European Convention. Boyle identifies the core issue raised by the discussion in this case of religion and secularism as follows:

> Can religion, democracy and human rights guarantees relate in ways that neither require the strict secularism as espoused in Turkey, nor the subordination of individual human rights to unchallengeable religious rules such as would result from shariah? Or may democracy and plurality of religion be accommodated only through the endorsement of secularism and the complete divorce of the religions of the electorate from political affairs? These questions undoubtedly constitute a new frontier of human right study, not just in multi-cultural Europe, but in the Middle East and in particular in the new Iraq.[74]

OTHER ASSOCIATIONS

The Strasbourg Court has interpreted Article 11 to include rights aimed at creating and preserving genuine democracy and freedom, not just in a political party sense, but also the freedom of citizens to pursue a vast array of interests such as culture, sport, and social and humanitarian assistance. Freedom of association includes the right to receive formal recognition for an association: an unreasonable refusal of registration, where this is required, will constitute a violation of Article 11. In assessing such cases, the Strasbourg Court has enunciated a number of general principles.[75] While Contracting Parties have a right to satisfy themselves that the aims and activities of an association are within the national law providing the scheme for registration, the decision on the application must be taken in a manner compatible with the Convention rights under Article 11. Inherent in the proper consideration of applications is recognition of the importance of pluralism to the proper functioning of democracy. This applies just as much in the case of associations formed other than for political purposes as for political parties. The implementation of the principle of pluralism must also recognize that unpopular or unorthodox expressions of opinion are a feature of the Convention right for individuals, and associations to which they belong, to express freely their ideas and opinions. Only convincing and compelling reasons can justify restrictions on freedom of association. As with political parties, refusal of recognition must always be grounded in conclusions based on convincing evidence that the

---

[72] As noted by Judge Kovler in his concurring opinion.
[73] K. Boyle, 'Human Rights, Religion and Democracy: The Refah Party Case' (2004) 1 *Essex Human Rights Review* 1, 12.
[74] Ibid., 16.
[75] Summarized in *Zhechev v Bulgaria*, (App. 57045/00), 21 June 2007, §§34–6.

association advocates the use of violence or undemocratic and unconstitutional means to secure its aims.[76]

The same position has been adopted where the conduct of the authorities in persistently returning documents seeking registration of an association amounts to a *de facto* refusal of registration. Blatant cases of delay in processing applications for registration are likely to be very difficult to defend, since the conduct will almost certainly not be 'prescribed by law'.[77]

Freedom of association includes the right not to join an association as well as the right to form an association. The *Chassagnou* case[78] concerned membership of hunting associations in France. The applicants complained that, despite their opposition to hunting, they had been obliged to join a local hunting association. The effect was to permit hunting on their land. The Strasbourg Court considered the complaint under Article 11, when read with Article 9 because of the personal beliefs of the applicants that hunting was wrong. Given the French love of hunting, the issues before the Grand Chamber were sensitive. The Grand Chamber recognized the ethical issues raised by hunting, and therefore the need to strike a balance between rural tradition in France, and personal convictions. Detailed examination of the national law on the establishment of hunting associations showed considerable variation in practice and application. By twelve votes to five, the Grand Chamber concluded that there was a violation of Article 11:

To compel a person by law to join an association such that it is fundamentally contrary to his own convictions to be as member of it, and to oblige him, on account of his membership of the association, to transfer his rights over the land he owns so that the association in question can attain objectives of which he disapproves, goes beyond what is necessary to ensure that a fair balance is struck between conflicting interests and cannot be considered proportionate to the aim pursued.[79]

Improper interference in the activities of an association may also breach Article 11. In the *Piroğlu and Karakaya* case,[80] the second applicant was convicted following a refusal to annul the membership of thirteen members of the Izmir Branch of the Human Rights Association. None of those named had been convicted of offences which would affect their membership of the association. It was conceded that those whose membership was required to be annulled had been taken into custody, but no charges had been brought. In such circumstances, the Strasbourg Court concluded that the authorities had not shown any legitimate reason why annulment of membership was required. It

---

[76] *Emin and others v Greece*, (App. 341344/05), 27 March 2008; and *Tourkiki Enosis Xanthis and others v Greece*, (App. 26698/05), 27 March 2008.

[77] *Ramazanova and others v Azerbaijan*, (App. 44363/02), 1 February 2007, (2008) 47 EHRR 407; and *Ismayilov v Azerbaijan*, (App. 4439/04), 17 January 2008.

[78] *Chassagnou and others v France*, (Apps. 25088/94, 28331/95, and 28443/95), 29 April 1999 [GC], (2000) 29 EHRR 615, ECHR 1999-III.

[79] §117. See also *Schneider v Luxembourg*, (App. 2113/04), 10 July 2007.

[80] *Piroğlu and Karakaya v Turkey*, (Apps 36370/02 and 37581/02), 18 March 2008.

was a requirement of the Convention that national law afford a measure of protection against arbitrary interference by the public authorities with Convention rights.[81]

TRADE UNIONS

FREEDOM FOR FORM AND JOIN TRADE UNIONS

The right to form and join trade unions is an aspect of the wider right to freedom of association set out in Article 11(1). It includes a positive obligation on the State to protect, through legislation, the union rights of workers in the private sector, as well as those employed by the State.[82] Article 11 is binding on the State as employer.[83] Inherent in any exercise of trade union rights is recognition of the legal personality of the union. In the *Tüm Haber Sen* case[84] the applicants, who were a trade union for public sector workers in the postal and telecommunications sector and its former president, complained that the dissolution of the union and consequent enforced cessation of its activities constituted a breach of Article 11. The Turkish authorities had ordered its dissolution on the grounds that it had been founded by civil servants and its members were civil servants.[85] The Strasbourg Court could find no pressing social need to prohibit the formation of trade unions by public sector workers and civil servants. There was a violation of Article 11.[86]

The Strasbourg Court has held that the words in that paragraph, 'for the protection of his interests' cannot be devoid of meaning, and that it follows therefore that members of a trade union have a right, in order to protect their interests, that the union be heard.[87] The union and its members must, moreover, be free, in one way or another, to seek to persuade the employer to listen to what it has to say on behalf of its members.[88] One way of forcing the employer to take notice is, of course, to strike.[89] The Court has, however, adopted an extremely cautious attitude, allowing a very wide margin of

---

[81] §65.

[82] *Gustafsson v Sweden* (App. 15573/89), of 25 April 1996, (1996) 22 EHRR 409, ECHR 1996-II, §45; Revision ECHR 1998-V.

[83] *Demir and Baykara v Turkey*, (App. 34503/97), 12 November 2008 [GC], (2009) 48 EHRR 1272, ECHR 2008-nyr, §109; and *Tüm Haber Sen and Çinar v Turkey*, (App. 28602/95), 21 February 2006, (2008) 46 EHRR 374, ECHR 2006-II, §29.

[84] *Tüm Haber Sen and Çinar v Turkey*, (App. 28602/95), 21 February 2006, (2008) 46 EHRR 374, ECHR 2006-II.

[85] See below on the question of whether civil servants are members of the administration of the State within the final sentence of Article 11(2).

[86] See also *Demir and Baykara v Turkey*, (App. 34503/97), 12 November 2008 [GC], (2009) 48 EHRR 1272, ECHR 2008-nyr.

[87] *National Union of Belgian Police v Belgium*, 22 October 1975, Series A No 19, (1979–80) 1 EHRR 578.

[88] *Wilson and the National Union of Journalists and others v United Kingdom*, (Apps. 30668/96, 30671/96, and 30678/96), 2 July 2002, (2002) 35 EHRR 523, ECHR 2002-V, §44.

[89] *Schmidt and Dahlström v Sweden*, 6 February 1976, Series A No 21, (1979–80) 1 EHRR 637; *Wilson and the National Union of Journalists and others v United Kingdom*, (Apps. 30668/96, 30671/96, and 30678/96), 2 July 2002, (2002) 35 EHRR 523, ECHR 2002-V, §45.

appreciation to Contracting Parties to decide the extent to which union rights should be recognized and protected under national law.[90] Thus, the Strasbourg Court has not been prepared until recently to hold that Article 11 includes a right for a union to be consulted or recognized for collective bargaining.[91] In the United Kingdom, for example, it is entirely a matter of choice for the employer to decide whether or not to negotiate over pay and conditions collectively with a union, or directly with the individual employees, and this is compatible with Article 11. However, where there is no obligation under domestic law for the employer to deal with the union, if the right to organize collectively is to have any meaning:

it must be possible for a trade union which is not recognized by an employer to take steps including, if necessary, organising industrial action, with a view to persuading the employer to enter into collective bargaining with it on those issues which the union believes are important for its members' interests. Furthermore, it is of the essence of the right to join a trade union for the protection of their interests that employees should be free to instruct or permit the union to make representations to their employer or to take action in support of their interests on their behalf. If workers are prevented from so doing, their freedom to belong to a trade union, for the protection of their interests, becomes illusory. It is the role of the State to ensure that trade union members are not prevented or restrained from using their union to represent them in attempts to regulate their relations with their employers.[92]

It follows, therefore, that the absence of any rule in English law to prevent an employer from bribing employees into giving up their Article 11 rights with a higher pay deal for those prepared to renounce union representation was in breach of the Convention.[93]

The right to strike and the consequences of doing so were considered in the *Schmidt and Dahlström* case[94] in which the applicants were a professor of law at the University of Stockholm and an officer in the Swedish army. They were members of unions which called selective strikes after the expiry of a collective agreement and the negotiation of its replacement. Neither went on strike, but as members of the 'belligerent' unions, they were denied certain retrospective benefits which were paid to members of other trade unions and to non-union employees who had not participated in the strikes. The Strasbourg Court concluded, first, that the rights enshrined in Article 11 did not include any rights to retroactivity of benefits, such as salary increases, resulting from a new collective agreement. Secondly, though the right to strike represents one of the

---

[90] *Schmidt and Dahlström v Sweden*, 6 February 1976, Series A No 21, (1979–80) 1 EHRR 637; *Wilson and the National Union of Journalists and others v United Kingdom*, (Apps. 30668/96, 30671/96, and 30678/96), 2 July 2002, (2002) 35 EHRR 523, ECHR 2002-V, §45.

[91] *National Union of Belgian Police v Belgium*, 22 October 1975, Series A No 19, (1979–80) 1 EHRR 578; *Swedish Engine Drivers' Union v Sweden*, 6 February 1976, Series A No 20, (1979–80) 1 EHRR 617; *Wilson and the National Union of Journalists and others v United Kingdom*, (Apps. 30668/96, 30671/96, and 30678/96), 2 July 2002, (2002) 35 EHRR 523, ECHR 2002-V, §44. See now *Demir and Baykara v Turkey*, (App. 34503/97), 12 November 2008 [GC], (2009) 48 EHRR 1272, ECHR 2008-nyr, §§154.

[92] *Wilson and the National Union of Journalists and others v United Kingdom*, (Apps. 30668/96, 30671/96, and 30678/96), 2 July 2002, (2002) 35 EHRR 523, ECHR 2002-V, §46   [93] Ibid.

[94] *Schmidt and Dahlström v Sweden*, 6 February 1976, Series A No 21, (1979–80) 1 EHRR 637.

most powerful means of protecting the interests of its members, such a right is subject to 'regulation of a kind that limits its exercise in certain instances'. There was thus no violation of Article 11 in the treatment accorded to the applicants.

CLOSED SHOP ARRANGEMENTS

Article 11 did not originally prohibit the 'closed shop' system, whereby workers cannot be employed in a particular trade unless they are members of a particular union. The preparatory work on the Convention shows that, on account of the difficulties raised by the 'closed shop' system, it was considered undesirable to include the principle set out in Article 20(2) of the Universal Declaration of Human Rights, that no one may be compelled to belong to an association.

In the *Young, James and Webster* case[95] the applicants complained that they had lost their jobs when they refused to join any of the unions within the closed shop agreement and that this amounted to a violation of Article 11. The arrangement had been introduced after they had begun their employment with British Rail.[96] In this case, the Strasbourg Court sidestepped the question whether Article 11 encompassed the right not to be compelled to join a trade union, though it noted that the *travaux préparatoires* suggested that such a right had been deliberately excluded from the Convention. The closed shop agreement at British Rail did, however, interfere with the applicants' right to form or join a trade union, since:

a threat of dismissal involving loss of livelihood is a most serious form of compulsion and, in the present instance, it was directed against persons engaged by British Rail before the introduction of any obligation to join a particular trade union.[97]

In the Court's opinion, such a form of compulsion 'strikes at the very substance of the freedom guaranteed by Article 11'[98] and gave rise to a violation.

The issue was revisited in the *Sigurjónsson* case[99] where the applicant complained that the obligation on him to become a member of '*Frami*' in order to retain his licence to operate a taxicab violated his rights under Article 11. The Strasbourg Court reviewed the current statements on the right *not* to join an association and noted a 'growing measure of common ground' both within the Council of Europe and internationally. This led it to conclude:

[T]he Convention is a living instrument which must be interpreted in the light of present-day conditions.... Accordingly, Article 11 must be viewed as encompassing a negative right of association. It is not necessary for the Court to determine in this instance whether this right is to be considered on an equal footing with the positive right.[100]

---

[95] *Young, James and Webster v United Kingdom*, 13 August 1981, Series A No 44, (1982) 4 EHRR 38.

[96] Sometimes referred to as post-entry requirements, as distinct from employments where it was known that there was a closed shop before the employment was taken up, which have been referred to as pre-entry arrangements.   [97] §55.   [98] Ibid.

[99] *Sigurdur A Sigurjónsson v Iceland*, 30 June 1993, Series A No 264-A, (1993) 16 EHRR 462.

[100] §35. But note that the Strasbourg Court did not, in this case, decide that '*Frami*' was a trade union.

The Court clearly disliked the degree of compulsion embedded in the provision and was not convinced that membership of '*Frami*' was necessary in order to achieve its objectives. It concluded that, notwithstanding Iceland's margin of appreciation, the measures complained of were disproportionate to the legitimate aim pursued.

The *Sibson* case[101] concerned an employee who resigned from his union following allegations of dishonesty and joined another union. His fellow employees voted in favour of a closed shop and threatened strike action if he continued to work at their depot. The employers sought to resolve the problem by transferring the applicant to another place of work. Another option was that he rejoin the union from which he had initially resigned. The applicant refused both options and resigned with immediate effect. The Strasbourg Court distinguished the *Young, James and Webster* case and found no violation of Article 11: the applicant had no strong objection to rejoining the union (he simply wanted an apology), and could, in any event, have kept his job by moving to another depot.

In the *Gustafsson* case[102] the applicant was an employer and restaurant owner, who refused to join one of the employers' associations established in Sweden for the purposes of collective bargaining with employees. Because of his refusal to enter into a collective agreement, his restaurant was the object of a union blockade which had a negative effect on his business. He complained that the respondent State should have provided some mechanism under national law whereby he could have terminated the union action.

The Strasbourg Court observed that in order to comply with the Swedish law on collective bargaining, it would not have been necessary for the applicant to join an employers' association. The law would have been satisfied, and the union action called off, if he had consented to sign a substitute agreement with his employees, recognizing their right to collective bargaining. The Court noted the special role and importance of collective agreements in the regulation of labour relations in Sweden, and the recognition of the legitimate character of collective bargaining included in a number of international instruments, including Article 6 of the European Social Charter, Article 8 of the 1966 International Covenant on Economic, Social and Cultural Rights, and Conventions nos. 87 and 98 of the International Labour Organisation. It concluded that the requirement on an employer to enter into a collective wage agreement fell within the respondent State's margin of appreciation under Article 11.

The distaste for closed shop arrangements has been reinforced by a decision of the Grand Chamber in the *Sørensen and Rasmussen* case.[103] Both applicants had objected to being required to join a trade union as a condition of their employment. The judgment does not totally outlaw closed shop arrangements but will make it very difficult for Contracting Parties to sustain such arrangements:

---

[101] *Sibson v United Kingdom*, 20 April 1993, Series A No 258-A, (1994) 17 EHRR 193.

[102] *Gustafsson v Sweden* (App. 15573/89), 25 April 1996, (1996) 22 EHRR 409, ECHR 1996-II; Revision, ECHR 1998-V.

[103] *Sørensen and Rasmussen v Denmark*, (Apps. 52562/99 and 52620/99), 11 January 2006 [GC], (2008) 46 EHRR 572, ECHR 2006-I.

In assessing whether a Contracting State has remained within its margin of appreciation in tolerating the existence of closed-shop agreements, particular weight must be attached to the justifications advanced by the authorities for them and, in any given case, the extent to which they impinge on the rights and interests protected by Article 11. Account must also be taken of changing perceptions of the relevance of closed-shop agreements for securing the effective enjoyment of trade union freedom. The Court sees no reason not to extend these considerations to both pre-entry and post-entry closed-shop agreements.[104]

That view is reinforced by the Strasbourg Court's conclusions following its survey of developments in Europe on the use of the closed shop:

it appears that there is little support in the Contracting States for the maintenance of closed-shop agreements and that the European instruments referred to above clearly indicate that their use in the labour market is not an indispensable tool for the effective enjoyment of trade union freedoms.[105]

In the case of Sørensen, the Grand Chamber found by twelve votes to five, and in the case of Rasmussen by fifteen votes to two, that the respondent State had breached Article 11 in that it had failed to protect the applicants' right not to join a trade union.

THE CURRENT STATE OF THE LAW

The Strasbourg Court has summarized the development of its case-law on trade union rights as follows:

144. As a result of the foregoing, the evolution of case-law as to the substance of the right of association enshrined in Article 11 is marked by two guiding principles: firstly, the Court takes into consideration the totality of the measures taken by the State concerned in order to secure trade-union freedom, subject to its margin of appreciation; secondly, the Court does not accept restrictions that affect the essential elements of trade-union freedom, without which that freedom would become devoid of substance. These two principles are not contradictory but are correlated. This correlation implies that the Contracting State in question, whilst in principle being free to decide what measures it wishes to take in order to ensure compliance with Article 11, is under an obligation to take account of the elements regarded as essential by the Court's case-law.

145. From the Court's case-law as it stands, the following essential elements of the right of association can be established: the right to form and join a trade union...the prohibition of closed-shop agreements...and the right for a trade union to seek to persuade the employer to hear what it has to say on behalf of its members....

146. This list is not finite. On the contrary, it is subject to evolution depending on particular developments in labour relations. In this connection it is appropriate to remember that the Convention is a living instrument which must be interpreted in the light of present-day conditions, and in accordance with developments in

---

[104] §58.   [105] §75.

international law, so as to reflect the increasingly high standard being required in the area of the protection of human rights, thus necessitating greater firmness in assessing breaches of the fundamental values of democratic societies. In other words, limitations to rights must be construed restrictively, in a manner which gives practical and effective protection to human rights....[106]

There is also a right to bargain collectively:

...the Court considers that, having regard to the developments in labour law, both international and national, and to the practice of Contracting States in such matters, the right to bargain collectively with the employer has, in principle, become one of the essential elements of the 'right to form and to join trade unions for the protection of [one's] interests' set forth in Article 11 of the Convention, it being understood that States remain free to organize their system so as, if appropriate, to grant special status to representative trade unions. Like other workers, civil servants, except in very specific cases, should enjoy such rights, but without prejudice to the effects of any 'lawful restrictions' that may have to be imposed on 'members of the administration of the State' within the meaning of Article 11 §2—a category to which the applicants in the present case do not, however, belong....[107]

RESTRICTIONS ON PARTICULAR GROUPS OF WORKERS

Paragraph (2) of Article 11 contains the standard limitations which are common to Articles 8 to 11.[108] Additionally, it provides that:

This article shall not prevent the imposition of lawful restrictions on the exercise of these rights by members of the armed forces, of the police or of the administration of the State.

The concept of 'lawfulness' in this provision is the same as that elsewhere in the Convention, requiring, in addition to conformity with domestic law, that the domestic law must be accessible, certain, and not arbitrary.[109]

There is a distinction to be drawn between members of the administration of the State, and civil servants, especially those employed in the municipalities.[110] It is not clear, however, whether interferences with the rights of association of civil servants in the specified groups must pursue a legitimate aim and be proportionate. The Commission, examining an application arising from the prohibition of trade union membership among civilian workers at the United Kingdom Government Communications

---

[106] *Demir and Baykara v Turkey*, (App. 34503/97), 12 November 2008 [GC], (2009) 48 EHRR 1272, ECHR 2008-nyr, §§144–6.

[107] §154.   [108] See ch.14 above.

[109] *Rekvényi v Hungary* (App. 25390/94), 20 May 1999 [GC], (2000) 30 EHRR 519, ECHR 1999-III.

[110] *Demir and Baykara v Turkey*, (App. 34503/97), 12 November 2008 [GC], (2009) 48 EHRR 1272, ECHR 2008-nyr, §97.

Headquarters (GCHQ) in Cheltenham,[111] took the view that the sole requirements in such cases were that the restrictions be in accordance with national law and be free from arbitrariness.[112] In the *Vogt* case[113] the Strasbourg Court appeared to imply that such a measure would need to be proportionate, but left the question open, as it did in a case brought by a Hungarian police officer, who complained about an amendment to the Constitution prohibiting the police and members of the armed forces from joining political parties or engaging in political activities.[114] The Court did not need to consider the question under Article 11(2) since it had already determined that the restriction was proportionate under Article 10, given in particular the problems Hungary had suffered in the past with a politicized police force.

The leading authority is now the decision of the Grand Chamber in the *Demir and Baykara* case.[115] This concerned the right of civil servants to form trade unions. Having regard to provisions in a number of international instruments, the Grand Chamber concluded that members of the administration of the State cannot be excluded from the scope of Article 11; at most they may be subject to lawful restrictions beyond those provided for elsewhere in the article. Municipal civil servants will not normally fall within the special category and so any interference with their trade union rights will have to be justified under the usual limitations set out in Article 11(2).

The Court has held that it is permissible for a Contracting Party to restrict the political activity of local government officials,[116] but not to require them to renounce Freemasonry.[117] In the *Vogt* case[118] it found violations of Articles 10 and 11 where a West German teacher had been dismissed for membership of the Communist Party, given that she had not let her political beliefs affect her professional conduct in any way.

CONCLUDING REMARKS

The case-law under Article 11 can, very broadly, be divided into two categories. The first, concerned with 'political' or 'democratic' rights—such as the freedom to take part in a demonstration or to join a political party—which are closely linked to freedom

---

[111] App. 11603/85, *Council of Civil Service Unions and others v United Kingdom*, Decision of 20 January 1987, (1987) 50 DR 228.

[112] 240 and 241.

[113] *Vogt v Germany*, 26 September 1995, Series A No 323, (1996) 21 EHRR 205, §67.

[114] *Rekvényi v Hungary* (App. 25390/94), 20 May 1999 [GC], (2000) 30 EHRR 519, ECHR 1999-III.

[115] *Demir and Baykara v Turkey*, (App. 34503/97), 12 November 2008 [GC], (2009) 48 EHRR 1272, ECHR 2008-nyr.

[116] *Ahmed and others v United Kingdom* (App. 22954/93), 2 September 1998, (2000) 29 EHRR 1, ECHR 1998-VI.

[117] *Grande Oriente d'Italia di Palazzo Giustiniani v Italy* (App. 35972/97), 2 August 2001, (2002) 34 EHRR 629, ECHR 2001-VIII.

[118] *Vogt v Germany*, 26 September 1995, Series A No 323, (1996) 21 EHRR 205. Contrast the admissibility decision in *Erdel v Germany*, (App. 30067/04), 13 February 2007, ECHR 2007-II.

of expression, draws heavily on the principles developed by the Strasbourg Court under Article 10. The second type of case which arises under Article 11 relates to the employment-based rights to join, or refuse to join, a trade union. Here the Strasbourg Court's judgments were initially somewhat less confident, sometimes allowing the Contracting Parties such a wide margin of appreciation that it is difficult to discern any real content to the rights for practical purposes.

It must be remembered, however, that there is other international machinery for dealing with complaints concerning trade union rights, in particular under the conventions of the International Labour Organisation[119] and under the European Social Charter. The provisions of the other international instruments are naturally more detailed, and within the International Labour Organisation, in particular, a substantial body of law has been developed.

The Strasbourg Court could react to this in one of two ways. Either it could decide that it does not have the expertise, and that the Convention is not the most appropriate vehicle, for settling complex socio-economic labour law questions.[120] In this case, the Strasbourg Court will continue to interpret Article 11 as affording a wide margin of appreciation to the Contracting Parties, and disgruntled trade unionists might be better advised to address their complaints to another forum. Alternatively, the Court might begin to look more closely at the case-law built up under other treaties, and apply the principles developed there to promote uniformity of approach in this field. There are signs in recent decisions of the Grand Chamber that the Court is adopting the latter approach.

---

[119] See L. Swepston, 'Human Rights Law and Freedom of Association: Development through ILO Supervision' (1998) 137 *International Labour Review* 169.

[120] See the separate opinions in the *Gustafsson v Sweden* case, 25 April 1996, (1996) 22 EHRR 409, ECHR 1996-II; Revision, ECHR 1998-V.

20

PROTECTION OF PROPERTY

INTRODUCTION

The protection of property rights as human rights presents particular problems, and it is therefore not surprising that agreement could not be reached on their inclusion in the Convention as originally drafted.[1] A right to property is included in Article 1 of Protocol 1, but its content is broadly framed and the permissible restrictions are broad in scope. The beneficiaries of the guarantees in the article are both individuals and business entities, including corporations. The article has, consequently, taken on a commercial character and been used extensively by business in the advancement of its interests.

All the provisions of the Convention, including Articles 13 to 18, apply equally to the rights guaranteed by the First Protocol.[2] These rights are also subject in the same way to the control of the organs set up by the Convention.

Article 1 of the First Protocol provides:

Every natural or legal person is entitled to the peaceful enjoyment of his possessions. No one shall be deprived of his possessions except in the public interest and subject to the conditions provided for by law and by the general principles of international law.

The preceding provisions shall not, however, in any way impair the right of a State to enforce such laws as it deems necessary to control the use of property in accordance with the general interest or to secure the payment of taxes or other contributions or penalties.

Though drafted rather differently, the structure of the provision is similar to that found in Articles 8 to 11. There is a general right to peaceful enjoyment of possessions.

---

[1] See generally, A. Grgic and others, *The right to property under the European Convention on Human Rights: a guide to the implementation of the European Convention on Human Rights and its Protocols*, Human Rights Handbooks No. 4 (Council of Europe Publishing, Strasbourg 2007); H.G. Schermers, 'The International Protection of the Right of Property' in F. Matscher and H. Petzold (eds.), *Protecting Human Rights: The European Dimension. Essays in honour of Gérard J. Wiarda* (Carl Heymanns, Köln 1988), at 565; J. Frowein, 'The Protection of Property' in R. Macdonald, F. Matscher, and H. Petzold, *The European System for the Protection of Human Rights* (Martinus Nijhoff, Dordrecht 1993) at 515; A. Riza Coban, *Protection of Property Rights within the European Convention on Human Rights* (Ashgate, Aldershot 2004); and G. Ress, 'Reflections on the Protection of Property under the European Convention on Human Rights' in S. Breitenmoser and others, *Human Rights, Democracy and the Rule of Law. Liber amicorum Luzius Wildhaber*, (Nomos, Baden Baden 2007), 625.

[2] Protocol 1, Art. 5.

Interferences can, however, be justified on the conditions set out in the article which include references both to the 'public interest' and the 'general interest'; this is the test of proportionality that pervades the Convention's consideration of interferences and requires the balancing of the interests of the individual against the collective interest.

There is also a requirement in the article that deprivations are 'subject to the conditions provided for by law'[3] and so the discussion of the notion of interferences being in accordance with law in relation to Articles 8 to 11 will also be relevant here.[4] The article makes express provision for certain deprivations of property, though these must be in accordance with national law, in accordance with the general principles of international law, and in the public interest. It is also acknowledged that public authorities can control the use of property either in the general interest, or specifically to secure the payment of taxes or other contributions or penalties.

The Strasbourg Court has come to approach the protection of property rights using much the same methodology as it adopts in relation to complaints of violations of the rights protected by Articles 8 to 11. This secures a certain uniformity of approach in cases where a Contracting Party interferes with rights protected in the Convention, and seeks to offer a justification for this. However, the range of rights which falls within the concept of the 'public interest' and the 'general interest' is very wide indeed.[5]

The Court has repeatedly said that the article comprises three distinct rules.[6] First, everyone is entitled to peaceful enjoyment of their possessions. Secondly, deprivation of possessions is subject to certain conditions. Finally, Contracting Parties are entitled to control the use of property where it is in the general interest. But these are not distinct rules, since the second and third rules relate to interferences with the peaceful enjoyment of possessions which may be justified in the general interest. This can be illustrated by the facts of the *Pye* case.[7] The applicants complained that the operation of the English land law rules on adverse possession meant that they had been deprived of property when land registered in their name was to be registered in the names of a couple who had occupied the land for twelve years. The Strasbourg Court categorizes the situation as one involving control over the use of land, whereas it might easily have been categorized as a deprivation.[8]

---

[3] *Prévues par la loi* in the French text.

[4] See ch.14 above. For an example of a discussion of legality in the context of this Article, see *Bozcaada Kimisis Teodoku Rum Ortodoks Kilisesi Vafki v Turkey No. 2)* (Apps 37639/03, 37655/03, 26736/04 and 42670/04), 3 March 2009.

[5] Encompassing for example, the protection of nature and forests: *Turgut and others v Turkey*, (App. 1411/03), 8 July 2008, ECHR 2008-nyr; and the protection of natural heritage: *Anonymos Touristiki Etairia Xenodocheia v Greece*, (App. 35332/05), 21 February 2008.

[6] *Sporrong and Lönnroth v Sweden*, (Apps. 7151–2/75), 23 September 1982, Series A No 52, (1983) 5 EHRR 35, §61. See, more recently, *Jahn and others v Germany*, (Apps. 46720/99, 72203/01, and 72552/01), 30 June 2005 [GC], (2006) 42 EHRR 1084, ECHR 2005-VI, §78; and *Hutten-Czapska v Poland*, (App. 35014/97), 19 June 2006 [GC], (2007) 45 EHRR 52, ECHR 2006-VIII, §157.

[7] *JA Pye (Oxford) Ltd and JA Pye (Oxford) Land Ltd v United Kingdom*, (App. 44302/02), 30 August 2007 [GC], (2008) 46 EHRR 1083, ECHR 2007-X.

[8] A point made in the joint dissenting opinion of Judges Rozakis, Bratza, Tsatsa-Nikolovska, Gyulumyan, and Šikuta, §6.

In the *Marckx* case,[9] the Strasbourg Court stated some general propositions on the scope of Article 1 of Protocol 1. It applies only to a person's existing possessions and gives no guarantee of a right to acquire possessions.[10] But the right to property does include the right to dispose of one's property.[11]

Once it has been established that the applicant has an interest which can be classified as a possession, the general approach of the Strasbourg Court is to consider first whether there has been a deprivation of possessions, followed by consideration of whether there has been a control of the use of possessions, since these are matters specifically dealt with by the article. Only if there has been neither deprivation of possessions nor a control of their use[12] does the Court consider, as a separate issue, whether there has been some other interference with the peaceful enjoyment of possessions. Such interferences will, however, only be unlawful if they are not in the general interest. In its more recent case-law, the Court has brought together the tests it applies in relation to deprivations, the control of the use of property, and to other interferences with property, so that the questions the Court will ask in each of these circumstances raise essentially the same issues.

A series of applications relating to the consequences of the reunification of Germany and the transition from totalitarian regimes to democratic structures in the countries of central and eastern Europe has threatened to overwhelm the Court. The law on the protection of property rights is now replete with judgments of the Grand Chamber seeking to establish the obligations of States in fairly managing a whole variety of schemes seeking to reverse injustices which arose from the regime in place before the advent of democracy.

POSITIVE OBLIGATIONS

The *Öneryildiz* case[13] concerned the loss of life and destruction of property as a result of unsafe conditions in a refuse tip, for which the respondent State was responsible. The Grand Chamber concluded that there was an obligation on States to take practical steps to avoid loss of property.[14] The obligation is very similar to that arising under Article 2. The *Budayeva* case[15] concerned a natural disaster rather than a disaster flowing from dangerous activities. There had been a mudslide which caused loss of life, and destruction of property. The authorities had known of the risk of mudslides in the

---

[9] *Marckx v Belgium*, (App. 6833/74), 13 June 1979, Series A No 31, (1979–80) 2 EHRR 330.

[10] §50.   [11] §63.

[12] Or where the circumstances of the case are such that detailed categorization in this way is inappropriate: see, for example, *Solodyuk v Russia* (App. 67099/01), 12 July 2005, §29; and *Broniowski v Poland* (App. 31443/96), 22 June 2004 [GC], (2005) 40 EHRR 495, ECHR 2004-V.

[13] *Öneryildiz v Turkey* (App. 48939/99), 30 November 2004 [GC], (2005) 41 EHRR 325, ECHR 2004-XII.

[14] §136.

[15] *Budayeva and others v Russia*, (Apps. 15339/02, 21166/02, 20058/02, 11673/02, and 15343/02), 20 March 2008, ECHR 2008-nyr.

area, but had not established any form of early warning system. This led the Court to conclude that a distinction should be drawn between the positive obligation to protect life and to protect property. Where there is a risk to life, the authorities must do everything to mitigate the risk, but where the risk is of destruction of property, 'the authorities enjoy a wider margin of appreciation.'[16] In the particular circumstances of the case, the respondent State had failed to comply with its positive obligations under Article 2, but not under Article 1 of Protocol 1. A similar distinction was drawn in respect of the obligation to conduct an enquiry into the disaster; there was a lesser obligation where destruction of property was involved.

Issues arising from the reunification of Germany, and from attempts to recover formerly-owned property in some of the countries of central and eastern Europe, have generated a new line of case-law on positive obligations. The Grand Chamber of the Court recapitulated the relevant principles in its judgment in the *Kopecký* case.[17] There is no duty falling on Contracting Parties to restore property taken by an earlier regime to its original owners; nor is there any restriction on their doing so. However, any scheme which is established will create a property right for those who meet the conditions of entitlement under the scheme, and will require that the scheme is Convention compliant. This will also be the case with any legislative scheme established prior to entry into force of the Convention which is continued in operation following accession. The positive obligation has been stated to be to take timely and consistent action, which avoids an atmosphere of general uncertainty.[18]

Increasingly, the Strasbourg Court is adopting a similar approach in cases involving positive obligations to that which it adopts when negative obligations are in issue. In the *Broniowski* case, the Grand Chamber said:

> …the boundaries between the State's positive and negative obligations under Article 1 of Protocol 1 do not lend themselves to precise definition. The applicable principles are nonetheless similar. Whether the case is analysed in terms of a positive duty on the State or in terms of an interference by a public authority which requires to be justified, the criteria to be applied do not differ in substance. In both contexts regard must be had to the fair balance to be struck between the competing interests of the individual and of the community as a whole. It also holds true that the aims mentioned in that provision may be of some relevance in assessing whether a balance between the demands of the public interest involved and the applicant's fundamental right of property has been struck. In both contexts the State enjoys a certain margin of appreciation in determining the steps to be taken to ensure compliance with the Convention.…[19]

Indeed in the *Broniowski* case, the Strasbourg Court declined to classify the contested measures as engaging either positive or negative obligations, indicating

---

[16] *Budayeva*, §175.

[17] *Kopecký v Slovakia* (App. 44912/98), 28 September 2004 [GC], (2005) 41 EHRR 944, ECHR 2004-IX. The 'restitution' cases are considered in more detail below.

[18] *Păduraru v Romania*, (App. 63252/00), 1 December 2005, §§92–3.

[19] *Broniowski v Poland* (App. 31443/96), 22 June 2004, (2005) 40 EHRR 495, ECHR 2004-V, §144.

that the Court would simply determine whether the conduct of the respondent State was justifiable.[20]

DEFINING POSSESSIONS

THE BASIC APPROACH

Possessions have been defined in broad terms by both the Commission and the Court. In this context, it is worth noting that the French text of the Convention uses the term '*biens*' which connotes a very broad range of property rights. The term has an autonomous meaning; it extends beyond physical goods, and covers a wide range of rights and interests which may be classified as assets.[21]

It is for the Strasbourg organs to determine what falls within the concept of possessions in the article having regard to the classification of the matter under national law. Clearly both real and personal property[22] are within the notion of possessions, but the concept extends far beyond to all manner of things which have an economic value. So the Strasbourg organs have held that company shares are possessions.[23] A patent is also a possession,[24] as is an internet domain name.[25] Indeed, the provision is applicable to all intellectual property as such, including applications for registration of a trade mark.[26] Goodwill in a business constitutes possessions,[27] as does a licence to serve alcoholic beverages where this is vital to an applicant's business.[28] Telecommunications licences for providing internet and fixed telephony services are possessions.[29] Similarly a licence to extract gravel was regarded by the Strasbourg Court as a possession,[30] as was a licence to run a bonded warehouse.[31] Fishing rights

---

[20] §146.

[21] *Gasus Dosier- und Fördertechnik GmbH v Netherlands*, 23 February 1995, Series A No 306-B, (1995) 20 EHRR 403, §53.

[22] Often referred to as immovable and movable property.

[23] Apps. 8588/79 and 8589/79, *Bramelid & Malmström v Sweden*, Decision of 12 October 1982, (1982) 29 DR 64, and App. 11189/84, *Company S. & T. v Sweden*, Decision of 11 December 1988, (1987) 50 DR 121.

[24] App. 12633/87, *Smith Kline and French Laboratories Ltd v Netherlands*, Decision of 4 October 1990, (1990) 66 DR 70.

[25] *Paeffgen GmbH v Germany*, (Apps. 25379/02, 21688/05, 21722/05, and 21770/05), Decision of 18 September 2007.

[26] *Anheuser-Busch Inc. v Portugal*, (App. 73049/01), 11 January 2007 [GC], (2007) 45 EHRR 830, ECHR 2007-I.

[27] *Van Marle and others v Netherlands*, 26 June 1986, Series A No 101, (1986) 8 EHRR 483, §41. But see also App. 10438/83, *Batelaan & Huiges v Netherlands*, Decision of 3 October 1984, (1985) 41 DR 170 to the effect that expectations lack the degree of certainty needed to constitute possessions.

[28] *Tre Traktörer Aktiebolag v Sweden*. 7 July 1989, Series A No 159, (1991) 13 EHRR 309, §53.

[29] *Megadat.com SRL v Moldova*, (App. 21151/04), 8 April 2008, ECHR 2008-nyr, §§62–3.

[30] *Fredin v Sweden*, 18 February 1991, Series A No 192 (1991) 13 EHRR 784, §40.

[31] *Rosenweig and Bonded Warehouses Ltd v Poland*, (App. 51728/99), 28 July 2005.

are possessions.[32] A planning permission is a possession.[33] But a driving licence is not a possession.[34] Tips paid to waiters were held in one case not to constitute possessions of the waiters,[35] but compulsory deductions from the wages of those who are not members of the union for trade union activities will constitute an interference with possessions.[36] In another case, it was suggested that royal property may have a special status, but since the State had consistently treated the property in issue as private property, and had not established a distinct set of rules relating to royal property, the case was decided by the application of ordinary principles.[37]

In the *Öneryildiz* case,[38] the respondent State argued that unlawfully occupying land and building a home on it could not give rise to property rights within the article. The applicant's home and its contents had been destroyed in a landslide following a methane explosion in a refuse tip; the authorities knew of the risks posed by the tip, but had taken no steps to make it safe. The Court rather sidestepped the issue by concluding that, although the applicant could show no property interest in the land, nevertheless he had a property interest in the house itself and its contents.

The Strasbourg Court has also read Article 1 of Protocol 1 with Article 6 to provide a property right in an enforceable judgment against the State.[39]

LEASES AND LICENCES TO OCCUPY PROPERTY

Rights flowing from leases are accepted as possessions. In the *Mellacher* case,[40] it was not disputed that reductions in contractually agreed rents under rent control legislation constituted an interference with the applicants' enjoyment of their rights as owners of the rented properties.

Somewhat inconsistently with the broad interpretation of possessions taken in other contexts, the Court has drawn a narrow distinction between the basis on which individuals occupy property as their homes. In an admissibility decision[41] the Court was faced with a situation in which a soldier in the provisional reserve force was allocated

---

[32] App. 11763/85, *Banér v Sweden*, Decision of 9 March 1989, (1989) 60 DR 128; *Posti and Rahko v Finland*, (App. 27824/95), 24 September 2002, (2003) 37 EHRR 158, ECHR 2002-VII; and *Alatulkkila and others v Finland*, (App. 33538/96), 28 July 2005.

[33] *Pine Valley Developments Ltd and others v Ireland*, (App. 12742/87), 29 November 1991, Series A No 222, (1992) 14 EHRR 319.

[34] App. 9177/80, *X v Federal Republic of Germany*, Decision of 6 October 1981, (1982) 26 DR 255.

[35] *Nerva and others v United Kingdom*, (App. 42295/98), 24 September 2002, (2003) 36 EHRR 31, ECHR 2002-VIII.

[36] *Evaldsson and others v Sweden*, (App. 75252/01), 13 February 2007.

[37] *The Former King of Greece and others v Greece*, (App. 25701/94), 23 November 2000 [GC], (2001) 33 EHRR 516, ECHR 2000-XII, §§65–6.

[38] *Öneryildiz v Turkey*, (App. 48939/99), 30 November 2004 [GC], (2005) 41 EHRR 325, ECHR 2004-XII.

[39] *Burdov v Russia*, (App. 59498/00), 7 May 2002, (2004) 38 EHRR639, ECHR 2002-III, and the pilot judgment in *Burdov v Russia (No. 2)*, (App. 33509/04), 15 January 2009, (2009) 49 EHRR 22.

[40] *Mellacher v Austria*, (Apps. 10522/83, 11011/84, and 11070/84), 19 December 1989, Series A No 169, (1990) 12 EHRR 391, §43.

[41] *JLS v Spain*, (App. 41917/98), Decision of 27 April 1999, ECHR 1999-V.

housing by the army. Following a change in the system for housing members of the military, the applicant was required to vacate the property and was evicted. The Court observed that the applicant did not have a lease, and that the arrangement could not be equated to 'an agreement under private law'. The Court went on to say:

[The Court] points out that a right to live in a particular property not owned by the applicant does not constitute a 'possession' within the meaning of Article 1 of Protocol 1…. Furthermore, allowing a 'user' such as the applicant (who was not even a tenant) to remain indefinitely in premises belonging to the State would prevent the authorities from performing their obligation to administer State property in accordance with their statutory and constitutional duties.[42]

The Court accordingly found the application to be inadmissible. It is suggested that a more satisfactory approach would have been to recognize the applicant's property right in his housing, but to find that the interference was justified in the general interest.[43]

In the *Larkos* case,[44] the Strasbourg Court sidestepped the issue when faced with a complaint by a government tenant that the differences in the levels of protection afforded under national law to private tenants and government tenants on termination of the lease violated Article 1 of Protocol 1 when read with Article 14 of the Convention.[45] The respondent State had argued that the applicant did not possess any interest in the property which constituted a possession falling within the scope of Article 1 of Protocol 1. The Court disposed of the case by finding a violation of Article 14 when read in conjunction with Article 8.

The English law of property makes a clear distinction between tenants and licensees, but would regard licensees as entitled to protection of their property rights, though to a lesser extent than tenants. It is accordingly odd that the Court should seemingly draw a distinction between a mere (lawful) user[46] who has nothing which constitutes a possession within the article, and a tenant who has a possession.

SOCIAL SECURITY PAYMENTS AND PENSIONS

Entitlements arising under pension and social security schemes have proved difficult to classify; the position was for some time unclear. A distinction had been drawn in the case-law between benefits which were paid on the basis of contributions, and those which were paid without reference to contributions. But the case-law did not always seem to maintain this distinction. However, the admissibility decision of the Grand Chamber in the *Stec* case[47] has clarified matters.

---

[42] §2.

[43] The applicant does not appear to have complained of a violation of his right to a home under Art. 8, presumably because an alternative home was made available to him.

[44] *Larkos v Cyprus*, (App. 29515/95), 18 February 1999 [GC], (2000) 30 EHRR 597, ECHR 1999-I.

[45] Art. 14 provides protection against discrimination in matters within the scope of the Convention: see ch.24 below.

[46] Likely to be characterized as a licensee under English law.

[47] *Stec and others v United Kingdom*, (Apps. 65731/01 and 65900/01), Decision of 6 July 2005 [GC], (2005) 41 EHRR SE18, ECHR 2005-X.

An example of the ambiguity caused by the earlier case-law can be found in the *Gaygusuz* case.[48] Gaygusuz was a Turkish national who had worked in Austria, where he had paid contributions under the Austrian social security scheme. He had experienced periods of unemployment and periods when he was unfit for work. He applied for an advance on his retirement pension as a form of emergency assistance, but was refused because he was not an Austrian national. He complained that there had been a violation of Article 14 when read in conjunction with Article 1 of Protocol 1. The first question was whether the substance of the claim was a matter within the scope of the article, since otherwise Article 14 could not be brought into play. Both the Commission and the Court concluded that the article was applicable but for different reasons. The Commission concluded that the article was brought into play because the obligation to pay 'taxes or other contributions' falls within its field of application.[49] The Court, however, concluded that the link with the obligation to pay taxes or other contributions was not required.[50] That was sufficient to engage the anti-discrimination provision in Article 14 and to find a violation since the discrimination between nationals and non-nationals was blatant. The Court took the same approach in the *Koua Poirrez* case.[51]

In the *Stec* case, the Grand Chamber accepted that the *Gaygusuz* case was ambiguous on the significance of contributions in bringing a claim within the scope of Article 1 of Protocol 1 for the purpose of claiming discriminatory treatment which breached Article 14 of the Convention. The Grand Chamber lays down a new approach which is to be applied in future cases, relying on an interpretation which renders the rights in the Convention practical and effective rather than theoretical and illusory.[52] The Grand Chamber also referred to the Court's case-law under Article 6 which had brought disputes concerning all forms of social security within the scope of that article. The Court concluded that, whenever persons can assert a right to a welfare benefit under national law, Article 1 of Protocol 1 applies.[53] The Court goes on to note that the bringing of social security fairly and squarely within the scope of Article 1 of Protocol 1 does not create any right to acquire property. However, if a Contracting Party does create rights to social security benefits, the benefit schemes must be operated in a manner which is compatible with the prohibition of discrimination set out in Article 14.[54]

---

[48] *Gaygusuz v Austria*, (App. 17371/90), 16 September 1996, (1997) 23 EHRR 364, ECHR 1996-IV.

[49] §47 of the Commission Opinion.

[50] §41 of the Judgment.

[51] *Koua Poirrez v France*, (App. 40892/98), 30 September 2003, (2005) 40 EHRR 34, ECHR 2003-X, §37. Other cases in the earlier line of authority include *Meyne-Moskalczuk and others v The Netherlands*, (App. 53002/99), Decision of 9 December 2003; *Van Den Bouwhuijsen and Schuring v The Netherlands*, (App. 44658/98), Decision of 16 December 2003; and *Kjartan Ásmundsson v Iceland*, (App. 60669/00), 12 October 2004, (2005) 41 EHRR 927, ECHR 2004-IX.

[52] See ch.4 above.

[53] *Stec and others v United Kingdom*, (Apps. 65731/01 and 65900/01), Decision of 6 July 2005 [GC], (2005) 41 EHRR SE18, ECHR 2005-X, §§50–1.

[54] See ch.24 below.

LEGAL CLAIMS, ASSETS, AND LEGITIMATE EXPECTATIONS

Various types of legal claims have been treated as possessions. Some of these cases are complex in their factual situations, making it difficult to draw general principles from them. What is clear is that there must be something which can be regarded as a legal claim. Thus a judgment debt will be a possession, so that quashing the judgment after it has become final will constitute an interference with the peaceful enjoyment of possessions.[55] Similarly a sufficiently established claim to a social tenancy agreement following disablement as a result of involvement in the emergency operations at the Chernobyl Nuclear Plant disaster of 1986 constituted a possession for the purposes of the article.[56] Retrospective variation of the claimable heads of damages in the law of obligations constitutes an interference with possessions in relation to those with pending proceedings.[57]

In the *Van der Mussele* case,[58] the Court found that the absence of remuneration for legal services where a pupil lawyer had been required to represent a client without payment did not constitute an interference with possessions because no legal duty to pay remuneration ever arose, and the client's indigence meant that no assessment of fees could take place.[59]

The *Pine Valley Developments* case[60] concerned the impact of the annulment of a planning permission.[61] The Court in determining that there had been no violation of Article 1 of Protocol 1 was influenced by the element of risk inherent in a commercial venture in considering the proportionality of the State action which had resulted in the annulment of an earlier planning permission relating to an area 'zoned for the further development of agriculture so as to preserve a green belt'.[62]

In the *Stretch* case,[63] a local authority had granted an option to renew a lease, which was void since the local authority exceeded is powers in granting such an option. The act in excess of its powers was only discovered late in the day, and the applicant was in the later stages of negotiations with his sub-tenants. The Court regarded him as having a possession which could be protected by Article 1 of Protocol 1, since he had

---

[55] *Rybakh v Russia*, (App. 52854/99), 24 July 2003, (2005) 40 EHRR 615, ECHR 2003-IX.

[56] *Malinovskiy v Russia*, (App. 41302/02), 7 July 2005; and *Shpakovskiy v Russia*, (App. 41307/02), 7 July 2005.

[57] *Draon v France*, (App.1513/03), 6 October 2005 [GC], (2006) 42 EHRR 807, ECHR 2005-IX; and *Maurice v France*, (App. 11810/03), 6 October 2005 [GC], (2006) 42 EHRR 885.

[58] *Van der Mussele v Belgium*, 23 November 1983, Series A No 70, (1984) 6 EHRR 163.

[59] Contrast the case of *Ambruosi v Italy*, (App. 31227/96), 19 October 2000, (2002) 35 EHRR 125, where a change in the rules on recovery of legal costs deprived a lawyer of fees, costs, and expenses due to him.

[60] *Pine Valley Developments Limited and others v Ireland*, (App. 12742/87), 29 November 1991, Series A No 222, (1992) 14 EHRR 319.

[61] It was an interference case rather than a deprivation case.

[62] *Pine Valley Developments Limited and others v Ireland*, (App. 12742/87), 29 November 1991, Series A No 222, (1992) 14 EHRR 319, §59. See also *Håkansson and Sturesson v Sweden*, (App. 11855/85), 21 February 1990, Series A No 171, (1991) 13 EHRR 1, §53.

[63] *Stretch v United Kingdom*, (App. 44277/98), 24 June 2003, (2004) 38 EHRR 196.

a legitimate expectation of exercising the option to renew which could be regarded as attached to the property rights he held under the lease.

In the *Gasus* case[64] the Court was faced with a situation in which the Dutch tax authorities had seized a concrete mixer from a buyer in order to enforce tax debts. The buyer had not yet paid the full price to the applicant company, which had the benefit of a retention of title clause. The Court considered that it made no difference whether the applicant company's right to the concrete mixer was a right of ownership or a 'security right *in rem*'. Whatever view was taken, there was an interference with the peaceful enjoyment of its possessions.

The *Stran Greek Refineries* case[65] involved very large sums of money arising in connection with disputes surrounding the building of an oil refinery. Arbitration proceedings eventually took place, and an award was made. The arbitration award was subsequently declared void. The applicants complained of a violation of, among other articles, Article 1 of Protocol 1, in that they had been deprived of the benefit of the award made in the arbitration proceedings. The Greek Government argued that there was no 'possession' involved here, since the arbitration award had a precarious legal basis and the award could not be equated with any right which might be recognized by such an award. The Court felt that the test was whether 'the arbitration award had given rise to a debt…that was sufficiently established to be enforceable.'[66] In the particular circumstances of the case, the Court concluded that the arbitration award was a final and binding award and did give rise to an enforceable debt, even though that right was revocable through the process of annulment of the award. There was therefore a possession within the meaning of Article 1 of Protocol 1.[67]

The *Pressos Compania Naviera* case revisited the issue in the context of claims in tort.[68] The dispute centred around claims arising following a collision at sea. Various parties concluded that the collision had arisen as the result of the negligence of the Belgian pilots on board the ships in question. A number of proceedings were brought. Legislation subsequently removed their causes of action retrospectively. The applicants claimed that this constituted an interference with their 'possessions'. The Commission concluded that there was nothing which constituted a possession; an action for damages simply raised the possibility of securing payment. Until there was an enforceable judgment, there was no debt and so no possession within the meaning of Article 1 of Protocol 1.

The Court disagreed, ruling that, having regard to the national law in issue, under the rules of tort, claims to compensation come into existence as soon as the damage occurs, and that a claim constituted an asset which was a possession within the meaning of Article 1 of Protocol 1.[69] The Court does not refer to its decision in *Stran Greek*

---

[64] *Gasus Dosier- und Fördertechnik GmbH v Netherlands*, 23 February 1995, Series A No 306-B, (1995) 20 EHRR 403.

[65] *Stran Greek Refineries and Stratis Andreadis v Greece*, 9 December 1994, Series A No 301-B, (1994) 19 EHRR 293.

[66] §59.   [67] §§60–2.

[68] *Pressos Compania Naviera SA and others v Belgium*, (App. 17849/91), 20 November 1995, Series A No 332, (1996) 21 EHRR 301.

[69] §31.

Refineries, and it is difficult to see a distinction between the two cases which would justify different decisions. The mere expectation that a claim in tort will be determined in accordance with the general law of tort and give rise to an award of damages was sufficient to constitute a possession. A mere expectation is usually not sufficient to constitute a possession.

The Court could have resolved the uncertainty in the *National & Provincial Building Society* case,[70] but did not do so. The case concerned claims that changes to the system for the taxation of interest paid to savers with building societies deprived them of the possibility of securing refunds of taxation paid by them when the regulations were invalidated. Certain regulations were declared invalid, giving rise in the view of the building societies to claims for restitution of tax paid to the Government. These regulations were later retrospectively validated by subsequent legislation, which deprived the building societies of their claims for restitution.

The issue was whether undetermined claims to restitution of monies paid constituted a possession. The Court, clearly aware of the case-law in the two earlier cases, sidesteps the definitional problem, and expresses 'no concluded view as to whether any of the claims asserted by the applicant societies could properly be considered to constitute possessions'.[71] The Court, however, proceeds 'on the working assumption that... the applicant societies did have possessions in the form of vested rights to restitution'.[72] Ultimately no breach of Article 1 of Protocol 1 was found. But a failure to pay default interest on overpaid tax over a period in excess of five years will constitute a violation of Article 1 of Protocol 1, even where the national law made no provision for payment of interest in such situations.[73]

Where does this leave the authorities? The best that can be hazarded in response to this question is that a legally acknowledged and enforceable debt is an asset (and so constitutes a possession within Article 1 of Protocol 1),[74] and that a legitimate expectation that an award of damages will be forthcoming on the application of the general law of obligations will also fall within the notion. Distinguishing the *Pressos Compania Naviera* case from the *National & Provincial Building Society* case requires the conclusion that in the former the expectation was 'legitimate' whereas in the latter it was not. In the *Gratzinger* case, the Grand Chamber said:

...there is a difference between a mere hope of restitution, however understandable that hope may be, and a legitimate expectation, which must be of a nature more concrete than a mere hope and be based on a legal provision or a legal act such as a judicial decision....[75]

---

[70] *National & Provincial Building Society, the Leeds Permanent Building Society and the Yorkshire Building Society v United Kingdom*, (Apps. 21319/93, 21449/93, and 21675/93), 23 October 1997, (1998) 25 EHRR 127, ECHR 1999-VII.

[71] §70.   [72] Ibid.

[73] *Eko-Elda AVEE v Greece*, (App. 10162/02), 9 March 2006, ECHR 2006-IV.

[74] See *Almeida Garrett, Mascarenhas Falcão and others v Portugal*, (Apps. 29813/96 and 30229/96), 11 January 2000, (2002) 34 EHRR 642, ECHR 2000-I.

[75] *Gratzinger and Gratzingerova v Czech Republic*, (App. 39794/98), Decision of 10 July 2002 [GC], ECHR 2002-VII, §73. See also *Von Maltzan and others v Germany*, (Apps. 71916/01, 71917/01, and 10260/02), Decision of 2 March 2005 [GC], ECHR 2005-V.

Indeed, the case-law concerning the restitution of property following the change from a totalitarian to a democratic regime in the countries of central and eastern Europe has led to something of a restatement of the law in this tricky area. The interest in issue in the *Pressos Compania Naviera* case has been explained in later case-law as being a legitimate expectation intimately linked to something which can be described as an asset, and the way in which the asset would be treated in the national legal order. What is required is a claim which is sufficiently established in the national legal order to constitute an asset for the applicant.[76] The Strasbourg Court now summarizes the position as follows:

…in certain circumstances, a 'legitimate expectation' of obtaining an 'asset' may also enjoy the protection of Article 1 of Protocol 1. Thus, where a proprietary interest is in the nature of a claim, the person in whom it is vested may be regarded as having a 'legitimate expectation' if there is a sufficient basis for the interest in national law, for example where there is settled case-law of the domestic courts confirming its existence (*Kopecký v Slovakia* [GC], no. 44912/98, §52, ECHR 2004-IX). However, no legitimate expectation can be said to arise where there is a dispute as to the correct interpretation and application of domestic law and the applicant's submissions are subsequently rejected by the national courts (*Kopecký v Slovakia*, judgment cited above, §50).[77]

In the *Veselinski and Djidrovski* cases,[78] the application of legislation, which had not been made retrospective, removing a benefit for former officers of the Yugolsav army under which they could buy their apartments at reduced prices without taking account of previous contributions to the army apartment construction fund and the agreements in force at the time, was held to defeat their legitimate expectations that they would be able to buy their apartments at a discount.

DEPRIVATION OF PROPERTY

WHAT CONSTITUTES DEPRIVATION?

The essence of deprivation of property is the extinction of the legal rights of the owner.[79] This can arise in a number of circumstances. Where a claim is made that there has been a deprivation of property in the absence of a formal transfer of ownership,

---

[76] *Kopecký v Slovakia*, (App. 44912/98), 28 September 2004 [GC], (2005) 41 EHRR 944, ECHR 2004-IX, §§45–52. See also *Vilho Eskelinen and others v Finland*, (App. 63235/00), 19 April 2007 [GC], (2007) 45 EHRR 985, ECHR 2007-IV.

[77] *Anheuser-Busch Inc. v Portugal*, (App. 73049/01), 11 January 2007 [GC], (2007) 45 EHRR 830, ECHR 2007-I, §65.

[78] *Veselinski v 'the former Yugoslav Republic of Macedonia'*, (App. 45658/99), and *Djidrovski v 'the former Yugoslav Republic of Macedonia'*, (App. 46447/99), 24 February 2009.

[79] See M. Pellonpää, 'Reflections on the notion of "deprivation of possessions" in Article 1 of the First Protocol of the European Convention on Human Rights', in P. Mahoney and others, *Protecting Human Rights: The European Perspective. Studies in Memory of Rolv Ryssdal* (Carl Heymanns, Köln 2000), 1087.

the Court will examine the realities of the situation in order to determine whether there has been a de facto expropriation.[80] An interference which does not constitute a formal or *de facto* expropriation may nevertheless constitute a means of control of the property which falls within Article 1 of Protocol 1. An obvious illustration is where a Contracting Party subjects property to a continuing tenancy at terms set by the State.[81]

In the *Sporrong and Lönnroth* case,[82] the presence of expropriation permits had the effect of imposing a long-term planning blight on the property in question and of reducing the selling price below normal market prices, but the Court concluded that the adverse impact on the property rights was not such as to make them disappear. There was accordingly no deprivation of property in this case. The *Holy Monasteries* case has complex facts relating to the ownership of monasteries in Greece.[83] Many monasteries in Greece date their foundations to periods between the ninth and thirteenth centuries, and over the centuries they have accumulated considerable landholdings. In May 1987 a Greek law provided that the State would become the owner of the monasteries' property unless the monasteries proved their title to it in one of a number of specified ways. In some cases, the requirements would have been difficult for the monasteries to meet. In effect, there was a presumption that the property belonged to the State unless this was rebutted by the monasteries. One essential issue before the Court was whether this was a procedural device, as the respondent State argued, relating to the burden of proof of title to property, or whether it was, as the monasteries argued, a substantive provision whose effect is to transfer full ownership of the land in question to the Greek State.[84] The Court concluded that there had been a deprivation.[85]

In a series of cases against Italy,[86] taking possession of land with a view to its appropriation and starting building works on it without formal expropriation measures being taken constituted a deprivation of property which was incompatible with the applicants' Convention rights.

In the *Pressos Compania Naviera* case,[87] retrospective legislation which operated to deny the claimants an opportunity to sue in respect of claimed negligence by pilots which had led to collisions at sea was treated as a deprivation of property.

---

[80] *Sporrong and Lönnroth v Sweden*, (Apps. 7151–2/75), 23 September 1982, Series A No 52, (1983) 5 EHRR 35, §63.

[81] As in *Ghigo v Malta*, (App. 31122/05), 26 September 2006.

[82] *Sporrong and Lönnroth v Sweden*, (Apps. 7151–2/75), 23 September 1982, Series A No 52, (1983) 5 EHRR 35.

[83] *Holy Monasteries v Greece*, (Apps. 13092/87 and 13984/88), 9 December 1994, Series A No 301-A, (1995) 20 EHRR 1.

[84] §61.   [85] §66.

[86] *Carletta v Italy*, (App. 63861/00); *Colacrai v Italy* (App. 63868/00); *Donati v Italy*, (App. 63242/00); and *La Rosa and Alba v Italy (No. 6) and (No. 8)*, (Apps. 63240/00 and 63285/00), 15 July 2005.

[87] *Pressos Compania Naviera SA and others v Belgium*, (App. 17849/91), 20 November 1995, Series A No 332, (1996) 21 EHRR 301; and see discussion of this case earlier in this chapter.

DESTRUCTION

Destruction of property plainly constitutes a deprivation of property.[88] A whole series of cases against Turkey related to the destruction of property in the course of clashes between the security forces and PKK sympathizers. A friendly settlement was reached on 22 March 2001 in 201 applications.[89]

The *Ayubov* case[90] concerned the alleged destruction of the applicant's house, its contents, and two cars which had been set on fire by armed men in camouflage uniforms who had arrived in military trucks. The Court concluded that they were agents of the State. The destruction of the applicant's property was a clear violation of Article 1 of Protocol 1.

EXPROPRIATIONS

As already noted, no formal expropriation is required for a deprivation of property to arise. But the distinction between deprivation and interference will be subtle. For a de facto deprivation through expropriation to arise, there must effectively be an extinction of property rights. That did not arise in the *Sporrong and Lönnroth* case discussed above.[91] A similar conclusion was reached where rent control legislation limited the rental income of the owners of the property in question.[92]

The *Papamichalopoulos* case[93] is a good example of a de facto deprivation. The Greek Government had transferred land to the Greek Navy. Court proceedings had resulted in decisions that the land was not for disposal, but the Navy nevertheless established a naval base and holiday resort for officers on the land. The whole area was designated as a 'naval fortress'. The Court considered that the applicants remained the lawful owners of the land, but that there had been a de facto expropriation. Despite attempts to make amends after the restoration of democracy in Greece, no substitute land had been allocated to the applicants and this continued the violation of the right to peaceful enjoyment of their land.

Similarly in the *Hentrich* case,[94] a French law which permitted the revenue authorities to buy property which had been sold at below market value in order to discourage the practice was a de facto expropriation.

---

[88] See also *Handyside v United Kingdom*, (App. 5493/72), 7 December 1976, Series A No 24, (1979–80) 1 EHRR 737, §§62–3 (destruction of a book); *Akdivar v Turkey*, (App. 21893/93), 16 September 1996, (1997) 23 EHRR 143, ECHR 1996-IV, §88 (destruction of a home); and *Isayeva, Yusupova and Bazayeva v Russia*, (Apps. 57947/00, 57948/00 and 57949/00), 24 February 2005, (2005) 41 EHRR 847, §§230–4 (destruction of cars and personal possessions in an air strike on a civilian convoy Grozny).

[89] Court of Human Rights, Information Note No. 28, March 2001, at 33.

[90] *Ayubov v Russia*, (App. 7654/02), 12 February 2009.

[91] *Sporrong and Lönnroth v Sweden*, (Apps. 7151–2/75), 23 September 1982, Series A No 52, (1983) 5 EHRR 35.

[92] *Mellacher v Austria*, (Apps. 10522/83, 11011/84, and 11070/84), 19 December 1989, Series A No 169, (1990) 12 EHRR 391, §44.

[93] *Papamichalopoulos and others v Greece*, (App. 14556/89), 24 June 1993, Series A No 260-B, (1993) 16 EHRR 440.

[94] *Hentrich v France*, (App. 13616/88), 22 September 1994, Series A No 296-A, (1994) 18 EHRR 440.

TEMPORARY OR PROVISIONAL DEPRIVATION

The *Handyside* case[95] establishes that temporary seizures do not constitute deprivations of property, though they may well constitute controls on the use of the property seized. In this case the material seized was a book which was considered to be obscene. Other examples of temporary seizures are provisional property confiscations in criminal proceedings;[96] provisional transfers of land as part of agricultural land consolidation proceedings;[97] and the seizure of an aircraft in which a consignment of cannabis had been found with a view to its forfeiture.[98]

CONDITIONS FOR PERMITTED DEPRIVATIONS

A deprivation falling within the first paragraph of Article 1 of Protocol 1 must meet three conditions to be justifiable under the provision:

- the measure providing for the deprivation must be in accordance with the conditions provided for by national law;
- the general principles of international law must be respected;
- the deprivation must be in the public interest, and this will require a balancing of the public interest against individual rights.

The requirement that the measure must be in accordance with the conditions provided for by national law raises issues similar to those raised in relation to Articles 8 to 11.[99] This does not merely involve the identification of a national law authorizing the taking, but also involves some consideration of the quality of that law, so that there is protection against arbitrary action.[100] The law must accordingly be sufficiently precise and foreseeable in its consequences, and the deprivation must be surrounded by appropriate procedural guarantees. So in the *Hentrich* case,[101] which concerned the State's power to buy property sold at an undervalue, the absence of adversarial proceedings to challenge the State's right of pre-emption constituted a violation of Article 1 of Protocol 1.[102]

---

[95] *Handyside v United Kingdom*, (App. 5493/72), 7 December 1976, Series A No 24, (1979–80) 1 EHRR 737, §62.

[96] *Raimondo v Italy*, (App. 12954/87), 22 February 1994, Series A No 281-A, (1994) 18 EHRR 237, §§29–30. See also *Jucys v Lithuania*, (App. 5457/03), 8 January 2008.

[97] *Erkner and Hofauer v Austria*, (App. 9616/81), 23 April 1987, Series A No 117, (1987) 9 EHRR 464, §74, and *Wiesinger v Austria*, (App. 11796/85), 24 September 1991, Series A No 213, (1993) 18 EHRR 258, §72.

[98] *Air Canada v United Kingdom*, (App. 18465/91), 5 May 1995, Series A No 316, (1995) 20 EHRR 150, §§28–33. See also *Islamic Republic of Iran Shipping Lines v Turkey*, (App. 40998/98), 13 December 2007, (2008) 47 EHRR 573, ECHR 2007-nyr.

[99] See in general ch.14 above.

[100] *James v United Kingdom*, (App. 8793/85), 21 February 1986, Series A No 98, (1986) 8 EHRR 123, §67.

[101] *Hentrich v France*, (App. 13616/88), 22 September 1994, Series A No 296-A, (1994) 18 EHRR 440.

[102] §42.

Of course, any taking which is in breach of national law will amount to a violation of Article 1 of Protocol 1.[103] However, it may be the way in which national law is applied that places an 'individual and excessive burden' on a person. This can be illustrated by the *Allard* case.[104] Certain property in Sweden was jointly owned by members of a family. Without the permission of the co-owners, a house was built on the land. When the dispute came before a national court, it resulted in a judicial decision that the house was to be removed. It was subsequently demolished. The applicant claimed that this constituted a deprivation of her property in breach of Article 1 of Protocol 1. The Strasbourg Court reiterated that a deprivation of property could be in the public interest even if the community at large gained no direct benefit from the deprivation. Maintaining a functioning system of co-ownership was considered to further the public interest.[105] But the manner of application of the law in this case went beyond what was necessary to secure that interest.

Deprivations of property must also evince respect for the general principles of international law, which require that non-nationals are protected against arbitrary expropriations and, in the case of lawful expropriations, are entitled to compensation for the loss of their property. The rule provides no protection for nationals of a State deprived of property by that State.[106] Once the Court had adopted this position, this requirement has proved to have little application in cases involving Article 1 of Protocol 1.

The public interest test will be at the heart of many cases arising under Article 1 of Protocol 1 as it is under many other claims of violations of Convention rights. In property cases, there is almost a presumption that a national measure is in the public interest. In the *James* case,[107] which concerned United Kingdom leasehold enfranchisement legislation, the Court said:

The Court, finding it natural that the margin of appreciation available to the legislature in implementing social and economic policies should be a wide one, will respect the legislature's judgment as to what is 'in the public interest' unless that judgment be manifestly without reasonable foundation. In other words, although the Court cannot substitute its own assessment for that of the national authorities, it is bound to review the contested measures under Article 1 of Protocol 1 and, in doing so, to make an enquiry into the facts with reference to which the national authorities acted.

In this case, the Court concluded that the United Kingdom system of leasehold enfranchisement under the Leasehold Reform Act 1967 was compatible with Article 1 of Protocol 1. Indeed, it is difficult to find a case in which the Court has not recognized

---

[103] As in *Iatridis v Greece*, (App. 31107/96), 25 March 1999 [GC], (2000) 30 EHRR 97, ECHR 1999-II; and *Minasyan and Semerjyan v Armenia*, (App. 27651/05), 23 June 2009.

[104] *Allard v Sweden*, (App. 35179/97), 24 June 2003, (2004) 39 EHRR 321, ECHR 2003-VII.

[105] §52.

[106] Affirmed in *James v United Kingdom*, (App. 8793/85), 21 February 1986, Series A No 98, (1986) 8 EHRR 123, §§61-3; and in *Lithgow v United Kingdom*, (Apps. 9006/80, 9262/81, 9263/81, 9265/81, 9266/81, 9313/81, and 9405/81), 8 July 1986, Series A No 102, (1986) 8 EHRR 329, §§111-19.

[107] *James v United Kingdom*, (App. 8793/85), 21 February 1986, Series A No 98, (1986) 8 EHRR 123, §46.

the policy preferences of a State as providing a legitimate goal. But the Court has gone further than merely requiring the identification of a legitimate goal in determining whether a deprivation of property is in the public interest. The test of proportionality is also brought into play. A fair balance must be struck between the demands of the general interest of the community, and the individual's property rights. The latter cannot be expected to bear an individual and excessive burden in the particular circumstances of each case.[108]

The offering of compensation has come to play a crucial part of the consideration of proportionality, and is discussed below.

THE ISSUE OF COMPENSATION

Where there has been a deprivation of property, there is an expectation that compensation will be paid if the taking is to constitute a fair balance between the individual interest and the general interest,[109] and not to impose an excessive burden on the individual. A total lack of compensation will be justifiable only in exceptional circumstances.[110] In the *Holy Monasteries* case,[111] the Court restated the position established in its case-law:

Compensation terms under the relevant legislation are material to the assessment whether the contested measure respects the requisite fair balance and, notably, whether it does not impose a disproportionate burden on the applicants. In this connection, the taking of property without payment of an amount reasonably related to its value will normally constitute a disproportionate interference and a total lack of compensation can be considered justifiable under Article 1 only in exceptional circumstances. Article 1 does not, however, guarantee a right to full compensation in all circumstances, since legitimate objectives of 'public interest' may call for less than reimbursement of the full market value.[112]

The existence of safeguards by which the reasonableness of the compensation can be checked can be important in showing that the burden on the individual is not excessive. The Strasbourg Court has indicated that legitimate objectives in the public interest may result in less than full compensation; and the protection of the historical and cultural heritage has been accepted as one such objective. But the scheme for determining compensation must be even-handed between the State and the individual. A violation was found in a case where depreciation in value arising from the listing

---

[108] §50.

[109] See, for example, *NA v Turkey*, (App. 37451/97), 11 October 2005, (2007) 45 EHRR 287, ECHR 2005-X.

[110] As in *Jahn and others v Germany*, (Apps. 46720/99, 72203/01, and 72552/01), 30 June 2005 [GC], (2006) 42 EHRR 1084, ECHR 2005-VI; see below in this chapter. See also F. McCarthy, 'Deprivation without Compensation: the Exceptional Circumstance of *Jahn v Germany* [2007] EHRLR 295.

[111] *Holy Monasteries v Greece*, (Apps. 13092/87 and 13984/88), 9 December 1994, Series A No 301-A, (1995) 20 EHRR 1.

[112] §71.

property as having historical and cultural value could be taken into account but not an increase in its value arising from such classification.[113]

In a group of cases against Greece[114] an irrefutable presumption of benefit as a result of the compulsory purchase of property needed to build a new road which reduced the compensation payable was considered to place a disproportionate burden on the property owners. They were unable to argue that the work was of less, or even no, benefit to them.[115] Consideration of individual circumstances will not, however, always be a required feature of the calculation of compensation. In the *Lithgow* case,[116] the Court accepted that major nationalization programmes may require a standardized rather than an individual approach to the calculation of compensation, and, subject to the securing of a fair balance, a wide margin of appreciation will be allowed in the method for determining the calculation of the compensation payable. However, individual expropriations will require the Contracting Party to establish all the relevant factors for compensation, and must take into account the impact of the expropriation on the value of any remaining land.[117]

These principles apply just as much to situations where there is a transition from a planned economy to a market-oriented economy following the fall of communist regimes. So, in a case against Slovakia,[118] the compulsory leasing of allotments owned by an association of landowners at a very low rent, and their subsequent transfer to the tenants with compensation paid well below the market value of the land constituted a violation of Article 1 of Protocol 1. In relation to the calculation of compensation, the Strasbourg Court observed that there was a 'sliding scale' which balanced the scope and degree of importance of the public interest against the nature and amount of compensation provided to the owners.[119]

Long delays in the payment of compensation, particularly where there is high inflation or an inadequate payment of interest on the late payment, will also impose an excessive burden on the individual. In a line of cases against Turkey, violations were found where the land valuation was at a price obtaining at the date of the taking and where inflation was running at 70 per cent, but this had not been taken into account in the payments eventually made.[120]

---

[113] *Kozacioğlu v Turkey*, (App. 2334/03), 19 February 2009 [GC], ECHR 2009-nyr.

[114] *Katikaridis and others v Greece*, (App. 19385/92), 15 November 1996, (2001) 32 EHRR 113, ECHR 1996-V; *Tsomtsos and others v Greece*, (App. 20680/92), 15 November 1996, ECHR 1996-V; and *Papachelas v Greece* (App. 31423/96), 25 March 1999, (2000) 30 EHRR 923, ECHR 1999-II.

[115] *Papachelas v Greece*, (App. 31423/96), 25 March 1999 [GC], (2000) 30 EHRR 923, ECHR 1999-II, §54.

[116] *Lithgow and others v United Kingdom*, (Apps. 9006/80, 9262/81, 9263/81, 9265/81, 9266/81, 9313/81, and 9405/81),8 July 1986, Series A No 102, (1986) 8 EHRR 329, §§121–2.

[117] *Bistrovic v Croatia*, (App. 25774/05), 31 May 2007. The overall principles are recapitulated in *Scordino v Italy (No. 1)*, (App. 36813/97), 29 March 2006 [GC], (2007) 45 EHRR 207, ECHR 2006-V, §§93–8.

[118] *Urbárska Obec Trenčianske Biskupice v Slovakia*, (App. 74258/01), 27 November 2007, (2009) 48 EHRR 1139, ECHR 2007-XIII.

[119] §126.

[120] *Akkuş v Turkey*, (App. 19263/92), 9 July 1997, (2000) 30 EHRR 365; literally dozens of other cases have been taken on this ground against a number of countries.

RESTITUTION CASES

A line of case-law[121] has developed in recent years dealing with issues flowing from the reunification of Germany, and with restitution claims in the countries of central and eastern Europe. This justifies separate treatment of this class of case, which present challenges to the Court by reason not only of the volume of cases, but also of the complex legal issues which are raised.

Certain principles emerge from the Court's case-law in cases of this kind. First, the Court will only be competent to examine applications to the extent that they relate to events occurring after the entry into force of the Convention for the respondent Contracting Party. Expropriations or confiscations which occurred before this date are outside the competence of the Court. Nor does a completed taking before the entry into force of the Convention for the respondent State give rise to any continuing situation of deprivation of a property right.[122] Secondly, where there is a procedure in national law for seeking recovery, those proceedings will be taken into account in determining whether there has been an interference with the applicant's property rights. But applicants must show that they have a property right which is being pursued in the national proceedings.[123] The mere hope of recognition of a former property right is not enough.[124] Furthermore, where the procedure for recovery of property is conditional, failure to fulfil that condition will extinguish any claimed property right. So in the *Malhous* case,[125] it was fatal to the applicant's claim that restitution proceedings in the Czech Republic were not available where the property had been transferred to other individuals who could establish that they had acquired a legal title to the property. That was precisely the situation in relation to the property he was seeking to recover. Furthermore the Court will be reluctant to go behind conclusions of the national courts that a condition has not been met.[126] The Strasbourg Court will not find violations where there have been irregularities or abuse of national regulations for which the applicants were responsible.[127]

---

[121] The issues raised in restitution cases are not wholly new, since the Court has already had to consider some of the consequences of the Turkish intervention in Cyprus in terms of restitution of property: see *Loizidou v Turkey*, (App. 15318/89), 18 December 1996, (1996) 23 EHRR 513, ECHR 1996-VI; for a discussion see R. White, 'Tackling political disputes through individual applications' [1998] EHRLR 61. See also *Xenides-Arestis v Turkey*, (App. 46347/99), 22 December 2005.

[122] *Malhous v Czech Republic*, (App. 33071/96), Decision of 13 December 2000 [GC], ECHR 2000-XII; and *Prince Hans-Adam II of Liechtenstein v Germany*, (App. 42527/98), 12 July 2001 [GC], ECHR 2001-VI. See also *von Maltzan, von Zitzewitz, Man Ferrostaal and Töpfer Stiftung v Germany*, (Apps. 71916/01, 71917/01 and 10260/02), Decision of 2 March 2005 [GC], ECHR 2005-V.

[123] *Malhous v Czech Republic*, (App. 33071/96), Decision of 13 December 2000 [GC], ECHR 2000-XII.

[124] *Gratzinger and Gratzingerova v Czech Republic*, (App. 39794/98), Decision of 10 July 2002 [GC], ECHR 2002-VII, §73.

[125] *Malhous v Czech Republic*, (App. 33071/96), Decision of 13 December 2000 [GC], ECHR 2000-XII.

[126] *Jantner v Slovakia*, (App. 39050/97), 4 March 2003, where the issue was whether the applicant had, in fact, established a genuine permanent residence in Slovakia which was a condition of being able to obtain restitution.

[127] See *Velikovi and others v Bulgaria*, (Apps. 43278/98, 45437/99, 48014/99, 48380/99, 51362/99, 53367/99, 60036/00, 73465/01, and 194/02), 15 March 2007, (2009) 48 EHRR 640.

The *Wittek* case[128] concerned an attempt by the applicants to recover title to their house in Leipzig, which they had given up as a condition of being permitted to leave the former German Democratic Republic. Their attempts to recover the property under national law failed, since it was well established that an agreement for sale could not be challenged in the civil courts if the dispute was over the restitution of property in the German Democratic Republic.[129] There had been, in the opinion of the Strasbourg Court, a thorough review of all the circumstances of the case by the national courts, and it could not be said that the applicants had suffered a disproportionate burden. There was no violation of Article 1 of Protocol 1.

The *Zvolský and Zvolská* case[130] concerned claims made by applicants who had been required to transfer property to a former owner. The applicants had, in 1967, acquired a farmhouse on a sale for value and adjoining agricultural land which the vendor had transferred to them without consideration.[131] At the time, release from an obligation to work for the socialist cooperative could only be achieved by transferring the land being worked; this was said to have been the vendor's motivation for the transfer. The applicants as the new owners were obliged as a condition of the purchase to give an undertaking to work for the cooperative as a replacement for the vendor. In 1991 the vendor signed a declaration that he had transferred the property of his own free will, but in 1993 nevertheless sought to recover the agricultural land, and obtained an order for its return to him. The applicants claimed that the Czech Republic had interfered with their property rights in breach of Article 1 of Protocol 1. The Court concluded that there was a basis in law for the restitution order and that it was in the public interest in that its purpose was to redress infringements of property rights which had occurred under the communist regime. The key question was whether a fair balance had been struck between the individual and community interest. As has already been noted, the absence of any compensation for a taking will require special justification. The Czech legislation had elected to deal with this issue without any ability to re-examine the circumstances surrounding individual transfers which had taken place. Cases such as this required some possibility for considering the competing claims of the former owner and the current owner in order to determine whether the transfer had genuinely infringed the former owner's property rights such that they should be given priority over the property rights of the current owner. There was a violation of the applicants' Convention rights.

The *Broniowski* case[132] concerned the long-term consequences of the re-drawing of the eastern border of Poland after the Second World War, which had resulted in the movement of large numbers of Polish citizens. Those who lost land were entitled to buy land from the State and to have the value of the abandoned land taken into account

---

[128] *Wittek v Germany*, (App. 37290/97), 12 December 2002, (2005) 41 EHRR 1060, ECHR 2002-X.

[129] §48.

[130] *Zvolský and Zvolská v Czech Republic*, (App. 46129/99), 12 November 2002, ECHR 2002-IX.

[131] Though it was argued that the applicants had paid a sum on top of the sale price of the farmhouse as compensation for his loss of the agricultural land.

[132] *Broniowski v Poland*, (App. 31443/96), 22 June 2004, (2005) 40 EHRR 495, ECHR 2004-V; 28 September 2005 [GC] (friendly settlement), ECHR 2005-IX.

in the purchase price. However, the pool of land available to satisfy these claims was restricted by the exclusion of State agricultural and military property. This exclusion was subsequently held to be unconstitutional. Poland then sought to close off all such claims by deeming those who had received some compensation to be fully compensated, and to award 15 per cent of their entitlement to those who had received no compensation. The applicant was in this group and received only 2 per cent of the value of the property abandoned by his grandmother. No issue over the temporal application of the Convention arose, since the applicant clearly had an entitlement to compensation which was continuing, and which had been foreclosed by the Polish legislation in 2004. The Court decided this case as an interference with the applicant's peaceful enjoyment of possessions rather than as a deprivation of property. The Court accepted that a wide margin of appreciation was available to the State in circumstances such as this. In enunciating the general principles applicable in this case, the Grand Chamber said:

...the notion of 'public interest' is necessarily extensive. In particular, the decision to enact laws expropriating property or affording publicly funded compensation for expropriated property will commonly involve considerations of political, economic and social issues. The Court has declared that, finding it natural that the margin of appreciation available to the legislature in implementing social and economic policies should be a wide one, it will respect the legislature's judgments as to what is 'in the public interest' unless that judgment is manifestly without reasonable foundation. This logic applies to such fundamental changes of a country's system as the transition from a totalitarian regime to a democratic form of government and the reform of the State's political, legal and economic structure, phenomena which inevitably involve the enactment of large-scale economic and social legislation.[133]

The Court accepted that, in complex political and economic circumstances such as those prevailing in Poland, entitlement to compensation may be severely restricted, but also indicated that the more stringent the restrictions the more compelling must be the reasons for the adoption of a particular scheme. In this case, the applicant's right to compensation had been rendered illusory, and then extinguished, by State conduct which could not be justified.

The Court went on to note that it had a further 167 applications relating to the same set of circumstances, and it was known that the scheme in issue affected nearly 80,000 people. The volume of potential cases was said to represent a 'threat to the future effectiveness of the Convention machinery'.[134] There was a systemic failure of the national legal order, which must be remedied as a consequence of the Court's judgment in this case.[135]

The *Hutten-Czapska* case[136] also concerned a situation which potentially affected very many people: around 100,000 landlords and between 600,000 and 900,000

---

[133] §149.   [134] §193.

[135] The just satisfaction phase of the case was concluded with a judgment of 28 September 2005, ECHR 2005-IX.

[136] *Hutten-Czapska v Poland*, (App. 35014/97), 19 June 2006 [GC], (2007) 45 EHRR 52, ECHR 2006-VIII; see also 28 April 2008 (friendly settlement), ECHR 2008-nyr.

tenants, and resulted in a pilot judgment. It concerned the imposition of tenancy agreements at very low levels of rent on property owners, which had occurred after the Second World War and had been maintained thereafter in one form or another. The applicant complained that the imposition of the tenancy agreements and the system of rent control deprived her of the opportunity to derive an income from the property, to cover the costs of the landlord's obligations, or to regain possession of her property (though she could sell it subject to any tenancy). The Strasbourg Court examined the claim as one involving the imposition of controls on the use of the property.[137] The Court considered that the measures had a proper legal base, and had a legitimate aim in the general interest. The Court then examined in considerable detail the issue of whether a fair balance had been struck. In concluding that there was a violation of the applicant's Convention rights, the Court was clearly influenced by a decision of the Polish Constitutional Court some five years earlier which had concluded that the rent control scheme had resulted in a disproportionate, unjustified, and arbitrary distribution of the social burden involved in housing reform, which had been effected mainly at the expense of landlords.

The *Jahn* case[138] concerned land in the former German Democratic Republic. In September 1945, owners of more than 100 hectares of land in the Soviet Occupied Zone of Germany had their property expropriated. This land was then distributed in plots averaging eight hectares to farmers who had little or no land of their own. Certain portions of the land had to be used for food production. The applicants were the heirs of such farmers. Following the fall of the Berlin Wall in November 1989, the negotiations on the reunification of Germany included the enactment of a law which permitted those to whom land had been distributed to acquire full title to it and to be able to dispose of it. This law became part of the law of the Federal Republic. The applicants' claims arose out of amendments to this law which required them to assign the property they had inherited to the German tax authorities without compensation, since they had not carried on an activity in the agricultural, forestry, or food-industry sector. This was a deprivation of property case. The Grand Chamber readily concludes that there was a legal basis for the deprivation, and that the law served the legitimate aim of correcting what the German Government viewed as unfair effects of the law that was amended. There was, accordingly, a need to consider whether a fair balance had been struck between the individual interest and the community interest. The Grand Chamber of the Court, differing from the decision of the Chamber, concluded that this was a case in which the absence of compensation was justifiable, since the application of the law which had been amended was to give the applicants a windfall gain rather than to deprive them of property they held.

The *Kopecký* case[139] concerned an attempt to recover gold and silver coins. The applicant's father had been convicted in 1959 for keeping gold and silver coins, and

---

[137] See below in this chapter.
[138] *Jahn and others v Germany*, (Apps. 46720/99, 72203/01, and 72552/01), 30 June 2005 [GC], (2006) 42 EHRR 1084, ECHR 2005-VI.
[139] *Kopecký v Slovakia*, (App. 44912/98), 28 September 2004 [GC], (2005) 41 EHRR 944, ECHR 2004-IX.

the coins had been confiscated. In 1992 the conviction and all consequential decisions had been quashed by the Supreme Court under the Judicial Rehabilitation Act 1990. The applicant then claimed restitution of the coins under a 1991 statute, which provided for restitution of the specific property taken, not any substitute property. This statute contained a condition that the person seeking restitution must show where the coins were deposited as at 1 April 1991, the date on which the 1991 Act entered into force. Though the applicant had been successful at first instance, ultimately his claim failed because he could not meet the burden of proof in showing the location of the property sought as at 1 April 1991, though he had been able to show that the coins had been deposited with the Regional Administration of the Ministry of the Interior on 12 December 1958. The Grand Chamber concluded that this was a case which turned on whether the applicant had an 'asset', that is, a proprietary interest which has a sufficient basis in national law. The Court specifically disagreed with the Chamber that such an interest could arise where there was a 'genuine dispute' or an 'arguable case'. The Grand Chamber concluded that the applicant had no interest which constituted a 'possession' within the meaning of Article 1 of Protocol 1. Four dissenting judges took a different view. Three of them considered that the test applied by the Chamber was a proper one. Furthermore, the annulment of the confiscation order itself gave rise to a legitimate expectation that the applicant would be able to recover the confiscated property. Judge Strážnická considered that it was contrary to the purpose of restitution laws, on the one hand, to declare the existence of a remedy in respect of past infringements of the law, and, on the other hand, to eliminate the legitimate interest of entitled persons by burdening them with requirements that were impossible to fulfil. Other cases which had failed because a necessary condition had not been fulfilled could be distinguished from the present case; they had involved situations in which immovable property was in issue, the applicants did not meet the criteria for being treated as entitled persons, and the conditions (such as citizenship and residence) were ones with which they had a fair chance to comply.

The *Străin* case[140] was a rather more straightforward case. The applicants had been the owners of a house which was nationalized in 1950. In 1993 they brought an action seeking a declaration that the taking of the property was unlawful and an order for its restitution. Although it knew of the action for the recovery of the property (which had been converted into four apartments), the State-owned company which managed the property sold one of the apartments. The applicants sought, unsuccessfully, to have the sale declared void. They claimed that the sale in these circumstances constituted a taking of their property without compensation. The Court found a number of deficiencies: the Romanian law which had been applied did not meet the requirements established by the Court for it to constitute a proper legal base for the sale to a third party, and the Romanian Government had not put forward any legitimate aim for the

---

[140] *Străin and others v Romania*, (App. 57001/00), 21 July 2005, ECHR 2005-VII. See also *Zwierzynski v Poland*, (App. 34049/96), 19 June 2001, (2004) 38 EHRR 122, ECHR 2001-VI.

measure;[141] nor had it adduced any exceptional circumstances justifying the absence of any compensation.

An excessive delay in paying compensation awarded for the nationalization of property will also engage Article 1 of Protocol 1 since it constitutes an interference with the right to peaceful enjoyment of possession. Lack of funds was not a justification for the delay in meeting awards of compensation.[142]

CONTROLLING THE USE OF PROPERTY

SCOPE

The second paragraph of Article 1 of Protocol 1 preserves the power of the State to control the use of property whether in the general interest or 'to secure the payment of taxes or other contributions or penalties'. Many of the examples discussed earlier in this chapter on what constitutes a deprivation of property (and which fall short of deprivation) are examples of control on the use of property. So, seizure of obscene publications,[143] rent controls,[144] planning restrictions,[145] temporary seizure of property in criminal proceedings,[146] temporary seizure of an aircraft in connection with drugs enforcement legislation,[147] the withdrawal of a licence,[148] limitations on fishing rights,[149] retrospective tax legislation,[150] refusal to register applicants as certified accountants with adverse effects for their business,[151] limitation periods relating to adverse possession,[152] and the excessive length of bankruptcy proceedings during

[141] Though the Court seems to have been prepared to accept that it could have been for the protection of the rights of others, namely a purchaser in good faith.

[142] *Scutari v Moldova*, (App. 20864/03), 26 July 2005.

[143] *Handyside v United Kingdom*, (App. 5493/72), 7 December 1976, Series A No 24, (1979–80) 1 EHRR 737.

[144] *Mellacher v Austria*, (Apps. 10522/83, 11011/84, and 11070/84), 19 December 1989, Series A No 169; (1990) 12 EHRR 391.

[145] *Pine Valley Developments Limited and others v Ireland*, (App. 12742/87), 29 November 1991, Series A No 222, (1992) 14 EHRR 319.

[146] *Raimondo v Italy*, (App. 12954/87), 22 February 1994, Series A No 281-A, (1994) 18 EHRR 237; and *Vendittelli v Italy*, (App.14804/89), 18 July 1994, Series A No 293-A, (1994) 19 EHRR 464.

[147] *Air Canada v United Kingdom*, (App. 18465/91), 5 May 1995, Series A No 316, (1995) 20 EHRR 150.

[148] *Tre Traktörer Aktiebolag v Sweden*, (App. 10873/84), 7 July 1989, Series A No 159, (1991) 13 EHRR 309; and App.12033/86), *Fredin v Sweden (No.1)*, 18 February 1991, Series A No 192, (1991) 13 EHRR 784.

[149] *Posti and Rahko v Finland*, (App. 27824/95), 24 September 2002, (2003) 37 EHRR 158, ECHR 2002-VII.

[150] *National & Provincial Building Society, the Leeds Permanent Building Society and the Yorkshire Building Society v United Kingdom*, (Apps. 21319/93, 21449/93, and 21675/93), 23 October 1997, (1998) 25 EHRR 127, ECHR 1997-VII.

[151] *Van Marle and others v Netherlands*, (Apps. 8543/79, 8674/79, 8675/79, and 8685/79), 26 June 1986, Series A No 101, (1986) 8 EHRR 483.

[152] *JA Pye (Oxford) Ltd and JA Pye (Oxford) Land Ltd v United Kingdom*, (App. 44302/02), 30 August 2007 [GC], (2008) 46 EHRR 1083, ECHR 2007-nyr.

which time the applicant's ability to deal with his property was severely restricted,[153] and rendering a television set unusable when the compulsory subscription to the public television service is cancelled,[154] all constitute measures of control on the use of property. The Strasbourg Court also regards measures of confiscation, which amount to a deprivation of property, also constitute control of the use of the property. This will involve consideration of whether a fair balance has been struck in confiscating the property between the interests of the community a respect for peaceful enjoyment of possessions.[155] The Strasbourg Court found the confiscation of a substantial sum of lawfully acquired United States dollars smuggled into Russia in breach of a requirement to declare such sums was a disproportionate penalty in the light of the imposition of a suspended prison sentence also imposed on the applicant.[156]

JUSTIFYING THE CONTROLS

As with all interferences with Convention rights, the measure which constitutes the interference must have a basis in national law, which will include European Union law. In a case concerning the impounding of an aircraft as part of the sanctions regime against Serbia and Montenegro, the Grand Chamber concluded that the underlying legal base for measures which interfere with property rights may lie in European Union law.[157]

Some of the early case-law suggested that, where a State can bring its actions within the scope of the second paragraph, there is no need for the balancing of interests to take place.[158] But later case-law has moved to a position where the fair balance test which applies to deprivations and other interferences is also applied to matters within the second paragraph of Article 1 of Protocol 1.[159]

The forfeiture and destruction of obscene materials is a justifiable measure within this second paragraph of Article 1.[160]

A similar view was taken of the forfeiture within the United Kingdom of Krügerrands.[161] In this case, the company had the misfortune to engage in business transactions in which they sold Krügerrands in exchange for a dishonoured cheque. They had the transaction declared void under German law and sought the recovery

---

[153] *Luordo v Italy*, (App. 32190/96), 17 July 2003, ECHR 2003-IX.

[154] *Faccio v Italy*, (App. 33/04), Decision of 17 April 2009.

[155] *Ismayilov v Russia*, (App. 30352/03), 6 November 2008, §30.

[156] Ibid. See also *Grifhorst v France*, (App. 28336/02), 26 February 2009; and *Moon v France*, (App. 39973/03), 9 July 2009.

[157] *'Bosphorus Airways' v Ireland*, (App. 45036/98), 30 June 2005 [GC], (2006) 42 EHRR 1, ECHR 2005-VI.

[158] *Handyside v United Kingdom*, (App. 5493/72), 7 December 1976, Series A No 24, (1979–80) 1 EHRR 737, §62.

[159] See *Pine Valley Developments Limited and others v Ireland*, (App. 12742/87), 29 November 1991, Series A No 222, (1992) 14 EHRR 319, §§57–59.

[160] See *Handyside v United Kingdom*, (App. 5493/72), 7 December 1976, Series A No 24; (1979–80) 1 EHRR 737, §63.

[161] *AGOSI v United Kingdom*, (App. 9118/80), 24 October 1986, Series A No 108, (1987) 9 EHRR 1.

of the gold coins from the British customs authorities which had seized them. The Court considered the case one in which forfeiture did constitute a deprivation of property but was essentially a consequence of their illegal importation, the prohibition of which was a constituent element in a measure for the control of their use in the United Kingdom. Therefore it was necessary to consider only whether there had been compliance with the second paragraph of Article 1.

Finally, the *Gasus* case[162] concerned the seizure by the Dutch tax authorities of property from a company the title in which remained with its seller in Germany, since a retention of title clause prevented the passing of the property until all instalments of the purchase price had been paid. Such seizure was in accordance with the provisions of Dutch tax law. The complaint of the applicant company was that they had been deprived of their property in payment of a tax debt owed by a third party, that they were in no way responsible for causing the tax debt, and that they could not have been aware of it in agreeing to accept the price of the concrete mixer and ancillary equipment by instalments. Nevertheless, the Court concluded that this was a deprivation falling within the second paragraph of Article 1 of Protocol 1.

More recent case-law has placed greater emphasis on the need to secure a fair balance between the individual interest and the general interest, though it has been acknowledged that a wide margin of appreciation will be accorded to States.[163] The modern approach can be illustrated by the *Chassagnou* case.[164] The applicants were opposed to hunting on ethical grounds. They had, nevertheless, been obliged to transfer hunting rights over their land to local hunters' associations, had been made members of the local association, and had been unable to prevent hunting on their land. The measures were treated as falling within the second paragraph of Article 1, and are categorized as 'an interference with the…enjoyment of their rights as owners of property'.[165] The Court restates its established case-law that the second paragraph must be construed in the light of the principle laid down in the first sentence of Article 1, and goes on to say that the interference must achieve a fair balance between the demands of the general interest of the community and the requirements of the protection of individuals' fundamental rights. The Court once again emphasized the wide margin of appreciation which the Contracting Parties enjoy, but tempered this with a restatement of the requirement of proportionality.[166] A violation of Article 1 of Protocol 1 was found in the case since the measures lacked proportionality.

---

[162] *Gasus Dosier- und Fördertechnik GmbH v Netherlands*, (App. 15375/89), 23 February 1995, Series A No 306-B, (1995) 20 EHRR 403.

[163] *National & Provincial Building Society, the Leeds Permanent Building Society and the Yorkshire Building Society v United Kingdom*, (Apps. 21319/93, 21449/93, and 21675/93), 23 October 1997, (1998) 25 EHRR 127, ECHR 1997-VII, §80; and *Mellacher v Austria*, (Apps. 10522/83, 11011/84, and 11070/84), 19 December 1989, Series A No 169; (1990) 12 EHRR 391, §53.

[164] *Chassagnou and others v France*, (Apps. 25088/94, 28331/95, and 28443/95), 29 April 1999 [GC], (2000) 29 EHRR 615, ECHR 1999-III.

[165] §74.   [166] §75.

The *Spadea and Scalabrino* case[167] concerned the Italian system of postponing, suspending, or staggering the enforcement of eviction orders in order to avoid an upsurge in tenants having to find alternative homes because of the large number of leases which expired in 1982 and 1983. The Court concluded that the system operated as a control on the use of the property by the freeholders, but accepted that the legislation authorizing the delays in the enforcement of the eviction orders served the social purposes of protecting tenants on low incomes and of avoiding a risk of public disorder. A fair balance had been struck between the interests of the individual and the collective interest. But where the delays imposed an excessive burden amounting to some eleven years when the freeholders were kept out of their property, and where there was no possibility of getting compensation for the losses arising from their inability to gain possession of their property, that balance was not met and a breach of Article 1 of Protocol 1 was found.[168]

In summary, three conditions need to be satisfied for a control on the use of property to be permissible under Article 1:

- the measure must have the character of law;
- the measure must be in the general interest, or be for the purpose of securing the payment of taxes or other contributions or penalties; and
- the measure must be deemed necessary by the State.

This modern approach has blurred somewhat the distinction between those measures constituting control of the use of property and those measures which are in the residual category of other interferences with peaceful enjoyment of possessions. It is also very close to the test for the permissibility of deprivation of property. Thus a unity of approach has developed in relation to all interferences with property rights.

OTHER INTERFERENCES WITH PEACEFUL ENJOYMENT OF POSSESSIONS

There remain cases which fall for consideration under a residual category of other interferences with peaceful enjoyment of possession. Although this right is guaranteed in the first sentence of the article, the practice of the Court is to consider first whether there has been a deprivation, and then whether there has been a control on the use of property before considering whether there has been some other interference with the peaceful enjoyment of possessions. As indicated above, the Court has come

---

[167] *Spadea and Scalabrino v Italy*, (App. 12868/87), 28 September 1995, Series A No 315-B, (1996) 21 EHRR 481.

[168] *Immobiliare Saffi v Italy*, (App. 22774/93), 28 July 1999 [GC], ECHR 1999-V. See also *Lunari v Italy*, (App. 21463/93), 11 January 2001; *PM v Italy* (App. 24650/94), 11 January 2001; and *Tanganelli v Italy*, (App. 23424/94), 11 January 2001.

to adopt a broad approach to the concept of the control of the use of property, leaving comparatively few cases to be considered under this head. The earlier case-law in which certain measures were considered to fall within this head would now almost certainly be considered as measures of control of the use of property. This is because the earlier case-law on the second paragraph of Article 1 did not require the State to show that the measure of control struck a fair balance between the individual and the collective interest.

For example, the system of expropriation permits in issue in the *Sporrong and Lönnroth* case[169] was considered to be an interference with the peaceful enjoyment of possessions, whereas now it would probably be regarded as a measure for the control of the use of property. A similar view would probably now be taken of land use plans,[170] though perhaps land consolidation plans might still be regarded as interferences with peaceful possessions rather than measures for the control of their use.[171] In a case against Greece,[172] the applicants bought a plot of land and proposed to develop it by building a shopping centre, but the local authority decided to block the development though it did not have the funds to expropriate the land. A freeze on new building licences followed. Eventually the land was expropriated. The Court did not consider the early stages to constitute a deprivation of the property, since the owners' rights remained unaffected, nor was it a control of the use of property since the measures did not pursue such an aim. What was in issue was an interference with the peaceful use of possessions. There was no reasonable balance in this case between the rights of the owners and the environmental concerns of the local authority. Consequently, there was a violation of Article 1 of Protocol 1.

In a case where pension payments were made late in circumstances where their value had reduced significantly by the time of actual payment as a result of inflation and the devaluation of the Russian rouble, the Court found that there had been a violation of the right to peaceful enjoyment of possessions. An individual and excessive burden had fallen on the applicants.[173]

In determining whether an interference with the peaceful enjoyment of possessions is permissible, the Court now applies the same test as it has developed in relation to cases involving a deprivation of property, though this is articulated in somewhat different terms. In the *Broniowski* case, the Grand Chamber articulated the test in the following terms:

---

[169] *Sporrong and Lönnroth v Sweden*, (Apps. 7151–2/75), 23 September 1982, Series A No 52, (1983) 5 EHRR 35.

[170] *Katte Klitsche de la Grange v Italy*, (App. 12539/86), 27 October 1994, Series A No 293-B, (1994) 19 EHRR 368.

[171] See *Erkner and Hofauer v Austria*, (App. 9616/81), 23 April 1987, Series A No 117, (1987) 9 EHRR 464; and *Wiesinger v Austria*, (App. 11796/85), 24 September 1991, Series A No 213, (1993) 18 EHRR 258.

[172] *Pialopoulos and others v Greece*, (App. 37095/97), 15 February 2001, (2001) 33 EHRR 977.

[173] *Solodyuk v Russia*, (App. 67099/01), 12 July 2005.

Both an interference with the peaceful enjoyment of possessions and an abstention from action must strike a fair balance between the demands of the general interest of the community and the requirement of the protection of the individual's fundamental rights.

The concern to achieve this balance is reflected in the structure of Article 1 of Protocol 1 as a whole. In particular, there must be a reasonable relationship of proportionality between the means employed and the aim sought to be realised by any measures applied by the State, including measures depriving a person of his or her possessions. In each case involving the alleged violation of that Article the Court must, therefore, ascertain whether by reason of the State's action or inaction the person concerned had to bear a disproportionate and excessive burden.[174]

CONCLUDING REMARKS

The early case-law suggested a need to define with some precision the nature of the interference with property rights, because there were differences in the standards demanded of Contracting Parties, but the more modern case-law takes a very similar approach to all forms of interferences with property rights. Though the conditions for a lawful interference with the rights protected by Article 1 of Protocol 1 are perhaps not as stringent as those arising in relation to the rights protected by Articles 8 to 11, the Strasbourg Court has been influenced by the approach adopted there, and has required any measures of interference to meet a legitimate aim and to be proportionate in that it strikes a fair balance between the individual interest and the collective interest, and does not impose a disproportionate and excessive burden on the individual.

The rights protected in Article 1 of Protocol 1 have developed organically into something which is close to a general protection of property rights for both individuals and business enterprises. Contracting Parties are required to justify acts or omissions which interfere with freedom of property in terms of a fair balance between an individual interest and a collective interest, though establishing a legitimate and proportionate justification for the measures in issue has not proved to be particularly difficult for Contracting Parties. The Grand Chamber has been particularly active in this area and in developing the principles to be applied in a wide variety of situations, including major programmes in the countries of central and eastern Europe to provide redress for infringements of property rights which arose in earlier times. However, just like Article 8, the development of the rights protected by Article 1 of Protocol 1 is almost certainly not yet complete.

---

[174] *Broniowski v Poland*, (App. 31443/96), 22 June 2004 [GC], (2005) 40 EHRR 495, ECHR 2004-V, §150.

21

THE RIGHT TO EDUCATION

INTRODUCTION

Article 2 of the Protocol 1 provides:

No person shall be denied the right to education. In the exercise of any functions which it assumes in relation to education and teaching, the State shall respect the right of parents to ensure such education and teaching in conformity with their own religious and philosophical convictions.

As with the right to property, the inclusion of a right to education among the Convention rights proved to be controversial and complicated.[1] Even when agreement could be reached on the inclusion of the right in Article 2 of Protocol 1, a large number of reservations were entered in respect of it.[2]

All the provisions of the Convention, including Articles 13 to 18, apply equally to the rights guaranteed by the First Protocol.[3] These rights are also subject in the same way to the control of the organs set up by the Convention.

Article 2 of Protocol 1 has resulted in comparatively few decisions of the Strasbourg Court, despite being invoked in applications under the Convention with some regularity. A number of general propositions can be made by way of introduction to the right enshrined in this article. Though drafted as a negative formulation, it has been accepted that there is a right to education within existing provision, which applies to primary, secondary, and further or higher education. The concept of education is considered broadly. Most of the rights are enjoyed by the pupil or student, but parents have a separate right to respect for their own religious and philosophical convictions in the education of their children.

---

[1] A.H. Robertson, 'The European Convention on Human Rights—Recent Developments' (1951) BYBIL 359; and L. Wildhaber, 'Right to Education and Parental Rights' in R. Macdonald, F. Matscher, and H. Petzold (eds.), *The European System for the Protection of Human Rights* (Martinus Nijhoff, Dordrecht 1993), 531.

[2] Including a reservation by the United Kingdom. Even in 2009 there are reservations to Article 2 of Protocol 1 by Andorra, Azerbaijan, Bulgaria, Georgia, Germany, Ireland, Malta, Moldova, The Netherlands, Romania, the former Yugoslav Republic of Macedonia, Turkey, and the United Kingdom. See http://conventions.coe.int for a current list of reservations of Council of Europe instruments.

[3] Art. 5 of Protocol 1.

The main focus of the case-law has been on primary education, but it is now clear that the rights also relate to secondary and higher education,[4] and probably also professional education.[5] The Strasbourg Court has recognized that the right to education has links with the rights protected by Articles 8 to 10 of the Convention and needs to be interpreted consistently with the general spirit of the Convention as an instrument designed to maintain and promote the ideals and values of a democratic society.[6]

Positive obligations are inherent in the obligations provided for in Article 2. This was recognized, in part, in the *Valsamis* case,[7] where the Strasbourg Court said that the obligation in the second sentence of the article implies 'some positive obligations on the part of the State'. So, it would seem that Contracting Parties must strive to accommodate parental wishes flowing from religious or philosophical convictions. Whether that would extend to the funding, or even partial funding, of private schools where this is the only way in which respect for particular convictions could be secured is, as yet, an unanswered question. In a number of cases, the reservation filed in respect of the article would, if found to be legitimate, protect the State.[8]

Where there is differential treatment in the provision of education, the anti-discrimination provision in Article 14 frequently comes into play.[9]

THE RIGHT TO EDUCATION

The first and leading case on the right to education was the *Belgian Linguistic* case.[10] Six groups of applicants claimed that various aspects of the Belgian legislation governing the use of languages in schools were inconsistent with the Convention. The applicants, who were French-speaking residents in the Dutch-speaking part of Belgium and in the Brussels periphery, wanted their children to be educated in French. The Strasbourg Court decided that Article 2 did not include a right to be taught in the language of parents' choice, nor a right of access to a particular school of the parents' choice. Ultimately, the Court found that the Belgian legislation failed to comply

---

[4] *Leyla Şahin v Turkey*, (App. 44774/98), 10 November 2005 [GC], (2007) 44 EHRR 99, ECHR 2005-IX, §141; *Mürsel Eren v Turkey*, (App. 60856/00), 7 February 2006, (2007) 44 EHRR 619, ECHR 2006-II, §41; and *Irfan Temel and others v Turkey*, (App. 36458/02), 3 March 2009, §39.

[5] *Kök v Turkey*, (App. 1855/02), 19 October 2006.

[6] *Kjeldsen, Busk Madsen and Pedersen v Denmark*, (Apps. 5095/71, 5920/72, and 5926/72), 7 December 1976, Series A No 23, (1979–80) 1 EHRR 711, §54. See also *Valsamis v Greece*, (App. 21787/93), 18 December 1996, (1997) 24 EHRR 314, ECHR 1996-VI, §25.

[7] *Valsamis v Greece* (App. 21787/93), 18 December 1996, (1997) 24 EHRR 294, ECHR 1996-VI, §27.

[8] Where the reservation indicates that the provision of education was subject to national resource constraints.

[9] See ch.24 below.

[10] *Case relating to certain aspects of the laws on the use of languages in education in Belgium (Belgian Linguistic Case (No. 2)*, (Apps. 1474/62, 1677/62, 1691/62, 1769/63, 1994/63, and 2126/64), 23 July 1968, Series A No 6, (1979–80), 23 July 1968, Series A No 6, (1979–80) 1 EHRR 252 (cited in this chapter as the *'Belgian Linguistic* case').

with the provisions of the Convention and Protocol in only one respect. It infringed Article 14 of the Convention,[11] read in conjunction with the first sentence of Article 2 of the First Protocol, in so far as it prevented certain children, solely on the basis of the residence of their parents, from having access to the French-language schools in certain communes on the periphery of Brussels. The law provided that the language of instruction in these communes was Dutch, but that French-speaking classes should be provided at the nursery and primary levels, on condition that it was asked for by sixteen heads of family. However, this education was not available to children whose parents lived outside these communes, even though there were no French-speaking schools in the communes where they lived. The Dutch classes, on the other hand, accepted all children, whatever the place of residence of the parents. Applying the criteria of discrimination which it elaborated in this case, the Court held that this differential treatment could not be justified under Article 14.

Although the wording of the article is that 'no person shall be denied the right to education', the Strasbourg Court stated in the merits phase of the *Belgian Linguistic* case that the negative formulation meant that there was no obligation for the Contracting Parties to 'establish at their own expense, or to subsidize, education of any particular type or at any level'.[12] The Court went on to note that all the Contracting Parties have public education systems, and that Article 2 guaranteed the right, in principle, for pupils to 'avail themselves of the means of instruction existing at a given time'.[13] What this means is that the article guarantees a right of access to existing educational provision, but Contracting Parties have a wide margin of appreciation as to the resources they devote to the system of education and as to its organization.

The right of access is to the educational provision existing at any given time. The choice of provision is a matter for the Contracting Party, though it would seem that there is a right of persons to establish private schools.[14] Commission decisions establish that there is no obligation on a Contracting Party to provide selective education,[15] or schools offering education in the context of particular religious affiliations,[16] single-sex schools,[17] or separate schools for those with special educational needs.[18]

In the *Belgian Linguistic* case, the Strasbourg Court defined the scope of the right to education in the following terms:

---

[11] The prohibition on discrimination: see ch.24 below.
[12] §3 under the heading 'B. Interpretation adopted by the Court'.   [13] Ibid.
[14] *Kjeldsen, Busk Madsen and Pedersen v Denmark*, (Apps. 5095/71, 5920/72, and 5926/72), 7 December 1976, Series A No 23, (1979–80) 1 EHRR 711, §50. See also App. 11533/85, *Jordebo Foundation of Christian Schools and Jordebo v Sweden*, Decision of 6 March 1987, (1987) 51 DR 125; and App. 23419/94, *Verein Gemeinsam Lernen v Austria*, Decision of 6 September 1995, (1995) 82-A DR 41.
[15] Apps. 10228/92 and 10229/82, *W and others v United Kingdom*, Decision of 6 March 1984, (1984) 37 DR 96.
[16] App. 7728/77, *X v United Kingdom*, Decision of 2 May 1978, (1979) 14 DR 179.
[17] Apps. 10228/82 and 10229/82, *W and others v United Kingdom*, Decision of 6 March 1984, (1984) 37 DR 96.
[18] App. 14688/89, *Simpson v United Kingdom*, Decision of 4 December 1989, (1989) 64 DR 188; and App. 28915/95, *SP v United Kingdom*, Decision of 17 January 1997.

The first sentence of Article 2 of the Protocol consequently guarantees, in the first place, a right of access to educational institutions existing at a given time, but such access constitutes only a part of the right to education. For the 'right to education' to be effective, it is further necessary that, inter alia, the individual who is the beneficiary should have the possibility of drawing profit from the education received, that is to say, the right to obtain, in conformity with the rules in force in each State, and in one form or another, official recognition of the studies which he has completed.[19]

Dicta of the Court in the *Belgian Linguistic* case support the view that the right to 'effective education' implies a duty on the state to provide schooling at least in the official language. In *Cyprus v Turkey*[20] the Cypriot Government complained that, although primary education was available in Greek in northern Cyprus, the 'Turkish Republic of Northern Cyprus' had closed down Greek secondary schools and that Greek Cypriot children living there had either to continue their secondary education in Turkish or English or to travel to the southern part of the island to attend Greek language schools. The Court observed that in the strict sense there was no denial of the right to education. Nonetheless, it found a violation of Article 2 of Protocol 1 because it considered that, having provided for primary education in Greek, it was unrealistic to expect children to switch to learning in another language once they reached secondary age. Having assumed responsibility for the provision of Greek-language primary schooling, the failure of the 'Turkish Republic of northern Cyprus' authorities to make continuing provision for it at the secondary-school level had to be considered in effect to be a denial of the substance of the right at issue. The Court also rejected the idea that the availability of Greek-language schools in southern Cyprus would be sufficient to comply with the obligation under Article 2 of Protocol 1.[21]

Issues relating to access to education have also been raised in a number of recent cases against the new democracies of central and eastern Europe. The *Timishev* case[22] concerned a forced migrant who was an ethnic Chechen. His property in Grozny had been destroyed as a result of military operations and he was living in Nalchik. He was refused permanent residence in Nalchik by reason of his being a former resident of the Chechen Republic. His children were refused admission to a school in Nalchik, which they had previously attended, on the grounds that he had no lawful right to remain in Nalchik, and that, since the schools were overcrowded, his request for admission of his

---

[19] *Case relating to certain aspects of the laws on the use of languages in education in Belgium (Merits) Belgian Linguistic Case (No. 2)*, (Apps. 1474/62, 1677/62, 1691/62, 1769/63, 1994/63, and 2126/64), 23 July 1968, Series A No 6, (1979–80) 1 EHRR 252, §4 under the heading 'B. Interpretation adopted by the Court'.

[20] *Cyprus v Turkey*, (App. 25781/94), 10 May 2001 [GC], (2002) 35 EHRR 731, ECHR 2001-IV.

[21] In relation to the first sentence of Article 2, a discontinuance of provision may constitute a violation. This means that there may be a positive obligation to continue educational provision in, for example, the language of a minority once that has been provided, even though there is no obligation to provide education in minority languages: *Cyprus v Turkey*, (App. 25781/94), 10 May 2001 [GC], (2002) 35 EHRR 731, ECHR 2001-IV, §§273–80.

[22] *Timishev v Russia*, (Apps. 55762/00 and 55974/00), 13 December 2005, (2007) 44 EHRR 776, ECHR 2005-XII.

children constituted an encroachment on the rights of other children. The Strasbourg Court considered this to be serious violation of Article 2.

In a group of cases involving the removal of gypsies from land where they had set up homes in breach of planning laws,[23] it was argued that the refusal to allow the families to remain on their own land resulted in their children being denied access to satisfactory education. In all three cases the Strasbourg Court found that the applicants had failed to substantiate their claims under this provision of the Convention and so there was no violation. The applications, however, signal the potential linkage between provisions of the Convention, though in most cases a requirement that a family moves its home would not result in schooling being unavailable to them if they were within the age range for which attendance at school was required by the State.

This linkage with other provisions of the Convention is also illustrated by the *Leyla Şahin* case,[24] which concerned the prohibition of the wearing of the Islamic headscarf in Turkish universities. The Grand Chamber found that there was no violation of Article 9 here and no separate violation of Article 2 of Protocol 1. The requirement not to wear a headscarf did not impair the essence of the right to education.

REGULATING EDUCATION

In the *Campbell and Cosans* case,[25] the Strasbourg Court noted that the rights enshrined in the article involved a duty on the State to regulate the provision of education:

The right to education guaranteed by the first sentence of Article 2 by its very nature calls for regulation by the State, but such regulation must never injure the substance of the right nor conflict with other rights enshrined in the Convention or its Protocols.[26]

The *Belgian Linguistic* case recognized that effective education may require a Contracting Party to regulate education by requiring compulsory attendance at school. The Strasbourg organs have, however, consistently accorded to the Contracting Parties a wide margin of appreciation in the measures of regulation taken.[27] Comments in the *Belgian Linguistic* case to the effect that the right to education involves a right to an effective education would seem to require Contracting Parties to maintain certain standards in education. This means that, whereas there may be universal entitlement to education up to a certain age, education beyond that age may be dependent upon the

---

[23] *Coster v United Kingdom*, (App. 24876/94), (2001) 33 EHRR 479; *Lee v United Kingdom*, (App. 25289/94), (2001) 33 EHRR 677; and *Smith (Jane) v United Kingdom*, (App. 25154/94), (2001) 33 EHRR 712, all 18 January 2001 [GC].

[24] *Leyla Şahin v Turkey*, (App. 44774/98), 10 November 2005 [GC], (2007) 44 EHRR 99, ECHR 2005-IX.

[25] *Campbell and Cosans v United Kingdom*, (Apps. 7511/76, and 7743/76), 25 February 1982, Series A No 48, (1982) 4 EHRR 293.

[26] §41.

[27] For example, as to the setting of the curriculum: see *Kjeldsen, Busk Madsen and Pedersen v Denmark*, (Apps. 5095/71, 5920/72, and 5926/72), 7 December 1976, Series A No 23, (1979–80) 1 EHRR 711, §53.

attainment of qualifications deemed necessary for the pursuit of more advanced education.[28] However, where the regulation operates as a denial of education, there will be a violation of the article. So a provision in Scotland excluding a pupil from a State school because of a refusal to submit to corporal punishment exceeded the scope for reasonable regulation of education and amounted to a violation of the right to education in the first sentence of the article.[29]

Basic procedural fairness prohibits a Contracting Party from acting in a totally arbitrary manner in relation to examination results within an established educational system. So, in the *Mürsel Erem* case,[30] it was a breach of Article 2 to refuse to accept some good results following a series of poor results solely on the basis that they could not be explained by the prior poor results, and in the absence of any proof of cheating.

Similarly, the system for the allocation of children to special schools must be fair, otherwise it runs the risk of violating Article 2 of Protocol 1 when read with Article 14 requiring equal treatment. The *DH* case[31] concerned the system in the Czech Republic for educating the children of Roma families. The applicants were children of Roma origin who had been assigned to special schools. The test which they had undertaken to establish their educational needs had been criticized by the European Commission against Racism and Intolerance (ECRI),[32] and by the Council of Europe Commissioner for Human Rights.[33] The applicants argued that the very high number of Roma children allocated to special schools as a result of the test provided strong evidence of indirect discrimination against this particular group. The Grand Chamber accepted that the statistical data did give rise to a strong presumption of indirect discrimination, which meant that it was for the respondent State to show that the difference in impact of the scheme was the result of objective factors unconnected with the racial origins of the applicants.[34] The Grand Chamber did not find the evidence of the respondent State satisfactory. Indeed the evidence suggested that there was bias in the educational tests, and that the parental consent to the allocation of places for their children in special schools was not an informed one, but in any event it was not possible to waive the right not to be subjected to racial discrimination.[35] The Grand Chamber concluded that the applicants, as members of a class, had suffered discrimination prohibited by

---

[28] App. 11655/85, *Glasewska v Sweden*, Decision of 10 October 1985; (1985) 45 DR 300.

[29] *Campbell and Cosans v United Kingdom*, (Apps. 7511/76, and 7743/76), 25 February 1982, Series A No 48, (1982) 4 EHRR 293.

[30] *Mürsel Eren v Turkey*, (App. 60856/00), 7 February 2006, (2007) 44 EHRR 619, ECHR 2006-II.

[31] *DH and others v Czech Republic*, (App. 57325/00), 13 November 2007 [GC], (2008) 47 EHRR 59, ECHR 2007-nyr. See also *Sampanis and others v Greece*, (App. 32526/05), 5 June 2008; and *Orşuş and others v Croatia*, (App. 15766/03), 17 July 2008. (2009) 49 EHRR 572. For a wide-ranging discussion of the human rights of travellers, see R. Sandland, 'Developing a Jurisprudence of Difference: The Protection of the Human Rights of Travelling Peoples by the European Court of Human Rights' (2008) 8 HRLRev 475; Section D of the article discusses the *DH* case.

[32] See www.coe.int/t/e/human_rights/ecri/ for information on its work.

[33] See ch.1 above.

[34] *DH and others v Czech Republic*, (App. 57325/00), 13 November 2007 [GC], (2008) 47 EHRR 59, ECHR 2007-nyr, §195.

[35] §204.

the Convention, thus making it unnecessary to consider their cases on an individual basis.[36] There was a violation of Article 2 of Protocol 1 when read with Article 14.

SAFEGUARDING PLURALISM IN EDUCATION

The scope of the second sentence of the article is much wider than the first, although it must be recalled that the Strasbourg Court has indicated that the two sentences of the article must be read in the light of each other and of other provisions of the Convention. Indeed the Court has said that Article 2 is 'dominated' by its first sentence.[37] Its scope is wide because it is delimited by reference to the functions which a Contracting Party assumes in relation to education; many governments assume wide functions in relation to the regulation of education offered by both the State and by the private sector. The Court has described the purpose of the second sentence of Article 2 as follows:

The second sentence of Article 2 aims in short at safeguarding the possibility of pluralism in education, which possibility is essential for the preservation of the 'democratic society' as conceived by the Convention.[38]

The rights protected by the second sentence are rights of parents, and so the focus will be on education provided before the children reach adulthood and can make their own decisions. The Strasbourg Court has also indicated that one of the purposes of the provision is to operate as a check against possible indoctrination:

The State is forbidden to pursue an aim of indoctrination that might be considered as not respecting parents' religious and philosophical convictions. That is the limit that must not be exceeded.[39]

The effect of the second sentence of the article on parental choice allows parents either to enrol their children in State education, to withdraw their children from the State system and educate them privately whether at a private school or at home,[40] or to enforce respect for their religious and philosophical convictions by alleging a violation of the second sentence of Article 2. It allows a significant parental influence on both the organization and content of educational provision.

---

[36] *DH*, §209.

[37] *Kjeldsen, Busk Madsen and Pedersen v Denmark*, (Apps. 5095/71, 5920/72, and 5926/72), 7 December 1976, Series A No 23, (1979–80) 1 EHRR 711, §53. All the principles described in this section have been re-stated in *Folgerø v Norway*, (App. 15472/02), 29 June 2007 [GC], (2008) 46 EHRR 1147, ECHR 2007-VIII.

[38] *Kjeldsen, Busk Madsen and Pedersen v Denmark*, (Apps. 5095/71, 5920/72, and 5926/72), 7 December 1976, Series A No 23, (1979–80) 1 EHRR 711, §50.

[39] §53.

[40] Though this may be regulated by a Contracting Party, see App. 10233/83, *Family H v United Kingdom*, Decision of 6 March 1984, (1984) 37 DR 105.

The Strasbourg Court has ruled that the duty applies not to education viewed narrowly, but to the performance of all the functions assumed by the State, which will include the internal administration of the school.[41]

THE NATURE OF RELIGIOUS AND PHILOSOPHICAL CONVICTIONS

The leading authority on the nature of religious convictions is the *Valsamis* case,[42] which arose in the context of objections raised by a family of Jehovah's Witnesses. The Strasbourg Court recalled its case-law under Article 9 and acknowledged that Jehovah's Witnesses 'enjoy both the status of a "known religion" and the advantages flowing from that as regards observance'.[43] Thus, any person whose convictions can be described as those of a 'known religion' will be able to argue that they have religious convictions.

The leading authority on the nature of philosophical convictions is the *Campbell and Cosans* case.[44] The Strasbourg Court said:

In its ordinary meaning the word 'convictions', taken on its own, is not synonymous with the words 'opinions' and 'ideas', such as are utilized in Article 10 of the Convention, which guarantees freedom of expression; it is more akin to the term 'beliefs'…appearing in Article 9—which guarantees freedom of thought, conscience and religion—and denotes views that attain a certain level of cogency, seriousness, cohesion and importance.

As regards the adjective 'philosophical', it is not capable of exhaustive definition and little assistance as to its precise significance is to be gleaned from the travaux préparatoires.…

Having regard to the Convention as a whole…, the expression 'philosophical convictions' in the present context denotes, in the Court's opinion, such convictions as are worthy of respect in a 'democratic society' and are not incompatible with human dignity; in addition, they must not conflict with the fundamental right of the child to education, the whole of Article 2 being dominated by its first sentence.[45]

THE NATURE OF THE DUTY TO RESPECT RELIGIOUS AND PHILOSOPHICAL CONVICTIONS

In the *Valsamis* case,[46] the Strasbourg Court explained its view of the nature of the duty to respect religious and philosophical convictions. The duty arose in relation not only to the content of education and the manner of its provision but also to the

---

[41] *Campbell and Cosans v United Kingdom*, (Apps. 7511/76, and 7743/76), 25 February 1982, Series A No 48, (1982) 4 EHRR 293, §33.

[42] *Valsamis v Greece* (App. 21787/93), 18 December 1996, (1997) 24 EHRR 294, ECHR 1996-VI, re-affirmed in *Folgerø v Norway*, (App. 15472/02), 29 June 2007 [GC], (2008) 46 EHRR 1147, ECHR 2007-VIII.

[43] *Valsamis v Greece* (App. 21787/93), 18 December 1996, (1997) 24 EHRR 294, ECHR 1996-VI, §25.

[44] *Campbell and Cosans v United Kingdom*, (Apps. 7511/76, and 7743/76), 25 February 1982, Series A No 48, (1982) 4 EHRR 293.

[45] §36.

[46] *Valsamis v Greece* (App. 21787/93), 18 December 1996, (1997) 24 EHRR 294, ECHR 1996-VI, re-affirmed in *Folgerø v Norway*, (App. 15472/02), 29 June 2007 [GC], (2008) 46 EHRR 1147, ECHR 2007-VIII.

performance of all of the functions assumed by a Contracting Party.[47] Respect, said the Court, involves more than acknowledgement. Quite how this will convert into practice will involve the judgment of national authorities, but it would seem to require that genuine consideration is made to the possibility of accommodations which will avoid conflicts in the delivery and organization of education with the religious or philosophical convictions of parents.

The Strasbourg Court re-affirmed its earlier case-law that respect for democratic values did not mean that the views of the majority must always prevail. Although individual interests had to be subordinated to the views of the majority in some circumstances, a balance had to be achieved which ensured the fair and proper treatment of minorities and avoided any abuse of the position of the majority group.[48]

APPLICATION OF THE DUTY

The *Kjeldsen* case[49] concerned compulsory sex education in Denmark. Sex education had been an optional subject in Danish state schools for many years. In 1970 a law was enacted to make it obligatory in these schools. According to the law, sex education would not be presented as a separate subject, but would be integrated with the teaching of other subjects. The parents of a number of children objected that this law infringed their right to ensure education and teaching in conformity with their own religious and philosophical convictions. The Strasbourg Court concluded that compulsory sex education did not violate Article 2 in failing to respect the wishes of the parents. The Court stressed that there must be no attempt at indoctrination that might be regarded as not respecting the parents' religious or philosophical convictions. The information must be presented in 'an objective, critical and pluralistic manner'. The sex education programme in Denmark was considered to be 'within the bounds of what a democratic State may regard as the public interest'.

A different view was taken in relation to parents' objections to corporal punishment in the *Campbell and Cosans* case.[50] At issue here was what, at best, was a philosophical belief. The Strasbourg Court stated that a philosophical belief must relate to 'a weighty and substantial aspect of human life and behaviour'. The parental objection to corporal punishment met this standard since it concerned 'the integrity of the person, the propriety or otherwise of the infliction of corporal punishment and the exclusion of the distress which risk of such punishment entails'. The Court concluded that the United Kingdom had violated Article 2 of the Protocol when the school offered the parents in question no guarantee that their son would not be beaten, and no alternative education was available for him.

---

[47] *Valsamis v Greece* (App. 21787/93), 18 December 1996, (1997) 24 EHRR 294, ERCHR 1996-VI, §27.
[48] Ibid.
[49] *Kjeldsen, Busk Madsen and Pedersen v Denmark*, (Apps. 5095/71, 5920/72, and 5926/72), 7 December 1976, Series A No 23, (1979–80) 1 EHRR 711.
[50] *Campbell and Cosans v United Kingdom*, (Apps. 7511/76, and 7743/76), 25 February 1982, Series A No 48, (1982) 4 EHRR 293.

Compulsory attendance at a school parade to mark National Day in Greece[51] was at issue in the *Valsamis* case.[52] The applicants were a family of Jehovah's Witnesses; part of their religious beliefs involved opposition to events with military overtones. The daughter was punished by the school for not attending the school parade, even though the school had been advised that attendance would be inconsistent with the child's religious beliefs. Her parents complained that their wishes in respect of the family's religious convictions had not been respected. Though there is little that can be criticized in the Strasbourg Court's discussion of the content of religious convictions, their application to the facts of this case, which resulted in a finding that there was no violation of the article, is unsatisfactory. The Court noted that the school had exempted the daughter from religious classes at the school, and went on to express surprise that 'pupils can be required on pain of suspension...to parade outside the school precincts on a holiday.'[53] It concluded that there was nothing in the requirement to attend the school parade which 'could offend the applicants' pacifist convictions to an extent prohibited by the second sentence of Article 2 of Protocol 1', because such celebrations serve both pacifist objectives and the public interest.[54] Perhaps the Court wished to send out a signal in this case that respect for religious and philosophical convictions would depend on an objective assessment of the situation, rather than simply seeking to ascertain whether the beliefs and the consequences of them were genuinely held.

The view of the two dissenting judges is to be preferred. They indicated that there was nothing to suggest that the beliefs of the family were unfounded and unreasonable. In the light of those beliefs the requirement of attendance was disturbing to the family and humiliating to the daughter. The applicant family was under no obligation to share the views of the majority on the value of the commemorative events of 28 October. Participation was not a neutral act, and it could not be said that attendance formed part of the usual school curriculum. The minority concluded that there had been a violation of the article.

The possibility of exemptions from certain parts of the school curriculum as a means of respecting parental wishes has arisen in two cases.

The *Hasan and Eylem Zengin* case[55] concerned classes in religious culture and ethics. The predominant form of Islam followed in Turkey is Hanafism, one of the four theological schools of Sunni Islam. The applicants, a father and his daughter, were adherents of Alevism, which is more closely related to Sufism. The practice of Alevism differs significantly from that of Hanafism. Classes in religious culture and ethics

---

[51] On 28 October each year, which marks the outbreak of war between Greece and Fascist Italy on 28 October 1940, and so recognizes Greek attachment to values of democracy, liberty, and human rights.

[52] *Valsamis v Greece* (App. 21787/93), 18 December 1996, (1997) 24 EHRR 294, ECHR 1996-VI. See also *Efstratiou v Greece* (App. 24095/94), 18 December 1996.

[53] *Valsamis v Greece* (App. 21787/93), 18 December 1996, (1997) 24 EHRR 294, §31.

[54] Ibid.

[55] *Hasan and Eylem Zengin v Turkey*, (App. 1448/04), 9 October 2007, (2008) 46 EHRR 1060, ECHR 2007-XI.

taught in Turkish schools are deeply rooted in the Sunni tradition. The request of the applicants for exemption from such classes was unsuccessful.

The Strasbourg Court concluded that the complaint required it to consider, first, whether the syllabus for religious culture and ethics was taught in an objective, critical and pluralist manner, and, secondly, whether appropriate accommodations were available to respect the religious beliefs of parents. Examination of the aims of the syllabus and, to a certain extent, its content led the Strasbourg Court to conclude that the syllabus failed to respect the religious diversity which prevailed in Turkish society in that there was no teaching relevant to the Alevi faith, which had a significant following in Turkey. As such, the education failed to meet the criteria of objectivity and pluralism. This led to the question of exemptions. In Turkey the subject is compulsory, although there is a possibility for exemption for children 'of Turkish nationality who belong to the Christian or Jewish religion'.[56] The unanimous view of the Court was that the exemption procedure was not an appropriate means of addressing the structural problem with the religious education which had been identified by the Court.

The circumstances of the *Folgerø* case[57] concerned a revision to the way in which Christianity, other forms of religious belief, and various philosophies were taught in Norway. An integrated approach was adopted, but it was established that preponderant weight was given to Christianity in the form of cultural heritage and the Evangelical Lutheran Religion, which was the official State religion in Norway, of which 86 per cent of the population were members. The applicants were parents of children in primary schools who were members of the Norwegian Humanist Association. Partial exemption from the integrated subject was possible. The applicants had sought unsuccessfully to have their children exempted from the whole subject. The Grand Chamber decided to deal with the case under Article 2 of Protocol 1 rather than Article 9, which the applicants had also pleaded. The key issue was whether the possibility of partial exemption was sufficient to afford respect for the philosophical convictions of the parents. The question sharply divided the Grand Chamber by nine votes to eight. The majority noted that partial exemption gave rise to considerable problems. It required clear communication about the delivery of the content of the revised curriculum, and, more particularly, required the parents to disclose in some detail 'intimate aspects of their own religious and philosophical convictions'.[58] The possibility of separating activity from knowledge also concerned the majority, since the idea behind the exemption was to offer exemption from an activity but not from the underlying knowledge. The majority also rejected the alternative of the parents educating their children in the private sector, since 'the existence of such a possibility could not dispense the State from its obligation to safeguard pluralism in State schools which are open to everyone.'[59] The outcome was as follows:

Against this background, notwithstanding the many laudable legislative purposes stated in connection with the introduction of the [the integrated] subject in the ordinary primary and lower secondary schools, it does not appear that the respondent State took sufficient care that information and knowledge included in the curriculum be conveyed in an objective, critical and pluralistic manner for the purposes of Article 2 of Protocol 1.[60]

The minority of eight judges disagreed both on the substance of the teaching of religion and other philosophies (which they did not feel gave an over-preponderance to Christianity) in the new syllabus, and on the intrusiveness into the beliefs of the objecting parents in relation to the securing of partial exemption. They concluded:

Against this background, we are satisfied that the respondent State, in fulfilling its functions in respect of education and teaching, had taken care that information or knowledge included in the curriculum of the [integrated] subject was conveyed in an objective, critical and pluralistic manner. It could not be said to have pursued an aim of indoctrination contrary to the parents' right to respect for their philosophical convictions and thereby transgressing the limits implied by Article 2 of Protocol 1.[61]

The case-law is now rather muddled and it is not easy to provide a rational explanation for the outcomes. In the *Belgian Linguistic* case, the Strasbourg Court declined to guarantee education in a particular language. In the *Kjeldsen* case, the Court declined to strike down compulsory sex education in the light of parental objections. In the *Valsamis* case, the Strasbourg Court declined to strike down compulsory attendance at a national commemorative occasion with military overtones found to be objectionable to those with religious beliefs a central part of which included pacifism. However, in the *Campbell and Cosans* case, the Court upheld the parental objections to corporal punishment. One possible explanation is that corporal punishment involves the physical integrity of the individual, whereas sex education reflects the duty of the State to provide children with information. Language education arouses great political and constitutional sensitivities in some regions of Europe, and parading as part of a national commemoration was not considered inconsistent with pacifist beliefs when the overall objectives of the National Day were taken into consideration. Finally the *Folgerø* case indicates how fine the lines will be between permissible and impermissible accommodations to the religious and philosophical beliefs of parents.

---

[59] §101.   [60] §102.
[61] Joint dissenting opinion of Judges Wildhaber, Lorenzen, Bîrsan, Kovler, Steiner, Borrego Borrego, Hajiyev, and Jebens.

EDUCATION FOR CONVICTED PRISONERS

Special difficulties may arise in relation to the right to education of convicted prisoners, especially since Article 2 contains no escape clause allowing interference in the interests of public order, security, or otherwise. The question has not yet been fully examined. In the *Golder* case,[62] the applicant referred to certain examination facilities which he was trying to obtain, but did not make any specific complaint in this respect. An application against Austria[63] which put the question clearly was rejected for non-exhaustion of domestic remedies. The applicant alleged that his right to further education was being denied by the prison authorities. Although the Austrian law on the Execution of Sentences provided that prisoners should be given the opportunity for further education, such provisions were ineffective because prisoners were required to pay for their books and other educational material, which they could not afford out of their prison earnings.

Again, it may be possible to apply by analogy the reasoning of the Strasbourg Court in the *Belgian Linguistic* case and to argue that Contracting Parties have no positive obligation to subsidize prisoners' education, but may not take steps to interfere with it. In this sense, the obligation under the first sentence of Article 2 may be much less susceptible to positive obligations on a Contracting Party than the obligation in the second sentence of the article.

CONCLUDING REMARKS

The interpretation of the Convention as a living instrument may result in further significant developments in the scope and protection of the article in the future, particularly in clarification of the accommodations to parental preferences based on their religious and philosophical convictions.

---

[62] *Golder v United Kingdom*, (App. 4451/70), 21 February 1975, Series A No 18, (1979–80) 1 EHRR 524. For a discussion of the case in relation to Article 8, see ch.16 above.

[63] App. 4511/70, *X v Austria*, Decision of 24 May 1971, (1972) 38 CD 84.

22

THE RIGHT TO FREE ELECTIONS

INTRODUCTION

Article 3 of Protocol 1 provides:

The High Contracting Parties undertake to hold free elections at reasonable intervals by secret ballot, under conditions which will ensure the free expression of the opinion of the people in the choice of the legislature.

All the provisions of the Convention, including Articles 13 to 18, apply equally to the rights guaranteed by the First Protocol.[1] Article 3, like Articles 1 and 2 of Protocol 1, but to a lesser extent, reflects the difficulties which prevented these rights from being incorporated in the original text of the Convention. Those difficulties are preserved in an unsatisfactory text, which is the result of a compromise, and which continues to give rise to problems of interpretation.[2]

Article 3 of Protocol 1 'presupposes the existence of a representative legislature, elected at reasonable intervals, as the basis of a democratic society'.[3] It goes further than requiring free elections; it requires that the exercise of political power be subject to a freely elected legislature. Examination of the rights and freedoms guaranteed by the Convention has shown the importance of all those rights and freedoms being guaranteed by law, and of all restrictions on them being subject to the law. Article 3 of Protocol 1 underpins the whole structure of the Convention in requiring that laws should be made by a legislature responsible to the people.[4] Free elections are thus a condition of the 'effective political democracy' referred to in the Preamble, and of the concept of a democratic society which runs through the Convention. The Strasbourg

---

[1] Art. 5 of Protocol 1.

[2] Contrast the drafting of Article 25 of the International Covenant on Civil and Political Rights. See also J. Cremona, 'The right to free election in the European Convention of Human Rights' in P. Mahoney and others, *Protecting Human Rights: The European Perspective. Studies in Memory of Rolv Ryssdal*, (Carl Heymanns, Köln 2000), 309.

[3] App. 3321/67, *Denmark v Greece*; App. 3322/67, *Norway v Greece*; App. 3323/67, *Sweden v Greece*; and App. 3344/67, *Netherlands v Greece* ('the *Greek* case'), Report of 18 November 1969, (1969) 12 *Yearbook* 1, 179.

[4] Article 3 is in force for 45 Contracting Parties. Monaco and Switzerland are not parties to Protocol 1.

Court has repeatedly stated that Article 3 of Protocol 1 'enshrines a characteristic of an effective political democracy.'[5]

The obligation in Article 3 is expressed as an undertaking by the Contracting Parties rather than in the form of a right or prohibition. This had led to suggestions that, unlike other provisions of the Convention, it was intended that it should only be invoked by States and not by individuals. But the Strasbourg Court has ruled that the interpretation of the provision requires the recognition of individual rights:[6] the right to vote[7] and the right to stand as a candidate for election.[8]

Free elections imply a genuine choice. Hence, as the Commission stated in the *Greek case*, the suspension of political parties is also contrary to Article 3.[9] On the other hand, it is consistent with the Convention, in accordance with Article 17, to prohibit political parties with totalitarian aims. The Strasbourg Court has also said that Article 11 does not protect political parties whose aims are incompatible with the Convention:

It necessarily follows that a political party whose leaders incite violence or put forward a policy which fails to respect democracy or which is aimed at the destruction of democracy and the flouting of the rights and freedoms recognized in a democracy cannot lay claim to the Convention's protection against penalties imposed on those grounds.[10]

The Grand Chamber of the Strasbourg Court has summarized the nature of the Court's test under Article 3 of the First Protocol as follows:[11]

103. The rights guaranteed under Article 3 of Protocol No. 1 are crucial to establishing and maintaining the foundations of an effective and meaningful democracy governed by the rule of law. Nonetheless, these rights are not absolute. There is room for 'implied limitations', and Contracting States must be given a margin of appreciation in this sphere. The Court re-affirms that the margin in this area is wide.... There are numerous ways of organising and running electoral systems and a wealth of differences, *inter alia*, in historical development, cultural diversity and political

---

[5] *Mathieu-Mohin and Clerfayt v Belgium*, 2 March 1987, Series A No 113, (1988) 10 EHRR 1, §47; *United Communist Party of Turkey and others v Turkey*, (App. 19392/92), 30 January 1998, (1998) 26 EHRR 121, ECHR 1998-I, §45; and *Matthews v United Kingdom*, (App. 24833/94), 18 February 1999, (1999) 28 EHRR 361, ECHR 1999-I, §42. See also *Refah Partisi (The Welfare Party) v Turkey*, (Apps. 41340/98, 41342/92, 41343/98, and 41344/98), 13 February 2003 [GC], (2003) 37 EHRR 1, ECHR 2003-II, §§86–95; and *Ždanoka v Latvia*, (App. 58278/00), 16 March 2006 [GC], (2007) 45 EHRR 478, ECHR 2006-IV, §§96–101.

[6] *Ždanoka v Latvia*, (App. 58278/00), 16 March 2006 [GC], (2007) 45 EHRR 478, ECHR 2006-IV, §102, affirming *Mathieu-Mohin and Clerfayt v Belgium*, 2 March 1987, Series A No 113, (1988) 10 EHRR 1. But note the dissention opinion of Judge Rozakis in *Ždanoka*, which argues that Article 3 does not imply the individual rights but actually provides for them.

[7] Referred to as the active element of the individual rights arising under the provision.

[8] Referred to as the passive element of the individual rights arising under the provision.

[9] App. 3321/67, *Denmark v Greece*; App. 3322/67, *Norway v Greece*; App. 3323/67, *Sweden v Greece*; and App. 3344/67, *Netherlands v Greece* ('the *Greek* case'), Report of 18 November 1969, (1969) 12 *Yearbook* 1, 180.

[10] *Refah Partisi (The Welfare Party) v Turkey*, (Apps. 41340/98, 41342/92, 41343/98, and 41344/98), 13 February 2003 [GC], (2003) 37 EHRR 1, ECHR 2003-II, §98. See also discussion of these issues in ch.19 above.

[11] *Ždanoka v Latvia*, (App. 58278/00), 16 March 2006 [GC], (2007) 45 EHRR 478, ECHR 2006-IV.

thought within Europe, which it is for each Contracting State to mould into its own democratic vision....

104. It is however for the Court to determine in the last resort whether the requirements of Article 3 of Protocol No. 1 have been complied with; it has to satisfy itself that the conditions imposed on the rights to vote or to stand for election do not curtail the exercise of those rights to such an extent as to impair their very essence and deprive them of their effectiveness; that they are imposed in pursuit of a legitimate aim; and that the means employed are not disproportionate.... In particular, any such conditions must not thwart the free expression of the people in the choice of the legislature—in other words, they must reflect, or not run counter to, the concern to maintain the integrity and effectiveness of an electoral procedure aimed at identifying the will of the people through universal suffrage....

The number of complaints of violations of Article 3 of Protocol 1 is increasing, and there is evidence that the Strasbourg Court is giving fresh emphasis to this provision as essential to the foundations of democratic legitimacy of the State. Many, but by no means all, of these cases come from the new democracies of central and eastern Europe. Issues arising from new democratic rights have often related to eligibility both to vote and to stand for election having regard to a person's past history within a totalitarian regime.

IMPLIED RESTRICTIONS

Although there is no room for implied limitations under Articles 8 to 11,[12] the Strasbourg Court has established that implied limitations have a central role to play in the application and interpretation of all aspects of Article 3 of Protocol 1.[13] No assistance can really be drawn from the list of express limitations in Article 8 to 11; any limitation compatible with the principle of the rule of law and the general objectives of the Convention will be permitted.[14] In assessing the compatibility of such restrictions with the provisions of Article 3, the Strasbourg Court does not apply the tests of necessity and a pressing social need, but rather considers whether there has been arbitrariness or a lack of proportionality, and whether the restriction has interfered with the free expression of the opinion of the people.[15]

Depriving persons of their vote simply by reason of being declared bankrupt was found to serve no purpose other than to belittle persons who had been made bankrupt irrespective of whether they had committed an offence. Such a provision was found not to serve any legitimate aim within Article 3 of the First Protocol.[16]

---

[12] See ch.14 above.

[13] *Ždanoka v Latvia*, (App. 58278/00), 16 March 2006 [GC], (2007) 45 EHRR 478, ECHR 2006-IV, §115.

[14] *Yumak and Sadak v Turkey*, (App. 10226/03), 8 July 2008 [GC], (2009) 48 EHRR 61, ECHR 2008-nyr, §119.

[15] Ibid.   [16] *Campagnano v Italy*, (App. 77955/01), 23 March 2006, ECHR 2006-IV.

WHAT IS THE LEGISLATURE?

The wording of Article 3 only encompasses elections to the legislature. This raises the question of what constitutes the legislature. The Commission consistently stated that the term must be interpreted in the light of both the institutions established by the constitutions of the Contracting Parties and the international undertakings affecting the legislative powers of the body under consideration.[17] The Strasbourg Court takes a similar view.[18]

Article 3 does not apply to the appointment of the Head of State, such as the Federal President of Austria.[19] Nor does it apply to elections to organs of a professional body, such as the Royal Society for the Cultivation of Flower Bulbs, even if certain legislative power has been conferred on it.[20]

Much more problematic are issues of whether regional authorities constitute the legislature. Of the Member States of the Council of Europe, Switzerland is the clearest proof that Article 3 cannot be confined to the central power. It must extend to the Swiss cantons, which have a very high degree of autonomy, and to all provincial legislatures where there is a measure of decentralization of power. The only federal States apart from Switzerland in the Council of Europe are Austria, Bosnia and Herzegovina, Germany, and Russia.

In one case where a convicted prisoner was refused permission to vote, his complaints related both to *Land* elections and to federal elections in Germany, and the Commission did not distinguish between them.[21] It would certainly be incorrect to exclude *Land* elections from the scope of Article 3.

Local government in the non-federal Contracting Parties may lack the necessary autonomy to constitute the legislature. However, it should be noted that the Strasbourg Court's decision in the *Ahmed* case is expressly stated to be without prejudice to the question of whether local government elections in the United Kingdom are within the scope of Article 3.[22] By contrast, the position of the

---

[17] For example, in App. 11123/84, *Tête v France*, Decision of 9 December 1987, (1987) 54 DR 52.

[18] *Mathieu-Mohin and Clerfayt v Belgium*, 2 March 1987, Series A No 113, (1988) 10 EHRR 1, §53; and *Matthews v United Kingdom* (App. 24833/94), 18 February 1999, (1999) 28 EHRR 361, ECHR 1999-I, §40.

[19] App. 15344/89, *C-L and L Habsburg-Lothringen v Austria*, Decision of 14 December 1989, (1990) 64 DR 210, 219. See also *Guliyev v Azerbaijan* (App. 35584/02), Decision of 27 May 2004 concerning the election of the President of Azerbaijan; and *Boškoski v the former Yugoslav Republic of Macedonia* (App. 11676/04), Decision of 2 September 2004 concerning the election of the President of the Republic. Note, however, that in the latter case the Strasbourg Court said that it did not exclude 'the possibility of applying [Article 3] to presidential elections.'

[20] App. 9926/82, *X v Netherlands*, Decision of 1 March 1983, (1983) 32 DR 274.

[21] App. 2728/66, *X v Federal Republic of Germany*, Decision of 6 October 1967, (1967) 10 *Yearbook* 336.

[22] *Ahmed and others v United Kingdom*, (App. 22954/93), 2 September 1998, (2000) 29 EHRR 1, ECHR 1999-VI, §76. In *Hirst v United Kingdom (No.2)*, (App. 74025/01), Chamber Judgment of 30 March 2004, this judgment says in passing that local elections fall outside the scope of the Article: §37. The judgment of the Grand Chamber of 6 October 2005 does not address this issue.

devolved parliaments of Scotland and Wales would seem to be clearly within the concept of a legislature.[23]

A distinction can be drawn in all modern States between the legislative bodies which have supreme legislative powers, and subordinate authorities which are empowered only to enact subordinate legislation, however general it may be in its application. The term 'legislature', used without qualification in Article 3, should be interpreted as extending to a provincial legislature which has a degree of autonomy, but not to such subordinate authorities. This was the view taken by the Commission in the case of English Metropolitan county councils[24] which could not be considered the legislature, since their powers are derivative and are defined by legislation with certain activities requiring approval or consent. They did not 'possess an inherent primary rulemaking power'.[25]

The status of the European Parliament and the application of Article 3 to elections to it arose in the *Matthews* case.[26] The applicant was a British citizen living in Gibraltar, which is a dependent territory of the United Kingdom with its own legislature. The EC Treaty applies to Gibraltar, although the operation of parts of the EC Treaty is excluded in relation to Gibraltar under the terms of the Treaty of Accession. Elections to the European Parliament are governed by the Act Concerning the Election of the Representatives of the European Parliament by Universal Suffrage of 20 September 1976; this was signed by the ministers of foreign affairs of the Member States of the European Communities and attached to Council Decision 76/787.[27] The Act provided for elections to take place only in the territory of the United Kingdom but not in Gibraltar. The Strasbourg Court rejected the argument of the respondent State that the European Parliament should be excluded from the ambit of elections within the scope of Article 3 on the ground that it is a supranational rather than a national representative organ. The respondent State then argued that it lacked the attributes of a legislature, which they defined as the power to initiate and adopt legislation.[28] After analysing the powers of the European Parliament and their impact upon Gibraltar, the Strasbourg Court concluded that the European Parliament constitutes 'part of the legislature of Gibraltar for the purposes of Article 3 of Protocol 1'.[29]

---

[23] Belgium and Spain are also among the Contracting Parties which operate systems of devolved government.

[24] App. 11391/85, *Booth-Clibborn and others v United Kingdom*, Decision of 5 July 1985, (1985) 43 DR 236.

[25] 248.

[26] *Matthews v United Kingdom*, (App. 24833/94), 18 February 1999; (1999) 28 EHRR 361, ECHR 1999-I. For a discussion of the case, see K. Muylle, 'Is the European Parliament a "Legislator"?' (2000) 6 EPL 243; and T. King, 'Ensuring human rights review of inter-governmental acts in Europe' (2000) 25 ELRev 79; and I. Canor, '*Primus inter pares*. Who is the ultimate guardian of fundamental rights in Europe?' (2000) 25 ELRev 3.

[27] [1976] OJ L278/5.

[28] The Parliament's most extensive legislative functions arise under the co-decision procedure set out in Article 251 EC, under which the European Parliament can block the progress of legislative measures proposed by the Commission and supported by the Council.

[29] *Matthews v United Kingdom*, (App. 24833/94), 18 February 1999; (1999) 28 EHRR 361, ECHR 1999-I, §54. For the 2004 and 2009 elections to the European Parliament, Gibraltar was attached to the constituency covering Cornwall.

ELECTORAL SYSTEMS

The Grand Chamber has summarized the requirements of Article 3 in relation to the choice of electoral system as follows:

The Court reiterates that the Contracting States enjoy a wide margin of appreciation when it comes to determination of the type of ballot through which the free expression of the opinion of the people in the choice of the legislature is mediated. In that regard, Article 3 of Protocol No. 1 goes no further than prescribing 'free' elections held at 'reasonable intervals' 'by secret ballot' and 'under conditions which will ensure the free expression of the opinion of the people'. Subject to that reservation, it does not create any 'obligation to introduce a specific system' such as proportional representation or majority voting with one or two ballots....[30]

A fair and proper electoral system under Article 3 requires a fair and proper system of voter registration, supported by effective electoral commissions.[31] Very weighty considerations will be needed to justify the disenfranchisement of sections of the electorate.[32] The way in which the outcome of elections is reviewed must also be fair and not arbitrary.[33] So the decision to annul the vote in four electoral divisions in elections in Ukraine in response to complaints about certain irregularities within those divisions was considered arbitrary and not proportionate to any legitimate aim.[34]

Although Article 3, in contrast to Article 21(3) of the Universal Declaration of Human Rights, does not refer expressly to universal suffrage, the Commission, reversing an earlier position, expressed the view that Article 3 implies recognition of universal suffrage.[35] The Strasbourg Court has agreed.[36] On the other hand, Article 3 is somewhat different in form from that in which the other rights in the Convention and Protocol are expressed. It does not provide in absolute terms that everyone has the right to vote. If a person complains that he or she is disqualified from voting, the Strasbourg Court's task is to consider whether such disqualification affects the free expression of the opinion of the people under Article 3.[37]

The formulation is important, if only because of the question of the effect of Article 14. The Commission accepted that certain categories of citizen may be excluded from voting, without the free expression of the opinion of the people being prejudiced. Thus,

---

[30] *Yumak and Sadak v Turkey*, (App. 10226/03), 8 July 2008 [GC], (2009) 48 EHRR 61, ECHR 2008-nyr, §110.

[31] *Georgian Labour Party v Georgia*, (App. 9103/04), 8 July 2008.

[32] Ibid.

[33] See, for example, *Paschalidis, Koutmeridis and Zaharakis v Greece*, (Apps. 27863/05, 28422/05, and 28028/05), 10 April 2008.

[34] *Kovach v Ukraine*, (App. 39424/02), 7 February 2008, ECHR 2008-nyr.

[35] App. 2728/66, *X v Federal Republic of Germany*, Decision of 6 October 1967, (1967) 10 *Yearbook* 336, at 338; see also App. 5302/71, *X & Y v United Kingdom*, Decision of 11 October 1973, (1973) 44 CD 29, at 48.

[36] *Mathieu-Mohin and Clerfayt v Belgium*, 2 March 1987, Series A No 113; (1988) 10 EHRR 1, §51.

[37] *Gitonas and others v Greece*, (Apps. 18747/91, 19376/92, 19379/92, 28208/95, and 27755/95), 1 July 1997, (1998) 26 EHRR 691, ECHR 1997-IV, §39.

Belgians resident in the Congo complained unsuccessfully that they were denied the right to vote in the metropolis.[38] On the other hand, wider disqualifications, such as, for example, the disqualification of women, might be considered as affecting the free expression of the opinion of the people, even without regard to Article 14. An argument to this effect might be based on the general spirit of the Convention as well as the modern understanding of a democratic society.

In any event, it is clear that Switzerland regarded as an obstacle to ratification of the Convention and First Protocol the fact that women had only recently acquired the right to vote in federal legislative elections and did not have this right in certain of the cantons.[39] The former disability was removed by revision of the federal constitution.[40]

The scope of the rights embedded in Article 3 was considered in the *Mathieu-Mohin and Clerfayt* case.[41] The case concerned the complex rules operating in Belgian elections to ensure appropriate representation of the French-speaking and Dutch-speaking communities. Before considering the application of Article 3 to the particular facts of the case, the Strasbourg Court provided authoritative guidance on the scope of the rights protected by the Article. The Strasbourg Court approved the Commission's decisions in which it had held that the provision included a right of universal suffrage,[42] which embraced both the right to vote and the right to stand for election to the legislature.[43] But the Court went on to confirm that these rights are not absolute and that there is room for implied limitations. States enjoy a wide margin of appreciation as to the conditions they attach to the exercise of the right. However, the Court:

has to satisfy itself that the conditions do not curtail the rights in question to such an extent as to impair their very essence and deprive them of their effectiveness; that they are imposed in pursuance of a legitimate aim; and that the means employed are not disproportionate. ... In particular, such conditions must not thwart 'the free expression of the opinion of the people in the choice of the legislature'.[44]

The Strasbourg Court went on to declare that Article 3 does not create any obligation to introduce a specific system of elections and States enjoy a wide margin of appreciation in the choice of voting system. The key test is whether the chosen system provides for the free expression of the opinion of the people in the choice of the legislature.

The dissenting opinions related to the specific facts of the case, but a concurring opinion of Judge Pinheiro Farinha expressed reservations about the Court's approach to legislative systems which have two chambers. The majority had said that Article 3

---

[38] App. 1065/61, *X v Belgium*, Decision of 30 May 1961, (1961) 4 *Yearbook* 260.

[39] Federal Council's Report to the Federal Assembly on the Convention, (1969) 12 *Yearbook* 502, 509–10.

[40] But note that Switzerland is not a party to Protocol 1.

[41] *Mathieu-Mohin and Clerfayt v Belgium*, 2 March 1987, Series A No 113, (1988) 10 EHRR 1.

[42] App. 2728/66, *X v Federal Republic of Germany*, Decision of 6 October 1967, (1967) 10 *Yearbook* 336.

[43] Apps. 6745–46/76, *W, X, Y and Z v Belgium*, Decision of 30 May 1975, (1975) 18 *Yearbook* 244.

[44] *Mathieu-Mohin and Clerfayt v Belgium*, 2 March 1987, Series A No 113, (1988) 10 EHRR 1, §52.

applies 'to the election of the "legislature", or at least one of its chambers if it has two or more'.[45] Judge Pinheiro Farinha considered this wording 'inadequate and dangerous':

As it stands, it would allow of a system at variance with 'the opinion of the people in the choice of the legislature' and might even lead to a corporative, elitist or class system which did not respect democracy.

In my opinion, we should say 'or at least of one of its chambers if it has two or more, on the twofold condition that the majority of the membership of the legislature is elected and that the chamber or chambers whose members are not elected does or do not have greater powers than the chamber that is freely elected by secret ballot.'

Some years ago the Liberal Party in the United Kingdom sought to challenge the simple majority voting system used in British elections on the grounds that it violated Article 3 when read in conjunction with Article 14 in that the effect of the chosen voting system was to give less weight to votes cast for Liberal Party candidates than for the Conservative or Labour Party candidates.[46] It was conceded by the applicants that the simple majority voting system could not be a violation of Article 3 when read alone, and the Commission noted that this concession was rightly made. But the Commission, in deciding that the application was manifestly ill-founded, also concluded that Article 3 when read in conjunction with Article 14 did not admit of the argument that there was any entitlement to the protection of equal voting influence for all voters.

The extent of Strasbourg supervision of electoral systems has been revisited by the Grand Chamber of the Strasbourg Court in the *Yumak and Sadak* case.[47] The applicants challenged the requirement in the Turkish electoral system for parties to reach a 10 per cent threshold of the national vote before they became entitled to representatives in the national Parliament. It was claimed that this threshold was the highest in Europe. The legitimacy of any national system will be judged in the context of 'the historical and political factors specific to each State.'[48] In the context of proportional representation systems, the Strasbourg Court acknowledged that thresholds served the purpose of avoiding excessive fragmentation and ensuring the emergence of a sufficiently clear and coherent political will.

In the context of the Turkish electoral system, the Grand Chamber accepted that the rules on thresholds served a legitimate aim: avoiding excessive and debilitating parliamentary fragmentation and strengthening governmental stability.[49] In considering the proportionality of the requirement, the Strasbourg Court noted that the threshold was the highest in Europe, but appears to conclude that the outcome of the elections of which the applicants complained was, in part, determined by the electoral strategy which had been adopted by their parties. The Court also noted certain observations made by the Constitutional Court in Turkey. The outcome was a finding by thirteen

---

    45 *Mathieu-Mohin and Clerfayt*, §53.
    46 App. 8765/79, *Liberal Party, R and P v United Kingdom*, Decision of 18 December 1980, (1981) 21 DR 211.
    47 *Yumak and Sadak v Turkey*, (App. 10226/03), 8 July 2008 [GC], (2009) 48 EHRR 61, ECHR 2008-nyr.
    48 §111.   49 §125.

votes to four that there was that no violation of Article 3. However, there is a veiled warning that the threshold should be lowered.

Issues related to the funding of political parties are more likely to give rise to issues under Article 11 than under Article 3 of the First Protocol.[50]

THE RIGHT TO VOTE

It has long been the position of the Commission that the right to vote and the right to stand for election to the legislature may be subject to legitimate restrictions imposed by the State.[51] The Strasbourg Court has adopted the same position.[52] It takes a more rigorous approach to restrictions of the right to vote (the active aspect of the rights under Article 3), than in relation to the passive aspect of the right to stand for election. The Grand Chamber summarized the position in this way in the *Ždanoka* case:[53]

…while the test relating to the 'active' aspect of Article 3 of Protocol No. 1 has usually included a wider assessment of the proportionality of the statutory provisions disqualifying a person or a certain group of persons from the right to vote, the Court's test in relation to the 'passive' aspect of the above provision has been limited largely to a check on the absence of arbitrariness in the domestic procedures leading to disqualification of an individual from standing as a candidate....

Depriving persons abroad of the right to vote in their country of origin is permissible.[54] However, it is not open to a Contracting Party to use residence in an arbitrary or discriminatory manner in determining a person's eligibility to stand for election.[55] Nor can permissible language requirements be set at a disproportionately high level or be operated in an arbitrary manner with the effect that individuals are disenfranchised.[56] Any question of disqualification must be surrounded by procedural fairness and legal certainty.[57]

---

[50] See, for example, *Parti Nationaliste Basque—Organisation Régionale D'Iparralde v France*, (App. 71251/01), 7 June 2007, (2008) 47 EHRR 1037, ECHR 2007-VII.

[51] App. 6850/74, *X, Y and Z v Federal Republic of Germany*, Decision of 18 May 1976, (1976) 5 DR 90 and App. 11391/85, *Booth-Clibborn and others v United Kingdom*, 5 July 1985, (1985) 43 DR 236.

[52] *Mathieu-Mohin and Clerfayt v Belgium*, 2 March 1987, Series A No 113, (1988) 10 EHRR 1, §52.

[53] *Ždanoka v Latvia*, (App. 58278/00), 16 March 2006 [GC], (2007) 45 EHRR 478, ECHR 2006-IV.

[54] App. 7730/76, *X v United Kingdom*, Decision of 28 February 1979, (1979) 15 DR 137.

[55] See *Melnychenko v Ukraine* (App. 17707/02), 19 October 2004, (2006) 42 EHRR 784, ECHR 2004-X, discussed below in this chapter. See also *Py v France* (App. 66289/01), 11 January 2005, (2006) 42 EHRR 548, ECHR 2005-I.

[56] *Podkolzina v Latvia* (App. 46726/99), 9 April 2002, ECHR 2002-II. The applicant was a member of the Russian-speaking minority, whose language competence was in issue.

[57] *Podkolzina v Latvia* (App. 46726/99), 9 April 2002, ECHR 2002-II; *Russian Conservative Party of Entrepreneurs and others v Russia*, (Apps. 55066/00 and 55638/00), 11 January 2007, (2008) 46 EHRR 863, ECHR 2007-I; *Krasnov and Skuratov v Russia*, (Apps. 17864/04 and 21396/04), 19 July 2007, (2008) 47 EHRR 1016, ECHR 2007-IX; and *Sarukhanyan v Armenia*, (App. 38978/03), 27 May 2008.

In the *Aziz* case[58] the Strasbourg Court found a violation of Article 3 where a Turkish Cypriot resident in the non-occupied south of the island was denied a vote on the ground that the constitutional arrangements[59] had provided for separate representation of the Greek Cypriot and Turkish Cypriot communities. The Court referred to a 'manifest lack of legislation resolving the ensuing problems.'[60]

In an early case,[61] the Commission considered that depriving convicted prisoners of the right to vote did not violate the Convention. This was so even if the conviction is for conscientious objection to military service by a person who has refused to comply with the formalities for acquiring objector status.[62]

The fresh consideration of the issues arising from an automatic statutory ban on voting imposed on convicted prisoners ultimately came before the Grand Chamber in the *Hirst* case.[63] The applicant[64] complained that the blanket ban on voting in elections in the United Kingdom violated his rights under Article 3 of Protocol 1. The applicant argued that little thought had been given by the respondent State to the justification for the ban on voting, and earlier legislation had been consolidated without any debate on the question. The blanket ban was disproportionate and arbitrary. The respondent State noted that, among the Contracting States, 18 countries imposed no restriction on the right of prisoners to vote, 13 countries had a blanket ban, and 12 countries imposed some restrictions. It was argued that the purpose of the ban in the United Kingdom was a combined one in order to prevent crime, to punish offenders, and to enhance civic responsibility and respect for the rule of law. It only operated where an immediate custodial sentence was imposed and so was not disproportionate in effect since it was linked to the seriousness of the criminal conduct.

In determining that a blanket ban on voting went beyond a State's margin of appreciation, the Court took note of the discussion of similar issues in the Canadian Supreme Court.[65] The Strasbourg Court noted that the loss of voting rights plays no part in the sentencing process in the United Kingdom, and the Court could see no rational link between the deprivation of the vote and punishment for a crime. Nor was the Court convinced that the claim that the loss of the vote enhanced civic responsibility had merit; no similar bar was applied to those whose crime might be considered to be equally anti-social or 'uncitizen-like' upon whom no immediate custodial sentence was imposed. Though the Court clearly had serious doubts about the legitimacy of the aims put forward by the United Kingdom, it nevertheless refrained from determining

---

[58] *Aziz v Cyprus*, (App. 69949/01), 22 June 2004, (2005) 41 EHRR 164, ECHR 2004-V.

[59] Which had long since ceased to operate.

[60] *Aziz v Cyprus*, (App. 69949/01), 22 June 2004, (2005) 41 EHRR 164, ECHR 2004-V, §29. The Court also found a separate violation of Article 14 when read in conjunction with Article 3 of Protocol 1.

[61] App. 2728/66, *X v Federal Republic of Germany*, Decision of 6 October 1967, (1967) 10 *Yearbook* 336.

[62] App. 9914/82, *H v Netherlands*, Decision of 4 July 1983, (1983) 33 DR 274.

[63] *Hirst v United Kingdom (No. 2)*, (App. 74025/01), 6 October 2005 [GC], (2006) 42 EHRR 849, ECHR 2005-IX.

[64] Who was serving a discretionary life sentence following his conviction for manslaughter.

[65] In *Sauvé v Attorney General of Canada (No.2)*, [2002] 3 SCR 519.

that they were not legitimate, preferring to decide that the blanket ban was a disproportionate response to meeting those aims:

The Court would observe that there is no evidence that the legislature in the United Kingdom has ever sought to weigh the competing interests or to assess the proportionality of a blanket ban on the right of convicted prisoners to vote.[66]

The Grand Chamber concluded that:

a general, automatic and indiscriminate restriction on a vitally important Convention right must be seen as falling outside any acceptable margin of appreciation, however wide that margin might be....[67]

There had accordingly been a violation of Article 3.

The *Santoro* case[68] concerned the loss of voting rights by an individual regarded as 'socially dangerous' whom the Italian authorities had placed under special police supervision. One consequence was that the individual lost his right to vote. The Strasbourg Court does not take issue with the application of the provisions under which the applicant became disenfranchised, but does require that the administrative machinery for implementing the disqualification and for reinstating the individual on the electoral role does not involve undue delay. Where it does, there will be a violation of Article 3, as in this case.

THE RIGHT TO STAND FOR ELECTION

The Strasbourg Court, in the *Mathieu-Mohin and Clerfayt* case,[69] confirmed the long-held view of the Commission that States may impose certain restrictions on the right to stand for election. So a requirement that a certain number of signatures be obtained as qualification to stand as a candidate is a reasonable requirement.[70] A fair system of deposits will not violate the Convention.[71] Nor will restriction on the return of deposits and the reimbursement of election expenses in a system of proportional representation where the lists do not obtain 5 per cent of the vote.[72] Restrictions which amount

---

[66] *Hirst v United Kingdom (No. 2)*, (App. 74025/01), 6 October 2005 [GC], (2006) 42 EHRR 849, ECHR 2005-IX, §79.

[67] §82.

[68] *Santoro v Italy*, (App. 36681/97), 1 July 2004, (2006) 42 EHRR 705, ECHR 2003-I.

[69] *Mathieu-Mohin and Clerfayt v Belgium*, 2 March 1987, Series A No 113, (1988) 10 EHRR 1, §52.

[70] App. 6850/74, *X, Y and Z v Federal Republic of Germany*, Decision of 18 May 1976, (1976) 5 DR 90.

[71] *Sukhovetskyy v Ukraine*, (App. 13716/02), 28 March 2006, (2007) 44 EHRR 1185, ECHR 2006-VI.

[72] App. 11406/85, *Fournier v France*, Decision of 10 May 1988, (1988) 55 DR 130. See also *Gorizdra v Moldova*, (App. 53180/99), Decision of 2 July 2002. But note that refusal to return a deposit where a party has been improperly disqualified from an election will violate Article 1 of Protocol 1: *Russian Conservative Party of Entrepreneurs and others v Russia*, (Apps. 55066/00 and 55638/00), 11 January 2007, (2008) 46 EHRR 863, ECHR 2007-I, §§95–7.

effectively to retrospective disqualifications from standing as a candidate will violate Article 3.[73]

The Greek rules prohibiting public officials from standing for election within a period of thirty-three months of holding public office were considered by the Strasbourg Court in the *Gitonas* case.[74] The applicants had stood for election, been elected, and had their election annulled by the Greek courts. The applicants argued that the Greek rules were imprecise and incoherent, and that far more senior posts did not carry the exclusion which applied to them. In a strongly factually based judgment, the Strasbourg Court disagreed with the Commission[75] in finding that there was no violation of Article 3.

Restrictions on the ability of certain local government officials to stand in local government elections in the United Kingdom were challenged in the *Ahmed* case.[76] In order to retain their posts in local government, the applicants all had to give up their political activities on behalf of political parties. They claimed that the requirement to do so breached, among other provisions, their right to full participation in the electoral process as guaranteed by Article 3 of Protocol 1. The regulations, they argued, had the effect of limiting without justification the electorate's choice of candidates. But the Court found no violation, accepting that the restrictions served the legitimate purpose of securing the political impartiality of civil servants.

Where the right to stand for election touches on the issue of individuals forming a political party, the Strasbourg Court has generally determined these issues under Article 11 and has, until recently, avoided addressing the question of whether the right to form and maintain a political party falls within the scope of Article 3 of Protocol 1.[77] However, in the *Sadak* case[78] the Strasbourg Court did consider the impact of Article 3 of Protocol 1 in a situation in which the dissolution of a political party[79] in Turkey had the automatic effect that the applicants forfeit their parliamentary seats. The Court found that such an immediate and automatic consequence of dissolution could not be regarded as 'proportionate to any legitimate aim relied on by the Government' and was 'incompatible with the very substance of the applicants' right to be elected and sit

---

[73] *Lykourezos v Greece*, (App. 33554/03), 15 June 2006, (2008) 46 EHRR 74, ECHR 2006-VIII.

[74] *Gitonas and others v Greece*, (Apps. 18747/91, 19376/92, 19379/92, 28208/95, and 27755/95), 1 July 1997; (1998) 26 EHRR 691, ECHR 1997-IV.

[75] Which had found a violation of Art. 3 by 9 votes to 8.

[76] *Ahmed and others v United Kingdom*, (App. 22954/93), 2 September 1998, (2000) 29 EHRR 1, ECHR 1998-VI.

[77] See discussion of cases involving political parties in ch.19 above. For examples of cases where the Court has not felt the need to consider applications under Art. 3 of Protocol 1, see *United Communist Party of Turkey and others v Turkey*, (App. 19392/92), 30 January 1998; (1998) 26 EHRR 121, ECHR 1998-I; *The Socialist Party and others v Turkey*, (App. 21237/93), 25 May 1998; (1999) 27 EHRR 51; and *Refah Partisi (The Welfare Party) v Turkey*, (Apps. 41340/98, 41342/92, 41343/98 and 41344/98), 13 February 2003 [GC], (2003) 37 EHRR 1, ECHR 2003-II.

[78] *Sadak and others v Turkey (No. 2)*, (Apps. 25144/94, 26149/95 to 26154/94, 27100/95 and 27101/95), 11 June 2002, (2003) 36 EHRR 396, ECHR 2002-IV. See also *Kavakçi v Turkey*, (App. 71907/01), 5 April 2007; *Silay v Turkey*, (App. 8691/02), 5 April 2007; and *Ilicak v Turkey*, (App. 15394/02), 5 April 2007.

[79] The Democracy Party *Demokrasi Partisi*.

in Parliament under Article 3 of Protocol 1'. It infringed the 'sovereign power of the electorate who elected them as member of parliament.'[80]

The *Melnychenko* case[81] concerned rules operating in Ukraine for determining eligibility to stand for election. The authorities insisted upon residence in Ukraine as a condition of eligibility. The applicant was living in the United States, where he had applied for political asylum, but his officially registered address (*propiska*) remained in Ukraine. This was the standard basis for registration as a candidate in the elections. In the particular circumstances of the case, the Strasbourg Court concluded that the refusal to register his candidacy to stand for election was in breach of Article 3. A ban on eligibility to stand for election of those holding a nationality additional to that of the country in which the elections are being held will also violate the Convention.[82] A significant number of Moldovans have acquired Romanian nationality.[83]

The *Ždanoka* case[84] concerned the ineligibility of Tatjana Ždanoka to stand for election in Latvia by reason of her former membership of the Latvian Communist Party. This party had been declared unconstitutional by the Latvian authorities with the result that former active members of that party could not stand for election to the national parliament. The ban was indefinite in duration. The Latvian Government sought to justify the measure as meeting three aims: (1) it was a punitive measure for past conduct which displayed a lack of civic responsibility; (2) it was a preventive measure where past activities evidenced a risk of conduct likely to endanger democracy; and (3) her election might create an imminent danger for the State's constitutional order.

The Chamber judgment, finding a violation of Article 3 by five votes to two, was over-turned on reference to the Grand Chamber in a thirteen votes to four judgment.

The Chamber[85] had accepted that barring a person's candidacy could be a legitimate punitive measure, but that the barring order should normally be temporary if it is to meet the requirement of proportionality. The aims relating to the protection of democratic values and the perceived threat to the State's constitutional order related to historical events in Latvia. The Court did not wish to become embroiled in historical controversy but did take as read the totalitarian and anti-democratic nature of the ruling Communist parties in the States of central and eastern Europe before 1990. However, there had been no ban on the activities of the political parties to which the applicant belonged until August 1991, and the Latvian Government had not taken legislative powers to provide for electoral ineligibility until the 1995 elections. This

---

[80] *Sadak and others v Turkey (No. 2)*, (Apps. 25144/94, 26149/95 to 26154/94, 27100/95 and 27101/95), 11 June 2002, (2003) 36 EHRR 396, ECHR 2002-IV, §40.

[81] *Melnychenko v Ukraine*, (App. 17707/02), 19 October 2004, (2006) 42 EHRR 784, ECHR 2004-X.

[82] *Tănase and Chirtoacă v Moldova*, (App. 7/08), 18 November 2008.

[83] The Chamber judgment has been referred to the Grand Chamber, which heard oral argument in September 2009.

[84] *Ždanoka v Latvia*, (App. 58278/00), 16 March 2006 [GC], (2007) 45 EHRR 478, ECHR 2006-IV. Contrast the judgment in *Ādamsons v Latvia*, (App. 3669/03), 24 June 2008, and see *Petkov and others v Bulgaria*, (Apps. 77568/01, 178/02 and 505/02), 11 June 2009.

[85] *Ždanoka v Latvia*, (App. 58278/00), 17 June 2004, (2005) 41 EHRR 659, ECHR 2004-IV.

inevitably coloured the Court's view of the nature of the threat to democracy and the State's constitutional order arising from the activities of these parties. The evidence supplied did not indicate that the activities of the applicant were anti-democratic, though her ideas were diametrically opposed to certain policies of the Latvian Government. It followed that permanent ineligibility to stand for election was disproportionate to the aims pursued by the national measures, and its necessity in a democratic society had not been established. The Chamber found a violation of Article 3 of Protocol 1.

The Grand Chamber took a different view. This was not a punitive measure, but a preventive measure designed to:

> protect the integrity of the democratic process by excluding from participation in the work of a democratic legislature those individuals who had taken an active and leading role in a party which was directly linked to the attempted violent overthrow of the newly established democratic regime.[86]

The national legislation was considered to be narrowly drafted by excluding only those who had 'actively participated' in the objectionable conduct. There was no reason to question the appreciation of the Latvian authorities that there was a threat to the new democratic order posed by a resurgence of ideas which could lead to the restoration of the former regime. In summary, the Strasbourg Court takes the view that this was a democracy defending itself. The dissenting judges considered that the indefinite ban on standing for election was problematic, but the majority too were alert to this question. The judgment of the Court notes that the Latvian Constitutional Court had indicated that a time limit should be placed on the restriction, and said that the Latvian Parliament 'must keep the statutory restriction under constant review, with a view to bringing it to an early end.'[87]

CONCLUDING REMARKS

After some initial uncertainty about the availability of individual petitions under Article 3 of Protocol 1, a significant case-law is developing on the nature of the legislature to which the article refers, on the control of elections, on the circumstances in which individuals can be disenfranchised, and on the right to stand for election.

There remain issues relating to which bodies within the national legal order fall within the scope of the term 'legislature', but there has been considerable narrowing of the wide margin of appreciation referred to in the early cases now that the Strasbourg Court seems to be adopting a more robust test for interferences which States impose. As with other articles of the Convention, the Strasbourg Court requires that procedural fairness surrounds decisions affecting the rights protected by the provision.

---

[86] *Ždanoka*, §122.   [87] §135.

23

FREEDOM OF MOVEMENT

INTRODUCTION

Provisions of the Fourth and Seventh Protocols concern freedom of movement in the broadest sense. Article 2 of Protocol 4 concerns liberty of movement and freedom to choose a residence. Article 3 of the same Protocol prohibits the expulsion of nationals and enshrines the right of nationals to enter their own country, while Article 4 prohibits the collective expulsion of aliens. The provisions of Protocol 4, which are controversial in some States since they touch on issues of immigration policy, have not been ratified by all the parties to the Convention.[1] Finally, Article 1 of Protocol 7 provides that aliens are not to be expelled without due process of law.

As between the States parties to Protocol 4, its provisions are to be regarded as additional articles of the Convention, and all the provisions of the Convention are to apply accordingly.[2] Article 5 of Protocol 4 and Article 6 of Protocol 7 make provision for a declaration concerning the application of the Protocol to dependent territories on the model of Article 56 of the Convention.

In addition, however, Article 5(4) of Protocol 4 provides that, for the purposes of Articles 2 and 3 of the Protocol, the territory of a State to which the Protocol applies by virtue of ratification, and each territory to which it applies by a declaration under Article 5, shall be treated as separate territories. The effect of this provision is that a State which ratifies the Protocol, and extends its application under Article 5 to its dependent territories, guarantees freedom of movement within each of those territories without also guaranteeing freedom of movement from one territory to another. The Committee of Experts explains paragraph 4 as follows:

The Committee decided to add a paragraph 4 to Article 5 in order to take account of a problem which may arise in connection with States which are responsible for the international relations of overseas territories. Thus, for example, insofar as nationality is concerned, there is no distinction between the United Kingdom and most of the territories for whose international relations it is responsible; in relation to these territories and the

---

[1] As at 1 September 2009, there are 42 parties to Protocol 4. Three countries (Spain, Turkey, and the United Kingdom) have signed but not ratified the Protocol. Greece and Switzerland have not even signed the Protocol. See, for an example of a case where this was an issue, *Eugenia Michaelidou Developments Ltd and Michael Tymvios v Turkey*, (App. 16163/90), 31 July 2003.

[2] Art. 6(1) of Protocol 4.

United Kingdom there is a common citizenship, designated as 'citizenship of the United Kingdom and Colonies'.

Persons who derive the common nationality from a connection with one such territory do not, however, have the right to admission to, or have immunity from expulsion from, another such territory. Each territory has its own laws relating to admission to and expulsion from its territory. Under these laws admission can be refused to persons who, though they possess the common nationality, do not derive it from connection with the territory in question, and in certain circumstances such persons can be expelled from that territory. Equally, persons who derive the common nationality from a connection with a dependent territory can in certain circumstances be refused admission to the United Kingdom or, if admitted, be expelled from the United Kingdom. What is said above is relevant to Article 3 of this Protocol, but a similar situation would arise as regards the interpretation of 'territory' for the purposes of Article 2.

Accordingly, it is desirable that the references in Articles 2 and 3 to the territory of a State should relate to the metropolitan territory and each non-metropolitan territory separately, and not to a single geographical entity comprising the metropolitan and other territories.

This interpretation would apply only to Article 2(1), and to Article 3 of Protocol 4.[3]

Article 6(5) of Protocol 7 contains similar provisions.

MOVEMENT AND RESIDENCE

Article 2 of Protocol 4 provides:

1. Everyone lawfully within the territory of a State shall, within that territory, have the right to liberty of movement and freedom to choose his residence.
2. Everyone shall be free to leave any country, including his own.
3. No restrictions shall be placed on the exercise of these rights other than such as are in accordance with law and are necessary in a democratic society in the interests of national security or public safety, for the maintenance of the *ordre public*, for the prevention of crime, for the protection of health or morals, or for the protection of the rights and freedoms of others.
4. The rights set forth in paragraph 1 may also be subject, in particular areas, to restrictions imposed in accordance with law and justified by the public interest in a democratic society.

These provisions are based on Article 13(1) and (2) of the Universal Declaration of Human Rights, whose wording they follow closely. The right to return to the country of nationality, which is also included in Article 13(2) of the Universal Declaration, is

---

[3] Explanatory Reports on the Second to Fifth Protocols to the Convention, Strasbourg 1971, 55.

dealt with separately by Article 3 of Protocol 4. While Article 2 deals with freedom of movement within a country, and the right to leave it, Article 3 precludes a State from expelling, or refusing to admit, its own nationals. Thus Article 2 applies to everyone, in relation to any country, but Article 3 applies only to nationals in relation to their own State.

The reference, in Article 2(1), to 'Everyone lawfully within the territory of a State' includes all that State's nationals present within its territory, since it follows from the provisions of Article 3 that, subject to the possible exception of extradition, the presence of persons in the State of which they are a national cannot be unlawful. As for persons who are not nationals, they are lawfully within the territory so long as they comply with any conditions of entry that may have been imposed. Such conditions may, of course, include restrictions as to the length of stay, after the expiry of which their presence will be unlawful. But it is argued that, subject to the limitations permitted under paragraphs 3 and 4, these conditions cannot, under Article 2(1), include any restrictions on their liberty of movement, or on their freedom to choose their residence.[4]

The position is a little different in the case of asylum seekers, as the *Omwenyeke* case makes clear.[5] The freedom of movement of asylum seekers can be limited pending determination of their status under provisional authorizations. Presence in the territory is only lawful where the asylum seeker complies with the terms of the provisional authorization. So an asylum seeker present in Germany under a provisional authorization conditional on his remaining in the city of Wolfsburg did not have a right to freedom of movement outside that city. The asylum seeker would not be lawfully present in Germany when in breach of his provisional authorization.

The freedom to leave a country, under Article 2(2), is subject to the restrictions set out in paragraph 3. These restrictions are, of course, sufficient to preclude convicted prisoners from leaving the country in which they are detained. The reference to 'the maintenance of *ordre public*' in paragraph 3 was included, as is shown by the preparatory work, expressly to allow for the case of persons lawfully detained under Article 5.[6] Similarly, a person who has been detained with a view to deportation or extradition under Article 5(1)(f)[7] cannot claim the right to leave the country freely.[8]

The approach adopted by the Strasbourg Court in dealing with restrictions or limitations on the rights granted in Article 2(1) and (2) is very similar to that adopted when the Strasbourg Court is considering the limitations to be found in Articles 8 to 11.[9]

---

[4] See to the contrary, Explanatory Reports on the Second to Fifth Protocols to the Convention, Strasbourg 1971, 41.

[5] *Omwenyeke v Germany*, (App. 44294/04), Decision of 20 November 2007, ECHR 2007-XII.

[6] Explanatory Reports on the Second to Fifth Protocols to the Convention, Strasbourg 1971, 41.

[7] See ch.11 above.

[8] App. 4436/70, *X v Federal Republic of Germany*, Decision of 26 May 1970, (1970) 13 *Yearbook* 1029.

[9] See ch.14 above.

In the *Baumann* case,[10] the Strasbourg Court said:

The Court reiterates that the right of free movement as guaranteed by paragraphs 1 and 2 of Article 2 of Protocol 4 is intended to secure to any person a right of liberty of movement within a territory and to leave that territory, which implies a right to leave for such a country of the person's choice to which he may be admitted.... It follows that liberty of movement prohibits any measure liable to infringe that right or to restrict the exercise thereof which does not satisfy the requirement of a measure which can be considered as necessary in a democratic society in the pursuit of the legitimate aims referred to in the third paragraph of the above-mentioned Article.[11]

In a later case, the Strasbourg Court said:

Any measure restricting [the rights in Article 2] must be lawful, pursue one of the legitimate aims referred to in the third paragraph... and strike a fair balance between the public interest and the individual's rights....[12]

Article 2 has been pleaded in a variety of circumstances, some of which appear quite fanciful. For example, admissibility decisions of the Strasbourg Court have ruled as inadmissible claims that security controls at airports constitute a restriction on free movement,[13] and that the need to avoid cigarette smoke in public restricts freedom of movement.[14] Rather more obvious situations have involved such matters as compulsory residence orders imposed in connection with criminal investigations, orders prohibiting a person's presence in a particular area, and passport confiscations.

In one case,[15] an applicant who was subject to a compulsory residence order, which involved placing him under special police supervision complained of a violation of the provision. The Commission ruled that the measures were an interference with his right of freedom of movement, but they were measures provided by law, which were necessary in a democratic society for the prevention of crime and maintenance of the *ordre public*. The measures were proportionate to a legitimate aim and the application was declared inadmissible.

In the *Raimondo* case,[16] the applicant, who was suspected of being a member of the Mafia, had been put under house arrest and placed under special police supervision. He complained that the special police supervision breached his rights under Article 2 of Protocol 4. The Strasbourg Court concluded that the measures fell short of a deprivation of liberty within the meaning of Article 5(1) and fell to be considered under Article 2 of the Protocol. The measures were, however, in its view justified as serving the aim of maintaining public order and for the prevention of crime; there was no lack of proportionality. However, for reasons which are not explained, there was a delay of

---

[10] *Baumann v France* (App. 33592/96), 22 May 2001, (2002) 34 EHRR 1041, ECHR 2001-V.
[11] §61.
[12] *Riener v Bulgaria*, (App. 46343/99), 23 May 2006, (2007) 45 EHRR 723, §109.
[13] *Phull v France* (App. 35753/03), Decision of 11 January 2005.
[14] *Botti v Italy* (App. 77360/01), Decision of 2 December 2004.
[15] App. 12541/86, *Ciancimino v Italy*, Decision of 27 May 1991, (1991) 70 DR 103.
[16] *Raimondo v Italy*, 22 February 1994, Series A No 281-A; (1994) 18 EHRR 237.

eighteen days before the revocation of the special police supervision was notified to the applicant. For this period the interference with his rights under Article 2 of the Protocol was not in accordance with law nor was it necessary. There was to this extent a violation of the article.[17]

The *Labita* case is a more dramatic example of a violation.[18] The applicant had been tried and acquitted of certain offences connected with Mafia-type activities. But the respondent State continued to keep in place special police supervision notwithstanding the acquittal, arguing that these were preventive measures to guard against the risk of future offences.[19] The Strasbourg Court concluded:

[T]he Court considers that it is legitimate for preventive measures, including special supervision, to be taken against persons suspected of being members of the Mafia, even prior to conviction, as they are intended to prevent crimes being committed. Furthermore, an acquittal does not necessarily deprive such measures of all foundation, as concrete evidence gathered at trial, though insufficient to secure a conviction, may nonetheless justify reasonable fears that the person concerned may in the future commit criminal offences.[20]

However, in this case, the Strasbourg Court concluded that there was no such basis for the continuation of the measures, which were, consequently, a breach of Article 2 of Protocol 4.

The *Baumann* case[21] concerned the seizure of a German passport in France by French police officers. At the time the passport holder was in Germany; he had been taken ill while staying in an hotel and moved from France to Germany for treatment. His passport was still in his hotel room and was seized when the police searched the hotel room. The passport was retained for some considerable time, but shortly after its seizure, the applicant was arrested by the German authorities, kept in custody by them, and subsequently tried and sentenced to imprisonment. The respondent State argued that the arrest and subsequent imprisonment in Germany meant that there had been no actual restriction on the applicant's freedom of movement. The Strasbourg Court considered that denial of the use of his passport constituted an interference with his right of movement. Since no action was taken by the French authorities against the applicant there was no justification for the continuing seizure of his passport. Though justified for a short initial period, the failure to return the passport thereafter constituted a violation of Article 2 of Protocol 4. Three judges added a partly dissenting opinion. For them, the factual situation presented by the applicant did not show any loss of movement in France; when the passport was seized in France, the applicant was already in Germany. The dissenting judges seem to take the view that the applicant could easily have obtained a replacement German passport from the German authorities, and so would not have suffered any restriction on his freedom of movement.

---

[17] §§37–40.
[18] *Labita v Italy* (App. 26772/95), 6 April 2000, (2008) 46 EHRR 1228, ECHR 2000-IV.
[19] As in the *Raimondo* judgment above.
[20] *Labita v Italy* (App. 26772/95), 6 April 2000, (2008) 46 EHRR 1228, ECHR 2000-IV, §195.
[21] *Baumann v France* (App. 33592/96), 22 May 2001, (2002) 34 EHRR 1041, ECHR 2001-V.

The *Napijalo* case[22] concerned the confiscation of a passport by the Croatian customs authorities at a border check when the applicant was crossing from Bosnia and Herzegovina into Croatia. He was alleged to have failed to declare certain goods he was bringing into Croatia; it was clear that this was a minor infringement, since a fixed penalty notice was issued for a sum equal to about €30.00, but the applicant could not pay this on the spot. It took the applicant just over two years to secure the return of his passport. He complained that this amounted to a violation of his freedom of movement under Article 2 of Protocol 4. The Strasbourg Court concluded that an unjustified confiscation of a passport constituted a violation of the rights protected by the article. To be justifiable, such a measure must be in accordance with law and be a necessary measure in a democratic society for securing a legitimate aim. In this case, it was the continuing deprivation of the passport which amounted to a violation of Convention rights. No proceedings were ever instigated against the applicant in relation to customs violations.

Barring someone from having a passport without good reason may also constitute a violation of Article 2 of Protocol 4.[23] Where a ban was put in place for a good reason, it must be subject to periodic reassessment.

The *Riener* case[24] concerned a restriction on leaving Bulgaria arising from a tax debt. The Strasbourg Court accepted that this had a legal basis in Bulgarian law,[25] and was for a legitimate purpose, since Article 1 of Protocol 1 permits States parties to that Protocol to enact laws for the purpose of securing payment of taxes. The respondent State, however, failed to persuade the Strasbourg Court that the lengthy restriction on movement was proportionate, since it was applied automatically, was not systematically reviewed, and there was little evidence of attempts to recover the tax debt. The measure could only be justified as long as it served the aim of securing recovery of the tax debt; the restriction had become a de facto punishment.

Extending measures beyond the period for which restrictions on movement are strictly necessary recurs in the case-law. So, in the *Luordo* case[26] restricting the movement of a bankrupt beyond the period needed to secure assets for creditors constituted a violation of the article.[27] But a more generous view of the conduct of a Contracting Party will be taken where the proceedings relate to criminal offences. In the *Federov and Federova* case,[28] the applicants had been charged with fraud, and the case had ping-ponged backwards and forwards between trial courts and the appellate courts for some years during which the applicants' movement was restricted. There was evidence that they had been given special permission to leave the district on two occasions. The

---

[22] *Napijalo v Croatia*, (App. 66485/01), 13 November 2003, (2005) 40 EHRR 735.

[23] *Ignatov v Bulgaria*, (App. 50/02), 2 July 2009.

[24] *Riener v Bulgaria*, (App. 46343/99), 23 May 2006, (2007) 45 EHRR 723.

[25] Though whether the law met the tests of foreseeability and clarity was regarded as closely linked to the issue of proportionality on which the case turned.

[26] *Luordo v Italy*, (App. 32190/96), 17 July 2003, (2005) 41 EHRR 547, ECHR 2003-IX.

[27] See also *Ciaramella v Italy*, (App. 6597/03), Decision of 23 September 2004.

[28] *Federov and Federova v Russia*, (App. 31008/02), 13 October 2005, (2006) 43 EHRR 943. See also *Ivanov v Ukraine*, (App. 15007/02), 7 December 2006.

Strasbourg Court did not consider that the actions of the Russian authorities to be disproportionate in this case.

In the *Hajibeyli* case, the Strasbourg Court provided guidance on the approach to be taken in cases where restrictions on movement were connected with the investigation of criminal conduct. It is not simply a matter of considering the duration of the restriction:

...the Court considers that, in the present case, the comparative duration of the restriction, in itself, cannot be taken as the sole basis for determining whether a fair balance was struck between the general interest in the proper conduct of criminal proceedings and the applicant's personal interest in enjoying freedom of movement. The issue must be assessed according to all the special features of the case. The restriction may be justified in a given case only if there are clear indications of a genuine public interest which outweighs the individual's right to freedom of movement.[29]

The Strasbourg Court has accepted that a proportionate restriction on leaving a country may be imposed for reasons of national security.[30] The applicant complained of the five year ban on his travel abroad following his work on developing rocket and space devices. The Court indicated that the same tests applied where national security was in issue as in other cases of restrictions on travel abroad. Here the applicant had surrendered all classified material prior to his application to travel abroad, and was proposing to travel for the purely private purpose of visiting his father in Germany who was ill. The review available against a refusal to issue a passport in such circumstances was concerned with form rather than the merits of the reasons for the visit, and the respondent State failed to indicate how the restriction served the interests of national security. The Court clearly considered the ban on travel for this purpose as belonging to an earlier era in Russia, when interpersonal communications could be controlled much more easily. There was a violation of Article 2 of Protocol 4.

Two cases with very similar facts concern the ability of the Burgomaster of Amsterdam to impose a prohibition order restricting a person's presence in a particular area of Amsterdam as part of the crackdown on the public use of hard drugs.[31] There were some doubts about whether these orders were 'in accordance with law'[32] though the majority was satisfied that the appropriate tests were met. The applicant argued that the long-standing nature of these orders[33] impugned the pressing social need for such measures. The Strasbourg Court disagreed. In the particular circumstances of these cases, the imposition of the measures on the applicants did not violate the rights protected by Article 2 of Protocol 4.

---

[29] *Hajibeyli v Azerbaijan*, (App. 16528/05), 10 July 2008, §63.

[30] *Bartik v Russia*, (App. 55565/00), 21 December 2006, ECHR 2006-XV.

[31] *Landvreugd v The Netherlands*, (App. 37331/97), 4 June 2002, (2003) 36 EHRR 1039; and *Olivieira v The Netherlands*, (App. 33129/96), 4 June 2002, ECHR 2002-IV.

[32] See the joint dissenting opinions in both cases.

[33] The provisions had been available as emergency measures for some eleven years at the time of their imposition on the applicants.

The unjustified monitoring of movements and expulsion to a specific part of the national territory will be a violation of Article 2 of Protocol 4. The *Denizci* case[34] concerned restrictions on the movement of the applicants in the southern part of Cyprus and subsequent expulsion to the northern part of Cyprus. No lawful basis for the restrictions on the applicants' movements was put forward by the respondent State, and the Court concluded that there was an interference with the rights in Article 2 which were neither provided by law nor necessary.[35]

Similar circumstances have arisen in Russia in relation to residence registration. A requirement to report to the police every time a person wishes to change their place of residence or to visit family or friends away from their home constitutes an interference with the right to liberty of movement.[36] Local practices in violation of a ruling of the Constitutional Court which had stated that there was a legal duty to certify an applicant's intention to live at a specified address on presentation of a completed application also constituted violations of the right to free movement.[37]

A number of other cases have concerned freedom of movement within the Russian Federation, and among the countries of central and eastern Europe. In the *Timishev* case,[38] the applicant, who was an ethnic Chechen, complained that he had been stopped at a particular checkpoint en route to Nalchik, refused entry to a part of Russia, and had been obliged to make a 300-kilometre detour to complete his journey within the country. He argued that this was part of a policy of refusing entry to Chechens travelling by car. The Russian authorities claimed that he had tried to jump the queue at the checkpoint and been turned back for that reason. The Strasbourg Court found that the restriction on the applicant's movement was not 'in accordance with law', and there was a violation of Article 2 of Protocol 4. The Strasbourg Court went on to find a violation of Article 14 when read with Article 2 of Protocol 4 in that the restriction was based on ethnic considerations; he had been treated in a discriminatory manner.

THE PROHIBITION OF EXPULSION
OF NATIONALS

As already stated, Article 3 precludes a State from expelling, or refusing to admit, its own nationals. Article 3(1) provides:

No one shall be expelled, by means either of an individual or of a collective measure, from the territory of the State of which he is a national.

---

[34] *Denizci and others v Cyprus*, (Apps. 25316–25321/94, and 27207/95), 23 May 2001, ECHR 2001-V.

[35] §400–6. The Strasbourg Court decided that its conclusions on the violation of Article 2 of Protocol 4 made it unnecessary to consider the complaint as a violation of Art. 3 of Protocol 4.

[36] *Tatishvili v Russia*, (App. 1509/02), 22 February 2007, (2007) 45 EHRR 1246, ECHR 2007-III, §45.

[37] Ibid.

[38] *Timishev v Russia*, (Apps. 55762/00 and 55974/00), 13 December 2005, (2007) 44 EHRR 776, ECHR 2005-XII. See also *Gartukayev v Russia* (App. 71933/01), 13 December 2005; and *Bolat v Russia* (App. 14139/03), 5 October 2006, (2008) 46 EHRR 354, ECHR 2006-XI.

There is no provision for any restrictions to the rights guaranteed by Article 3, which is curious since the provision makes no exception for the practice of extradition. It is extraordinary that the explanatory report on Protocol 4 merely says that 'It was understood that extradition was outside the scope of this paragraph.'[39] Such understandings are not an adequate basis for drafting a legal text. In any event, on the accepted principles of treaty interpretation, this explanatory report cannot be invoked to interpret the text, since the text is clear and unambiguous.[40]

The European Convention on Extradition does not preclude the extradition of nationals, but provides that a Contracting Party shall have the right to refuse extradition of its nationals.[41] The extradition of nationals is prohibited by the law of many Member States of the Council of Europe.[42] But the Convention on Extradition permits a State to refuse the extradition of its nationals even if this would not be contrary to its own law. It would seem that States Parties to Protocol 4 are precluded from extraditing their nationals in the absence of a reservation to the contrary.[43]

The Commission has defined what constitutes expulsion, which occurs when a 'person is obliged permanently to leave the territory of the State ... without being left the possibility of returning later'.[44] This definition neatly excludes extradition from the compass of expulsion under the Article.

It appears that the Committee of Experts which drafted Protocol 4 also considered the hypothesis of a State expelling one of its nationals after first depriving them of their nationality, but 'thought it was inadvisable in Article 3 to touch on the delicate question of the legitimacy of measures depriving individuals of nationality'.[45]

However, the effect of Article 3(1) must be to preclude a State from depriving persons of their nationality in order to expel them. Otherwise it would offer no adequate protection. The Commission, indeed, has gone further, and has considered whether it may be contrary to Article 3(1) to refuse to grant a person nationality if the object of the refusal is to be able to expel them. An applicant complained both of his imminent expulsion, and of the refusal of the German authorities to recognize him as a German citizen. The Commission stated that, although the Convention confers no right to a nationality as such, the question arose whether there existed, between the decision to refuse him nationality and the order for his expulsion, a causal connection creating the presumption that the refusal had as its sole object his expulsion from German territory. There was no evidence of that, however, in the case before them.[46]

---

[39] Explanatory Reports on the Second to Fifth Protocols to the Convention, Strasbourg 1971, 47.

[40] Art. 31, Vienna Convention on the Law of Treaties, and see generally ch.4 above.

[41] ETS 24, Art. 6(1).

[42] For example, Cyprus, Germany, the Netherlands, and Switzerland.

[43] This view is not supported by J. Merrills and A. Robertson, *Human Rights in Europe* (MUP, Manchester 2001), 256.

[44] App. 6189/73, *X v Federal Republic of Germany*, Decision of 13 May 1974, (1974) 46 CD 214.

[45] Explanatory Reports on the Second to Fifth Protocols to the Convention, Strasbourg 1971, 47–8.

[46] App. 3745/68, *X v Federal Republic of Germany*, Decision of 15 December 1969, (1970) 31 CD 107.

In its admissibility decision in the *Slivenko* case,[47] the Strasbourg Court ruled that, while Article 3 secures an absolute and unconditional freedom from expulsion of a national, the grant of nationality was a matter for the national legal orders. While an arbitrary denial of nationality may under certain circumstances amount to an interference with rights under Article 8, no 'right to nationality' similar to that under Article 15 of the Universal Declaration of Human Rights is guaranteed by the Convention or its Protocols.[48]

THE RIGHT OF ENTRY TO THE TERRITORY OF THE STATE OF NATIONALITY

Similar considerations relating to the withdrawal of nationality apply to paragraph 2, which provides that:

No one shall be deprived of the right to enter the territory of the State of which he is a national.

A State could not refuse persons nationality if they fulfil the conditions laid down by its law, or deprive such persons of their nationality, in order to be able to refuse them admission.

PROHIBITING THE COLLECTIVE EXPULSION OF ALIENS

Article 4 simply states, 'Collective expulsion of aliens is prohibited.' The article does not regulate in any way the individual expulsion of aliens. Its scope is thus extremely limited.[49] The reasons given for this omission by the Committee of Experts are set out in the explanatory report.[50] One reason was that the matter had already been dealt with in the European Convention on Establishment. However, that Convention does not deal with the expulsion of aliens in general; it deals only with the expulsion of nationals of other States parties to that Convention.[51] Possibly a difficulty for the governments was that if any rights were recognized in the Protocol in relation to the expulsion of aliens generally, then the rights granted on a reciprocal basis, under

---

[47] *Slivenko and others v Latvia* (App. 48321/99), Decision of 23 January 2002, ECHR 2002-II.

[48] §77.

[49] Issues relating to this provision are raised in *Georgia v Russia (I)*, (App. 13255/07). See Decision of 3 July 2009.

[50] Explanatory Reports on the Second to Fifth Protocols to the Convention, Strasbourg 1971, 50–1.

[51] ETS 19, Art. 3.

the Establishment Convention or under other treaties, to the nationals of other States parties to those instruments might have had to be extended, through the effect of Article 14, to all aliens.

One issue which remains controversial is what constitutes a collective expulsion. This poses the question of when a series of individual expulsions can be regarded as a collective expulsion. The Commission appears to have concluded that where persons are expelled with others without their cases having received individual treatment, the expulsion will be collective.[52] The Strasbourg Court, citing its admissibility decision in an earlier case,[53] offers the following definition of collective expulsions:

The Court reiterates its case-law whereby collective expulsion, within the meaning of Article 4 of Protocol No. 4, is to be understood as any measure compelling aliens, as a group, to leave a country, except where such a measure is taken on the basis of a reasonable and objective examination of the particular case of each individual alien of the group.... That does not mean that where the latter condition is satisfied the background to the execution of the expulsion orders plays no further role in determining whether there has been compliance with Article 4 of Protocol No. 4.[54]

In the *Čonka* case, four members of a single family had been expelled from Belgium; they were Slovakian nationals of Roma origin who had come to Belgium and claimed asylum. There had been some specific consideration of their individual circumstances, but it was clear from public statements that official arrangements had been made for the 'collective repatriation' to Slovakia of substantial numbers of Slovak nationals. Furthermore, a group of Slovak nationals had been required to attend at the police station at the same time; the orders requiring them to leave Belgium were couched in identical circumstances; there had been difficulties in the aliens making contact with a lawyer; and the asylum procedure had not been completed. All these factors led the Court to conclude that this was a case of collective expulsion rather than a series of individual expulsions; there were insufficient guarantees demonstrating that the personal circumstances of each of those concerned had been genuinely and individually taken into account. In a partly dissenting opinion, Judge Velaers did not find a violation of Article 4 of Protocol 4. In essence, he felt that the factors which gave rise to doubt about the genuineness of the consideration of the individual circumstances of each case did not lead to the conclusion that this was a collective expulsion:

Repatriation as a group, an option the national authorities are free to choose for reasons of efficiency and economy, clearly cannot take place without prior preparation.[55]

A partly dissenting opinion by two other judges shares this view.[56]

---

[52] App. 7011/75, *Becker v Denmark*, Decision of 30 October 1975, (1976) 19 *Yearbook* 416; App. 14209/88, *A and others v Netherlands*, Decision of 16 December 1988, (1989) 59 DR 274.

[53] *Andric v Sweden* (App. 45917/99), Decision of 23 February 1999.

[54] *Čonka v Belgium* (App. 51564/99), 5 February 2002, (2002) 34 EHRR 1298, ECHR 2002-I, §59.

[55] §8 of Judge Velaers' partly dissenting opinion.

[56] Partly dissenting opinion of Judge Jungwiert, joined by Judge Kuris.

Where a case has been individually examined before a decision to remove a person from the territory is taken, it will be very difficult to establish that there is, in reality, a decision to expel a group of persons.[57]

EXPULSION ONLY TO FOLLOW DUE PROCESS

Article 1 of Protocol 7 provides:

1. An alien lawfully resident in the territory of a State shall not be expelled therefrom except in pursuance of a decision reached in accordance with law and shall be allowed:

   a. to submit reasons against his expulsion

   b. to have his case reviewed; and

   c. to be represented for these purposes before the competent authority or a person or persons designated by that authority.

2. An alien may be expelled before the exercise of his rights under paragraph 1.a, b and c of this article, when such expulsion is necessary in the interests of public order or is grounded on reasons of national security.

This article[58] provides certain limited procedural guarantees for those who are lawfully resident in one of the States which has ratified this provision in respect of decisions to expel them. Expulsion, according to the Explanatory Memorandum, is any measure compelling the departure of the person from the territory except extradition.[59] It is arguable that to be lawfully resident, a person must have passed through the necessary immigration procedures and have been admitted for residence rather than some more limited purpose, such as, perhaps a person admitted for a limited period as a student or a visitor. However, an admissibility decision under Article 2 of Protocol 4 suggests that a broader view may be taken, even though the words of Article 2 refer to a person as 'lawfully within the territory' while Article 1 of Protocol 7 uses the term 'lawfully resident in the territory'. The *Omwenyeke* case[60] suggests that a person is lawfully present where they are compliant with the terms of entry. So it would follow that a visitor is lawfully present while complying with the terms of any leave to enter for that purpose, but not thereafter. It remains to be seen whether the Strasbourg Court will define lawful residence under Article 1 of Protocol 7 differently from lawful presence under Article 2 of Protocol 4.

---

[57] *Sultani v France*, (App. 45223/05), 20 September 2007, ECHR 2007-X.

[58] Protocol 7 has attracted 41 ratifications as at 1 September 2009; a further five countries (Belgium, Germany, The Netherlands, Spain, and Turkey) have signed but not yet having ratified the Protocol. The United Kingdom is the only country not to sign this Protocol.

[59] Explanatory Memorandum on the Seventh Protocol, 7.

[60] *Omwenyeke v Germany*, (App. 44294/04), Decision of 20 November 2007, ECHR 2007-XII.

The *Lupsa* case[61] appears to be the first judgment under Article 1 of Protocol 7 by the Strasbourg Court. Lupsa was a national of Serbia who had lived in Romania for fourteen years, where he ran a business selling coffee. He was summarily deported on his return from travel outside Romania. In subsequent proceedings it was alleged that he was an undesirable person engaged in activities capable of endangering national security. The Strasbourg Court found that the legal basis for his deportation had not afforded the minimum guarantees against arbitrary action.[62] In addition, the Romanian authorities had infringed the guarantees under Article 1(1)(a) and (b) of the provision; he had not been provided with the slightest intimation of the national security ground on which the authorities purported to base their decision, and his lawyer had not been afforded sufficient opportunity to study the case in order to guarantee a proper review of the decision.

Article 1 of Protocol 7 will be violated where there is no legal base for the deportation order.[63] The concept of action 'in accordance with law' has the same meaning as in other provisions of the Convention.[64]

The procedural guarantees are set out in self-explanatory manner in the article,[65] which provides no protection of substance,[66] that is, relating to the grounds on which their expulsion might be sought. Nevertheless, the due process requirements themselves almost certainly operate to preclude arbitrary decisions to expel.

CONCLUDING REMARKS

Issues of free movement have begun to throw up a number of interesting and controversial issues, especially in relation to free movement in the new democracies of the Council of Europe. Complaints of violations of the freedom of movement provisions of Protocols 4 and 7 are frequently attached to complaints of violations of other provisions of the Convention. The Strasbourg Court tends to consider them towards the end of its decisions and judgments, often finding either that there is no substance to the complaint or that the factual context is the same as that considered under some other provision of the Convention. There will undoubtedly continue to be further developments in the case-law arising, in particular, from the policies and practices of some of the countries of central and eastern Europe.

---

[61] *Lupsa v Romania*, (App. 10337/04), 8 June 2006, (2008) 46 EHRR 810, ECHR 2006-VII. See to similar effect *Kaya v Romania*, (App. 33970/05), 12 October 2006; and *CG v Bulgaria*, (App.1365/07), 24 April 2008, (2008) 47 EHRR 1117, ECHR 2008-nyr.

[62] See also *Nolan and K v Russia*, (App. 2512/04), 12 February 2009.

[63] *Bolat v Russia* (App. 14139/03), 5 October 2006, (2008) 46 EHRR 354, ECHR 2006-XI.

[64] *CG v Bulgaria*, (App.1365/07), 24 April 2008, (2008) 47 EHRR 1117, ECHR 2008-nyr, §73.

[65] For further explanation, see Explanatory Memorandum on the Seventh Protocol.

[66] Other provisions of the Convention might assist, such as Arts. 3, 5(1)(f), 8, and 13.

24

FREEDOM FROM DISCRIMINATION

INTRODUCTION

Article 14 is an autonomous provision of the Convention, which contains a general prohibition of both direct and indirect discrimination in relation to the enjoyment of the rights guaranteed by the Convention and Protocols.[1] It is joined—for those Contracting Parties which have ratified it—by a more general equality provision in Protocol 12.[2]

Article 14 provides that:

The enjoyment of the rights and freedoms set forth in this Convention shall be secured without discrimination on any ground such as sex, race, colour, language, religion, political or other opinion, national or social origin, association with a national minority, property, birth or other status.

The term 'Convention' includes the First, Fourth, Sixth, and Seventh Protocols, which themselves provide that all the provisions of the Convention apply to them.[3]

The enunciation of the principle of equality, and the prohibition of discrimination, were considered so fundamental as to be placed at the beginning of the Universal Declaration of Human Rights,[4] and of the United Nations Covenants on Economic, Social and Cultural Rights and on Civil and Political Rights.[5] These principles also have a prominent place in many national constitutions, for example in Article 3 of the German Basic Law, in the 'equal protection' clauses of the United States Constitution, and in the constitutions of many Commonwealth countries. Several international instruments prohibiting particular forms of discrimination, or discrimination in particular fields, have been drawn up, in the United Nations, in the International Labour

---

[1] See K. Partsch, 'Discrimination' in R. Macdonald, F. Matscher, and H. Petzold, (eds.) *The European System for the Protection of Human Rights* (Martinus Nijhoff, Dordrecht 1993), 571; and R. O'Connell, 'Cinderella comes to the Ball: Article 14 and the right to non-discrimination in the ECHR' (2009) 29 *Legal Studies* 211.

[2] ETS 177; in force since 1 April 2005. As at 1 September 2009 in force for 17 Contracting Parties. For current ratifications see http://conventions.coe.int. See further below in this chapter.

[3] Art. 5 of Protocol 1; Art. 6(1) of Protocol 4; Art. 6 of Protocol 6; and Art. 7 of Protocol 7.

[4] Arts. 1 and 2.   [5] Arts. 2 and 3 of each Covenant.

Organisation, in UNESCO, and elsewhere. There is thus a substantial body of law on the subject.

In considering allegations of violations of Article 14, there are four key questions. First, is the complaint within the 'scope' or 'ambit' of one of the substantive provisions of the Convention? Secondly, is the alleged reason for the discrimination one of the grounds listed in Article 14? Thirdly, can the applicants properly compare themselves with another class of persons which is treated more favourably? Fourthly, is the difference in treatment reasonably and objectively justified?

POSITIVE OBLIGATIONS

The issue of positive obligations is somewhat different under Article 14 because of the requirement for the allegation of discrimination to fall within the ambit of one of the substantive articles of the Convention. However, the Strasbourg Court has indicated that, whether the discrimination arises by positive action or by a failure to ensure non-discrimination, the justification for the differential treatment must meet a legitimate aim and there must be a reasonable relationship of proportionality between that aim and its realization.[6] It is also inherent in the scheme of the article that Contracting Parties are obliged to take steps to prevent discrimination falling within the ambit of the article. This obligation manifests itself in the Court's conclusion that the right not to be discriminated against in the enjoyment of rights falling within the scope of the Convention will be violated where Contracting Parties fail to treat persons in different situations differently without any objective and reasonable justification for doing so.[7] However, in this context the Contracting Parties enjoy a considerable margin of appreciation in assessing whether and to what extent differences in otherwise similar situations justify a difference in treatment.[8]

An example of discrimination arising where there is a failure to treat different individuals or groups differently can be found in the *Thlimmenos* case, which concerned a conviction for refusal to serve in the armed forces by a Jehovah's Witness.[9] The applicant complained that, as a result of his conviction for the offence, he had been excluded from the profession of chartered accountant, and that the law failed to make any distinction between those convicted as a result of their religious beliefs and those convicted on other grounds. The applicant complained of a violation of Article 14 when taken together with Article 9 on freedom of thought, conscience, and religion. The Court, in finding a violation of Article 14 taken in conjunction with Article 9, extended its earlier case-law to situations where, without any objective and reasonable

---

[6] *Posti and Rahko v Finland* (App. 27824/95), 24 September 2002, (2003) 37 EHRR 158, ECHR 2002-VII.

[7] *Thlimmenos v Greece* (App. 34369/97), 6 April 2000, (2001) 31 EHRR 411, ECHR 2000-IV.

[8] *Sommerfeld v Germany* (App. 31871/96), 8 July 2003 [GC], (2004) 38 EHRR 756, ECHR 2003-VIII, §92.

[9] *Thlimmenos v Greece* (App. 34369/97), 6 April 2000, (2001) 31 EHRR 411, ECHR 2000-IV.

justification, a Contracting Party fails to treat differently persons whose situations are significantly different.

CONCEPTUAL ISSUES

Until the judgment of the Strasbourg Court in the *Belgian Linguistic* case,[10] there was some doubt as to the relationship between Article 14 and the articles which define the other rights and freedoms guaranteed. Article 14 does not prohibit discrimination as such, in any context, but only in 'the enjoyment of the rights and freedoms set forth in this Convention'. On the other hand, did Article 14 only come into play if there had been a violation of one of those rights? The view that Article 14 had such a subsidiary role, advanced by the respondent State before the Court in the *Belgian Linguistic* case, derived some support from certain earlier decisions of the Commission.[11] However, this interpretation would, as the Commission itself argued in the *Belgian Linguistic* case, have deprived Article 14 of its effectiveness, and it was rejected by the Court. The breach of Article 14 does not presuppose the violation of the rights guaranteed by other Articles of the Convention. While it is true that this guarantee has no independent existence in the sense that under the terms of Article 14 it relates solely to 'rights and freedoms set forth in the Convention', a measure which in itself is in conformity with the requirements of a substantive article enshrining the right or freedom in question may nevertheless infringe Article 14 when read in conjunction with it for the reason that it is of a discriminatory nature.

Thus, persons subject to the jurisdiction of a Contracting Party cannot draw from Article 2 of Protocol 1 the right to obtain from the public authorities the creation of a particular kind of educational establishment. Nevertheless, a Contracting Party which had set up such an establishment could not, in laying down entrance requirements, take discriminatory measures within the meaning of Article 14. To recall a further example, cited in the course of the proceedings, Article 6 of the Convention does not compel Contracting Parties to institute a system of appeal courts. A Contracting Party which does set up such courts consequently goes beyond its obligations under Article 6. However, it would violate Article 6, read in conjunction with Article 14, were it to debar certain persons from these remedies without a legitimate reason while making them available to others in respect of the same type of actions.

In such cases there would be a violation of a guaranteed right or freedom as it is proclaimed by the relevant article read in conjunction with Article 14. It is as though

---

[10] *Case relating to certain aspects of the laws on the use of languages in education in Belgium (Belgian Linguistic Case (No. 20)*, (Apps. 1474/62, 1677/62, 1691/62, 1769/63, 1994/63, and 2126/64), 23 July 1968, Series A No 6, (1979–80), 23 July 1968, Series A No 6, (1979–80) 1 EHRR 252 (cited in this chapter as the *'Belgian Linguistic* case').

[11] See M. Eissen, 'L'autonomie de l'article 14 de la Convention européenne des droits de l'homme dans la jurisprudence de la Commission', in *Mélanges Modinos* (Paris, 1968), 122.

the latter formed an integral part of each of the substantive articles laying down rights and freedoms. No distinctions should be made in this respect according to the nature of these rights and freedoms and of their correlative obligations, and for instance as to whether the respect due to the right concerned implies positive action or mere abstention. This is, moreover, clearly shown by the very general nature of the terms employed in Article 14 'the enjoyment of the rights and freedoms set forth in this Convention shall be secured'.[12]

Thus, to put the matter differently, while there can never be a violation of Article 14 considered in isolation, there may be a violation of Article 14, considered together with another article of the Convention, in cases where there would be no violation of that other article taken alone. The right of appeal, however, in the example given by the Court, is as such outside the scope of the Convention altogether, whether in civil or in criminal cases. Nevertheless, Article 14 together with Article 6 prohibits discrimination in access to the courts throughout the whole of the judicial system. The conclusion is, therefore, that discrimination is prohibited, not only in the restrictions permitted, but also in laws implementing the rights guaranteed, even if those laws go beyond the obligations expressly provided by the Convention.

A second, and more difficult, problem of interpretation raised by Article 14 was also dealt with by the Court in the *Belgian Linguistic* case. What forms of differential treatment constitute 'discrimination'? To argue that Article 14 prohibits all inequalities of treatment based on the grounds stated would lead to manifestly unreasonable results, since the inequality might actually be designed to benefit the less privileged class. For example, the provision of additional educational facilities for the children of poorer families would not necessarily constitute discrimination. On the other hand, if only certain forms of inequality are prohibited, by what objective criteria can they be identified? On this issue, the Court said:

In spite of the very general wording of the French version ('*sans distinction aucune*'), Article 14 does not forbid every difference in treatment in the exercise of the rights and freedoms recognized. This version must be read in the light of the more restrictive text of the English version ('without discrimination'). In addition, and in particular, one would reach absurd results were one to give Article 14 an interpretation as wide as that which the French version seems to imply. One would, in effect, be led to judge as contrary to the Convention every one of the many legal or administrative provisions which do not secure to everyone complete equality of treatment in the enjoyment of the rights and freedoms recognized. The competent national authorities are frequently confronted with situations and problems which, on account of differences inherent therein, call for different legal solutions; moreover, certain legal inequalities tend only to correct factual inequalities. The extensive interpretation mentioned above cannot consequently be accepted.

It is important, then, to look for the criteria which enable a determination to be made as to whether or not a given difference in treatment, concerning of course the exercise of one of the rights and freedoms set forth, contravenes Article 14. On this question the Court,

---

[12] *Belgian Linguistic* case, (Apps. 1474/62, 1677/62, 1691/62, 1769/63, 1994/63, and 2126/64), 23 July 1968, Series A No 6, (1979–80) 1 EHRR 252, Section IB, §9.

following the principles which may be extracted from the legal practice of a large number of democratic States, holds that the principle of equality of treatment is violated if the distinction has no objective and reasonable justification. The existence of such a justification must be assessed in relation to the aim and effects of the measure under consideration, regard being had to the principles which normally prevail in democratic societies. A difference of treatment in the exercise of a right laid down in the Convention must not only pursue a legitimate aim; Article 14 is likewise violated when it is clearly established that there is no reasonable relationship of proportionality between the means employed and the aim sought to be realised.[13]

The Court thus adopted, and applied in its examination of the legislation in question, the weaker of two alternative theses on the meaning of discrimination. On this weaker thesis, differential treatment is justified if it has an objective aim, derived from the public interest, and if the measures of differentiation do not exceed a reasonable relation to that aim.

A stronger thesis would be that differential treatment is justified only if, *without regard to the purpose of the measures in question*, the facts themselves require or permit differential treatment. This view of Article 14 was clearly formulated by a member of the Commission, Mr Balta, in an individual opinion in the *Grandrath* case.[14] He stated:

In my view, the intention of Article 14 is to establish the principle of complete equality in the enjoyment of the rights and freedoms set forth in the Convention. This being so, enjoyment of those rights and freedoms may not be made subject to any kinds of discrimination other than those which are either inherent in the nature of the right in question or are designed to remedy existing inequalities.

The two theses both start from the idea that a difference of status, of sex, race, language, and so on, cannot of itself justify differential treatment; but whereas on the first thesis differential treatment might be justified by the purpose of the measures in question, on the second thesis it could only be justified if the difference of status implied certain objective factual differences which required or permitted different legal treatment. The distinction is of considerable practical importance, since, on the thesis adopted by the Strasbourg Court in the *Belgian Linguistic* case, it found a violation on only one aspect of the Belgian legislation; on the stronger thesis, other provisions might also have been inconsistent with the Convention.

Some examples of discrimination on certain of the grounds referred to in Article 14 has already been mentioned in earlier chapters: for example, in relation to sex, under Article 8; to race, under Article 3; to language, under Article 2 of Protocol 1; and to religion, under Article 9; and in relation to property under Article 1 of Protocol 1. Complaints under Article 14 are most frequently paired with Article 8, followed by Article 1 of Protocol 1, and Articles 10 and 6.

---

[13] *Belgian Linguistic* case, Section IB, §10.

[14] App. 2299/64, *Grandrath v Federal Republic of Germany*, Report of Commission, 12 December 1966; Decision of Committee of Ministers, 29 June 1967, (1967) 10 *Yearbook* 626.

Finally, it should be noted that the grounds listed in Article 14 are not exhaustive. Discrimination based on any 'other status' is also prohibited. The French text, *toute autre situation*, seems to go even further in this respect. It is sometimes said that, where consideration of discrimination with regard to 'other status' is in issue, the basis of comparison must relate to a personal characteristic.[15] But precisely what is meant by a personal characteristic is one of the troublesome aspects of Article 14. There is no direct authority which provides that the ground of differentiation must be based on the narrow view of what constitutes a personal characteristic. The better view, therefore, is that there is no formal requirement flowing from the Strasbourg case-law which requires that the party seeking to show discrimination falling within Article 14 is based upon a personal characteristic.[16] For example, in the *Carson* case, the Strasbourg Court accepted that residence, like domicile and nationality, is an aspect of personal status, and will ground a complaint of differential treatment.[17] It will generally be easier to establish a situation as falling within Article 14 where the ground of differentiation is a personal characteristic. It is probably also true that different treatment which is based other than on a personal characteristic may be easier for the Contracting Party to justify.[18]

THE COURT'S METHODOLOGY

Over the years, the Strasbourg Court's methodology in dealing with complaints under Article 14 has developed considerably. At one time, there was much focus on whether there had been a violation of the substantive provision of the Convention claimed to be within the ambit of Article 14 before consideration of whether there was discrimination. If a violation of the substantive provision was found, there was a tendency not to consider that provision in conjunction with Article 14 in what one commentator describes as for 'reasons of procedural economy.'[19] The signal for a

---

[15] See *Kjeldsen, Busk Madsen and Pedersen v Denmark*, (App. 5095/71, 5920/72, and 5926/72), 7 December 1976, Series A No 23, (1979–80) 1 EHRR 711, §56. See also *Budak v Turkey*, (App. 57345/00), Decision of December of 7 September 2004, §4.

[16] See *Stubbings and others v United Kingdom*, (Apps. 22083/93 and 22095/93), 22 October 1996, (1997) 23 EHRR 213, ECHR 1996-IV, where the differential treatment related to the legal system's approach to providing a remedy for psychological harm resulting from child abuse and other types of actionable wrong; and *National & Provincial Building Society and others v United Kingdom*, (Apps. 21319/93, 21449/93, and 21675/93), 23 October 1997, (1998) 25 EHRR 127, ECHR 1997-VII, which concerned recovery of tax paid under invalidated tax regulations.

[17] *Carson and others v United Kingdom*, (App. 42184/05), 4 November 2008, §76. The Chamber judgment has been referred to the Grand Chamber.

[18] As in the *Carson* case, which concerned differential treatment of pensioners in terms of the annual increase in their pensions according to the country of their residence. The Court noted that residence can be changed as a matter of choice: §80.

[19] K. Partsch, 'Discrimination' in R. Macdonald, F. Matscher, and H. Petzold (eds.), *The European System for the Protection of Human Rights* (Martinus Nijhoff, Dordrecht 1993), 583.

change to that approach was reinforced in an early decision of the Grand Chamber in the *Chassagnou* case:[20]

Where a substantive Article of the Convention has been invoked both on its own and together with Article 14 and a separate breach has been found of the substantive Article, it is not generally necessary for the Court to consider the case under Article 14 also, though the position is otherwise if a clear inequality of treatment in the enjoyment of the right in question is a fundamental aspect of the case.[21]

This approach addresses a criticism which could be levelled at some early decisions of the Strasbourg organs where clear inequality of treatment had been ignored to the detriment of the development of the case-law on the prohibition of discrimination. When an allegation of a violation of a substantive provision of the Convention is coupled with an allegation that there has also been a violation of that article when read with Article 14, there remain many cases where the Strasbourg Court does not find it necessary to address the complaint under Article 14, but there is an increasing number of cases in which the Court does choose to deal with this aspect of the applicant's complaints. Sometimes the Strasbourg Court does not consider the additional complaint involving discrimination because its response to the complaint under the substantive question would constitute reasonable and objective justification in relation to discrimination within Article 14.[22]

Where the essence of the complaint of a violation of the substantive provision is an act of discrimination, the Strasbourg Court begins by considering the allegation of a violation of Article 14 when read with the substantive provision. This can render it unnecessary to consider whether there has been a separate violation of the substantive article. So, in the *Burghartz* case,[23] the applicants complained under Article 8 taken alone, and in conjunction with Article 14, that they had been refused consent to change their family surname and the husband's surname. The Court considered whether there had been a violation of Article 8 taken in conjunction with Article 14 first. The basis for doing so was said to be 'the nature of the complaints',[24] which was essentially a difference of treatment on the grounds of sex in relation to the use of names. The Court found a violation.

Sometimes, the Strasbourg Court finds a violation both of the substantive provision, and of that provision when read with Article 14. In the *Marckx* case,[25] the Court found violations of Article 8 taken alone in the process of recognition required of an unmarried mother to establish her maternity, and then went on to consider whether

---

[20] *Chassagnou and others v France*, (Apps. 25088/94, 28331/95, and 28443/95), 29 April 1999 [GC], (2000) 29 EHRR 615, ECHR 1999-III.

[21] §89, although similar statements can be found in much earlier cases, see, for example, *Dudgeon v United Kingdom*, (App. 7525/76), 22 October 1981, Series A No 45, (1982) 4 EHRR 149, §67.

[22] As in *Evans v United Kingdom*, (App. 6339/05), 10 April 2007 [GC], (2008) 46 EHRR 728, ECHR 2007-IV.

[23] *Burghartz v Switzerland*, (App. 16213/90), 22 February 1994, Series A No 280-B, (1994) 18 EHRR 101.

[24] §21.

[25] *Marckx v Belgium*, (App. 6833/74), 13 June 1979, Series A No 31, (1979–80) 2 EHRR 330.

violations had occurred under Article 8 taken in conjunction with Article 14. It is difficult to see how these complaints were not in substance the same as those taken under Article 8 alone, but this was presumably one of those cases in which a 'clear inequality of treatment in the enjoyment of the right in question' arose as 'a fundamental aspect of the case'. A more recent example of a case in which a violation was found both of the substantive provision and of Article 14 is the *Bączkowski* case.[26] Members of an association whose objectives were to campaign on behalf of homosexual people were refused permission to organize a march in Warsaw. While the application was pending, the Mayor of Warsaw had made remarks in a newspaper interview to the effect that he would ban the march and that 'propaganda about homosexuality is not tantamount to exercising one's freedom of assembly.' The subsequent refusal of permission purported to be based on concerns over road traffic management. The Strasbourg Court found that the decision was influenced by the remarks of the Mayor in the interview. A violation of Article 11 was found, but a violation of Article 14 read with Article 11 was also found on the grounds that the Mayor's statements indicated unlawful discrimination in the exercise of public powers.

In the *Aziz* case,[27] the Strasbourg Court found a violation of Article 3 of Protocol 1, and a violation of that article when read with Article 14. The applicant was a Turkish Cypriot living in Nicosia who had been deprived of the opportunity to vote. After finding a violation of Article 3 of Protocol 1, the Court went on to consider the complaint under Article 14, noting that the complaint was 'not a mere restatement of the applicant's complaint' under the substantive article.[28] There was discrimination between members of the Greek Cypriot and Turkish Cypriot communities for which there was no reasonable and objective justification. The case might usefully be contrasted with the *Eugenia Michaelidou Developments Ltd* case,[29] where the complaint concerned continuing denial of access to property in the occupied north of Cyprus. Having found a violation of Article 1 of Protocol 1, the Court declined to pronounce on allegations of violations of Article 14 when read with Article 1 of Protocol 1 since these allegations amounted to essentially the same complaints.[30]

In the *Nachova* case,[31] the Grand Chamber found violations both of Article 2 when read alone, and of Article 14 when read with Article 2. The applicants were relatives of two Roma men who had been shot and killed when they were on the run from the police. It was alleged that the killings were racially motivated, and that the authorities had failed in their duty to investigate the possible racist motivations in their killing. The Grand Chamber found that the investigation of the killings was inadequate and

---

[26] *Bączkowski and others v Poland*, (App. 1543/06), 3 May 2007, (2009) 48 EHRR 475, ECHR 2007-VI.

[27] *Aziz v Cyprus*, (App. 69949/01), 22 June 2004, (2005) 41 EHRR 164, ECHR 2004-V.

[28] §36.

[29] *Eugenia Michaelidou Developments Ltd and Michael Tymvios v Turkey*, (App. 16163/90), 31 July 2003.

[30] Following the approach it had adopted in *Cyprus v Turkey* (App. 25781/94), 10 May 2001 [GC], (2002) 35 EHRR 731, ECHR 2001-IV, §199, but note the partly dissenting opinion of Judge Costa.

[31] *Nachova and others v Bulgaria*, (Apps. 43577/98 and 43579/98), 6 July 2005 [GC], (2006) 42 EHRR 933, ECHR 2005-VII.

that this constituted a violation of the procedural aspect of Article 2.[32] In considering whether there was also a violation of Article 14 when read with Article 2, the Grand Chamber commented as follows:

Owing to the interplay between the two provisions, issues such as those in the present case may fall to be examined under one of the two provisions only, with no separate issue arising under the other, or may require examination under both Articles. This is a question to be decided in each case on its facts and depending on the nature of the allegation made.[33]

The motivation for dealing with the complaint under Article 14 when read with Article 2 is not articulated beyond that statement, though it seems that the background of 'many published accounts of the existence in Bulgaria of prejudice and hostility against Roma'[34] may have been a significant factor. It is, however, not difficult to view this separate consideration as merely a recapitulation of the issues raised in relation to the procedural aspect of Article 2 itself. Subsequent cases have made the racial component much more explicit.[35]

In very many cases, the Strasbourg Court concerns itself with four questions in making decisions on complaints under Article 14:[36]

- Does the complaint of discrimination fall within the scope of a protected right?
- Is the alleged reason for the discrimination one of the grounds listed in Article 14?
- Can the applicants properly compare themselves with another class of persons which is treated more favourably?
- Is the difference of treatment capable of objective and reasonable justification?

Each of these questions will now be considered.

DOES THE COMPLAINT OF DISCRIMINATION FALL WITHIN THE SCOPE OF A PROTECTED RIGHT?

Article 14 only applies in respect of 'the enjoyment of the rights and freedoms as set forth' in the Convention, including its Protocols. But there is no requirement that there is a breach of another Convention right. An example of the modern formula used by the Strasbourg Court can be found in the *Kafkaris* case:[37]

---

[32] See ch.8 above.   [33] §161.

[34] §163. See below in this chapter for further comments on cases involving discrimination against minorities.

[35] See, for example, *Angelova and Iliev v Bulgaria*, (App. 55523/00), 26 July 2007, (2008) 47 EHRR 236; and *Cobzaru v Romania*, (App. 48254/99), 26 July 2007, (2008) 47 EHRR 288.

[36] See the Grand Chamber's statement of general principles in *Kafkaris v Cyprus*, (App. 21906/04), 12 February 2008 [GC], (2009) 49 EHRR 877, ECHR 2008-nyr, §§159–61.

[37] *Kafkaris v Cyprus*, (App. 21906/04), 12 February 2008 [GC], (2009) 49 EHRR 877, ECHR 2008-nyr.

The Court reiterates that Article 14 of the Convention has no independent existence, since it has effect solely in relation to the rights and freedoms safeguarded by the other substantive provisions of the Convention and its Protocols. However, the application of Article 14 does not presuppose a breach of one or more of such provisions and to this extent it is autonomous.... . A measure which in itself is in conformity with the requirements of the Article enshrining the right or freedom in question may however infringe this Article when read in conjunction with Article 14 for the reason that it is of a discriminatory nature.... . Accordingly, for Article 14 to become applicable it suffices that the facts of a case fall within the ambit of another substantive provision of the Convention or its Protocols.... .[38]

In the *Stec* case,[39] the Court made it clear that there was no requirement under, for example, Article 1 of Protocol 1, to set up a system of social security or to pay welfare benefits of any particular kind or amount. However, if a State did decide to exceed its Convention commitments, and provide for the payment of a welfare benefit, it had to ensure that the terms of entitlement to the benefit were not discriminatory. The applicants in that case were complaining that different amounts of an industrial injury benefit were paid to men and women. When women reached the statutory retirement age of 60, they became entitled to a lower rate of benefit. The statutory retirement age was 65 for men, however, so that men continued to be entitled to the higher rate of industrial injury benefit for a longer period. The Strasbourg Court held that although there was no obligation on the State under the Convention to provide for an industrial injury benefit, if such a benefit did exist, a person who was entitled to it under the terms of national law could claim it as a 'possession' within the meaning of Article 1 of Protocol 1. It therefore fell within the 'scope' of the Convention and Article 14 therefore applied.

Another example is the *Runkee and White* case.[40] The applicants here were men whose wives had died. They complained that female widows in the United Kingdom received a widow's pension, whereas male widowers did not. The Court held that the complaint about the non-payment of widow's pension fell within the scope of Article 1 of Protocol 1. The Court has held that, in such cases, concerning a complaint that the applicant has been denied all or part of a particular benefit on a discriminatory ground covered by Article 14, the relevant test is whether, but for the condition of entitlement about which the applicant complains, he or she would have had a right, enforceable under domestic law, to receive the benefit in question.[41]

Similarly, in the *Belgian Linguistic* case,[42] the Strasbourg Court held that, although Article 2 of Protocol 1 did not place an obligation on the State to set up a publicly-funded school of any particular kind, if the State did create such a school, it could

---

[38] §159.

[39] *Stec and others v United Kingdom*, (Apps. 65731/01 and 65900/01), 12 April 2006 [GC], (2006) 43 EHRR 1017, ECHR 2006-VI. See also ch.20 above.

[40] *Runkee and White v United Kingdom*, (Apps. 42949/98 and 53134/99), 10 May 2007.

[41] *Stec and others v United Kingdom*, (Apps. 65731/01 and 65900/01), Decision of 5 September 2005 [GC], (2005) 41 EHRR SE18, ECHR 2005-X, §55.

[42] *Belgian Linguistic* case, (Apps. 1474/62, 1677/62, 1691/62, 1769/63, 1994/63, and 2126/64), 23 July 1968, Series A No 6, (1979–80) 1 EHRR 252.

not, in laying down entrance requirements, take discriminatory measures within the meaning of Article 14. In the same case, the Court gave as another example of this principle the right of access to a court of appeal. Article 6 does not require a State to create an appeal system in civil or criminal proceedings. But if a right of appeal is created, the guarantees of fairness under Article 6 will apply. The right to an appeal therefore falls within the 'scope' of Article 6 and access to it must not be limited on discriminatory grounds in breach of Article 14.

An example of a complaint which was not found to fall within the scope of a Convention right is the *Haas* case.[43] The applicant was an illegitimate child; he knew who his father was, though his father had never recognized him as his son. Nevertheless, his father made regular payments towards his maintenance, visited him, and went on day trips with him. The father died intestate and his estate went to his nephew. The applicant claimed part of the estate, but the national courts refused to accept his claim to be the unrecognized son. The Court concluded that the complaint was not within the scope of Article 8; he had never lived with his father and the sporadic contacts did not constitute 'family life', nor had he taken steps to have his paternity recognized during his father's life.[44] Since the claim was not within the scope of Article 8, Article 14 issues could not be considered.

The Strasbourg Court generally takes a broad brush approach as to whether a claim falls within the ambit of one of the substantive articles, and this can sometimes lead to considerable confusion about the outer limits of the operation of a particular article.[45]

IS THE ALLEGED REASON FOR THE DISCRIMINATION ONE OF THE GROUNDS LISTED IN ARTICLE 14?

Article 14 includes a list of prohibited grounds of discrimination: 'sex, race, colour, language, religion, political or other opinion, national or social origin, association with a national minority, property, birth'. The list of prohibited grounds is not exhaustive, however, as the article also states that discrimination based on 'other status' is prohibited. The French version, 'toute autre situation', is even broader.

In the *Kjeldsen, Busk Madsen and Pedersen* case, the Strasbourg Court established that to fall within the concept 'other status', the difference in treatment had to be based

---

[43] *Haas v The Netherlands*, (App. 36983/97), 13 January 2004, (2004) 39 EHRR 897, ECHR 2004-I. Contrast *Merger and Cros v France*, (App. 68864/01), 22 December 2004, dealing with the rights of an illegitimate child to inherit in a different situation.

[44] Which the Court, in the *Haas* case, hints might have brought the claim within the scope of 'private life' since it concerned the son's personal identity: §42.

[45] See A. Baker, 'The Enjoyment of Rights and Freedoms: A New Conception of the "Ambit" under Article 14 ECHR' (2006) 65 MLR 714.

on 'a personal characteristic by which persons or groups of persons are distinguishable from each other'.[46] The Court and Commission have held that such characteristics as sexual orientation,[47] marital status,[48] country of domicile or residence,[49] and the suffering from the psychological harm caused by child abuse,[50] all constitute 'other status'.

The open-ended nature of the phrase 'other status' can make it difficult to apply in some cases. The *Sidabras and Džautas* case[51] illustrates the differences of view which can arise. The case concerned the application of laws in Lithuania designed to restrict the activities of former KGB officers. Both had been dismissed from Government employment when it was established that they were former KGB employees. A consequence of the application of the legislation to them was a restriction on their applying for various jobs in the private sector for a period of ten years. They argued that this breached their rights under Article 8 either taken alone or when read with Article 14. The Strasbourg Court chose to consider the claims under Article 8 when read with Article 14 because the applicants 'alleged discrimination in this respect'.[52] The Court concluded that the complaints were within the scope of Article 8, and so considered the Contracting Party's compliance with Article 14. The Court recognized the legitimate interest of the Contracting Party in regulating employment conditions both in the public and private sectors, though the Convention does not guarantee a right of access to a particular profession. The Court also acknowledged that under Article 10 of the Convention a democratic State had 'a legitimate interest in requiring civil servants to show loyalty to the constitutional principles on which the society was founded.'[53] As it had in other cases,[54] the Court recognized the political context of the emergence of countries of central and eastern Europe from totalitarian regimes. The restrictions on the employment of former KGB employees could be seen as pursuing the aim of protecting national security, public safety, the economic well-being of the country, and the rights and freedoms of others. However, the restrictions which applied to employment in the private sector went beyond what was reasonably needed to secure those aims. The scheme lacked 'the necessary safeguards for avoiding discrimination and for guaranteeing adequate and appropriate judicial supervision of the imposition of such

---

[46] *Kjeldsen, Busk Madsen and Pedersen v Denmark*, (App. 5095/71, 5920/72, and 5926/72), 7 December 1976, Series A No 23, (1979–80) 1 EHRR 711, §56.

[47] *Sutherland v United Kingdom*, (App. 25186/94), Report of the Commission adopted on 1 July 1997, §51.

[48] *McMichael v United Kingdom*, (App. 16424/90), 24 February 1995, Series A No 307-B, (1995) 20 EHRR 205.

[49] *Johnston v Ireland*, (App. 9697/82), 18 December 1986, Series A No 112, (1987) 9 EHRR 203, §§59–61; *Darby v Sweden*, (App. 11581/85), 23 October 1990, Series A No 187, (1991) 13 EHRR 774, §§ 31–4.

[50] *Stubbings and others v United Kingdom*, (Apps. 22083/93 and 22095/93), 22 October 1996, (1997) 23 EHRR 213, ECHR 1996-IV.

[51] *Sidabras and Džautas v Lithuania*, (Apps. 55480/00 and 59330/00), 27 July 2004, (2004) 42 EHRR 104, ECHR 2004-VIII. See also *Žickus v Lithuania*, (App. 26652/02), 7 April 2009.

[52] §37. The discrimination was between those who were former KGB employees and those who were not: see §41.

[53] §52.

[54] Notably in cases concerning property rights: see ch.20 above.

restrictions.'[55] No separate consideration of a violation of Article 8 was undertaken. There were two dissenting opinions. Judge Loucaides did not consider that people who had worked for the KGB and people who had not worked for the KGB could be said to be in 'analogous', 'similar', or 'relevantly similar' situations. Judge Thomassen took a similar view:

The principle of non-discrimination, as it is recognized in European Constitutions and in International Treaties, refers above all to a denial of opportunities on grounds of personal choices in so far as these choices should be respected as element's of someone's personality, such as religion, political opinion, sexual orientation and gender identity, or, on the contrary, on grounds of personal features in respect of which no choice at all can be made, such as sex, race, disability and age.

Working for the KGB in my opinion does not fall within either of those categories.

Both dissenting judges would have found a violation of Article 8 read alone in the circumstances of this case. Judge Mularoni appended a partly concurring opinion; she too would have preferred the Court to have considered the case under Article 8 when read alone, and would have found a violation. The case displays both some uncertainty about the nature of 'other status', the choice of comparator, and the circumstances in which it will be appropriate to take first the allegation of discrimination.

CAN THE APPLICANTS PROPERLY COMPARE THEMSELVES WITH ANOTHER CLASS OF PERSONS WHICH IS TREATED MORE FAVOURABLY?

The third question, in determining whether there has been a breach of Article 14, is whether the applicants can properly compare themselves with a class of persons who are treated more favourably. The Strasbourg Court has not developed a single statement which it repeats in this regard. Over time, it has referred to the comparators being in 'similar situations',[56] or in 'relevantly similar situations',[57] or in 'analogous situations'.[58] The purpose of this test is to enable the Court to determine whether the less favourable treatment is attributable to one of the Article 14 prohibited grounds of discrimination, and not to other factors. For the test to function, the situation of the applicant and the comparator must be analogous in all material respects so that it

---

[55] *Sidabras and Džautas*, §59.

[56] *Marckx v Belgium*, (App. 6833/74), 13 June 1979, Series A No 31, (1979–80) 2 EHRR 330, §32.

[57] *Fredin v Sweden*, (App. 12033/86), 18 February 1991, Series A No 192, (1991) 13 EHRR 784, §60. This appears to be the currently favoured formulation: see *Burden v United Kingdom*, (App. 13378/05), 29 April 2008 [GC], (2008) 47 EHRR 857, ECHR 2008-nyr, §60.

[58] *Stubbings and others v United Kingdom* (Apps. 22083/93 and 22095/93), 22 October 1996, (1997) 23 EHRR 213, ECHR 1996-IV, §71.

can properly be concluded that the difference between them arises from an Article 14 ground.

The problem of comparing like with like is illustrated in the *Van der Mussele* case,[59] where the applicant argued unsuccessfully that the comparators were different professional groups. The Court considered that there were fundamental differences in the regulation of different professions that precluded their use as comparators in the case. The Court can perhaps be criticized for sometimes passing over detailed consideration of whether the comparators are in an analogous situation to the applicants, particularly where it seems likely that the Contracting Party will be able to show justification for the differential treatment. In fairness, it should be noted that the issue of whether the compared groups are truly in analogous situations can sometimes only be answered by considering whether their differential treatment can be justified.

In the *Burden* case,[60] the applicants were sisters who were living together in the same house. They argued that they were victims of discrimination, because they could not pass property between them on death free of inheritance tax, whereas property passing between spouses or civil partners was exempt. The issue was whether siblings, on the one hand, and spouses and civil partners, on the other hand, were in analogous positions. The Grand Chamber[61] concluded that they were not, because the relationship are qualitatively different. The relationship between siblings is a blood tie, and marriage or civil partnership is prohibited for those with such close blood ties. The relationship between couples who are married or register a civil partnership is a matter of choice, and a special status is thereby conferred upon that relationship. Since the sisters could not compare themselves with married couples or civil partners, they could not show any discrimination in breach of Article 14. The two dissenting judges considered that the justification for the inheritance tax exemption was the proximity of the relationship between the affected parties. That being so, it could not be the justification for refusing the exemption to the two sisters while allowing it for married couples and civil partners.

The starting point is to consider whether applicants can show that they have been treated less favourably than the comparator group by reason of the characteristics identified. However, Article 14 also applies where there is indirect discrimination. This occurs where the same requirement applies to both groups, but where a significant number of one group is unable to comply with the requirement. As early as the *Belgian Linguistic* case, the Court indicated that the existence of discrimination might relate to the *effects* of State measures.[62] The Court's analysis does not use the terms direct and indirect discrimination, but rather focuses on whether the differential treatment

---

[59] *Van der Mussele v Belgium*, (App. 8919/80), 23 November 1983, Series A No 70, (1984) 6 EHRR 163.

[60] *Burden v United Kingdom*, (App. 13378/05), 29 April 2008 [GC], (2008) 47 EHRR 857, ECHR 2008-nyr.

[61] The Chamber judgment of 12 December 2006 had found no violation, but had left open the question of whether the sisters were in an analogous position to married couples or civil partners, indicating that, even if they were, the differential treatment could be justified.

[62] *Belgian Linguistic* case, (Apps. 1474/62, 1677/62, 1691/62, 1769/63, 1994/63, and 2126/64), 23 July 1968, Series A No 6, (1979–80) 1 EHRR 252, §10 of Section IB.

alleged has no objective and reasonable justification.[63] That Article 14 covers indirect discrimination has been established beyond doubt in the *DH* case.[64]

IS THE DIFFERENCE OF TREATMENT CAPABLE OF OBJECTIVE AND REASONABLE JUSTIFICATION?

In the *Burden* case, the Grand Chamber said

...a difference of treatment is discriminatory if it has no objective and reasonable justification; in other words, if it does not pursue a legitimate aim or if there is not a reasonable relationship of proportionality between the means employed and the aim sought to be realised. The Contracting State enjoys a margin of appreciation in assessing whether and to what extent differences in otherwise similar situations justify a different treatment, ...[65]

In asserting a legitimate aim for the differential treatment, the respondent State must not only show the nature of the legitimate aim it is pursuing, but must also show by convincing evidence the link between the legitimate aim pursued and the differential treatment challenged by the applicant.[66] As with the requirement to establish a legitimate claim under Article 8 to 11,[67] this is not generally a difficult hurdle for the respondent State to clear, particularly since the Court has held that the purpose of saving public money can be a legitimate aim under Article 14.[68]

In the *Gillow* case,[69] the Strasbourg Court accepted that preferential treatment for those with a strong attachment to Guernsey reflected in the island's restrictive housing laws was a legitimate aim, and found no breach of Article 14 read with Article 8. In the *Darby* case,[70] the Court concluded that the refusal to grant exemption from a church tax to a claimant not formally registered as a resident in Sweden on the grounds that their case for exemption was less strong than for those registered as formally resident and would give rise to administrative inconvenience, did not meet the requirement of being a legitimate aim, and accordingly found a violation of Article 14 read with Article 1 of Protocol 1.

---

[63] See, for example, *Abdulaziz, Cabales and Balkandali v United Kingdom*, (Apps. 9214/80, 9473/81, and 9474/81), 28 May 1985, Series A No 94, (1985) 7 EHRR 471, §72.

[64] *DH and others v Czech Republic*, (App. 57325/00), 13 November 2007 [GC], (2008) 47 EHRR 59, ECHR 2007-nyr, §§175 and 184.

[65] *Burden v United Kingdom*, (App. 13378/05), 29 April 2008 [GC], ECHR 2008-nyr, §60. Compare *Korelc v Slovenia*, (App. 28456/03), 12 May 2009.

[66] *Larkos v Cyprus* (App. 29515/95), 18 February 1999, (2000) 30 EHRR 597, ECHR 1999-I, §31.

[67] See ch.14 above.

[68] *Andrejeva v Latvia* (App. 55707/00) 18 February 2009 [GC], ECHR 2009-nyr, §86.

[69] *Gillow v United Kingdom*, (App. 9063/80), 24 November 1986, Series A No 109, (1989) 11 EHRR 335.

[70] *Darby v Sweden*, (App. 11581/85), 23 October 1990, Series A No 187, (1991) 13 EHRR 774.

In the *PM* case,[71] the Court did not accept that provisions of United Kingdom tax law which permitted married fathers to claim tax relief on maintenance payments after the breakdown of a marriage but did not allow unmarried fathers to claim such relief following the breakdown of a relationship outside marriage served a legitimate aim. The respondent State had sought to rely on the special regime of marriage as conferring specific rights and obligations for married persons. The Court responded by ruling that as a general rule unmarried fathers who have established family life with their children can claim equal rights of contact and custody with married fathers; the equal treatment requirement would extend to tax deductibility of maintenance payments.

In the *Abdulaziz, Cabales and Balkandali* case,[72] the Court concluded that the construction of immigration rules in such a way as to protect the domestic labour market was 'without doubt legitimate'[73] but that in its application the need to apply rules for this purpose which discriminated on grounds of sex could not be regarded, in fact, as sufficiently important to justify the difference of treatment.[74]

Again, as with Article 8 to 11, the breadth of the margin of appreciation allowed to the State—and thus the level of justification required from the State—will vary according to the circumstances, the subject matter and its background. The case-law of the Court shows that not all grounds of discrimination are equally potent.[75] There are echoes of the case-law of the United States Supreme Court when it is dealing with the equal protection clause in the Fourteenth Amendment to the Constitution. Certain grounds of discrimination are inherently suspect and will be subject to particularly careful scrutiny. These include discrimination on grounds of sex, race, nationality, legitimacy, religion, and sexual orientation, where there is recognition that discrimination on such grounds is especially demeaning for those affected.

Where the differential treatment is between men and women,[76] on grounds of nationality,[77] on grounds of race,[78] on grounds of religion,[79] on grounds of legitimacy,[80]

---

71 *PM v United Kingdom* (App. 6638/03), 19 July 2005, (2006) 42 EHRR 1015.

72 *Abdulaziz, Cabales and Balkandali v United Kingdom*, (Apps. 9214/80, 9473/81, and 9474/81), 28 May 1985, Series A No 94, (1985) 7 EHRR 471.

73 §78.   74 §79.

75 *Inze v Austria*, 28 October 1987, Series A No 126, (1988) 10 EHRR 394.

76 *Abdulaziz, Cabales and Balkandali v United Kingdom*, (Apps. 9214/80, 9473/81, and 9474/81), 28 May 1985, Series A No 94, (1985) 7 EHRR 471, §78. See also *Van Raalte v Netherlands* (App. 20060/92), 21 February 1997, (1997) 24 EHRR 503, ECHR 1997-I, §39.

77 *Gaygusuz v Austria* (App. 17371/90), 16 September 1996, (1997) 23 EHRR 364, ECHR 1996-IV, §42; and *Andrejeva v Latvia* (App. 55707/00) 18 February 2009 [GC], ECHR 2009-nyr.

78 *Timishev v Russia*, (Apps. 55762/00 and 55974/00), 13 December 2005, (2007) 44 EHRR 776, ECHR 2005-XII, §58.

79 *Hoffmann v Austria*, (App. 12875/87), 23 June 1993, Series A No 255-C, (1994) 17 EHRR 293, §36. See also *Palau-Martinez v France* (App. 64927/01), 16 December 2003, ECHR 2003-XII.

80 *Inze v Austria*, (App. 8695/79), 28 October 1987, Series A No 126, (1988) 10 EHRR 394, §41. See also *Mazurek v France* (App. 34406/97), 1 February 2000, ECHR 2000-II, §49; *Camp and Bourimi v The Netherlands* (App. 28369/95), 3 October 2000, (2002) 34 EHRR 1446, ECHR 2000-X, §38; and *Sommerfield v Germany* (App. 31871/96), 8 July 2003 [GC], (2004) 38 EHRR 756, ECHR 2003-VIII, §93.

and on grounds of sexual orientation,[81] very weighty reasons are required to justify the differential treatment.

Where the basis for the difference of treatment is grounds of sex, the Contracting Parties enjoy no margin of appreciation and will find it very difficult to establish object-ive and reasonable justification. This can be illustrated by the *Karlheinz Schmidt* case.[82] The applicant complained that the system of requiring men to serve in the fire brigade or to pay a fire service levy in lieu violated Article 4 taken together with Article 14. The Court looked at the practicalities of the situation which was that men were not in prac-tice required to serve, since there was no shortage of volunteers. But there remained the liability to pay the levy, which bore only on men and not on women. This difference of treatment on grounds of sex could hardly be justified.[83]

In contrast, in the *Stec* case,[84] the Strasbourg Court held that it was permissible for the State authorities to treat men and women differently for the purposes of positive discrimination, in order to 'correct factual inequalities between them'. The Court accepted that the reason for introducing a differential age of entitlement to the state pension for men and women in the United Kingdom (65 for men and 60 for women) was to compensate women for the fact that, in general, they tended to spend longer periods of time than men out of paid employment and looking after children and other family members. It was therefore harder for women to build up the required number of qualifying years of National Insurance contribu-tions. The difference in pensionable ages continued to be justified until such time as social conditions had changed so that women were no longer substantially preju-diced because of a shorter working life. This change, must, by its very nature, have been gradual, and it would be difficult or impossible to pinpoint any particular moment when the unfairness to men caused by differential pensionable ages began to outweigh the need to correct the disadvantaged position of women. According to the evidence before the Court, the State authorities had been within their margin of appreciation in deciding to wait until December 1991 before starting to move towards an equal pension age and in deciding to introduce the changes very gradu-ally over a long period of time.

---

[81] At least where there is significant common ground among the Contracting Parties. See *Salgueiro da Silva Mouta v Portugal* (App. 33290/96), 21 December 1999, (2001) 31 EHRR 1055, ECHR 1999-IX, (a cus-tody case by the father of a daughter: violation found). See also *SL v Austria* (App. 45330/99), 9 January 2003, (2003) 37 EHRR 799, ECHR 2003-I, (criminalization of certain homosexual conduct: violation found); *Karner v Austria* (App. 40016/98), 24 July 2003, (2004) 38 EHRR 528, ECHR 2003-IX, (succession of tenan-cies between homosexual men: violation found); *BB v United Kingdom* (App. 53760/00), 10 February 2004, (2004) 39 EHRR 635, (different ages of consent for homosexual and heterosexual acts: violation found); and *EB v France*, (App. 43546/02), 22 January 2008 [GC], ECHR 2008-nyr (over-reliance on sexual orientation in authorization by single person to adopt: violation found).

[82] *Karlheinz Schmidt v Germany*, (App. 13580/88), 18 July 1994, Series A No 291-B, (1994) 18 EHRR 513.

[83] See also *Burghartz v Switzerland*, (App. 16213/90), 22 February 1994, Series A No 280-B, (1994) 18 EHRR 101, §27; and *Schuler-Zgraggen v Switzerland*, (App. 14518/89), 24 June 1993, Series A No 263, (1993) 16 EHRR 405, §67.

[84] *Stec and others v United Kingdom*, (Apps. 65731/01 and 65900/01), 12 April 2006 [GC], (2006) 43 EHRR 1017, ECHR 2006-VI.

The Strasbourg Court is taking an increasingly robust approach to cases where racial or ethnic motivation is involved.[85] As the Court has indicated, these are overlapping concepts. In the *Timishev* case, the Court said:

Whereas the notion of race is rooted in the idea of biological classification of human beings into subspecies according to morphological features such as skin colour and facial characteristics, ethnicity has its origins in the idea of societal groups marked by common nationality, tribal affiliation, religious faith, shared language, or cultural and traditional origins and backgrounds.[86]

Discrimination on grounds of ethnicity is a form of racial discrimination, which is seen as a particularly serious form of discrimination. As a consequence, Contracting Parties are required to 'use all available means to combat racism', and no difference of treatment based on race or ethnicity is capable of being objectively justified.[87] The increasingly robust approach of the Strasbourg Court can be illustrated by the *Šečič* case.[88] The applicant was a Croatian national of Roma origin. He was attacked and injured; his attackers shouted racist abuse at him while attacking him. The police investigation was extremely dilatory, lasting more than seven years. No one was brought to trial for the attack. The Strasbourg Court affirmed the positive obligation of Contracting Parties to use their best endeavours to investigate attacks, even by private parties, which involved racial hatred. A failure to make any distinction between such attacks and 'ordinary' violence was a failure to make a vital distinction, and may constitute unjustified treatment which breaches Article 14 when read with Article 3.[89] Such a violation was found in addition to a violation of Article 3 alone concerning the lack of an effective investigation.[90]

Even in less dramatic factual situations, the Strasbourg Court requires very weighty reasons for distinctions between nationals and non-nationals. In the *Andrejeva* case,[91] the Strasbourg Court held that, in the field of social security, differences in treatment between nationals and non-nationals would require very weighty reasons.

In contrast, where the difference of treatment is not based on an 'inherent' characteristic, such as sex or race, it is likely that the Strasbourg Court will require a lower level of justification and allow a wider margin of appreciation to the State. Similarly, the

---

[85] See further below in this chapter in relation to minorities.

[86] *Timishev v Russia*, (Apps. 55762/00 and 55974/00), 13 December 2005, (2007) 44 EHRR 776, ECHR 2005-XII, §55.

[87] §56–7.

[88] *Šečič v Croatia*, (App. 40116/02), 31 May 2007, (2009) 49 EHRR 408, ECHR 2007-VI. See also *97 members of the Gldani Congregation of Jehovah's Witnesses & 4 others v Georgia*, (App. 71156/01), 3 May 2007, (2008) 46 EHRR 30, ECHR 2007-V.

[89] §67. See also *Angelova and Iliev v Bulgaria*, (App. 55523/00), 26 July 2007, (2008) 47 EHRR 236; and *Cobzaru v Romania*, (App. 48254/99), 26 July 2007, (2008) 47 EHRR 288.

[90] See also *Bekos and Koutropoulos v Greece*, (App. 15250/02), 13 December 2005, (2006) 43 EHRR 22, ECHR 2005-XIII.

[91] *Andrejeva v Latvia* (App. 55707/00) 18 February 2009 [GC], ECHR 2009-nyr.

margin of appreciation is usually wide when it comes to general measures of economic or social strategy.[92] The Court has held that:

> Because of their direct knowledge of their society and its needs, the national authorities are in principle better placed than the international judge to appreciate what is in the public interest on social or economic grounds, and the Court will generally respect the legislature's policy choice unless it is 'manifestly without reasonable foundation'.[93]

So, as has been seen, there is little room for choice where the discrimination is based on sex, race, nationality, religion, legitimacy of children, and sexual orientation. However, in matters of, for example, housing policy designed to ensure an adequate supply of housing for the poorer section of the community, there will be a wide margin.[94] There is a similarly wide margin of appreciation in relation to policies in the area of taxation,[95] and social security.[96]

DISCRIMINATION AND MINORITIES

The Strasbourg Court's increasingly tough approach to discrimination cases involving differential treatment based to a decisive extent on race or ethnicity has already been noted. Those cases were decided on the individual circumstances presented.[97] The focus of attention in a number of cases has been systematic ill-treatment of those of Roma origin, where evidence of their ill-treatment in a number of Contracting Parties has come before the Strasbourg Court. A development in the case-law, which may be based upon recognition that minorities need special and collective protection if their human rights are to be respected, warrants a discussion distinct from reference to individual cases involving discrimination on racial or ethnic grounds.

The seminal case is the *DH* case.[98] The complaints arose in the context of the attempts by the respondent State to address the question of the education of children of Roma

---

[92] As in, for example, *Stec and others v United Kingdom*, (Apps. 65731/01 and 65900/01), 12 April 2006 [GC], (2006) 43 EHRR 1017, ECHR 2006-VI; *Burden v United Kingdom*, (App. 13378/05), 29 April 2008 [GC], (2008) 47 EHRR 857, ECHR 2008-nyr; and *Andrejeva v Latvia* (App. 55707/00) 18 February 2009 [GC], ECHR 2009-nyr.

[93] *Stec and others v United Kingdom*, (Apps. 65731/01 and 65900/01), 12 April 2006 [GC], (2006) 43 EHRR 1017, ECHR 2006-VI, §52.

[94] *Gillow v United Kingdom*, (App. 9063/80), 24 November 1986, Series A No 109, (1989) 11 EHRR 335, §66.

[95] *National & Provincial Building Society and others v United Kingdom*, (Apps. 21319/93, 21449/93, and 21675/93), 23 October 1997; (1998) 25 EHRR 127, §88.

[96] *Carson and others v United Kingdom*, (App. 42184/05), 4 November 2008. The Chamber judgment has been referred to the Grand Chamber.

[97] See, for example, *Timishev v Russia*, (Apps. 55762/00 and 55974/00), 13 December 2005, (2007) 44 EHRR 776, ECHR 2005-XII; *Angelova and Iliev v Bulgaria*, (App. 55523/00), 26 July 2007, (2008) 47 EHRR 236; and *Cobzaru v Romania*, (App. 48254/99), 26 July 2007, (2008) 47 EHRR 288.

[98] *DH and others v Czech Republic*, (App. 57325/00), 13 November 2007 [GC], (2008) 47 EHRR 59, ECHR 2007-nyr. On this case, see R. Sandland, 'Developing a Jurisprudence of Difference: The Protection of the

origin. The adopted solution was the creation of special schools. These were not, however, limited to Roma children; they were schools designated for children with learning difficulties who were unable to follow the ordinary school curriculum. Allocation to a special school was determined by an assessment made by a head teacher on the basis of tests which measured the child's intellectual capacity, and required the consent of the child's parent or guardian. Statistical evidence showed that more than half the pupils in the special schools were of Roma origin, and that in one of the school districts involved a child of Roma origin was 27 times more likely to be in a special school than a child not of Roma origin. The applicants complained that the tests were not reliable, and that the parents had not been sufficiently informed to give consent to placement in a special school.

The Chamber judgment looked at the cases on an individual basis, and found no violation of the Convention. The Grand Chamber judgment takes an entirely different approach to the case, treating the problem as a collective or systemic issue affecting Roma children in general, exemplified by the situations of the applicants in the case before them.

The Grand Chamber does not find that the authorities were motivated to discriminate; indeed there is some praise for the efforts made in the Czech Republic to address the issue.[99] But the segregated educational system was seen to be a source of concern. The Grand Chamber considered that the tests might well be culturally biased, and was influenced by critical reports from the European Commission against Racism and Intolerance (ECRI) and the Council of Europe's Commissioner for Human Rights. On the issue of parental consent, the Grand Chamber finds that there can be no waiver of the right not to be subjected to racial discrimination, even when that discrimination arose indirectly. By thirteen votes to four, the Grand Chamber finds a violation of Article 14 when read in conjunction with Article 2 of Protocol 1. This finding did not relate to individual cases, but to the applicants in general as members of the Roma community.[100] A key significance in this case is in treating indirect discrimination as a phenomenon and in addressing the phenomenon rather than focusing on individual complaints. This collective rather than individual approach could have implications for many areas of the Court's caseload.

It remains to be seen whether this case signals a new approach to discrimination affecting minorities, and potentially to systemic problems of discrimination. It does appear to open the door to something close to a class action before the Strasbourg Court. If this analysis is correct, it may not be too long before the first pilot judgment in respect of discrimination is handed down by the Strasbourg Court.

Human Rights of Travelling Peoples by the European Court of Human Rights' (2008) 8 HRLRev 475; and G. Hobcraft, 'Roma Children and Education in the Czech Republic: DH v Czech Republic: opening the door to indirect discrimination findings in Strasbourg' [2008] EHRLR 245.

[99] By the time of the judgment of the Grand Chamber legislation had abolished the system of special schools.

[100] There are strongly worded dissenting opinions, which castigate the Court for its collective approach and accuse it of usurping the functions of ECRI.

THE BURDEN OF PROOF UNDER ARTICLE 14

Establishing differential treatment of a group in relevantly similar or analogous situations raises issues of evidence and proof. The practice of the Court is that it is for the applicant to show that there has been a difference of treatment, but that it is then for the respondent State to show that the difference in treatment can be justified.[101] There is, however, no formal burden of proof; nor are there formal rules of evidence. The Court will adopt conclusions that are supported by the free evaluation of all the evidence before it.[102] In the *DH* case,[103] the Grand Chamber observed:

According to its established case-law, proof may follow from the coexistence of sufficiently strong, clear and concordant inferences or of similar unrebutted presumptions of fact. Moreover, the level of persuasion necessary for reaching a particular conclusion and, in this connection, the distribution of the burden of proof are intrinsically linked to the specificity of the facts, the nature of the allegation made and the Convention right at stake.[104]

The Grand Chamber also went on to note that a respondent State might be required to disprove an arguable allegation of discrimination.[105] Although statistics alone will not generally constitute evidence of discriminatory practices, in some cases the Court has relied upon statistics to establish a difference in treatment, especially in relation to discrimination between men and women.[106] In the *Zarb Adami* case,[107] statistical imbalances between the numbers of men and women serving as jurors was used to show differential treatment, even though the Maltese law made no distinction between the eligibility of men and women to serve as jurors. In the *DH* case, the Grand Chamber said that less strict evidential rules should apply in cases of alleged indirect discrimination,[108] and stressed the relevance of official statistics.[109] The Grand Chamber added:

...the Court considers that when it comes to assessing the impact of a measure or practice on an individual or group, statistics which appear on critical examination to be reliable and significant will be sufficient to constitute the prima facie evidence the applicant is required to produce. This does not, however, mean that indirect discrimination cannot be proved without statistical evidence.[110]

---

[101] *Chassagnou and others v France* (Apps. 25088/94, 28331/95, and 28443/95), 29 April 1999 [GC], (2000) 29 EHRR 615, ECHR 1999-III, §§91–2.

[102] *Nachova and others v Bulgaria*, (Apps. 43577/98 and 43579/98), 6 July 2005 [GC], (2006) 42 EHRR 933, ECHR 2005-VII, §147, re-affirmed in *DH and others v Czech Republic*, (App. 57325/00), 13 November 2007 [GC], (2008) 47 EHRR 59, ECHR 2007-nyr, §178.

[103] *DH and others v Czech Republic*, (App. 57325/00), 13 November 2007 [GC], (2008) 47 EHRR 59, ECHR 2007-nyr.

[104] §178.   [105] §179.   [106] §180.

[107] *Zarb Adami v Malta*, (App. 17209/02), 20 June 2006, (2007) 44 EHRR 49, ECHR 2006-VIII.

[108] *DH and others v Czech Republic*, (App. 57325/00), 13 November 2007 [GC], (2008) 47 EHRR 59, ECHR 2007-nyr, §186.

[109] §187.   [110] §188.

PROTOCOL 12: A GENERAL PROHIBITION OF DISCRIMINATION

Protocol 12 adds a general prohibition of discrimination to the prohibition of discrimination in relation to rights within the ambit of the Convention currently to be found in Article 14 of the Convention.[111] There is, as yet, no case-law on Protocol 12.

Article 1 of Protocol 12 reads:

1. The enjoyment of any right set forth by law shall be secured without discrimination on any ground such as sex, race, colour, language, religion, political or other opinion, national or social origin, association with a national minority, property, birth or other status.

2. No one shall be discriminated against by any public authority on any ground such as those mentioned in paragraph 1.

The emphasis under Protocol 12 moves from a prohibition of discrimination to a recognition of a right of equality. The preamble to the Protocol refers to all persons being equal before the law and being entitled to the equal protection of the law, and expresses a commitment to the promotion of the equality of all persons through the collective prohibition of discrimination.

The Explanatory Report[112] states that the additional scope of the protection of Protocol 12 when compared with Article 14 relates to cases where a person is discriminated against:

(1) in the enjoyment of any right specifically granted to an individual under national law;

(2) in the enjoyment of a right which may be inferred from a clear obligation of a public authority under national law, that is, where a public authority is under an obligation under national law to behave in a particular manner;

(3) by a public authority in the exercise of discretionary power (for example, granting certain subsidies);

(4) by any other act or omission by a public authority (for example, the behaviour of law enforcement officers when controlling a riot).

---

[111] For some background to Protocol 12, see G. Moon, 'The Draft Discrimination Protocol to the European Convention on Human Rights: A Progress Report' [2000] EHRLR 49. See also N. Grief, 'Non-discrimination under the European Convention on Human Rights: a Critique of the United Kingdom's Refusal to Sign and Ratify Protocol 12' (2002) 27 ELRev *Human Rights Survey* 3.

[112] Explanatory Report to Protocol No. 12 to the Convention for the Protection of Human Rights and Fundamental Freedoms. See also administrative opinion of the European Court of Human Rights of 6 December 1999 on the Protocol.

The Explanatory Report goes on to note that it is unnecessary to specify which of the four examples given above comes within the first or second paragraph of Article 1 of Protocol 12, since the two paragraphs are complementary and their combined effect is to include all the circumstances listed. The Explanatory Report also notes that the emphasis on acts or omissions of public authorities should not be taken to exclude the possibility of positive obligations emerging from the new rights protected, just as they have emerged under many articles of the current Convention.

Though there is significant overlap between the provisions, Article 1 of Protocol 12 is not drafted as a replacement for Article 14, and there is intended to be harmony of interpretation across the two provisions. Article 14 requires the applicant to show that there is differential treatment in an area within the ambit of the Convention rights. Article 1 of Protocol 12 requires the applicant to show that there is differential treatment in the enjoyment of any right set forth in national law. This will include rights granted by legislative measures, as well as rights granted by common law rules and by international law.[113] As with Article 14, the list of comparators given in the article is illustrative only and not exhaustive.

Until Protocol 12 is ratified by a much broader group of Contracting Parties, it is unlikely to play a significant role in the development of equality law under the Convention.

CONCLUDING REMARKS

Article 14 is an important provision of the Convention, but remains replete with difficulty in its application. The lack of signatures and the range of ratifications to Protocol 12 does not suggest that the development of a generic equality law under the Convention is foreseeable.

As the case-law develops, it becomes less easy to predict when a matter will be regarded as falling within the scope of the Convention, what constitute relevantly similar situations, and when objective and reasonable justification can be established. There are cases where Contracting Parties seem to have an easy time in explaining the challenged measures, and others where they face an uphill struggle to escape condemnation under Article 14.

There is now also the prospect of a collective approach to discrimination at least in the field of the protection of minorities, and possibly in other cases where the discrimination is systemic.

One of the difficulties of Article 14 is the range of enumerated grounds of discrimination coupled with its open-ended nature by adding the words 'or other status'.

---

[113] The Explanatory Report states that, in the case of international law, this does mean that the Court of Human Rights will sit in judgment on compliance with international treaties.

The case-law shows the beginnings of a delimitation between discrimination which can never, or hardly ever, be justified, and other areas of differential treatment where the heart of the debate will be about the legitimacy of choices made by Contracting Parties in State policies. Perhaps those conceptual issues which surrounded the *Belgian Linguistic* case need to be revisited in the hope of providing greater clarity outside those areas of discrimination which are regarded as deeply suspect.

PART 3

REFLECTIONS

25

RESULTS AND PROSPECTS

INTRODUCTORY REMARKS

The European Convention on Human Rights has attained a leading place in the development of international human rights protection. Over sixty years, the Strasbourg organs have built an admired human rights discourse from scratch. It has been regarded as a 'chapter in a developing European constitution'.[1] In its judgments, the Court itself has described the Convention as 'a constitutional instrument of European public order.'[2] The Convention system has become an integral part of the Council of Europe system; States wishing to become parties to the Statute of the Council of Europe are required to sign the Convention. Following the entry into force of Protocol 11, there is now a pan-European judicial system for the protection of human rights which applies to over 800 million people in forty-seven countries. The Court is also excellent value for money. The budget for 2009 is a little under €57 million,[3] or €0.07 per head of population for the year.

The expansion of the Convention system to the new democracies of central and eastern Europe has brought with it new challenges.[4] Many of those countries had weak traditions of human rights protection, and in some of them, old traditions have led to a slow transition to respect for Convention rights within the national legal order. The result has been large numbers of applications made to the Strasbourg Court. Four countries,[5] three of which are from central and eastern Europe, account for some 35 per cent of the total population of Council of Europe countries, but are the source of nearly

---

[1] F. Jacobs, 'Human Rights in Europe: New Dimensions' (1992) 3 KCLJ 49, 50. See also R. Ryssdal, *Forty Years of the European Convention on Human Rights*, Address at Vienna on 18 January 1991, Council of Europe document Cour (91) 61, at 12; and Ryssdal, 'On the Road to a European Constitutional Court' in *Collected Courses of the Academy of European Law*, ii. bk. 2 (Martinus Nijhoff, Dordrecht 1993), 1.

[2] See, for example, *Loizidou v Turkey*, 23 March 1995, Series A No 310, (1995) 20 EHRR 99, §75; and *Banković and others v Belgium and sixteen other States* (App. 52207/99), Decision of 12 December 2001, (2007) 44 EHRR SE5, ECHR 2001-XII, §80.

[3] Source: www.echr.coe.int.

[4] See C. Dupré, 'After Reforms: Human Rights Protection in Post-Communist States' [2008] EHRLR 621.

[5] Russia, Turkey, Romania, and Ukraine.

60 per cent of applications to the Strasbourg Court. The cultural shift enlargement has brought is significant. Greer comments:

No longer does [the Convention] express the identity of western European liberal democracy in contrast with the rival communist model of central and eastern Europe; it now provides an 'abstract constitutional identity' for the entire continent, especially for the former communist states recently received into membership.[6]

The principal achievement of the Convention has been the establishment of a formal system of legal protection available to individuals covering a range of civil and political rights, which has become the European standard. As arguably the most developed system of legal protection worldwide, it has also contributed to the development of the global definition and understanding of the substantive content of the rights it protects. It has been the model for the American Convention on Human Rights of 1969 and was a key text to which reference was made in the drafting of the African Charter on Human and Peoples' Rights. It has also been a reference point for courts in countries such as Australia, Canada, and India.[7]

The key challenge the system faces is coping with an ever-increasing caseload. This is calling into question the role of the Strasbourg Court, and, in particular, the continuance of a system under which there is a judicial determination of all applications, and a determination on the merits of all those declared admissible. There remains a reluctance to review such an arrangement,[8] which somewhat flies in the face of a system under which around 94 per cent of applications are currently declared inadmissible, and two-thirds of judgments represent the application of well-established Convention principles. Huge amounts of judicial time are taken in determining that applications do not come within the current admissibility rules. The Court has adopted administrative procedures designed to prioritize the more important and more serious cases.[9] Has the time come for the Court to seek changes which would embed its constitutional function more firmly in its institutional structures? Could Contracting Parties do more within their own national legal orders to reduce the flow of cases to the Strasbourg Court?

---

[6] S. Greer, *The European Convention on Human Rights. Achievements, Problems and Prospects*, (CUP, Cambridge 2006), 170–1. This book is a penetrating analysis of what the author calls in his preface the key successes and a cluster of systemic problems concerning the Convention and its application.

[7] R. Ryssdal, *Europe: the Roads to Democracy. The Council of Europe and the 'architecture' of Europe*, speech at Colloquy organized by the Secretary-General of the Council of Europe in Strasbourg, 18–19 September 1990, Council of Europe document Cour (90) 223, at 2.

[8] The President of the Court has said, 'I have repeatedly declared that it is quite simply inconceivable to abandon the right of individual petition …'. Speech by Jean-Paul Costa, President of the Court, Solemn hearing of the European Court of Human Rights on the occasion of the opening of the judicial year, 30 January 2008, 6.

[9] Speech by Jean-Paul Costa, President of the Court, Solemn hearing for the European Court of Human Rights on the occasion of the opening of the judicial year, 30 January 2009, 8.

RESULTS

SUBSTANTIVE PROVISIONS

The catalogue of human rights in the European Convention is a statement of legal human rights,[10] that is, it consists of a system of rules, decisions, and principles. It confers rights, imposes duties, and establishes institutions to monitor and implement the specified rights and duties. The catalogue of rights in the European Convention is generally of civil and political rights based on liberal democratic ideals, though there are some rights, such as the provisions relating to education and property, and aspects of freedom of association, which touch on economic, social, and cultural rights.[11]

In November 1950, when the Convention was signed, there was little existing material defining the content of human rights. The key document was the Universal Declaration of Human Rights which had been adopted by the General Assembly of the United Nations in December 1948.[12] It would be many years before the United Nations International Covenant on Civil and Political Rights introduced a more detailed statement of civil and political rights coupled with measures of implementation. The Strasbourg system accordingly became a pioneer in the elaboration of the content of the rights declared in the Convention. The contribution to an understanding of the content and extent of the rights protected by the case-law of the Strasbourg Court, and to a lesser extent the decisions and reports of the European Commission, should not be underestimated both within the legal systems of the Contracting Parties to the Convention and beyond.

Every article of Section I of the Convention has now spawned a significant case-law defining and clarifying the content of the rights protected. There is now a body of case-law imposing procedural requirements on Contracting Parties under Article 2 which provide additional guarantees that there will be proper respect for the right to life. Such requirements apply not only to those difficult circumstances where States face increasing threats of terrorist activity, but also to deaths arising in prisons and hospitals. Similar procedural requirements have been imposed on Contracting Parties under Article 3. The definitions of torture and inhuman and degrading treatment under Article 3 have shaped State conduct, particularly in the methods for dealing with the threats of terrorist activity, and in procedures for considering the deportation or extradition of individuals.

---

[10] On the distinction between legal, political, and moral human rights, see D. Meuwissen, 'Human Rights and the End of History' in R. Lawson and M. de Blois (eds.), *The Dynamics of the Protection of Human Rights in Europe: Essays in Honour of Henry G. Schermers* (Martinus Nijhoff, Dordrecht 1994), at 293.

[11] Under the Council of Europe system, such rights are primarily the province of the European Social Charter; see D. Harris and J. Darcy, *The European Social Charter* (Transnational Publishers, New York 2001).

[12] General Assembly Resolution 217A of 10 December 1948, UNGAOR, 3rd session.

In certain areas of internal military conflict, such as the conflicts in Chechnya and south-east Turkey, where national courts have for political reasons been unwilling or unable to defend human rights, the Strasbourg Court has been the only effective forum for establishing the facts relating to large numbers of extremely serious abuses, often amounting to war crimes, including murder, disappearances, torture and the destruction of entire villages.[13]

Other examples of the impact of the Convention case-law can be found in the development of standards relating to the imposition of corporal punishment, and the conditions of detention. Various provisions of the Convention have interacted to produce a body of new protections for prisoners, for mental patients, and for transsexuals. The tendencies of the modern State to subject some within its jurisdiction to covert surveillance have been controlled by standards developed under the emerging case-law under Article 8. Even in areas where State regulation has a clear role to play, the Court has insisted that such basic rights as freedom of expression are given equal weight with the urge to regulate and restrict. There is hardly an area of State regulation untouched by standards which have emerged from the application of Convention provisions to situations presented by individual applicants. For example, nationalizations and planning regulation must respect the right to property spelled out in the Convention. There is emerging case-law giving coherence and substance to the right to an effective remedy in the national legal order under Article 13. The Court has not shirked the call to address systems in the countries of central and eastern Europe, and in the unified Germany, for dealing with property restitution issues which potentially affect many thousands of people.

National courts, even among the new Contracting Parties, frequently apply Convention case-law in determining issues before them. For example, recent research suggests that in Russia judges increasingly make reference to the Convention and the Court's case-law, despite a host of pressures to do otherwise.[14]

Since the Convention is subsidiary to the protection of human rights in national law, the task of the Strasbourg organs involves treading a delicate path between developing and enhancing the standards inherent in the Convention text, and respect for the choices which individual States must make in the face of specific situations. Many of the rights protected are subject to limitations. Setting the boundaries of those limitations has proved to be one of the most contentious aspects of the enforcement of the Convention provisions. Critics of the Court accuse it of accommodating States too readily; others recognize the value of the doctrine of the margin of appreciation as a valuable tool in allowing some differences in the standards adopted in Contracting

---

[13] P. Leach, C. Paraskeva, and G. Uzelac, *International Human Rights and Fact-Finding. An analysis of the fact-finding missions conducted by the European Commission and Court of Human Rights* (London 2009), available at www.londonmet.ac.uk/research-units/hrsj/.

[14] A. Trochev, 'All appeals lead to Strasbourg? Unpacking the impact of the European Court of Human Rights on Russia' (2009) 17 *Demokratizatsiya* 145, available at ssrn.com/abstract=1421342. See also H. Keller and A. Stone Sweet (eds.), *A Europe of Rights. The Impact of the ECHR on National Legal Systems* (OUP, Oxford 2008).

States reflecting the absence of common values even among Council of Europe countries.[15] It should, however, be remembered that the purpose of the Convention system is not to generate uniformity in the protection of human rights in the Contracting Parties, but rather to set minimum standards. It is to be hoped that many Contracting Parties will exceed the minimum standards set by the Convention.

PLACING THE INDIVIDUAL CENTRE STAGE IN ENFORCING CONVENTION RIGHTS

The European Convention system has succeeded in securing the acceptance of a machinery for the consideration of complaints from individuals, where they believe that their rights have been violated and where no remedy has been provided by the State. The willingness of States to become party to an exclusively judicial system served by a Court with automatic jurisdiction to receive complaints from individuals is remarkable. It is the more so when it is recalled that acceptance of any form of judicial settlement was initially very hesitant and that until comparatively recently reference to the Court was very much the exception. In its first forty years, the Court handed down 800 judgments; in its next ten years, it handed down 9,200 judgments. The total number of judgments as at 1 September 2009 stands at 11,596 judgments. Finally, the maturing of the system has to be set in a context where the Court has at times been bold in its interpretation of the substantive provisions of the Convention.

The role of the individual applicant before the Strasbourg Court has been improved. Initially, the individual was little more than a bystander when cases came before the Court, but individuals are now the main enforcers of Convention rights. However, the success of the Convention has brought with it an increase in the volume of individual applications, which has resulted in excessive delays in the determination of applications from high case-count countries. The volume of applications to the Court threatens to overwhelm the institution, and that itself poses a threat to the protection of human rights in Europe.

In virtually all Contracting States, the Convention provisions have been incorporated into national law, although this has not, on the whole, reduced the incidence of applications to the Court. The system may be the victim of its own success, and the number of applications an indication that more than half a century after the introduction of the Convention's catalogue of fundamental rights, there remain serious threats to their guarantee in very many Contracting States. Indeed, reactions to the terrorist attacks in the United States in September 2001, in Spain in March 2004, and in London in July 2005, show quite how fragile some rights which had come to be taken for granted are in times of international crisis.[16] In some Contracting Parties, national reflexes have kicked in which fallaciously suggest that human rights protections

[15] R. Ryssdal, *The Future of the European Court of Human Rights*, Public lecture given at the Centre of European Law, King's College, London on 22 March 1990, Council of Europe document Cour (90) 296, at 6.

[16] See generally Council of Europe, *Human Rights and the Fight against Terrorism. The Council of Europe Guidelines* (Council of Europe Publishing, Strasbourg 2005).

need to be lowered or removed in order to respond to the threat of terrorist outrages. The Strasbourg Court has stood firm in not allowing fundamental protections to be watered down.[17]

MAKING JUDGMENTS MORE EFFECTIVE

The Strasbourg Court, with the support of the Parliamentary Assembly and the Committee of Ministers, has developed pilot judgments which seek to address systemic abuses which come to light as a result of individual applications.[18] In two seminal cases against Poland,[19] the Grand Chamber of the Court extended the requirements the Convention imposes on Contracting Parties. In the first case, the Court ruled that Article 13 requires States to have a remedy in the national legal order for either avoiding excessive delays in the administration of justice, or for providing redress where such delays occur.[20] In the second case, the Court indicated, in the context of a property restitution case, that the remedy required in an individual application where a violation was found would extend to a requirement to provide a remedy for a class of individuals in the same situation. In both cases, the Court was requiring a remedy to a systemic defect in the national legal order; the effect of such decisions should be to reduce the number of repetitive claims[21] that are made to the Strasbourg Court. Pilot judgments have been used on a number of occasions; they are likely to be used with greater frequency as the Strasbourg Court identifies applications which evidence systemic or structural problems within a national legal order which produces multiple applications. Pilot judgments raise new issues related to their enforcement, which, in turn, imposes new burdens on the Committee of Ministers. Despite these difficulties, and the controversy which surrounds the legal base for pilot judgments, they are, without question, examples of the imaginative development of effective procedures within the Strasbourg Court which can be introduced without the need for treaty reform with its attendant problems of delay in implementation.

The contribution of the Grand Chamber is becoming increasingly significant. By the end of 2008, the Grand Chamber had delivered 182 judgments and one Advisory Opinion. Roughly half of the judgments were the result of relinquishment by a Chamber and half as a result of an application by one of the parties for review of a Chamber judgment. Despite the frequency with which the Grand Chamber is less than

---

[17] For example, in re-affirming its judgment in the *Chahal* case in *Saadi v Italy*, (App. 37201/06), 28 February 2008 [GC], (2009) 49 EHRR 730, ECHR 2008-nyr, and in requiring basic procedural guarantees for terrorist suspects in *A and others v United Kingdom*, (App. 3455/05), 19 February 2009 [GC], (2009) 49 EHRR 29, ECHR 2009-nyr.

[18] See ch.2 above.

[19] *Kudła v Poland*, (App. 30210/96), 26 October 2000 [GC], (2002) 35 EHRR 198, ECHR 2000-XI; and *Broniowski v Poland*, (App. 31443/96), 22 June 2004 [GC], (2005) 40 EHRR 495, ECHR 2004-V.

[20] See above ch.23.

[21] Sometimes referred to as 'manifestly well-founded cases': see address by Luzius Wildhaber at the high level seminar on the reform of the European human rights system, held at Oslo on 18 October 2004: available at www.echr.coe.int.

unanimous,[22] judgments of the Grand Chamber are making a significant contribution to clarifying the requirements of the Convention.[23]

PROSPECTS

EXTENDING THE RIGHTS PROTECTED

The rights protected in the Convention and its Protocols are traditional civil and political rights. Yet even this restricted range of rights has not found universal acceptance among the existing Contracting Parties. A significant number of rights for which provision is made in the Protocols to the Convention have not been ratified by all Contracting Parties.

Within the Council of Europe, and despite the Strasbourg Court, through its recognition that the Convention is a living instrument, seeking to ensure the relevance of the Convention rights to contemporary concerns, there is certain to be a debate concerning the content of the Convention, which very much reflects the agenda of civil and political rights in 1950. Already, there is evidence of specialist arrangements providing for more detailed treatment of particular areas. The range of rights protected under the developing case-law under Article 8 of the Convention suggests that there is a place for more detailed rules on the protection of privacy, and on environmental rights. There are also important rights, which are not touched upon by the Convention. One example is women's rights to equal pay and equal treatment,[24] though there is extensive coverage of these rights in European Community law.

In his speech on the opening of the 2009 judicial year, which also marked the fiftieth anniversary of the Court, President of the Court, Jean-Paul Costa, noted that human rights are today more fragile and more complex than ever. He called for a special conference in 2010 to reflect upon the rights and freedoms the Contracting Parties wish to guarantee for their citizens for the future, and to give human rights 'a second wind' by seeing human rights in today's context which is different from that which faced the framers of the Convention.[25]

---

[22] See A. Mowbray, 'No violations but interesting: a study of the Strasburg Court's Jurisprudence in cases where no breach of the Convention has been found' (2008) 14 EPL 237; and R. White and I. Boussiakou, 'Separate Opinions in the European Court of Human Rights' (2009) 9 HRLRev 37, 50–1.

[23] Excellent examples are the development of the law on indirect discrimination in *DH and others v Czech Republic*, (App. 57325/00), 13 November 2007 [GC], (2008) 47 EHRR 59, ECHR 2007-nyr, on the use of embryos without consent in *Evans v United Kingdom*, (App. 6339/05), 10 April 2007 [GC], (2008) 46 EHRR 728, ECHR 2007-IV; and on the extension of the protection against removal from a country of those with a network of personal relationships within a Contracting Party in *Slivenko v Latvia*, (App. 48321/99), 9 October 2003 [GC], (2004) 39 EHRR 490, ECHR 2003-X.

[24] Some of these may be addressed by Protocol 12.

[25] Speech by Jean-Paul Costa, President of the Court, Solemn hearing for the European Court of Human Rights on the occasion of the opening of the judicial year, 30 January 2009, 6–7.

RELATIONSHIPS WITH OTHER INTERNATIONAL
HUMAN RIGHTS PROCEDURES

The development of European standards runs the risk of producing conflict with other international agreements. The majority of the Contracting Parties to the European Convention are also party to international conventions on human rights protection having a global character.[26] The conflict has so far been avoided because generally the European standards have been more explicit and better developed than any global counterpart. It is also true that where other international bodies have been called upon to determine the content of rights protected, they have made reference to the deliberations of the European Court of Human Rights on similar issues; the Strasbourg Court is also making increasing reference to the text of corresponding human rights instruments, and to judgments and rulings in other procedures. The result has been that, to date, the other international regimes have provided a baseline of protection which the European Convention system has further developed as the minimum guarantee of protection in each of the Contracting States.[27] These, in turn, have been able in many cases to provide a higher level of protection than the minimum level required by the European Convention. Louise Arbour, speaking as United Nations Commissioner of Human Rights, has observed:

In international law, there is a real risk of unnecessary fragmentation of the law, with different interpretative bodies taking either inconsistent, or worst, flatly contradictory views of the law, without proper acknowledgment of differing views, and proper analysis in support of the stated better position. In the field of human rights, these effects can be particularly damaging, especially when differing views are taken of the scope of the same State's obligations. Given the wide degree of overlap of substantive protection between the European Convention and, in particular, the International Covenant on Civil and Political Rights, the [Strasbourg] Court's use of UN materials diminishes the risk of inconsistent jurisprudence and enhances the likelihood of a better result in both venues.[28]

Despite such optimistic statements, there remains a risk of divergent interpretations of what appear at first sight to be the same human rights obligation expressed in different treaty texts.

Conflict can also arise as a result of judgments of the Court of Justice of the European Communities. Where these involve possible conflict with judgments of the Strasbourg Court, they are readily resolved as a result of judicial comity. Although the Luxembourg Court ruled that Article 8 did not provide for the inviolability of the home in regard to the business premises of undertakings in the *Hoechst* case,[29] it would

---

[26] See T. Opsahl, 'Ten years' coexistence Strasbourg—Geneva' in F. Matscher and H. Petzold (eds.), *Protecting Human Rights: The European Dimension. Essays in honour of Gérard Wiarda* (Carl Heymanns, Köln 1990), 431.

[27] See address by L. Arbour on the opening of the judicial year 2008 of the European Court of Human Rights, 25 January 2008.

[28] Ibid.

[29] Joined Cases 46/87 and 227/88, *Hoechst v Commission*, [1989] ECR 2859.

almost certainly follow the judgments of the Strasbourg Court[30] to the opposite effect if the point were to come before it directly today. But there is also potential for differential interpretations of the requirements of human rights arising from judgments of the Luxembourg Court in relation to international regimes other than the Strasbourg system. An example is the controversial conclusion in the *Kadi and Al-Barakat* case[31] that the European Union could review procedures within the United Nations institutions for compliance with the right to be heard before being included in a list of persons whose assets were to be frozen because of association with terrorist activities.[32] The decision is arguably at odds with the Strasbourg Court's conclusions in the *Behrami and Seramati* case,[33] where the Strasbourg Court declined to become involved in any human rights review of activities of Contracting Parties when acting within a United Nations mandate.[34]

RELATIONSHIP WITH THE EUROPEAN UNION

A subset of Contracting Parties to the European Convention constitute the European Union, which is increasingly seeing itself as a human rights organization. This calls for consideration of the relationship between the two organizations and their courts.

The development of the protection of human rights within the European Community is well documented.[35] The early steps involved the development of the protection of fundamental rights as general principles of Community law.[36] The approach taken in the case-law of the Luxembourg Court was endorsed by the political institutions in their Joint Declaration of 5 April 1977 which stressed the importance they attached to the protection of fundamental rights as derived from the constitutions of the Member States and from the European Convention, and confirmed the respect of all the institutions for such rights. This was followed by the inclusion in the Preamble to the Single European Act of 17 February 1986 of a reference to the European Convention. The Treaty on European Union, which entered into force on 1 November 1993, incorporated reference to the European Convention in Article F.2, which reads:

---

[30] *Chappell v United Kingdom*, (App. 10461/83), 30 March 1989, Series A No 152, (1990) 12 EHRR 1; *Niemetz v Germany*, (App. 13710/88), 16 December 1992, Series A No 251-B, (1993) 16 EHRR 97; and *Funke v France*, (App. 10828/84), 25 February 1993, Series A No 256-A, (1993) 16 EHRR 297.

[31] Joined Cases C-402/05 P and C-415/05 P, *Yassin Abdullah Kadi and Al Barakat International Foundation*, 3 September 2008, [2008] ECR I-6351.

[32] See B. Kunoy and A. Dawes, 'Plate tectonics in Luxembourg: the *ménage à trois* between EC Law, International Law and the European Convention on Human Rights following the UN sanctions cases' (2009) 46 CMLRev 73.

[33] *Behrami v France*, (App. 71412/01), Decision of 2 May 2007 [GC]; and *Saramati v France, Germany and Norway*, (App. 78166/01), Decision of 2 May 2007 [GC], (2007) 45 EHRR SE10.

[34] See discussion in ch.5 above.

[35] See, for example, G. Harpaz, 'The European Court of Justice and its relations with the European Court of Human Rights: the quest for enhanced reliance, coherence and legitimacy' (2009) 46 CMLRev 105, and the literature cited there.

[36] In such cases as Case 29/69, *Stauder v Ulm*, [1969] ECR 419; Case 11/70, *Internationale Handelsgesellschaft*, [1970] ECR 1125; Case 4/73, *Nold v Commission*, [1974] ECR 491; Case 36/75, *Rutili*, [1975] ECR 1219; and Case 44/79, *Hauer*, [1979] ECR 3727.

The Union shall respect fundamental rights, as guaranteed by the European Convention for the Protection of Human Rights and Fundamental Freedoms signed in Rome on 4 November 1950 and as they result from the constitutional traditions common to the Member States, as general principles of Community law.

This provision takes over the language of the Court itself in its case-law.[37] Despite this progress, the context in which human rights questions have arisen in Community law remains rather meagre, although the recent, and controversial, judgment of the Grand Chamber of the Luxembourg Court in the *Kadi and Al Barakat* case[38] suggests a new impetus. But whatever the long-term significance of that case, it is now the position that the Luxembourg Court will review measures of the institutions for their compatibility with fundamental rights protected by the European Convention.

The Luxembourg Court has, however, not ignored the question of the extent to which the conduct of Member States may also be subject to review for compatibility with human rights standards when they are acting within the field of Community law. In such cases, the conduct of Member States can be called to account by the Luxembourg Court where they are directly implementing Community provisions.[39] Where the Member States are implementing Community law, the review may go further. So in the *ERT* case,[40] which concerned a Greek television monopoly, the Court took the view that any derogation by a Member State from the freedom to provide services under the EEC Treaty had to be compatible with the freedom of expression recognized under the European Convention on Human Rights. This formulation suggests that in any regulation by Member States of matters falling within the scope of Community, measures taken by Member States must as a matter of *Community law* comply with the Convention.

The cumulative effect of the case-law of the Luxembourg Court is that the Luxembourg Court must have regard to national constitutions and to international instruments, especially the European Convention. The Convention is not formally binding on the Community, but its provisions can and must be given effect as general principles of Community law. The result is much the same as if the Community were bound by the Convention.

The Strasbourg Court has ruled that action by a Member State of the European Union in implementation of obligations under Community law is capable of giving rise to a violation by that State of provisions of the Convention.[41] In the *Bosphorus*

---

[37] The location of this provision in the Treaty on European Union (rather than its insertion into the EC Treaty) coupled with the limitations on the Luxembourg Court's jurisdiction under Art. L of the Treaty on European Union, avoids the incorporation of the European Convention (at least in relation to matters within the scope of the EC Treaty) by the back door.

[38] Joined Cases C-402/05 P and C-415/05 P, *Yassin Abdullah Kadi and Al Barakat International Foundation*, 3 September 2008, [2008] ECR I-6351.

[39] See Case C-5/88, *Wachauf*, [1989] ECR 2609, and cf. Case C-2/92, *Bostock*, [1994] ECR I-955.

[40] Case C-260/89, *ERT*, [1991] ECR I-2925. See also Opinion of Advocate General Jacobs in Case C-168/91, *Konstantinidis v Altensteig-Standesamt*, [1993] ECR I-2755.

[41] *Dangeville SA v France*, (App. 36677/97), 16 April 2002, (2004) 38 EHRR 699.

Airways case,[42] the Grand Chamber was called upon to consider the relationship between the protection of human rights in the European Community and such protection under the European Convention. The context was the seizure in Ireland of an aircraft in compliance with the EC Regulation imposing sanctions against Serbia and Montenegro. The Grand Chamber concluded that the Member States of the European Union remain individually responsible for compliance with Convention rights where competence has passed to the European Union, but the Strasbourg Court would only interfere where the protection afforded by the Union was not equivalent to that provided under the Convention. Equivalence was regarded as comparability rather than congruence. There was a presumption that protection within the Union was equivalent to that under the Convention, and the Strasbourg Court would only interfere if it considered that the protection within the Union was 'manifestly deficient'.[43] The Grand Chamber found that the systems for the protection of human rights under Community law were equivalent to those offered under the European Convention. Hence the presumption of compliance applied, and it had not been rebutted in the case before the Court.

The decisions of the Luxembourg Court on respect for fundamental rights inevitably led to the question of whether the Community should accede to the European Convention, which was proposed by the Union's European Commission. The Council of the European Union responded by asking the Luxembourg Court, in accordance with the procedure in Article 228 of the EC Treaty,[44] for an Opinion on certain questions in connection with the proposed accession.[45] The Luxembourg Court ruled that 'as Community law now stands, the Community has no competence to accede to the European Convention.' The only possible basis for competence was Article 235 (now 308) of the EC Treaty.[46] Some Member States had argued that the Community was competent to accede to the European Convention because of the penetration of the protection of fundamental rights through the general principles of law. This is referred to in the Court's reasoning, but accession would, in the Court's view, require the integration of two separate systems for the protection of human rights. Such changes 'would be of constitutional significance and would therefore be such as to go beyond the scope of Article 235' and could only be brought about by way of amendments to the EC Treaty. The Opinion is very clever; it is argued that the response is legally correct in

---

[42] *'Bosphorus Airways' v Ireland*, (App. 45036/98), 30 June 2005 [GC], (2006) 42 EHRR 1, ECHR 2005-VI; for a penetrating commentary, see C. Costello, 'The *Bosphorus* ruling of the European Court of Human Rights: fundamental rights and blurred boundaries in Europe' (2006) 6 HRLRev 87. See also *Cooperatieve Producentorganisatie van de Nederlandse Kokkelvisserij UA v The Netherlands*, (App. 13546/05), Decision of 5 February 2009.

[43] §§154–5.

[44] Now Art. 300 of the EC Treaty.

[45] Opinion 2/94 on accession by the Community to the European Convention on Human Rights, [1996] ECR I-1759.

[46] This provides: 'If action by the Community should prove necessary to attain, in the course of the operation of the common market, one of the objectives of the Community and this Treaty has not provided the necessary powers, the Council shall, acting unanimously on a proposal from the Commission and after consulting the European Parliament, take the appropriate measures.'

the context of the timing and the question asked. It serves to preserve in full the power of protection of fundamental rights by way of the application of the general principles of law. Few reading the Opinion can be left in any doubt about the complexities of integrating the European Community system and the Strasbourg system.[47]

Provision is now made in the Treaty of Lisbon on the European Union side, and in Protocol 14 on the Council of Europe side for the Union to accede to the European Convention.[48] Both treaties currently await ratification. The Treaty of Lisbon will also give legal status to the European Union's Charter of Fundamental Rights of the European Union. This Charter was adopted by solemn proclamation on 7 December 2000[49] at the Nice Council. This document currently has no legally binding force and there remain intriguing questions about its impact on the protection of fundamental rights within the European Union. It is divided into six sections[50] and includes rights for citizens of the European Union as well as certain rights which are to be applicable to all within the jurisdiction of the Member States. The rights are said to be based on the rights guaranteed by the European Convention, but in many cases there are significant differences of wording.[51] Its scope is considerably wider than the rights protected in the European Convention. A limited welcome can be offered to the EU Charter. As a declaratory document standing behind the legal recognition of fundamental rights, it is probably as good as it could be given that its purpose was not formally decided in advance of the Nice Council and given the manner in which it was constructed.[52]

The European Union has also established an Agency for Fundamental Rights in March 2007 with the remit to provide:

the relevant institutions and authorities of the Community and its Member States when implementing Community law with assistance and expertise relating to fundamental rights

---

[47] See also Study of the Technical and Legal Issues of a Possible EC/EU Accession to the European Convention on Human Rights. Report adopted by the Steering Committee for Human Rights (CDDH) at its 53rd meeting 25–28 June 2002, DG-II(2002)006 (CDDH(2002)010 Addendum 2). See also below in this chapter on the Treaty establishing a Constitution for Europe.

[48] Article I-9(2) of the Treaty of Lisbon, and Article 17 of Protocol 14. The Treaty of Lisbon entered into force on 1 December 2009. On whether accession is really necessary, see R. White, 'The Strasbourg Perspective and its Effect on the Court of Justice: Is Mutual Respect Enough?', in A. Arnull and others, *Continuity and Change in EU Law. Essays in Honour of Sir Francis Jacobs* (OUP, Oxford 2008), 130.

[49] Referred to in this chapter as 'the EU Charter'. See, generally, S. Peers and A. Ward, *The EU Charter of Fundamental Rights. Politics, Law and Policy* (Hart, Oxford 2004). See also speech by P-H. Imbert, Director General of Human Rights of the Council of Europe at the Judge's [sic] Symposium on the relationship between the European Convention on Human Rights and the Charter of Fundamental Rights of the European Union, 16 September 2002: available at www.coe.int.

[50] Dignity, freedoms, equality, solidarity, citizens' rights, and justice.

[51] For example, Art. 9 of the EU Charter provides, 'The right to marry and the right to found a family shall be guaranteed in accordance with the national laws governing the exercise of these rights.' This could be interpreted as decoupling the right to marry and the right to found a family which are coupled in Article 12 of the Convention. Elsewhere there is a more sweeping approach to limitations which may be applied to certain rights.

[52] See G. de Búrca, 'The drafting of the European Union Charter of Fundamental Rights' (2001) 26 ELRev 126.

in order to support them when they take measures or formulate courses of action within their respective spheres of competence to fully respect fundamental rights.[53]

Whether such a body is really needed is questionable.

PROTOCOL 14 AND PROTOCOL 14BIS

The limitations of what Protocol 11 could achieve, coupled with the continuing rise in the caseload and the accession of the countries of central and eastern Europe, led to a further round of reform proposals being started in 2000 in order to secure the long-term effectiveness of the machinery of protection offered by the Convention.[54] The Steering Committee for Human Rights set up a Reflection Group on the Reinforcement of Human Rights Protection Mechanisms. The issue was also taken up in the Report of the Evaluation Group to the Committee of Ministers on the European Court of Human Rights.[55]

In making proposals for addressing the management of workloads, the Evaluation Group adopted a number of premises, which informed its recommendations:

- There should be no reduction in the substantive rights protected by the Convention.
- The right of individual petition should be maintained, since it lies at the heart of the Strasbourg machinery.
- The Court must be in a position to dispose of applications in a reasonable time while maintaining the quality and authority of its decisions and judgments.

The Steering Committee concluded that a number of strategies were needed to address the problem.[56] The first is to seek to prevent violations at national level and to improve domestic remedies where such violations are alleged. The second is to optimize the effectiveness of the filtering of application to the Strasbourg Court. The third is improving and accelerating the execution of the Court's judgments. In addition, there should be improvements in the systems in the national legal orders for testing the compatibility of new legislation with the standards required by the Convention. Finally, it was recognized that human rights education both in higher education and in professional training had an important role to play in ensuring proper respect for Convention

---

[53] www.fra.europe.eu. See also E. Howard, 'The European Agency for Fundamental Rights' [2006] EHRLR 445; and, more generally, S. Besson, 'The European Union and human rights: towards a post-national human rights institution?' (2006) 6 HRLRev 323.

[54] Council of Europe, *Reforming the European Convention on Human Rights. A work in progress* (Council of Europe Publishing, Strasbourg 2009).

[55] EG Court (2001) 1 of 27 September 2001. The Evaluation Group consisted of Justin Harman, Irish Ambassador to the Council of Europe, Luzius Wildhaber, President of the Court of Human Rights, and Hans Krüger, Deputy Secretary-General of the Council of Europe.

[56] See generally Council of Europe, *Applying and Supervising the ECHR. Guaranteeing the Effectiveness of the European Convention on Human Rights. Collected Texts* (Council of Europe Publishing, Strasbourg 2004). This publication includes Protocol 14 and its Explanatory Memorandum, as well as the text of the Convention as amended by Protocol 14.

standards in the national legal orders. Those measures which require amendment of the Convention can be found in Protocol 14 of 13 May 2004.[57]

The most controversial provision in Protocol 14 is the introduction of a new admissibility criterion.[58] Article 12 of Protocol 14 amends Article 35(3) of the Convention to read as follows:

The Court shall declare inadmissible any individual application submitted under Article 34 if it considers that:

> (a) the application is incompatible with the provisions of the Convention or the Protocols thereto, manifestly ill-founded, or an abuse of the right of individual application; or
>
> (b) the applicant has not suffered a significant disadvantage, unless respect for human rights as defined in the Convention and the Protocols thereto requires an examination of the application on the merits and provided that no case may be rejected on this ground which has not been duly considered by a domestic tribunal.

The Explanatory Report stresses that the new provision in Article 35(3)(b) does not restrict the right of individuals to apply to the Court, but it is seen as providing the Court with 'an additional tool which would assist in its filtering work'.[59] There are twin safeguards in the application of this ground of inadmissibility; it cannot be used where an examination of the application on the merits is required; and it cannot be used unless the complaint has already been duly considered by a court or tribunal in the national legal order. What constitutes 'significant disadvantage' and when 'respect for human rights...requires an examination of the application on the merits' are not spelled out in the Protocol. For a period of two years following the entry into force of the Protocol, Article 20 reserves to the Court's Chambers and the Grand Chamber the application of the new criterion. This means that single-judge formations[60] and committees of judges will not be able to rule an application inadmissible on this ground during the initial period after the entry into force of the Protocol when it is expected that the Court's Chambers and Grand Chamber will be providing guidance on the circumstances when it is appropriate to use the new inadmissibility criterion.

Other changes are made to the system for filtering applications. Article 26 of the Convention is amended to add the use of single-judge formations to the existing formations of the Court.[61] The new single-judge formations have competence to declare inadmissible or to strike out applications. In this work they are to be assisted

---

[57] Protocol 14 to the Convention for the Protection of Human Rights and Fundamental Freedoms, amending the Control System of the Convention, of 13 May 2004, ETS 194. As at 1 September 2009 the Protocol had been ratified by all Contracting Parties except the Russian Federation.

[58] See X-B. Ruedin, 'De minimis non curat the European Court of Human Rights: the introduction of a new admissibility criterion (Article 12 of Protocol No. 14)' [2008] EHRLR 80.

[59] Explanatory Report, §77.

[60] See below in this chapter.

[61] Committees of three judges, Chambers of seven judges (under an amendment made by the Protocol, these may by decision of the Committee of Ministers and for a fixed period only be reduced to Chambers of five judges), and a Grand Chamber of seventeen judges.

by rapporteurs.[62] Committees of three judges will be able to go on to consider the merits of applications considered admissible where the interpretation of application of the Convention and its Protocols is well established in the case-law of the Court.[63] This provision is designed to enable repetitive cases[64] to be determined rapidly and efficiently.

Article 16 of the Protocol gives new powers to the Committee of Ministers which are designed to make the execution of judgments of the Court more effective. The Committee of Ministers may apply for an interpretation of a judgment where execution of the judgment is hindered by a problem of interpretation. The Committee of Ministers may also bring infringement proceedings against a Contracting State which it alleges has violated Article 46 of the Convention by failing to implement a judgment of the Court.[65] The Committee must first serve a notice on the recalcitrant State. Such proceedings will be heard by a Grand Chamber. They are also seen as necessary only in 'exceptional circumstances.'[66]

All but one of the Contracting Parties has ratified Protocol 14, but to enter into force it requires ratification by all. The continuing failure of the Russian Federation to ratify Protocol 14 has been a source of frustration for some time. The interim solution adopted in 2009 is Protocol 14bis, which takes the provisions on the use of judicial resources from Protocol 14 and enables them to be applied on a party by party basis.[67] In relation to applications from those Contracting Parties that ratify Protocol 14bis, the extended jurisdiction of single judges and three-judge Committees can be used. The new Protocol entered into force on 1 October 2009. Since 46 Contracting Parties have ratified Protocol 14, it is anticipated that these Contracting Parties will all ratify Protocol 14bis without undue delay, which will mean that for all but applications from Russia, judicial resources will be able to be used as economically as possible in dealing with applications to the Strasbourg Court. Indeed Article 7 of the Protocol allows for very speedy implementation through the process of making declarations permitting the provisional application of the Protocol from the first day of the month following the filing of the declaration; a number of Contracting Parties have made use of this provision, and the Court began to use the new procedures for those countries in July 2009. It should, however, be noted that the Russian Federation alone accounts for more than a quarter of pending applications; for these cases three-judge Committees will continue to consider admissibility, and for those applications declared admissible

---

[62] Who will not be judges of the Court, but will be attached to the Court's Registry. See Article 4 of the Protocol.

[63] Article 8 of Protocol 14, amending Article 28 of the Convention.

[64] Which may well constitute up to 70 per cent of admissible applications.

[65] But note the ability of an applicant to complain that in a further application that a judgment has not been implemented, as in *Verein Gegen Tierfabriken Schweiz (VgT) v Switzerland (No. 2)*, (App. 32772/02), 30 June 2009 [GC], ECHR 2009-nyr, in which the Grand Chamber found a violation of Article 10 arising from the continuing failure of the respondent State to permit the broadcasting of the commercial following an earlier judgment of the Court.

[66] Explanatory Memorandum, §100.

[67] The overall objective remains to secure ratification of Protocol 14.

Chambers or a Grand Chamber will determine whether or not a violation of the Convention has occurred.

IMPROVING NATIONAL IMPLEMENTATION

The Evaluation Group had considered that the better the system of protection within the national legal orders, both in securing the rights guaranteed by the Convention, and in the machinery available in the national legal order for remedying violations of those rights, the fewer cases there will be that need determination by the Strasbourg Court. The Evaluation Group stressed the need for Contracting Parties to have effective domestic remedies to prevent and redress violations of Convention rights. Emphasis is placed, in this context, on the machinery for the proper investigation and establishment of facts. The Evaluation Group also calls for the systematic screening of draft legislation and administrative procedures to ensure that they meet Convention standards.

These themes are taken up in the Final Activity Report of the Steering Committee,[68] and remain an important adjunct of developments in the Strasbourg process if the number of applications to the Court is to be reduced. Indeed, the President of the Court at the time said that the implementation of Protocol 14 would not itself reduce the volume of cases brought to Strasbourg, and that action within the national legal orders of the Contracting States is an essential ingredient in ensuring that the Strasbourg Court is not overwhelmed by individual applications brought before it.[69]

LONG-TERM REFORMS

Protocol 14 and Protocol 14bis, like Protocol 11, represent only a partial remedy to the problems presented by the exponential increase in applications to the Strasbourg Court.[70] For this reason the Declaration at the end of the Third Summit of the Council of Europe held in Warsaw in May 2005 included a commitment to the establishment of a group of 'wise persons to draw up a comprehensive strategy to secure the effectiveness of the system in the longer term' but these proposals are to preserve the basic philosophy underlying the Convention.

This group presented its report to the Committee of Ministers in November 2006.[71] Much of its work is predicated on the implementation of the changes set out in Protocol 14. In summary the key proposals in the report are the establishment of a Judicial

---

[68] CM(2004)65 of 8 April 2004.

[69] See address by Luzius Wildhaber at the high level seminar on the reform of the European human rights system, held at Oslo on 18 October 2004: available at www.echr.coe.int.

[70] See address by Luzius Wildhaber at the at the high level seminar on the reform of the European human rights system, held at Oslo on 18 October 2004: available at www.echr.coe.int. See also Final Declaration of the Heads of State and Government of the Member States of the Council of Europe, and its accompanying Action Plan (CM(2005)80 final), of 17 May 2005.

[71] The report is available on the Court's website and in Council of Europe, *Reforming the European Convention on Human Rights. A work in progress* (Council of Europe Publishing, Strasbourg 2009), 609.

Committee composed of those qualified for appointment to high judicial office. This body would have competence to determine all applications raising admissibility issues and all cases whose determination could be based on well-established case-law of the Strasbourg Court. The Judicial Committee would be attached to the Court, but there would be no onward appeal to the Court from decisions of the Judicial Committee.

A group of proposals related to the relations between the Court and the Contracting Parties. The report considers that there could be improvements in the dissemination of judgments of particular importance; that there is scope for the introduction of a system under which national constitutional courts or courts of last instance could seek advisory opinions on matters of interpretation of Convention rights,[72] but oddly the proposal is that opinions given by the Strasbourg Court would not be binding. Unsurprisingly, the report sees much scope for improved enforcement of Convention rights within national legal orders.[73] It is also suggested that the issue of just satisfaction could be referred back for implementation within the national legal orders rather than being determined by the Strasbourg Court. The pilot judgment procedure gets much praise and there is an exhortation to make the fullest possible use of the procedure.

Alternative dispute resolution also plays its role. Friendly settlements and mediation, where the parties agree, are seen as having a role in sidestepping the need for adjudication by the Strasbourg Court. It is envisaged that the Commissioner for Human Rights could assist in this context.

A CHANGING ROLE

The report of the wise persons did not address any fundamental change to the system of Convention supervision, because its terms of reference required it to preserve the basic philosophy underlying the Convention. Yet the thrust of many of the proposals made by the wise persons, and indeed other proposals, would be to enhance the constitutional role of the Strasbourg Court.[74] The dilemma arises from the need to manage the docket while retaining the system of individual application. Any long-term consideration of the development of the role of the Strasbourg Court has to grapple with the issue of its constitutional role. No other constitutional court is so open to applicants. The paradigm of national constitutional courts is that they determine for

---

[72] This proposal does not have the support of the Strasbourg Court.

[73] See also L. Helfer, 'Redesigning the European Court of Human Rights: Embeddedness as a Deep Structural principle of the European Human Rights Regime' (2008) 19 EJIL 125.

[74] See W. Sadurski, 'Partnering with Strasbourg: Constitutionalization of the European Court of Human Rights, the Accession of Central and Eastern European States to the Council of Europe, and the Idea of Pilot Judgments' (2009) HRLRev 397, and S. Greer, *The European Convention on Human Rights. Achievements, Problems and Prospects* (CUP, Cambridge 2006), ch.7. For an overview of reform of the system under both the European Convention and the European Social Charter, see V. Mantouvalou and P. Voyatzis, 'The Council of Europe and the Protection of Human Rights: A System in Need of Reform' in S. Joseph and A. McBeth, *Research Handbook on International Human Rights Law* (Edward Elgar, Cheltenham 2010), available at http://ssrn.com/abstract=1360250.

themselves which cases they will hear. The underlying purpose is to enable finite judicial resources to be matched to cases of the greatest significance.[75] The most attractive of the proposals made by the wise persons is for the separation of 'routine' cases, which would be heard by the Judicial Committee, and 'serious' cases which would be heard by the Strasbourg Court. Whether the political will and willingness to fund a dual system exists among the Contracting Parties remains doubtful. If no such willingness is present, then the alternative solution is to make changes to the admissibility criteria which would make admission a matter of discretion rather than entitlement. How might such a system work? Here perhaps something can be learned from the way in which the United States Supreme Court filters applications for certiorari to bring cases before the Supreme Court.[76] The nine-judge Supreme Court serves a population of 304 million people, and receives around 7,500 petitions for certiorari each year. Around 100 to 150 will be admitted for a hearing. Rule 10 of the Rules of the Supreme Court states:[77]

Review on a writ of certiorari is not a matter of right, but of judicial discretion. A petition for a writ of certiorari will be granted only for compelling reasons.

There follows, in the rule, some guidance on the exercise of the discretion. The final decision on all applications is taken by the justices in closed session,[78] and four votes[79] in favour of granting certiorari are needed in order for certiorari to be granted. The views of the justices are informed by memoranda produced by the law clerks; there are four appointed for each justice. The law clerks are among the brightest students of their graduating classes, but lack experience in practice.[80] By contrast the lawyers in the Registry of the Strasbourg Court are highly experienced and well versed in handling applications to the Court. A system of selection of cases as a result of some variant of this system would be very novel, but is arguably the way in which applications for a hearing before the Strasbourg Court could be managed. It is worth observing that the consistently avowed position of the Supreme Court is that a denial of certiorari has no meaning other than that the Supreme Court will not hear the case, and a denial should not be viewed as any indication as to the correctness, or otherwise, of the

---

[75] See discussion of this issue in the light of comments by some Strasbourg judges in R. White and I. Boussiakou, 'Voices from the European Court of Human Rights' (2009) 27 NQHR 167.

[76] This is now the process by which virtually all cases come before the Supreme Court. See generally H. Perry, *Deciding to Decide: Agenda Setting in the United States Supreme Court* (Harvard University Press, Cambridge, Mass. 1991); K. Hall, *The Oxford Companion to the Supreme Court of the United States*, (OUP, Oxford 1992); R. McKeever, *The United States Supreme Court. A Political and Legal Analysis*, (MUP, Manchester 1997); and D. O'Brien, *Storm Center. The Supreme Court and American Politics* (6th edn W.W. Norton & Co, London 2002).

[77] See www.supremecourtus.gov/ctrules/.

[78] On Friday afternoons. Most cases are not discussed; the Chief Justice prepares a discuss list which forms the basis of the Friday afternoon deliberations.

[79] The so-called 'rule of four' is an informal rule observed by the Supreme Court.

[80] Typically, they will have a spent a year clerking in a court of appeals prior to appointment to be one of four clerks for each justice of the Supreme Court.

decision of the court below. The process of selection has not gone without criticism,[81] particularly since a substantial part of the decision-making turns on memoranda produced by law clerks. But the law clerks are expected to write impartially about the merits of applications.

The transplantation of a system such as that operating in the Supreme Court would require some modification in a court of 47 judges, but something akin to one or more Grand Chambers[82] could be responsible for the final determination of which cases would be admitted for hearing under a discretionary system, informed by memoranda prepared by Registry lawyers.

It is argued that an amendment to the admissibility criteria would readily facilitate a move from mandatory determination of all admitted appeals to a system under which admissibility was a matter of the Court's discretion. The jurisdiction of the Court as set out in Article 32 would not need to change. The Strasbourg Court might wish to retain a system under which inter-State cases are always heard. It is, however, readily conceded that the political will among the Contracting Parties to move to such a system, coupled with the ambivalence of the current Strasbourg judiciary to a move away from the current system of admissibility, means that such change is unlikely to be effected.

FINAL REMARKS

A former President of the European Court of Human Rights described the Court as emerging as a 'fully fledged international tribunal' which deals with diverse grievances brought to it by individuals which not only allege violations of the right to liberty or the right to the proper administration of justice, but also touch on 'some aspect of social, political or even economic life in the respondent Convention country.'[83]

Though there are certain to be conventions setting detailed standards in particular areas, there will remain a central role for a more general catalogue of rights, which provides the essential core of fundamental rights which surrounds everyone within the jurisdiction of the Contracting States. That catalogue will be extended, and there will come a time when the substantive provisions of the Convention and its Protocols will need to be consolidated.

Together the Commission and the Court have ensured that the European Convention now provides the most sophisticated regional judicial architecture for the protection of human rights. Substance has been given to the rights in Section I of the Convention

---

[81] See sources cited at n.76 above.

[82] There is easily scope for three configurations of Grand Chambers within the Strasbourg Court with overlapping membership to ensure a degree of consistency.

[83] R. Ryssdal, 'The European Court of Human Rights and Gérard Wiarda' in F. Matscher and H. Petzold (eds.), *Protecting Human Rights: The European Dimension. Essays in honour of Gérard Wiarda* (Carl Heymanns, Köln 1990), 1, 2.

and the accompanying Protocols. The Contracting Parties have all accepted that individuals within their jurisdiction can raise a complaint before the Strasbourg Court if they believe that the State has not accorded them the protection guaranteed by the Convention. The immediate past President of the Court has noted that 'impervious and imperious sovereignty has yielded to a culture of international accountability of States and indeed individuals.'[84] Those are huge achievements in the six decades since the Convention was signed. The signing of the European Convention on 4 November 1950 in the Palazzo Barberini represented a milestone in the protection of human rights in Europe. Sixty years later the system introduced by the Convention is at another milestone, facing the challenge of ensuring the continuing effectiveness and development of the protection of human rights for over 800 million people in forty-seven countries of a wider democratic Europe.

---

[84] Luzius Wildhaber, President of the Court of Human Rights speaking at the ceremony to commemorate the fiftieth anniversary of the European Convention, reproduced in *The European Convention on Human Rights at 50, Human Rights Information Bulletin No. 50, Special Issue*, 2000, at 41.

APPENDIX

TEXT OF THE EUROPEAN CONVENTION AND PROTOCOLS AS MODIFIED BY PROTOCOL 11

Entered into force: 1 November 1998

CONVENTION FOR THE PROTECTION OF HUMAN RIGHTS AND FUNDAMENTAL FREEDOMS

The governments signatory hereto, being members of the Council of Europe,

Considering the Universal Declaration of Human Rights proclaimed by the General Assembly of the United Nations on 10th December 1948;

Considering that this Declaration aims at securing the universal and effective recognition and observance of the Rights therein declared;

Considering that the aim of the Council of Europe is the achievement of greater unity between its members and that one of the methods by which that aim is to be pursued is the maintenance and further realisation of human rights and fundamental freedoms;

Reaffirming their profound belief in those fundamental freedoms which are the foundation of justice and peace in the world and are best maintained on the one hand by an effective political democracy and on the other by a common understanding and observance of the human rights upon which they depend;

Being resolved, as the governments of European countries which are like-minded and have a common heritage of political traditions, ideals, freedom and the rule of law, to take the first steps for the collective enforcement of certain of the rights stated in the Universal Declaration,

Have agreed as follows:

Article 1
Obligation to respect human rights

The High Contracting Parties shall secure to everyone within their jurisdiction the rights and freedoms defined in Section I of this Convention.

SECTION I RIGHTS AND FREEDOMS

Article 2
Right to life

(1) Everyone's right to life shall be protected by law. No one shall be deprived of his life intentionally save in the execution of a sentence of a court following his conviction of a crime for which this penalty is provided by law.

(2) Deprivation of life shall not be regarded as inflicted in contravention of this Article when it results from the use of force which is no more than absolutely necessary:

    (a) in defence of any person from unlawful violence;

    (b) in order to effect a lawful arrest or to prevent the escape of a person lawfully detained;

    (c) in action lawfully taken for the purpose of quelling a riot or insurrection.

Article 3
Prohibition of torture

No one shall be subjected to torture or to inhuman or degrading treatment or punishment.

Article 4
Prohibition of slavery and forced labour

(1) No one shall be held in slavery or servitude.

(2) No one shall be required to perform forced or compulsory labour.

(3) For the purposes of this Article the term 'forced or compulsory labour' shall not include:

    (a) any work required to be done in the ordinary course of detention imposed according to the provisions of Article 5 of this Convention or during conditional release from such detention;

    (b) any service of a military character or, in the case of conscientious objectors in countries where they are recognised, service exacted instead of compulsory military service;

    (c) any service exacted in case of an emergency or calamity threatening the life or well-being of the community;

    (d) any work or service which forms part of normal civic obligations.

Article 5
Right to liberty and security

(1) Everyone has the right to liberty and security of the person. No one shall be deprived of his liberty save in the following cases and in accordance with a procedure prescribed by law:

    (a) the lawful detention of person after conviction by a competent court;

    (b) the lawful arrest or detention of a person for non-compliance with the lawful order of a court or in order to secure the fulfilment of any obligation prescribed by law;

    (c) the lawful arrest or detention of a person effected for the purpose of bringing him before the competent legal authority on reasonable suspicion of having committed an offence or when it is reasonably considered necessary to prevent his committing an offence or fleeing after having done so;

(d) the detention of a minor by lawful order for the purpose of educational supervision or his lawful detention for the purpose of bringing him before the competent legal authority;

(e) the lawful detention of persons for the prevention of the spreading of infectious diseases, of persons of unsound mind, alcoholics or drug addicts or vagrants;

(f) the lawful arrest or detention of a person to prevent his effecting an unauthorised entry into the country or of a person against whom action is being taken with a view to deportation or extradition.

(2) Everyone who is arrested shall be informed promptly, in a language which he understands, of the reasons for his arrest and of any charge against him.

(3) Everyone arrested or detained in accordance with the provisions of paragraph (1)(c) of this article shall be brought promptly before a judge or other officer authorised by law to exercise judicial power and shall be entitled to trial within a reasonable time or to release pending trial. Release may be conditioned by guarantees to appear for trial.

(4) Everyone who is deprived of his liberty by arrest or detention shall be entitled to take proceedings by which the lawfulness of his detention shall be decided speedily by a court and his release ordered if the detention is not lawful.

(5) Everyone who has been the victim of arrest or detention in contravention of the provisions of this article shall have an enforceable right to compensation.

Article 6
Right to a fair trial

(1) In the determination of his civil rights and obligations or of any criminal charge against him, everyone is entitled to a fair and public hearing within a reasonable time by an independent and impartial tribunal established by law. Judgment shall be pronounced publicly but the press and public may be excluded from all or part of the trial in the interests of morals, public order or national security in a democratic society, where the interests of juveniles or the protection of the private life of the parties so require, or to the extent strictly necessary in the opinion of the court in special circumstances where publicity would prejudice the interests of justice.

(2) Everyone charged with a criminal offence shall be presumed innocent until proved guilty according to law.

(3) Everyone charged with a criminal offence has the following minimum rights:

(a) to be informed promptly, in a language which he understands and in detail, of the nature and cause of the accusation against him;

(b) to have adequate time and facilities for the preparation of his defence;

(c) to defend himself in person or through legal assistance of his own choosing or, if he has not sufficient means to pay for legal assistance, to be given it free when the interests of justice so require;

(d) to examine or have examined witnesses against him and to obtain the attendance and examination of witnesses on his behalf under the same conditions as witnesses against him;

(e) to have the free assistance of an interpreter if he cannot understand or speak the language used in court.

Article 7
No punishment without law

(1) No one shall be held guilty of any criminal offence on account of any act or omission which did not constitute a criminal offence under national or international law at the time when it was committed. Nor shall a heavier penalty be imposed than the one that was applicable at the time the criminal offence was committed.

(2) This Article shall not prejudice the trial and punishment of any person for any act or omission which, at the time when it was committed, was criminal according to the general principles of law recognised by civilised nations.

Article 8
Right to respect for private and family life

(1) Everyone has the right to respect for his private and family life, his home and his correspondence.

(2) There shall be no interference by a public authority with the exercise of this right except such as is in accordance with the law and is necessary in a democratic society in the interests of national security, public safety or the economic well-being of the country, for the prevention of disorder or crime, for the protection of health or morals, or for the protection of the rights and freedoms of others.

Article 9
Freedom of thought, conscience and religion

(1) Everyone has the right to freedom of thought, conscience and religion; this right includes freedom to change his religion or belief and freedom, either alone or in community with others and in public or private, to manifest his religion or belief, in worship, teaching, practice and observance.

(2) Freedom to manifest one's religion or beliefs shall be subject only to such limitations as are prescribed by law and are necessary in a democratic society in the

interests of public safety, for the protection of public order, health or morals, or for the protection of the rights and freedoms of others.

Article 10
Freedom of expression

(1) Everyone has the right to freedom of expression. This right shall include freedom to hold opinions and to receive and impart information and ideas without interference by public authority and regardless of frontiers. This article shall not prevent States from requiring the licensing of broadcasting, television or cinema enterprises.

(2) The exercise of these freedoms, since it carries with it duties and responsibilities, may be subject to such formalities, conditions, restrictions or penalties as are prescribed by law and are necessary in a democratic society, in the interests of national security, territorial integrity or public safety, for the prevention of disorder or crime, for the protection of health or morals, for the protection of the reputation or rights of others, for preventing the disclosure of information received in confidence, or for maintaining the authority and impartiality of the judiciary.

Article 11
Freedom of assembly and association

(1) Everyone has the right to freedom of peaceful assembly and to freedom of association with others, including the right to form and to join trade unions for the protection of his interests.

(2) No restrictions shall be placed on the exercise of these rights other than such as are prescribed by law and are necessary in a democratic society in the interests of national security or public safety, for the prevention of disorder or crime, for the protection of health or morals or for the protection of the rights and freedoms of others. This article shall not prevent the imposition of lawful restrictions on the exercise of these rights by members of the armed forces, of the police or of the administration of the State.

Article 12
Right to marry

Men and women of marriageable age have the right to marry and to found a family, according to the national laws governing the exercise of this right.

Article 13
Right to an effective remedy

Everyone whose rights and freedoms as set forth in this Convention are violated shall have an effective remedy before a national authority notwithstanding that the violation has been committed by persons acting in an official capacity.

Article 14
Prohibition of discrimination

The enjoyment of the rights and freedoms set forth in this Convention shall be secured without discrimination on any ground such as sex, race, colour, language, religion, political or other opinion, national or social origin, association with a national minority, property, birth or other status.

Article 15
Derogation in time of emergency

(1) In time of war or other public emergency threatening the life of the nation any High Contracting Party may take measures derogating from its obligations under this Convention to the extent strictly required by the exigencies of the situation, provided that such measures are not inconsistent with its other obligations under international law.

(2) No derogation from Article 2, except in respect of deaths resulting from lawful acts of war, or from Articles 3, 4 (paragraph 1) and 7 shall be made under this provision.

(3) Any High Contracting Party availing itself of this right of derogation shall keep the Secretary General of the Council of Europe fully informed of the measures which it has taken and the reasons therefor. It shall also inform the Secretary General of the Council of Europe when such measures have ceased to operate and the provisions of the Convention are again being fully executed.

Article 16
Restrictions on political activity of aliens

Nothing in Articles 10, 11 and 14 shall be regarded as preventing the High Contracting Parties from imposing restrictions on the political activities of aliens.

Article 17
Prohibition of abuse of rights

Nothing in this Convention may be interpreted as implying for any State, group or person any right to engage in any activity or perform any act aimed at the destruction of any of the rights and freedoms set forth herein or at their limitation to a greater extent that is provided for in the Convention.

Article 18
Limitation on use of restrictions on rights

The restrictions permitted under this Convention to the said rights and freedoms shall not be applied for any purpose other than those for which they have been prescribed.

SECTION II EUROPEAN COURT OF HUMAN RIGHTS

Article 19
Establishment of the Court

To ensure the observance of the engagements undertaken by the High Contracting Parties in the Convention and the protocols thereto, there shall be set up a European Court of Human Rights, hereinafter referred to as 'the Court'. It shall function on a permanent basis.

Article 20
Number of judges

The Court shall consist of a number of judges equal to that of the High Contracting Parties.

Article 21
Criteria for office

(1) The judges shall be of high moral character and must either possess the qualifications required for appointment to high judicial office or be jurisconsults of recognised competence.

(2) The judges shall sit on the Court in their individual capacity.

(3) During their term of office the judges shall not engage in any activity which is incompatible with their independence, impartiality or with the demands of a full-time office; all questions arising from the application of this paragraph shall be decided by the Court.

Article 22
Election of judges

(1) The judges shall be elected by the Parliamentary Assembly with respect to each High Contracting Party by a majority of votes cast from a list of three candidates nominated by the High Contracting Party.

(2) The same procedure shall be followed to complete the Court in the event of the accession of new High Contracting Parties and in filling casual vacancies.

Article 23
Terms of office

(1) The judges shall be elected for a period of six years. They may be re-elected. However, the terms of office of one-half of the judges elected at the first election shall expire at the end of three years.

(2) The judges whose terms of office are to expire at the end of the initial period of three years shall be chosen by lot by the Secretary General of the Council of Europe immediately after their election.

(3) In order to ensure that, as far as possible, the terms of office of one-half of the judges are renewed every three years, the Parliamentary Assembly may decide, before proceeding to any subsequent election, that the term or terms of office of one or more judges to be elected shall be for a period other than six years but not more than nine and not less than three years.

(4) In cases where more than one term of office is involved and where the Parliamentary Assembly applies the preceding paragraph, the allocation of the terms of office shall be effected by a drawing of lots by the Secretary General of the Council of Europe immediately after the election.

(5) A judge elected to replace a judge whose term of office has not expired shall hold office for the remainder of his predecessor's term.

(6) The terms of office of judges shall expire when they reach the age of 70.

(7) The judges shall hold office until replaced. They shall, however, continue to deal with such cases as they already have under consideration.

Article 24
Dismissal

No judge may be dismissed from his office unless the other judges decide by a majority of two-thirds that he has ceased to fulfil the required conditions.

Article 25
Registry and legal secretaries

The Court shall have a registry, the functions and organisation of which shall be laid down in the rules of the Court. The Court shall be assisted by legal secretaries.

Article 26
Plenary Court

The plenary Court shall:

(a) elect its President and one or two Vice-Presidents for a period of three years; they may be re-elected;

(b) set up Chambers, constituted for a fixed period of time;

(c) elect the Presidents of the Chambers of the Court; they may be re-elected;

(d) adopt the rules of the Court; and

(e) elect the Registrar and one or more Deputy Registrars.

Article 27
Committees, Chambers and Grand Chamber

(1) To consider cases brought before it, the Court shall sit in committees of three judges, in Chambers of seven judges and in a Grand Chamber of seventeen judges. The Court's Chambers shall set up committees for a fixed period of time.

(2) There shall sit as an *ex officio* member of the Chamber and the Grand Chamber the judge elected in respect of the State Party concerned or, if there is none or if he is unable to sit, a person of its choice who shall sit in the capacity of judge.

(3) The Grand Chamber shall also include the President of the Court, the Vice-Presidents, the Presidents of the Chambers and other judges chosen in accordance with the rules of the Court. When a case is referred to the Grand Chamber under Article 43, no judge from the Chamber which rendered the judgment shall sit in the Grand Chamber, with the exception of the President of the Chamber and the judge who sat in respect of the State Party concerned.

Article 28
Declaration of inadmissibility by committees

A committee may, by a unanimous vote, declare inadmissible or strike out of its list of cases an individual application submitted under Article 34 where such a decision can be taken without further examination. The decision shall be final.

Article 29
Decisions by Chambers on admissibility and merits

(1) If no decision is taken under Article 28, a Chamber shall decide on the admissibility and merits of individual applications submitted under Article 34.

(2) A Chamber shall decide on the admissibility and merits of inter-State applications submitted under Article 33.

(3) The decision on admissibility shall be taken separately unless the Court, in exceptional cases, decides otherwise.

Article 30
Relinquishment of jurisdiction to the Grand Chamber

Where a case pending before a Chamber raises a serious question affecting the interpretation of the Convention or the protocols thereto or where the resolution of a question before it might have a result inconsistent with a judgment previously delivered by the Court, the Chamber may, at any time before it has rendered its judgment, relinquish jurisdiction in favour of the Grand Chamber, unless one of the parties to the case objects.

Article 31
Powers of the Grand Chamber

The Grand Chamber shall

(a) determine applications submitted either under Article 33 or Article 34 when a Chamber has relinquished jurisdiction under Article 30 or when the case has been referred to it under Article 43; and

(b) consider requests for advisory opinions submitted under Article 47.

Article 32
Jurisdiction of the Court

(1) The jurisdiction of the Court shall extend to all matters concerning the interpretation and application of the Convention and the protocols thereto which are referred to it as provided in Articles 33, 34 and 47.

(2) In the event of dispute as to whether the Court has jurisdiction, the Court shall decide.

Article 33
Inter-State cases

Any High Contracting Party may refer to the Court any alleged breach of the provisions of the Convention and the protocols thereto by another High Contracting Party.

Article 34
Individual applications

The Court may receive applications from any person, non-governmental organisation or group of individuals claiming to be the victim of a violation by one of the High Contracting Parties of the rights set forth in the Convention and the protocols thereto. The High Contracting Parties undertake not to hinder in any way the effective exercise of this right.

Article 35
Admissibility criteria

(1) The Court may only deal with the matter after all domestic remedies have been exhausted, according to the generally recognised rules of international law, and within a period of six months from the date on which the final decision was taken.

(2) The Court shall not deal with any individual application submitted under Article 34 that

(a) is anonymous; or

(b) is substantially the same as a matter that has already been examined by the Court or has already been submitted to another procedure of international investigation or settlement and contains no relevant new information.

(3) The Court shall declare inadmissible any individual application submitted under Article 34 which it considers incompatible with the provisions of the Convention or the protocols thereto, manifestly ill-founded, or an abuse of the right of application.

(4) The Court shall reject any application which it considers inadmissible under this Article. It may do so at any stage of the proceedings.

Article 36
Third-party intervention

(1) In all cases before a Chamber or the Grand Chamber, a High Contracting Party one of whose nationals is an applicant shall have the right to submit written comments and to take part in the hearings.

(2) The President of the Court may, in the interest of the proper administration of justice, invite any High Contracting Party which is not a party to the proceedings or any person concerned who is not the applicant to submit written comments or take part in the hearings.

Article 37
Striking out applications

(1) The Court may at any stage of the proceedings decide to strike an application out of its list of cases where the circumstances lead to the conclusion that

(a) the applicant does not intend to pursue his application; or

(b) the matter has been resolved; or

(c) for any other reason established by the Court, it is no longer justified to continue the examination of the application.

However, the Court shall continue the examination of the application if respect for human rights as defined in the Convention and the protocols thereto so requires.

(2) The Court may decide to restore an application to its list of cases if it considers that the circumstances justify such a course.

Article 38
Examination of the case and friendly settlement proceedings

(1) If the Court declares the application admissible, it shall

(a) pursue the examination of the case, together with the representatives of the parties, and if need be, undertake an investigation, for the effective conduct of which the States concerned shall furnish all necessary facilities;

(b) place itself at the disposal of the parties concerned with a view to securing a friendly settlement of the matter on the basis of respect for human rights as defined in the Convention and the protocols thereto.

(2) Proceedings conducted under paragraph 1(b) shall be confidential.

Article 39
Finding of a friendly settlement

If a friendly settlement is effected, the Court shall strike the case out of its list by means of a decision which shall be confined to a brief statement of the facts and the solution reached.

Article 40
Public hearings and access to documents

(1) Hearings shall be public unless the Court in exceptional circumstances decides otherwise.

(2) Documents deposited with the Registrar shall be accessible to the public unless the President of the Court decides otherwise.

Article 41
Just satisfaction

If the Court finds that there has been a violation of the Convention or the protocols thereto, and if the internal law of the High Contracting Party concerned allows only partial reparation to be made, the Court shall, if necessary afford just satisfaction to the injured party.

Article 42
Judgments of Chambers

Judgments of Chambers shall become final in accordance with the provisions of Article 44, paragraph 2.

Article 43
Referral to the Grand Chamber

(1) Within a period of three months from the date of the judgment of the Chamber, any party to the case may, in exceptional cases, request that the case be referred to the Grand Chamber.

(2) A panel of five judges of the grand Chamber shall accept the request if the case raises a serious question affecting the interpretation or application of the Convention or the protocols thereto, or a serious issue of general importance.

(3) If the panel accepts the request, the Grand Chamber shall decide the case by means of a judgment.

Article 44
Final judgments

(1) The judgment of the Grand Chamber shall be final.

(2) The judgment of a Chamber shall become final.

    (a) when the parties declare that they will not request that the case be referred to the Grand Chamber; or

    (b) three months after the date of the judgment, if reference of the case to the Grand Chamber has not been requested; or

    (c) when the panel of the Grand Chamber rejects the request to refer under Article 43.

(3) The final judgment shall be published.

Article 45
Reasons for judgments and decisions

(1) Reasons shall be given for judgments as well as for decisions declaring applications admissible or inadmissible.

(2) If a judgment does not represent, in whole or in part, the unanimous opinion of the judges, any judge shall be entitled to deliver a separate opinion.

Article 46
Binding force and execution of judgments

(1) The High Contracting Parties undertake to abide by the final judgment of the Court in any case where they are parties.

(2) The final judgment of the Court shall be transmitted to the Committee of Ministers, which shall supervise its execution.

Article 47
Advisory opinions

(1) The Court may, at the request of the Committee of Ministers, give advisory opinions on legal questions concerning the interpretation of the Convention and the protocols thereto.

(2) Such opinions shall not deal with any question relating to the content or scope of the rights or freedoms defined in Section I of the Convention and the protocols thereto, or with any other question which the Court or the Committee of Ministers might have to consider in consequence of any such proceedings as could be instituted in accordance with the Convention.

(3) Decisions of the Committee of Ministers to request an advisory opinion of the Court shall require a majority vote of the representatives entitled to sit on the Committee.

Article 48
Advisory jurisdiction of the court

The Court shall decide whether a request for an advisory opinion submitted by the Committee of Ministers is within its competence as defined in Article 47.

Article 49
Reasons for advisory opinions

(1) Reasons shall be given for advisory opinions of the Court.

(2) If the advisory opinion does not represent, in whole or in part, the unanimous opinion of the judges, any judge shall be entitled to deliver a separate opinion.

(3) Advisory opinions of the Court shall be communicated to the Committee of Ministers.

Article 50
Expenditure on the Court

The expenditure on the Court shall be borne by the Council of Europe.

Article 51
Privileges and immunities of judges

The judges shall be entitled, during the exercise of their functions, to the privileges and immunities provided for in Article 40 of the Statute of the Council of Europe and in the agreements made thereunder.

SECTION III MISCELLANEOUS PROVISIONS

Article 52
Inquiries by the Secretary General

On receipt of a request from the Secretary General of the Council of Europe any High Contracting Party shall furnish an explanation of the manner in which its internal law ensures the effective implementation of any of the provisions of the Convention.

Article 53
Safeguard for existing human rights

Nothing in this Convention shall be construed as limiting or derogating from any of the human rights and fundamental freedoms which may be ensured under the laws of any High Contracting Party or under any other agreement to which it is a Party.

Article 54
Powers of the Committee of Ministers

Nothing in this Convention shall prejudice the powers conferred on the Committee of Ministers by the Statute of the Council of Europe.

Article 55
Exclusion of other means of dispute settlement

The High Contracting Parties agree that, except by special agreement, they will not avail themselves of treaties, conventions or declarations in force between them for the purpose of submitting, by way of petition, a dispute arising out of the interpretation or application of this Convention to a means of settlement other than those provided for in this Convention.

Article 56
Territorial application

(1) Any State may at the time of its ratification or at any time thereafter declare by notification addressed to the Secretary General of the Council of Europe that the present Convention shall, subject to paragraph 4 of this Article, extend to all or any of the territories for whose international relations it is responsible.

(2) The Convention shall extend to the territory or territories named in the notification as from the thirtieth day after the receipt of this notification by the Secretary General of the Council of Europe.

(3) The provisions of this Convention shall be applied in such territories with due regard, however, to local requirements.

(4) Any State which has made a declaration in accordance with paragraph 1 of this Article may at any time thereafter declare on behalf of one or more of the territories to which the declaration relates that it accepts the competence of the Court to receive applications from individuals, non-governmental organisations or groups of individuals as provided in Article 34 of the Convention.

Article 57
Reservations

(1) Any State may, when signing this Convention or when depositing its instrument of ratification, make a reservation in respect of any particular provision of the Convention to the extent that any law then in force in its territory is not in conformity with the provision. Reservations of a general character shall not be permitted under this Article.

(2) Any reservation made under this Article shall contain a brief statement of the law concerned.

Article 58
Denunciation

(1) A High Contracting Party may denounce the present Convention only after the expiry of five years from the date on which it became a party to it and after six months' notice contained in a notification addressed to the Secretary General of the Council of Europe, who shall inform the other High Contracting Parties.

(2) Such a denunciation shall not have the effect of releasing the High Contracting Party concerned from its obligations under this Convention in respect of any act which, being capable of constituting a violation of such obligations, may have been performed by it before the date at which the denunciation became effective.

(3) Any High Contracting Party which shall cease to be a member of the Council of Europe shall cease to be a Party to this Convention under the same conditions.

(4) The Convention may be denounced in accordance with the provisions of the preceding paragraphs in respect of any territory to which it has been declared to extend under the terms of Article 56.

Article 59
Signature and ratification

(1) This Convention shall be open to the signature of the members of the Council of Europe. It shall be ratified. Ratifications shall be deposited with the Secretary General of the Council of Europe.

(2) The present Convention shall come into force after the deposit of ten instruments of ratification.

(3) As regard any signatory ratifying subsequently, the Convention shall come into force at the date of the deposit of its instrument of ratification.

(4) The Secretary General of the Council of Europe shall notify all the members of the Council of Europe of the entry into force of the Convention, the names of the High Contracting Parties who have ratified it, and the deposit of all instruments of ratification which may be effected subsequently.

Done at Rome, 4 November 1950.

Protocol to the Convention for the Protection of Human Rights and Fundamental Freedoms, as amended by Protocol No. 11

The governments signatory hereto, being members of the Council of Europe *Being resolved* to take steps to ensure the collective enforcement of certain rights and freedoms other than those already included in Section I of the Convention for the Protection of Human Rights and Fundamental Freedoms signed at Rome on 4 November 1950 (hereinafter referred to as 'the Convention'),

Have agreed as follows:

Article 1
Protection of property

Every natural or legal person is entitled to the peaceful enjoyment of his possessions. No one shall be deprived of his possessions except in the public interest and subject to the conditions provided for by law and by the general principles of international law.

The preceding provisions shall not, however, in any way impair the right of a State to enforce such laws as it deems necessary to control the use of property in accordance with the general interest or to secure the payment of taxes or other contributions or penalties.

Article 2
Right to education

No person shall be denied the right to education. In the exercise of any functions which it assumes in relation to education and to teaching, the State shall respect the right of parents to ensure such education and teaching in conformity with their own religious and philosophical convictions.

Article 3
Right to free elections

The High Contracting Parties undertake to hold free elections at reasonable intervals by secret ballot, under conditions which will ensure the free expression of the opinion of the people in the choice of the legislature.

Article 4
Territorial application

Any High Contracting Party may at the time of signature or ratification or at any time thereafter communicate to the Secretary General of the Council of Europe a declaration stating the extent to which it undertakes that the provisions of the present Protocol shall apply to such of the territories for the international relations of which it is responsible as are named therein. Any High Contracting Party which has communicated a declaration in virtue of the preceding paragraph may from time to time communicate a further declaration modifying the terms of any former declaration or terminating the application of the provisions of this Protocol in respect of any territory. A declaration made in accordance with this Article shall be deemed to have been made in accordance with paragraph 1 of Article 56 of the Convention.

Article 5
Relationship to the Convention

As between the High Contracting Parties the provisions of Articles 1, 2, 3 and 4 of this Protocol shall be regarded as additional articles to the Convention and all the provisions of the Convention shall apply accordingly.

Article 6
Signature and ratification

This Protocol shall be open for signature by the members of the Council of Europe, who are the signatories of the Convention; it shall be ratified at the same time as or after the ratification of the Convention. It shall enter into force after the deposit of ten instruments of ratification. As regards any signatory ratifying subsequently, the Protocol shall enter into force at the date of the deposit of its instrument of ratification.

The instruments of ratification shall be deposited with the Secretary General of the Council of Europe, who will notify all members of the names of those who have ratified.

Done at Paris, 20 March 1952.

[Protocol No. 2 becomes otiose, since the provisions on the Court's competence to give advisory opinions are incorporated in Articles 47 to 49 of the Convention]

[Protocol No. 3 has become otiose; it modified the procedure of the Commission by abolishing the system of sub-commissions]

Protocol No. 4 to the Convention for the Protection of Human Rights and Fundamental Freedoms securing certain rights and Freedoms other than those already included in the Convention and in the first Protocol thereto, as amended by Protocol 11

The governments signatory hereto, being members of the Council of Europe, *Being resolved* to take steps to ensure the collective enforcement of certain rights and freedoms other than those already included in Section I of the Convention for the Protection of Human Rights and Fundamental Freedoms signed at Rome on 4th November 1950 (hereinafter referred to as 'the Convention') and in Articles 1 to 3 of the First Protocol to the Convention, signed at Paris on 20th March 1952,

Have agreed as follows:

Article 1
Prohibition of imprisonment for debt

No one shall be deprived of his liberty merely on the ground of inability to fulfil a contractual obligation.

Article 2
Freedom of movement

(1) Everyone lawfully within the territory of a State shall, within that territory, have the right to liberty of movement and freedom to choose his residence.

(2) Everyone shall be free to leave any country, including his own.

(3) No restrictions shall be placed on the exercise of these rights other than such as are in accordance with law and are necessary in a democratic society in the interests of national security or public safety, for the maintenance of the *ordre public*, for the prevention of crime, for the protection of health or morals, or for the protection of the rights and freedoms of others.

(4) The rights set forth in paragraph 1 may also be subject, in particular areas, to restrictions imposed in accordance with law and justified by the public interest in a democratic society.

Article 3
Prohibition of expulsion of nationals

(1) No one shall be expelled, by means either of an individual or of a collective measure, from the territory of the State of which he is a national.

(2) No one shall be deprived of the right to enter the territory of the State of which he is a national.

Article 4
Prohibition of collective expulsion of aliens

Collective expulsion of aliens is prohibited.

Article 5
Territorial application

(1) Any High Contracting Party may, at the time of signature or ratification of this protocol, or at any time thereafter, communicate to the Secretary General of the Council of Europe a declaration stating the extent to which it undertakes that the provisions of this Protocol shall apply to such of the territories for the international relations of which it is responsible as are named therein.

(2) Any High Contracting Party which has communicated a declaration in virtue of the preceding paragraph may, from time to time, communicate a further declaration modifying the terms of any former declaration or terminating the application of the provisions of this Protocol in respect of any territory.

(3) A declaration made in accordance with this Article shall be deemed to have been made in accordance with paragraph 1 of Article 56 of the Convention.

(4) The territory of any State to which this Protocol applies by virtue of ratification or acceptance by that State, and each territory to which this Protocol is applied by virtue of a declaration by that State under this Article, shall be treated as separate territories for the purpose of the references in Articles 2 and 3 to the territory of a State.

(5) Any State which has made a declaration in accordance with paragraph 1 or 2 of this Article may at any time thereafter declare on behalf of one or more of the territories to which the declaration relates that it accepts the competence of the Court to receive applications from individuals, non-governmental organisations or groups of individuals as provided in Article 34 of the Convention in respect of all or any of Articles 1 to 4 of this Protocol.

Article 6
Relationship to the Convention

As between the High Contracting Parties the provisions of Articles 1 to 5 of this Protocol shall be regarded as additional Articles to the Convention, and the provisions of the Convention shall apply accordingly.

Article 7
Signature and ratification

(1) This Protocol shall be open for signature by the members of the Council of Europe who are signatories of the Convention; it shall be ratified at the same time as or after the ratification of the Convention. It shall enter into force after the deposit of five instruments of ratification. As regards any signatory ratifying subsequently, the Protocol shall enter into force at the date of the deposit of its instrument of ratification.

(2) The instruments of ratification shall be deposited with the Secretary General of the Council of Europe, who will notify all members of the names of those who have ratified.

Done at Strasbourg, 16 September 1963.

[Protocol No. 5 has become otiose; it concerned the procedure for the election of members of the Commission and Court]

Protocol No. 6 to the Convention for the Protection of Human Rights and Fundamental Freedoms Concerning the Abolition of the Death Penalty, as amended by Protocol 11

The Member States of the Council of Europe, signatory to this Protocol to the Convention for the Protection of Human Rights and Fundamental Freedoms, signed at Rome on 4 November 1950 (hereinafter referred to as 'the Convention'),

Considering that the evolution that has occurred in several Member States of the Council of Europe expresses a general tendency in favour of the abolition of the death penalty;

Have agreed as follows:

Article 1
Abolition of the death penalty

The death penalty shall be abolished. No-one shall be condemned to such penalty or executed.

Article 2
Death penalty in time of war

A State may make provision in its law for the death penalty in respect of acts committed in time of war or of imminent threat of war; such penalty shall be applied only in the instances laid down in the law and in accordance with its provisions. The State shall communicate to the Secretary General of the Council of Europe the relevant provisions of that law.

Article 3
Prohibition of derogations

No derogation from the provisions of this Protocol shall be made under Article 15 of the Convention.

Article 4
Prohibition of reservations

No reservation may be made under Article 57 of the Convention in respect of the provisions of this Protocol.

Article 5
Territorial application

(1) Any State may at the time of signature or when depositing its instrument of ratification, acceptance or approval, specify the territory or territories to which this Protocol shall apply.

(2) Any State may at any later date, by a declaration addressed to the Secretary General of the Council of Europe, extend the application of this Protocol to any other territory specified in the declaration. In respect of such territory the Protocol shall enter into force on the first day of the month following the date of receipt of such declaration by the Secretary General.

(3) Any declaration made under the two preceding paragraphs may, in respect of any territory specified in such declaration, be withdrawn by a notification addressed to the Secretary General. The withdrawal shall become effective on the first day of the month following the date of receipt of such notification by the Secretary General.

Article 6
Relationship to the Convention

As between the States Parties the provisions of Articles 1 to 5 of this Protocol shall be regarded as additional articles to the Convention and all the provisions of the Convention shall apply accordingly.

Article 7
Signature and ratification

The Protocol shall be open for signature by the Member States of the Council of Europe, signatories to the Convention. It shall be subject to ratification, acceptance or approval. A member State of the Council of Europe may not ratify, accept or approve this Protocol unless it has, simultaneously or previously, ratified the Convention. Instruments of ratification, acceptance or approval shall be deposited with the Secretary General of the Council of Europe.

Article 8
Entry into force

(1) This Protocol shall enter into force on the first day of the month following the date on which five Member States of the Council of Europe have expressed their consent to be bound by the Protocol in accordance with the provisions of Article 7.

(2) In respect of any member State which subsequently expresses its consent to be bound by it, the Protocol shall enter into force on the first day of the month following the date of the deposit of the instrument of ratification, acceptance or approval.

Article 9
Depositary functions

The Secretary General of the Council of Europe shall notify the Member States of the Council of:

(a) any signature;

(b) the deposit of any instrument of ratification, acceptance or approval;

(c) any date of entry into force of this Protocol in accordance with Articles 5 and 8;

(d) any other act, notification or communication relating to this Protocol.

Done at Strasbourg, 28 April 1983.

Protocol No. 7 to the Convention for the Protection of Human Rights and Fundamental Freedoms, as amended by Protocol No. 11

The Member States of the Council of Europe signatory hereto,

Being resolved to ensure the collective enforcement of certain rights and freedoms by means of the Convention for the Protection of Human Rights and Fundamental Freedoms signed at Rome on 4 November 1950 (hereinafter referred to as 'the Convention'),

Have agreed as follows:

Article 1
Procedural safeguards relating to expulsion of aliens

(1) An alien lawfully resident in the territory of a State shall not be expelled therefrom except in pursuance of a decision reached in accordance with law and shall be allowed:

    (a) to submit reasons against his expulsion;

    (b) to have his case reviewed; and

    (c) to be represented for these purposes before the competent authority or a person or persons designated by that authority.

(2) An alien may be expelled before the exercise of his rights under paragraph 1 (a), (b) and (c) of this Article, when such expulsion is necessary in the interests of public order or is grounded on reasons of national security.

Article 2
Right of appeal in criminal matters

(1) Everyone convicted of a criminal offence by a tribunal shall have the right to have his conviction or sentence reviewed by a higher tribunal. The exercise of this right, including the grounds on which it may be exercised, shall be governed by law.

(2) This right may be subject to exceptions in regard to offences of a minor character, as prescribed by law, or in cases in which the person concerned was tried in the first instance by the highest tribunal or was convicted following an appeal against acquittal.

Article 3
Compensation for wrongful conviction

When a person has by a final decision been convicted of a criminal offence and when subsequently his conviction has been reversed, or he has been pardoned, on the ground that a new or newly discovered fact shows conclusively that there has been a miscarriage of justice, the person who has suffered punishment as a result of such conviction shall be compensated according to the law or the practice of the State concerned, unless it is proved that the non-disclosure of the unknown fact in time is wholly or partly attributable to him.

Article 4
Right not to be tried or punished twice

(1) No one shall be liable to be tried or punished again in criminal proceedings under the jurisdiction of the same State for an offence for which he has already been finally acquitted or convicted in accordance with the law and penal procedure of that State.

(2) The provisions of the preceding paragraph shall not prevent the reopening of the case in accordance with the law and penal procedure of the State concerned, if there is evidence of new or newly discovered facts, or if there has been a fundamental defect in the previous proceedings, which could affect the outcome of the case.

(3) No derogation from this Article shall be made under Article 15 of the Convention.

Article 5
Equality between spouses

Spouses shall enjoy equality of rights and relationships of a private law character between them, and in their relations with their children, as to marriage, during marriage and in the event of its dissolution. This Article shall not prevent States from taking such measures as are necessary in the interests of the children.

Article 6
Territorial application

(1) Any State may at the time of signature or when depositing its instrument of ratification, acceptance or approval, specify the territory or territories to which the Protocol shall apply and state the extent to which it undertakes that the provisions of this Protocol shall apply to such territory or territories.

(2) Any State may at any later date, by a declaration addressed to the Secretary General of the Council of Europe, extend the application of this Protocol to any other territory specified in the declaration. In respect of such territory the Protocol shall enter into force on the first day of the month following the expiration of a period of two months after the date of receipt of such notification by the Secretary General.

(3) Any declaration made under the preceding two paragraphs may, in respect of any territory specified in such declaration, be withdrawn or modified by a notification addressed to the Secretary General. The withdrawal or modification shall become effective on the first day of the month following the expiration of a period of two months after the date of receipt of such notification by the Secretary General.

(4) A declaration made in accordance with this Article shall be deemed to have been made in accordance with paragraph 1 of Article 56 of the Convention.

(5) The territory of any State to which this Protocol applies by virtue of ratification, acceptance or approval by that State, and each territory to which this Protocol is applied by virtue of a declaration by that State under this Article, may be treated as separate territories for the purpose of the reference in Article 1 to the territory of a State.

(6) Any State which has made a declaration in accordance with paragraph 1 or 2 of this Article may at any time thereafter declare on behalf of one or more of the territories to which the declaration relates that it accepts the competence of the Court to receive applications from individuals, non-governmental organisations or groups of individuals as provided in Article 34 of the Convention in respect of Articles 1 to 5 of this Protocol.

Article 7
Relationship to the Convention

As between the States Parties, the provisions of Article 1 to 6 of this Protocol shall be regarded as additional Articles to the Convention, and all the provisions of the Convention shall apply accordingly.

Article 8
Signature and ratification

This Protocol shall be open for signature by Member States of the Council of Europe which have signed the Convention. It is subject to ratification, acceptance or approval. A member State of the Council of Europe may not ratify, accept or approve this Protocol without previously or simultaneously ratifying the Convention. Instruments of ratification, acceptance or approval shall be deposited with the Secretary General of the Council of Europe.

Article 9
Entry into force

(1) This Protocol shall enter into force on the first day of the month following the expiration of a period of two months after the date on which seven Member States of the Council of Europe have expressed their consent to be bound by the Protocol in accordance with the provisions of Article 8.

(2) In respect of any member State which subsequently expresses its consent to be bound by it, the Protocol shall enter into force on the first day of the month following the expiration of a period of two months after the date of the deposit of the instrument of ratification, acceptance or approval.

Article 10
Depositary functions

The Secretary General of the Council of Europe shall notify all the Member States of the Council of Europe of:

(a) any signature;

(b) the deposit of any instrument of ratification, acceptance or approval;

(c) any date of entry into force of this protocol in accordance with Articles 6 and 9;

(d) any other act, notification or declaration relating to this Protocol.

Done at Strasbourg, 22 November 1984.

[Protocol No. 8 has become otiose; it concerned procedure of the 'old' Commission and Court]

[Protocol No. 9 has become otiose; it amended certain provisions of the Convention to improve the position of individual applicants]

[Protocol No. 10 has become otiose; it changes the majority required for a decision of the Committee of Ministers under the original Article 32]

[Protocol No. 11 is omitted; it amended the Convention and made transitional arrangements for the transfer of work from the Commission and Court to the 'new' Court]

Protocol No. 12 to the Convention for the Protection of Human Rights and Fundamental Freedoms

Entered into force on 1 April 2005

The Member States of the Council of Europe signatory hereto,

Having regard to the fundamental principle according to which all persons are equal before the law and are entitled to the equal protection of the law;

Being resolved to take further steps to promote the equality of all persons through the collective enforcement of a general prohibition of discrimination by means of the Convention for the Protection of Human Rights and Fundamental Freedoms signed at Rome on 4 November 1950 (hereinafter referred to as 'the Convention');

Reaffirming that the principle of non-discrimination does not prevent States Parties from taking measures in order to promote full and effective equality, provided that there is an objective and reasonable justification for those measures,

Have agreed as follows:

Article 1
General prohibition of discrimination

(1) The enjoyment of any right set forth by law shall be secured without discrimination on any ground such as sex, race, colour, language, religion, political or other opinion, national or social origin, association with a national minority, property, birth or other status.

(2) No one shall be discriminated against by any public authority on any ground such as those mentioned in paragraph 1.

Article 2
Territorial application

(1) Any State may, at the time of signature or when depositing its instrument of ratification, acceptance or approval, specify the territory or territories to which this Protocol shall apply.

(2) Any State may at any later date, by a declaration addressed to the Secretary General of the Council of Europe, extend the application of this Protocol to any other territory specified in the declaration. In respect of such territory the Protocol shall enter into force on the first day of the month following the expiration of a period of three months after the date of receipt by the Secretary General of such declaration.

(3) Any declaration made under the two preceding paragraphs may, in respect of any territory specified in such declaration, be withdrawn or modified by a notification addressed to the Secretary General of the Council of Europe. The withdrawal or modification shall become effective on the first day of the month following the expiration of a period of three months after the date of receipt of such notification by the Secretary General.

(4) A declaration made in accordance with this article shall be deemed to have been made in accordance with paragraph 1 of Article 56 of the Convention.

(5) Any State which has made a declaration in accordance with paragraph 1 or 2 of this article may at any time thereafter declare on behalf of one or more of the territories to which the declaration relates that it accepts the competence of the Court to receive applications from individuals, non-governmental organisations or groups of individuals as provided by Article 34 of the Convention in respect of Article 1 of this Protocol.

Article 3
Relationship to the Convention

As between the States Parties, the provisions of Articles 1 and 2 of this Protocol shall be regarded as additional articles to the Convention, and all the provisions of the Convention shall apply accordingly.

Article 4
Signature and ratification

This Protocol shall be open for signature by Member States of the Council of Europe which have signed the Convention. It is subject to ratification, acceptance or approval. A member state of the Council of Europe may not ratify, accept or approve this Protocol without previously or simultaneously ratifying the Convention. Instruments of ratification, acceptance or approval shall be deposited with the Secretary General of the Council of Europe.

Article 5
Entry into force

(1) This Protocol shall enter into force on the first day of the month following the expiration of a period of three months after the date on which ten Member States of the Council of Europe have expressed their consent to be bound by the Protocol in accordance with the provisions of Article 4.

(2) In respect of any member state which subsequently expresses its consent to be bound by it, the Protocol shall enter into force on the first day of the month following the expiration of a period of three months after the date of the deposit of the instrument of ratification, acceptance or approval.

Article 6
Depositary functions

The Secretary General of the Council of Europe shall notify all the Member States of the Council of Europe of:

(a) any signature;

(b) the deposit of any instrument of ratification, acceptance or approval;

(c) any date of entry into force of this Protocol in accordance with Articles 2 and 5;

(d) any other act, notification or communication relating to this Protocol.

In witness whereof the undersigned, being duly authorised thereto, have signed this Protocol.

Done at Rome, 4 November 2000.

Protocol No. 13 to the Convention for the Protection of Human Rights and Fundamental Freedoms, Concerning the Abolition of the Death Penalty in all Circumstances, Signed at Vilnius on 3 May 2002

Entered into force on 1 July 2003

Preamble

The Member States of the Council of Europe signatory hereto,

Convinced that everyone's right to life is a basic value in a democratic society and that the abolition of the death penalty is essential for the protection of this right and for the full recognition of the inherent dignity of all human beings;

Wishing to strengthen the protection of the right to life guaranteed by the Convention for the Protection of Human Rights and Fundamental Freedoms signed at Rome on 4 November 1950 (hereinafter referred to as 'the Convention');

Noting that Protocol No. 6 to the Convention, concerning the Abolition of the Death Penalty, signed at Strasbourg on 28 April 1983, does not exclude the death penalty in respect of acts committed in time of war or of imminent threat of war;

Being resolved to take the final step in order to abolish the death penalty in all circumstances,

Have agreed as follows:

Article 1
Abolition of the death penalty

The death penalty shall be abolished. No one shall be condemned to such penalty or executed.

Article 2
Prohibition of derogations

No derogation from the provisions of this Protocol shall be made under Article 15 of the Convention.

Article 3
Prohibition of reservations

No reservation may be made under Article 57 of the Convention in respect of the provisions of this Protocol.

Article 4
Territorial application

1. Any State may, at the time of signature or when depositing its instrument of ratification, acceptance or approval, specify the territory or territories to which this Protocol shall apply.

2. Any State may at any later date, by a declaration addressed to the Secretary General of the Council of Europe, extend the application of this Protocol to any other territory specified in the declaration. In respect of such territory the Protocol shall enter into force on the first day of the month following the expiration of a period of three months after the date of receipt of such declaration by the Secretary General.

Any declaration made under the two preceding paragraphs may, in respect of any territory specified in such declaration, be withdrawn or modified by a notification addressed to the Secretary General. The withdrawal or modification shall become effective on the first day of the month following the expiration of a period of three months after the date of receipt of such notification by the Secretary General.

Article 5
Relationship to the Convention

As between the States Parties the provisions of Articles 1 to 4 of this Protocol shall be regarded as additional articles to the Convention, and all the provisions of the Convention shall apply accordingly.

Article 6
Signature and ratification

This Protocol shall be open for signature by Member States of the Council of Europe which have signed the Convention. It is subject to ratification, acceptance or approval. A Member State of the Council of Europe may not ratify, accept or approve this Protocol without previously or simultaneously ratifying the Convention. Instruments of ratification, acceptance or approval shall be deposited with the Secretary General of the Council of Europe.

Article 7
Entry into force

1. This Protocol shall enter into force on the first day of the month following the expiration of a period of three months after the date on which ten Member States of the Council of Europe have expressed their consent to be bound by the Protocol in accordance with the provisions of Article 6.

2. In respect of any member State which subsequently expresses its consent to be bound by it, the Protocol shall enter into force on the first day of the month following the expiration of a period of three months after the date of the deposit of the instrument of ratification, acceptance or approval.

Article 8
Depositary functions

The Secretary General of the Council of Europe shall notify all the Member States of the Council of Europe of:

(a) any signature;

(b) the deposit of any instrument of ratification, acceptance or approval;

(c) any date of entry into force of this Protocol in accordance with Articles 4 and 7;

(d) any other act, notification or communication relating to this Protocol.

In witness whereof the undersigned, being duly authorised thereto, have signed this Protocol.

Protocol No. 14 to the Convention for the Protection of Human Rights and Fundamental Freedoms, amending the Control System of the Convention, Signed at Strasbourg on 13 May 2004

Not yet in force

Preamble

The Member States of the Council of Europe, signatories to this Protocol to the Convention for the Protection of Human Rights and Fundamental Freedoms, signed at Rome on 4 November 1950 (hereinafter referred to as 'the Convention'),

Having regard to Resolution No. 1 and the Declaration adopted at the European Ministerial Conference on Human Rights, held in Rome on 3 and 4 November 2000;

Having regard to the Declarations adopted by the Committee of Ministers on 8 November 2001, 7 November 2002 and 15 May 2003, at their 109th, 111th and 112th Sessions, respectively;

Having regard to Opinion No. 251 (2004) adopted by the Parliamentary Assembly of the Council of Europe on 28 April 2004;

Considering the urgent need to amend certain provisions of the Convention in order to maintain and improve the efficiency of the control system for the long term, mainly in the light of the continuing increase in the workload of the European Court of Human Rights and the Committee of Ministers of the Council of Europe;

Considering, in particular, the need to ensure that the Court can continue to play its pre-eminent role in protecting human rights in Europe,

Have agreed as follows:

Article 1
Paragraph 2 of Article 22 of the Convention shall be deleted.

Article 2
Article 23 of the Convention shall be amended to read as follows:

'Article 23—Terms of office and dismissal

1. The judges shall be elected for a period of nine years. They may not be re-elected.

2. The terms of office of judges shall expire when they reach the age of 70.

3. The judges shall hold office until replaced. They shall, however, continue to deal with such cases as they already have under consideration.

4. No judge may be dismissed from office unless the other judges decide by a majority of two-thirds that that judge has ceased to fulfil the required conditions.'

Article 3
Article 24 of the Convention shall be deleted.

Article 4
Article 25 of the Convention shall become Article 24 and its text shall be amended to read as follows:

'Article 24—Registry and rapporteurs

1. The Court shall have a registry, the functions and organisation of which shall be laid down in the rules of the Court.

2. When sitting in a single-judge formation, the Court shall be assisted by rapporteurs who shall function under the authority of the President of the Court. They shall form part of the Court's registry.'

Article 5

Article 26 of the Convention shall become Article 25 ('Plenary Court') and its text shall be amended as follows:

1. At the end of paragraph d, the comma shall be replaced by a semi-colon and the word 'and' shall be deleted.

2. At the end of paragraph e, the full stop shall be replaced by a semi-colon.

3. A new paragraph f shall be added which shall read as follows:

'(f) make any request under Article 26, paragraph 2.'

Article 6

Article 27 of the Convention shall become Article 26 and its text shall be amended to read as follows:

'Article 26—Single-judge formation, committees,
Chambers and Grand Chamber

1. To consider cases brought before it, the Court shall sit in a single-judge formation, in committees of three judges, in Chambers of seven judges and in a Grand Chamber of seventeen judges. The Court's Chambers shall set up committees for a fixed period of time.

2. At the request of the plenary Court, the Committee of Ministers may, by a unanimous decision and for a fixed period, reduce to five the number of judges of the Chambers.

3. When sitting as a single judge, a judge shall not examine any application against the High Contracting Party in respect of which that judge has been elected.

4. There shall sit as an *ex officio* member of the Chamber and the Grand Chamber the judge elected in respect of the High Contracting Party concerned. If there is none or if that judge is unable to sit, a person chosen by the President of the Court from a list submitted in advance by that Party shall sit in the capacity of judge.

5. The Grand Chamber shall also include the President of the Court, the Vice-Presidents, the Presidents of the Chambers and other judges chosen in accordance with the rules of the Court. When a case is referred to the Grand Chamber under Article 43, no judge from the Chamber which rendered the judgment shall sit in the Grand Chamber, with the exception of the President of the Chamber and the judge who sat in respect of the High Contracting Party concerned.'

Article 7

After the new Article 26, a new Article 27 shall be inserted into the Convention, which shall read as follows:

'Article 27—Competence of single judges

1. A single judge may declare inadmissible or strike out of the Court's list of cases an application submitted under Article 34, where such a decision can be taken without further examination.

2. The decision shall be final.

3. If the single judge does not declare an application inadmissible or strike it out, that judge shall forward it to a committee or to a Chamber for further examination.'

Article 8
Article 28 of the Convention shall be amended to read as follows:

'Article 28—Competence of committees

1. In respect of an application submitted under Article 34, a committee may, by a unanimous vote,

    (a) declare it inadmissible or strike it out of its list of cases, where such decision can be taken without further examination; or

    (b) declare it admissible and render at the same time a judgment on the merits, if the underlying question in the case, concerning the interpretation or the application of the Convention or the Protocols thereto, is already the subject of well-established case-law of the Court.

2. Decisions and judgments under paragraph 1 shall be final.

3. If the judge elected in respect of the High Contracting Party concerned is not a member of the committee, the committee may at any stage of the proceedings invite that judge to take the place of one of the members of the committee, having regard to all relevant factors, including whether that Party has contested the application of the procedure under paragraph 1(b).'

Article 9
Article 29 of the Convention shall be amended as follows:

1. Paragraph 1 shall be amended to read as follows:

'If no decision is taken under Article 27 or 28, or no judgment rendered under Article 28, a Chamber shall decide on the admissibility and merits of individual applications submitted under Article 34. The decision on admissibility may be taken separately.'

2. At the end of paragraph 2 a new sentence shall be added which shall read as follows:

'The decision on admissibility shall be taken separately unless the Court, in exceptional cases, decides otherwise.'

3. Paragraph 3 shall be deleted.

Article 10
Article 31 of the Convention shall be amended as follows:

1. At the end of paragraph a, the word 'and' shall be deleted.

2. Paragraph b shall become paragraph c and a new paragraph b shall be inserted and shall read as follows:

    '(b) decide on issues referred to the Court by the Committee of Ministers in accordance with Article 46, paragraph 4; and'.

Article 11

Article 32 of the Convention shall be amended as follows:

At the end of paragraph 1, a comma and the number 46 shall be inserted after the number 34.

Article 12

Paragraph 3 of Article 35 of the Convention shall be amended to read as follows:

'3. The Court shall declare inadmissible any individual application submitted under Article 34 if it considers that :

> (a) the application is incompatible with the provisions of the Convention or the Protocols thereto, manifestly ill-founded, or an abuse of the right of individual application; or

> (b) the applicant has not suffered a significant disadvantage, unless respect for human rights as defined in the Convention and the Protocols thereto requires an examination of the application on the merits and provided that no case may be rejected on this ground which has not been duly considered by a domestic tribunal.'

Article 13

A new paragraph 3 shall be added at the end of Article 36 of the Convention, which shall read as follows:

'3. In all cases before a Chamber or the Grand Chamber, the Council of Europe Commissioner for Human Rights may submit written comments and take part in hearings.'

Article 14

Article 38 of the Convention shall be amended to read as follows:

'Article 38—Examination of the case

The Court shall examine the case together with the representatives of the parties and, if need be, undertake an investigation, for the effective conduct of which the High Contracting Parties concerned shall furnish all necessary facilities.'

Article 15

Article 39 of the Convention shall be amended to read as follows:

'Article 39—Friendly settlements

1. At any stage of the proceedings, the Court may place itself at the disposal of the parties concerned with a view to securing a friendly settlement of the matter on the basis of respect for human rights as defined in the Convention and the Protocols thereto.

2. Proceedings conducted under paragraph 1 shall be confidential.

3. If a friendly settlement is effected, the Court shall strike the case out of its list by means of a decision which shall be confined to a brief statement of the facts and of the solution reached.

4. This decision shall be transmitted to the Committee of Ministers, which shall supervise the execution of the terms of the friendly settlement as set out in the decision.'

Article 16

Article 46 of the Convention shall be amended to read as follows:

'Article 46—Binding force and execution of judgments

1. The High Contracting Parties undertake to abide by the final judgment of the Court in any case to which they are parties.

2. The final judgment of the Court shall be transmitted to the Committee of Ministers, which shall supervise its execution.

3. If the Committee of Ministers considers that the supervision of the execution of a final judgment is hindered by a problem of interpretation of the judgment, it may refer the matter to the Court for a ruling on the question of interpretation. A referral decision shall require a majority vote of two thirds of the representatives entitled to sit on the Committee.

4. If the Committee of Ministers considers that a High Contracting Party refuses to abide by a final judgment in a case to which it is a party, it may, after serving formal notice on that Party and by decision adopted by a majority vote of two thirds of the representatives entitled to sit on the Committee, refer to the Court the question whether that Party has failed to fulfil its obligation under paragraph 1.

5. If the Court finds a violation of paragraph 1, it shall refer the case to the Committee of Ministers for consideration of the measures to be taken. If the Court finds no violation of paragraph 1, it shall refer the case to the Committee of Ministers, which shall close its examination of the case.'

Article 17

Article 59 of the Convention shall be amended as follows:

1. A new paragraph 2 shall be inserted which shall read as follows:

    '2. The European Union may accede to this Convention.'

3. Paragraphs 2, 3 and 4 shall become paragraphs 3, 4 and 5 respectively.

Final and transitional provisions

Article 18

1. This Protocol shall be open for signature by Member States of the Council of Europe signatories to the Convention, which may express their consent to be bound by

    (a) signature without reservation as to ratification, acceptance or approval; or

    (b) signature subject to ratification, acceptance or approval, followed by ratification, acceptance or approval.

2. The instruments of ratification, acceptance or approval shall be deposited with the Secretary General of the Council of Europe.

Article 19

This Protocol shall enter into force on the first day of the month following the expiration of a period of three months after the date on which all Parties to the Convention have expressed their consent to be bound by the Protocol, in accordance with the provisions of Article 18.

Article 20

1. From the date of the entry into force of this Protocol, its provisions shall apply to all applications pending before the Court as well as to all judgments whose execution is under supervision by the Committee of Ministers.

2. The new admissibility criterion inserted by Article 12 of this Protocol in Article 35, paragraph 3.b of the Convention, shall not apply to applications declared admissible before the entry into force of the Protocol. In the two years following the entry into force of this Protocol, the new admissibility criterion may only be applied by Chambers and the Grand Chamber of the Court.

Article 21

The term of office of judges serving their first term of office on the date of entry into force of this Protocol shall be extended *ipso jure* so as to amount to a total period of nine years. The other judges shall complete their term of office, which shall be extended *ipso jure* by two years.

Article 22

The Secretary General of the Council of Europe shall notify the Member States of the Council of Europe of:

  (a) any signature;

  (b) the deposit of any instrument of ratification, acceptance or approval;

  (c) the date of entry into force of this Protocol in accordance with Article 19; and

  (d) any other act, notification or communication relating to this Protocol.

In witness whereof, the undersigned, being duly authorised thereto, have signed this Protocol.

Protocol No. 14bis to the Convention for the Protection of Human Rights and Fundamental Freedoms

Entered into force on 1 October 2009

Preamble

The Member States of the Council of Europe, signatories to this Protocol to the Convention for the Protection of Human Rights and Fundamental Freedoms, signed at Rome on 4 November 1950 (hereinafter referred to as 'the Convention'),

Having regard to Protocol No. 14 to the Convention for the Protection of Human Rights and Fundamental Freedoms, amending the control system of the Convention, opened for signature by the Committee of Ministers of the Council of Europe in Strasbourg on 13 May 2004;

Having regard to Opinion No. 271 (2009), adopted by the Parliamentary Assembly of the Council of Europe on 30 April 2009;

Considering the urgent need to introduce certain additional procedures to the Convention in order to maintain and improve the efficiency of its control system for the long term, in the light of the continuing increase in the workload of the European Court of Human Rights and the Committee of Ministers of the Council of Europe;

Considering, in particular, the need to ensure that the Court can continue to play its pre-eminent role in protecting human rights in Europe,

Have agreed as follows:

Article 1
In relation to High Contracting Parties to the Convention which are bound by this Protocol, the Convention shall read as provided in Articles 2 to 4.

Article 2
1. The title of Article 25 of the Convention shall read as follows:

'Article 25—Registry, legal secretaries and rapporteurs'

2. A new paragraph 2 shall be added at the end of Article 25 of the Convention, which shall read as follows:

'2. When sitting in a single-judge formation, the Court shall be assisted by rapporteurs who shall function under the authority of the President of the Court. They shall form part of the Court's registry.'

Article 3
1. The title of Article 27 of the Convention shall read as follows

'Article 27—Single-judge formation,
committees, Chambers and Grand Chamber'

2. Paragraph 1 of Article 27 of the Convention shall read as follows:

'1. To consider cases brought before it, the Court shall sit in a single-judge formation, in committees of three judges, in Chambers of seven judges and in a Grand Chamber of seventeen judges. The Court's Chambers shall set up committees for a fixed period of time.'

3. A new paragraph 2 shall be inserted in Article 27 of the Convention, which shall read as follows:

'2. When sitting as a single judge, a judge shall not examine any application against the High Contracting Party in respect of which that judge has been elected.'

4. Paragraphs 2 and 3 of Article 27 of the Convention shall become paragraphs 3 and 4 respectively.

Article 4

Article 28 of the Convention shall read as follows:

'Article 28—Competences of single judges and of committees

1. A single judge may declare inadmissible or strike out of the Court's list of cases an application submitted under Article 34, where such a decision can be taken without further examination.

2. The decision shall be final.

3. If the single judge does not declare an application inadmissible or strike it out, that judge shall forward it to a committee or to a Chamber for further examination.

4. In respect of an application submitted under Article 34, a committee may, by a unanimous vote,

    a. declare it inadmissible or strike it out of its list of cases, where such decision can be taken without further examination; or

    b. declare it admissible and render at the same time a judgment on the merits, if the underlying question in the case, concerning the interpretation or the application of the Convention or the Protocols thereto, is already the subject of well-established case-law of the Court.

5. Decisions and judgments under paragraph 4 shall be final.

6. If the judge elected in respect of the High Contracting Party concerned is not a member of the committee, the committee may at any stage of the proceedings invite that judge to take the place of one of the members of the committee, having regard to all relevant factors, including whether that Party has contested the application of the procedure under paragraph 4.b.'

Article 5

1. This Protocol shall be open for signature by Member States of the Council of Europe signatories to the Convention, which may express their consent to be bound by :

    a. signature without reservation as to ratification, acceptance or approval; or

    b. signature subject to ratification, acceptance or approval, followed by ratification, acceptance or approval.

2. The instruments of ratification, acceptance or approval shall be deposited with the Secretary General of the Council of Europe.

Article 6

1. This Protocol shall enter into force on the first day of the month following the expiration of a period of three months after the date on which three High Contracting Parties to the Convention have expressed their consent to be bound by the Protocol in accordance with the provisions of Article 5.

2. In respect of any High Contracting Party to the Convention which subsequently expresses its consent to be bound by this Protocol, the Protocol shall enter into force for that High Contracting Party on the first day of the month following the expiration of a period of three months after the date of expression of its consent to be bound by the Protocol in accordance with the provisions of Article 5.

Article 7
Pending the entry into force of this Protocol according to the conditions set under Article 6, a High Contracting Party to the Convention having signed or ratified the Protocol may, at any moment, declare that the provisions of this Protocol shall apply to it on a provisional basis. Such a declaration shall take effect on the first day of the month following the date of its receipt by the Secretary General of the Council of Europe.

Article 8
1. From the date of the entry into force or application on a provisional basis of this Protocol, its provisions shall apply to all applications pending before the Court with respect to all High Contracting Parties for which it is in force or being applied on a provisional basis.

2. This Protocol shall not apply in respect of any individual application brought against two or more High Contracting Parties unless, in respect of all of them, either the Protocol is in force or applied on a provisional basis, or the relevant corresponding provisions of Protocol No. 14 are applied on a provisional basis.

Article 9
This Protocol shall cease to be in force or applied on a provisional basis from the date of entry into force of Protocol No. 14 to the Convention.

Article 10
The Secretary General of the Council of Europe shall notify the Member States of the Council of Europe of:

a. any signature;

b. the deposit of any instrument of ratification, acceptance or approval;

c. the date of entry into force of this Protocol in accordance with Article 6;

d. any declaration made under Article 7; and

e. any other act, notification or communication relating to this Protocol.

In witness whereof, the undersigned, being duly authorised thereto, have signed this Protocol.

Done at Strasbourg, this 27th day of May 2009, in English and in French, both texts being equally authentic, in a single copy which shall be deposited in the archives of the Council of Europe. The Secretary General of the Council of Europe shall transmit certified copies to each member State of the Council of Europe.

INDEX